THE PAPERS OF
THOMAS JEFFERSON

RETIREMENT SERIES

THE PAPERS OF
Thomas Jefferson

RETIREMENT SERIES

Volume 16
1 June 1820 to 28 February 1821

J. JEFFERSON LOONEY,
THE DANIEL P. JORDAN EDITOR

ROBERT F. HAGGARD AND JULIE L. LAUTENSCHLAGER,
SENIOR ASSOCIATE EDITORS
ELLEN C. HICKMAN, ASSOCIATE EDITOR
ANDREA R. GRAY, ASSISTANT EDITOR
LISA A. FRANCAVILLA, MANAGING EDITOR
KERRY DAHM, GARY SELLICK, AND PAULA VITERBO,
EDITORIAL ASSISTANTS
SUSAN SPENGLER, TECHNICAL SPECIALIST

PRINCETON AND OXFORD
PRINCETON UNIVERSITY PRESS

2019

Published by Princeton University Press, 41 William Street,
Princeton, New Jersey 08540
IN THE UNITED KINGDOM:
Princeton University Press, 6 Oxford Street,
Woodstock, Oxfordshire OX20 1TR

Library of Congress Cataloging-in-Publication Data

Jefferson, Thomas, 1743–1826

The papers of Thomas Jefferson. Retirement series / J. Jefferson Looney, editor . . .
[et al.] p. cm.

Includes bibliographical references and index.

Contents: v. 1. 4 March to 15 November 1809—[etc.]—
v. 16. 1 June 1820 to 28 February 1821

ISBN 978-0-691-19727-2 (cloth: v. 16: alk. paper)

1. Jefferson, Thomas, 1743–1826—Archives. 2. Jefferson, Thomas, 1743–1826—
Correspondence. 3. Presidents—United States—Archives.
4. Presidents—United States—Correspondence. 5. United States—
Politics and government—1809–1817—Sources. 6. United States—Politics and
government—1817–1825—Sources. I. Looney, J. Jefferson.
II. Title. III. Title: Retirement series.

E302.J442 2004b

973.4'6'092—dc22   2004048327

This book has been composed in Monticello

Princeton University Press books are printed on
acid-free paper and meet the guidelines for permanence
and durability of the Committee on Production
Guidelines for Book Longevity of the
Council on Library Resources

Printed in the United States of America

THIS EDITION was made possible by a founding grant from The New York Times Company to Princeton University.

The Retirement Series is sponsored by the Thomas Jefferson Foundation, Inc., of Charlottesville, Virginia. It was created with a six-year founding grant from The Pew Charitable Trusts to the Foundation and to Princeton University, enabling the former to take over responsibility for the volumes associated with Jefferson's retirement. Initial leadership gifts from Richard Gilder, Mrs. Martin S. Davis, and Thomas A. Saunders III, as well as subsequent generous gifts from Janemarie D. and Donald A. King, Jr., Alice Handy and Peter Stoudt, Harlan Crow, Mr. and Mrs. E. Charles Longley, Jr., and the Abby S. and Howard P. Milstein Foundation have assured the continuation of the Retirement Series. For these essential donations, and for other indispensable aid generously given by librarians, archivists, scholars, and collectors of manuscripts, the Editors record their sincere gratitude.

The position of Editor of the Papers of Thomas Jefferson at Monticello is named in honor of Dr. Daniel P. Jordan, who served as the President of the Thomas Jefferson Foundation and guided Monticello from 1985 to 2008. Dr. Jordan's vision and leadership led to the establishment in 1999 of The Papers of Thomas Jefferson: Retirement Series, part of Monticello's Robert H. Smith International Center for Jefferson Studies, which was also founded during Dr. Jordan's tenure. A challenge grant, generously provided by the Abby S. and Howard P. Milstein Foundation in 2017, made this recognition possible, with matching support from many donors, including John and Renee Grisham, Roger and Susan Hertog, Mrs. Walter H. Helmerich III, Richard Gilder and Lois Chiles, J.F. and Peggy Bryan, Charles T. Cullen, Grady and Lori Durham, Brent and Lindsay Halsey, Janemarie D. and Donald A. King, Jr., and John L. Nau III.

FOREWORD

THE 571 DOCUMENTS in this volume cover the period from 1 June 1820 to 28 February 1821. During this time Jefferson continued to show concern over the question of Missouri statehood but observed that "the boisterous sea of liberty is never without a wave." He argued that geographically limiting slavery would not relieve the country of that great evil but would instead lead to increased national division, while spreading the enslaved "over a larger surface adds to their happiness and renders their future emancipation more practicable." Seeking to persaude the Virginia General Assembly to allocate further funds to the University of Virginia and thus enable it to open sooner, Jefferson invoked fears that young southern men who went north for their university education would be indoctrinated with northern values. The school's delayed opening due to inadequate funding caused the Board of Visitors to cancel the contract that would have made Thomas Cooper its first professor, and Jefferson arranged for his own grandson Francis Eppes to study under Cooper at South Carolina College (later the University of South Carolina) in Columbia. Still hopeful that the University of Virginia would open during his lifetime, Jefferson called his work on the school "the Hobby of my old age" and envisioned an institution dedicated to seeking truth through "the illimitable freedom of the human mind." When his fellow university visitor Joseph C. Cabell, whose lobbying for the institution as a state senator had been invaluable, announced his intention to retire from the legislature, Jefferson changed his mind by reminding the much-younger man that he would "die in the last ditch" for the university and that his colleagues ought to be similarly committed.

Jefferson also kept abreast of revolutionary movements in Europe and South America and approvingly observed to Lafayette that "the disease of liberty is catching." At the same time, however, he believed that the United States should preserve its neutrality. Facing what he and other republicans believed to be dangerous encroachment by the federal judiciary on the constitutional rights of individual states, Jefferson recommended John Taylor of Caroline's new work, *Construction Construed, and Constitutions Vindicated*, as required reading for all congressmen, particularly those from Virginia. Jefferson rejoiced to learn that Carlo Botta's history of the American Revolution had been translated into English while agreeing with criticisms of the original work expressed by John Adams and John Jay to George Alexander Otis, its translator and himself a Jefferson correspondent. Jefferson also sent the American Philosophical Society a Nottoway-language vocabulary recently procured from a woman of that nation of Virginia Indians. Peter S. Du Ponceau then used the word list to compare Nottoway to Onondaga and Mohawk numerals and to Iroquois dialects, research he shared with Jefferson. Constantine S. Rafinesque presented his archaeological research on the Alligewi Indians in Kentucky in a series of published letters addressed to Jefferson.

Amidst continued economic depression and low prices obtained for his flour and tobacco, Jefferson struggled to pay his debts and satisfy increasing calls for payment by his creditors. Particularly painful was the debt he had incurred by acting as security for Wilson Cary Nicholas, who died in October 1820. To help aid his immediate financial situation, Jefferson accepted a $4,000 loan from his son-in-law John Wayles Eppes to be repaid two years later through a transfer of slaves. Early in 1821 Jefferson also turned over the management of his Monticello and Poplar Forest plantations to his grandson Thomas Jefferson Randolph, explaining that he found himself to be greatly "declining by age and ill health in the attention and energy necessary for business."

Jefferson discussed religion with trusted correspondents. He wrote to William Short of the historical Jesus, whose morality he admired but whose miracles he doubted. Jefferson expounded on materialism and the soul as physical matter in letters to Cooper and Adams, and he shared his thoughts on Unitarianism with Timothy Pickering in his first correspondence since his presidency with that Federalist. Jefferson wrote to Maria Cosway of the experience of aging and the dwindling number of their old friends, likening himself to "a solitary trunk in a desolate field, from which all it's former companions have disappeared." One particular friend lost to a move abroad was José Corrêa da Serra, who paid one last visit in the summer of 1820 to Jefferson and his household at Monticello, remarking that it was "the family i am the most attached to in all America."

ACKNOWLEDGMENTS

MANY INDIVIDUALS and institutions provided aid and encouragement during the preparation of this volume. Those who helped us to locate and acquire primary and secondary sources and answered our research questions include our colleagues at the Thomas Jefferson Foundation, especially Anna Berkes, Jack Robertson, and Endrina Tay of the Jefferson Library and Christine Devine of the Department of Archaeology; Vincent L. Golden, Marie E. Lamoureux, and Kimberly Toney at the American Antiquarian Society; Brian Carpenter and Earle E. Spamer from the American Philosophical Society; Brooke Guthrie of Duke University's David M. Rubenstein Rare Book & Manuscript Library; Sarah Funke Butler of Glenn Horowitz Bookseller in New York; Lisa Caprino, Andrew Kettler, and Olga Tsapina at the Huntington Library; Sara Rivers Cofield of the Jefferson Patterson Park & Museum; Joseph Lasala from New Port Richey, Florida; Eric Frazier, Julie Miller, Marianna Stell, and their colleagues at the Library of Congress, especially the helpful staffs of the Manuscripts Division and the Rare Books and Special Collections Reading Room; Virginia Dunn and Brent Tarter at the Library of Virginia; Dan Goodrich from the Maryland Historical Society; Anna J. Clutterbuck-Cook, Theresa Mitchell, and Erin Weinman of the Massachusetts Historical Society; Emily Zurlo at the National Archives and Records Administration; Deborah Shapiro from the Smithsonian Institution; Tom Kanon of the Tennessee State Library and Archives; Betty Jean Gooch at the Special Collections & Archives Library, Transylvania University; Pastor Darrell Davis from the Uniontown United Methodist Church in Westminster, Maryland; Susan Lintelmann of the United States Military Academy at West Point; Peyton Brown, Jamison Davis, Matthew Guillen, and John McClure at the Virginia Historical Society; Anne P. Causey, Edward F. Gaynor, Heather Riser, Penny White, and David R. Whitesell of the Albert and Shirley Small Special Collections Library at the University of Virginia; and Jay Gaidmore, Kimberly Sims, and Carolyn Wilson at the College of William and Mary. As always, we received advice, assistance, and encouragement from many of our fellow documentary editors, including Neal Millikan of the Adams Papers; Amy Jacarusco from the Papers of Benjamin Franklin; James P. McClure and his colleagues at Princeton University's Papers of Thomas Jefferson; and Robert Karachuk of the Papers of James Monroe. Genevieve Moene and Roland H. Simon transcribed and translated the

ACKNOWLEDGMENTS

French letters included in this volume; Coulter George assisted us with passages in Greek; Jonathan T. Hine lent his aid for Italian documents; and John F. Miller provided his expertise for Latin quotations. The maps of Jefferson's Virginia, Jefferson's Albemarle, and the University of Virginia were created by Rick Britton. The other illustrations that appear in this volume were assembled with the assistance of Isabella Donadio of Harvard University; Roger Hull at the Liverpool Record Office in England; Carolyn Cruthirds from the Museum of Fine Arts in Boston; Jenette Parish of the National Archives and Records Administration; Graham Greer at the Newberry Library in Chicago; John McKee from the Thomas Jefferson Foundation; and Robert D. Smith of the University of Virginia. We thankfully acknowledge the efforts of the capable staff at Princeton University Press, including Leslie Flis, Meghan Kanabay, Dimitri Karetnikov, and our production editor, Lauren Lepow. The volume's complex typesetting needs were ably addressed by Bob Bartleson and his colleagues at Integrated Publishing Solutions.

The Editors deeply regret the sudden and untimely passing on 19 May 2019 of Mark H. Saunders, a valued member of our Advisory Committee. During his tenure at the University of Virginia Press, of which he was director when he died, Mr. Saunders played a leading role in the digitization and online publication of the Retirement Series, along with many other scholarly documentary editions, and in so doing ensured an exponential increase in their present and future readership. For this and his many other achievements, he will be greatly missed.

EDITORIAL METHOD AND APPARATUS

1. RENDERING THE TEXT

From its inception *The Papers of Thomas Jefferson* has insisted on high standards of accuracy in rendering text, but modifications in textual policy and editorial apparatus have been implemented as different approaches have become accepted in the field or as a more faithful rendering has become technically feasible. Prior discussions of textual policy appeared in Vols. 1:xxix–xxxiv, 22:vii–xi, 24:vii–viii, and 30:xiii–xiv of the First Series.

The textual method of the Retirement Series will adhere to the more literal approach adopted in Volume 30 of the parent edition. Original spelling, capitalization, and punctuation are retained as written. Such idiosyncrasies as Jefferson's failure to capitalize the beginnings of most of his sentences and abbreviations like "mr" are preserved, as are his preference for "it's" to "its" and his characteristic spellings of "knolege," "paiment," and "recieve." Modern usage is adopted in cases where intent is impossible to determine, an issue that arises most often in the context of capitalization. Some so-called slips of the pen are corrected, but the original reading is recorded in a subjoined textual note. Jefferson and others sometimes signaled a change in thought within a paragraph with extra horizontal space, and this is rendered by a three-em space. Blanks left for words and not subsequently filled by the authors are represented by a space approximating the length of the blank. Gaps, doubtful readings of illegible or damaged text, and wording supplied from other versions or by editorial conjecture are explained in the source note or in numbered textual notes. Foreign-language documents, the vast majority of which are in French during the retirement period, are transcribed in full as faithfully as possible and followed by a full translation.

Two modifications from past practice bring this series still closer to the original manuscripts. Underscored text is presented as such rather than being converted to italics. Superscripts are also preserved rather than being lowered to the baseline. In most cases of superscripting, the punctuation that is below or next to the superscripted letters is dropped, since it is virtually impossible to determine what is a period or dash as opposed to a flourish under, over, or adjacent to superscripted letters.

Limits to the more literal method are still recognized, however, and readability and consistency with past volumes are prime considerations. In keeping with the basic design implemented in the first volume of the Papers, salutations and signatures continue to display in large and small capitals rather than upper- and lowercase letters. Expansion marks over abbreviations are silently omitted. With very rare exceptions, deleted text and information on which words were added during the process of composition is not displayed within the document transcription. Based on the Editors' judgment of their significance, such emendations are either described in numbered textual notes or ignored. Datelines for letters are consistently printed at the head of the text, with a comment in the descriptive note when they have been moved. Address information, endorsements, and dockets are quoted or described in the source note rather than reproduced in the document proper, and in most cases line breaks, underscoring, and horizontal lines in such material are not preserved.

2. TEXTUAL DEVICES

The following devices are employed throughout the work to clarify the presentation of the text.

[. . .]   Text missing and not conjecturable. The size of gaps longer than a word or two is estimated in annotation.

[   ]   Number or part of number missing or illegible.

[roman]   Conjectural reading for missing or illegible matter. A question mark follows when the reading is doubtful.

[*italic*]   Editorial comment inserted in the text.

<*italic*>   Matter deleted in the manuscript but restored in our text.

3. DESCRIPTIVE SYMBOLS

The following symbols are employed throughout the work to describe the various kinds of manuscript originals. When a series of versions is included, the first to be recorded is the one used for the printed text.

Dft   draft (usually a composition or rough draft; multiple drafts, when identifiable as such, are designated "2d Dft," etc.)

Dupl   duplicate

MS   manuscript (arbitrarily applied to most documents other than letters)

PoC polygraph copy
PrC press copy
RC recipient's copy
SC stylograph copy
Tripl triplicate

All manuscripts of the above types are assumed to be in the hand of the author of the document to which the descriptive symbol pertains. If not, that fact is stated. The following types of manuscripts are assumed not to be in the hand of the author, and exceptions will be noted:

FC file copy (applied to all contemporary copies retained by the author or his agents)

Tr transcript (applied to all contemporary and later copies except file copies; period of transcription, unless clear by implication, will be given when known)

4. LOCATION SYMBOLS

The locations of documents printed in this edition from originals in private hands and from printed sources are recorded in self-explanatory form in the descriptive note following each document. The locations of documents printed or referenced from originals held by public and private institutions in the United States are recorded by means of the symbols used in the *MARC Code List for Organizations* (2000) maintained by the Library of Congress. The symbols DLC and MHi by themselves stand for the collections of Jefferson Papers proper in these repositories. When texts are drawn from other collections held by these two institutions, the names of those collections are added. Location symbols for documents held by institutions outside the United States are given in a subjoined list. The lists of symbols are limited to the institutions represented by documents printed or referred to in this volume.

A-Ar Alabama Department of Archives and History, Montgomery
CLU-C William Andrews Clark Memorial Library, University of California, Los Angeles
CSmH Huntington Library, San Marino, California
  JF Jefferson File
  JF-BA Jefferson File, Bixby Acquisition

CtY Yale University, New Haven, Connecticut

DCHi Historical Society of Washington, D.C., Washington, D.C.

DLC Library of Congress, Washington, D.C.

NPT Nicholas Philip Trist Papers

TJ Papers Thomas Jefferson Papers (this is assumed if not stated, but also given as indicated to furnish the precise location of an undated, misdated, or otherwise problematic document, thus "DLC: TJ Papers, 213:38071–2" represents volume 213, folios 38071 and 38072 as the collection was arranged at the time the first microfilm edition was made in 1944–45. Access to the microfilm edition of the collection as it was rearranged under the Library's Presidential Papers Program is provided by the *Index to the Thomas Jefferson Papers* [1976])

DNA National Archives, Washington, D.C., with identifications of series (preceded by record group number) as follows:

CRL Consular Records, Leghorn

CS Census Schedules

DIDC Declarations of Intention to the United States Circuit Court for the District of Columbia

DL Domestic Letters

LAR Letters of Application and Recommendation

LRSW Letters Received by the Secretary of War

MLR Miscellaneous Letters Received

NPM Naturalization Petitions to the United States Circuit and District Courts for Maryland

PW1812 War of 1812 Papers

W1812PAFI War of 1812 Pension Application Files Index

DNT National Trust for Historic Preservation, Washington, D.C.

ICN Newberry Library, Chicago, Illinois

ICU University of Chicago, Chicago, Illinois

IGK Knox College, Galesburg, Illinois

L-Ar	Louisiana State Archives, Baton Rouge
L-M	Louisiana State Museum, New Orleans
LN	New Orleans Public Library, New Orleans, Louisiana
LNT	Tulane University, New Orleans, Louisiana
MBBS	Bostonian Society, Boston, Massachusetts
MdHi	Maryland Historical Society, Baltimore
MH	Harvard University, Cambridge, Massachusetts
MHi	Massachusetts Historical Society, Boston
MoSHi	Missouri History Museum, Saint Louis
	TJC-BC Thomas Jefferson Collection, text formerly in Bixby Collection
MWA	American Antiquarian Society, Worcester, Massachusetts
NBiSU	State University of New York, Binghamton
NBuHi	Buffalo History Museum, Buffalo, New York
NcD-MC	Medical Center, Duke University, Durham, North Carolina
NcU	University of North Carolina, Chapel Hill
	NPT Southern Historical Collection, Nicholas Philip Trist Papers
NHi	New-York Historical Society, New York City
NjP	Princeton University, Princeton, New Jersey
NN	New York Public Library, New York City
NNC	Columbia University, New York City
NNGL	Gilder Lehrman Institute of American History, New York City
NNPM	Pierpont Morgan Library, New York City
NWM	United States Military Academy, West Point, New York
OClWHi	Western Reserve Historical Society, Cleveland, Ohio
OhCiUAR	University of Cincinnati Archives and Rare Books Library, Cincinnati, Ohio
OHi	Ohio History Connection, Columbus
OOxM	Miami University, Oxford, Ohio
PHi	Historical Society of Pennsylvania, Philadelphia
PMA	Allegheny College, Meadville, Pennsylvania
PPAmP	American Philosophical Society, Philadelphia, Pennsylvania
PPL	Library Company of Philadelphia, Philadelphia, Pennsylvania

RHi	Rhode Island Historical Society, Providence
T	Tennessee State Library and Archives, Nashville
THi	Tennessee Historical Society, Nashville
TxDaHCL	Harlan Crow Library, Dallas, Texas
TxU	University of Texas, Austin
Vi	Library of Virginia, Richmond
ViCMRL	Jefferson Library, Thomas Jefferson Foundation, Inc., Charlottesville, Virginia
ViHi	Virginia Historical Society, Richmond
ViU	University of Virginia, Charlottesville

FWG	Francis Walker Gilmer Papers
JCC	Joseph C. Cabell Papers
JHC	John Hartwell Cocke Papers
JRTFP	Jefferson, Randolph, and Trist Family Papers
PP	Papers from the Office of the Proctor and Papers of the Proctor of the University of Virginia
TJP	Thomas Jefferson Papers
TJP-CT	Thomas Jefferson Papers, text formerly in Carr-Terrell Papers
TJP-ER	Thomas Jefferson Papers, text formerly in Edgehill-Randolph Papers
TJP-PC	Thomas Jefferson Papers, text formerly in Philip B. Campbell Deposit
TJP-PP	Thomas Jefferson Papers, text formerly in Papers of the Proctor of the University of Virginia
TJP-VMJB	Thomas Jefferson Papers, Visitors Minutes, University of Virginia and its predecessors, copy prepared after 7 Oct. 1826 for James Breckinridge
TJP-VMJCC	Thomas Jefferson Papers, Visitors Minutes, University of Virginia and its predeces-

		sors, copy prepared after 7 Oct. 1826 for Joseph C. Cabell
	TJP-VMJHC	Thomas Jefferson Papers, Visitors Minutes, University of Virginia and its predecessors, copy prepared after 7 Oct. 1826 for John H. Cocke
	TJP-VMTJ	Thomas Jefferson Papers, Visitors Minutes, University of Virginia and its predecessors, original manuscript largely in Thomas Jefferson's hand during the period of his service
ViW	College of William and Mary, Williamsburg, Virginia	
	TC-JP	Jefferson Papers, Tucker-Coleman Collection
	TJP	Thomas Jefferson Papers

The following symbols represent repositories located outside of the United States:

FrM	Archives Municipales de Marseille, France
ItT	Biblioteca civica centrale di Torino, Italy
Ne	Nationaal Archief, The Hague, the Netherlands
NeAA	Stadsarchief Amsterdam, the Netherlands
UkLA	Lancashire Archives, Preston, United Kingdom
UkLi	Liverpool Record Office, United Kingdom
UkNA	National Archives, Kew, United Kingdom

5. OTHER ABBREVIATIONS AND SYMBOLS

The following abbreviations and symbols are commonly employed in the annotation throughout the work.

Lb   Letterbook (used to indicate texts copied or assembled into bound volumes)

RG   Record Group (used in designating the location of documents in the Library of Virginia and the National Archives)

SJL   Jefferson's "Summary Journal of Letters" written and received for the period 11 Nov. 1783 to 25 June 1826 (in DLC: TJ

Papers). This epistolary record, kept in Jefferson's hand, has been checked against the TJ Editorial Files. It is to be assumed that all outgoing letters are recorded in SJL unless there is a note to the contrary. When the date of receipt of an incoming letter is recorded in SJL, it is incorporated in the notes. Information and discrepancies revealed in SJL but not found in the letter itself are also noted. Missing letters recorded in SJL are accounted for in the notes to documents mentioning them, in related documents, or in an appendix

TJ Thomas Jefferson

TJ Editorial Files Photoduplicates and other editorial materials in the office of the Papers of Thomas Jefferson: Retirement Series, Jefferson Library, Thomas Jefferson Foundation, Inc., Charlottesville

d Penny or denier

f Florin or franc

£ Pound sterling or livre, depending on context (in doubtful cases, a clarifying note will be given)

s Shilling or sou (also expressed as /)

tt Livre Tournois

℗ Per (occasionally used for pro, pre)

„ Old-style guillemet (European quotation mark)

6. SHORT TITLES

The following list includes short titles of works cited frequently in this edition. Since it is impossible to anticipate all the works to be cited in abbreviated form, the list is revised from volume to volume.

Acts of Assembly *Acts of the General Assembly of Virginia* (cited by session; title varies over time)

ANB John A. Garraty and Mark C. Carnes, eds., *American National Biography*, 1999, 24 vols.

Annals *Annals of the Congress of the United States: The Debates and Proceedings in the Congress of the United States . . . Compiled from Authentic Materials*, Washington, D.C., Gales & Seaton, 1834–56, 42 vols. (All editions are undependable and pagination varies from one printing to another. Citations given below are to the edition mounted on the American Memory website of the Library of Congress and give the date of the debate as well as page numbers.)

APS American Philosophical Society

ASP   *American State Papers: Documents, Legislative and Executive, of the Congress of the United States*, 1832–61, 38 vols.

Axelson, *Virginia Postmasters*   Edith F. Axelson, *Virginia Postmasters and Post Offices, 1789–1832*, 1991

BDSCHR   Walter B. Edgar and others, eds., *Biographical Directory of the South Carolina House of Representatives*, 1974– , 5 vols.

Betts, *Farm Book*   Edwin M. Betts, ed., *Thomas Jefferson's Farm Book*, 1953 (in two separately paginated sections; unless otherwise specified, references are to the second section)

Betts, *Garden Book*   Edwin M. Betts, ed., *Thomas Jefferson's Garden Book, 1766–1824*, 1944

Biog. Dir. Cong.   *Biographical Directory of the United States Congress, 1774–Present*, online resource, Office of the Clerk, United States House of Representatives

Biographie universelle   *Biographie universelle, ancienne et moderne*, new ed., 1843–65, 45 vols.

Black's Law Dictionary   Bryan A. Garner and others, eds., *Black's Law Dictionary*, 7th ed., 1999

Botta, *History of the War*   Carlo Botta, *History of the War of the Independence of the United States of America*, trans. George Alexander Otis, Philadelphia, 1820–21; Poor, *Jefferson's Library*, 5 (no. 151), 3 vols.

Brigham, *American Newspapers*   Clarence S. Brigham, *History and Bibliography of American Newspapers, 1690–1820*, 1947, 2 vols.

Bruce, *University*   Philip Alexander Bruce, *History of the University of Virginia 1819–1919: The Lengthened Shadow of One Man*, 1920–22, 5 vols.

Bush, *Life Portraits*   Alfred L. Bush, *The Life Portraits of Thomas Jefferson*, rev. ed., 1987

Cabell, *University of Virginia*   [Nathaniel Francis Cabell], *Early History of the University of Virginia, as contained in the letters of Thomas Jefferson and Joseph C. Cabell*, 1856

Callahan, *U.S. Navy*   Edward W. Callahan, *List of Officers of the Navy of the United States and of the Marine Corps from 1775 to 1900*, 1901, repr. 1969

Chambers, *Poplar Forest*   S. Allen Chambers, *Poplar Forest & Thomas Jefferson*, 1993

Clay, *Papers*   James F. Hopkins and others, eds., *The Papers of Henry Clay*, 1959–92, 11 vols.

CVSP   William P. Palmer and others, eds., *Calendar of Virginia State Papers . . . Preserved in the Capitol at Richmond*, 1875–93, 11 vols.

DAB   Allen Johnson and Dumas Malone, eds., *Dictionary of American Biography*, 1928–36, 20 vols.

DBF   *Dictionnaire de biographie française*, 1933– , 22 vols.

Destutt de Tracy, *Treatise on Political Economy*   Destutt de Tracy, *A Treatise on Political Economy; to which is prefixed a supplement to a preceding work on the understanding, or Elements of Ideology*, Georgetown, 1817 [1818]; Poor, *Jefferson's Library*, 11 (no. 700)

Dexter, *Yale Biographies*   Franklin Bowditch Dexter, *Biographical Sketches of the Graduates of Yale College*, 1885–1912, 6 vols.

Doc. Hist. Ratification   Merrill Jensen, John P. Kaminski, and others, eds., *The Documentary History of the Ratification of the Constitution*, 1976– , 29 vols.

DSB   Charles C. Gillispie, ed., *Dictionary of Scientific Biography*, 1970–80, 16 vols.

DVB   John T. Kneebone, Sara B. Bearss, and others, eds., *Dictionary of Virginia Biography*, 1998– , 3 vols.

EG   Dickinson W. Adams and Ruth W. Lester, eds., *Jefferson's Extracts from the Gospels*, 1983, *The Papers of Thomas Jefferson, Second Series*

Fairclough, *Horace: Satires, Epistles and Ars Poetica*   *Horace: Satires, Epistles and Ars Poetica*, trans. H. Rushton Fairclough, Loeb Classical Library, 1926, repr. 2005

Fairclough, *Virgil*   *Virgil*, trans. H. Rushton Fairclough, Loeb Classical Library, 1916–18, rev. by G. P. Goold, 1999–2000, repr. 2002–06, 2 vols.

Ford   Paul Leicester Ford, ed., *The Writings of Thomas Jefferson*, Letterpress Edition, 1892–99, 10 vols.

Franklin, *Papers*   Leonard W. Labaree and others, eds., *The Papers of Benjamin Franklin*, 1959– , 43 vols.

Harvard Catalogue   *Harvard University Quinquennial Catalogue of the Officers and Graduates, 1636–1925*, 1925

HAW   Henry A. Washington, ed., *The Writings of Thomas Jefferson*, 1853–54, 9 vols.

Heitman, *Continental Army*   Francis B. Heitman, comp., *Historical Register of Officers of the Continental Army during the War of the Revolution, April, 1775, to December, 1783*, rev. ed., 1914, repr. 1967

Heitman, *U.S. Army*   Francis B. Heitman, comp., *Historical Register and Dictionary of the United States Army*, 1903, repr. 1994, 2 vols.

Hening   William Waller Hening, ed., *The Statutes at Large; being a Collection of all the Laws of Virginia*, Richmond, 1809–23, 13 vols.; Sowerby, no. 1863; Poor, *Jefferson's Library*, 10 (no. 573)

Hoefer, *Nouv. biog. générale*   J. C. F. Hoefer, *Nouvelle biographie générale depuis les temps les plus reculés jusqu'a nos jours*, 1852–83, 46 vols.

Hortus Third   Liberty Hyde Bailey, Ethel Zoe Bailey, and the staff of the Liberty Hyde Bailey Hortorium, Cornell University, *Hortus Third: A Concise Dictionary of Plants Cultivated in the United States and Canada*, 1976

Jackson, *Papers*   Sam B. Smith, Harold D. Moser, Daniel Feller, and others, eds., *The Papers of Andrew Jackson*, 1980– , 10 vols.

Jefferson Correspondence, Bixby   Worthington C. Ford, ed., *Thomas Jefferson Correspondence Printed from the Originals in the Collections of William K. Bixby*, 1916

JEP   *Journal of the Executive Proceedings of the Senate of the United States*

JHD   *Journal of the House of Delegates of the Commonwealth of Virginia*

JHR   *Journal of the House of Representatives of the United States*

JS   *Journal of the Senate of the United States*

JSV   *Journal of the Senate of Virginia*

Kimball, *Jefferson, Architect*   Fiske Kimball, *Thomas Jefferson, Architect*, 1916

L & B   Andrew A. Lipscomb and Albert E. Bergh, eds., *The Writings of Thomas Jefferson*, Library Edition, 1903–04, 20 vols.

LCB   Douglas L. Wilson, ed., *Jefferson's Literary Commonplace Book*, 1989, *The Papers of Thomas Jefferson*, Second Series

Leavitt, *Poplar Forest*   Messrs. Leavitt, *Catalogue of a Private Library . . . Also, The Remaining Portion of the Library of the Late Thomas Jefferson . . . offered by his grandson, Francis Eppes, of Poplar Forest, Va.*, 1873

Leitch Daybook   MS daybook of Charlottesville merchant James Leitch, 2 Mar. 1820–8 May 1823, ViCMRL on deposit ViU, bound volume with ruled paper, in a clerk's hand

Leonard, *General Assembly*   Cynthia Miller Leonard, comp., *The General Assembly of Virginia, July 30, 1619–January 11, 1978: A Bicentennial Register of Members*, 1978

List of Patents   *A List of Patents granted by the United States from April 10, 1790, to December 31, 1836*, 1872

Litchfield Law School   *The Litchfield Law School, 1784–1833*, 1900

Longworth's New York Directory   *Longworth's American Almanac, New-York Register, and City Directory*, New York, 1796–1842 (title varies; cited by year of publication)

MACH   *Magazine of Albemarle County History*, 1940– (title varies; issued until 1951 as *Papers of the Albemarle County Historical Society*)

Madison, *Papers*   William T. Hutchinson, Robert A. Rutland, John C. A. Stagg, and others, eds., *The Papers of James Madison*, 1962– , 41 vols.
> *Congress. Ser.*, 17 vols.
> *Pres. Ser.*, 10 vols.
> *Retirement Ser.*, 3 vols.
> *Sec. of State Ser.*, 11 vols.

Malone, *Jefferson*   Dumas Malone, *Jefferson and his Time*, 1948–81, 6 vols.

Marshall, *Papers*   Herbert A. Johnson, Charles T. Cullen, Charles F. Hobson, and others, eds., *The Papers of John Marshall*, 1974–2006, 12 vols.

MB   James A. Bear Jr. and Lucia C. Stanton, eds., *Jefferson's Memorandum Books: Accounts, with Legal Records and Miscellany, 1767–1826*, 1997, 2 vols., *The Papers of Thomas Jefferson, Second Series*

Nichols, *Architectural Drawings*   Frederick Doveton Nichols, *Thomas Jefferson's Architectural Drawings*, 1961, 5th ed., 1984

Notes, ed. Peden   Thomas Jefferson, *Notes on the State of Virginia*, ed. William Peden, 1955, repr. 1995

OCD   Simon Hornblower and Antony Spawforth, eds., *The Oxford Classical Dictionary*, 2003

ODNB   H. C. G. Matthew and Brian Harrison, eds., *Oxford Dictionary of National Biography*, 2004, 60 vols.

OED   James A. H. Murray, J. A. Simpson, E. S. C. Weiner, and others, eds., *The Oxford English Dictionary*, 2d ed., 1989, 20 vols.

Peale, *Papers*   Lillian B. Miller and others, eds., *The Selected Papers of Charles Willson Peale and His Family*, 1983– , 5 vols. in 6

Pierson, *Jefferson at Monticello*   Hamilton W. Pierson, *Jefferson at Monticello: The Private Life of Thomas Jefferson, From Entirely New Materials*, 1862

Poor, *Jefferson's Library*   Nathaniel P. Poor, *Catalogue. President Jefferson's Library*, 1829

Princetonians   James McLachlan and others, eds., *Princetonians: A Biographical Dictionary*, 1976–90, 5 vols.

PTJ   Julian P. Boyd, Charles T. Cullen, John Catanzariti, Barbara B. Oberg, James P. McClure, and others, eds., *The Papers of Thomas Jefferson*, 1950– , 43 vols.

PW   Wilbur S. Howell, ed., *Jefferson's Parliamentary Writings*, 1988, *The Papers of Thomas Jefferson*, Second Series

Randall, *Life*   Henry S. Randall, *The Life of Thomas Jefferson*, 1858, 3 vols.

Randolph, *Domestic Life*   Sarah N. Randolph, *The Domestic Life of Thomas Jefferson, Compiled from Family Letters and Reminiscences by His Great-Granddaughter*, 1871

Report and Documents for 1820   *Report and Documents respecting the University of Virginia*, Richmond, 1820, containing a 2 Oct. 1820 report by the Board of Visitors and supporting documents

Scharf, *Western Maryland*   J. Thomas Scharf, *History of Western Maryland*, 1882, repr. 2003, 2 vols.

Shackelford, *Descendants*   George Green Shackelford, ed., *Collected Papers . . . of the Monticello Association of the Descendants of Thomas Jefferson*, 1965–84, 2 vols.

Sowerby   E. Millicent Sowerby, comp., *Catalogue of the Library of Thomas Jefferson*, 1952–59, 5 vols.

Sprague, *American Pulpit*   William B. Sprague, *Annals of the American Pulpit*, 1857–69, 9 vols.

Stein, *Worlds*   Susan R. Stein, *The Worlds of Thomas Jefferson at Monticello*, 1993

Terr. Papers   Clarence E. Carter and John Porter Bloom, eds., *The Territorial Papers of the United States*, 1934–75, 28 vols.

TJR   Thomas Jefferson Randolph, ed., *Memoir, Correspondence, and Miscellanies, from the Papers of Thomas Jefferson*, 1829, 4 vols.

True, "Agricultural Society"   Rodney H. True, "Minute Book of the Agricultural Society of Albemarle," *Annual Report of the American Historical Association for the Year 1918* (1921), 1:261–349

U.S. Reports   *Cases Argued and Decided in the Supreme Court of the United States*, 1790– (title varies; originally issued in distinct editions of separately numbered volumes with *U.S. Reports* volume numbers retroactively assigned; original volume numbers here given parenthetically)

U.S. Statutes at Large   Richard Peters, ed., *The Public Statutes at Large of the United States . . . 1789 to March 3, 1845*, 1845–67, 8 vols.

Va. Reports   *Reports of Cases Argued and Adjudged in the Court of Appeals of Virginia*, 1798–   (title varies; originally issued in distinct editions of separately numbered volumes with *Va. Reports* volume numbers retroactively assigned; original volume numbers here given parenthetically)

VMHB   *Virginia Magazine of History and Biography*, 1893–

Washington, *Papers*   W. W. Abbot and others, eds., *The Papers of George Washington*, 1983–   , 65 vols.

    Colonial Ser., 10 vols.

    Confederation Ser., 6 vols.

    Pres. Ser., 19 vols.

    Retirement Ser., 4 vols.

    Rev. War Ser., 26 vols.

William and Mary Provisional List   *A Provisional List of Alumni, Grammar School Students, Members of the Faculty, and Members of the Board of Visitors of the College of William and Mary in Virginia. From 1693 to 1888*, 1941

WMQ   *William and Mary Quarterly*, 1892–

Woods, *Albemarle*   Edgar Woods, *Albemarle County in Virginia*, 1901, repr. 1991

CONTENTS

·⸨ {1820} ⸩·

CONTENTS

CONTENTS

CONTENTS

CONTENTS

CONTENTS

CONTENTS

CONTENTS

CONTENTS

CONTENTS

CONTENTS

CONTENTS

{1821}

CONTENTS

CONTENTS

CONTENTS

MAPS

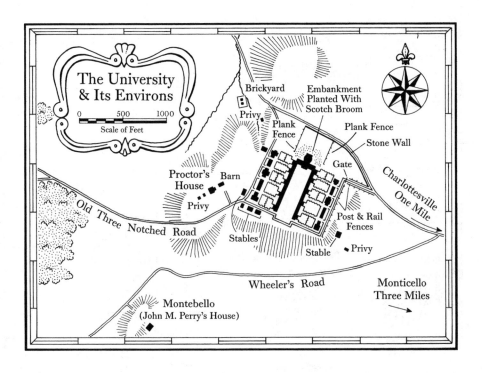

The University & Its Environs

0   500   1000
Scale of Feet

Brickyard

Embankment
Planted With
Scotch Broom

Privy

Plank Fence

Plank Fence

Stone Wall

Proctor's House   Barn

Gate

Privy

Charlottesville
One Mile

Old Three Notched Road

Stables

Post & Rail
Fences

Stable

Privy

Wheeler's Road

Monticello
Three Miles

Montebello
(John M. Perry's House)

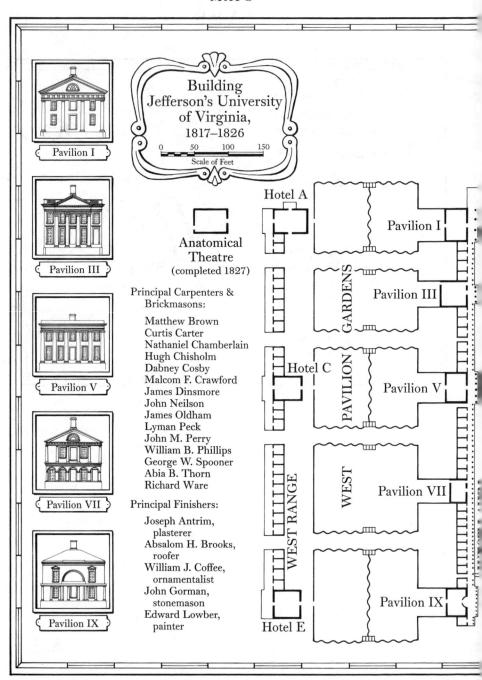

Building
Jefferson's University
of Virginia,
1817–1826

0   50   100   150
Scale of Feet

Anatomical
Theatre
(completed 1827)

Principal Carpenters &
Brickmasons:

Matthew Brown
Curtis Carter
Nathaniel Chamberlain
Hugh Chisholm
Dabney Cosby
Malcom F. Crawford
James Dinsmore
John Neilson
James Oldham
Lyman Peck
John M. Perry
William B. Phillips
George W. Spooner
Abia B. Thorn
Richard Ware

Principal Finishers:

Joseph Antrim,
    plasterer
Absalom H. Brooks,
    roofer
William J. Coffee,
    ornamentalist
John Gorman,
    stonemason
Edward Lowber,
    painter

Pavilion I

Pavilion III

Pavilion V

Pavilion VII

Pavilion IX

Hotel A

Hotel C

Hotel E

GARDENS

PAVILION

WEST

WEST RANGE

Pavilion I

Pavilion III

Pavilion V

Pavilion VII

Pavilion IX

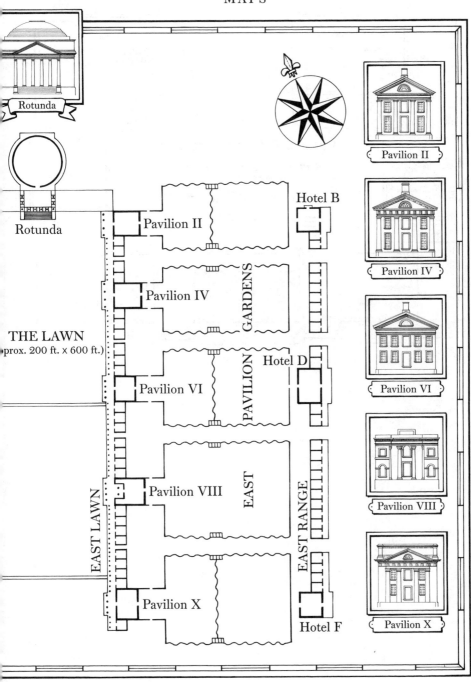

Rotunda

Rotunda

THE LAWN
(approx. 200 ft. x 600 ft.)

EAST LAWN

Pavilion II

Pavilion IV

Pavilion VI

Pavilion VIII

Pavilion X

PAVILION GARDENS

EAST

EAST RANGE

Hotel B

Hotel D

Hotel F

Pavilion II

Pavilion IV

Pavilion VI

Pavilion VIII

Pavilion X

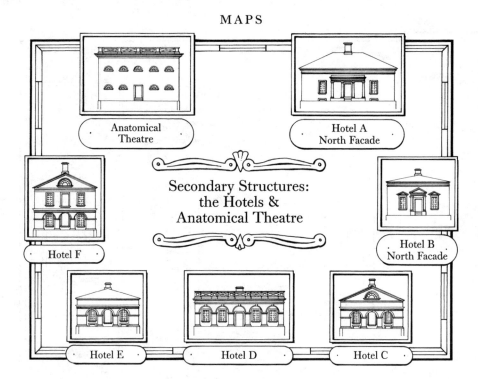

Anatomical
Theatre

Hotel A
North Facade

Secondary Structures:
the Hotels &
Anatomical Theatre

Hotel F

Hotel B
North Facade

Hotel E

Hotel D

Hotel C

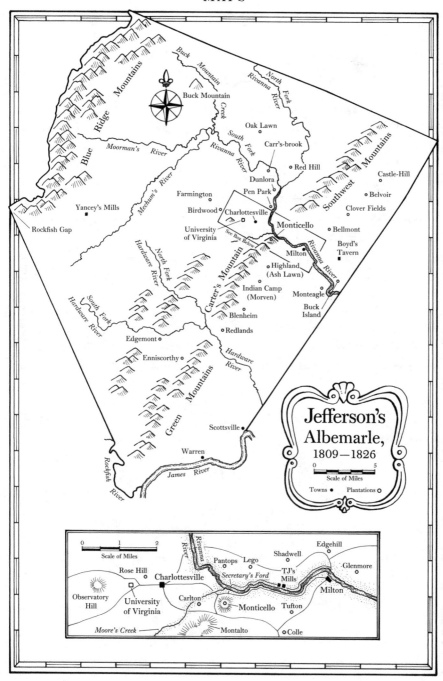

Jefferson's
Albemarle,
1809—1826

0   5
Scale of Miles

Towns ●   Plantations ○

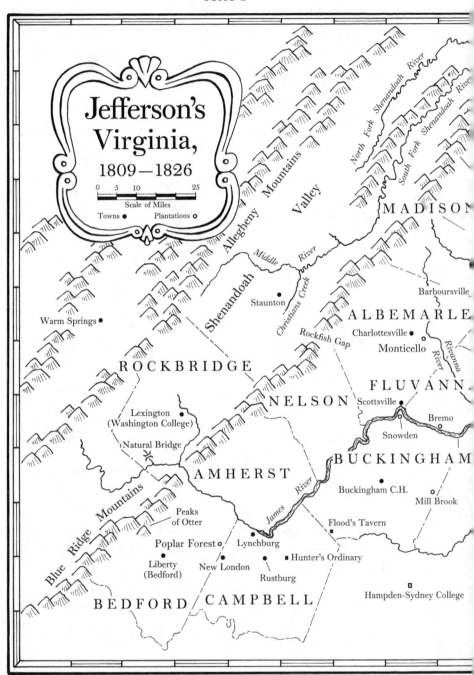

Jefferson's Virginia, 1809–1826

Scale of Miles
0 5 10 25

Towns ●   Plantations ○

North Fork Shenandoah River

South Fork Shenandoah River

Allegheny Mountains

Valley

MADISON

Middle River

Christians Creek

Staunton

Barboursville

Warm Springs ●

ALBEMARLE

Shenandoah

Rockfish Gap

Charlottesville ●

Monticello

Rivanna River

ROCKBRIDGE

NELSON

Scottsville ●

FLUVANNA

Bremo

Lexington
(Washington College) ●

Snowden

Natural Bridge

BUCKINGHAM

AMHERST

James River

Buckingham C.H. ●

Mill Brook ○

Peaks
of Otter

Flood's Tavern ■

Blue Ridge Mountains

Poplar Forest ○

Lynchburg ●

Liberty
(Bedford) ●

New London ●

Hunter's Ordinary ■

Rustburg

Hampden-Sydney College □

BEDFORD

CAMPBELL

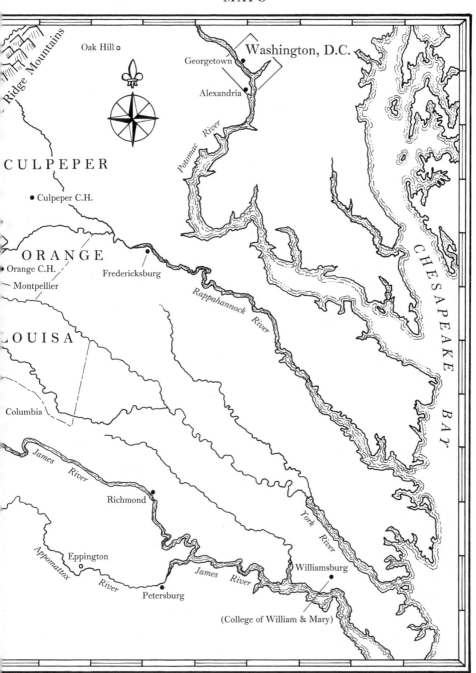

ILLUSTRATIONS

Following page 348

JARED SPARKS BY REMBRANDT PEALE

The noted American artist Rembrandt Peale (1778–1860) probably painted this $20\frac{1}{8}$-by-$15\frac{1}{4}$-inch oil-on-canvas portrait of the historian, documentary editor, and author Jared Sparks shortly after the latter's ordination in 1819 as pastor of Baltimore's First Independent Church, a Unitarian congregation to which Peale also belonged. Sparks visited Monticello in August 1820. The artwork descended through Sparks's daughter Elizabeth Sparks Pickering to her husband, Edward C. Pickering, a longtime professor at Harvard University and the director of its astronomical observatory. It was bequeathed to the school in 1919 (Theodore E. Stebbins Jr. and others, eds., *American Paintings at Harvard* [2008–   ], 1:392; *Harvard Catalogue*, 104).
Courtesy of Harvard Art Museums, Harvard University, Cambridge, Massachusetts.

HARPSICHORD

Jefferson wrote his friend John Paradise from Paris in May 1786 that he wished to have the London instrument manufacturer Jacob Kirckman "make for me one of his best harpsichords with a double set of keys, and the machine on the top resembling a Venetian blind for giving a swell. The case to be of mahogany, solid not vineered, without any inlaid work but deriving all it's beauty from the elegance of the wood." Following his return from Europe, Jefferson placed the instrument in the parlor at Monticello, where it gradually fell into disrepair and was discarded. In 1798 he purchased a second Kirckman harpsichord, this time for his recently married younger daughter, Maria (Mary) Jefferson Eppes. Although it was also "double-keyed," "one of Kirckman's highest priced, and of a fine silver tone," this harpsichord had fewer pedals than the one at Monticello. Following stays at the Eppes's Eppington and Mill Brook residences, the instrument was sent in 1820 to Poplar Forest. By this time, however, Jefferson's granddaughter Ellen W. Randolph (Coolidge) described it as being "in a very bad state." Like its Monticello counterpart, it has since gone missing. The image shown here depicts a mahogany harpsichord produced in 1798 by Jacob Kirckman's successor, Joseph Kirckman (Stein, *Worlds*, 425; *PTJ*, 9:579, 30:215; John Wayles Eppes to TJ, 6 Feb., 8 July 1820; Extract from Ellen W. Randolph [Coolidge] to Martha Jefferson Randolph, 13 Sept. 1820).
Courtesy of the Museum of Fine Arts, Boston, Massachusetts.

THEATER ADVERTISEMENT

On Saturday, 19 Aug. 1820, a traveling troupe of actors performed Elizabeth Inchbald's comedy *Animal Magnetism* and Thomas Knight's farce *The Turnpike Gate* at the Swan Tavern in Charlottesville. Sandwiched between the two productions was a eulogy on George Washington and the comic song

{ xlix }

ILLUSTRATIONS

"Paddy Leary." Tickets costing one dollar for adults and fifty cents for children could be had "at the bar of the tavern, and at the door the night of performance." Although it is uncertain which members of Jefferson's family attended the theater on the night in question, the ex-president noted in his financial records the expenditure of four dollars on 19 August for "Tickets to the play" (*MB*, 2:1367; Charlottesville *Central Gazette*, 18 Aug. 1820; John Hammond Moore, *Albemarle: Jefferson's County, 1727–1976* [1976; repr. 1986], 97).

Courtesy of the Albert and Shirley Small Special Collections Library, University of Virginia.

BUST OF WILLIAM ROSCOE

In June 1820 Jefferson's lifelong friend James Maury happened upon a small bust of the English historian, poet, and botanist William Roscoe in a "Porcelain Warehouse" in Liverpool, England. He purchased the piece as a gift for the former president and had it shipped to Richmond. Even before it arrived at Monticello in 1821, Jefferson informed Roscoe, with whom he had previously corresponded on shared scientific and literary interests, that he looked forward "with great pleasure" to receiving the artwork and planned to place it in his home "in honorable file" with those of other "cherished characters." The porcelain sculpture is $10\frac{1}{2}$ inches tall and was likely produced by one of the firms operated by the Franceys family of Liverpool (Maury to TJ, 26 June 1820; TJ to Roscoe, 27 Dec. 1820; Bernard Peyton to TJ, 19 Mar. 1821; Stein, *Worlds*, 228; *The Stranger in Liverpool; or, an historical and descriptive view of the Town of Liverpool and its environs* [Liverpool, 1820], 164–5).

Courtesy of the Thomas Jefferson Foundation, Inc.

"THE ILLIMITABLE FREEDOM OF THE HUMAN MIND": THOMAS JEFFERSON TO WILLIAM ROSCOE, 27 DECEMBER 1820

Jefferson informed his friend William Roscoe on 27 Dec. 1820 that the nascent University of Virginia would "be based on the illimitable freedom of the human mind," a place where the faculty and students were "not afraid to follow truth wherever it may lead, nor to tolerate any error so long as reason is left free to combat it." With these words, now often quoted as the institution's unofficial mission statement, Jefferson expressed concepts that were both typical of and important to him. The first was that no limits should be placed on freedom of thought, belief, and expression, especially at an institution of higher learning. In Jefferson's view such restrictions retard, where they do not entirely subvert, the sorts of intellectual inquiry and educational development that colleges ought to foster. Second, Jefferson regarded objective truth as a realizable goal that can be attained, however slowly and imperfectly, through the exercise of rational thought. Those who were prevented from employing their reason to its fullest extent could neither be expected to solve the errors of the past nor even to recognize what needed to be corrected.

Courtesy of the Liverpool Record Office, United Kingdom.

ILLUSTRATIONS

1820 UNITED STATES CENSUS

Article 1, section 2, of the United States Constitution mandates the taking of a census "within three years after the first meeting of the Congress of the United States, and within every subsequent term of ten years." Enumerations have accordingly taken place every decade beginning in 1790. In the 1810 census Jefferson appears in Albemarle County, and ten years later he is listed in entries for both Albemarle and Bedford counties. On 1 Aug. 1820 Jefferson tabulated the number of persons living at Monticello. Relying in part on information supplied by his overseer Edmund Bacon, Jefferson's count included his own family and slaves and those of Bacon, Youen Carden, his sister Anne Scott Marks, Edmund Meeks, and his son-in-law Thomas Mann Randolph. Jefferson determined that 26 free whites and 107 slaves resided at his Albemarle County estate. His enumeration was accepted in toto when the census was officially taken six days later. That same month, Jefferson's Bedford County properties were found to contain 8 free whites and 98 slaves. The comparable figure for Albemarle in 1810 was 51 free whites and 147 slaves (Bacon to TJ, [before 1 Aug. 1820]; TJ's Monticello Census Record, 1 Aug. 1820 [MS in ViU: TJP], entirely in TJ's hand; DNA: RG 29, CS, Albemarle Co., 1810, 1820, Bedford Co., 1820).
Courtesy of the National Archives, Washington, D.C.

JEFFERSON'S NOTES FOR A BIOGRAPHY OF GEORGE WYTHE
(FIRST AND LAST PAGES)

Jefferson was often asked during his retirement for biographical information about people he had known and with whom he had worked. While he did not always comply with these requests, he did pass along his recollections on a number of occasions. In 1812 Jefferson sent William Wirt detailed notes about the famed Virginia orator and politician Patrick Henry. A year later he forwarded to Paul Allen facts about the life of the explorer Meriwether Lewis, and in 1816 he dispatched his reminiscences of Peyton Randolph (ca. 1723–75) to the revolutionary's namesake nephew. When John Sanderson solicited data from Jefferson about George Wythe and John Hancock for the multivolume *Biography of the Signers to the Declaration of Independence* (Philadelphia, 1820–27; Poor, *Jefferson's Library*, 5 [no. 152]), Jefferson was glad to oblige, at least with regard to Wythe. He demurred concerning Hancock, of whom he knew far less. Sanderson, for his part, used and in places quoted extensively from Jefferson's portrait of his mentor, friend, and colleague in the second volume of the *Biography of the Signers* (TJ to Wirt, 12 Apr. 1812, and enclosure; TJ to Allen, 18 Aug. 1813; TJ to Peyton Randolph [d. 1828], 26 July 1816, and enclosure; Sanderson to TJ, 19 Aug. 1820; TJ to Sanderson, 31 Aug. 1820, and enclosure).
Courtesy of the Newberry Library, Chicago, Illinois.

HAND TELESCOPE

Jefferson owned various telescopes and famously used one to observe the approach of invading British forces in Richmond and Charlottesville during the Revolutionary war. When he acquired this particular "pocket telescope" or "Spy-glass" is unclear. Manufactured by the well-known English scientific-instrument maker Jesse Ramsden during the final third of the eighteenth century, it is made of mahogany and silver plate. Measuring $7\frac{1}{2}$ inches in length when closed and $20\frac{1}{2}$ when fully extended, Jefferson's name is inscribed on the upper silver band. He likely used it late in life to view the construction of the University of Virginia from Monticello's North Terrace. Having descended through Thomas Jefferson Randolph's family, the instrument was donated to the Thomas Jefferson Foundation in 1986 (James A. Bear Jr., ed., *Jefferson at Monticello* [1967; repr. 1994], 6–7; Randolph, *Domestic Life*, 55–6; TJ to George Jefferson, 1 May 1809; *MB*, 2:1368; Stein, *Worlds*, 352).

Courtesy of the Thomas Jefferson Foundation, Inc.

JOSÉ CORRÊA DA SERRA BY REMBRANDT PEALE

Rembrandt Peale probably executed this $28\frac{1}{2}$-by-$23\frac{1}{4}$-inch oil-on-canvas portrait of the Portuguese botanist and diplomat José Corrêa da Serra (1751–1823) in Philadelphia shortly after the latter arrived in the United States in 1812. It was, apparently, at Charles Willson Peale's Philadelphia Museum the following year. Corrêa da Serra, who impressed Jefferson as "one of the most learned men of the age"; the "best digest of science in books, men, and things that I have ever met with"; and the possessor of a "most amiable and engaging character," visited Monticello on multiple occasions between July 1813 and August 1820. Shortly thereafter he returned to Portugal (*Historical Catalogue of the Paintings in the Philadelphia Museum, consisting chiefly of portraits of revolutionary patriots and other distinguished characters* [(Philadelphia), 1813], 52; TJ to Josef Yznardy, 6 Aug. 1813; TJ to Caspar Wistar, 17 Aug. 1813; TJ to Christopher Clark, 14 Sept. 1815; TJ to William Short, 4 Aug. 1820).

Courtesy of the Thomas Jefferson Foundation, Inc.

MONTICELLO'S NORTH SQUARE ROOM

José Corrêa da Serra became a favorite of the Jefferson and Randolph families and often seems to have stayed in Monticello's 15-by-15-foot North Square Room, which is located next to the front portico and boasts a fireplace, alcove bed, overhead closet, and interior window shutters for privacy and insulation. This room is rarely open to the public (Cornelia J. Randolph's Plan of Monticello's First Floor, [after 4 July 1826] [ViU: JRTFP]).

Courtesy of the Thomas Jefferson Foundation, Inc.

Volume 16

1 June 1820 to 28 February 1821

JEFFERSON CHRONOLOGY

1743 • 1826

1743	Born at Shadwell, 13 April (New Style).
1760–1762	Studies at the College of William and Mary.
1762–1767	Self-education and preparation for law.
1769–1774	Albemarle delegate to House of Burgesses.
1772	Marries Martha Wayles Skelton, 1 January.
1775–1776	In Continental Congress.
1776	Drafts Declaration of Independence.
1776–1779	In Virginia House of Delegates.
1779	Submits Bill for Establishing Religious Freedom.
1779–1781	Governor of Virginia.
1782	Martha Wayles Skelton Jefferson dies, 6 September.
1783–1784	In Continental Congress.
1784–1789	In France on commission to negotiate commercial treaties and then as minister plenipotentiary at Versailles.
1790–1793	Secretary of State of the United States.
1797–1801	Vice President of the United States.
1801–1809	President of the United States.

RETIREMENT

1809	Attends James Madison's inauguration, 4 March.
	Arrives at Monticello, 15 March.
1810	Completes legal brief on New Orleans batture case, 31 July.
1811	Batture case dismissed, 5 December.
1812	Correspondence with John Adams resumed, 1 January.
	Batture pamphlet preface completed, 25 February; printed by 21 March.
1814	Named a trustee of Albemarle Academy, 25 March.
	Resigns presidency of American Philosophical Society, 23 November.
1815	Sells personal library to Congress.
1816	Writes introduction and revises translation of Destutt de Tracy, *A Treatise on Political Economy* [1818].
	Named a visitor of Central College, 18 October.
1817	Cornerstone laid for first structure at Central College (later Pavilion VII, University of Virginia), 6 October.
1818	Attends Rockfish Gap conference to choose location of proposed University of Virginia, 1–4 August.
	Visits Warm Springs, 7–27 August.
1819	University of Virginia chartered, 25 January; named to Board of Visitors, 13 February; elected rector, 29 March.
	Debts greatly increased by bankruptcy of Wilson Cary Nicholas.
1820	Likens debate over slavery and Missouri statehood to "a fire bell in the night," 22 April.
1821	Writes memoirs, 6 January–29 July.
1823	Visits Poplar Forest for last time, 16–25 May.
1824	Lafayette visits Monticello, 4–15 November.
1825	University of Virginia opens, 7 March.
1826	Writes will, 16–17 March.
	Last recorded letter, 25 June.
	Dies at Monticello, 4 July.

THE PAPERS OF
THOMAS JEFFERSON

·◖━━━━━━◗·

From Bernard Peyton

DEAR SIR, Rich'd 1ˢᵗ June 1820

I was duely favor'd with yours covering a note for the renewal yours for $3,000 at the Farmers Bank, which was accordingly done this day, & I am requested by the cashier to inform you that a curtail of $500 will be required on it at the renewal <u>after the next</u>, to wit, on the 4th: of October.—This is done I understand in consequence of the loan being considered <u>temporary</u> in the beginning, & an indisposition on the part of the Directors to increase their <u>accomodation</u> debt.

Your last note I observed was filled up with Sixty <u>five</u> days, which was incorrect, & I was obliged to date it back five days in order to make it discountable, 60 days being the longest period either of the Banks in this City can discount for—the 3 days grace allowed does not effect the time to be expressed in the body of the note, of course all notes are filled up with 60 days only.

I am glad of every occasion to be servicable to you, & beg you will accept assurances of the sincere regard & attachment of

Dear sir Yours Mo: Truely BERNARD PEYTON

RC (MHi); endorsed by TJ as received 3 June 1820 and so recorded in SJL. RC (CtY: Franklin Collection); address cover only; with PoC of TJ to Katherine Duane Morgan, 26 Jan. 1822, on verso; addressed: "Mʳ Thomas Jefferson Monticello Milton"; franked; postmarked Richmond, 1 June.

TJ's recent communication to Peyton enclosing a NOTE FOR THE RENEWAL of his loan at the Farmers' Bank of Virginia has not been found and is not recorded in SJL.

From Thomas Appleton

DEAR SIR— Leghorn 2ⁿᵈ June 1820—

The unexpected departure of a vessel in the course of the day, Affords me but a short time to reply to your letter of 15ᵗʰ of febʸ receiv'd by me on the 5ᵗʰ of may—at the same time, I receiv'd a bill of exchᵃ from m[r] Vaughan, on Paris, which produc'd here, precisely four hundred dollars, and has been paid equally between the wives of the Raggi's.— The wife of Giacomo, who is advanc'd in years, infirm, and has a daughter on the point of being married, has determin'd not to leave her native place; the younger m[rs] Raggi, is greatly desirous of joining her husband with her infant-child; but the obstacles are great & numerous—to pay her small debts, & purchase what She would require before embarking, would consume nearly the 200 D[rs].—then there is no vessel in port, bound nearer to her husband, than Boston; for since the failure of Purviance & nicholas, not a vessel has arriv'd from Baltimore—but the greatest of all the obstacles is, considering that history furnishes but one Joseph,[1] that she should find a second.— on the whole, there is no probability, that she will embark this year; and I am inclin'd to beleive, her husband will approve her[2] determination, considering that the elder woman, has absolutely refus'd to leave her country.—I hope shortly to receive your remittances for mesdames mazzei and Pini, as their frequent inquiries, strongly indicate their wants.—I shall be gratified to learn the safe arrival of the seeds I sent you to Richmond; as likewise, if you shall require any architectural works in marble from Italy, for the edifices you are erecting; for, as I presume, they could be imported free of duties, there would only be the freight to add to the cost at Carrara.—

accept, Sir, the renewal of my invariable esteem & respect—

TH: APPLETON

RC (DLC); at foot of text: "Thomas Jefferson esq[r] Monticello"; endorsed by TJ as received 21 Aug. 1820 and so recorded in SJL. FC (Lb in DNA: RG 84, CRL); in Appleton's hand; at foot of text: "Sent by Ship Francis for Boston 2. June."

HISTORY FURNISHES BUT ONE JOSEPH: Appleton apparently alludes to the biblical story of Joseph, Mary, and the virgin birth of Jesus, thereby implying that Michele Raggi was not the biological father of his wife's infant child.

[1] Remainder of sentence in FC reads "he might Still <remain> continue the Solitary example of mere admiration."

[2] Remainder of sentence in FC reads "resolution, considering the elder woman will not leave her native country."

From George S. Gibson
(for Patrick Gibson)

SIR   Richmond 2nd June 1820

Yours of the 22nd inclosing Blank Notes for renewal in the Banks, was duly received, the last Hhd of your Crop has been received & sold it was refused on acc[t] of its being very much stained & in too high order

T.J. 1710. 160. 1550. Refus^{d} at \$5.10 = 79.05 it brought the highest price that refused Tob^{o} has been sold for in this Market for some time past.—Flour is now \$4 to $4\frac{1}{8}$ I am

Yours Respectfully

Patrick Gibson
P^{R} George S Gibson

As soon as Mr Gibson has recovered he will write you in answer to what you say respecting his remaining under advances to you

Wth respect

G S Gibson

RC (DLC); entirely in George S. Gibson's hand; postscript adjacent to first signatures; endorsed by TJ as a letter from Patrick Gibson received 6 June 1820 and so recorded in SJL. RC (MoSHi: TJC-BC); address cover only; with PoC of TJ to Rufus Woodward, 7 July 1820, on verso; addressed in a different hand: "Thomas Jefferson Esquire Monticello"; franked; postmarked Richmond, 2 June.

George Sanderson Gibson (1800–72), physician, was the second son of Patrick Gibson, TJ's business agent and frequent correspondent. Born in Richmond, he was educated in England and Holland. Gibson returned to the United States by 1819, took up the study of medicine, and received his medical degree from the University of Maryland in 1823. He settled thereafter in Baltimore, where he remained in private practice for forty years, reportedly declining a number of professorial positions in order to concentrate on his patients. Gibson was active in both the temperance and colonization movements, and he served as treasurer of the Medical and Chirurgical Faculty of Maryland, 1836–38. He owned two slaves in 1840, and his estate was estimated to be worth \$85,000 in 1860 and \$150,000 a decade later. Gibson died in Baltimore (American Medical Association, *Transactions* 23 [1872]: 590–1; Vi: Gibson Family Papers; Eugene Fauntleroy Cordell, *Historical Sketch of the University of Maryland School of Medicine* [1891], 176; *Baltimore Patriot & Mercantile Advertiser*, 23 Apr. 1823, 21 Dec. 1831; Maryland State Colonization Society, Board of Managers, *Annual Report* 7 [1839]: 2; Cordell, *The Medical Annals of Maryland, 1799–1899* [1903], 734; DNA: RG 29, CS, Md., Baltimore, 1840–70; Baltimore *Sun*, 1 Feb. 1872; gravestone inscription in Westminster Burial Ground, Baltimore).

Transactions with James Leitch

[*Leitch Daybook, p. 63, 2 June 1820:*]

·395.	Thomas Jefferson ℘ Mr Eppes				
	1 Co. Blairs Lectures \$3.25. 1 Adams Antiquities $\$3^{50}$		6	75	
	1 " Baileys English Dictionary \$4.50		4	50	
	1 " Keith on the Globes \$2.75. 1 do. Italian Grammar $\$2^{50}$		5	25	
	1 " Moore's Poems	6/9	1	13	17.63

[*p. 67, 5 June 1820:*]

'395. Thomas Jefferson ℔ self
    5½ yds drab Cotton Cassimere 3/6
      2 hanks Silk 6ᵈ   3 | 38
    1 doz. buttons   1/6 | 25   3.63

Ref	Description		£	s/¢	$
'395.	Thomas Jefferson ℔ self				
	5½ yds drab Cotton Cassimere 3/6				
	2 hanks Silk 6ᵈ		3	38	
	1 doz. buttons	1/6		25	3.63

[*p. 68, 7 June 1820:*]

Ref	Description		£	s/¢	$
'395.	Thomas Jefferson				
	Dr to Sundries ℔ Order				
	2 doz button moulds 9ᵈ. 2 Small do				
	4½ᵈ			38	
	13½ ℔s Blister Steel 6ᵈ.		1	13	
'460.	Bramham & Jones for 1 Lock	1/6		25	1.76

[*p. 69, 9 June 1820:*]

Ref	Description		£	s/¢	$
'395.	Thomas Jefferson ℔ Order				
	1 Sack Salt	$8			8

[*p. 71, 10 June 1820:*]

Ref	Description		£	s/¢	$
'395.	Thomas Jefferson ℔ Order				
	6 ℔s Shot 1/. 1 ℔ Powder 6/. 1 pr				
	Brass Butts 2/3				2.38

[*p. 73, 13 June 1820:*]

Ref	Description		£	s/¢	$
'395.	Thomas Jefferson ℔ Order				
	5 yds Olive Cotton Cassimere 3/6. 1 doz				
	buttons 3/.		3	42	
	2 Skeins Silk 6ᵈ. 2 hanks thread 3ᵈ. 1 Stkˡ				
	Twist 6ᵈ			34	3.76

[*p. 78, 22 June 1820:*]

Ref	Description		£	s/¢	$
'395.	Thomas Jefferson ℔ Mrs Randolph				
	15 yds blue Cotton Cassimere	3/.	7	50	
	1 ps Short Nankeen 6/. 4 yds Brown				
	Holland	3/.	3		
	⅓ ℔ Black thread 10/6. 2 doz Common				
	Buttons 1/6		1	08	
	3 yds Calico 3/6. 2 yds Cambric Muslin				
	5/3		3	50	
	2 doz bullet buttons 2/3			75	

	2. 14 Inch Dishes. $2.60 ℔ pair. 4. 12						
	Inch do $2 ℔ do			6	60		
	1 Salad Bowl			2	82		25.25

[*p. 88, 13 July 1820:*]

˙395.	Thomas Jefferson ℔ Order						
	2½ yds Irish linen	7/6					3.13

[*p. 88, 14 July 1820:*]

˙395.	Thomas Jefferson ℔ Order						
	1 M. ½ Inch sprigs	2/3					38

[*p. 97, 28 July 1820:*]

˙395.[2]	Thomas Jefferson ℔ Order E[d] Bacon						
	42 ℔s. 20[d] wrought nails	1/.					7.

[*p. 97, 29 July 1820:*]

˙395.	Thomas Jefferson ℔ Order						
	3 Bed cords	3/9					1.88

[*p. 100, 31 July 1820:*]

	Sundries D[r] to Interest Acct. amt from						
	Page (99)[3]						
395	Thomas Jefferson			353	88		

[*p. 101, 31 July 1820:*]

	Interest Acct D[r] to Sundries brought						
	forward[4]						
395.	Thomas Jefferson			2	50		

[*p. 106, 2 Aug. 1820:*]

˙395.	Thomas Jefferson ℔ Order						
	To ½ gross. Inch Screws	7/6					63

[*p. 107, 3 Aug. 1820:*]

˙395.	Thomas Jefferson ℔ Order						
	71 ℔s Iron 6[d]. 11 ℔s Blister						
	Steel 9[d]			7	30		
	14 ℔s German Steel	1/6		3	50		10.80

[*p. 114, 16 Aug. 1820:*]

	˙395.	Thomas Jefferson ⅌ Order						
		15 yds Ticklenburg	2/.					5.

[*p. 115, 17 Aug. 1820:*]

	˙395.	Thomas Jefferson ⅌ Mʳ Crenshaw						
		2 ℔s. 5ᵈ Cut Nails	1/1½					38

[*p. 115, 18 Aug. 1820:*]

	˙395.	Thomas Jefferson ⅌ Order for Burrell						
		4¼ yds Stripᵈ Jeans 4/6. 1¼ fine B.						
		Holland 3/6			3	92		
		4 hanks thread 3ᵈ. 3¾ yds. B. Stuff 4/.						
		2 hks Silk 6ᵈ			2	83		
		1 yd B. Holland 2/6. 1 Stick Twist 6ᵈ.						
		1 " Silk 6ᵈ				50		
						8⁵		7.33

[*p. 117, 23 Aug. 1820:*]

	˙395.	Thomas Jefferson ⅌ Order						
		55 ℔s Iron (Plow Plates)	9 cts					4.95

[*p. 118, 24 Aug. 1820:*]

	˙395.	Thomas Jefferson ⅌ Order T J. Randolph						
		22 ℔s. 8ᵈ Cut Nails 1/. 5 ℔s. 20ᵈ do 10ᵈ						4.37

[*p. 119, 29 Aug. 1820:*]

	˙395.	Thomas Jefferson ⅌ Order T J Rand.						
		12 ℔s. 8 Cut Nails 1/. 10 ℔s. 20ᵈ 1/.						3.67

[*p. 119, 29 Aug. 1820:*]

	˙395.	Thomas Jefferson ⅌ Order						
		1 ℔ Lamp black 1/6. 1 M. 1¾ Inch. Sprigs						
		6/9			1	38		
		13 ℔s. 8ᵈ Brads 1/.			2	17		3.55

[*p. 120, 30 Aug. 1820:*]

	˙395.	Thomas Jefferson ⅌ Overseer T J Ran.						
		1½ ℔ 8ᵈ Cut Nails	1/.					25

[*p. 121, 31 Aug. 1820:*]

	˙395.	Thomas Jefferson ℞ Order E Bacon							
		30 ℔s. 20ᵈ Cut Nails	1/.					5.00

[*p. 122, 2 Sept. 1820:*]

	˙395.	Thomas Jefferson ℞ Miss R							
		3¾ yds. Spotted Pelise flannel 7/6.							
		2 doz Pearl buttˢ	3/9					5.94

[*p. 127, 13 Sept. 1820:*]

	˙395.	Thomas Jefferson ℞ Order E. Bacon							
		27ᶜᵗˢ Iron.	6ᵈ					2.25

[*p. 128, 15 Sept. 1820:*]

	˙395.	Thomas Jefferson ℞ Mʳˢ Randolph							
		1¼ yd Lustring 6/. 4 yds Riband 1/. 1 ℔							
		G. Salts 1/6						2.17

[*p. 130, 21 Sept. 1820:*]

	˙395.	Thomas Jefferson ℞ Order E. Bacon							
		15¼ ℔s, Iron plough plates	9 cts					1.38

[*p. 131, 22 Sept. 1820:*]

	˙395.	Thomas Jefferson Dʳ							
		paid for Waggoning Tin & Sheet Iron							
		from Richmond			2	63		

[*p. 132, 26 Sept. 1820:*]

	˙395.	Thomas Jefferson ℞ Overseer of T. J.							
		Randolphs							
		4 ℔s. 12ᵈ Cut Nails	1/.					67

[*p. 132, 26 Sept. 1820:*]

	˙395.	Thomas Jefferson ℞ Mʳˢ Randolph							
		6 yds white Marsielles 4/6. 7 yds white							
		Flannel 5/3			10	63		
		2 hanks Silk. 6ᵈ. 2 pr. Worsted Stockings						
		9/.			3	08		
						08⁶	13.79

[p. 135, 30 Sept. 1820:]

	˙395.	Thomas Jefferson ⅌ Order					
		½ doz Wine Glasses (Cut) 27/. ½ doz do					
		long Stem 30/.			4	75	
		2 bottles Mustard	1/6			50	5.25

[p. 139, 7 Oct. 1820:]

˙44.	˙395.	Thomas Jefferson D^r to Cash					
		paid Carriage of a bundle W^t 32 ℔s					
		@ 4/6 ⅌ Cwt from Richm^d				25	

[p. 140, 10 Oct. 1820:]

	˙395.	Thomas Jefferson ⅌ Order					
		28½ lbs Iron	6^d				2.38

[p. 141, 11 Oct. 1820:]

	˙395.	Thomas Jefferson ⅌ Order					
		10 ℔s. 10^d Wrought Nails	1/1½				1.88

[p. 141, 12 Oct. 1820:]

	˙395.	Thomas Jefferson					
		D^r to Sundries ⅌ Order					
		Merchandise for 2 ℔s Copperas 9^d. 1 ℔					
		Alum 1/6				50	50

[p. 148, 25 Oct. 1820:]

	˙395.	Thomas Jefferson ⅌ Order					
		10^{lb} 10^d Cut Nails 1/. 2 Ozs. Nutmegs 3/.			2	67	
		2 Best double bolted padlocks 7/6. 1^{lb}					
		Allspice 3/.			3		
˙460.		Bramham & Jones for 2 Ozs Cloves 1/6.				50	6.17

[p. 148, 25 Oct. 1820:]

	˙395.	Thomas Jefferson ⅌ Self					
		1 Co. Neilsons Greek Exercises	$2				2

[p. 149, 28 Oct. 1820:]

	˙395.	Thomas Jefferson ⅌ Order					
		4½ yds blue forest Cloth @ 7/6. 1¾ yd					
		Brown Holland 3/.					6.51

		8 hanks thread 3^{cts} 1½ doz buttons 1/6. 4^{lbs} Putty 1/.					1.29[7]

[*p. 150, 30 Oct. 1820:*]

	˙395.	Thomas Jefferson ⅌ Order					
		15 yds Blue forest Cloth 7/6 3 yds Brown Holland 2/6		20			
		2 yds Green Baize 6/. 16 hanks thread 2^d. 2 Sticks Twist 6^d		2	62		
		3 doz Plated Buttons	3/.	1	50		24.12

[*p. 153, 4 Nov. 1820:*]

	˙395.	Thomas Jefferson ⅌ Order				
		1 yd green baize 6/. 1 yd Blue plains 7/6	2	25		
		1 doz small buttons 1/6. 1 Slip thread 1/6		50		2.75

[*p. 156, 7 Nov. 1820:*]

	˙395.	Thomas Jefferson ⅌ Order				
		4^{lbs} 10^d wrought nails	1/1½			75

[*p. 160, 10 Nov. 1820:*]

	˙395.	Thomas Jefferson ⅌ Order E. Bacon				
		20^{lbs} 10^d wrought Nails 1/1½. 15^{lbs} 16^d do 1/–				6.25

[*p. 163, 16 Nov. 1820:*]

	˙395.	Thomas Jefferson ⅌ Mrs Randolph				
		1½ yd Spotted Bambazette 7/6. 2 papers pins 1/6		2	38	
		2 pairs black worsted Stockings	7/6	2	50	4.88

[*p. 171, 4 Dec. 1820:*]

	˙395.	Thomas Jefferson ⅌ Joe				
		13 ℔s German Steel 1/6. 2½ Gallons A. Brandy ⅌ Order 6/–				5.75

[*p. 176, 13 Dec. 1820:*]

	˙395.	Thomas Jefferson ⅌ Order E Bacon				
		1 Sack Salt	$7			7.—

[p. 179, 18 Dec. 1820:]

˙395.	Thomas Jefferson ⅌ Order E Bacon						
	51ˡᵇˢ Bar Iron 6ᵈ. 1 Sack Salt ⅌ Order $7						11.25

[p. 182, 23 Dec. 1820:]

˙395.	Thomas Jefferson ⅌ Self					
	3 yds fine white flannel	6/.	3			
	½ " Olive velvet 6/– 1 Ream letter					
	paper	$6	6	50		
	4 quires fine writing paper	2/–	1	34		
	1 Almanac 9ᵈ					13⁸
	6 Silver wired tooth Brushes	2/.	2			12.84

[p. 184, 27 Dec. 1820:]

˙395.	Thomas Jefferson ⅌ Order					
	7⅛ gallons of French Brandy	15/–				17.81

[p. 187, 2 Jan. 1821:]

˙395.	Thomas Jefferson ⅌ Order					
	24 large striped Blankets 17/– 2					
	ditto	13/6	72	50		
	460 yds Ticklenburg @ 30ᶜᵗˢ 55 yds					
	Hempen Linen 25ᶜᵗˢ		151	75		
	2 ⅌s. each⁹ 21 yds No 3. Kendal					
	Cotton	3/9	26	25		
	4 papers needles 1/– 6ˡᵇ Oznaburg thread					
	7/6		8	17		
	135 yds Blue plains 5/3. 1 Bunch plough					
	lines 1/–		118	30		
	23 " White Kerseys	6/.	23			399.97

[p. 188, 2 Jan. 1821:]

˙395.	Thomas Jefferson ⅌ Order					
	2½ Bushels Salt 9/– 6 Bottles Mustard					
	1/6					5.25

[p. 189, 5 Jan. 1821:]

˙395.	Thomas Jefferson ⅌ Order T J Ran					
	7ˡᵇˢ 20ᵈ Cut nails	10ᵈ				97

[*p. 190, 8 Jan. 1821:*]

	˙395.	Thomas Jefferson ℔ Order E Bacon					
		1¼ galls. whiskey	4/6				94

[*p. 191, 11 Jan. 1821:*]

	˙395.	Thomas Jefferson ℔ Order					
		3 yds steam loom shirting 3/9. 1^{lb} Powder					
		5/3. 4^{lbs} Shot 1/–					3.42

[*p. 192, 15 Jan. 1821:*]

	˙395.	Thomas Jefferson ℔ Order E Bacon					
		20^{lbs} 10^d Cut nails 1/– 6^{lbs} 20^d wrought do					
		18^{cts}					4.41

[*p. 194, 22 Jan. 1821:*]

	˙395.	Thomas Jefferson ℔ Order					
		120^{lbs} Iron	6^d				10

[*p. 195, 23 Jan. 1821:*]

	˙395.	Thomas Jefferson ℔ Self					
		5 Ozs Wafers 3/– 3. 6/4 Blue Cloth 13/6			9	25	
		3 slips thread 1/6. 3 doz gilt Buttons 3/			2	25	
		9 yds Blue plains 5/3. 4^{lbs} Shot 1/–			8	55	
		1^{lbs} Powder	5/3			88	20.93

[*p. 196, 26 Jan. 1821:*]

	˙395.	Thomas Jefferson ℔ Order					
		1 Sack salt $7. 1^{lb} Saltpetre 4/6					7.75

[*p. 197, 27 Jan. 1821:*]

	˙395.	Thomas Jefferson ℔ Order					
		2 yds fine white flannel	5/3				1.75

[*p. 199, 2 Feb. 1821:*]

	˙395.	Thomas Jefferson ℔ Order					
		6 yds 6/4 Blue cloth 13/6. 1 Slip thread					
		1/6			13	75	
		2 doz buttons 1/6. 3 doz plated Buttons					
		2/3			1	63	15.38

[*p. 200, 5 Feb. 1821:*]

˙395.	Thomas Jefferson ℔ Edm^d Bacon					
	3 Cross cut saw files 2/. 3 Handsaw do 1/.					1.50

[*p. 203, 7 Feb. 1821:*]

˙395.	Thomas Jefferson ℔ Order					
	20^lbs 8^d Cut nails	1/.				3.34

[*p. 204, 9 Feb. 1821:*]

˙395.	Thomas Jefferson ℔ Mr Colclaser					
	2 ℔s Tape 1/6. 1 Hank thread 1/6			75		
	3 Skeins thread 3^d 1¼ yd Ticklenburgs 2/3			58		1.33

[*p. 207, 20 Feb. 1821:*]

˙395.	Thomas Jefferson ℔ Order E. Bacon					
	95^lb Iron 6^d 5^lbs German Steel 1/6					9.17

[*p. 208, 21 Feb. 1821:*]

˙395.	Thomas Jefferson ℔ Order					
	30^lbs 20^d Cut nails	10^d				4.17

[*p. 209, 28 Feb. 1821:*]

˙395.	Thomas Jefferson ℔ Order					
	9^lb Putty 1/. 1 Clamp Brush 5/3					1.38[10]

The Leitch Daybook in ViU, Leitch's bookkeeping methods and frequently used abbreviations, and the methods by which the Editors present the above extracts detailing entries involving TJ are described above at 6 Mar. 1820 in an editorial note on Extracts from James Leitch's Daybook.

BULLET BUTTONS: two- and three-piece brass buttons spherical in shape (Stanley J. Olsen, "Dating Early Plain Buttons by Their Form," *American Antiquity* 28 [1963]: 552; Martin A. Wyckoff, *United States Military Buttons of the Land Services, 1787–1902* [1984]: xix, 64). BURRELL: probably Burwell Colbert. LUSTRING: "lutestring." G. SALTS: "Glauber's salts." FOREST CLOTH is a woolen fabric (*OED*). BAMBAZETTE: "bombazine." A. BRANDY is probably apple brandy.

[1] Manuscript: "Slk."
[2] Manuscript: "397," here and in next entry.
[3] Preceding line written as part of running head at top of page.
[4] Preceding line written as part of running head at top of page.
[5] Number interlined, with total reworked from "7.25."
[6] Number interlined.
[7] To the left of this amount is interlined "7.80."
[8] Line interlined.
[9] Word interlined.
[10] The correct amount is $2.38.

From Edward Postlethwayt Page

To the venerable Thomas Jefferson:,
whom I and other fools did whilom[1]
contemptuously brand as the sage of
Monticello.

Father!   [by 3 June 1820]

   Conscious of the injustice I have done you by the influence of priest craft my judgment having been misled—I do sincerely recant. I was, when <u>12</u> a midshipman on board the <u>Leviathan</u> 74 in the West Indies.—Afterwards I was a Lieut^t in H.B.M. <u>12</u>th reg^t in India— But the liver complaint & Mercury in excess for 3 years drove me to Eng^d. Thence, after being accepted as a missionary to Africa & the East by the Episcopal society in London—my nervous system being greatly impaired & unfitting me for the requisite study—I came to America just after the Chesapeake was fired into designing to proceed to India at my own expence & act independent of Societies.—I hid myself in Little York Pennsyl^a with an Irishman Henry Coxe a Quaker—& have travelled much & been very unsteady as to residence, all over the United States, teaching school every now & then—I had always been very prudent with my property till I came to Ohio—but here in a few months I have lost 3000 dollars at least by all of a sudden becoming infatuated & a speculator—& withal—I e'en thought to be possessed of half a silver-mine being duped[2] by another Englishman who played me a yankee trick—Suddenly, my neighbour D^r McIntosh, the only man acquainted with divine Urim & Thummim that ever seceded from the Slave mason lodge developed to me (who never was one) their error about 3 months ago—Since I addressed you on the same subject 10 thousand other arguments to verify the number 12 as the standard measure of the true spiritual Temple have broke upon my mind & 3 days since I found that the[3] Magic <u>circle</u> of <u>circles</u> & Square of Squares discovered by Dr Franklin had their <u>then</u> <u>latent</u> but now to me at least evident correspondency & connexion with the seven attributes of Jehovah & the 5 of man—for when the whole world of men shall harmonize & become subject to such a government as that of the slave masons (oaths excepted) then the whole aggregate is Jehovah's agent or <u>hand</u> & divine magic shall be fully restored—& there will be the Saviour found.—Sir I have seen a 3 headed monster in Bombay harbour on the Isle of Elephanta when I went there with my uncle (then a Member of the B-bay Council) to dine in the Cave of which history is as much in ignorance as of the Mounds & fortifications here—about him were Covra Capells or <u>hooded</u> snakes Genl Putnam[4] says that the rattle, black & copper head snakes he has seen in <u>one</u> hole coiled up <u>together</u> in winter quarters—Sir in Europe King-craft was a viper <u>blind</u>—here is become a <u>rattle</u> snake—priest craft is a black snake & Slave oath[5] masonry a copper headed Sodomite loving strange flesh & you never see a woman in the hellish lodge the infamous Babylon the mother of all spiritual[6] whoredom & thraldom—The Jew is Adam Slave mason Eve—Selfishness the forbidden fruit—Every abomination has been hatched in that detestable sink of perdition— By masons Kings have reigned & Priests decreed injustice—Popery, Slavery, death, hell itself was begotten here in this Magic lanthorn of sorcery where you may behold the imp inverted till I and McIntosh reflect him upon Belshazzar's wall—See Daniel 5th Chapter—See also Ezekiel 8, 9, 10 chapt. See Esther—See <u>in</u> <u>the Allegory</u> all scripture We totally contradict Emanuel Swedenborg as it respects hell[7]— he was among monarchs and had no divine Urim & Thummim key wherewith[8] to unlock the temple—he knew no virtue in Numbers associated with letters & the planets & stars.—Sir—I beseech you to regard me—You have one foot in the grave—Your worldly cares are over—You partly penned & you signed the little book John in the Apocalypse ate, viz our precious <u>leaven</u> the Constitution—Sir—I predicted 2 months ago that not a monarch would exist in Europe (Emperor of Russia perhaps excepted) by the 7th of next Jan[y] certainly not by the 7th of the year ensuin[g] that—& in[9] 1826 we, in North Ameri[ca] would have neither President Senate nor Congress—but simply the regulations of Masonry oaths excepted—That this year commences the day of judgment[10]—that <u>all</u> are finally saved—not any one damned to all eternity that the Mexican Indians in their astronomy <u>13</u> must scalp our pride—that we must drink tea in the hieroglyphic temple of China (80,000 characters) that the North & South poles are open & some Dragon or wonder there—that we must have all things in common & resemble patriarchal & Indian simplicity & love—that God <u>is</u> <u>Love</u>.—<u>equity</u>—<u>truth</u>, and all <u>Scripture</u> is <u>true</u>. that the book of Nature is the greatest of all books—and rightly to associate the arts and sciences and history & Nations & all things in one aggregate pile for holy blazing[11] is to perform miracles—and restore Divine Magic and raise our fathers from the dead—And Sir I call upon you in the name of suffering humanity to send me forthwith every thing in your power relative to numbers and association of them in Magical form & immediately to penetrate into these things & cease not—for it is life to the world—By their making merchandize of holy things, and their sorceries they have bewitched all the world to run after kings & black priests—feeding upon husks—The world must

[16]

be levelled—<u>All</u> <u>men</u> <u>are</u> <u>equal</u> says Eternal Truth—whether Black White or copper—Sir—All nations & this America too shall immediately become bankrupt—their <u>lice</u> is <u>money</u> (see about the plagues of Egypt)[12]—If encouraged I will deluge you with arguments—In all humility   EDWARD POSTLETHWAYT PAGE
alias, King David's Page
Alias,   EDWARD PUZZLEPATE PAGE

At the town of Marietta, <u>N</u>:<u>B</u>: Mary, mother of Jesus[13]
I had supposed (till I brought this to the office this[14] 3ᵈ of June) that all went free to you—and I rather think I should not have written it if I had been apprised of my mistake—It goes—& I know the Truth is with it I will not intrude upon you again without permission—Your silence will forbid me I regret to find that I am imposing upon you the expence of Postage

RC (DLC: TJ Papers, 217:38827–8); undated, with dated postscript; torn at seal; postscript oriented upside down to body of letter; addressed: "Thomas Jefferson Esqʳᵉ Late President of the U: States Montecello Virginia"; franked; postmarked Marietta, 7 June; endorsed by TJ as a letter of 3 June 1820 received nineteen days later and so recorded (with additional bracketed notation: "insane") in SJL.

The British warship *Leviathan* carried 74 guns. URIM & THUMMIM are Hebrew words, sometimes translated as "light" and "truth," which appear on a number of occasions in the Bible (Albert G. Mackey, *An Encyclopædia of Freemasonry* [1874], 848–9). Benjamin Franklin's description of the MAGIC CIRCLE OF CIRCLES & SQUARE OF SQUARES had first been published in 1767 (Franklin, *Papers*, 4:392–403). A magic circle, in this context, is "an arrangement of numbers in concentric circles with radial divisions, with arithmetical properties similar to those of the magic square" (*OED*). Cobras de capello

(COVRA CAPELLS) are particularly venomous snakes native to India and nearby countries (*OED*). The biblical story of Adam, Eve, the serpent, and the FORBIDDEN FRUIT is in Genesis 2–3. EMANUEL SWEDENBORG gives a detailed description of both heaven and hell in *De Cælo Et ejus Mirabilibus, et de Inferno, ex Auditis & Visis* (London, 1758).

The Aztecs (MEXICAN INDIANS) used a ritual calendar based on multiples of the number thirteen (Elizabeth Hill Boone, *Stories in Red and Black: Pictorial Histories of the Aztecs and Mixtecs* [2000], 39–41). TJ neither PARTLY PENNED nor SIGNED the United States Constitution. Saint John in the biblical Book of Revelation took a LITTLE BOOK "out of the angel's hand, and ate it up," finding it sweet in the mouth but bitter in the belly (10.8–10). In the Bible, the phrase GOD IS LOVE appears in 1 John 4.8, 16, while the story of the prodigal son reduced to FEEDING UPON HUSKS usually given to swine is in Luke 15.16. ALL MEN ARE EQUAL is a variant of a phrase in the Declaration of Independence (*PTJ*, 1:413–33, quote on

p. 429). LICE (or gnats), one of the biblical PLAGUES OF EGYPT, appear in Exodus 8.16–8. ƎʇⱯꓭꓣZZⴖd (puzzlepate): "A puzzle-headed person; a person confused in his or her mind or ideas" (*OED*). Marietta, Ohio, was named after the French queen Marie Antoinette, not MARY, MOTHER OF JESUS.

[1] Manuscript: "whilon."
[2] Manuscript: "dupeed."
[3] Page here canceled "little."
[4] Manuscript: "Putnan."
[5] Word interlined.
[6] Word interlined.
[7] Preceding four words interlined.

[8] Unmatched opening single quotation mark preceding this word editorially omitted.
[9] Word interlined in place of "by."
[10] Unmatched closing single quotation mark editorially omitted.
[11] Preceding two words interlined in place of "burning."
[12] Omitted closing parenthesis editorially supplied.
[13] Text in graphic above this line reads "King   Priest   Mason" and "Holy   Spirit   Father   Son."
[14] Unmatched opening parenthesis preceding this word editorially omitted.

Promissory Note from Thomas Jefferson Randolph and Thomas Jefferson to John Neilson

$900‖

On or before the first day of August one thousand eight hundred & twenty one we promise to pay to John Nelson of the county of Albemarle the sum of nine hundred dollars with legal interest thereon from the date hereof for the true payment of which we[1] bind ourselves our heirs executors & administrators. Witness our hand and seal, this sixth day of June one thousand eight hundred & twenty

TH J RANDOLPH   (seal)

TH: JEFFERSON   (seal)

MS (Mrs. A. Slater Lamond, Alexandria, 1976; photocopy in ViU: TJP); in Randolph's hand, signed by Randolph and TJ; with 7 Mar. 1823 receipt on verso, in Randolph's hand, signed by Neilson (edge trimmed): "Recieved from Th J Randolph two hundre[d] dollars on account of the within bond."

This note apparently replaced one that TJ had sent Neilson six days previously. The earlier note was for $843.50, stipulated two years for repayment, and probably listed only TJ as Neilson's debtor (*MB*, 2:1365; TJ to Neilson, 31 May 1820).

[1] Manuscript: "be."

From Arthur S. Brockenbrough

DEAR SIR,   University June 7th 1820

I am sorry I was out of place yesterday when you were here, as I wished to see and take your, wishes & opinion on several subjects, Viz. 1st On the propriety of substituting tin gutters for Wood over the

Dormitories & Flat roofed Pavilions—it takes 26 Feet of gutter to go over the dormitory & that at about 25 cents p^r foot for Materials & workmanship will cost $6.50 for each gutter—a box of tin will make 8 gutters which at 15 $ ℔ box will be say $2. for the tin necessary for each gutter, the workmanship for puting in the same 1$ more p^r gutter all other work preparing, will not be more than $2.34—makg in all $ 5.34 the cost of each tin gutter for the dormitories—1. D. 16 C. less than the wooden gutter—Tin under the floor will in all probability last longer than the wood, & may be so laped or sodered as to prevent leaks—2nd Subject, do you wish the ornaments for the metop layed down by Nicholson put in the Frize of Pavilion N° 2 E. Range—3^d Would not the Cornice & Entablature of the Pavilions look better to be of a stone colour than perfectly white?—4th the expence of Hotel windows[1] may be very considerably reduced by substituting 10 by 12 Glass for 12 by 12—the first will cost p^r light 25 cents including Glass & 2 coat puntey the 2nd about 55 cents p^r light—5th I send you a small peice of marble brought from Philadelphia by G. Raggi, would it not be well to enquire what it can be had for per foot in Philadelphia, also the freight of it to Richmond? M. Raggi complains much of this stone—6th The Mr Raggis will be looking in a short time for their families, and are frequently at me to have a small house put up for each one, must I do so? I would adopt the cheapest possible plan for them—Our pipe borers are laying down the logs they are down for 300 yards—I have conveyed it 300 yards in a covered ditch at the end of which is a reservoir, 6 by 7 feet & 5 feet deep from whence I take the water—the contract for brick work is made at 10$ for common & place bricks 16$ for the front or rubed stretchers—C. Carter has Pav: N° 3 & Hotel **A**—Perry & Thorn Pav: N° 4 & Hotel **B**—W. Phillips Pav: N° 5 & Hotel **C**—& the dormitories divided amongst them—in haste

I am Sir respectfully
your Ob^t sev^t

A. S. BROCKENBROUGH

RC (ViU: TJP-PP); between dateline and salutation: "Thomas Jefferson Esqr"; endorsed by TJ as received 14 June 1820 and so recorded in SJL.

PAVILION N° 2 E. RANGE at the University of Virginia was later redesignated as Pavilion IV.

PLACE BRICKS were "made of soft clay, and laid on a prepared surface to harden before being burnt." FRONT bricks were used for the fronts of buildings. Rubbed (RUBED) brick is "a soft clay brick with a smooth polished surface, chiefly used for ornamental and high-quality brickwork" (*OED*).

Pavilions N° 3, N° 4, and N° 5 were later redesignated as pavilions VI, VIII, and X, respectively. The East Range hotels in question later became known as hotels B, D, and F, respectively.

[1] Word interlined.

To Patrick Gibson

DEAR SIR   June 7. 20.

Your favor of the 2ᵈ inst. came to hand yesterday and I percieve that the sale of the last hhd of tob° 79.05 with the balance of 400.81 D stated in yours of May 16. enables me to request you to remit to mr Vaughan the sum of 444.D. this sum will answer a particular portion of the objects of my letters of Apr. 23. and May 12., which I wish to be expedited, and I shall shortly be able to make him the additional remittance for the other objects proposed. I salute you with friendship and respect.   TH: JEFFERSON

PoC (DLC); on verso of reused address cover of James H. McCulloch to TJ, 6 Dec. 1819; at foot of text: "Mʳ Gibson"; endorsed by TJ.

Gibson's letter to TJ OF MAY 16, not found, is noted at TJ to Gibson, 22 May 1820.

Benjamin J. Barbour's Account of a Visit to the University of Virginia and Monticello

DEAR TOM   Barboursville June 8ᵗʰ 1820

Your last letter I received just as I was leaving Winʳ and owing to my being busy there, and since my arrival, I have failed to answer it. I visited Charloˡˡᵉ for the purpose of seeing the University, and had expected to have the pleasure of seeing you, but as you will testify, was dissappointed, the buildings however I saw, and felt much pleased with; as to the design there is something truly beautiful, and somewhat grand; the effect produced on every friend to literature and his state must of course be pleasing; — the elegant edefices crowning our hills and associating with them the idea of their being as a mighty fountain from which thousands will drink knowledge, is sufficient to excite the deepest interest.

I then paid my first visit to the <u>sage of the mountain</u> but he was from home, and I enjoyed but a poor view of the curiosities of his house, so much so that I shall go again. The old fellow has something of design in fixing his seat on that mountain, for illustrious as he is now, and dying covered with fame as having been the chief architect in this beautiful temple of liberty, his tomb will in after ages be as eagerly sought after by the classic and patriotic as was ever the holy sepulchre of Jerusalem by the deluded pilgrim, riding up the other

[20]

day, and suffering my imagination[1] to fly beyond the swiftness of time, glancing my eye over a neglected tomb stone, persuading myself that I was viewing the grave of Jefferson, some centuries hence, I felt myself inspired with a holy reverence.

MS (ViHi: Barbour Family Papers); consisting of a letter in Barbour's hand addressed to an unidentified correspondent; apparently unfinished, given lack of signature and abrupt end in the middle of a page.

Benjamin Johnson Barbour (1802–20), the son of TJ's correspondent and United States senator James Barbour, died at the family's Barboursville estate less than a month after dating the above letter. His obituary describes him as possessing a "sincere, liberal and honorable heart" and a "fine native capacity, cultivated and expanding under an assiduous application to literary and scientific pursuits." A brother of the same name, born just under a year after Barbour's death, was rector of the University of Virginia, 1866–72 (Barbour to Lucy M. Barbour, Winchester, 27 June 1819, 29 Feb. 1820 [ViHi: Barbour Family Papers]; *Richmond Enquirer*, 11 July 1820; "Elegy on the Death of Benjamin Johnson Barbour" by "Condolius," Washington *Daily National Intelligencer*, 9 Aug. 1820; gravestone inscription in family cemetery at Barboursville; *DVB*, 1:328–31).

WIN[R]: Winchester. The Church of the HOLY SEPULCHRE in Jerusalem is believed by many Christians to be located on the site of Jesus's crucifixion and resurrection.

[1] Manuscript: "imgination."

From George S. Gibson
(for Patrick Gibson)

Sir   Richmond 10th June 1820

Since mine of the 2nd Inst[l] I have received on your acc[t] 5 Bbls Flour from M[r] Cradock & a promise of 15 more;—The market price is now from $3\frac{7}{8}$ to 4\$ I am

    Yours Respectfully   Patrick Gibson
                                     P[R] George S Gibson

RC (DLC); entirely in George S. Gibson's hand; endorsed by TJ as a letter from Patrick Gibson received 16 June 1820 and so recorded in SJL. RC (DLC); address cover only; with PoC of TJ to John H. James, 7 July 1820, on verso; addressed in a clerk's hand: "Thomas Jefferson Esquire Monticello," with "Milton" added in another hand; franked; postmarked Richmond, 10 June.

[1] Reworked from "Ult."

From John Quincy Adams

SIR,   Department of State, Washington, 12. June, 1820.

By a Resolution of Congress, of the 19th of January last, the Secretary of State has been instructed to furnish each College and University in the United States with one copy of the Journal of the Federal Convention, recently printed by Order of Congress. Being uncertain whether a selection of a Principal or President has been made for the Virginia University, I beg leave to confide the copy of the Journal intended for that Seminary to your friendly care, and will be indebted to your kindness for placing the Volume in such a situation, that it may, either immediately or ultimately, become appertinent to the Library of the University: And, at the same time, I have the pleasure of transmitting to you a copy of the Journal for yourself.

I have the honour to be, very respectfully,

sir, your most humble and obedient servant—

JOHN QUINCY ADAMS.

RC (DLC); in a clerk's hand, signed by Adams; at foot of text: "Thomas Jefferson, Esqr"; endorsed by TJ as received 18 June 1820 but recorded in SJL as received a day earlier. FC (Lb in DNA: RG 59, DL); at head of text: "Thomas Jefferson Esquire Milton. Virginia." Enclosure: two copies of the *Journal, Acts and Proceedings, of the Convention, assembled at* *Philadelphia . . . 1787, which formed the Constitution of the United States* (Boston, 1819; Poor, *Jefferson's Library*, 11 [no. 647]).

APPERTINENT is a variant of "appurtenant" that is "used especially in the non-legal sense," meaning appertaining or "properly belonging or relating" (*OED*).

From John Wayles Eppes

DEAR SIR,   Buckingham Near Raines Tavern June 12th 1820.

Since my visit to Monticello I have written to you frequently and although I do not know it I presume of course some of my letters have been received. My anxiety about Francis induces me again to write to you—He is now advancing to an age when the only controul which either of us can exercise over him must depend on his own feelings. From every thing I hear I conclude with certainty that the University will not be in operation in time for him—The question often presents itself to my[1] mind where shall we send him after the present year?—If it was possible for him to complete his Education within the limits of Virginia I should greatly prefer it.

The sentiments I entertain on this subject are perhaps illiberal and many of them founded on prejudice. I have however a decided preference for the Virginia character and principles. All the science in the world would not to me as a parent compensate the loss of that open, manly, character which Virginians possess and in which the most liberal and enlightened of the Eastern people are deplorably deficient. I have known many of their conspicuous men intimately, and I have never yet seen one who could march directly to his object. Some view at home or at the seat of Government entered all their projects & subjected them continually to the commission of acts which would tinge with shame the face of a Virginian. So far too as my observation has extended many of those who have been educated at Yale have embibed enough of the Eastern leven to destroy the confidence which under other circumstances would be justly due to their Talents. Your means of information are superior to mine—Perhaps (on this subject) to those of any other man in the United States. Will you be so good as to turn your attention in due time to this subject and inform me to what place I had better send Francis the next year—

I have heard whether correctly or not that you have been unfortunate with Colo: Nicholas and will probably have to dispose of Negroes for the purpose of meeting his debt—It has occurred to me if such should be the fact that it would probably be in my power to propose to you an arrangement which might be acceptable to yourself & at the same time an accomodation to me—I have at this place a very large body of woodland to open and it would suit me very well to exchange United States bank Stock for Negroe men—Say 12. for which I would either give their valuation in stock or such price as we might agree on—I would employ them here a couple of years and afterwards send them to Bedford to Francis's land there—The stock I expect would be as acceptable to the United States Bank as the cash. at any rate it can be converted into cash—The Negroes if drawn from Bedford would in fact only be in the same situation as if hired to me for a couple of years after which they would be returned to their connections in Bedford together with such as I can add to them. It was my intention as soon as an opportunity offered to exchange the Bank stock for labouring men. as I intend the Negroes for Francis, I thought if the information I had received was correct, it would be more agreeable to you to dispose of them in this way than to sell them to strangers, and much more for Francis's interest thus to acquire them—If you have no intention of selling you will I know pardon the liberty I have taken, and consider it as originating solely in the idea that the arrangement I have proposed might be a mutual accomodation to us and ultimately be advantageous to Francis—In the event of exchange it would suit my arrangements to take the Negroes at the end of the

[23]

year & the stock if you find it can be employed in the mode I have suggested will be immediately at your service.

Francis in his last letter mentions having left Laporte with your approbation—I have stated to him in reply that any arrangement which meets your approbation will not be objected to by me. I enclosed him also a draft on Richmond to meet the expences attendant on his change of situation and to pay a small balance for 15. days board due Laporte.

With sincere affection & respect I am yours.

JNO: W: EPPES

RC (Mrs. Francis Eppes Shine, Los Angeles, 1946; photocopy in ViU: TJP); addressed: "Thomas Jefferson Esq' Monticello Near Charlottesville Vᵃ"; endorsed by TJ as received 22 June 1820 and so recorded in SJL.

Elizabeth Trist wrote her grandson Nicholas P. Trist from Monticello on 15 June 1820 that the debt arising out of TJ's decision to act as security for Wilson Cary NICHOLAS "will be a serious injury to him," with the annual interest alone amounting to $1,250. After describing Nicholas's conduct as "abominable," she lamented that to meet the obligation TJ's "land in poplar Forest and Negroes must be sacrafised for our friend has never any thing before hand; an expensive establishment to support." Further on in the letter she reported that "Mʳ Jefferson thinks the Banking System has been the ruin of this Country" (RC in DLC: NPT).

[1] Manuscript: "my my."

From James Gibbon

SIR   Custom House Richmond June 12. 1820

The inclos'd came to my hand only a few minutees since—the vessall in which the package of seed, is said to be, is now at Wowick having enterd here early in the last week in ballast—on examineg her manifest, I find no such box: this the Capᵗ may have omitted as I have & shall retain the bill of loading which was within the letter & shall send on board the vessall for the purpose of having it forwarded according to Mʳ Beasleys desire if on board—   Im Sir

very Respᶜ Yo Mᵒ Ob   J GIBBON
                               Collᶜ

RC (DLC); endorsed by TJ as received 16 June 1820 and so recorded in SJL. RC (DLC); address cover only; with PoC of TJ to Peter S. Du Ponceau, 7 July 1820, on verso; addressed: "Thᵒ Jefferson Esqᵉ Monticello near Charotts Ville"; franked; postmarked Richmond, 12 June. Enclosure: Reuben G. Beasley to the Customs Collector at City Point or Norfolk, American Consulate, Le Havre, 25 Mar. 1820, which reads "Be pleased to receive and to forward the small Box 'for which you have Bill Lading' herewith for mʳ Jefferson which contains seeds from the Royal Garden of Plants in Paris. It is important that it get to hand early" (RC in DLC; addressed: "To the Collector of the Customs at City Point or Norfolk Vᵃ ℔

l'Agnes"; redirected in an unidentified hand to "the port of Richmond"; stamped; postmarked Hampton, 26 May, and Norfolk, 10 June; with possibly unrelated notation by Beasley on address leaf: "Havre, March 23rd 1820").

Warwick (WOWICK) was located on the James River about five miles below Richmond.

The BILL OF LOADING, which eventually found its way to TJ, stated that on 25 Mar. 1820 the shipmaster Dumont Pallier received from Beasley a shipment to be carried from Le Havre to Richmond on the brig *Agnes*, consisting of a box of seeds addressed to TJ at Monticello, with Pallier due to receive from the customs collector in Virginia a total of five francs for carriage from Paris and customhouse and shipping fees, plus fifty cents in freight charges (MS in MHi; printed form, with blanks filled in by an unidentified hand and signed by Pallier; in English).

To John Laval

SIR   Monticello June 12. 20

Being engaged at this time in reading Euripides the possession of Potter's translation is of much more importance now than at any future day. I must therefore relinquish the objection of price, and pray you to send me the copy you have, stated at 10.D. if well wrapped in strong paper, and each volum[e] singly, it will come safely by the mail, only observing an interval of 4. days between the transmission of the two volumes. I salute you with esteem and respect.

TH: JEFFERSON

P.S. the little Aeschylus was safely recieved.

PoC (DLC); on verso of reused address cover of James H. McCulloch to TJ, 23 Dec. 1819; edge trimmed; at foot of text: "Mr Laval"; endorsed by TJ.

From Opie Norris

DR SIR   Charlottesville 12 June 1820

Above you have a statement of your acct with the Charlottesville Female Academy, for rent last year—

The board of Stock holders will have a meeting in a few days, when, this acct will be Obliged to be rendered to the board, and if it is convenient for you to discharge it, before[1] the meeting of the board it will greatly Oblige

Your friend & Humble servt   O NORRIS. B.F.A.

RC (MHi); subjoined to enclosure; addressed: "Thomas Jefferson Esqe Montichello"; endorsed by TJ as received 14 June 1820 and so recorded in SJL; additional notation by TJ beneath endorsement: "June 29. pd by ord. for 36. D on

P. Gibson," with TJ's financial records indicating that the payment was "for my assumpsit of rent to Female academy for Stack's schoolhouse" (*MB*, 2:1365).

A group of local parents founded the CHARLOTTESVILLE FEMALE ACADEMY in 1819. As the building purchased for its use at the time of its establishment was needed in 1819–20 by Gerard E. Stack for the Charlottesville Academy and by Peter Laporte for his boardinghouse, during that period classes for the girls' school were held instead in a structure located on the corner of Third and High streets. Courses were taught in English grammar,

reading, composition, geography, history, astronomy, and arithmetic. French and music lessons could also be obtained for an additional charge. The school's STOCK HOLDERS included TJ's correspondents Alexander Garrett, James Leitch, and John Winn. The institution was active well into the 1820s (John Hammond Moore, *Albemarle: Jefferson's County, 1727–1976* [1976; repr. 1986], 102–3; TJ to John H. Cocke, 3 May 1819; Washington *Daily National Intelligencer*, 10 Jan. 1821).

A missing letter from TJ to Norris of 15 June 1820 is recorded in SJL.

[1] Manuscript: "befor."

Account with Charlottesville Female Academy

[ca. 12 June 1820]

M[r] Tho[s] Jefferson

In acct with Female Academy

1819
Dec[r] 25 To 7 Mo rent of the Office belonging to the said ⎱ $35.00
    Academy at the rate of 60$ ℔ annum— ⎰
    Int on the same from 1 Jan[y] till 1 June   85
                                       $35.85

MS (MHi); in Opie Norris's hand; undated; with covering letter subjoined.

From John H. James

SIRE   Cincinnati 13th June 1820

You will no doubt be much surprized at being addressed by one totally unknown to you—It was with reluctance that I prevailed on myself to take this step, as I feared and do still fear that it can be viewed in no other aspect than that of an intrusion on your retirement and leisure. Be assured Sire, it is not to gratify the vanity of a young man that incites me to address one so distinguished as yourself, but the humble desire of acquiring knowledge for which I knew not elsewhere to apply—

For a year past I have been engaged at intervals in collecting materials and composing memoirs of Kosciusko. My success has not been commensurate with my desires. Notwithstanding all my exertions, I have been unable to discover in the American Histories & Journals any thing of value or interest relative to his services in this country.[1] Disappointed in my first exertion I was near abandoning it altogether— It however occurred to me that[2] many valuable and interesting facts might possibly be obtained from individuals,[3] which if not collected now, would in a few years be entirely lost. Several hints gleaned from newspapers and conversations have induced me to believe that you were personally acquainted with Kosciusko. I have therefore made my first and principal application to you, in hopes that you would be able to furnish some facts with regard to him or to direct me to other sources of information—

The amount of the information I possess relative to that part of his life spent in America is this. That he arrived in America about the commencement of the revolution, volunteered his services to Genl Washington and received a Colonel's commission: and that after the conclusion of the war he returned to France with Fayette. That after his liberation by the Emperour Paul, he made a second voyage to America and after a short sojourn returned again to Europe—

The points on which I solicit information are these 1. the year and place of his first arrival in America. 2. In what section of the country he was employed during the war—in what battles he fought—and in what year and from what place he took his departure for Europe— 3. In what year he landed in America the second time—how received— and at what time and from what port he took his passage on returning to Europe—

These are points on which I have no information whatever. I have looked the American Histories over in vain to receive some account of his services—Judge Marshall as well as I recollect does not mention him once—Mrs Warren notices him very slightly—I think his memory has been treated with unmerited neglect.—indeed I am certain of it:—for all who speak of him say that he was serviceable to our cause.—and Dr Franklin declared in Paris that the Americans stood highly indebted to him for their independence.[4] And that man would never have made such a declaration had such not been the fact—

It is the consciousness[5] of this unjust neglect that urges me (weak as I am in abilities, poor in resources of intelligence and fettered by my studies) to attempt to put in practice that design so long conceived. If I succeed in collecting materials I shall at some future period present them to the public in the form of a Biography. And[6] should I be unable to compose a work capable of me[riting?] the rigid Critic's "Bene et Recte" at the least I can produce one that will be useful to the future Historian & Biographer—

Should it agree with your leisure, your pursuits, or what in this case must be more powerful your inclinations, to give me any information on the above points, or to direct me in making further applications, I shall esteem it a great favour as well as a condescension. And any additional anecdotes and facts will increase my obligations the more.— My thanks and my Gratitude will be but a poor recompense for your trouble: yet they are the only one I can make, which you can receive.[7] And those I can now only declare—tho believe me distance and length of time shall never make me cease to feel them—

I am Sire with the most profound Respect yours

JOHN H JAMES

RC (DLC); torn at seal; addressed: "Hon. Thomas Jefferson Monticello Va"; franked; postmarked Cincinnati, 15 June; endorsed by TJ as received 6 July 1820 and so recorded in SJL.

John Hough James (1800–81), attorney, businessman, and public official, was born in Virginia and moved with his family to Cincinnati in 1813. He matriculated at Cincinnati College (later the University of Cincinnati) when it was founded in 1819, and he graduated in 1821. Over the next four years, James tutored students at his alma mater, passed the bar, and established a law office. He relocated his legal practice permanently in 1826 to Urbana, Ohio, where he also served as a militia colonel, bank president, and railroad director. A political ally of William Henry Harrison and Henry Clay, James supported both internal improvements and, after 1836, the reestablishment of the Bank of the United States. He held a seat in the Ohio senate, 1835–39, and he helped found a Swedenborgian school, Urbana University, around 1850. James's net worth, much of it in real estate, was estimated to be

$267,500 in 1860 and $212,000 a decade later (William E. Smith and Ophia D. Smith, *A Buckeye Titan* [1953]; OOxM: James Papers; W. E. Halley and John P. Maynard, comps., *Legislative Manual of the State of Ohio, 1919–1920* [1920], 80, 82; DNA: RG 29, CS, Ohio, Urbana, 1830–80; gravestone inscription in Oak Dale Cemetery, Urbana).

FAYETTE: the marquis de Lafayette.

While James seems never to have published his research on Tadeusz Kosciuszko IN THE FORM OF A BIOGRAPHY, his "Life of Thaddeus Kosciusko," appended to his "Retrospective View of Poland," survives in manuscript (OhCiUAR).

BENE ET RECTE: "good and correct."

[1] Omitted period at right margin editorially supplied.

[2] Manuscript: "me that <*my*> me that."

[3] Manuscript: "indiviuals."

[4] Omitted period at right margin editorially supplied.

[5] Manuscript: "consciusness."

[6] Manuscript: "And And."

[7] Omitted period at right margin editorially supplied.

From Fernagus De Gelone

SIR.   N. York June 14. 1820

herein is an advertisement which I very respectfully beg you to look at. I should be proud to receive your advice on the Subject, and I would esteem myself peculiarly happy by being honored with your visit, if You come to this place—I had Just now the pleasure to receive two poor Boys. After few days, I Shall have Judged Their faculties.

I am most respectfully—Sir. Your very humble obedient Servant

FERNAGUS DE GELONE

30. Pine S^t

RC (MHi); endorsed by TJ as received 21 June 1820 and so recorded in SJL. RC (ViU: TJP); address cover only; with PoC of final page of TJ to Thomas Cooper, 4 July 1820, on verso; addressed: "Thomas Jefferson Esqr—Monticelo. Milton.—Virginia"; franked; inconsistently postmarked New York, 13 June.

The enclosed ADVERTISEMENT was probably that printed in the New York *Commercial Advertiser* from 12 to 20 June 1820 under the title "*Mutual Teaching of Languages, and of the Mechanical Arts. Foreign Book store, Library, etc.*" It reads "F. De Gelone, No. 30 Pine-street, New-York, invites his friends and the public to visit his apparatus, which is calculated to teach a language and the liberal arts to the Deaf and Dumb. The Latin, French and Spanish tongues are indispensable to Gentlemen. The French is spoken in all the Courts and by the trad-

ing class in Europe—treaties were written in that language for centuries past. This method of Teaching, which was imitated from the formal plan by Lancaster and Bell, extends to the study of Mathematics.—It may be applied to the practice of the Fine Arts, such as Drawing, Statuary, Sculpture, Engraving, and to that of the Mechanical Arts, as Turning, Carpentry, Joinery, Forging, Dorimartics, etc. Any sort of instruments shall be *thankfully* received, as they are for the use of the Poor.—Each utensil presented, shall be marked *City of New-York*, and *will be, of course, considered as its property*. Two poor boys of 10 years of age, shall be taught without any compensation. As there is a lady in the house, two young girls may also apply." "Dorimartics" is probably a typographical error for "Docimastics," a variant of "docimasy," the "art or practice of assaying metallic ores" (*OED*).

From Joseph Gilmore

SIR   [ca. 14 June 1820]

I made a trial the other morning to Raise The End of the house to Get it off the hurst floore and Raised it about 3 Inches with one prise with the weight of Twelve men on it all of which I suppose weighed about 1500 w with A prise of about 24 feet in length Giveing about 18 Inches power & I thought it quite Practicable to Raise it with about 4 more Prises of the same power provided that I had a Good Foundation to Raise on I think that Peirs of [Stone?] will do as time is scarce but I Think my first plan best of haveing a wall But I find time will not[1] admit of it I shoul be Glad to have the hands on monday morning to Get in the hurst & tell them to bring all the Spades they have to Clean out the pit to get in the Back Sill

RC (DLC: TJ Papers, 235:42108); undated, with conjectural date based on beginning of Gilmore's work repairing TJ's

mill; one word illegible; at head of text: "J Gilmore To Thos Jefferson"; addressed: "Mr Thos Jefferson Esqr Montocello";

endorsed by TJ: "Mill. power necessary to raise it."

Joseph Gilmore (d. 1821), boatman and millwright at Milton, may have served for a time as interim miller at TJ's Shadwell mills while Thomas Mann Randolph was away on military service during the War of 1812. He transported goods to and from Richmond for TJ from at least 1816 and, from 14 June to 23 Oct. 1820, worked for TJ, at a rate of $30 a month, repairing damage to TJ's mills caused by settling walls and sinking floors. Gilmore also rented a piece of land in Albemarle County from TJ during the last year of his life (TJ to Randolph, 14 Nov. 1813; Betts, *Farm Book*, pt. 1, p. 107; TJ to Patrick Gibson, 2 Jan. 1816; *MB*; TJ to Joel Yancey, 15 Aug. 1821; Woods, *Albemarle*, 401).

A HURST is the "frame of a pair of millstones," while a PRISE is a lever (*OED*).

[1] Word interlined.

From Samuel Garland

SIR   Lynchburg June 15th 1820

You have heard no doubt, that the Copartnership of Mess. A Robertson & C[o] was disolved on the 31st of August last—

Your bond to them on a divission of the debts &[a] has fallen to me in right of M[r] B Miller the foreign partner, all of whose debts at this place have been put into my hands as attorney for collection, I shall be happy to hear from you on this subject stating particularly when I may expect payment—my instructions are preremptory to close the collections with all dispatch—

Respectfully Yr. obt. St.   S, GARLAND

RC (MHi); endorsed by TJ as received 22 June 1820 from "E." Garland and so recorded (with initial corrected to "S.") in SJL. RC (MHi); address cover only; with PoC of TJ to Garland, 13 July 1820, on verso; addressed: "Thomas Jefferson esqr Monticello Charlottesville"; stamped; postmarked Lynchburg, 16 June.

Samuel Garland (1789–1861), attorney and plantation owner, was a native of Albemarle County who relocated by 1813 to Lynchburg, where he served in the county militia during the War of 1812 and established a legal practice. During his long and successful business career, he lived in a mansion on Garland Hill, supported railway expansion into the western part of the state, and was a founding trustee of the Lynchburg Manufacturing Company, which was incorporated in 1829 for the purpose of making fabric from cotton, flax, hemp, and wool. Although Garland owned relatively few slaves in Virginia, he deployed hundreds at three plantations he operated in the state of Mississippi during the latter part of his life. Virginia census records credit him with real estate worth $50,000 in 1850 and real estate and personal property valued at $27,000 a decade later. Estate inventories taken shortly after his death in Coahoma County, Mississippi, indicate that Garland's holdings there were worth far more than the latter figure (Woods, *Albemarle*, 199; DNA: RG 15, W1812PAFI; TJ to Archibald Robertson, 23 May 1815; S. Allen Chambers Jr., *Lynchburg: An Architectural History* [1981], 114; *Richmond Enquirer*, 30 Mar. 1832, 23 Oct. 1835; William Asbury Christian, *Lynchburg and Its People* [1900], 91–2; *Acts of Assembly* [1828–29 sess.], 118–9 [9 Feb. 1829]; DNA: RG 29, CS, Lynchburg,

1820, 1840–50, 1850 slave schedules, Campbell Co., 1860; Lynchburg Hustings and Corporation Court Will Book, E:65–7, 106–10; gravestone inscription in Presbyterian Cemetery, Lynchburg; *Southeastern Reporter* 4 [1887/88]: 334–9).

From Levett Harris

SIR,   Philadelphia 15. June 1820.

After having spent fourteen years of my life in the service of my Country, and having had so distinguished a share in the establishment of our relations with the Emperor of Russia, I returned to the US, under a full conviction of enjoying, as I felt I deserved, the countenance & confidence of my Government at home, as I had done abroad. But I had not been long here before I was apprized by Mr. Adams, Secretary of State, that he was in possession of certain reports which implicated my Consular character, and which he made known to me, as he stated, with friendly dispositions towards me, and with a view of enabling me to afford such explanations on the subject as I might think proper.

To this Communication I immediately replied, and I have good reason to know, that the explanations furnished were, at the time, satisfactory to every body, except perhaps Mr Adams; who, since his return from Europe, has evinced on my subject, an inexorable & an unceasing ill will, and which his credit has been employed to extend even beyond the limits of his department.

A Young man of the name of Lewis, almost a stranger to me, brother to an American trader established at St Petersburg, arrived here last Autumn, & uttered, in the Shape of anonymous handbills, which he clandestinely and industriously circulated, both here and at Washington, a new edition of the self Same calumnies, which had been previously reported to me by Mr Adams.

I immediately instituted a Suit against this libeller, and to the astonishment of every body here, did it soon afterwards appear, that he was upon a footing of intimacy, and of friendly correspondence with the Secretary of State; and that an union of feeling and of action existed between them on this occasion!

A conduct so extraordinary, and at the same time so unworthy, necessarily excited in me and my friends, the livliest indignation. It was deemed expedient however to remain silent on this discovery. Mr Adams, in his active determination to defeat all my supposed views of further advancement in the diplomatic service, having been led into the wildest indiscretions, I was encouraged to wait the Slow but certain issue of events, and especially of the law, in the Suit I had just commenced.

It is now ascertained that it may be of importance to me to proceed to Russia in order to collect evidence necessary to this prosecution. I have therefore resolved, and have deemed it an imperious duty, to lose no further time in making you fully known to the conduct observed towards me in this conjuncture, and to leave you ignorant of nothing, either as to the merits of the occurrence itself, or the machinations of my Enemies.

You will witness in these disclosures, the manner in which the honor of the Executive Government has been committed, and how the man, whom you protected Sir, in early life, and whose acts, far from having dishonored your Administration, are full of evidences to the Contrary, has recently been treated by one, who owes, I have it in my power to prove, a no inconsiderable share of his present credit, to my successful efforts in the public service.

As I am hence exceedingly anxious to have as early an interview with you, as it may be agreeable to you to honor me with, I shall repair to Monticello the moment I am apprized of the time, that it will be Suitable to you to receive me.

Mr Madison having had, as you know, a like interest in the course of my public life, and feeling also I flatter myself some concern for my future welfare I have deemed it due to him to address him a letter of a corresponding tenor with the present.

I am, with Sentiments of the most profound respect, Sir, Your most obedient & very humble Servant   LEVETT HARRIS.

RC (DLC); endorsed by TJ as received 21 June 1820 and so recorded in SJL. RC (ViU: TJP); address cover only; with first two pages of PoC of TJ to Thomas Cooper, 4 July 1820, on recto and verso; addressed: "Thomas Jefferson (late President of the United States) Monticello"; franked; postmarked Philadelphia, 16 June.

On 5 Mar. 1819 Secretary of State John Quincy Adams stated in his diary that the charges against Harris's CONSULAR CHARACTER amounted to "a case of corruption . . . so gross, that the only scruple I have ever had with regard to my own conduct, in relation to it—a doubt, whether I ought not to have reported it to the Government at the time, and broken off all friendly intercourse with him forever." Nearly a year later, on 20 Jan. 1820 Adams recorded the receipt of a letter from William D. LEWIS "mentioning that Levitt Harris had brought an action against him for defamation, and that a Rule of Court would issue to take my deposition in the cause—And he requests me to state in my deposition all the circumstances which I had related to him, in the conversation which I had with him at my house" (MHi: Adams Papers).

Harris's letter to James Madison OF A CORRESPONDING TENOR is also dated 15 June 1820 (Madison, *Papers, Retirement Ser.*, 2:68–9).

From Robert Mills

My dear Sir   Baltimore June 16. 1820

May I be permitted to present myself to your remembrance,—and in the first place enquire respectfully after your health?—It is now some years since I had the pleasure of seeing you, but have frequently had the satisfaction of hearing of your welfare—

The activity of your valuable life displays itself in the great work you are now engaged in, to found a seat of learning in the center of your native state—I trust that its success will exceed your most sanguine expectations, and that this institution will remain to future ages a monument of the wisdom & philanthropy of the mind that projected and has carried it into execution—May this institution be famed for the correctness of its principles, as well in morals as physicks, and the light of its knowledge spread its influence thro'out our country—

Since your kindness first directed me in my professional pursuits, I have been aiming to advance as far as lay in my power the interests of my country in the useful arts—For the sixteen years that I have been in the exercise of my profession, both as an Engineer & Architect, I have (thank God) been scarcely a moment idle—Since I removed to Baltimore (where I was invited to put my design for the Washington Monument into execution) I have been engaged in various public works especially in the Engineering department.—Being under the impression from the circumstance of the disposition of our people, and the local situation of our country that a better prospect opened for the encouragement of the Engineer than the Architect, I have since my engagements in the Delaware & Chesapeake Canal with Mr Latrobe, turned my studies & practice particularly to this branch of my business, and as I have nearly completed my engagements here I would wish to look forward in time to some situation in this department—Finding that the state of Virginia is making considerable exertions towards improving their internal navigation, I would take the liberty, my dear Sir to interest your good opinion in my favor—& to request you to mention me in nomination to the Governor for the situation of Engineer when any such business should require the appointment of one and no appointment being already made.

I have a preference to Virginia from my having married there— Should there be no prospect of an engagement in this state soon, and you should become acquainted with any works of this nature intended to be prosecuted by either the general government or any neighboring[1] state or Company, I should be much indebted to your attentions in a remembrance of me.—I wish not to be idle whilst there is so much

[33]

to be done, & the prospects here, from the great depression of commerce leads me to anticipate, comparatively, nothing to do soon—

I hope from the experience I have had in my profession that I should be able to do justice to whatever business is put into my hands, and I trust that in every other respect I shall not be found wanting to secure the confidence you may please to honor me with.—The kindness you have already manifested to me induces me to hope you will excuse this intrusion—

I h[a]ve directed my attention also a good deal to the subject of <u>Bridges</u>, and was fortunate enough to have a design of mine executed of a <u>single arch</u> of the greatest chord line in the world, being 340 feet & upwards—versed sine only 19 feet. you will find a brief notice of it in the last edition of Gregory's Encyclopedia under the head of Schuylkill—with a plate.

It has been my intention for some time to send you a drawing of the Washington Monument as executing,—the undecission respecting the character of the decorations has occasioned a delay—this will be determined soon, and if acceptable I will send you a view of this Colossal Column, which, without having a reference to others executed, happens to be the greatest in the world, and differs entirely in the style of its design from either Trajans, Antoninus' Pompeys, the National Column at Paris or the London Monument.—In making the design originally, I had a reference rather to the character of a <u>Monument</u> than simply to a Column.—The proportions of the <u>Column</u> are purely of the greek Doric—

Excuse the length of this letter, and permit me to salute you with sentiments of the highest respect & esteem   Robt Mills

Will you allow me to ask if the professors chairs of the University are filled?—There is a Gentleman here (G. Blackburn Esqr professor of Mathematics[2] &c) whose talents are no doubt well known to you—he has an intention of leaving this City—Such are his acknowledged merits as a teacher that I believe he would prove a valuable acquisition to any literary institution—he has some peculiarities, but these appear to be generally allied to genius.—He is much attached to Virginia, & would prefer an engagement there—His daughters too are well qualified to educate young ladies—I have not mentioned the subject to him. I thought I would take the liberty of making this N.B—

RC (DLC); mutilated at seal; addressed: "Thomas Jefferson Esqr Monticello Albemarle C° Virginia" by "Mail"; stamp canceled; franked; postmarked Baltimore, 16 June; endorsed by TJ as received 21 June 1820 and so recorded in SJL.

In bridge building, a VERSED SINE is "the rise of an arch" (OED). The BRIEF

NOTICE and PLATE of the "*Upper ferry or Lancaster* SCHUYLKILL BRIDGE," which was designed by Mills and constructed by Lewis Wernwag in 1812–13 just above the city of Philadelphia, were printed in George Gregory's *New and Complete Dictionary of Arts and Sciences* (Philadelphia, 1819), vol. 3. The NATIONAL COLUMN AT PARIS is located in the Place Vendôme, and the LONDON MONUMENT commemorating the Great Fire of 1666 is near the northern end of the modern London Bridge.

[1] Manuscript: "neghboring."
[2] Manuscript: "Mathmatics."

From Archibald Stuart

DEAR SIR   Staunton 16ᵗʰ June 1820—

The bearer Mʳ Hobson on his Way from Mississippi to Richmond called upon me with the enclosed letter from Govʳ Holmes—He is desirous of seeing Monticello before his Return to England—

I have understood he came to this Country in Company with Mʳ Lowndes who has recommended him to Govʳ Holmes with some other of his friends—

I am with respecᵗ & regard your Obᵗ Serᵗ   ARCHᴰ STUART

RC (MHi); endorsed by TJ as delivered 17 June 1820 "by mr Hobson" and so recorded in SJL. RC (MHi); address cover only; with PoC of TJ to Louis H. Girardin, 8 July 1820, on verso; addressed: "The honᵇˡᵉ Thomas Jefferson Esqr Monticello." Enclosure: David Holmes to Stuart, Natchez, 10 May 1820, in which the former Mississippi governor states that "Mʳ Hodson from Liverpool Englᵈ will hand you this letter, He is a respectable intelligent Gentleman, with whose acquaintance I feel confident you will be gratified I therefore recommend him to your friendly attention   It is probable that on his way to Richmond he may pass through Albemarle, If that should be his determination, you will oblige me by giving him a letter to some Gentleman in the Neighbourhood of Monticello" (RC in MHi; addressed: "Archᵈ Stuart Esq— Staunton Virginia" by "Mʳ Hodson").

Mᴿ HOBSON: Adam Hodgson.

Adam Hodgson's Account of
a Visit to Monticello

[17 June 1820]

———. I FEAR, however, that I am leaving no room for an account of my very interesting visit to Monticello. I went nearly 25 miles out of my way to obtain a letter of introduction to Mr. Jefferson, from his friend, Judge ——, of Staunton, to whom I was recommended by the late amiable and very popular Governor of the State of Mississippi.

On the 18th instant, I left Hayes's tavern, at the foot of the Blue ridge . . . We shortly afterwards passed through Charlottesville, where General Tarleton was near capturing Mr. Jefferson and the State

Legislature, being prevented only by a private intimation, sent by a female relation of one of[1] the officers, a few miles distant, at whose house the General and his suite had invited themselves to breakfast. Here we saw an extensive university, which the State is erecting under Mr. Jefferson's auspices, and to which it is intended to invite the ablest Professors which Europe can supply.

We arrived at Monticello, three miles farther, about eleven o'clock, ascending the South West Mountain, on which the house is situated, by a winding carriage-road through the wood. I sent in my letter to Mr. Jefferson, who soon afterwards came out and gave me a polite reception, leading me through the hall, hung with mammoth bones and Indian curiosities, to a room, ornamented with fine paintings. A young lady was playing on a piano-forte, but retired when we entered. Our conversation turned principally on the Indians, and the fine timber of the United States. With respect to the former, he considers them quite on a level, as respects intellectual character, with the Whites, and attributes the rapid civilization of the Choctaws, compared with that of the Creeks, on whom, perhaps, greater efforts have been bestowed, to the advantages possessed by the former for the growth of cotton, which had gradually induced them to spin and weave. He observed, that notwithstanding the fine specimens which have been preserved of Indian eloquence, the Indians appear to have no poetic genius; and that he had never known an Indian discover a musical taste; that, on the contrary, the Africans almost universally possess fine voices and an excellent ear, and a passionate fondness for music. With this I have often been struck, as I passed through the Southern States, especially when I have seen them assembled at public worship, or packing cotton at New Orleans. Mr. Jefferson said that he never knew a person who had resided long among the Indians, return and settle among the Whites; and I understood him to say also, that he never knew a person who left the coast for the western country, or his descendants, return to the Atlantic States. After sitting about an hour, I rose to take leave, when Mr. J. pressed me to stay to dinner, to which I assented, on condition that he would not allow me to be any restraint upon him. He said he must leave me for an hour to ride, as his health had a few months since begun to fail, for the first time. I found no difficulty, however, in amusing myself in the museum and the grounds and garden. In the former, was the only upper jaw ever yet discovered, as I was told, of a large animal now extinct, and some maps traced by the Indians on leather. The view on every side of the house, except one, where a small arc of the horizon is intercepted by a hill, is very extensive and beautiful. The Blue ridge affords an interesting variety of romantic scenery in a broken curve, extending, I believe, above 100 miles; one peak at the distance, I understood, of more than 120 miles, being sometimes visible. The horizon, on the Atlantic side, is about 40 miles distant; and bounds a flat well-wooded country, which appeared tame, when contrasted with the sublimity of the mountains. These, and especially a hill of the shape and dimensions of the largest pyramid in Egypt, which gives Mr. Jefferson a meridian line of 40 miles, frequently exhibit the phenomenon of looming.

On Mr. Jefferson's return from his ride, we had some interesting conversation respecting the university, and a favourite plan of his of dividing every county into districts, in which there should be schools, and a humble sort of college at convenient distances, a superior college, with every possible advantage, being established in the State. After dinner, when the ladies had retired, and we were quite alone, he expressed his sentiments very freely on the present situation of England, and the character of many of her public men. He then stated the views and feelings which he had entertained with respect to her while President, as well as those which had been generally entertained by the American Government; the various causes which had contributed to the unhappy misunderstanding between the two countries, and the grounds for believing that many of them were of a nature which rendered their recurrence improbable. He then described, with a good deal of spirit and minuteness, the character of the different ministers we have sent to Washington, and concluded with an earnest hope, that as the two Governments at length understood each other perfectly, the people might gradually be soothed into better humour with one another. The particulars of this very interesting conversation, which lasted two hours, and of which I have preserved a memorandum, I will give you when we meet.*

Mr. Jefferson's appearance is rather prepossessing. He is tall and very thin, a little bent with age, with an intelligent and sprightly countenance. His manners are dignified, but courteous and gentlemanly; and he enters into conversation with great ease and animation.

After two hours téte-à-téte, I rose about six o'clock to take my leave. He invited me to stay all night; but I thought I had already encroached

---

* It is with great regret that I feel myself constrained to omit what would, perhaps, have been more generally interesting than any thing these volumes contain. It is not, indeed, probable, that Mr. Jefferson would object to the publication of any thing which he saw fit to communicate in conversation with a stranger; but there is not time to obtain his permission, and without it, delicacy imposes a restraint, which I feel unwilling to break through.

[37]

sufficiently on his time, and I was not sure that we should withdraw to the ladies, of whom I had just seen enough to feel persuaded that I should have passed a very agreeable evening with them. While sitting with this philosophical legislator and his polished family,[2] in a handsome saloon, surrounded by instruments of science, valuable specimens of the fine arts, and literary treasures of every nation, and every age, I could not help contrasting my situation with some of those which I had occupied during the preceding month, when sleeping on a bear-skin, on the floor of an Indian hut, listening to the traditions of my Chickasaw or Choctaw host, or dandling on my knee a young Indian warrior, with his miniature belt and mocassins, his necklaces and feathers, and his little bow and arrow, doomed to provoke nothing but a smile. In the course of a few weeks, I had passed from deep forests, whose silence had never been broken by the woodman's axe, to a thickly settled country, where cattle were grazing in extensive meadows, and corn fields waving in the wind; where commerce was planting her towns, science founding her universities, and religion rearing her heaven-directed spires. In the same period, I had traced man through every successive stage of civilization, from the roaming savage, whose ideas scarcely extend beyond the narrow circle of his daily wants, to the statesman who has learnt to grasp the complicated interests of society, and the philosopher, to contemplate the system of the universe.

Crossing the Rivannah, at the bottom of Mr. Jefferson's grounds, the water up to our saddle-skirts, we proceeded to Mr. Boyd's tavern, about eight miles distant. On Monday, the 19th, we resumed our journey . . .

I forgot to say, that at Mr. Jefferson's, I saw the belt and shot pouch of the famous Tecumseh . . .

Printed in Hodgson, *Letters from North America, written During a Tour in the United States and Canada* (London, 1824; Poor, *Jefferson's Library*, 7 [no. 349]; TJ's copy in IGK), 1:313–9, 320; at head of text: "Richmond, 21st June, 1820." Different version of one paragraph previously printed in Hodgson, *Remarks during a Journey through North America in the years 1819, 1820, and 1821* (New York, 1823), 261 (see note 2 below).

Adam Hodgson (1789–1862), merchant, banker, and author, was born in Liverpool, England. He was a partner from at least 1814 in Rathbone, Hodgson & Company, an enterprise that traded widely in both Europe and North America. In 1819 Hodgson crossed the Atlantic to gather information for his firm and meet potential trading partners. He left the company a few years after his return to Liverpool in 1821 and made his living thereafter as a cotton and insurance broker and banker. Hodgson helped found the Liverpool and Manchester Railroad in 1824 and was an organizer and the longtime managing director of the Bank of Liverpool. He served as an officer of numerous charitable and religious organizations and was an unwavering opponent of the slave trade. Besides works on his

North American travels, Hodgson wrote *A Letter to M. Jean-Baptiste Say, on the Comparative Expense of Free and Slave Labour* (Liverpool, 1823), and *A Letter to the Right Honorable Sir Robert Peel, Bart., on the Currency* (1848). He was also a justice of the peace from 1835 until his death and a borough magistrate during his final years. Hodgson died near Lancaster, England (UkLA: Lancashire Anglican Parish Registers; Kevin J. Hayes, ed., *Jefferson in His Own Time* [2012], 88; Hodgson to TJ, 13 Sept. 1824; *Gore's Directory of Liverpool and Its Environs* [1827]: 73, 78, 82, 182, 357; [1853]: 128, 130–3, 675; [1860]: 73, 75–7, 81, 84, 302; Henry Booth, *An Account of the Liverpool and Manchester Railway* [1831], 11; UkNA: 1851, 1861 England census, Lancashire; *Liverpool Mercury*, 19 Aug. 1814, 30 Dec. 1862).

Although Hodgson indicates above that he arrived at Monticello on 18 June, TJ's receipt of a letter of introduction of 16 June 1820 from Archibald Stuart (JUDGE ——, OF STAUNTON) a day earlier suggests that his visit actually took place on 17 June. The former GOVERNOR OF THE STATE OF MISSISSIPPI was David Holmes.

The INTIMATION that TJ and the legislators assembled at Charlottesville in June 1781 should flee the oncoming British force commanded by Banastre Tarleton was conveyed to both by John (Jack) Jouett, a young militia captain, who, as TJ later reported, "seeing them pass his father's house in the evening of the 3d. and riding through the night along by-ways, brought the notice" (*PTJ*, 4:261; *MB*, 1:510).

The LARGE ANIMAL NOW EXTINCT was the mastodon. The ARC OF THE HORIZON IS INTERCEPTED at Monticello by Montalto. The geographic feature in the SHAPE AND DIMENSIONS OF THE LARGEST PYRAMID IN EGYPT was Willis's Mountain in Buckingham County.

[1] Printed text: "of of."
[2] Remainder of paragraph printed with some variations in Hodgson, *Remarks*, preceded by "Monticello, the well-known seat of Mr. Jefferson, is finely situated on an eminence which commands a magnificent prospect. Here I experienced a very polite and hospitable reception, from this retired and philosophic Statesman; whose urbanity and intelligence can scarcely fail to make a favourable impression on a stranger. While conversing with him."

From Arthur S. Brockenbrough

RESPECTED SIR,   June 19th 1820

You are under a mistake as to any remittance being made to M[r] Vaughan in September last for the two M[r] Raggis, our funds were at so low a state at that time the remittance of 300 D. could not be made, no remittance was made untill Feb: & that for $400—by yourself. I have never had any correspondence with M[r] Vaughan on the subject, the $400 in Feb: as I understand was to bring in the wives of the two M[r] Raggis—I am Sir

your Ob[t] sev[t]   A. S. BROCKENBROUGH

RC (DLC); addressed: "Thomas Jefferson Esq[r] Monticello"; with apparently unrelated calculation by TJ on verso; endorsed by TJ: "Brockenbrough A. S."

From John Holmes

Dear Sir   Alfred Maine, 19 June 1820
I have taken the liberty to shew your excellent letter on the Missouri question, to a few select friends & they unite in urging its publication. The influence of your name, opinion & reasons in preventing or at least delaying the evils which you apprehend & seem to predict, is most important. Always disposed to make personal sacrifices where your country's safety required it, it is hoped that in the evening of your days, you will condescend to shed light & consolation on your country & gratify the wishes of your friends & admirers—

In this section of the United States, the Missouri excitement is subsiding. My election to the Senate of the US, was opposed on this ground with much zeal & more expectation. But it succeeded 95 to 50 in the H.R. & 16 to 4 in the Senate—I am, Sir, with the highest respect & esteem
Your friend & servt   J Holmes

RC (DLC); endorsed by TJ as received 2 July 1820 and so recorded in SJL. RC (MHi); address cover only; with PoC of TJ to Martin Dawson, 21 July 1820, on verso; addressed: "Hon. Thos Jefferson Monticello Va"; franked; postmarked Alfred, 21 June.

From John Laval

Sir,   Philada June 19th 1820
Agreeably to your Order of the 12th instt I have deposited in the Post-Office, to be forwarded by to-morrow's mail, the first Volume of Potter's Euripides, Russia Calf, $10= the 2d Volume will be Sent, according to your direction, on the 24th—

I am with the highest Consideration & respect
Sir,   your very humble Servant   John Laval

RC (DLC); dateline at foot of text; endorsed by TJ as received 28 June 1820 and so recorded in SJL; additional notation by TJ beneath endorsement: "1820. Mar. 23. remitted 72.D. in full," presumably TJ's reminder to himself that prior to the above purchase he was not in debt to Laval. RC (MHi); address cover only; with PoC of TJ to Charles Everette, 21 July 1820, on verso; addressed: "Thos Jefferson, Esq. Monticello—Va"; stamp canceled; franked; postmarked Philadelphia, 19 June.

From Bernard Peyton

D<small>EAR SIR</small>,   Rich'd 19 June. 20.

By Mr Johnson you will receive a small Bag of Seeds ford^d by the Collector at Petersburg.—if delivered in good order please pay freight as customary—

Say to Mrs Randolph if you please that her Bll: Haws by Mr Johnson for Mrs Morris are safely to hand & shall be dispatched by the first Vessel to N. York—in haste—

Your Mo: Obd: Servt: B. P<small>EYTON</small>

---

1 Bag

RC (MHi); addressed: "Mr Thomas Jefferson Monticello"; endorsed by TJ as received 3 July 1820 and so recorded in SJL.

The <small>COLLECTOR AT PETERSBURG</small> was Joseph Jones.

From Bernard Glenn

H<small>ON</small>^{<small>BLE</small>} S<small>IR</small>   South Carolina Union District June 20th 1820

I beg leave to address you, on a subject, Relitive to the war, worn, Officers and Soldiers of Virginia of the Revolutionary war, on State establishment, and Solicite what information you may think proper to give me, on the leading and preceeding errors, which occasion'd the Officers & Soldiers of Virginia on State establishment from Locateing their military Land warrants, and obtaining their Lands, promised them, by the General Assembly of the State of Virginia—

For some cause I have been barred from Locateing my Military Land warrant ever sence Kentucky has become a seperate State from the State of Virginia, I have waited with Sympathy a number of years for the Honble Congress, of the United States, to rectify the preceeding errors, (but in vain,) I solicite your Opinion whether you, think, that those warrants aluded to above, will be Valid, and be Suffered to be Located, or become Nugatary and of no account—or whether the State of Virginia, will not in Justice make Remuneration, to the War worn Officers and Soldiers of the Revolution, any Information you should think proper to give me will be thankfully, received and remain in confidence with an Officer of the Revolution—

I am, Dear Sir, with sentiments of esteem, and respects your Mo^t Ob^t Servt—   B<small>ERN</small>^D G<small>LENN</small>

P.S. if you should be so good as to write me, direct to me Wrightsboro, Union District South Carolina

RC (MHi); endorsed by TJ as received 6 July 1820 from Wrightsboro, S.C., and so recorded in SJL. RC (DLC); address cover only; with PoC of TJ to Joseph C. Cabell, 3 Jan. 1822, on verso; addressed: "Honble Thomas Jefferson Esqr near Charlotteville State of Virginia Albermarle County" by "Mail"; stamped; postmarked Wrightsboro, 21 June.

Bernard Glenn (1757–1831), planter and public official, was a native of Virginia. A low-ranking officer in the Virginia militia "on State establishment" during the Revolutionary War, after hostilities ended Virginia awarded him a military land warrant for 2,666 acres on the Cumberland River in what would later become the state of Kentucky. Following its admission into the Union in 1792, however, Kentucky prohibited the location within its boundaries of land warrants issued by any other state. Although Glenn took his case to Congress in 1802, his claim was apparently not honored during his lifetime, either at the federal or state level. Having relocated permanently during the 1780s to Union County, South Carolina, he served as a justice of the peace and sat in the state's House of Representatives for five consecutive terms, 1806–15. Glenn owned seven slaves in 1800, twenty-nine in 1820, and thirty-six in 1830. Shortly after his death his personal estate was valued at just over $18,000 (*BDSCHR*, 4:235; John H. Gwathmey, *Historical Register of Virginians in the Revolution* [1938], 311; *JHR*, 4:256 [21 Dec. 1802]; *ASP, Public Lands*, 1:119; DNA: RG 29, CS, S.C., Union District/Co., 1800–30; Union Co. Probate Court records; gravestone in Rice Cemetery, Union Co.).

From George Alexander Otis

Philadelphia 20 June 1820 215. Market Street.

The translator of de Pradt's Europe for 1819. hopes it may find acceptance as an apology for addressing the revered author of the declaration of American Independence, & of the Notes on Virginia, and the twice elected Chief Magistrate of the only free Nation on Earth.

This Greatness already appreciated by Contemporaries, and destined to acquire increase of Splendour with the lapse of Ages, certainly fills him with a certain awe; but as it is united with the reassuring attribute of patron of literature and domestic industry, the writer is encouraged to Solicit the patronage of Mr Jefferson for the work in which he is now engaged, the translation of Botta.

He is the more confident of excuse for this great liberty, as his friend General Brown, on returning from a visit to Monticello, assured him that Mr Jefferson was desirous that our literature Should receive such an addition. The first Volume of the work is now forwarded: which if it Should be So fortunate as to meet the approbation of the most distinguished of Americans, it cannot fail of success.

One word of encouragement from such a source would be more precious to the writer than fame; and at the same time its presage.

That Heaven may prolong the days of a fellow citizen So justly[1] venerated is the earnest prayer

of his respectful humble Servant   GEO. A. OTIS.

RC (MHi); at foot of text: "To Thomas Jefferson late President of the United States of America"; endorsed by TJ as received 2 July 1820 and so recorded in SJL.

George Alexander Otis (1781–1863), merchant, broker, and translator, was born in Scituate, Massachusetts. He moved by 1802 to Boston, where he established himself as a vendor of merchandise from England and India. Three years later Otis went into business with his father-in-law, Barney Smith. An accomplished linguist, he spent four years in Europe before returning in 1817 to Boston. Otis resumed his career as a trader there, attempted unsuccessfully to obtain a number of federal appointments, and published translations of three works: Dominique Dufour, baron de Pradt, *Europe after the Congress of Aix-la-Chapelle. Forming the Sequel to the Congress of Vienna* (Philadelphia, 1820; Poor, *Jefferson's Library*, 11 [no. 643]), Botta, *History of the War*, and *The Tusculan Questions of Marcus Tullius Cicero* (1839). He became a member of the American Philosophical Society in 1821.

Otis later worked as a broker in Boston for a number of years. When his father-in-law died in 1828, Otis came into considerable wealth. Thereafter, he scaled back his business activities and devoted himself to the management of his estate and to his literary studies. Otis died in Boston (*Vital Records of Scituate Massachusetts to the Year 1850* [1909], 1:280; Boston *Columbian Centinel. Massachusetts Federalist*, 25 Dec. 1802; Boston *Democrat*, 3 Apr. 1805; *Boston Commercial Gazette*, 11 Aug. 1817; *Independent Chronicle & Boston Patriot*, 15 Oct. 1817; DNA: RG 59, LAR, 1817–25; APS, Minutes, 20 Apr. 1821 [MS in PPAmP]; *The Boston Directory* [Boston, 1825], 200; *Stimpson's Boston Directory* [1832], 252; DNA: RG 29, CS, Mass., Boston, 1840, 1850; *Boston Daily Advertiser*, 25, 26 June 1863).

On this day Otis sent similar letters to John Adams, John Quincy Adams, and James Madison (MHi: Adams Papers; DNA: RG 59, MLR; Madison, *Papers, Retirement Ser.*, 2:70–1).

[1] Word added in margin.

From Rufus Woodward

HONORED SIR,   New-Haven Con. June 20th 1820.

Having heard that Professors are soon to be appointed in the Virginia University, & that you have a principal part in the management of its Concerns, I take the liberty of addressing a line to you, for the purpose of ascertaining what is your mode of proceeding in making these appointments. I am informed it is a practice in some parts of the Southern States [i]n such cases, to publish a request that candidates should themselves make application. Whether this has been done in regard to your University, I have not heard. I hope you will pardon me, Sir, for troubling you with a communication to me on the subject, should you have no objections. I am at present a tutor in Yale-College, & having a partiality for literary & scientific pursuits, I have thought that a situation in your University would accord very well with my inclinations. I say nothing at present of my preference as to the branches to be[1] taught, it being my object rather to make <u>enquiries</u>, than to offer myself as a candidate.

With great respect I am, Sir, Your Obed^t ser^{vt}

RUFUS WOODWARD

RC (ViU: TJP); torn at seal; endorsed by TJ as received 2 July 1820 and so recorded in SJL. RC (DLC); address cover only; with PoC of TJ to George Watterston, 27 July 1820, on verso; addressed: "Thomas Jefferson Esq. late President of the U. States Monticello Virginia"; stamped; postmarked New Haven, 20 June.

Rufus Woodward (1793–1823), educator, was born in Torringford (later a district of Torrington), Connecticut, and graduated from Yale College (later Yale University) in 1816. A member of Phi Beta Kappa, at his commencement he participated in a "Dialogue, on the Force of Flattery." Following teaching stints in Stratford and Wethersfield, Connecticut, Woodward secured an appointment as a tutor at Yale in 1818 and served until his resignation late in 1822. Having long suffered from dyspepsia, he traveled to Europe in the summer of 1823 to further his education and restore his health. After visiting England, Scotland, and France, Woodward died in Edinburgh (*Christian Spectator* 7 [1825]: 113–26; Franklin Bowditch Dexter, *Biographical Notices of Graduates of Yale College* [1913], 15; *Catalogue of the Members of the Connecticut Alpha of the ΦBK* [New Haven, 1818], 22; *Norwich* [Conn.] *Courier*, 25 Sept. 1816; *Historical Register of Yale University 1701–1937* [1939], 554; *Hartford Connecticut Mirror*, 9 Feb. 1824; gravestone inscription in Saint Cuthbert's churchyard, Edinburgh).

[1] Preceding two words interlined.

From Samuel Garland

SIR   Lynchburg June 21. 1820.

I had this pleasure by the last weeks mail to which I beg leave to call your attention—

Mr Jacob W. White has just put into my hands your assumset for $143:56. due 19th July 1819. for collection—he request me to say to you that he is in great want of the money, so much indeed that if it be not paid in a few weeks he must sustain great inconveniance if not a sacrifise—

With Sentiments of Respect
Yr obt St   S, GARLAND

RC (MHi); endorsed by TJ as a letter from "Garland <E> S." received 26 June 1820 and so recorded in SJL. RC (DLC); address cover only; with PoC of TJ to Patrick Gibson, 14 July 1820, on verso; addressed: "Thomas Jefferson esq^r near Charlottesville"; franked; postmarked Lynchburg, 23 June.

From George S. Gibson
(for Patrick Gibson)

SIR   Richmond 21ˢᵗ June 1820

I wrote you on the 10ᵗʰ Instᵗ & have since received your favor of the 7ᵗʰ—finding it impracticable to remit to Philadelphia owing to the difficulty of obtaining dfts on the North I wrote to Mʳ Vaughan desiring him to draw which he informs me he has done for $444.—as directed.—Your dfts for $35.68 & $50 in favor of Joel Wolfe & Alex Hepburn have been paid—I have sold 13 Bbls Sfine flour of yours at $4⅛ & 5 fine at 3¾ I have one yet on hand which is condemned on account of the Bbl—Mʳ Craddock has sent down only 19 instead of 20 Bbls as he promised.—Mʳ Wᵐ Hening has left with me, the 4ᵗʰ 5ᵗʰ & 6ᵗʰ Volumes of his Statutes, for you, you will please inform me, how I am to send them up to you.—Flour is selling at from $4 to 4⅛.

I am Yours Respectfully   PATRICK GIBSON
                                 Pᴿ GEORGE S GIBSON

RC (DLC); entirely in George S. Gibson's hand; endorsed by TJ as a letter from Patrick Gibson received 28 June 1820 and so recorded in SJL. RC (MHi); address cover only; with PoC of TJ to Bernard Peyton, 21 July 1820, on verso; addressed in a different clerk's hand: "Thomas Jefferson Esquire Monticello"; franked; postmarked Richmond, 23 June.

SFINE: "superfine."

To John Quincy Adams

                                 Monticello. June 22. 20.

Th: Jefferson presents his respectful salutations to mr Adams, and his thanks for the copy of the journals of the Convention which he has been so kind as to send him. [t]hat also presented to the University of Virginia, has been properly addressed to Th:J. as Rector of that institution and shall be carefully preserved until the proper depository shall be provided. he prays mr Adams to be assured of his great friendship and respect.

PoC (DLC); on verso of reused address cover of William Short to TJ, 2 May 1820; dateline at foot of text; one word faint; endorsed by TJ.

From Arthur S. Brockenbrough

DEAR SIR,   June 22rd 1820

I must ask the favor of you to permit us to advance the Eastern
range of Hotels & Dormitories about 17 feet—in order to save much
labor in diging & removing earth, we shall still have the same front,
& the earth from the back of the dormitories & Hotels will be sufficient
to widen the street to its proper width & the assent to the back of the
pavilions will also be a little more moderate, the distance then from
the front of the Eastern range of Pavilions to the front of the Hotels
& dormitories will only be 300 feet

I am Sir respectfully your obt sevt   A. S. BROCKENBROUGH

RC (CSmH: JF-BA); addressed: "Thomas Jefferson Esqr Monticello."

To Fernagus De Gelone

SIR   Monticello June 22. 20.

I recieved yesterday your favor of the 14th and have duly noted the
advertisement it covered. altho' age & ill health have obliged me to
withdraw as much as possible from the transactions passing in the
world, yet they have not extinguished in me all interest in the good[1]
establishments arising among us, of which I deem that mentioned in
your advertisement to be one. the same powerful causes forbid me to
expect ever again to pass the limits of my own state, or to have the
pleasure of visiting your institution. I can only therefore pray for it's
success and your prosperity and assure you personally of my great
esteem & respect.   TH: JEFFERSON

PoC (MHi); on verso of reused address
cover of Thomas Cooper to TJ, 3 May
1820; at foot of text: "Mr Fernagus de
Gelone"; endorsed by TJ. Printed in New
York *Commercial Advertiser*, 29 June
1820.

[1] Word not in *Commercial Advertiser*.

To James Gibbon

Monticello June 22. 20.

Th: Jefferson presents[1] his compliments to Majr Gibbons and his
thanks for his attention to the box of seeds sent him from the Royal
garden of Paris, which he has now safely recieved. it is a trust committed to him annually by the Director of that garden to be passed on
to some of the botanical gardens of our country. within the course of

a couple of years he hopes to have these missions[2] usefully employed at our own university. if any expence has been incurred for the box, mr Gibson will be so good as to refund it, on recieving the bill. he prays Maj[r] Gibbons to accept his friendly & respe[ctful sa]lutations.

PoC (DLC); on verso of a reused address cover from Thomas Mann Randolph to TJ; dateline beneath closing; torn at seal; at foot of text: "Maj[r] James Gibbons"; endorsed by TJ.

André Thoüin was the longtime DIRECTOR of the Jardin des plantes et Muséum National d'Histoire Naturelle.

[1] Manuscript: "prents."
[2] Preceding two words interlined in place of "it."

To Patrick Gibson

DEAR SIR   Monticell[o] June.[1] 22. 20.
Your letter of June 10. has been duly recieved. the 5. barrels of flour lately delivered by Craddock are a part of 20. barrels which he purloined out of a boatload sent from here in Octob. but which by a fall of the water did not get to Richm[d] until December. he withheld & sold 20. barrels & forged your reciept for the whole load. this parcel has been missing in our accounts until producing your[2] reciept the alteration of the figures was discovered, and to avoid prosecution[3] he promised to replace it immediately.

I am extremely anxious to hear that the remittance of 444 D. has been made to mr Vaughan; because until I know that fact I cannot write to him how to dispose of it. my letter of the 7th inst. stated the grounds on which this was requested, to wit, the balance of 400.81 D of your acc[t] of May 16. and the 79.05 proceeds of the hhd of tob[o] last sold as mentioned in yours of June 2. I will thank you therefore for this information. it was not till lately that I learned with certainty the afflicting state of your health it's severity & long continuance. I sincerely sympathise in it and pray for it's relief being with real affection and respect

Your friend & serv[t]   TH: JEFFERSON

PoC (DLC); on verso of reused address cover of John Adams to TJ, 12 May 1820; dateline faint; at foot of text: "M[r] Gibson"; endorsed by TJ.

[1] Reworked from "Jul."
[2] Word interlined in place of "the."
[3] Manuscript: "posecution."

To Levett Harris

Dear Sir   Monticello June 22. 20.

I recieved yesterday your favor of the 15. and sincerely regret the misunderstanding mentioned in it, of which that letter was the first notice. I can say conscientiously that your services gave me, while in office, the most perfect satisfaction. not apprised of the service I can render you at the interview proposed, retired as I am from all intermedling with the transaction[s] of the government I shall on every consideration be happy to recieve your proposed visit to Monticello at your own convenience[.] to prevent disappointment by my own absences, I must observe that some important works in which I am engaged here, will keep me at home three weeks certainly, and possibly a little more; and the moment they are done I am obliged to visit a possession I have 90. miles S.W. from this, where I shall make a stay of some weeks. in the mean time, or after my return, I shall be happy to recieve your visit as most convenient to yourself and to assure you personally of my high respect & esteem.

Th: Jefferson

PoC (DLC); on verso of reused address cover to TJ; edge trimmed; at foot of text: "Levitt Harris esq."; endorsed by TJ.

To Robert Mills

Dear Sir   Monticello June 22. 20.

Your favor of the 16th came to hand yesterday. with respect to the operations in which this state is engaged in the engineering line, they are placed in the hands of Thomas Moore and Isaac Briggs jointly appointed engineers to the state, and they are now, and have for some time been engaged in the work. retired as I entirely am from the business of the world, I know nothing of the similar works going on in the other states.   with respect to my health after which you are so kind as to enquire it is much impaired and very uncertain. I am thankful to you for the copy of the design of the Washington monument which you offer to send me. but these subjects also, once the delight of my life, have ceased to excite a sufficient interest in me to be willing to give you the trouble of drawing it. I accept therefore the kindness of the offer as quite equivalent with me to the actual performance. the time at which our university may open is too uncertain for us as yet to look out for professors. a stiffening wrist which renders writing slow & painful, disables me from adding more than my sincere wishes for your prosperity and assurances of my great esteem and respect.   TH: JEFFERSON

RC (ViU: TJP); at foot of text: "M[r] Robert Mills." PoC (DLC); on verso of reused address cover of William H. Crawford to TJ, 22 Mar. 1820; endorsed by TJ.

To Jesse Wharton

SIR   Monticello June 22. 20.

Your letter of May 30. came to hand yesterday. the transactions of which it asks information, are of 40. years date. the crowded scenes thro' which I have passed within that period, with a memory in the wane of age, have so far obliterated them from[1] my mind as to be quite unable to give any account of them which would merit attention. I can only say in general that my best recollections concur with the statement you have sent me from Gen[l] Smith. I think that is accurate. the instruction given by myself as Governor to D[r] Walker and Smith I well remember. an apprehension that a peace was patching up in Europe on the principle of Uti possidetis, induced us hastily to ascertain where our boundary struck the Missisipi, and to take possession by a fort which we directed Gen[l] Clarke to build & garrison. more than this my memory does not enable me to say. Accept the assurances of my esteem & respect   TH: JEFFERSON

RC (Mrs. James O. Murdock, Washington, D.C., 1951); addressed: "M[r] J. Wharton Nashville. Ten."; franked; postmarked Charlottesville, 25 June. PoC (CSmH: JF); on verso of reused address cover of William Wirt to TJ, 9 Mar. 1820; endorsed by TJ.

For TJ's 29 Jan. 1780 INSTRUCTION as governor of Virginia to Thomas Walker and Daniel Smith, see *PTJ*, 3:278–9. UTI POSSIDETIS is the "doctrine that old administrative boundaries will become international boundaries when a political subdivision achieves independence" (*Black's Law Dictionary*). Also on 29 Jan. 1780, TJ authorized George Rogers Clark (GEN[L] CLARKE) to construct an army post "as near the mouth of Ohio as can be found fit for fortification and within our own lines." The resulting installation, located in present-day Kentucky, was named Fort Jefferson in TJ's honor (*PTJ*, 3:273, 277n).

[1] Reworked from "in."

From John Vaughan

D SIR   Philad. 23 June 1820

M[r] Patrick Gibson has desired me to draw upon him for y/a for 444. D[s] which I have done.[1] I shall expect your Special Directions for the appropriation of it—

I have the pleasure of inclosing an extract made from a letter I have rec[d] from M. Dessaus[sure] under date 5 May—which cannot fail being of a very Satisfactory nature to all who have advocated his cause, particularly to you who knew & fully appreciated his Merit— He has just arrived in Good health & returns in the fall

 I remain with great respect Your friend   JN VAUGHAN

 PS

Upon refering to your favor of 22 April I observe that 444$ are to be rem[d] to Tho[s] appleton Leghorn.[2] The 206$ for Marseilles are not yet rec[d]—

RC (MHi); on a sheet folded to form four pages, with letter on p. 1, address on p. 2, and enclosure on pp. 3–4; mutilated at seal; postscript adjacent to closing and signature; addressed in a clerk's hand: "Thomas Jefferson Monticello Virginia"; franked; postmarked Philadelphia, 23 June; endorsed by TJ as received 6 July 1820 and so recorded in SJL.

Y/A: "your account." TJ's FAVOR OF 22 APRIL to Vaughan was actually dated 24 Apr. 1820. REM[D]: "remitted."

[1] Omitted period at right margin editorially supplied.
[2] Omitted period at right margin editorially supplied.

ENCLOSURE

Extract from Henry William DeSaussure to John Vaughan

[Columbia, S.C., 2 May 1820]

"Ever[1] since Dr Cooper has been here, he has performed the duties of his professor-ship—so ably & so faithfully, that there has been a Strong desire on the part of the Trustees who reside here to retain him altogether—That desire has been greatly increased by the pleasure derived from personal intercourse with him.

His mind is wonderfully Stored with learning & wisdom, communicated[2] frankly, but modestly & unpresumingly—His whole deportment has been such as to give entire satisfaction, & to procure him many friends warmly attached to him—You know that we children of the Sun have warm feelings, 'tho' mixed with many faults—The distant Trustees who attended the meetings of the board, soon learn't the character of Dr Cooper & appreciated it—It was proposed to establish a professor-ship of mineralogy—& Geology, to annex it to that of Chemistry with a salary of 1000$ in addition to the 2000$ already given him—And the proposition was unanimously[3] agreed to—

Dr Cooper himself prefered the Union of those studies to Chemistry, to any other which could be named—He has besides a good house furnished him free from rent—The salaries of our professors are paid quarterly, out of the State Treasury—"

Tr (MHi); dateline supplied from note at head of text: "Extract of a letter from Henry W DeSaussure to John Vaughan

Philad—dated Columbia So Ca 2 May 1820"; with Vaughan's signed attestation as a "true Extract" at foot of text, dated

Philadelphia, 23 June 1820; conjoined with covering letter.

Henry William DeSaussure (1763–1839), attorney and public official, was born in Pocotaligo in Old Granville County (later Jasper County), South Carolina, and educated at private schools in Beaufort and Charleston. Having assisted in the defense of Charleston, he was captured when the city fell into British hands in May 1780, confined on a prison ship, and then sent north to Philadelphia for exchange. Following his arrival there, DeSaussure studied law under Jared Ingersoll and was admitted to the Pennsylvania bar in 1784. He returned to Charleston the following year and established a legal practice. A Federalist, defender of Low-Country interests, opponent of protective tariffs, and a Unionist during the Nullification crisis early in the 1830s, DeSaussure attended South Carolina's 1790 constitutional convention and sat for seven terms in the state legislature between 1791 and 1808. He served briefly as director of the United States Mint in 1795 and was a presidential elector for John Adams the following year. DeSaussure sat on the five-person South Carolina Court of Equity, 1808–24, was one of two chancellors of the succeeding tribunal, the Court of Appeals in Equity, 1824–37, and published four volumes of court reports, 1817–19. A longtime supporter of South Carolina College (later the University of South Carolina), he was a member of its board of trustees, 1801–05 and 1808–37. Although DeSaussure moved to Columbia in 1812, he died during a visit to Charleston (*DAB*; *BDSCHR*, 4:154–6; John Belton O'Neall, *Biographical Sketches of the Bench and Bar of South Carolina* [1859], 1:243–52; Walter Edgar, ed., *The South Carolina Encyclopedia* [2006], 260–1; Heitman, *Continental Army*, 195; Dorothy Twohig, ed., *Journal of the Proceedings of the President, 1793–1797* [1981], 331; *JEP*, 1:194 [10 Dec. 1795]; *Charleston Courier*, 1 Apr. 1839; gravestone inscription in First Presbyterian Churchyard, Columbia).

[1] Omitted opening quotation mark editorially supplied.
[2] The word "freely" is here canceled.
[3] Manuscript: "unimously."

From Peter Poinsot

MONSIEUR   Cette 24th June 1820

Je profite de la Goëlette Fénélon C[a]pitaine Mayhew de Fairhaven faisant voile pour Norfolk, pour avoir lhonneur de vous écrire. Je n'ai pas été assez heureux d'être favorisé du Succés de la demande que je vous ai addressée par ma lettre du 7 Juin 1819 [à] Son Excellence M[r] Le Président des EU, & de celle a lui adressée par feu mon ami le General Kosciuszko, Sollicitant pour [m]oi le Consulat du Port & Ville de Cette. Plusieurs Batimens Sont venus prendre des produits du Languedoc & il [. . .] arriver de votre Continent. Cette place a besoin d'une personne de confiance pour protéger vos Nationnaux. [. . .] digne, sous tous les rapports, de la mériter & dêtre à même d'occuper cette place, de la representer avec honneur & dist[in]ction. Mon cousin le General Poinsot étant à Paris S'est offert à Monsieur Gallatin pour la caution des $2000– exigible for [. . .] execution of the office. Permettez moi de vous donner une Copie litérale que M[r] Barnet, Consul à Paris, me dit [. . .] à Mons[r] Le Secrétaire dEtat

=to my letter to the Secretary of the Sta[te o]f the 19 June 1819 I [. . .] compliance with the request of Mr Peter Poinsot now at Cette and a naturalized Citysen of the U.S. to [repeat?] his desire of being appointed Consul of the United States for the district of Cette. You may recollect how Strongly M Poinsot [was] recommended by the late Gal Kosciuszko his particular friend, in a letter to the Président written a Short time before his death [. . .] Officer. Mr Cuming of Georgia (a friend of M^r J Forsyth) who was lately in the South of France, represent M. Poinsot as being a man of respectable character. I presume no native Citysen will offer for the Consulship of Cette as long as no Salary is allowed, and as the duties on french Wine are reduced, there will probably be[1] some trade from that port to the U.S. had I possessed the authority Gal Kosciuszko's recommandation could, long ago have induced me to comply your wishes.=[2]

Je m'etais flaté d'esperance, d'aprés la lettre de mon ami [. . .] Kosciuszko, envoyée par Monsr Barnet à Monsieur le Président, d'obtenir ce quil lui demandait avec instance, & quil regardait co[m]me une faveur en accomplissant ses désirs pour Le Consulat de Cette. Sil fallait meme une recommandation de M^r Le Marquis de Lafayette [. . .] serait aisée de l'avoir. Mais vous Seul, Mon cher Monsieur, pouvez tout. Je m'addresse à vous avec une pleine confiance, e[t] l'esperance qu'il vous plaira prendre la peine de renouveller à Monsieur le President la priere que mon ami le Général Kosciu[szk]o lui a faite par ses deux lettres, dont la derniere lui a été remise par vos Soins—Je compte Sur votre protection—Je la reclame [à la] mémoire de notre ami commun—Soyez mon bienfaiteur, ma reconnaissance Sera éternelle. Mon fils ayant resté 4 ans dans [. . .] comptoir à Londres revient ici le mois prochain, dans l'esperance d'aller a New York. la place de Consul me conviendrait & me do[nne]rait plus de rapports avec le Continent. des amis de Bordeaux m'ont recommandé a Messrs Thompson & Cie de Baltimore [. . .] les tems dont je vous ai entretenus, & dont enfin, Jai trouvé le titre original à Marseille deposé chez un Notaire—ah, [. . .] Monsieur, quelle Satisfaction n'aurais-je pas Si je pouvais trouver l'occasion de vous témoigner ma reconnaissance & de pouvoir [d']etre utile. oserais-je encore vous prier de m'instruire de ce quil vous aura plu de faire pour moi, Cest la derniere que je vous fais, v[ous pr]iant de m'excuser pour tous ce que vous faites pour moi—

& Croyez aux Sentimens d'Estime & de la plus haute Venéra[tion] avec lesquels j'ai lhonneur d'être

Monsieur   Votre trés humble & trés obeissant serviteur

POINSOT

EDITORS' TRANSLATION

SIR   Cette 24th June 1820

I have the honor of writing you, benefitting from the departure of the schooner *Fénelon*, Captain Mayhew, of Fairhaven, which is sailing for Norfolk. I was not so fortunate as to succeed in the request I addressed to you, in my letter of 7 June 1819 to His Excellency the president of the United States, and in the one my friend the late General Kosciuszko sent him, by soliciting for me the consulship for the port and city of Cette. Several ships have come to pick up products of Languedoc and the [. . .] arrive from your continent. This place needs a trustworthy person to protect your citizens, someone who is worthy in every respect, ready to fill the position and represent them with honor and distinction. My cousin General Poinsot, being in Paris, offered Mr. Gallatin the $2,000 deposit due for the execution of the office. Permit me to give you an exact copy of what Mr. Barnet, the consul in Paris, tells me [he wrote] to the secretary of state:

"to my letter to the Secretary of the Sta[te o]f the 19 June 1819 I [. . .] compliance with the request of Mr Peter Poinsot now at Cette and a naturalized Citysen of the U.S. to [repeat?] his desire of being appointed Consul of the United States for the district of Cette. You may recollect how Strongly M Poinsot [was] recommended by the late Gal Kosciuszko his particular friend, in a letter to the Président written a Short time before his death [. . .] Officer. Mr Cuming of Georgia (a friend of M^r J Forsyth) who was lately in the South of France, represent M. Poinsot as being a man of respectable character. I presume no native Citysen will offer for the Consulship of Cette as long as no Salary is allowed, and as the duties on french Wine are reduced, there will probably be some trade from that port to the U.S. had I possessed the authority Gal Kosciuszko's recommandation could, long ago have induced me to comply your wishes."

The letter my friend General Kosciuszko sent through Mr. Barnet to the president gave me the flattering hope of obtaining what he insistently requested, and which he considered as a favor that would fulfill his wishes for the Cette consulate. If a recommendation from the marquis de Lafayette was needed, [it] would also be easy to obtain. But you alone, my dear Sir, can do everything. I write you with complete confidence and hope that you will take the trouble of renewing the request that my friend General Kosciuszko made to the president in the two copies of his letter, the last of which was delivered through you. I count on your protection and claim it [in] memory of our mutual friend. If you act as my benefactor, my gratitude will know no end. My son, having been in a London countinghouse for 4 years, returns here next month in the hope of proceeding to New York. The position of consul would both suit me and give me more contact with your continent. Some friends from Bordeaux, [whom] I mentioned to you some time ago and through whom I finally found the original deed deposited with a notary in Marseille, have recommended me to Messrs. Thompson & Company, of Baltimore. Ah, [. . .] Sir, what satisfaction I would have if I had the opportunity of proving my gratitude and being useful to you. Dare I ask you again to let me know what you have decided to do for me? This is the last favor I will request of you, and I beg you to forgive me for troubling you for all your prior assistance—

And believe in the sentiments of esteem and highest veneration with which I have the honor to be

Sir   Your very humble and very obedient servant   POINSOT

RC (ViW: TC-JP); mutilated at fold; endorsed by TJ as received 29 Sept. 1820 and so recorded in SJL. RC (DLC); address cover only; with PoC of TJ to John Patterson, 15 May 1821, on verso; addressed: "Thomas Jefferson Esqre late President of the United States of America Monticello"; stamped "SHIP"; franked; postmarked Norfolk, 23 Sept. Translation by Dr. Genevieve Moene.

For Poinsot's letter to President James Monroe (MA LETTRE), see note to Poinsot to TJ, 6 June 1819. For the recommendation that Tadeusz Kosciuszko (GENERAL KOSCIUSZKO) sent Monroe, see note to Poinsot to TJ, 12 Sept. 1818.

[1] Manuscript: "will be probably be."
[2] Omitted closing quotation mark editorially supplied.

From Thomas B. Robertson

DEAR SIR   New Orleans June 24th 1820

I yesterday had the pleasure of receiving your letter of the 26th ult[o] and have made some enquiries concerning M[r] Bostwick—

I find by the records of our Parish court that he was formerly a Merchant of this place, and failed in the year 1818 as the inclosed certificate will shew.

From what I can learn from other sources I have reason to believe him to be an impostor, not only unworthy of credit, but of that hospitality and attention which are due to strangers of respectability—

I am very respectfully yo. ob. s[t]   THO[s] B ROBERTSON

RC (MHi); at foot of text: "Tho[s] Jefferson Esq"; endorsed by TJ as received 11 Aug. 1820 and so recorded in SJL. Enclosure not found.

From Francis Adrian Van der Kemp

DEAR AND RESPECTED SIR!   Oldenbarneveld 25 June 1820.

Your former kind indulgence make me presume, that a few lines— after So long a Silence—to renew the assurance of my unabated respect Shall not be unacceptable, although I have it not in my power, to make these interesting. I hope that your health remains comfortable, and domestic happiness your lot—   enjoy this happiness— during your last days—and I am persuaded, very many will take a Share in it—   My high respected friend John Adams—enjoy's the Same blessing—although his trembling hand, does [no][1] longer permit him, to make use of his pen—I expect—to pay him my last visit next month. How I regret—that So much must remain in the Escritoires of Both—by which the Literary world would be benefitted—and—is there nothing from your hand, for which you feel a lurking wish in your bosom—to hear the impartial judgment of the Publick?—and—my Dear Sir! would it require a greater confidence, than which you placed in me before—or here or in England—I would execute your trust, and return—if desired—the original—

I have nearly lost my eyes—in pouring on the State-Records—of which I accomplished ten volumes—in Folio—many of those containing an invaluable treasure—relative—to commerce—Police—History—in Several branches—and I Shall not be Surprised—as it happens with my N— England correspondents—Virginia might possess valuable Documents—to illustrate our State Annals—I have now two vol. before me—with regard to the Dutch Government on the Delaware (South river in N. Netherland) and before—I met different mercantile transactions—and intercourses of Individuals—of Dutch vessels—taking ladings of Tobacco in Virginia—and Sailing under English colours to London.   Perhaps[2]—you might through your friends discover the proofs of commercial or Political intercourse—between the years 1640—and 1670. by whose communications, you would lay our State under a great obligation, and I might glory, that in your opinion I had deserved to obtain this boon—

The prospects—with regard to the progress of pure undefiled religion become brighter every day So here as in Europe—even in our State its progress is Sensible—it must eventually be crowned with Success—I am confident—many riches—with regard to the gradual progress of the enlightened human mind may be collected in Italy and the Northern parts of Germany, and I continue to use my utmost exertions to Spurr my friends to discover these buried treasures—The expulsion of the Jews from the environs of Babylon by the Saracens—and their Spreading over Europe—is an important feature in this History—Is the mission of mahomet not another?

A Splendid church is build in N. york—under the name of First congregational Church—and I doubt—or Cambridge Shall provide it with an enlightened prudent Pastor—

I dare not—however[3] persuaded of your indulgence—to take more of your precious moments, and Shall be Satisfied—if—what I wrote—is not taken amiss—and if I am permitted, grateful of your kind regards, to recommend myself further in your good opinion—and assure you, that I remain, with the highest respect—

Dear and respected Sir! Your obed. and obliged—

FR. ADR. VAN DER KEMP

[55]

RC (DLC); dateline adjacent to closing; endorsed by TJ as received 6 July 1820 and so recorded in SJL; with TJ's notes on the above letter beneath endorsement: "his health

> visit to mr A.
> our escrutoires.
> religion
> Jews." RC (DLC); address cover

only; with PoC of TJ to John D'Wolf, 26 Jan. 1822, on verso; addressed: "Thomas Jefferson. LL.D. at his Seat Monticello Virginia"; franked; postmarked Trenton, N.Y., 27 June.

New York City's First Congregational Church was Unitarian in doctrine and incorporated in 1819. Installed at the end of 1821, William Ware, its first pastor, was indeed a graduate of Harvard University in CAMBRIDGE, Massachusetts (Sprague, *American Pulpit*, 8:xix, 511–2; *Harvard Catalogue*, 193, 924; *New-York Evening Post*, 20 Dec. 1821).

[1] Omitted word editorially supplied.
[2] Manuscript: "Perphaps."
[3] Manuscript: "howewer."

From de Bure Frères

MONSIEUR   paris ce 26 juin 1820.

Nous avons l'honneur de vous prevenir que nous venons de vous expedier par l'entremise de M Beaslie, votre consul au havre, une petite Caisse, dont nous vous donnons la facture de l'autre coté. Nous sommes fachés de n'avoir point pu vous avoir tout ce que vous demandiez, mais notre correspondant a Leipsick, a qui nous avions demandé le Dion Cassius de Sturz, nous a dit qu'il n'avoit point paru. l'hesiode de heinrich, n'est point complet, ce n'est que le Scutum herculis; les autres ouvrages d'hesiode n'y sont point. nous avons eu le xenophon d'Edinbourg que vous nous marquiez, vous en serez Content, Monsieur, cette edition est tres bien imprimée, et tres agreable a lire. nous avons pu vous trouver le volume du ciceron variorum que vous nous demandiez, nous sommes bien aises d'avoir pu vous completter cet ouvrage, qui est tres estimé, et que l'on trouve difficilement complet.

la premiere livraison de la collection des moralistes francois, pour la quelle vous nous aviez ecrit de souscrire, vient de paroitre, vous la trouverez dans votre caisse, nous garderons les autres volumes a mesure qu'ils paroitront, pour votre premier envoi.

nous deduisons comme vous le verrez, Monsieur, l'argent que vous nous aviez envoyé de trop l'année derniere, sur le compte de cette année, de sorte que vous ne nous redevez maintenant que 38^{francs} 40 Cent. cette somme pourra entrer dans le prochain compte, a moins qu'il ne vous soit plus commode de nous la faire remettre.

nous esperons, Monsieur, que cette petite caisse vous arrivera a bon port, nous l'avons bien recommandée a M Beaslie, et nous lui en avons marqué la valeur, pour qu'elle n'eprouve point de retards, ni de difficultés a vos Douanes.

nous avons l'honneur d'etre,   Monsieur Vos tres humbles et tres obeissants serviteurs

DE BURE FRERES.

Libraires du Roi, et de la Bibliotheque du Roi.

p.s. la nouvelle edition du manuel du libraire paroitra vers la fin de cette année.

EDITORS' TRANSLATION

SIR   Paris 26 June 1820.

We have the honor of informing you that we just sent to you through Mr. Beasley, your consul at Le Havre, a small crate, for which we give you the invoice on the other side. We regret being unable to obtain everything you requested, but our correspondent in Leipzig, whom we had asked for Sturz's Cassius Dio, told us that it had not been published. Heinrich's Hesiod is incomplete. As it only includes the *Scutum Herculis*, Hesiod's other works are not in it. We obtained the Xenophon printed in Edinburgh as you indicated. You will be happy with it, Sir. This edition is very well printed and pleasant to read. We were able to find you the variorum volume you requested of Cicero. We are quite happy that we could complete this work, which is highly esteemed and hard to locate complete.

The first volume of the *Collection de Moralistes Français*, to which you had asked us to subscribe, has just come out; you will find it in your crate. As the other volumes appear we will retain them for inclusion in your next shipment.

As you will see, Sir, we are deducting the surplus money you sent us last year from this year's account. In consequence, you now owe us only 38 francs and 40 centimes. This sum can be included in your next account, unless it is more convenient for you to remit it to us sooner.

We hope, Sir, that this little crate will reach you safely. We have commended it to Mr. Beasley's care and informed him of its value so as to avoid delays or difficulties from your customs.

We have the honor to be,   Sir, your very humble and very obedient servants   DE BURE FRERES.

Booksellers to the king, and to the royal library

P.S. The new edition of the *Manuel du Libraire* will appear toward the end of this year.

RC (MHi); in the hand of a representative of de Bure Frères; addressed on verso of enclosure: "A Monsieur Monsieur th. jefferson, a Monticello, en Virginie Etats unis D'Amerique"; mistakenly endorsed by TJ as received 6 Aug. 1820, but correctly recorded in SJL as received 26 Aug. 1820. Dupl (MHi); in the hand of a different representative of the firm, but signed in the same hand as RC; at head of text in signer's hand: "Duplicata"; addressed as above; with notation on address cover signed by Daniel Brent as TJ's "faithful & Respectful serv^t" and dated Department of State, 24 Sept. 1820, indicating that he had forwarded the letter to Milton; endorsed by TJ as a triplicate received 5 Oct. 1820. Tripl (MHi); on one sheet folded to form four pages, with enclosure on p. 1, letter on p. 3, and address on p. 4; with same signer as RC and Dupl and in hand of same representative as Dupl; at head of text in signer's hand: "triplicata"; addressed as above; stamp canceled; franked; stamped "SHIP"; postmarked New York, 21 Sept.; endorsed by TJ as a duplicate received 28 Sept. 1820. Translation by Dr. Genevieve Moene. Enclosed in Reuben G. Beasley to TJ, 8 July 1820.

ENCLOSURE

Invoice of Books for Thomas Jefferson Purchased from de Bure Frères

facture des Livres remis en une caisse cordée et emballée en Toile grasse et maigre, marquée Libri. ⚹ 5. **M.TJ.** adressée au havre a M Beasly, consul americain, le 24 Juin 1820.

	f
Xenophontis opera. gr. et lat. ex edit. Schneideri et Zeunii, Edinburgi, 1811, 10 vol. in—12. cart	120.
histoire des republiques Italiennes, par Sismondi. in—8° br. les Tomes 12 a 16. 5 vol	30.
Ciceronis epistolæ ad quintum fratrem, et ad Brutum, cum not. var. hagæ comit. 1725, in—8° vel.	12.
Juliani Imperat. Cæsares. gr. lat. et gall. cum not. var. ed. J. M. heusinger. gothæ, 1741, in—8° dem. rel	8.
Collection des Moralistes françois, publiée par amaury Duval, paris, 1820, in—8° Tom. 1 et 2. br. cont. montaigne	10.
frais de Caisse, de Douane, d'Emballage, &c.	11. 50
	191.^{f}50^c

avoir,	
d'aprés le Compte de 1819	153. 10
Il Reste dû	38.^{f}40

MS (MHi); written in the hand of a representative of de Bure Frères on verso of address cover of covering letter. Dupl (MHi); in same hand; with notation by TJ at head of text: "1820. June." Tripl (MHi); in same hand; conjoined with Tripl of covering letter. Also enclosed in Reuben G. Beasley to TJ, 8 July 1820, TJ to David Gelston, 27 Aug. 1820, and Gelston to TJ, 2 Sept. 1820.

FACTURE DES LIVRES . . . LE 24 JUIN 1820: "Invoice for books delivered in a crate tied with rope and wrapped in a thin oilcloth, labeled Libri. ⚹ 5. **M.TJ.**, directed to Le Havre to Mr. Beasley, the American consul, on 24 June 1820."

For explanations of bookbinding terms and abbreviations, see note to Invoice of Books for TJ Purchased from de Bure Frères, 30 May 1816, enclosed in David Bailie Warden to TJ, 12 July 1816. CUM NOT. VAR. HAGÆ COMIT. ("cum notis variorum. hagæ comitis"): "with notes by various people. The Hague." GALL.: "Gallic; Gaulish"; in this context, "French."

FRAIS DE CAISSE, DE DOUANE, D'EMBALLAGE, &C.: "cost of the crate, customs, packing, etc." AVOIR, D'APRÉS LE COMPTE DE 1819: "credit, from the 1819 account." IL RESTE DÛ: "The remainder due."

From William J. Matchet

Near Shelbyville,
Shelby County, Ky: June 26th 1820

WORTHY SIR,

Although I have not the honour of being personally acquainted with you; yet from the knowledge I have of your character, & the high opinion I have of you, I have bien induced to trouble you on this occasion with the hope that you will not pass this by unnotised—I wish you to express your opinion on the constutionallity or unconstutionallity of such laws as privilege the debtor to replevy the debt for years at the option of the state legislature; Or compel the creditor to take property at a certain proportion of its value—I wish to know particularly whether it is your opinion that the state legislatures are by the United States constitution vested with the power to privilege the debtor to delay the payment of acknowledged, just, & honourable debts for the term of one, two, ten, one hundred, or one thousand years—This is contended for by some of our leading characters—I enclose you an act of our legislature at their last session—A great many look forward to the next session of the legislature for an extention of the replevin law, & the passage of what is called a property law; which they argue can be effected without empairing the obligation of contracts—I wish to know what you think the true construction of the first paragraph in the tenth section of the first article of the United States constitution—

Hoping that you will not fail to give me a satisfactory answer, I shall conclude by assuring you that there is no person whose opinion would weigh more with me than yours—Your publick services command the respect, & deserve the thanks of your[1] fellow citizen

WM J. MATCHET—

RC (DLC); endorsed by TJ as received 27 July 1820 from William J. "Hatchet" and so recorded in SJL. RC (DLC); address cover only; with PoC of TJ to Archibald Thweatt, 24 Dec. 1821, on recto and verso; addressed: "Hon. Thomas Jefferson Esq. Montocello, Near Charlottesville, Albamarle County, Virginia"; stamped; postmarked Shelbyville, 28 June.

The enclosure was a copy, not found, of an 11 Feb. 1820 ACT "to regulate the sales of Property under Execution," which allowed defendants to replevy property taken in execution of their debts for one year. The replevin could be extended to a second year if the creditor refused to ac- cept payment in notes on the Bank of Kentucky (*Acts passed at the First Session of the Twenty-Eighth General Assembly for the Commonwealth of Kentucky* [Frankfort, 1820], 917–21).

The FIRST PARAGRAPH of article 1, section 10, of the United States Constitution reads "No state shall enter into any treaty, alliance, or confederation; grant letters of marque and reprisal; coin money; emit bills of credit; make anything but gold and silver coin a tender in payment of debts; pass any bill of attainder, ex post facto law, or law impairing the obligation of contracts, or grant any title of nobility."

[1] Manuscript: "you."

From James Maury

DEAR SIR,   Liverpool 26 June 1820

In passing a Porcelain Warehouse the other day, I was so struck with a correct likeness of Mr Roscoe in a small Bust that I thought it would be pleasing to you to have the opportunity of giving it a place in your Collection at Monticello & I have requested Mr Pollard of Richmond to forward it, of which I pray your acceptance with the best wishes of your old obliged friend   JAMES MAURY

RC (DLC); at foot of text: "Thomas Jefferson Monticello"; endorsed by TJ as received 13 Aug. 1820 and so recorded in SJL. Enclosed in TJ to Bernard Peyton, 16 Mar., and Peyton to TJ, 19 Mar. 1821.

An image of the SMALL BUST of William Roscoe sent to TJ is reproduced elsewhere in this volume.

To James Monroe

TH:J. TO THE PRESIDENT   June 27. 20.

Instead of the unintelligible sketch I gave you the other day, I send it drawn more at large. mrs Monroe & yourself may take some hints from it for a better plan of your own. this supposes 10.f. in front, and 8.f in flank added to your sills. a flat of 12.f. square is formed at the top, to make your present rafters answer, & to lighten the appearance of the roof. Affectionate and respectful salutations.

RC (Frank C. Littleton, Aldie, Va., 1944, on deposit ViU: TJP); dateline at foot of text; addressed: "President of the United States"; endorsed in an unidentified hand, with date of composition mis- takenly given as 20 June 1820. Not re- corded in SJL. Enclosure, not found, probably pertained to the construction of the main house at Monroe's Oak Hill es- tate in Loudoun County.

From Fernagus De Gelone

SIR.   New Yorck June 29. 1820

I have received the honour of your letter. It mentions what I did ex- pect, devoutedness to improvement and politeness. I did feel so proud, that I had it inserted in the Commercial Advertiser. I take the liberty of sending you a short part of the plan which I pursue. it is to embrace all the sections of human knowledge. I know nothing of the method of Laharpe, nor of those of Pestalozzi, Sicard, Lancaster, Bell. As mine is founded on Mathematics, it must have more or less anal- ogy with theirs. it is truth. I hope You will read the manuscript, and

Send it back at leisure. I would be happy even to know That You found me incorrect.

hoping that You are well and shall be long well, Sir. I am your most obedient servant   FERNAGUS DE GELONE

I had the delight of being understood by a Deaf and Dumb. Dr Mitchill introduced me to Dr Stansbury. his System, however good, is very limited.

RC (MHi); at head of text: "Thomas Jefferson, Esqr"; endorsed by TJ as received 6 July 1820 and so recorded in SJL. Enclosure not found.

From Levett Harris

SIR,   Philadelphia 29. June 1820.

I have had the honor to receive your very kind letter of the 22^d Inst., in reply to the one I addressed to you on the 15th and I return you my best acknowledgments for the expressions of interest & regard contained in it.

I shall profit of the time you have allotted Yourself at Monticello, previous to your departure for your distant Estate, to pay you my respects:—and Shall leave here for this purpose, in all the next week.

And I beg to tender you Sir, in advance, the renewed Assurances of my most profound Respect and Veneration.

LEVETT HARRIS

RC (DLC); dateline beneath signature; endorsed by TJ as received 6 July 1820 and so recorded in SJL. RC (DLC); address cover only; with PoC of TJ to Joseph C. Cabell, 25 Jan. 1822, on verso; addressed: "Thomas Jefferson late President of the United states Monticello"; franked; postmarked Philadelphia, 30 June.

A missing letter from Harris to TJ of 27 July 1820 (address cover only in DLC; with PoC of TJ to Mathew Carey, 11 Dec. 1821, on verso; addressed [with parentheses editorially changed to brackets]: "Thomas Jefferson [late President of the United States] Monticello"; franked; postmarked Philadelphia, 27 July) is recorded in SJL as received 4 Aug. 1820 from Philadelphia.

From William Short

DEAR SIR   Philad^a June 29. 1820

I had the pleasure of thanking you in part in my letter of May 2. for your most invaluable favor contained in yours of April. I say in part; for it would take more than one letter to contain the whole of my gratitude for this most acceptable mark of your friendship. I have read it over & over again; always with delight & instruction, & a renewed sense of my obligation to your amiable grandaughter as well as to yourself. I should have repeated my thanks to you ere this, but for the fear of adding to all the trouble of correspondence, which I know you are overloaded with by your friends & others.

I cannot however let Mr Harris go without carrying to you some mark of remembrance from one of your oldest, & certainly most attached friends. He has moreover requested me to do him the favor & pleasure of sending a letter by him. Without that, I should not probably have given you this trouble at this moment.

Mr Harris tells me that having heard from you, that you will still be at Monticello for three weeks, he has determined to avail himself of it to go & pay his respects to you—One of the motives seems to be his great anxiety to stand <u>rectus</u> in your eyes—by exposing to you the whole truth relative to his conduct, whilst acting abroad under a commission from Government—An attempt has been made by circulating anonymous & printed handbills, to stain him with corruption in his consular office. He has at length been able to fix these handbills on their author or distributor, & has instituted a suit against him. This is all that the most innocent man can do in such a case; as it evinces his desire to have the truth & the whole truth brought forward to the public knowlege.

This however is necessarily a slow process, & leaves a painful interval for public impressions. Mr Harris's delicacy & sensibility make him, I think, too much alive to this & too impatient under it. He is extremely anxious in the mean time, not to lose his fair standing in the public estimation & particularly in yours, & the other members of Government under whom he acted.

I am not acquainted with his adverse party who is a merchant that went to establish himself at St Petersburgh during the consulship of Mr Harris, & where probably the situation of Mr Harris gave him greater advantages in commercial speculations. And if this should have given rise to envy, hatred & malice, we need not be surprized at any consequences arising therefrom.

The first knowlege I ever had of Mr Harris was from Count Romanzow[1] at Paris. Every thing he said to me of him was of the most flattering kind, & shewed me that Mr Harris had by his good & proper & prudent conduct placed himself at St Petersburgh, in a situation very well calculated to excite envy—Count R. who took frequent opportunities of speaking to me of Mr Harris, assured me more than once that his conduct had been such as not only to acquire his (C^t R's) esteem, but also that of the Emperor—& he expressed to me an earnest desire that the American Government should be informed of this.

Mr Harris seems to have no doubt that Mr Adams, the present Sec. of State, is his most bitter enemy—If so, I should not be surprized if his envy also had been excited by the situation which he held in the estimation of C^t Romanzow; & which I am persuaded the Count took no pains to conceal from him. Yet if Mr Harris should be correct in supposing that Mr Adams has excited these calumnies, surely it would be acting a part very unworthy of the high office he now holds, & which should dispose him to protect the character of those who have acted worthily under that department rather than give his countenance towards destroying it. Since the return of Mr Harris to this country, he has passed a great part of his time in the same house with me. I have therefore seen a great deal of him—And I can say with great truth that every thing which I have seen, has been indicative of the most unexceptionable conduct, & highly honorable sentiments. And such I have no doubt he will appear before the tribunal which is to draw out the whole truth on his subject.

Mr Harris's departure at this moment for Monticello brings to my view in striking colors, the wish I have felt every year to carry into execution a similar project—& which has always been postponed by feelings that I know not how to explain—Whilst I feel a very sincere wish to visit the friends of my youth, yet this is always checked by a certain mixture of melancholy that I cannot account for. There is one friend at least there with whom I should feel no melancholy but at the moment of my separation from him—And then indeed if I should consider it a long & last farewell, the pain would be more than I should have courage to encounter.　　　　I have always also apprehended I should experience a certain degree of embarassment in a visit to that part of Virginia which I most wish to see. I may be wrong—but I have long felt a great change in my former disposition towards two persons in your part of the country—insomuch that I hope, & shall always endeavour, never to see them again. And yet it would be more pointed than I would wish to be, to avoid them if I were to be in their neighborhood. These men have both attained by one of those jeux du hazard, so often exhibited in elective Republics, the highest posts in the country. They may therefore laugh at my unfavorable disposition towards them, & certainly would laugh at it, if they knew it. I do not allow myself to carry this so far as to be their enemy—On the contrary I wish them both well—from the remains of old habit—although this sentiment is not entirely free of a certain degree of contempt for their metaphysical <u>charlatanerie</u>—& wch would have been greater probably if it had not been crowned with such unexpected success—For after all—It is certain that in this world, success in human affairs, tends more than anything else to diminish that contempt which they so often deserve.

God bless & preserve you my dear sir—long to enjoy health & happiness with those who are near & dear to you—This is the earnest prayer of your affectionate friend   W: Short

RC (DLC); endorsed by TJ as received 11 July 1820 and so recorded in SJL.

RECTUS: short for "rectus in curia," meaning "free from charge or offense" (*Black's Law Dictionary*). The AUTHOR OR DISTRIBUTOR of the charges against

Levett Harris was William D. Lewis. The TWO PERSONS IN YOUR PART OF THE COUNTRY were President James Monroe and his predecessor, James Madison. JEUX DU HAZARD: "games of chance."

[1] Manuscript: "Romazow."

To John Wayles Eppes

DEAR SIR   Monticello June 30. 20.
I am become quite delinquent in epistolary correspondence; my right wrist, from an antient dislocation, grows now so stiff, as to render writing a slow and painful operation, and has produced an aversion to the pen almost insuperable. I go therefore to the writing table under the spur of necessity alone.   The delay in the opening of our seminary in this neighborhood has proceeded entirely from it's conversion into a general and public University, instead of a local &[1] private college. the latter would have been ready and opened two years ago. the general institution requires more extensive preparation. the legislature, at their last session authorised us to borrow 60,000.D. on the pledge of our own funds, that is, of the annual public donation of 15,000.D. we have accordingly done so, and have so made our contracts as to ensure the completion of the whole of our buildings for the accomodation of Professors & students by autumn 12.month. this secures ultimately, and independently of all change of opinion an institution on a full scale embracing the whole circle of sciences; and we consider a compleat, tho' later institution, as preferable to an earlier, but defective one. if the legislature leaves us to repay our loan from our own funds they will be tied up by this object for 5. years to come: & so long all the buildings will remain empty and idle, & a standing mark of regret and reproach to those whose fault it will be. but we believe it impossible that this will be permitted either by the nation or it's representatives. and we have no doubt that this state of things

being reported to them, as it will be at their next session, they will remit the loan, and the more readily as it is from the literary fund we have obtained it, a fund ready raised, appropriated by law to the purpose of education, and therefore legitimately applied to the establishment of an University. in this event our funds will be liberated on the 1st day of Jan. next; and we shall then immediately take measures to procure our professors, which can certainly be done by autumn 12month. (1821.[2]) and the institution then be opened. if this takes place, which will be known early in the next session, then what I have thought best with respect to the object of our mutual care, Francis, is that he shall employ the intervening time in compleating himself in the antient languages with Stack, and the Mathematics with Ragland, an associate with Stack, & adequate to this object: and he already possesses the modern languages. with these acquisitions, he will enter the University, fall 12.month for Astronomy, Natural Philosophy, chemistry, natural history & Rhetoric, & finish them by the close of 22. this will be as compleat a course of education as the circumstances of our country call for, adding to it, after he leaves the University, ethics, history [and Law, if you please,] which can as well be acquired in his closet, as at an University. this is a view of one branch of our dilemma, that which supposes a remission of our debt by the legislature. let us now view the 2d possibility, that the University is to be locked up until our loan is redeemed by our own funds, which would remove the opening the University until beyond Francis's time.   After getting antient languages from Stack, and Mathematics from Ragland, he will want Astronomy, Natural philosophy, chemistry, nat^l history and Rhetoric. Where must he go for them? on the subject of Eastern seminaries and Eastern[3] character, I concur entirely with you. Francis's honorable mind, his fine dispositions and high promise ought not to be exposed to infection from the fanaticism, the hypocrisy the selfish morals, and crooked politics of the East. nor would the half way science of that quarter be equal to what he can get from a single character who happens to be in the South. for Nat^l philosophy, chemistry, nat^l history, no man in the US. is equal to Cooper, now professor of the College of Columbia S.C. he has more science in his single head than all the Colleges of New England New Jersey, and I may add Virginia put together. and I doubt[4] not there are other professors there, as adequate as elsewhere to Astronomy and Rhetoric, which would not be within Cooper's line. Columbia you know is in the center of S.C. a hilly & healthy country; and the state of society and morals there very much as our own, and much indeed of the society is of our own emigrated countrymen. should therefore the legislature leave our own establishment at a stand, I know no place so worthy of recommendation as Columbia.   But there is a 3^d possibility which must be thought of also. it is very possible that Stack's school may dissolve itself, by losing it's younger boys, and some even of the larger, who need more discipline than he has nerve to enforce, and who may therefore be withdrawn by their parents. in that case Columbia I think should be our immediate choice. these are my views on the subject of your enquiry, which I submit for your consideration. I will write to Cooper immediately to know the state of the sciences in that college (not within his line) and the terms of tuition & board.

My commitment for Mr Nicholas is still of uncertain issue. if a compromise, now in negociation, succeeds, of which it is said there is a good prospect, I shall be saved by the time it provides for the disposal of his estate as well as for the preference of bonâ fide creditors. 3. or 4 of the shavers only have held off, and it is believed they are now disposed to concur. this will be known in a few days. if this compromise fails it is very possible I may have to advance the money, and not certain that I shall be ever reimbursed. besides this I have considerable debts of my own, which the fall of produce, likely to be permanent, forbids me to count on paying from annual crops. I had therefore proposed to begin to prepare for these cases by selling some lands; having scruples about selling negroes but for delinquency, or on their own request. but your proposition gets me over these scruples as it is in fact to keep them in the family. and on that ground it will be acceptable, and indeed desirable, with some necessary modifications. for the negroes here being under engagement for 3. or 4. years to come, the sale must be from those in Bedford only. but there I could not part with 10. men without breaking up my plantations. I would spare 20. negroes in all from those plantations, men women and children in the usual proportions: and I should think this really more advantageous for Francis than all men. I know no error more consuming to an estate than that of stocking farms with men almost exclusively. I consider a woman who brings a child every two years as more profitable than the best man of the farm. what she produces is an addition to the capital, while his labors disappear in mere consumption. the agreement you propose therefore, with this modification would be really acceptable to me, and more salutary for my affairs than to sell land only. the selection of the individuals should be made with a fair and favorable eye to the interests of Francis, & the valuation left to any good and unconnected judges.

With respect to the lands in Bedford, those designated on a former occasion to you, at the South end of the tract, are not of the quality I expected. I had never at that time seen them, and was guided in their allotment[5] by information from others, and the consideration that those given to mr Randolph being in the North, it would be better to have in the middle of the tract those reserved for future appropriation. but having repeated opportunities afterwards of examining the lands I found the quality not what I had supposed. I determined therefore to substitute a better portion; and on that I have built a house exactly on the plan once thought of for Pantops, and intended from the beginning for Francis: and I have always purposed, as soon as he should come of age to put him into possession of the house and a portion of land including it, of which there is a sufficiency of open fields in good heart, and a large body of woodlands adjacent of the best quality and lying well; for some of which two years ago I was assured I might have 100.D. an acre if I would part with it. this disposition therefore you may consider as fixed, and may accomodate to it the provisions for him you may propose yourself. the beauty and healthiness of that country, his familiarity with it and it's society will I am sure make it an agreeable residence to him. if you should conclude to accede to my proposition, let me hear from you as soon as convenient, and immediately after the meeting of our visitors on the 2ᵈ of October, I shall be happy to meet you at Poplar Forest and carry the arrangement into execution.

In your letter of Feb. 6. you were so kind as to propose that we shᵈ remove to Poplar Forest the harpsicord of Millbrook, where you observed it was not in use. it would certainly be a relief to the heavy hours of that place to Martha and the girls. this offer therefore is thankfully accepted on the supposition it is not used where it is, and on the condition that we hold and leave it in it's new position in the hands of Francis, subject to your orders. on this ground I will take some occasion of sending a waggon for it's transportation.   In the mean time is it impossible that mrs Eppes yourself and family should pay a visit to Monticello where we could not be made happier than by seeing you. it is little over a day's journey whether by New Canton or Buckingham C.H. the former being the best road. and our University is now so far advanced as to be worth seeing. it exhibits already the appearance of a beautiful Academical village, of the finest models of building and of classical architecture, in the US. it begins to be much visited by strangers and admired by all, for the beauty, originality and convenience of the plan. by autumn 3 ranges of buildings will be erected 600.f. long, with colonnades and arcades of the same length in front for communication below, and terrasses of the same extent for communication above: and, by the fall of the next year, a 4ᵗʰ range will be done, which compleats the whole (the Library excepted) and will form an establishment of 10. Pavilions for professors, 6. hotels or boarding houses, and 100. Dormitories. these will have cost in the whole about 130,000 D. there will remain then nothing to be added at present but a building for the Library of about 40,000.D. cost. all this is surely worth a journey of 50. miles, and requires no effort but to think you can do it, and it is done. think so then, and give that gratification to the sincere affection with which I salute you.

TH: JEFFERSON

RC (ViU: TJP); brackets in original; edge torn, with missing text supplied from PoC; addressed: "John W. Eppes esq. Mill-brook." PoC (MHi); first four pages only; endorsed by TJ. PoC (ViU: TJP-ER); remaining two pages only; endorsed by TJ.

The Virginia General Assembly passed "An act authorising the Visitors of the University of Virginia to borrow money for finishing the buildings thereof" on 24 Feb. 1820, during its LAST SESSION (*Acts of Assembly* [1819–20 sess.], 14). Some of TJ's Monticello slaves were UNDER ENGAGEMENT to Thomas Jefferson Randolph FOR 3. OR 4. YEARS TO COME (see TJ's Notes on Lease of Tufton and Lego to Randolph, [after 1 Jan. 1818]). In October 1801 TJ had informed his sons-in-law, John Wayles Eppes and Thomas

Mann Randolph, that he was setting aside for each of them a portion of his LANDS IN BEDFORD County (*PTJ*, 35:414–5, 418–20). He had long INTENDED to give his grandson Francis Eppes the part containing the house at Poplar Forest (TJ to John Wayles Eppes, 18 Sept. 1812).

IN GOOD HEART, in this context, means "in excellent condition" (*OED*). MARTHA: Martha Jefferson Randolph. The 3 RANGES OF BUILDINGS under construction at the University of Virginia were located on the West Lawn, East Lawn, and East Range.

[1] Manuscript: "& and."
[2] Manuscript: "1721."
[3] RC: "Easttern." PoC: "Eastern."
[4] Manuscript: "dowbt."
[5] Preceding three words interlined.

To Samuel Garland

SIR   Monticello. June 30. 20.

Your two letters of the 15th and 21st inst. have been recieved. on the withdrawing of one half of our circulating medium, the prostration of commerce produced by it, and the fall in the price of produce which suddenly ensued and is likely to be permanent, I became sensible that the debts which I had expected to pay from annual crops as prices had been, could no longer be met in that way. I determined therefore at once, as soon as things [s]hould take their new stand, and a fair price could be obtained, to make a sale of property so as to pay every thing I owe. my expences of the last year having been on the usual scale, & the produce of the year selling but for one half the usual price, have added that much to the calls on me. I have just accomplished one sale which will free me from all minor calls. I am in treaty for another which I hope to close, and as soon as I can get to Bedford I shall endeavor to make a 3ᵈ sale sufficient to compleat the discharge of every thing I owe. not knowing what instalments I may be forced to admit, I am not able as yet to fix particular epochs of payment; but as soon as these sales can be accomplished, I will inform you & fix times. my present expectation is that I can discharge the bond to mr Millar at two instalments of the next spring, & the spring after that. of one thing I pray you to be assured that it shall be as early as the sale of either produce or property can enable me to effect it. mr White's money will be in my hands within a few days. if I do not go to Bedford within a fortnight I will inclose by mail either the cash, or an order for it on Richmond accordingly as the payment is made to me here or there. I pray you to accept the assurance of my great respect.

TH: JEFFERSON

PoC (MHi); on verso of reused address cover of William A. Burwell to TJ, 22 May 1820; one word faint; at foot of text: "Mʳ <E> S. Garland"; endorsed by TJ.

ONE SALE: TJ had recently sold his 400-acre Pouncey's tract in Albemarle County to Charles Everette, from whom he received his first installment on 13 July 1820 (*MB*, 2:1365). MR MILLAR: Boyd Miller.

From John Gorman

July 1ˢᵗ 1820

SIR

Mʳ Jefferson I had a message from Mʳ Randolf By Jmˢ Dinsmore yesterday Requesting Thrimston to go to the harvest for a week or two the Boy is Learning faster than I Expected he Would Do. it Would hinder his Progress to keep him longer away or Even that time if it Could be helped but as the harvest is Ripe you Can Do as you think Proper but I Wished to Let you know of his going first

=======

If you think Well of sending that other boy of 12 or 13 years old I will take him and find him If he is as willing to Learn as Thrimston his being younger will make him a Better hand.. I thought I would Mention it to you as I have had two people applying to me to take their Sons but as I Promised you I wished to Let you know

With respect your Humble Servant   JNᵒ GORMAN

RC (CSmH: JF); dateline at foot of text; addressed: "Mʳ Jefferson Montesella"; endorsed by TJ as received 2 July 1820.

A missing letter from Gorman to TJ of 7 Feb. 1820 is recorded in SJL as received the day it was written.

From James Deneale

Sir   Dumfries 2^d July 1820

altho there is no persons opinion I would prefer to yours on any Invention of mine as none If favourable Could be more Useful to me, I should not have Ventured to trouble you, If the particular Situation in which I am placed had not render^d it Neccessary. A few days past I Enclosed the Instrument (I now Enclose to you) to a Mr Goolrick of Fredricksburg, he on returning it writes me amongst other things in the following words to wit "the Idea of the mapper I am Inclined is not a new one Mr Girrardin was at my house 6 or Seven years ago he lived at that time in the neighbourhood of Montecello and was Intimate with Mr Jefferson as Near as my recollection Serves me at So remote a period I think I was Inform^d that Mr Jefferson used Something Similar to your mapper in platting fields &C" as I Could Consciencously have Sworn that I believed I was the original Inventor of the Enclosed Instrument before the Receipt of this letter: I Cannot now do it untill I hear from you. altho I believe Mr Goolrick has mistaken Mr Girrardins description of your Instrument I have deem^d it the Correct[1] Course to Enclose it. may I ask the favour of you after Examining of it and If not your Invention to Say your opinion of it and If favourable[2] whethr I may make that opinion Publick practical Surveyors here have born testimony to its usefulness. I have for many years platted by Latitude & departure instead of Course and distance. by this Means the distance was a Check upon my work. it occur^d to me that an Instrument on the plan Sent would facilitate mapping as Neither protractor, Sweep, Scale,[3] or Even dividers would be neccessary. after the mapping Sheet is prepared like the one Enclosed which by the by Should last a surveyor his life time as I have made dozens of maps on the same Sheet by drawing the outlines of the map with a black lead pencil when the map is prick^d off on a Clean Sheet with a rubber the lines are rubbed out and the pricks Stop^d by pressing on them the Sheet is ready for a new map. this Sheet Should be Carefully laid off[4] and to prevent Blunders in Calculating the Contents of your map Each Inch Should be a red line as the map lies before you you may in a few minutes add up the Contents of your map. the mapper is on a scale of Forty poles to an Inch but may be made to any Scale, in useing this Instrument you map by the Latitude & departure of your Course and not by the Course and distance If your Latitude is north the angle of the Instrument is Upwards. If South downward the perpendicular of the Instrument is the Latitude and the Base the Departure it has occur^d to me there is a possibility I am describing what you well know the thought has Stopt me your General Character assures me you will pardon this freedom

yours Respectfully   JAMES DENEALE

one word more. the Hypothenuse of this Instrument is intended as a ruler as it is on the same Scale as you rule the line you See If your distance is Correct   JD[5]

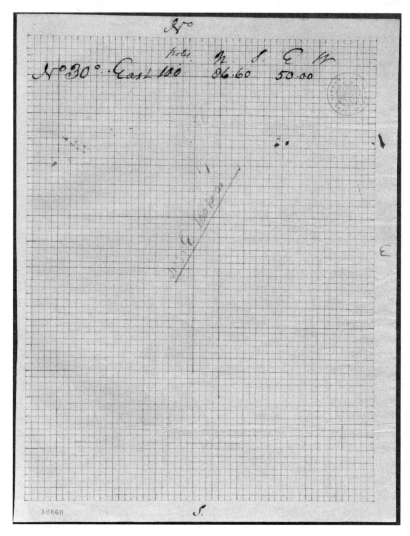

RC (DLC); endorsed by TJ as received 6 July 1820 and so recorded in SJL. RC   (DLC); address cover only; with PoC of TJ to David Easton, 14 Jan. 1822, on verso; addressed: "Thomas Jefferson Esqʳ Montecello"; franked; postmarked Dumfries, 2 July.

James Deneale (ca. 1765–1821), miller and inventor, was a native Virginian. He resided by 1800 in Prince William County, where for many years he operated a gristmill and a nearby manufacturing mill on Quantico Creek just outside of Dumfries. Deneale received five federal patents during his lifetime: for a "Kiln for drying grain" in 1800, an improved threshing machine in 1804, a "perpetual oven" in 1806, a "wheat rubber" machine in 1809, and an "Instrument for mapping lands, &c." on 3 Aug. 1820. He also served as county sheriff, 1816–17, and applied unsuccessfully to be principal engineer to the Virginia Board of Public Works in 1818. Having evidently lost both of his mills in 1821 at an auction for debt,

Deneale died later that year at his home near Dumfries (*Federal Gazette & Baltimore Daily Advertiser*, 5 Jan. 1801; *Alexandria Daily Advertiser*, 12 Dec. 1804; *Norfolk Gazette and Publick Ledger*, 14 Dec. 1810; *List of Patents*, 22, 48, 58, 74, 215; *Prince William Reliquary* 4 [2005]: 31; Deneale to Bernard Peyton, 31 May 1818 [Vi: RG 57, Board of Public Works, Applications for Position of Principal Engineer]; *Alexandria Gazette & Daily Advertiser*, 16 Apr. 1821; Washington *Daily National Intelligencer*, 18 Sept. 1821).

A SWEEP is "an instrument used for drawing curves at a large radius" (*OED*).

[1] Manuscript: "Corrct."
[2] Preceding two words interlined.
[3] Manuscript: "Scole."
[4] Manuscript: "of."
[5] Remainder on separate sheet.

From Benjamin B. Jackson

DEAR SIR,   (Perkinsonville) Amelia Cty. va. July 2nd. 1820

Fully convinced of the real and incalculable importance of an early and familiar acquaintance with our language, I have devoted much of my time to the study of it;—and, during one or two years, I have been charged with the delightful task of giving instruction on this useful branch of learning.[1] During my feeble but assiduous endeavours to enter the parts to me unknown and thence bring to my view the hidden value of the English Language, I found my progress greatly impeded by some insuperable difficulties. I mean, difficulties that I could not remove. Every construction that I can lay upon passages containing these difficulties, seems to be accompanied with ambiguity. In consequence of the absence of proper means, I live in a silent and unfrequented retirement, through the darkening shades of which there scarcely ever beams a single ray of instruction, to penetrate the film which nature has drawn over my eyes and to illumine my dark mind. I then in an awkward, but humble and sincere manner, beg you to lead me into the light of the method most proper to solve these difficulties attending the Etymological and Syntactical construction of a few sentences which I shall here introduce: "The compiler &C. hopes it will not be deemed inconsistent with the nature and design of his work, to make a short address &C." Now of what construction the infinitive "to make" and the <u>neuter</u> pronoun "it" are capable, I cannot, with certainty ascertain. But my low opinion is, that this member of the sentence; "to make a short address &C." stands independently and absolutely as the antecedent to the pronoun "it" or rather as the subject, for which this pronoun is substituded. In the following instance with regard to the Participle, my decision is equally dubious and uncertain: "He was sent to prepare the way by <u>preaching</u> repentance."

How shall I construe the participle "preaching?" as a participial noun governed by the foregoing preposition; agreeably to the 17th. rule of L. Murray's Syntax? Will this Participial Noun still retain the active power of its origin[?] If not on what principle of Syntax, can the Noun "repentance" be construed? Were the sentence to assume this form, "He was sent to prepare the way by the preaching of repentance[,"] that is, with the definite article "the" immediately[2] before and the preposition "of" immediately after the Participle "preaching["] all obscurity on that point would then vanish. I have also laboured under some misconception of the Subjunctive Mood. The general circumstances most necessary to a variation of the Indicative Mood to the Subjunctive, seem to be two: doubt and futurity. Yet it appears, that some of the tenses are invariably the same whether of the Indicative or Subjunctive form and some are different. Yr. instruction to me on the few points which I have awkwardly suggested, and many others which I could enumerate, were I disposed to encroach upon your peacfu[l] hours with my (I fear) intrusive and impertinent questions.—I say, a few hints from you in answer to my humble, candid requests, would be within my breast a source of much gratitude to my instructor.

Please accept this with the assurance of the respect and sincere esteem of yr. humble Servant   BENJAMIN B. JACKSON

P.S.

Direct yr. answers to Perkinsonville or to Amelia C.H.

RC (MHi); edge trimmed; postscript adjacent to closing; endorsed by TJ as a letter from "Jackson Benj. G." received 27 July 1820 and so recorded in SJL.

The FEW SENTENCES are from Lindley Murray, *English Grammar, adapted to the Different Classes of Learners, with An Appendix, containing Rules and Observations, for assisting the more advanced student to write with perspicuity and accuracy* (Philadelphia, 1800, and other eds.; Sowerby, no. 4851), pp. 310 and 172, respectively. The 17TH. RULE in Murray's book reads: "Prepositions govern the objective case: as, 'I have heard a good character *of her*;' '*From him* that is needy turn not away;' 'A word to the wise is sufficient *for them*;' 'Strength of mind is *with them* that are pure in heart'" (p. 177).

[1] Manuscript: "learnig."
[2] Manuscript: "inmediately."

[73]

From Joseph Marx

SIR   Richmond 3ᵈ July 1820—

I avail myself of the conveyance afforded me by Governor Randolph to transmit and to request Your acceptance, of the Volume containing the proceedings of the Sanhedrin, convened by order of the Emperor Buonaparte,

should any part of their Deliberations, or sentiments expressed by any member of that Body, tend to confirm the liberal and enlightned views, expressed by Yourself, for that persecuted Race, when last I had the honor and pleasure of an interview, it will prove to me a source of high gratification

I am with sentiments of profound Respect

sir Your most Obedient sevt   JOSEPH MARX

RC (DLC); at foot of text: "Thomas Jefferson Esqr"; endorsed by TJ as received 7 July 1820 and so recorded in SJL. Enclosure: Diogène Tama, *Transactions of the Parisian Sanhedrim, or Acts of the Assembly of Israelitish Deputies of* *France and Italy, convoked at Paris by an imperial and royal decree, dated May 30, 1806,* ed. and trans. F. D. Kirwan (London, 1807; Poor, *Jefferson's Library,* 9 [no. 522]).

From Charles Willson Peale

Belfield July[1] 3ᵈ 1820

In the hope, my dear Sir, of giving you some little amusement on what I concieve an interresting subject, which my Son Rembrandt has very nearly[2] completed for the Public Eye, Therefore I have made a Sketch of his Picture, enclosed, and trouble you once more with my address and a description of "Peale's great Moral Picture the Court of Death." From Portius Poem on Death.

The center figuers shew the certainty of Death—The lifeless trunk of man lies prostrate at the foot of the awful power which commands the period of life—Sublime in its obscurity.

Old Age, conscious of his approaching end, submits to the invitable and wise decree, And is supported by Virtue, whose pious thoughts are turned to heaven—"thy will be done."

The right hand Group represents War with soul inflamed by envy, revenge, Ambition, striding over helpless innocence and unprotected Weakness. Behind him lies a Youthful Warriour, the victim of Glory, breathing his last Gasp. The disolating torch precedes—Famine & Pestilence follow.

[74]

The left hand Group represents the effects of Vice. A hapless Youth, whose noble energies are blasted by intemperance, holding the fatal Cup, deceptive Pleasure smiling on his ruin & preparing another draught. The shadow of death rest on the Bowl. At his shoulder stands remorse—Frenzy at his feet & in his shadow revolting Suecide. Fever, Opoplexy, Palsey, Gout, consumption &c terminate the Scene.

When I made my sketch from the picture the latter figuers was not painted in, as may [be]³ seen by the enclosed slight drawing. it is a very rude and imperfect performance, and is only ment to give an Idea of the design, The Painting is powerful in its effect, The drawing and colouring fine—The picture is 24 feet long & 13 feet high, and the figures a little⁴ larger than life, so that [at]⁵ a proper distance to take in the whole of the Picture they⁶ appear of the proper size.   It is a great effort of the genius of Rembrandt, and he has made great exertions to make it worthy of Admiration, on which rests much of his pecuniary concerns, for under the Idea that a Museum would give considerable support to a wife & 9 children, he has been at more expence in its establishment, than our present population can justifie. His Museum is a pattern of neatness, but his Buildings are too expensive for the profits of exhibition in Baltemore. And if this great Picture does not give him relief he must double his deligence in the Portrait line to extricate himself from a heavy rent. for he has engaged to pay too high an Interest for the Monies he owes for making his House.

I love the Art of Painting, but the greatest merit of execution on subjects that have not a virtuous tendency, loose all their value in my estimation.

A Picture now Exhibiting in Philadᵃ attracts an abundance of Visitants, It is the inside of a Chapel of Capucens at Rome—The painting has been made on the spot, and is a very well painted picture. It was purchased by a gentleman of fortune on his travels⁷ at a high price it is said, & also that the income from its exhibition is to be applied to a charitable Institution. The Picture is placed in the most advantagous light, with art, and no other picture in the Room—Therefore the Illusion is improoved. I am greatly mistaken if my Sons picture is not more attractive—Can it be partiality in me? my feeling I think does not deceive me.   I would have given you some extracts from Portius Poem on Death. but I fear I have been too lenthy already, and perhaps you possess the Poem. I shall only remark that Rembrandt has endeavored to produce a speaking Picture, and to avoid all emblamatical signs.

Pardon my prolexity—I wish to serve not to oppress you.[8] May you long live enjoying perfect health, and any thing I can do to promote your amusement will be grateful to

your friend   C W PEALE

RC (DLC); endorsed by TJ as received 8 July 1820 and so recorded in SJL. RC (Edward Churchill, Haddonfield, N.J., 1991); address cover only; with PoC of TJ to Ellen W. Randolph (Coolidge), 16 Jan. 1822, on recto and verso; addressed: "Thomas Jefferson Esqr Monticlla Verginea"; franked; postmarked Germantown, Pa., 5 July. PoC (PPAmP: Peale Letterbook).

Charles Willson Peale's enclosed SKETCH OF HIS PICTURE may be the elder Peale's pencil-and-ink version of Rembrandt Peale's massive oil-on-canvas depiction of THE COURT OF DEATH reproduced from a private collection in Peale, Papers, 3:827. The painting has long been owned by the Detroit Institute of Arts and was inspired by Beilby Porteus (PORTIUS), Death: A Poetical Essay (Cambridge, Eng., 1759).

THY WILL BE DONE is from the Lord's Prayer in the Bible (Matthew 6.10; Luke 11.2).

The French artist François Marius Granet painted The Choir of the Capuchin Church in Rome (CHAPEL OF CAPUCENS) in 1814–15, and he copied it a number of times thereafter. The piece on display in Philadelphia was probably the one that had been recently "conveyed to the United States by an American merchant" (Boston Intelligencer & Evening Gazette, 15 Jan. 1820). The original is owned by the Metropolitan Museum of Art in New York.

[1] Reworked from "June."
[2] Manuscript: "nealy."
[3] Omitted word editorially supplied.
[4] Manuscript: "alittle."
[5] Omitted word editorially supplied.
[6] Manuscript: "thy."
[7] Preceding three words interlined.
[8] Omitted period at right margin editorially supplied.

To Thomas Cooper

DEAR SIR   Monticello. July 4. 20

I was about addressing a letter to you at Columbia, when I recieved information by Dr Caldwell that he had left you in Philadelphia. I learnt with great pleasure by your's of May 3. that our friends of S. Carolina had had the wisdom so readily to avail themselves of your disengagement with us. yet I could not, & cannot renounce the hope that it is not to be final. I had felt no concern at the bellowings of our pulpit mountebanks, half rogues, half dupes; having ever found that the only way to get along in any public concern is, first to decide wisely, then to persevere steadily, without regarding[1] the noise to right or left, assured that all will rally in the end, to what has been well devised in the beginning. but some of our younger colleagu[es,] not hardened as I had been to the currycomb, were skittish & restless under it, as young colts are at their first handling. I joined them however, in the general result, on another ground. we had borrowed of the literary fund 60,000.D. under the authority of the legislature and on the pledge of our annual donation; to comp[le]at all the building[s] for the accomodation of the Professors and students. if the legislatur[e] should really leave us to reimburse the loan from our own revenue that would be tied up for 5. years before we could open the Universit[y.] in this case every motive of justice and expediency made it a duty in us to release you from your engagement. and on that ground I concurred with my brethren: at the same time I consider it a certainty that the legislature, at their next meeting, will relinquish the deb[t,] and the more certainly as the loan is from a public fund, ready raised, and specifically appropriated to the purposes of education. if it is relinquished, our funds will be liberated on the 1st of Jan. ne[xt,] and we shall then immediately take measures to procure our profess[ors,] which we have no doubt of doing by the autumn of the next year. our board had been unanimous in the opinion that there would be no fear of attack on you, entering, en groupe, with the other professors: that the attacks in that case would be on the whole body or on ourselves which would not be regarded. my hope therefore is that your engagements at Columbia will be such as to leave you a free choice between them and us. the building intended for you has been compleated, and locked up for some time. and I can assure you that yourself and brethren will be as comfortably & handsomely lodged here as the professors of any University on either side of the Atlantic. my hope therefore is still kept alive that we may yet have your aid in giving the first forms to our University. all this is written to you in confidence and in my private capacity, and for a purpose now to be explained. Stack's school will, I fear, slip from under him. nobody doubts he is the able scholar whic[h yo]u represented him to be, and his correctne[ss,] morals, and inoffensiveness of character are obvious to all.[2] unfortunately he is hypocondriac, suspicious, indecisive and so totally without nerve as to be incapable of keeping up any order or discipline in his school. the younger boys generally therefore, and some of the older, are so idle and disorderly as to have brought the school into entire disrepute; and parents have consequently withdrawn several of the pupils; and it is feared that most will be taken away at their year's end. Laporte too, who kept the boarding house, for them; falls thro' from the want of funds, and perhaps of management to maintain it; and it is very doubtful if they can find board elsewhere in the place. if this school breaks up, I have no hesitation in advising those in whose education I feel an interest, to go to whatever seminary you will be in. my grandson Eppes I am particularly anxious about. he will possess the ant^t and modern languages, &

Mathematics but for Nat. philos. Chemistry & Nat. hist. I should look to you and I suppose there are other professors in Columbia college, qualified to give him Astron. & Rhetoric. this is as full a course a[s] he can accomplish before age. Ethics & Politics, which need not the aid of an instructor, must remain to be afterwards pursued in his closet. the object of this letter therefore is to ask of you the state of Columbia college as to the sciences not within your department; and what would be the expences of tuition and boarding? and to these enquiries I will ask as early an answer as convenient; for we may have early occasion to look out for another place.   I wish it were possible for yourself, mrs Cooper and family to take an upper route on your return to Columbia, by Washington, this place, Warren, Danville and Salisbury. it is direct and healthier than the lower one. making Monticello a station of rest, you would see our University far advanced beyond what you had seen it before. the two ranges of Pavilions & dormitorie[s] 600.f. long all but finished. a range of the same length, of hote[ls] and dormitories, on a backstreet to the East, advancing fast and preparations making for a like range of Hotels & dormitories on a Western back street.   but this way, that way, or any way my wishes are all for your success and happiness.

TH: JEFFERSON

PoC (ViU: TJP); first two pages on reused address cover of Levett Harris to TJ, 15 June 1820, and final page on verso of reused address cover of Fernagus De Gelone to TJ, 14 June 1820; edge trimmed; damaged at seal, with several words rewritten by TJ; at foot of first page: "Doct^r Cooper"; endorsed by TJ.

TJ's YOUNGER COLLEAGUES and MY BRETHREN were the other members of the University of Virginia Board of Visitors. EN GROUPE: "as a group."

Elizabeth Trist wrote to her grandson Nicholas P. Trist on this date from Monticello that "poor" Peter LAPORTE had "had all his furniture seized for debt," adding that Gerard E. Stack had "no control" over the students at his Charlottes-ville Academy, that they mostly did as they pleased, that many were planning to leave the school, and that Stack was "offended with Mr Jefferson because he dont come to the school to keep his Boys in order." Later in the letter she reported that "This being the Anneversary of our independence . . . Mr Jefferson had an invitation to a barbacue near Charlottesville which he declined as he had long given up attending those festivals" (RC in DLC: NPT).

ANT^T: "antient." COLUMBIA COLLEGE: South Carolina College (later the University of South Carolina).

[1] Manuscript: "rigarding."
[2] Omitted period at right margin editorially supplied.

To Peter S. Du Ponceau

D^R SIR   Monticello July 7. 20.

I have lately had an opportunity of procuring a copy of a Vocabulary of the Nottoway tribe of Indians. these with the Pamunkies and Mattaponies were component parts of the great Powhatan confederacy which covered all the lower part of this state, and probably spoke the general language of the Powhatans. this vocabulary was taken by mr John Wood formerly professor of mathematics in W^m & Mary college. I do not know whether vocabularies of these tribes or of some of them might not have been among those I formerly sent you. in that case this may still be of service by collating their orthographies. I tender you constant assurances of my friendship & respect.

TH: JEFFERSON

RC (PPAmP: Thomas Jefferson Papers); at foot of text: "Peter S. Duponceau esq." PoC (DLC); on verso of reused address cover of James Gibbon to TJ, 12 June 1820; endorsed by TJ.

ENCLOSURE

Edy Turner's Vocabulary of the Nottoway Language

Vocabulary of the language of the Nottoway Tribe of Indians, obtained from an old Indian Woman of the name of Edie Turner, the 4th of March 1820.

Nouns.

Of the Universe

1.	The Sun	Aheeta
2.	The Moon	Tethrăke
3.	The Stars	Deeshū[1]
4.	The Clouds	Uraseque[2]
5.	Thunder	Hahenū
6.	Lightning	Towatgeheterise
7.	Air	Yautatch
8.	God	Quakerhuntè
9.	Devil	Otkum
10.	Rain	Yountoutch[3]
11.	Snow	Kankaus[4]
12.	Ice	Owees
13.	Fire	Auteur
14.	Water	Auw̄a
15.	A River	Joke
16.	A great River	Onoschioke
17.	The Ocean	Owan-Fetchota.[5]
18.	A Mountain	Yenun-Tenuntè
19.	The Woods	Ora-racoon[6]

20.	Rocks	Oruntag
21.	Light	Youhanhū
22.	Darkness	Asuntā
23.	A Swamp	Reenu
24.	Sand	Oter
25.	Gold or Copper	Geekquan
26.	Silver	Wanee
27.	Iron	Owena
28.	Heaven	Quakeruntika.

Of the Human Species.

1.	Man	Enihā[7]
2.	An old man	Akuhor.
3.	A young man	Aquatio.
4.	A boy	Aqueianha
5.	A woman	Ekening.
6.	An old woman	Aquasquari
7.	A young woman	Chewasrisha
8.	Death	Anseehe
9.	A dead body	Wahehun
10.	The head	Setarakē[8]
11.	Marriage	Gotyāg[9]
12.	A husband	Gotyakum
13.	A wife	Dekes[10]
14.	A son	Wakatonta[11]
15.	A daughter	Eruhā[12]
16.	A King	Tirer
17.	The belly	Unkē[13]
18.	My belly	Setunke
19.	Your belly	Getunke
20.	The hand or fingers	Nunke[14]
21.	My hand	Sesnunke
22.	Your hand	Gesnunke
23.	The right hand	Panunkee
24.	The left hand	Matapanunkee
25.	The thigh	Otitchag
26.	The knee	Sunsheke
27.	The leg	Franseke
28.	The foot	Saseeke[15]
29.	The hair	Howerac
30.	The eyes	Unkoharac
31.	The mouth	Eskaharant
32.	The ears	Suntunke
33.	The tongue	Darsunke
34.	The teeth	Otosag
35.	The neck	Steereke
36.	The nose	Oteusag
37.	The lips	Oarāg
38.	The chin	Ochag
39.	The toes	Seeke

40.	Blood	Gātkūm
41.	Skin	Ohonag
42.	Flesh	Skeshunke
43.	Nails	Yetunke
44.	Heart	Sunke[16]
45.	The cheeks	Ekunsquare
46.	The breath	Untures
47.	The Eye-brows	Eskarunke
48.	A Shoemaker	Yuntaquaankum.

Of Animals

1.	A Cow	Tosherung
2.	A dog	Cheer
3.	A cat	Tose
4.	A hog	Waskarrow
5.	A boar	Garhusung
6.	A deer	Aquia[17]
7.	A mouse	Rosquenna[18]
8.	A rat	Oyentu
9.	A bull frog	Drakon
10.	Fish	Kaintu
11.	A Shad or Herring	Rohan
12.	An Eel	Kunte
13.	A crab	Sosune
14.	A snake	Antatum
15.	A bird	Cheeta
16.	A turkey	Kunum
17.	A Hen	Tawrettig[19]
18.	A Fox	Skeyu
19.	A Wolf	Huse
20.	A Squirrel	Osarst
21.	A Rabbit	Querū
22.	A house-fly	Dēēsrere
23.	A Bee	Ronuquam
24.	A Shell	Odorsag
25.	A Deer-skin	Aquia-ohonag
26.	A Wing	Ohuwistāg
27.	A Feather	Awonkrāg
28.	Wool	Ostoharag
29.	The tail	Orwisag
30.	Horns	Osherāg

The Vegetable Kingdom

1.	A Tree	Geree
2.	A Pine	Ohotee
3.	A red oak	Coree
4.	A Cypress	Rasso
5.	Grass	Oherag
6.	Firewood	Geka
7.	Ashes	Oquag
8.	Bread	Gotateru

9.	Potatoes	Anton
10.	Peaches	Rashēē
11.	Cherries	Ratung
12.	Apples	Quaharrag
13.	Strawberries	Weesrunt
14.	Briars	Oster
15.	A leaf	Oharrak

Division of Time

1.	A year	Wokenhu
2.	The new year	Unksawa-Wokenhu
3.	The new moon	Dotratung
4.	Spring	Shantaroswache
5.	Summer	Genheke
6.	Autumn	Basheke
7.	Winter	Goshera
8.	Morning	Suntetung
9.	Day-time	Antyeke.
10.	Mid-day	Anteneekal
11.	Evening	Gensake
12	Night-time	Asunta

Domestic Articles

1.	A House	Onushag
2.	The house of some individual.	Weynushag
3.	A door	Ototorag
4.	A chimney	Odeshag
5.	A Knife	Osakenta
6.	A Stick	Ocherura
7.	A Gun	Ata
8.	A Bed	Sattaak
9.	Milk	Canu
10.	Spirits	Anuqua
11.	Clothes	Aquast
12.	Smoke	Okyer
13.	Shoes	Otagwāg
14.	Stockings	Orisrāg
15.	Leather	Totierhiā
16.	Linen	Nikanrārā
17.	Fat meat	Oskaharag
18.	Lean meat	Oharag
19.	A Fiddle	Eruskarintita
20.	A Bottle	Chewak
21.	Paper	Orirag

Adjectives.

1.	White	Owheryakun[20]
2.	Black	Gahuntee[21]
3.	Red	Ganuntquare
4.	Green	Sekatequantain
5.	Long	Ewis

6.	Short	Newisha
7.	Great	Tatchanawihiē
8.	Little	Newisha
9.	Deep	Tatchanuwiras
10.	Sharp	Watchoka
11.	Round	Tatowenonte.[22]
12.	Smooth	Chuwatee
13.	Rough	Genuaquast
14.	Hard	Wokoste
15.	Strong	Wakoste
16.	Weak	Genuheha
17.	Dry	Yourha
18.	Wet	Yaorā
19.	Ugly	Yesaxa
20.	Beautifull	Yesaquast
21.	Good	Waquast[23]
22.	Bad	Wassa
23.	Hot	Tariha
24.	Cold	Watorae
25.	Angry	Thatcharore
26.	Happy	Thatchanunte
27.	Unhappy	Dodoitchewakeraksa
28.	Old	Onahahe
29.	Young	Osae

Numerals

1.	One	Unte[24]
2.	Two	Dekanee
3.	Three	Arsa
4.	Four	Hentag
5.	Five	Whisk
6.	Six	Oyag[25]
7.	Seven	Ohatag
8.	Eight	Dekra
9.	Nine	Deheerunk
10.	Ten	Washa
11.	Eleven	Unteskahr
12.	Twelve	Dekaneskahr
13.	Thirteen	Arsaskahr
14.	Fourteen	Hentagskahr
15.	Fifteen	Whiskahr
16.	Sixteen	Oyagskahr.
17.	Seventeen	Ohatagskahr
18.	Eighteen	Dekraskahr
19.	Nineteen	Deheerunkskahr
20.	Twenty	Dewartha-Unteskahr
21.	Thirty	Arseneewarsa
22.	Forty	Hentagneewarsa
23.	Fifty	Wiskaneewarsa
24.	Sixty	Oyagneewarsa

25. Seventy	Getaganeewarsa
26. Eighty	Dekraneewarsa
27. Ninety	Deheerunkneewarsa
28. A Hundred	Kaharsthree
29. A Thousand	Unteyoasthree.

Verbs.

1. To walk	Jā
2. To ride	Unksatā
3. To fly	Getya
4. To swim	Orerunte
5. To drink	Ararher
6. To eat	Untchore
7. To throw	Esungwisatae
8. To cry	Tehesuhand
9. To sleep	Kentus
10. To fight	Wauntrehu
11. To wound	Yahterund
12. To kill	Untatreeyou
13. To hear	Thrahunta
14. To see	Waskehee
15. To smell	Saharantoo
16. To touch	Swarore
17. To speak	Wasweke
18. To hunt	Kunun
19. To fish	Watchunund
20. To love	Tatchadanuste
21. To hate	Dotautche
22. To pray	Duntanharu
23. To stab	Untequaru
24. To cut	Untatren
25. To break	Wayetcherorag
26. To drown	Untoreesweg
27. To hang	Waharee
28. To strike	Untateuheerug
29. To shoot	Untatehag
30. To listen	Satuntatag
31. To wash	Gakuhar
32. To run	Sarioka
33. To leap	Deuntirasrag.

MS (PPAmP); in the hand of Ellen W. Randolph (Coolidge); beneath title, in Peter S. Du Ponceau's hand: "Communicated by Mr Jefferson"; numerous words translated in right margin by Du Ponceau into the Choctaw, Delaware, Naudowessie, Onondaga, Tuscarora, and Wyandot languages, with only those not included in the enclosure to his letter to TJ of 13 July 1820 noted below. Text bound with short works by John Heckewelder and Christian F. Kampman and also a newspaper clipping, apparently from the *Petersburg Intelligencer*, dated 17 Mar. [1820] and entitled "THE NOTTO-WAY INDIANS," which reads "The only remains in the state of Virginia, of the formidable tribes which once composed the Powhatan confederacy, are the Pamunkeys and Nottoways with a few Mottoponies. The Nottoway Indians in number about twenty seven, including men, women and children, occupy a tract of seven thousand acres of excellent land upon the west side of Nottoway river, two miles from Jerusalem, in the county of Southampton. The principal character among them is a woman, who is styled their Queen. Her name is Edie Turner. She is nearly sixty years of age, and extremely intelligent, for although illiterate, she converses and communicates her ideas with greater facility and perspicuity than women among the lower orders in society. She has a comfortable cottage well furnished, several horses and cows, and keeps her portion of the settlement in a good state of cultivation. The ancient Nottoway or Powhatan language is only known to the queen and two other old Indians. This language is evidently of Celtic origin; and appears equally harmonious and expressive as either the Erse, Irish, or Welch. It has two genders, masculine and feminine; three degrees of comparison, and two articles; but the verbs are extremely irregular."

Edy (Edie, Edith) Turner (also known as Wané Roonseraw) (ca. 1754–1838), leader of a dwindling group of residents on the reservation of the Nottoway Indians, was apparently a lifelong resident of Southampton County. She was described in 1808 as possessing a farm of thirty-four acres and being employed at "knitting, sewing and what is usual in common housewifery." Turner signed petitions to the Virginia General Assembly on behalf of her tribe, succeeded in obtaining title in her own right to part of the reservation in 1830, and provided information to a number of visitors about Nottoway language and culture. She owned one slave in 1830 and was the only Nottoway of her time to leave a will (Helen C. Rountree, "Edy Turner: The Nottoway Indians' 'Female Chief,'" in Cynthia A. Kierner and Sandra Gioia Treadway, eds., *Virginia Women: Their Lives and Times* [2015–16], 1:244–59; Nottoway Indian Trustees to William H. Cabell, 18 July 1808 [Vi: RG 3, Governor's Office, Executive Papers]; petitions by Nottoway Indians, 16 Dec. 1818, 11 Dec. 1821 [Vi: RG 78, Legislative Petitions, Southampton Co.]; *Gentleman's Magazine: and Historical Chronicle* 91 [1821]: 505–6; DNA: RG 29, CS, Southampton Co., 1830; Southampton Co. Will Book, 12:106–7).

[1] Du Ponceau here added "Del. Gischuh. Wyand. Tisuh (Moon)."
[2] Du Ponceau here added "Wyand: Teeshoo (Stars) Bart. App. 20" (Benjamin Smith Barton, *New Views of the Origin of the Tribes and Nations of America* [Philadelphia, 1798], appendix, p. 20).
[3] Du Ponceau here added "Tusc: Untuch."
[4] Du Ponceau here added "Tusc: Acaunque."
[5] Du Ponceau here added "Ganiatáre."
[6] Du Ponceau here added "Onond. Garonta, a wood."
[7] Du Ponceau here added "Onond. Etschinak."
[8] Du Ponceau here added "Anúwara."
[9] Next to this and following line Du Ponceau added "Tusc. Kateeouké, Wife."
[10] Du Ponceau here added "Chok: Tike."
[11] Du Ponceau here added "Onond. Hahawak."
[12] Du Ponceau here added "Onon. Echròyehawak."
[13] Du Ponceau here added "O. Otquænta Tuscar. Ootqueh."
[14] Du Ponceau here added (superfluous closing parenthesis after "hand" editorially omitted) "O. Eniáge (hand or finger)."
[15] Du Ponceau here added "O. Ochsitage."
[16] Du Ponceau here added "Aweriáchsa."
[17] Du Ponceau here added "Scænónto."
[18] Du Ponceau here added "Zinówa."
[19] Du Ponceau here added "Gitgit."
[20] Above this word Du Ponceau added "Onond: Orhestoku."
[21] Du Ponceau here added "On: Jahūntschi."
[22] Du Ponceau here added "On: Tiodwenóni."
[23] Du Ponceau here added "Naud. Washtaw."
[24] Du Ponceau here added "Naudow. Wonchaw."
[25] Du Ponceau here added "Tusc: Houeyoc. Bart. lxvii."

To Fernagus De Gelone

SIR   Monticello July 7. 20.

Your favor of June. 29. with the MS. accompanying it are recieved. the prostration of my health and the positive injunctions of my physician forbid to me all difficult applications of the mind. I am therefore constrained to return you your voluminous manuscript without indulging myself in observations on it as requested by you. I can only therefore repeat my good wishes for the success of your institution, and assurances of great respect & esteem.   TH: JEFFERSON

PoC (MHi); on verso of reused address cover of James Maury to TJ, 30 Mar. 1820; at foot of text: "Mr Fernagus de Gelone"; endorsed by TJ. Enclosure: enclosure to Fernagus De Gelone to TJ, 29 June 1820.

TJ's PHYSICIAN was Thomas G. Watkins.

To Bernard Glenn

SIR   Monticello July 7. 20.

I am sorry it is not in my power to give you any information on the subject of your letter of June 20. just now recieved but it is now 40 years since the transactions have passed after which you enquire, and during upwards of 20 of thos[e] years I was absent from the state and generally my attention[1] so occupied with other business as to prevent the mind ever recurring to the objects of your enquiry. every trace of them therefore is obliterated from my memory, and I can only express my regrets that I am unable to serve you, and assurances of my great respect.   TH: JEFFERSON

PoC (MHi); on verso of a reused address cover from Arthur S. Brockenbrough to TJ; edge trimmed; at foot of text: "Mr Bernard Glenn"; endorsed by TJ.

[1] Preceding two words interlined.

To John H. James

SIR   Monticello. July 7. 20.

I recieved last night your favor of June 13. and am sorry it is not in my power to give you any material information as to General Kosciuzko. my acquaintance with him was only during his last short visit to the US. about the year 1792. a mr St Julien, a writer of distinction in France has been engaged, ever since the General's death, in writing his life. he has full opportunities of being informed of all the minute circumstances of his life from his birth in Poland till he came here, of his return, his transactions as Commander in the Polish revolution till his second visit to us, of his 2ᵈ return to Europe and subsequent life. he can obtain also from Fayette and the French officers who served in America very full information probably of his transactions during our war. M. Sᵗ Julien wrote to me for aid in his enquiries as to the latter article & I sent him what Genˡ Armstrong of N. York could give, who having been his companion while aid to Genˡ Gates, was best qualified to give that portion of information. I think it probable mr Sᵗ Julien's book will appear soon if not already published. I have thought it a duty to inform you of these facts which happen to be within my knolege that you may judge for yourself how far they may interfere with your views, and I tender you the assurance of my respect.   TH: JEFFERSON

RC (OhCiUAR); addressed: "Mʳ John H. James. Cincinnati"; franked; postmarked Charlottesville, 9 July. PoC (DLC); on verso of reused address cover of George S. Gibson (for Patrick Gibson) to TJ, 10 June 1820; endorsed by TJ.

Tadeusz Kosciuszko last visited the United States and made TJ's acquaintance in 1797–98 rather than THE YEAR 1792. MR Sᵀ JULIEN was Marc Antoine Jullien.

To Benjamin Morgan

DEAR SIR   Monticello July 7. 20.

On the preceding page is the copy of a letter I took the liberty of addressing to you at it's date and of forwarding to N.[1] Orleans. learning since that that you are in Philadelphia I send a duplicate; for altho' no longer in the place where enquiry can be made, yet possibly you may be able to give of your own knolege some answer to the enquiries. I repeat to you the assurances of my friendship and respect

                                              TH: JEFFERSON

RC (L-M: Miscellaneous Manuscripts and Modern Ephemera); with enclosure on verso; addressed: "Benjamin Morgan esq. now in Philadelphia"; franked; postmarked Charlottesville, 8 July; endorsed by Morgan as received 11 (reworked from 12) July 1820 and answered the follow-

ing day. PoC (MHi); on verso of reused address cover to TJ; edge trimmed; endorsed by TJ. Enclosure: Dupl of TJ to Morgan and Thomas B. Robertson, 26 May 1820.

[1] PoC: "New."

To William G. Pendleton

SIR   Monticello July[1] 7. 20.

Will you have the goodness to order me a copy of a patent to Peter Jefferson for 400. acres of land in Albemarle dated Aug. 16. 1756. and described probably as on the waters of Carroll's creek? I presume your office to be the depository of the antient patents, and therefore take the liberty of addressing the request to you. the fee will be paid on presenting this letter to my correspondent mr Gibson, or on notifying it to myself, or to the Collector as you please. Accept the assurance of my esteem and respect.   TH: JEFFERSON

PoC (MHi); on verso of reused address cover of Daniel Call to TJ, 18 May 1820; at foot of text: "W. G. Pendleton esq. Register of the land office"; endorsed by TJ as a letter of 7 July 1820 and so recorded in SJL.

William Garland Pendleton (1788–1839), attorney and public official, was probably a native of Amherst County. By 1810 he had moved to Richmond, where he served as register of the Virginia Land Office, 1814–23, as clerk of the local chancery court, 1828–31, and as one of the commissioners of the Superior Court of Law and Chancery in 1832. Pendleton was also proctor of the University of Virginia, 1832–36. The owner of five slaves in 1820 and nine a decade later, he relocated late in life to Lynchburg, where he died (Joseph Saxton Pendleton's 1935 membership application in Sons of the American Revolution archive, Louisville, Ky.; Louise Pecquet du Bellet, *Some Prominent Virginia Families* [1907], 4:278–9; *JSV* [1814–15 sess.], 5–6 [15 Oct. 1814]; [1818–19 sess.], 43 [5 Jan. 1819]; [1821–22 sess.], 45–6 [11 Jan. 1822]; *JHD* [1816–17 sess.], 136 [7 Jan. 1817]; [1820–21 sess.], 117 [15 Jan. 1821]; *Richmond Enquirer*, 8 Apr. 1828, 6 May 1831, 11 Sept. 1832; DNA: RG 29, CS, Richmond, 1810–30; *A Sketch of the History of the University of Virginia together with a Catalogue* [1859], 13; *Lynchburg Virginian*, 4 Feb. 1839; gravestone inscription in Presbyterian Cemetery, Lynchburg).

James Gibbon was the COLLECTOR at Richmond.

[1] Word interlined in place of "June" after removal from polygraph, with missing RC left uncorrected (see Pendleton to TJ, 11 July 1820).

To Rufus Woodward

SIR   Monticello July 7. 20.

Your favor of June 20. is just now recieved. it havin[g] been deemed expedient to employ our whole funds, in the erecting the necessary buildings for our university, all determination[s][1] respecting professors are postponed until that object is accomplished. nor can the term of the opening of the University be at all ascertained at this time. accept the tender of my gre[at] respect.   TH: JEFFERSON

PoC (MoSHi: TJC-BC); on verso of reused address cover of George S. Gibson (for Patrick Gibson) to TJ, 2 June 1820; two words faint; at foot of text: "Mr Rufus Woodward Newhaven"; endorsed by TJ.

[1] Edge trimmed.

From Reuben G. Beasley

DEAR SIR,   Havre, July 8, 1820.

I have the pleasure to enclose a letter from your Booksellers in Paris, and to say that I have this day put on board of the American ship Comet, Hall master, directed to the care of the Collector at New York, the packet which came with the letter and requested him to forward the same to you.

With great respect & esteem I am Dear Sir, Your Obedient Servant.

R G BEASLEY

RC (MHi); at foot of text: "Thomas Jefferson Esqr &c. &c. &c."; endorsed by TJ as received 26 Aug. 1820 and so recorded in SJL. Enclosure: de Bure Frères to TJ, 26 June 1820, and enclosure.

To James Deneale

SIR   Monticello. July 8. 20.

Your favor of the 2ᵈ has been recieved with the mapping instrument for platting lands by latitude and departure. it bears no analogy at all to the method of platting explained by me to mr Girardin some years ago. that was in the usual mode of course and distance, and was merely a substitution of East & West lines instead of Meridians, transferring those lines from station to station by the triangled parallel ruler; & applying the protractor to the edge of the ruler, at the new station instead of drawing the line actually on the paper. this method is quicker, neater, and less liable to errors than the common, but is a mere manual abridgment of trouble, not at all claiming the honors of invention.   Having never been in the practi[ce of] platting in the way to which your instrument is applicable, [I am] not a judge of the degree of convenience to be derived from it's use. I return it with assurances of my respect.   TH: JEFFERSON

PoC (DLC); on verso of reused address cover to TJ; torn at seal, with two words rewritten by TJ; at foot of text: "Mʳ James Deneale"; endorsed by TJ.

TJ described his METHOD OF PLATTING in an 18 Mar. 1814 letter to Louis H. Girardin.

From John Wayles Eppes

I am happy to find that our opinions agree so well on the subject of Eastern Seminaries—Francis if he could have been educated at the Central University[1] would have had the advantage of being near you—At his period of life I consider this circumstance of great importance—If however contrary to our hopes and expectations this cannot be accomplished your selection of Columbia in preference to any Eastern Seminary meets my entire approbation—

From the reputation of Cooper and the favorable situation of Columbia; It is probable that many of the distinguished young men of South Carolina will finish their Education there—with these Francis will have an opportunity of forming that sort of friendship which is valuable because it continues through life—He would I hope have prudence enough to avoid their expensive habits and soon learn what to a Virginian is of great importance "That it is easier to reduce our wants than multiply beyond a certain extent the means of supplying them"[2]—Whatever is necessary and for his advantage I shall feel as much and indeed more pleasure in supplying than in appropriating money to any other object—I suppose he will at any event remain with Mr Stack to the end of the present year and some months previous notice will enable me to make such arrangements as his new location may require—

I have on my farm here at present about 90 negroes of which only 27. are Farm labourers—To add therefore to my establishment here a force consisting of many women and children would in part defeat the object I had in view—I presume that a large portion of the 20 which you propose to allott instead of the 12 will be worth their victuals & clothes—If so Suppose after the allotment was made you were to allow me to draw from them such as will answer my purpose for the ensuing year and you were to keep the residue two years for their victuals and clothes—This would accomodate me with a portion of the labour I want—Boys of a size to plough would to me be almost as valuable as men, as I am obliged at present from the want of this kind of force to keep men at the plough—

I will meet you in Bedford at the time you propose—If I find after the allotment is made that the description of force in toto will not answer the object I have in view and it will not suit your convenience for me to draw a portion leaving the residue with you for two years, I will loan you the stock for two years to be paid for in Negroes at that time—In doing this I should relinquish altogether my proje't of opening land which my farm requires—I should however accomodate you and ultimately promote in your opinion the interest of Francis—These motives combined are sufficient to induce me to relinquish any project of my own—If however it will suit your convenience for me to draw as I propose a portion of the force leaving the residue I should greatly prefer it as I should myself be on this arrangement accomodated[3] in part—

Nothing would give martha and myself more pleasure than to visit you—I have however been so unfortunate in Horses this year and the last that we are entirely out of fix for moving—I have lost two fine horses and purchased another who turns out to be useless for the carriage from being unsteady—at some time when we are in better fix we shall take great pleasure in paying you a visit—

The box in which I moved the Harpsicord from Eppington is still here—I will have it packed securely & with great pleasure deliver it whenever you send—It is almost entirely without strings—I do not know however that it has sustained any other injury—

Present me to the family and accept yourself my best wishes.

With sincere affection I am yours. JNO: W: EPPES

RC (MHi); addressed: "Thomas Jefferson Esq' Monticello"; endorsed by TJ as received 9 July 1820 and so recorded in SJL.

[1] Manuscript: "Univesity."
[2] Omitted closing quotation mark editorially supplied.
[3] Manuscript: "accomddated."

To Louis H. Girardin

DEAR SIR Monticello July 8. 20.

I am uncertain whether you know that you have been anticipated in the translation of Botta. the first information I had of it was the reciept of the 1ˢᵗ vol. three days ago from the translater mr Geo. A. Otis. it is to be in 3. v. 8ᵛᵒ and the 2ᵈ & 3ᵈ are promised as fast as they can be printed. should you consider this as a release from that labor, I should hope you would give the time it saves you to putting the last hand to your 2ᵈ vol. of the history of our own state. I salute you always with friendship and respect. TH: JEFFERSON

RC (PPAmP: Thomas Jefferson Papers); addressed: "Mʳ Girardin Staunton"; franked; postmarked Milton, 12 July. PoC (MHi); on verso of reused address cover of Archibald Stuart to TJ, 16 June 1820; endorsed by TJ.

To John Holmes

DEAR SIR   Monticello July 8. 20.

Your favor of June 19. is recieved and I congratulate, not yourself, but your state, on preserving to the councils of the nation your useful talents. their entrance into the Union is thus marked by an act of peculiar magnanimity, proving that in becoming a member of the nation, they will rise above local considerations, & think & act on the National scale.

You ask leave to publish my letter of apr. 22. but the wise man tells us there is a time for every thing; of course, for retiring from business as well a[s] for entering into it; and my time for retiring is long since arrived. I feel it most sensibly in all the faculties of mind and body: and in nothing more than in the wish to pass the remainder of life in tranquility, and in the peac[e] and goodwill of all mankind.—of all mankind, have I said?—No—that is impossible. it was my fortune, good or bad, to be placed at the head of the phalanx which entered first the breach in the federal ramparts. and our opponents, like Nero, wishing for a single neck, chose to consider mine as that of the whole body, and to spend on that all the hackings and hewings of their wrath. some, I know, have forgiven, some have forgotten me: but many still brood in silence over their angry recollections. and why should I rekindle these smoking embers? why call up from their cearments the ghosts of the dead? the letter, you think, would have weight. it might be acceptable to those who think with it; but otherwise to those of the opposit[e] sentiment. save me then, dear Sir, from this Arena of gladiators; from th[e] ridicule of Priam in juvenile arms: and perform rather the office of the good old Hecuba, who withdrew him to the asylum of the altar 'et sacrâ longaevum, in sede locavit.' for this good office, and for all your good services, I shall offer my prayers to heaven for your health & happiness   TH: JEFFERSON

PoC (DLC); edge trimmed; at foot of text: "The honble J. Holmes."

THERE IS A TIME FOR EVERY THING is from the Bible (Ecclesiastes 3.1). The Emperor Caligula, not NERO, reportedly cried out, "I wish the Roman people had but a single neck," presumably in order that he might easily sever the head (Suetonius, *Lives of the Caesars*, 4.30.2, trans. John C. Rolfe, Loeb Classical Library [1913–14; rev. ed. 1997–98], 1:464–5). CEARMENTS is a variant of "cerements" (*OED*).

When Hecuba, in Virgil's *Aeneid*, 2.517–25, saw her husband, King Priam of Troy, "harnessed in the armour of his youth" (IN JUVENILE ARMS) as his kingdom fell, she exclaimed, "what dreadful thought has driven you to don these weapons . . . Come hither, pray; this altar will guard us." Then she drew him to her "and placed him on the holy seat" (ET SACRÂ LONGAEVUM, IN SEDE LOCAVIT) (Fairclough, *Virgil*, 1:350–1).

To Joseph Marx

Monticello July 8. 20

Th: Jefferson presents to mr Marx his compliments & thanks for the Transactions of the Paris Sanhedrim, which he shall read with great interest, and with the regret he has ever felt at seeing, a sect the parent and basis of all those of Christendom, singled out by all of them for a persecution and oppression which prove they have profited nothing from the benevolent doctrines of him whom they profess to make the model of their principles and practice.

He salutes mr Marx with sentiments of perfect esteem [an]d respect.

PoC (DLC); on verso of reused address cover of otherwise unlocated letter from Thomas Jefferson Randolph to TJ, 12 June 1820 (addressed: "Thomas Jefferson Esqr Monticello"; franked; postmarked Richmond, 12 June; recorded in SJL as received 16 June 1820 from Richmond); dateline at foot of text; torn at seal; endorsed by TJ.

The MODEL OF THEIR PRINCIPLES AND PRACTICE: Jesus.

To George Alexander Otis

SIR   Monticello July 8. 20.

I thank you for De Pradt's book on the Congress of Aix la Chapelle. it is a work I had never seen, and had much wished to see. altho' his style has too much of Amphibology to be suited to the sober precision of Politics, yet we gather from him great outlines, and profound views of the new constitution of Europe, and of it's probable consequences. these are things we should understand to know how to keep clear of them.

I am glad to find that the excellent history of Botta is, at length translated. the merit of this work has been too long unknown with us. he has had the faculty of sifting the truth of facts from our own histories, with great judgment, of suppressing details which do not make a part of the general history, and of enlivening the whole with the constant glow of his holy enthusiasm for the liberty & independance of nations. neutral as an historian should be in the relation of facts he is never neutral in his feelings, nor in the warm expression of them, on the triumphs and reverses of the conflicting parties, and of his honest sympathies with that engaged in the better cause. another merit is in the accuracy of his narrative of those portions of the same war which passed in other quarters of the globe, and especially on the ocean. we must thank him too for having brought within the compass of 3. vols.

every thing we wish to know of that war, and in a style so engaging that we cannot lay the book down. he had been so kind as to send me a copy of his work, of which I shall manifest my acknolegement by sending him your volumes as they come out. My original being lent out, I have no means of collating it with the translation; but see no cause to doubt exactness. with my request to become a subscriber to your work be pleased to accept the assurance of my great respect.

TH: JEFFERSON

RC (Raab Collection, Ardmore, Pa., 2006); addressed: "Mʳ George A. Otis Philadelphia"; frank torn; postmarked Milton, 11 July. PoC (DLC); edge trimmed. Printed in Philadelphia *National Gazette and Literary Register*, 19 July 1820, and elsewhere; with editor's introductory comment that "It will be read with interest on account not only of the real importance of its subject, but of its happy style of expression and its vigorous tone of patriotic feeling so stimulative and exemplary in the composition of one seasoned by temperate, comprehensive philosophy, advanced far beyond the common term of human life, and long abstracted from active politics."

To Francis Adrian Van der Kemp

DEAR SIR   Monticello July 9. 20.

Your favor of June 25. is just now recieved, and I learn from it with much regret that too industrious an use of your eyes has seriously affected them. rest, during the visit you contemplate to Montezillo may perhaps restore them. I envy you that visit, or rather lament that I have not wings to participate in it. I owe my friend there a letter or two, not for want of inclination to pay the debt, but from a stiffening wrist, the consequence of an antient dislocation, which renders writing slow and painful. our fathers taught us 'never to put off to tomorrow what can be done to-day.' but this disorganisation of the writing hand is leading me to an inversion of the maxim, by never writing to-day what can be put off to tomorrow. Your conjecture that the scrutoires of mr Adams and myself may contain useful things is probably half true. mr Adams's I hope does; but mine I assure you does not. my life has been one of meer business. the duties of the various offices in which I have acted, have employed[1] my whole time too fully, to admit any collateral pursuit. the transactions of these offices have indeed been embodied chiefly in the letters they required me to write. but to look for any thing valuable in that pile, would be seeking a needle in a hay-stack.

I trust with you that the genuine and simple religion of Jesus will one day be restored: such as it was preached and practised by himself.

very soon after his death, it became muffled up in mysteries, and has been ever since kept in concealment from the vulgar eye. to penetrate and dissipate these clouds of darkness, the general mind must be strengthened by education. enlightened by it's torch the disciples of religion will see that, instead of abandoning their reason, as the superstitions of every country requires, and taking for the will of their god whatever their own hierophants declare it to be (and no two of them declaring it alike) that god has confided to them the talent of reason, not to hide under a bushel, but to render him account of it's employment.[1] I hope that that day of restoration is to come, altho' I shall not live to see it. and to my prayers that it may come soon, I add those for your health and happiness.   TH: JEFFERSON

RC (NBuHi: Van der Kemp Papers); addressed: "Mr Fr. Adr. Vanderkemp Oldenbarneveld near Trenton. Oneida. N.Y."; franked; postmarked Charlottesville, 13 July. PoC (DLC); edge trimmed.

John Adams gave the playful name of MONTEZILLO to his home in Quincy, Massachusetts. SCRUTOIRES: "escritoires" (*OED*).

In Jesus's biblical parable of the talents, a servant entrusted by his lord with a TALENT was severely punished for hiding it for safekeeping rather than investing it (Matthew 25.14–30; Luke 19.11–25). TJ here combines this story with a different parable about placing a candle UNDER A BUSHEL (Matthew 5.15; Mark 4.21; Luke 11.33).

[1]Manuscript: "employ-."

From Thomas G. Watkins

DEAR SIR,   Glenmore July 10. 1820.

Agreeably to your commands I have made out your acct for my medical services. The expences incident to a removal & reestablishment may have induced a belief, that early remuneration for my professional labours might be, necessarily, a desirable object—I assure you it is no way material—I have paid very little attention to collections with any—And so long as I may have the happiness to serve you—I shall always feel myself particularly obliged if you will consult your own most entire convenience in the discharge of any amts becoming due.

I am with the highest respect your most fthful & Obedient Servant
                                                    T G WATKINS

RC (MHi); addressed (trimmed): "Mr Jefferson Monticell[o]"; inconsistently endorsed by TJ as a letter of 10 July received 9 July 1820 and so recorded in SJL.

TJ's most recent extant account with Watkins (YOUR ACCT) is printed above at 1 Mar. 1820.

From Richard Young

Sir   Richmond July 10th 1820

I duly received your verry obligeing favour of the 22d of may last I am truely sorry to be informed of the ill[1] State of your health which I hope is better. In my communication of the 11th of that month I had no Sort of expectation that had your health permitted that you woul at that time engage in Meteological Subjects. This communication was intended to call your attention to our seasons[2] as you are the only writer that I have had the pleasure of prruseing who has attended to this climate in Such a manner as to exhibit a Table. This is a Science of recent date. I find that it is much practised in Eaurope There is Greate diversity in th quantity of water which falls in the different parts of the Globe according to these tables. I also find that the winds without the tropics no where prevail as they have done at this place for these two or three years (Say between east and South) for Such a length of tim[3] I hope that you will pardon the Suggestion of keeping a Register at the New Colleage and altho I make no doubt but that Should Such a design be in Contemplation the necessary apparatus will be fixed, yet I will Suggest a convenient method of assertaining the quantey of Rain This may be done by a cistern of metal Say Tin, cased with a cisten of wood lined with metal withn So as to leave a Space between these cistersns of about two inches the inner cistern Should have a cover to fit tight to which a meck Should be fixed about three feet in length* on the top of which a funnel to any proportionate Size of the cistern. The cistern being constructed with a flat bottom, the top and bottom of equal Size. in this a float with a Rod to pass through the neck of the cover into the funnel which is intended to receive the Rain; This Rod to have feet inches and line marked on it in such a way as to Shew by examination the quantity of Rain which may fall in any requrd time: These cisterns Should be placed in the earth and the better to Secure it whatever debth it may be constructed. the top of the cistern to Which the pipe thro which the foat Rod is intended to pass Should be about three feet below the Surface of the earth and the Space dug out to receive it about one food deeper than both together[4] and one foot larger in diametor than the cistern. and in placeing the cistern, one foot of clay well puddled Should be made at bottom and the cistern placed in the center on this puddle when it is about half Settled or Shrunk. It will be thene of a consistance hard

*it is propose to place the top of the cistern 3 feet below the Surface of the earth So that the frost will not injure the Surrounding Puddle wich Shoud be made of the best clay and well puddled

enought to Sustain the weight of the cistern it will then Stand erect, and theri Should[5] be placd over the cisten on the Surface weight Sufficient to Sustain the cistern in its place while the Space Round the cistern is puddled up to the Top of the cistern. This puddle when dry and the Space of confined air between the [ci]sten[6] will protect the cistern from decay (tho the outer be of wood) and protect it from the chainges of the humidity of the earth the distances in inches and lines[7] on the Rod attached to the float could be greaduated to the proportion of the diameter of the[8] mouth of the funnel with that of the cistern. an apparatus thius fixed will Shew the exact quantity of Rain that fall in any givin time with the least trouble as the water can be pumped out, to any particular gage, at any time, Should the Suggestion be worthy of your attention I will with pleasure Send you a drawing of this apparatus. The vaporating cistern is a thing with which I am told Greate care Should be taken; Should This institution conclude on keeping a Meteorological Register the other fixtures Such as the Barometer Thermometor and vane can be asily obtained. the latter has I find ben So fixed as to Shew on a dial plate in any Room of a house over which it is placed the course of the currant of air or wind[9] without attending to the vane itselfe. There is a remark which is common among those who I have conversed, who have observed the Barometor in America and Eaurope particularly, Britain that the canges in the Atmosphere do not affect it in the same proportion in America as there, I find that one writer Mr Copland in writein to the Royal Society of Manchester[10] in the year 1793 Says that one thing is certain with that Instrument that it indicates heat and cold in all climates. I find from a Meteorological Register kept at Calcutta in the year 1784 that the mean of the Tormometer was 70° and that of the Berometer about 30 That their fell 81 inches of Rain at that place in that year.[11] at or near Edinbrough in the year 1776 about 29 inches in the year 1792 there fell on the western coast of Greate Britain about 47. inches The medium of Rany days at Paris for a number of years is 126. the quantity of Rain about 20 inches each year, thus it will be found that in the Climate of paris the mean quantity of Rain is in the proportion of one fourth the quantity at Calcutta thus the orginozation of matter proceeds with time in their Several ordinations in perfect hormony without regard to the minute calculations which have come under our obserations. I formerly mentioned that from your Statement that the quantity of Rain at this place or its kneighbourhood was about 47 inches. This quantity If we calculated on the Small Streams is reduced, in 40 years in the proportion as 60 is to 100. This can only be accounted for from drawing a comparrison Between the quanty of Rain which fell previous to the decrease of these Streams and their present Supply of water and other matters worthy of a Serious investigation. In the consideration of this Subgect three things present themselves first that the quantity of Rain is less. Secon'd. that the Absorbsion or that the exelation is Greater or that each Combine to this fact we must of necessity conclude; To assertain the former is now made the Subject of this communcation This can be assertained by the Simplest capacity by Being previously provided with a Suitable apparatus. The Subject of exelation is a matter which in my humble oppinion requires ilisttration it will be found that the quantity of exelation is Greatier in proportion than the quantity of Rain, which falls this Seems to be admitted wherever Meteological observations have been made, These lead us to the enquiry wheether there is not a proportion absorbed by Such vessels as these trials have been made in or Whether the night dew Supply the difference I have not from the limited oppertunty I have had of research been able to make any calculation If a digression is proper I shall endeavour to Give you my crude Ideas on that Subject by caling to view the Observations of Doctor Hallie on the current wich makes from the Atlantick in to the Mediterrannean Sea This Greate man after haveing exhausted his Genious, has concluded by endeavouring to account for it by exelation. his process is familar to you; I shall confine my observations within the Small limits of my research he has endeavoured to account for this current on the principals of evoporation others by a counter current below the Surface. The latter is attempted to be proved[12] by the curveture of a Suspended cord below the Surface this is of all others the most absurd, fror in all runng[13] waters the particles Glide in proportion to their distance from the Surface, and it will ever be found that the curveture of a line thus Suspended will be in the proportion of its Size the Suspending weight and the motion of the current* with due diffidene to the former I take the liberty to offer to your my ideas on that Subjet[14] It is my oppinion from the best information I have been able to obtain that this is caused from absorbsion There being Such a portion of Africa a Sandy desert and a certain district wheron rain never falls† I have atributed this current to that cause I merely make these Suggestions to you for consideration   There is one other Subgect of Some moment to this State that is now under execu-

---

* all currants have been found to glide faster on the Surface as to their proportionabl debth

†Lower Egypt It is remarkable that Darien and this are the only parts of the Globe where it is known that no Rain falls and the former the most fertill part of Africa

tion That is a correct Map of this State It is a verry desirable object How fare this will be obtained in the present attemp I cannot Say withe certainty. I am inclined to believe that too much is required for the Sum apropiated of this I can only judge from my own litle experience I have some time pased published a Map of this city merely from compilation this cost but a Small Sum I have A Map of this city includeing Manchester and the Jurisdiction of the city in manuscrip[15] drawn from actual Survey The angels taken by one of Giberts most improved Theodelites and all the distances measured horizontal This on a Scale of 400 feet to an inch will require Six Sheets This works has occupied three or four years of my time and it will cost from four to five thousand dollars to have it engraved printed Shaded and mounted The limited demand for this Map requires the Subscription to come high from a comparrison I cannot believe that a correct Map of this State can be made for the Sum contemplated. in addition I have Substantial reasons to believe that the undertaker of this work is by no means quallifyed for this undertakeing hower well he may understand Mathematicks his vision is defective and all his facilties are thoretical I have the most Statifatory evidence that he is no Surveyor, According to my understanding of this law it was contemplated to lay down the latitude and Longitude of each court house in the State all the most remarkable mountains by celestual observations like wise their hight the latter could be easily accomplished With a Good Barometer this Should all ways where practicable by Triangles taken from a correctly measured Base this is the foundation of all calculations and a long experience has taught me that it requires not only time but Greate attention to measure correctly Triangles are hard to be correctly obtained among Mountains The Barometer must when they cannot be correctly obtained be depended on An instrument Such as could be depended on[16] to correctly take the angles of the havenly body's So as to lay down the latitude and Longitude of the places required would cost considrable and the transportation and fixing up at these places would require time and consideroble expence greate advantage is often derived by haveing two persons both for Observation and calculation at the same time and plac in order to ensure correctness[17] I am by no means quallifyed to say what it would cost to comply with what I understand was Contemplated by the Legislature but I cannot believe that three times the Sum apropiated woud have been more than Sufficient with the most Strict eoconomy, I cannot pretend to the united wisdom of the Legislature but withall due Submission it was to be expected that the piriod between the passuage of this law and the tim the contract was enterd into was

Sufficient, to enable them to examine this Subject with more Scrutiny than when this law was enacted. A Map of the State was a most desirable object to accomplish which I fear that the apropiation will be Spent without Otaining any part of the Object This in the event that the new Map Should not be found more correct than that published by M[r] Maddison and others, That it will not on the whole I am well Satisfied for while it may correct Some errours, it is more[18] likely to leade us into more and Greater ones[19] I had Suggested a more Simple method of obtaining a Map which tho it woud have cost considerably more than contemplated It would have been as correct as the nature of things at this time would require. This by assertaining the true latitude and Longitude[20] of the capitol and exstending intersecting lines at given distances across the State at parrallel distances from each other the two first through the capitol[21] these accurately measured would be the best correction on the Surveys of counties and if corretly measured any inacessiable distances could be taken by means of Rockets by haveing an observer at each end of the Base line* all the work could by this means be brought neare enoughf to correctness for the present mean[s] of the State and a greate deal of Local matter could have been obtained by way of key to the work tho not as copious as contemplated by this work It is but natura[l] for us to be partial to our own Suggestions and therefore I am a verry umproper Jude wheether it is not likely to obtain a more corret Map on this plan than is likely to be obtained for the means by the method proposed, errours by these means can be correctid by the other it will require a connection by a Series of Angles Some of the placs inaccessiable to the Sight even by Rockett the latter mithot would require more labour the former will be attended with Greate difficulty and if not done with the Greates accuracy confusion will be the result I am Satisfied that the most Skillfull Geographer Astronomer and Survey could not Say what Sum it would require to make a Survey and map of each county as contemplated by the Act of assemby by many thousand dollars it would So fare exeed his calculations. every mecessary exertion[22] precaution, and eoconemy used both in time and expence much depends on the Skill and exertions of the principal Surveyor who Shoud allways have the assistance of capablee persons to assist him in chaining Perambulateing observeing noteing and calculating two at least is necessary for the three[23] latter   When I get my map of Richmond published I will Send you one and the key which is

---

* it is contemplated to connect all prominent places with Some part of these lines making a part of them the Base

intended to accompany it I am Shure you will be much Surpriseed to find that the Jurisdiction line[24] of this city is upwards of 23 miles, larger than Paris or London The paper Towns which Surround this city has nearly evaporated its inhabitantse The Streets as named by you when you were a director of Publick buildings have been retained and the number aedded within the Jurisdiction had nearly exhausted my powers to find apropiate names as you will See when you Get this map the publication of which is protracted on account of the common Hall not haveing Subscribed towards it publication all the respecticable inhabitance who are intrested have Subscribed but a work of this kind local as it now is will need the aid of this city before it can go under the hand of the Engraver The Map the key and the plate are readey the former for the Engraver and the latter for the printer the Greate depression here is beyonn example If we take into view that we have neither been visited with the ellements fire or water without our controle or disease they are of a pecuiary nature ariseing mostly from the examples and designs of Some of our most infuencal citizens whoes ambition led them into wild and exstravagant Speculation in Lots Lands Tobacco and Flour and other things these have been fostered to a greate exstent by the Banks The example of these individuals have had a most lementable effect on the Scociety here I have had more amediate knowledge of the former as my profession led me to lay of a vas many Section of land for Sale. I often attended these sales and as often witnessed the Grocerr the Blacksmith the Shoemaker Carpenter Bricklayer even the Night watch become land Speculators, this by way of Geting rich as some few had done by the rise of property which according to the prevailing oppinion was never to obtain its medium in a cntry to come These follys were the effects of certain leading individuals to which the many look up to as samples the old habits of Industry are too slow for their purpose Those habits of Industry and frugallity are insippid in comparrison with immaginary weath of which we Supposed ourselves all these have[25] been fostered by the leading individuals in Scociety I fear it has had its influence in our publick councils most of the Chartered companys in this place have been managed in such a manmer as to defeat the design for which they were Granted making them a total loss of capital to the Stockholders Experien[ce] points out the necessity of more circumspection in granting charters to companys their Obsjects Should be well defined before they are granted their real objects have been kept behind the Sceen until obtained and thene are the means of Ruin to many.   I most sincearly have to ask your indugenc in detainig you so long on subjects the only motive I can have for writing is that if you can obtain any thing from them which you can makee usefull to Sceociety they are at your Service I am in the meantime

with high respect your Ob H Sev   RICHARD YOUNG

RC (DLC); edge chipped and trimmed; between dateline and salutation: "Mr Thomas Jefferson"; endorsed by TJ as received 16 July 1820 and so recorded in SJL.

In his *Notes on the State of Virginia*, TJ summarized his meteorological observations, including quantity of rainfall, in A TABLE (*Notes*, ed. Peden, 74). Alexander COPLAND stated in a 15 Jan. 1793 letter written at Dumfries, Scotland, "that the barometer is a most certain indication of heat and cold, however imperfect it may be with respect to wet or dry weather" (Literary and Philosophical Society of Manchester [England], *Memoirs* 4 [1793]: 269–72, quote on p. 269). Weather readings for CALCUTTA appeared in "A Meteorological Diary, Kept at Calcutta, by Henry Trail, Esq. From 1st February 1784, to 31st December 1785," *Asiatick Researches* 2 (1790): appendix, 470–1. Between 1687 and 1715 Sir Edmond Halley (DOCTOR HALLIE) published a series of papers demonstrating that evaporation (EVOPORATION) of seawater was adequate to replenish rivers and springs, thus helping to establish the concept of the hydrologic cycle (Asit K. Biswas, "Edmond Halley, F.R.S., Hydrologist Extraordinary," Royal Society of London, *Notes and Records* 25 [1970]: 47–57).

Young PUBLISHED A MAP of Richmond and Manchester in 1817 (copy in Vi). William Gilbert and Thomas Gilbert (the GIBERTS) were London instrument makers. TJ acquired one of their theodolites during his retirement (Silvio A. Bedini, *Jefferson and Science* [2002], 21).

John Wood was the UNDERTAKER hired to do the cartographic work authorized by "An Act to provide an accurate chart of each county and a general map of the territory of this Commonwealth" (THIS LAW), which the Virginia General Assembly approved on 27 Feb. 1816 (*Acts of Assembly* [1815–16 sess.], 39–42).

In May 1780 TJ was named a director for locating PUBLICK BUILDINGS and enlarging the town of Richmond (Hening, 10:317–20).

[1] Word interlined.
[2] Preceding three words interlined.
[3] Preceding six words interlined.
[4] Preceding three words interlined.
[5] Manuscript: "Should Should."
[6] Preceding nine words interlined.
[7] Preceding four words interlined.
[8] Preceding three words interlined.
[9] Preceding two words interlined.
[10] Preceding two words interlined.
[11] Preceding three words interlined.
[12] Preceding five words interlined.
[13] Word interlined.
[14] Preceding five words interlined in place of "more mature reflection that."
[15] Preceding two words interlined.
[16] Preceding four words interlined.
[17] Preceding eleven words interlined.
[18] Word interlined.
[19] Preceding two words interlined.
[20] Preceding two words interlined.
[21] Preceding nine words interlined.
[22] Word interlined.
[23] Word interlined.
[24] Manuscript: "line line."
[25] Manuscript: "have have."

From William G. Pendleton

SIR,   Land Office, 11 July, 1820.

I hand you, under cover, a copy of the patent to Peter Jefferson, for 400 acres of land in Albemarle, as requested by your letter under date June 7, received on yesterday. The fee of 75 Cents for this copy &

search will be received of Mr Gibson. With sentiments of high respect and esteem,

I am, Sir, Yr mo. ob. servant,   W^M G. PENDLETON.

RC (MHi); endorsed by TJ as received 16 July 1820 and so recorded in SJL. RC (MHi); address cover only; with PoC of TJ to Bernard Peyton, 18 Jan. 1822, on verso; addressed: "Thomas Jefferson, esq: Monticello, near Charlottesville, Albemarle"; franked; postmarked Richmond, 12 July.

The enclosed COPY OF THE PATENT for Pouncey's tract has not been found, but a different one reads "George the Second &c: To all &c: Know ye that for divers good Causes and Considerations but more especially for and in Consideration of the Sum of Forty Shillings of good and lawful Money for our Use paid to our Receiver General of our Revenues in this our Colony and Dominion of Virginia We have Given Granted and Confirmed and by these Presents for us our Heirs and Successors Do Give Grant & Confirm unto Peter Jefferson one certain Tract or parcel of Land containing Four hundred Acres lying and being in the County of Albemarle among the Branches of Carrel's Creek of the North Side of the Rivanna River and bounded as followeth to wit, Beginning at Pointers in Anthony Pouncey's Line running thence new Lines South seventy five degrees West two hundred and eighteen Poles to a red Oak Saplin North twenty eight Degrees West one hundred and twenty seven Poles to Pointers thence on Thomas James North eleven Degrees East two hundred & seventeen Poles thence on Anthony Pouncey East one hundred and fifty five Poles to a pine South fifteen Degrees East two hundred and eighty Poles to the first Station. With all &c: To have hold &c: To be held &c: Yielding and Paying &c: Provided &c: In Witness &c: Witness our Trusty and welbeloved Robert Dinwiddie Esquire our Lieutenant Governor and Commander in chief of our said Colony and Dominion at Williamsburgh Under the Seal of our said Colony the sixteenth Day of August one thousand seven hundred & fifty six In the thirtieth Year of our Reign Robt Dinwiddie" (FC in Vi: RG 4, Virginia Land Office Patent Book, 34:134; with marginal notes: "Peter Jefferson   400 Acres   Form Page 1" and "Ex^d").

TJ's misdated letter to Pendleton of JUNE 7 was actually written on 7 July 1820 and is printed above at that date.

From Edmund Bacon

DEARE SIR.   July 12th 1820.

for several weeks past I have been closely useing my best indeavours to make collections of my money. I have the sum of 1800 dollars divided out in the hands of five differant persons all of whom I considerd quite good to pay me at any moment. they now say they will pay me as soon as they can get their wheat in markit others say they will pay me if they can borrow money so that I cannot say that I have any certainty of geting money in time for my moove from any other person but yourself. this fixes me in a horrid situation for without money I cannot go and it will very badly soot me to leave any potion of my small sum behind for I shall have immedeate use for every dollar and my arraingments has been made with an expectation of recieveng all my money before I go. my arrangements with my brothers in Missouri is such as to Oblige me to convey to them money in some way and if I can moove it will be better than to put it off especially as I have prepard my waggons and most of my horsis. if I cannot Obtain all my money so as to moove intirely I have been thinking that rather than to leave money here that I may send on a part of my people this fall and waite myself with the balance of my family untill I can finish my collections in that case it may best soot me to remaine in your imploy for another yeare. but if it could soot you I would rather waite untill the 10th or 15th of August before we finally conclude which will best soot me because by that time I can see how my chance will be to collect a sum sufficient to answer my purpose

I am your Ob. St.   E: BACON

RC (MHi); addressed: "Mr Jefferson Monticello"; endorsed by TJ as received 12 July 1820.

To William Bain

SIR   Monticello July 12. 20.

My grandson has made a last effort to get hi[s][1] tenant to give up the grounds at the Secretary's ford. but the tenant[2] appears to be entirely unwilling to part with it and would requir[e] in exchange such a sacrifice of the adjacent fields as would destroy the value of the remainder. I fear therefore that that ground is not to be obtained. as you seemed anxious to have some certain resource on the approaching expiratio[n] of your term at Bleinheim, you may consider yourself as free to take the place at Ingraham's meadow of which we spoke. I should require 2.D. an acre for the meadow part only, and nothing for the highlands you might occupy. after the expiration of August I would assist you in erecting any log buildin[gs] you might need, and in the winter in enclosing the grounds. a lease for 5. years, no rent for the 1st year, and probab[ly] that for the following years would be taken out mostly in serv[ice] and vegetables. on all this you will determine as you please and when you please and accept my best wishes.

TH: JEFFERSON

PoC (MHi); on verso of a reused address cover from Thomas Mann Randolph to TJ; edge trimmed; damaged at seal, with one word rewritten by TJ; at foot of text: "Mr Baine"; endorsed by TJ as a letter to "Baine" and so recorded in SJL.

William Bain (b. ca. 1792), farmer and gardener, was a native of Scotland. In the summer of 1820 he was working at Blenheim, a plantation located about five miles south of Monticello. There is no evidence that Bain leased the nearby Ingraham's tract from TJ. He moved with his family to Maryland by the latter half of the 1820s, settled in Baltimore, and made his living there as a gardener and nursery-man from early in the 1840s until at least 1860 (*MB*, 1:76n, 372n; DNA: RG 29, CS, Albemarle Co., 1820, Md., Baltimore, 1850, Ga., Clarke Co., 1860 [entry for son William A. Bain]; *Matchett's Baltimore Director, or Register of Householders, cor-* rected up to June, 1842 [(1842)], 71; *Woods' Baltimore City Directory* [(1860)], 28).

TJ's GRANDSON was Thomas Jefferson Randolph.

[1] Word faint.
[2] Preceding two words reworked from "he."

From Thomas Cooper

DEAR SIR   July 12. 1820 Philadelphia.

I thank you for your kind letter of the 4th but I can give no decisive answer as to S. Carolina. The Trustees passed an unanimous resolution to apply to the Legislature for a new Professorship with 1000 Dlrs a year, giving me the option of Law or Geology and Mineralogy. I preferred the latter as more immediately connected with Chemistry, & they will apply for it. Whether the Legislature when it meets will agree to this proposal, is uncertain. If they do, I do not yet see how I can avoid making a permanent engagement. They will also purchase my minerals in that case, which must accompany me, wherever I fix, & to which I have added greatly within this 12month. I find by experience, that my exertions are not now equal to more than a course of chemistry and a course of Mineralogy. I gave a lecture 4 days a week in the former branch, and examined the Students on the 5th day. With a course of mineralogy I should occupy nearly as much time, so that connecting electricity and Galvanism with my chemical course, I could not go through more business than these branches would supply. Indeed it would be labour enough, (making the courses occupy at least 8 months) for me at my age.

If there should be any hesitation in the Legislature, I will not engage at Columbia for more than another 12month: in mean time my books & minerals, & apparatus (about 115 boxes) will remain here to await my final destination.

I am not fully prepared to answer your queries as to the expence of education at the S. Carolina College, but I have always understood it was very cheap, not exceeding 250 Dlrs for the session of 9 months; the particulars I do not know. Boarding in College is, I believe, $3\frac{1}{2}$ dlrs per week paid in advance: there is a tutor in Rhetoric & Metaphysics, in my view very useless studies: one in logic/ethics—a classical tutor—

a teacher of mathematics, nat. philosophy & astronomy (who I believe will be Mr Nulty)—and a teacher of Chemistry. The principal Dr Maxcey died the day after I left Columbia; I am in hopes[1] Mr Step. Elliot of the Charleston Bank will succeed him. If they send for a parson from New England, as the fashion is, I shall be strongly inclined to resign. I greatly dislike this combination of character, which promises little better, than a mixture of cunning, sciolism, canting, & bigotry.[2] I am aware that this may well be considered as an objectionable prejudice, but the experience of many years has forced it upon me, and I cannot help it.

Indeed I feel gloomy at the persevering, determined, unwearied march of religious intolerance among us. The clergy daily acquire more strength: they insinuate themselves among the females of the families, whose heads will not bend to their sway, & they exercise compleat controul over the ignorant every where. The bible and missionary societies, and the clerical propagandists, raise (chiefly from the females) at least a million and a half of dollars annually, & they begin now to threaten the most respectable men in society. For instance:

You know Mr Pet. St. DuPonceau; certainly the first jurist among us; and one of the most learned men this country can boast of: rich, regular, respectable, in his situation, his character, his public deportment, and his private manners. He told me yesterday this story: I make him speak.

"I married to my first wife, the daughter of the minister of the presbyterian church in Arch Street: I have had a pew there occupied by my family for these 30 Years: my second wife frequented that meeting: all my children were baptized there: I sent a few days ago to the present minister, the rev^d Mr Janeway, to baptize my daughter's child, as she was indisposed, and could not go out. He sent word he w^d see me. He called: complained that I was not a regular attendant at his church that I neglected my religious duties, that he could not avoid reproving the members of his congregation for remissness in religious exercises: he thought it therefore his duty to decline baptizing my grandchild. He then turned to my daughter, and began in my presence to catechise her, untill I stopped him, & requested that he would not employ his influence in creating dissention between a child & her parent. I did mean to apply for a mandamus, but I do not wish to be exposed to the marked hostility of these people, & become a subject of public observation."—

If this insolent domination can be exercised in Philadelphia, where can it be controuled? My opinion yet is, that the clergy will defeat all your schemes at Charlottesville, if you do not divide the professorships among them. I hope I may be mistaken. since I wrote to you, I have reviewed my publications, & I cannot find a syllable in opposition to Christianity: doubts I may have expressed particularly in my summary of Dr Priestley's opinions, but decided opposition nowhere. As to the doctrine of Materialism, it has been maintained in fact, or considered as doubtful, by so many divines of eminence of the church of England, & openly advocated by so many physicians & physiologists in that Country, as well as by Cabanis in France, & by Dr Rush here, that I think it a ground extremely tenable, & affording no <u>reasonable objection whatever</u> to the christianity of any professed Christian. But the reign of ignorance, bigotry and intolerance, is fast approaching: it will pass away, but not in my time. I have had too many melancholy occasions to remark, that in this country there is much of theoretical toleration, but far more of practical persecution; so much, that silence where public motives would urge to speak is forced upon every man who thinks on these subjects; and simulation & dissimulation become points of prudence, if not of duty. Adieu. May God bless you, & preserve you while you remain with us, in peace and in health.

THOMAS COOPER.

RC (ViU: TJP); addressed: "Thomas Jefferson Esq Montecello Virginia"; franked; postmarked Philadelphia, 12 July; endorsed by TJ as received 21 July 1820 and so recorded in SJL.

The GRANDCHILD for whom Peter S. Du Ponceau was denied baptism was Joseph Gabriel Du Ponceau Garesché (William A. Tieck, "In Search of Peter Stephen Du Ponceau," *Pennsylvania Magazine of History and Biography* 89 [1965]: 60). Cooper published a SUMMARY OF DR PRIESTLEY'S OPINIONS in the *Memoirs of*

Dr. Joseph Priestley, to the year 1795, written by himself: With a continuation, to the time of his decease, by his son, Joseph Priestley: and Observations on his Writings, by Thomas Cooper . . . and the Rev. William Christie, 2 vols. (Northumberland, Pa., 1806; Sowerby, no. 390).

[1] Cooper here canceled "D^r."
[2] Paragraph to this point extracted by TJ in his letter to John Wayles Eppes of 29 July 1820, with some alterations described there.

From Peter S. Du Ponceau

DEAR SIR   Philadelphia, 12th July 1820

I have received the letter you have done me the honor to write to me dated the 7th inst. enclosing a Vocabulary of the language of the Nottoway tribe of Indians, which I shall not fail to lay before the Historical Committee at their next meeting, & in the mean while, I am free to anticipate their cordial thanks for your unwearied & effectual exertions in promoting the great cause of American literature as well as the Committee's special objects. They will always be proud &

happy to acknowledge the great obligations which you have laid them under, & which Men truly devoted to the pursuit of Science can best appreciate.

I am at no loss to determine on the true character of this language. The moment I cast my eyes on this Vocabulary, I was Struck as well as astonished at its decided Iroquois Physiognomy, which habit has taught me easily to discriminate. I say I was astonished, because from the names of Rivers & places in Virginia, which in general are to be traced to the great & widely extended Lenni Lenape, or Delaware idiom, and also from the words of the Virginia Indians quoted by Capt Smith, which are all in close affinity with the Lenape, I did not expect to find, in what you consider as a branch of the general language of the Powhatans, an Iroquois Dialect; & yet nothing is clearer nor more incontrovertible, than that this Nottoway language is essentially Iroquois, & is compounded of the different Dialects of the Six Nations, in which the Tuscarora Seems to predominate. I have yet found but one word in which there appears Some affinity to the Lenape; it is <u>Deeshū</u>, (a Star) which appears derived from the Delaware <u>Gischuh</u> (the Sun). The Nottoway word <u>Aheeta</u>, which in the Vocabulary Signifies the great luminary, is evidently the Tuscarora <u>Heita</u>, which has the Same meaning. I shall take the liberty Some time hence of Sending you full proofs of the assertion which I have made; in the mean while I enclose the Nottoway numerals from one to ten, compared with the Onondago & Mohawk, the two principal Iroquois Dialects. I regret I have not the Tuscarora numerals as a further means of comparison. You will be thus far convinced of the great affinity which exists between those languages.

Whether the Nottoway is a Mother tongue, from which the Iroquois Dialects have branched out, or whether it is itself a derivative mixture, I dare not undertake to pronounce; but thus much appears to me certain, that Virginia has been inhabited by Nations of the two great Stocks which filled the Northern parts of this Country, the Lenape & the Iroquois, or Five & afterwards Six Nations. Of these last the Tuscaroras are the least known, having joined the Confederacy at a late period. It would be perhaps hazarding too much to Say, that their original Stock is found in the Nottoways. I content myself with stating facts, leaving it to those who are better informed than I am to draw inferences from them.

Among the Vocabularies which you have heretofore had the goodness to Send to the Historical Committee, there is none of this language, nor of any connected with it. They are all of various idioms of the Lenape & Floridian Stocks—There is not a Single one at all in affinity with the Iroquois or any of its Dialects. This Iroquois language appears to have been more extended in its branches than was imagined before Zeisberger & Pyrlæus made it known. I have found considerable affinity to it in the Osage.

If more Vocabularies could be procured of the Idioms of the Virginia Indians, it would be easy to trace them to their respective stocks, for I have no doubt they were all in affinity with one or other of the two great families[1] the Lenape & the Iroquois, & that the settlements of the Floridian Indians did not begin farther to the Northward than North Carolina. Yet I may be mistaken, I offer only a conjecture in which I think I am warranted by all that I have hitherto seen of the languages of the Northern Indians.

I have the honor to be With the greatest respect Sir Your most obedient & most humble servant   PETER S, DU PONCEAU

RC (DLC); at head of text: "Thomas Jefferson, Esqr"; endorsed by TJ as received 21 July 1820 and so recorded in SJL. FC (PPAmP: APS Historical and Literary Committee Letterbook); unsigned; with enclosure subjoined.

The explorer and colonist John SMITH (ca. 1580–1631) included a list of Algon-

quian words and phrases at the beginning of his *Map of Virginia. With a Description of the Countrey, the Commodities, People, Government and Religion* (Oxford, Eng., 1612).

[1] Preceding eight words interlined in place of "either."

ENCLOSURE

Peter S. Du Ponceau's Comparison of Indian Numerals

[ca. 12 July 1820]

Indian Numerals
The Onondago is taken from Zeisberger's Grammar
The Mohawk from Luther's Cathechism, Swedish & Delaware
with a Short Mohawk Vocabulary

	Nottoway	= Onondago	= Mohawk = Onskat
1.	Unte —	Skata	Onskat
2.	Dekánee	tekeni	Tiggene
3.	Arsa	Achso	Áxe
4.	Hentag	Gaȳeri	Rayéne
5.	Whisk	Wisk	Wisck
6.	Oyag	Achiak	Yayak
7.	Ohatag	Tchoatak	Tzadak
8.	Dekra	Tekiro	Tickerom
9.	Deheerunk	Watiro	Wáderom
10.	Washa.	Wasshé	Washa

Except in N°s 1. 4. 9. the analogy is evident=That of those three Numbers exists probably in the Tuscarora Dialect.=The German & Swedish spelling in the Onondago & Mohawk should be attended to—Dekánee with the English a͟ acute, considering the frequent German Substitution of t͟ for d͟, is exactly the Same as T͟e͟k͟e͟n͟i͟; the English a͟g͟ & the German a͟k͟ are the Same. The English frequently drop the gutturals in their Spelling of Indian Words. Hence they write A͟c͟h͟i͟a͟k͟ (ch guttural) O͟y͟a͟g͟, and A͟c͟h͟s͟a͟, Arsa.[1] More need not be said.

MS (DLC: TJ Papers, 218:38882); entirely in Du Ponceau's hand; undated. FC (PPAmP: APS Historical and Literary Committee Letterbook); subjoined to covering letter.

ZEISBERGER'S GRAMMAR: three manuscript grammars of the Onondaga language by the Moravian missionary David Zeisberger were on deposit at PPAmP at this time (APS, *Transactions of the Historical & Literary Committee* 1 [1819]: xlviii; *Catalogue of the Library of the American Philosophical Society* [Philadelphia, 1824], 231). Martin LUTHER'S CATHECHISM was *Lutheri Catechismus Öfwersatt på American-Virginiske Språket*, trans. John Campanius (Stockholm, 1696).

[1] Preceding three words interlined.

From Benjamin Morgan

DEAR SIR   Philad[a] July 12th 1820

Your letter of the 26th may and 7th Instant reached me last evening

A person named Bostwick came to New Orleans in 1815 or 16 & commenced business in the grocery line & after being in trade one or two years fail'd & quit our Country   I do not recollect the christian name of the person I describe but as I knew no other Bostwick in NO I think it must be the Grocer who is in treaty with your Kinsman & who in my opinion is not entitled to credit

There is no one here at present who can give me any information but as my Partners are instructed to open & reply to all letters address'd to me I presume you will hear from them in a few days after the receipt of this letter—I am with much respect

& esteem your Ob[t] Serv[t]   BENJ[A] MORGAN

RC (MHi); endorsed by TJ as received 21 July 1820 and so recorded in SJL. RC (MHi); address cover only; with PoC of TJ to Jonathan Thompson, [18] Jan. 1822, on verso; addressed: "Thomas Jefferson Esquire Monticello" by "Mail"; franked; postmarked Philadelphia, 13 July.

From Henry Orne

SIR.   Boston July 12th 1820

On an occasion which reminds us of the great authors of our independence, and more especially on an occasion when the principles are enquired into which lead to that independence, and by which it may be perpetuated, no American can forget the highly venerated author of the instrument by which that independence was declared. Impressed with a deep conviction that to no one is our country more indebted for the secure establishment, and increasing popularity of the fundamental principles of our national institutions, permit me to offer to you, sir, the accompanying feeble effort to render those principles more generally understood, and more profoundly cherished, by the great body of the American people.

That your services may be duly estimated by posterity, and that the decline of your life may be as tranquil and happy, as the meridian of it has been active and useful, seems, at this moment, to be almost the unanimous wish of the whole American people; but perhaps of no one, more than him, who subscribes himself,

With feelings of great respect, and profound veneration Your obediant servant.   HENRY ORNE

RC (MHi); endorsed by TJ as received 23 July 1820 and so recorded in SJL. RC (DLC); address cover only; with PoC of TJ to Henry A. S. Dearborn, 3 Jan. 1822, on verso; addressed: "Hon. Thomas Jefferson. late president of the U. States, Monticello, Virginia." Enclosure: Orne, *An Oration, pronounced at Boston, 4th July, 1820, at the request of the republican citizens of that place: in commemoration of American Independence* (Boston, 1820), which hails the founding generation for obtaining "greater political advantages, than society has ever before enjoyed" (p. 3); states that the American people are honor bound to defend the institutions passed down to them and transmit them, unimpaired and uncorrupted, to posterity; argues that political equality is best safeguarded by the spread of education and a wider distribution of wealth; insists that a free press is vitally important as a counterweight to tyranny; quotes the "divine sentiment" in TJ's First Inaugural Address that "Error of opinion may be tolerated with safety when reason is left free to combat it" (p. 18; *PTJ*, 33:149); criticizes Massachusetts for electing its senate on the basis of wealth rather than population and for its retention of religious tests for office; posits that all "honest men" have "a political and religious duty" to oppose the expansion of slavery (p. 20); and looks forward to a day, "not far distant, when the diffusion of knowledge, the distribution of property, and the

freedom of public opinion shall overturn all hereditary power, and erect the great temple of human liberty in every country, and in every age, on the *imperishable basis of political equality*" (p. 23).

Henry Orne (ca. 1791–1853), attorney, public official, and farmer, was born in Marblehead, Massachusetts. After attending Phillips Academy in Andover beginning in 1802, he embarked on a legal career in Boston. Orne was admitted to practice before the circuit court of common pleas in 1812 and the supreme judicial court four years later. He sat on the Boston common council in 1822 and was a director of both the North Bank and the Commonwealth Insurance Company later in the decade. Orne also saw service as a justice of the peace and a police-court judge in Boston. A longtime Republican and the author of several political works, he strongly supported Andrew Jackson's presidential aspirations. Late in the 1830s Orne moved permanently to Maine, where he farmed, operated a saw- and gristmill, and owned real estate worth $10,000 in 1850. He died in Orneville, Piscataquis County (James Spear Loring, *The Hundred Boston Orators appointed by the Municipal Authorities and Other Public Bodies, from 1770 to 1852* [1852], 393; *Biographical Catalogue of the Trustees, Teachers and Students of Phillips Academy, Andover, 1778–1830* [1903], 48; Elbridge Gerry to James Madison, 2 Sept. 1808 [DNA:

RG 107, LRSW]; Boston *New-England Palladium*, 20 Nov. 1812; *Boston Gazette*, 5 Dec. 1816; *Boston Daily Advertiser*, 10 Apr. 1822; *Massachusetts Register and United States Calendar* [1823]: 29, 197; [1827]: 29, 37, 178, 186; [1830]: 30; [1838]: 201; Washington *Daily National Intelligencer*, 30 Sept. 1829; *Sprague's Journal of Maine History* 1 [1913]: 131–6; DNA: RG 29, CS, Mass., Cambridge, 1820, Maine, Bradford, 1840, Orneville, 1850; *Bangor Daily Whig and Courier*, 10 Jan. 1853).

To Thomas Appleton

DEAR SIR   Monticello. July 13: 20.

My letters to you, within the last 12. months have been of May 28. 19. with the annual remittance to M. & Mᵉ Pini, Sep. 3. informing you of a remittance thro' mr Vaughan of 300.D. for the wives of the two Raggis, and Feb: 15. 20. announcing a remittance of 400.D. for the same persons to pay their passage and expences to the US. since the last of these your two of Jan. 15. & 21. have been recieved. I wonder much that the remittance of the 300.D. had not got to hand at the date of yours of Jan. 21. but that transaction having passed between mr Vaughan and our Proctor, I am not able to state the particulars of it's transmission. I hope however it is long since at hand.[1] as to the 400.D. of Feb. last, mr Vaughan in a letter of Mar. 3. says 'the 400.D. have been recieved, and I purchased S. Girard's bill on Jaˢ Lafite and co. Paris at 60. days to order of Thoˢ Appleton for $2135\frac{90}{100}$, equal to 403.D. which I have forwarded to him under cover to Bernard Henry, Gibralter by the Newburn, capᵗ Cushing viâ Madeira, & duplicate by the Pleiades Capᵗ West direct to Gibralter under care of a friend. the 3ᵈ I shall send viâ New York. by the Pleiades I sent your letter to mr Appleton.'   Since your information as to the post thro' Spain I much regret that this last remittance has gone by Gibralter. altho' I should have supposed opportunities from that to Leghorn by sea could not have been rare. however I shall caution mr Vaughan against it in future, and recommend London & Paris, perhaps also Marseilles where an opportunity to Leghorn direct does not occur.

In mine of Feb. 15. I mentioned that I should make my annual remittance to M. & Mᵉ Pini in April or May. I am however to this date before it could be done. the extraordinary embarrasments produced by the sudden withdrawing of one half of our circulating medium has in a great measure suspended money transactions. 9. out of 10. of the banks of the different states have blown up; the adventurers calling themselves merchants, who had been trading on bank credits, have been swept away; those who stood the ordeal still suspend their business, from caution, till the storm shall be over, so that from the want of medium, and the want of purchasers at market, property & produce are fallen one half. we had 18. month ago 6. millio[ns] of Dollars in circulation in this state, of paper; we have but 3. millions now. produce, say flour sold from 8. to 16.D. a barrel. it is now at 4.D. this extraordinary curtailment in the profits of the year has brought on a general distress, unknown before in the annals of our country. before this explosion in our commerce, I had hoped myself to have been able in good time to remit the principal of my debt to M. & Me Pini, from the annual profits of my estate: but the fall in the price of produce likely to continue some time yet, has induced me to give up that hope and to determine on the sale of property sufficient for that paiment. this I will certainly do as soon as the present suspension of buying and selling ceases, and bidders at a fair price return into the market. at this time nothing can be sold at half price.　　these difficulties have made me a little later than I had expected in the remittance of interest this year to M. & Me Pini. I have now placed in Mr Vaughan's hands 444.D. with a request to vest it in a bill of m^r Girard on Paris, (the most solid channel of remittance, and indulged to me as a favor) and to send it viâ Paris or London, or both; so that I hope it will have a safe and speedy passage to you.

The seeds mentioned in your two last letters are not yet at hand: they will probably come safe, but not in time for the present season

The quarry of stone near our University on which we had depended for the caps and bases of our columns, we find to answer for the bases of all the orders, and the capitels of the plainer ones; but not for the Ionic & Corinthian capitels. we have resorted to a distant quarry 70. miles off, for a better stone. but this is scarcely susceptible of the delicate sculpture of the Corinthian. it has occurred to me that, considering the low price of labor, and of the material with you, we might probably get them from Carrara, ready made and delivered at Richmond, cheaper than we can make them of stone. in this expectation, I will request you to inform me what will be the cost, delivered at Leghorn, and the probable freight thence to Richmond, of capitels of the following orders & dimensions, to wit

Corinthian capitels for columns whose diminished diameters are $20\frac{8}{10}$ English inches, and others of $25\frac{2}{10}$ Inches. to be copied from Palladio Book Ist pl. 26. Ionic capitels for columns whose diminished diameters are $26\frac{1}{8}$ English inches and others $26\frac{1}{2}$ inches to be copied from Palladio Book I. plate 20. and within what time after you recieve the order can they be delivered at Leghorn? the marble you know, for outside work, need be but of common quality; but our bases & columns being of a greyish stone the capitel should be of nearly the same hue. if we find the prices more advantageous than here, the money will be remitted you with the order. each capitel to be packed singly in a strong box. the sooner I can recieve your answer to this enquiry, the sooner we shall stop here, and the larger our order will be for Carrara. this is the only kind of work in marble we shall have occasion for. a future building proposed, on the model of the Pantheon, but on a smaller scale, may call hereafter for a larger supply of Corinthian capitels.

P.S. June[2] 30. 20. I had written thus far when your favor of May 18. came to hand. the remittance of 300.D. for the Raggis, mentioned in my letter from Poplar Forest, I find on enquiry was not carried into execution. the Proctor informs me that they soon after changed their mind, concluded to send for their wives, which requiring a larger sum, produced delay till the state of their accounts admitted it, this brought on winter and finally the remittance of 400.D. was made only in time for them to sail in spring. on the subject of what I owe to M[r] Mazzei's representatives I had already[3] made up my mind to clear it out as soon as possible. like thousands of others, I had sustained some losses by being security for a friend who failed under the late general bankruptcies. this not admitting the delay of annual crops I had come to the resolution of selling some unprofitable property to pay at once, and to make the sale sufficient to discharge the debt to M. & M[e] Pini. as yet however nothing can be sold. all confidence is suspended, and fear takes it's place. the grounds, for example, in Richm[d] of mr Mazzei which sold for 6432.D. could not now be sold for 1500.D.[4] it will probably be another year before the fair prices of things are settled and proportioned to the reduction of circulating medium. I shall certainly take advantage of the first possibilities of disposing of property to disengage myself. it is this same state of commerce which has delayed to this date the remittance of this year's interest.   I salute you with constant & affectionate friendship and respect.   TH: JEFFERSON

PoC (DLC); on reused address cover to TJ; mutilated, with one word rewritten by TJ; at foot of first page: "M[r] Appleton," and above that: "original by mr Vaughan"; at foot of text: "original to mr Vaughan"; endorsed by TJ. Recorded in SJL with additional bracketed notation: "by Vaughan & Gelston." Enclosed in TJ to John Vaughan, 13 July 1820, and TJ to David Gelston, 13 Aug. 1820.

Arthur S. Brockenbrough was OUR PROCTOR at the University of Virginia. Its Rotunda was to be modeled on the PANTHEON in Rome. Appleton's FAVOR OF MAY 18 was actually dated 18 Mar. 1820. TJ suffered a significant financial loss because of his service as SECURITY FOR A FRIEND, Wilson Cary Nicholas. The 1813 sale of Philip Mazzei's house and lot in Richmond actually netted

$6,342, not 6432.D. (TJ to Mazzei, 29 Dec. 1813).

[1] Omitted period at right margin editorially supplied.

[2] Thus in manuscript. TJ apparently wrote the body of this letter in May or June and inserted the 13 July 1820 dateline just before mailing it.

[3] Word interlined.

[4] Sentence interlined, with caret mistakenly placed in front of the period at the end of the preceding sentence.

From Mathew Carey & Son

Sir[1]   Phil. July 13. 1820

Agreeably to the request made by You[2] sometime since we now hand you statement of ⅌, & remain, very respectfully,

Your obed serv[ts]   M. Carey & Son

RC (MHi); on a sheet folded to form four pages, with letter on p. 1, enclosure on p. 3, and address on p. 4; in the hand of a representative of Mathew Carey & Son except where noted below; dateline at foot of text; addressed (in the hand of a different representative of the firm): "Thomas Jefferson. Eq[r] Monticello V[a]"; franked; postmarked Philadelphia, 16 July; endorsed by TJ as a letter from Mathew Carey received 21 July 1820 and so recorded in SJL; additional notation by TJ beneath endorsement: "July 31. 20. inclosed him 25.D."

[1] Salutation in Mathew Carey's hand.
[2] Manuscript: "Yo."

ENCLOSURE

Account with Mathew Carey & Son

[ca. 13 July 1820]

D[r]			Tho[s] Jefferson Esq[r] in A/C with M Carey & son			C[r]
1819					1819	
Mar	19 To	Merchdze[1]	75		Feb[y] 2 By Balance	25
sep	28 To	d[o2]	575		Balance card down	2125
Oct	7 To	d[o]	5—			
Nov	19 To	d[o3]	10—			
		$	2150		$	2150
	To Balance br[t] down		2125			
	To binding Baines Wars		2—			
		$	2325			

MS (MHi); in the hand of a representative of Mathew Carey & Son; undated; conjoined with covering letter; with some lines previously drawn in red ink.

[1] TJ here added "Price book" (i.e., *The House Carpenters' Book of Prices, and Rules for measuring and valuing all their different kinds of work* [Philadelphia, 1812; Poor, *Jefferson's Library*, 6 (no. 243)]).

[2] TJ here added "Carter's Epictetus."
[3] TJ here added "Thomson's Bible."

To Eulalie Cathalan

Monticello July 13. 20.

I learnt, Madam, with great sensibility, the death of my friend M^r
Cathalan, your estimable father. the information came first thro' the
public papers in the month of August; and it's confirmation by your
letter of that month recieved in October: and tho' late, I not the less
sincerely offer my cordial condolance. no one had more opportunity
than myself of knowing his value as a public officer; and a friendly
correspondence of 35. years, kept alive the personal esteem which his
kind hospitalities to me when at Marseilles, had strongly impressed
on my mind. we are to look for consolation only in the assurance that
when we meet again it will be to part no more. my recollection of
yourself, an infant in 1787. when I was of full years, admonishes me
that my own call cannot be long after that of my friend.

I am to thank you, Madam, for having put my letter of May 26. into
so good hands as those of mr Oliver. he executed my commissions to
my perfect satisfaction: and I am to add my approbation of your payment of the balance of my remittance to mr Dodge.   Having
long withdrawn all attention to the transactions of our government,
the particulars of mr Cathalan's advances for the squadron of the US.
in the Mediterranean, committed to mr Shaler, are unknown to me.
the President of the US. is my particular friend. his country seat ad-
joins that of my residence, and he is dayly expected on a visit to it. I
shall not fail to interest his just attentions to your case: and, if not
already done, I am sure he will do what is right.

I pray you to accept the assurance of my great respect & attachment

TH: JEFFERSON

RC (FrM); addressed: "Madame Cathalan veuve Samatan Marseilles." Recorded
in SJL with the additional notation: "by
Vaughan & Gelston." Enclosed in TJ to
Joshua Dodge, 13 July 1820, TJ to John

Vaughan, 13 July 1820, and TJ to David
Gelston, 13 Aug. 1820.

TJ addressed his letter OF MAY 26
1819 to Stephen Cathalan.

To Joshua Dodge

SIR   Monticello July 13. 20.

The season for asking my annual supply of wines being now come
about, I have first to acknolege the reciept of your letters of Oct. 9. &
Nov. 9., as likewise to inform you that the Nice wines you were so
kind as to forward, came safely to hand, as h[ave] also those forwarded

by mr Oliver. accepting with thankfulnes[s] your kind offers of service, I take the liberty of addressing to you my wants for the present
year. Mr Oliver sent me the last year half a dozen bottles of Clairette
wine of Limoux, bought of mr Chevalier, which we found so much to
our taste that I have asked 150. bottles of it this year. by applying to
the same gentleman, or to mr Oliver, you may probably be able to get
it for me exactly of the same quality, which is my wish. he sent me
from Mr Chevalier also a cask of a Muscat wine of Rivesalte; an excellent wine, for which I shall renew my application the next year, but
not the present. the vin sec of Rivesalte I now ask for is such as mr
Cathalan furnished me with for several years mad[e] by M. Durand
of Rivesalte, who will probably recollect the particular quality, and be
able to furnish it with exactness. the Ledanon which M. Cathalan
was used to send me, was made at a vineyard formerly the property
of his aunt, now held by M. Tourneron of that place. I first became
acquain[t]ed with it at M. Cathalan's table; and that furnished by mr
Tourneron, her successor, was equally good. mr Chevalier's of the last
year however was also good.

To meet this supply, I now place in the hands of my friend John
Vaughan of Philadelphia, 200.D. to be invested in a bill of mr Girard
on his correspondent of Paris. in estimating the wines E^tc called for,
I have governed myself by the prices of the same articles in mr Oliver's invoice of the last year. I suppose also that my last year's remittance fell short some 20. or 30.*f.* leaving me that much in your debt.
should the present remittance be inadequate to pay that balance &
the articles now required, be so good as to make a countervailing reduction on the number of bottles of Ledanon & Limoux wines.

I am later this year than usual in making my application. but if mr
Vaughan's remittance has a speedy passage, & an early opportunity
occurs for your shipping the articles, they may yet get into our ports
before they are shut up by ice. always address for me to the Collector of the port the vessel is bound to, recollecting that, if there be a
choice, the ports of the Chesapeak are most convenient, and next to
these New York, or Philadelphia but never send to any port South of
the Chesapeak.

1. gross (say 12. doz. bottles) of mr Bergasse's claret. taking care not
   to call it by that name on account of the high duties here on all
   Clarets.
150. bottles of Ledanon.
150. bottles of vin clairette de Limoux from mr Chevalier.
30. gallons vin sec de Rivesalte, de M. Durand.

24. bottles virgin olive oil of Aix.

50. ℔ Maccaroni. [those of Naples preferred][1]

6. bottles of Anchovies.

PoC (MHi); on reused address cover of Thomas Cooper to TJ, 18 Dec. 1819; edge trimmed; at foot of first page: "Mr Dodge"; with canceled notations by TJ written perpendicularly in left margin of last page: "original by J. Vaughan. Duplicate thro' Sec' of sta's office & mr Gallatin"; endorsed by TJ. Recorded in SJL as forwarded "by Vaughan & Gelston." Enclosures: (1) TJ to Eulalie Cathalan, 13 July 1820. (2) TJ to Julius Oliver, 13 July 1820. Enclosed in TJ to John Vaughan, 13 July 1820, and TJ to David Gelston, 13 Aug. 1820.

Made from the clairette grape, the white CLAIRETTE WINE was a popular Limoux vintage (John Hailman, *Thomas Jefferson on Wine* [2006], 359). VIN SEC: "dry wine." M. TOURNERON: Jean Jacques Tourneysen.

[1] Brackets in original.

From Peter S. Du Ponceau

13th July 1820

M^r Du Ponceau has the honor of enclosing to Mr Jefferson, a Short Comparative Vocabulary of the Nottoway & Iroquois idioms. Few words will be found in which the Analogy is not Striking. It may be carried farther, but he believes this will be Sufficient to Shew the affinity which exists between those languages. Mr D. regrets that his Stock of Tuscarora words is very Scanty, as these generally helped him, when the other idioms failed.

He begs Mr Jefferson will accept the assurance of his high Veneration & respect

RC (DLC); dateline at foot of text; endorsed by TJ as received 21 July 1820 and so recorded in SJL.

ENCLOSURE

Peter S. Du Ponceau's Comparison of the Nottoway and Iroquois Languages

[ca. 13 July 1820]

Affinities of the Nottoway language
with the Iroquois Dialects

	Nottoway	
The Sun	Aheeta,	Tuscarora. Heita
The Moon	Tethrake,	Onondago, Garáchqua
Ice	Owees,	Onond. Owissa, Tuscar: Oowisse

Fire	Auteur,	Onond. <u>Otshishta</u>, <u>Yotécka</u>. Huron, <u>Atsista</u> (Sagard).
Water	Auwa,	Tusc. <u>Auweah</u>
A Mountain	Yenun; Tenunte,	Tusc: <u>Yooneneeunte</u>, Wyandot or Huron (an Iroquois Dialect) Onunteh
Darkness,	Asunta,	Onond: <u>Achsonta</u>, Tusc: <u>Autsonneah</u>.
The Woods,	Oraracoon,	Tusc: Orenneh, a tree
A Swamp.	Keenu,	Tusc: <u>Keenah</u>, a river
God, Heaven,	Quakerhunte Quakeruntika	Onond: <u>Garochia</u>, Heaven, <u>ne Karong-yage</u>, in heaven, Huron, <u>haronhiaye</u>, au Ciel (Fath: Sagard).

<u>Kerhun</u>, <u>Karhon</u>, is found in these Nottoway words.

Man,	Eniha,	Tusc: Aneehhah
A young Man, a boy,	Aquatio Aqueianha	Onond: <u>Axhaa</u>, a boy Tusc: <u>Woccanookne</u>, a child <u>Aqua</u>, <u>Axa</u>, <u>Wocca</u>, may easily have been corrupted from one another
A Woman	Ekening,	Onond: <u>Echro</u>.
Death,	Anseehe,	Seneca, <u>Haneeh</u>, Tusc: <u>Aucreeah</u>.
Hand or finger =	Nunke,	Oneida, <u>Osnoongee</u>, hands
The foot =	Saseeke,	Tusc: <u>Auseekeh</u>
The hair =	Howerac,	Tusc: <u>Oowara</u>.
The eyes =	Unkoharac,	Tusc: <u>Okauhreh</u>, Cochnewago (an Iroq. Dial.) Okaraah.
The mouth =	Eskaharant,	Tusc: <u>Yeaskaren</u> Onond. <u>Ixhagachrænta</u>.
The ears =	Suntunke,	Oneid. <u>Ohuntah</u> Tusc. <u>Ohuntneh</u>.
The tongue =	Darsunke,	Huron, <u>Dachia</u> (Father Sagard) Wyandot, <u>Uskunsheeaw</u> (Prof. Barton)
The teeth =	Otosag,	Tusc: <u>Otoseh</u>.
The nose =	Oteusag,	Onond: <u>Oniochsa</u>, Tusc: <u>Ocheoossah</u> <u>Oteusag</u> & <u>Ocheoossah</u>, are evidently the Same word, pronounced <u>Otchoossach</u> (<u>ch</u>, Greek χ. guttural)
Blood,	Gātkum,	Tusc: <u>Kautkeh</u> <u>Gāt</u>, <u>Gaut</u>, <u>Kaut</u>, the Same, termination differs
Skin,	Ohonag,	Tusc: <u>Enunkeh</u>
Nails	Yetunke	Onond: <u>Eechta</u>.
A Cow =	Toskerung,	Onond: <u>Tionkósquæront</u>
A dog	Cheer,	Onond: <u>Tschiera</u> (Germ: pron. <u>Cheera</u>)[1] Tusc: <u>Cheeth</u>, Seneca, <u>Cheerah</u>.
A Cat	Tose,	Onond: <u>Taguh</u>.
Summer =	Genheke,	Onond. <u>Gagenhé</u> Oneida: Kau-waw-kun-heak-ke The termination <u>Kunheakke</u>, appears the Same with <u>Genheke</u>
Winter =	Goshera,	Tusc: Kooséhhea G. for. K:, r for the guttural <u>hh</u>.

A House,	Onushag,	Oneida, <u>Kanoughsaw</u>
		Mohawk, <u>Kanoughsagough</u>
		Onondago, <u>Ganochsáye</u>.
Meat,	Oskaharag,	Onond: Owáchra
Long (adj.)	Ewis,	Onond: Iòs (pron: <u>Eeos</u>)
Little	Newisha,	Onond: <u>Niwa</u>.
Cold	Watorae,	Onond: <u>Otohri</u>.

MS (DLC: TJ Papers, 218:38880–1); entirely in Du Ponceau's hand; undated; with internal running head of "Nottoway" at page breaks editorially omitted.

The French missionary Gabriel SAGARD appended an unpaginated dictionary containing the Huron words herein to his *Le Grand Voyage du Pays des Hurons, situé en l'Amerique vers la Mer douce, és derniers confins de la nouvelle France, dite Canada* (Paris, 1632; Sowerby, no. 3991). AU CIEL: "in the sky; in heaven." The 1798 edition of Benjamin Smith BARTON, *New Views of the Origin of the Tribes and Nations of America* (Philadelphia, 1797; rev. ed., Philadelphia, 1798; Sowerby, no. 3998; Poor, *Jefferson's Library*, 7 [no. 341]) lists "Undauchsheeau" as the Wyandot word for "tongue" (p. 111).

[1] Omitted closing parenthesis editorially supplied.

To Samuel Garland

SIR   Monticello July 13. 20.

Not being able as yet to proceed myself to Bedfo[r]d I according to promise inclose you a draught for mr White's debt[1] on Capt Peyton of Richmond for 152.90 D to wit 143.56 principal and 9.34[2] thirteen months interest from July 19. 1819. this will be paid on demand, the funds being in his hands. I salute you with esteem & respect.

TH: JEFFERSON

PoC (MHi); on verso of reused address cover of Garland to TJ, 15 June 1820; one word faint; at foot of text: "E. Garland esq."; endorsed by TJ. Enclosure not found.

[1] Preceding four words interlined.
[2] Preceding two numbers reworked from "143.57" and "9.33," respectively.

To Julius Oliver

SIR   Monticello July 13. 20.

The death of mr Cathalan, which happened about the date of my letter to him of May 26. was not known to me until 3. months after. I learned it with that deep regret which a friendship of 35. years was calculated to produce. his long and faithful services succeeding to those of his respected father, as Consul of the US. had proved his value to those who, like myself, had had occasions of official intercourse with him; and a personal, and intimate acquaintance with him had given me peculiar opportunities of knowing also his private worth. uninformed as I was, at the time of hearing of his death, of the persons who might succeed to his business, I wrote to mr Dodge, the chancellor of the Consulate, on the 22^d of August, to pray his attention to the subject of the letter I had addressed to mr Cathalan on the 26th of May. it was not until the 24th of Octob. that the reciept of Mad^e Samatan's letter informed me she had been so kind as to commit my commissions to you. and I have now the pleasure to [a]cknolege the reciept of your letters of Sep. 27. & Oct. 9. [and to?] thank you for the very satisfactory manner in which you have been so good as to execute what I had requested of my deceased friend. the wines and other articles arrived safely and in good condition and were entirely approved in their qualities and prices. I have to thank you too for your kind offers of service to me. my little wants are such as to give more trouble than profit, and having been previously committed to mr Dodge, the successor to the consulship, I address to him again my supply for this year. his official connections too with the vessels of the US. visiting your port, give him peculiar facilities for expediting my little commissions.   the vin clairette de Limoux of mr Chevalier having been peculiarly approved, a supply of it is among my commissions to mr Dodge, who would be aided perhaps by your kind information, should he be at a loss to find the quality of wine designated by that name.   I beg you to be assured that my best wishes will ever attend the family and friends of mr Cathalan, and I tender to yourself the assurance of my friendly and respectful salutations.

TH: JEFFERSON

PoC (MoSHi: TJC-BC); on reused address cover of Eulalie Cathalan to TJ, 28 Sept. 1819; mutilated at seal, with part of one word rewritten by TJ; at foot of first page: "Mr Julius Oliver. Marseilles. chez Messrs Clappier & co." and, evidently added separately, "original by mr Vaughan"; endorsed by TJ. Recorded in SJL as forwarded "by Vaughan & Gelston." Enclosed in TJ to Joshua Dodge, 13 July 1820, TJ to John Vaughan, 13 July 1820, and TJ to David Gelston, 13 Aug. 1820.

MAD^E SAMATAN'S LETTER: Eulalie Cathalan to TJ, 10 Aug. 1819, which reached Monticello on 24 Oct. 1819, contained nothing about Oliver. Her later letter of 28 Sept. 1819 notified TJ that she had chosen Oliver to procure the items he had requested from her father.

To Bernard Peyton

DEAR SIR   Monticello July 13. 20.

I have to ask the favor of you to dispose of the inclosed bill of ex-change for me. it is drawn by Dr Everitt on James Maury of Liverpool, being the nett proceeds of tobaccos consigned by the D^r to Maury, sold by the latter, and the account of sales acknoleging the balance of 240 £–15 s–8 d sterling in his hands and liable to order. these papers under Maury's hand Dr Everitt shewed to my grandson in whose favor the draft is; and should any doubt of it's solidity be apprehended, mr Anderso[n] of Richm^d the correspd^t of the D^r can vouch the facts.

As soon as sold I will pray you to remit 200.D. of the proceeds to mr John Vaughan of Philadelphia on my acc^t and to give me immedi-ate notice that I may draw on you for the balance: for so pressing are the calls for money that every day is an additional day of uneasiness, and so pressing in deed is a particular call for the sum of 152. D 90 cents that I have ventured to draw on you for it in favor of Jacob W. White. as this draught[1] is to go from hence to Bedford and thence to Richm^d my confiden[ce] has been that before it reaches you you will have effected the sale of the bill, or that it will in some way give you the means of honoring the draug[ht.] I will further pray of you, as soon as you recieve the proceeds to inclos[e] to me by post 225.D. and for the balance I shall give special draughts on you. ever and affec-tionately Yours   TH: JEFFERSON

PoC (MHi); on verso of reused address cover to TJ; edge trimmed; at foot of text: "Capt Peyton"; endorsed by TJ.

Earlier this day TJ received the en-closed BILL OF EXCHANGE, not found, from Charles Everette (DR EVERITT). Drawn in favor of TJ's GRANDSON Thomas Jefferson Randolph and worth

$1,070.15 when converted into United States currency, it represented a partial payment for the "400. as. land called Pouncey's" that Everette had recently purchased from TJ "@ 12.50 per acre" (*MB*, 2:1365).

[1] Word interlined in place of "bill."

To John Vaughan

DEAR SIR   Monticello July 13. 20.

I informed you some time ago that I should desire mr Gibson to remit you a sum of about 650.D. to be transmitted to Leghorn, and Marseilles. yet it was not till the 1st of June I could place in his hands the sum of 444.D. (for which your's of June 23. informs me you have drawn on him) nor till this day that I have been enabled to provide the further sum of 200.D. this I have done by inclosing a bill of exchange on London to Capt Bernard Peyton of Richmond to be sold there, and out of it's proceeds when sold to remit you the sum of 200.D. as soon as recieved I pray you to procure a bill on Paris for the whole sum (mr Girard's is safest if he will be kind enough to favor me with it) and that you will make 444.D. of it payable to mr Thomas Appleton of Leghorn and 200.D. payable to mr Joshua Dodge Consul of the US. at Marseilles, and advise these gentlemen of it. I trouble you with letters also to be forwarded to Leghorn and Marseilles on the subject of these remittances. during the long and severe illness of my habitual correspondent mr Gibson, I have occasionally used the agency of my friend Capt Peyton as I do now.

On the subject of the channels of transmitting letters to mr Appleton I must give you an extract from a letter of his of January 15. 'allow me to recommend to send your letters either thro' London or Paris, as certain conveyances and cheap. from Spain to Italy the letters are 6. weeks on the route, from London 2. weeks, and the postage by the former is just four times greater than the latter.' again in a letter of Jan. 21. he says 'your letter of Sep. 3. has been just delivered me.[1] thro' what avenues it has past in this period of time, I cannot say; I only percieve it last past thro' Germany.'

Mr Harris, who left me this morning, gives me a good account of your health, and of mr Correa's; and a hope that I may see the latter here before I leave home for Bedford which will be about the 7th Proximo.[2] ever and affectionately yours   Th: Jefferson

RC (PPAmP: Vaughan Papers); addressed: "John Vaughan esq. Philadelphia"; endorsed in an unidentified hand as received 19 July 1820 and by Vaughan as answered 7 Aug.; with notation in a second unidentified hand beneath first endorsement indicating that $444 was to be sent to Thomas Appleton and $200 to Joshua Dodge; notation by Vaughan on verso of address leaf stating that the letter for Appleton was dispatched to Leghorn on 23 July and the bill of exchange forwarded to London two days later. PoC (DLC); on verso of reused address cover to TJ; mutilated at seal; endorsed by TJ. Enclosures: (1) TJ to Thomas Appleton, 13 July 1820. (2) TJ to Eulalie Cathalan, 13 July 1820. (3) TJ to Joshua Dodge, 13 July 1820. (4) TJ to Julius Oliver, 13 July 1820.

[1] Omitted period at right margin editorially supplied.

[2] RC: "Proximi," reworked to "Proximo" in PoC.

To Patrick Gibson

DEAR SIR   Monticello July 14. 20.

The time for renewing my note in the bank of Virginia being at hand I now inclose one for that purpose. altho' I believe it should have been filled up with the sum of 1378.D. I have left it blank for fear of error. as the US. bank does not require a tow[n] endorser[1] I relieve you from continuing the indorsement on my note to that bank for 2250.D. which I do with great pleasure and extreme thankfulness for having so long continued it. my grandson endorses it and takes charge of it.

On the 29th of June I drew on you in favor of Joel Wolfe for 30.60 D and of Opie Norris for 36.D. which the last statement of accounts appeared to justify. I salute you with affection and respect

TH: JEFFERSON

PoC (DLC); on verso of reused address cover of Samuel Garland to TJ, 21 June 1820; edge trimmed, with one amount rewritten by TJ; at foot of text: "Mr P. Gibson"; endorsed by TJ. Enclosure not found.

Thomas Jefferson Randolph was TJ's GRANDSON.

TJ's financial records indicate that on 23 Apr. 1820 he received from Thomas Eston Randolph and Daniel Colclaser "George Millerway's draught on Edmund Anderson of Richmond for 30.60 D. which I inclosed to Isaac Raphael to have presented &, if paid, placed to my credit, or retd. if not pd." On 2 June Raphael returned to TJ "Millerway's note ante Apr. 23 refused to be pd. by Anderson," with TJ then passing it back to Colclaser (MB, 2:1364–5). A missing letter from Raphael to TJ of 2 June 1820, which presumably covered the failed draft, is recorded in SJL as received from Charlottesville the day it was written. Joel Wolfe was Raphael's brother-in-law and sometime business partner (MB, 2:1358n).

[1] Word interlined in place of "subscriber."

From John Hyder

Post Office, Union Town
SIR,   Frederick County Maryland, July 14th 1820.

Sometime in the summer of 1803, my father & self happened to be at Washington city, when we had the honor of a short interview with you at the presidents house.—You will have some recollection of this, by being reminded that my father prevailed on me to recite a valedictory address to you, which I had shortly before delivered to his patrons and a number of spectators as an assistant in his laudable labors; namely, the instruction of youth. I was then about fifteen years of age. My father has left this world nearly seven years ago. He frequently observed as an encouragement to me, "that he was satisfied I would some day be rewarded for my undaunted and firm conduct in making a speech before the president m^r Jefferson."—

From this circumstance, connected with others which I shall state, I have been induced to take the liberty of addressing you at this time.— My father was of the town of Anspach, in the circle of Franconia, Germany, and was forced to this happy land under Lord Cornwallis.

The mechanical business he acquired in his native country was the manufacture of porcelain. This he could not practice here, and therefore undertook to teach a country school in the English and German languages, at which he continued upwards of thirty years, the proceeds of which from time to time, however were scarcely sufficient to procure a decent living.—

He often said he very much regretted that he had it not in his power to procure me such books as would be really serviceable to me in life, particularly an edition of the cy—, or of the Encyclopedia, as them works embraced the most extensive stock of useful knowledge.

Having been raised in my fathers school, after I arrived to mature age I also taught a school for several years, when my health began to be impaired, and thro' the advice of a Physician I quit it. After which I commenced the practice of surveying land, and for several years done a tolerable good business, until the general stagnation of all business in these parts broke in, and which still continues.

In the fall of 1815 there was a Post Office established here, and thro' the recommendation of my neighbors I was appointed postmaster. The net proceeds of which does not exceed twelve dollars per quarter, there being five other offices within a circle of six miles from this.—

I have a wife and four children, the second a son named Euclid, in commemoration of the famous mathematician of Alexandria in Egypt.

The above is a short and correct account of my situation, and having for many years felt over anxious to get the works refered to, with some mathematical, Geographical and a course of natural history; I respectfully submit my desires, dear sir, to your generosity, agreeably to my dec^d father's wishes; with the assurance that if it should please you to realise them by affording me any works that you may deem proper, that they will be received and cherished as the greatest patrimony bestowed by a parent upon a child.

I should reproach myself, were I to conclude without offering an apology for intruding thus upon your goodness, altho' I am conscious of your liberal disposition in promoting scientific knowledge.—I shall also be grateful to see the receipt of this letter acknowledged.—

That your future days may be crowned with the blessings of health and happiness, and your exit sealed with lasting peace, are the first and sincerest wishes of my heart.—

I am sir, most respectfully your Obe^dt Servt   JNᵒ HYDER

P.S. I am also extremely desirous of having a copy of your own writings, such as have been published, particularly the Notes on your native state, as I could never get the use of one in these parts.—

Respy.   J. H.

RC (DLC); addressed: "Thomas Jefferson Esquire Monticello n^r Charlottesville Albemarle county Virginia"; franked; postmarked Uniontown, 14 July; endorsed by TJ as received 27 July 1820 and so recorded in SJL.

John Hyder (1787–1848), educator, surveyor, and postal official, was born in Frederick County, Maryland. The son of a German schoolteacher from Ansbach, he took students of his own for a time after leaving his father's academy. A Freemason and a resident of Uniontown from at least 1811, Hyder worked thereafter as a surveyor and a drafter of legal documents. Appointed the community's first postmaster in 1815, he served in that capacity for a third of a century ([Ella Beam], *A Family History* [1909], 5–7;

Scharf, *Western Maryland*, 2:854, 859; *Engine of Liberty and Uniontown Advertiser*, 23 Mar. 1815; *Table of Post Offices in the United States* [Washington, 1822], 81; *Table of the Post Offices in the United States* [1831], 111; *Register of all Officers and Agents, Civil, Military, and Naval, in the Service of the United States* [1847], 176; DNA: RG 29, CS, Md., Frederick Co., 1820, 1830, Carroll Co., 1840; gravestone inscription in Uniontown Methodist Cemetery).

Hyder's brief VALEDICTORY ADDRESS as he and his father gave up their school was delivered on 11 Apr. 1803 after final student exercises and subsequently printed in a local newspaper (Fredericktown [later Frederick], Md., *Bartgis's Republican Gazette*, 13 May 1803).

To Bernard Peyton

DEAR SIR   Monticello July 14. 20.

The periods for the renewal of my notes in the Farmer's & US. banks approaching I inclose you the two of 3000.D. each for those banks which you have heretofore been so kind as to attend to, to which I add another to the US. bank for 2250.D. heretofore endorsed by mr Gibson, but now by my grandson to relieve mr Gibson, mr Marx having informed me that this change would be admitted. I shall be ready for the curtailment in the Farmer's bank of which you have been so kind as to apprise me, and am thankful to you for doing it so long before hand, which can never be amiss & may sometimes be essential.   I have a little packet of books at mr Gibson's which he will have no chance now of forwarding by the boats and as you personally know the trusty Augusta waggons, I will thank you to ask for & forward them in that way to mr Lietch. affectionately yours

TH: JEFFERSON

P.S. if the 65. days in the US. notes is wrong you can strike out the 5. and correct me, but I think [it was that?] originally from their printed forms sent to me.

PoC (MHi); bottom torn; adjacent to signature: "Capt Peyton"; endorsed by TJ. Enclosures not found.

TJ's GRANDSON was Thomas Jefferson Randolph.

From George Alexander Otis

SIR,   Philadelphia 15 July 1820

I hasten to return my acknowledgements for the letter with which you have honoured me under date of 8th July, in which the character of Botta's work is traced with so much force and elegance, that Mr Walsh has persuaded me it would be an injustice to the Historian as well as to the people of this Union, as yet unacquainted with his[1] merit, to withhold it from the world, I have accordingly consented to its publication; for which I venture to anticipate your excuse; and for which I must frankly confess another motive, that my fellow citizens might not be ignorant of the delicate compliment with which you were pleased to express your approbation of my enterprise; and for this ambition I find an apology in the poet of philosophy: "Juvat novos excerpere flores

Atque meo capiti petere inde coronam."[2]

I pray you, Sir, to accept the homage of my profound veneration and grateful respect.

G. A. OTIS

RC (MHi); endorsed by TJ as received 31 July 1820 and so recorded in SJL. RC (MHi); address cover only; with PoC of TJ to John Hemmings, 18 Dec. 1821, on verso; addressed: "To the Honourable Thomas Jefferson late President of the U.S of America Monticello Virg^a"; franked; postmarked Philadelphia, 16 July.

A variant of the phrase JUVAT NOVOS EXCERPERE FLORES ATQUE MEO CAPITI PETERE INDE CORONAM ("I love to gather new flowers and to seek a chaplet for my head") appears in Lucretius, *On the Nature of Things*, 4.3–4 (*Lucretius De Rerum Natura*, trans. William Henry Denham Rouse, Loeb Classical Library [1924; rev. by Martin Ferguson Smith, 1992], 276–7).

[1] Reworked from "him."
[2] Omitted closing quotation mark editorially supplied.

From Edmund Bacon

DEARE SIR.   July 16th–1820.

Some time last yeare I proposed buying the little markit waggon of you I got Mr Randolph to look at it and to say what he considerd it to be worth he said that he considerd it worth 70 or 75 dollars I disremember which at the same time we discoverd that some parts of it required some little repairs which Mr Randolph said could be done which he included in the price then fixed on the waggon I disremember whither we informed You of his valueation on it or not. I asked Mr R. to do it but after wards I dont remember that I have ever herd any more from You about the waggon so that I dont know whither you still wish me to have it or not. one part of the repair is the puting on new tire on the hind wheels which was spoken of by Mr R and myself in this way that I would find the new tire and you take the old at what ever it ways and give the whole price of the waggon a credit of the amount of the old tire but I am not shore if the takeing off[1] & puting on new tire will not injure the fellows too much so that I dont no whither that part of the repairs had better be done the balance is very trifleing

as I mentioned in my note to You a day or too ago the slow progress of my Collections renders it very doubtfull whither I can get away in time. I shall use my best exirtion to go. but unless I can get in my money in course I cannot go and in that Case I should not want the waggon. but this I hope to asertain in 3 or 4 weeks at furthest and as you expect to leave home in a short time is the reason I wish our affars understood.

I am Yours &C   E: BACON

I have recievd your note requesting to send the men to the mill do You no that Beverly has been absent from the carpenters for about a week

RC (ViU: TJP-ER); adjacent to closing and dateline: "Mr Jefferson"; endorsed by TJ as received 16 July, with his additional notation next to endorsement: "Coachee" (i.e., a lightweight horse carriage [*OED*]).

Calling it a "stage waggon," Bacon seems to have purchased TJ's LITTLE MARKIT WAGGON for $75 later this year (ViU: Bacon Memorandum Book, 1802–22). YOUR NOTE: TJ's letter to Bacon from around this time has not been found and is not recorded in SJL.

[1] Manuscript: "of."

From Patrick Gibson

S<small>IR</small>   Richmond 17th July 1820.

After a painful and tedious indisposition, which has confined me to the house for nearly the last eight months, and, during much of this time either by a total deprivation of sight or most acute pain, render'd me incapable of attending to my affairs, I am once more enabled to devote myself to business—This will explain to you and I trust serve as an appology for the <u>manner</u> of the letter written in my name the 22^d of Feby and noticed in yours of the 22^d May, which I did not see until to-day,—There was no intention on the part of the writer to refer to any previous transaction, but simply to express his apprehension that he would not be able to meet any dfts which might be made— The truth is that too great a confidence in mankind has deprived me of <u>all</u> my means, and prevents my making even the trifling temporary advances generally required

This explanation I consider due to you—I come now to reply to your favor of the 14th Ins^t enclosing a blank note for renewal in the V^a bank—In consequence of an alteration in the discount day at that bank, your note due in May was put in for 57 ^d/. and fell due the 11th Ins^t—I was enabled to renew this with a blank I had in my possession, but only for $1307 instead of $1378 as you suppose—I am pleased that you have been able with so much facility to yourself to relieve me from my endorsement in the US: bank—as I find the actual loss of money is not all I shall have to contend with—Your dfts in favor of Wolfe and Norris have been paid—   With much respect and esteem I am

    Your ob Servt

                                              P<small>ATRICK</small> G<small>IBSON</small>

RC (DLC); endorsed by TJ as received 23 July 1820 and so recorded in SJL. RC (MHi); address cover only; with PoC of TJ to Joel Yancey, 2 Jan. 1822, on recto and verso; addressed in a clerk's hand: "Thomas Jefferson Esquire Monticello"; franked; postmarked Richmond, 18 July.

The letter of T<small>HE</small> 22^D <small>OF</small> F<small>EB</small>^Y written on Gibson's behalf may have been that to TJ of 24 Feb. 1820, not found (see note to TJ to Gibson, 15 Mar. 1820). ^D/.: "days' sight."

From Bernard Peyton

DEAR SIR,   Rich'd 17 July 1820

This morning's mail put me in rec^t your two esteemed favors of the 13th: & 14th: of this instant, together with their several enclosures— The Bill of Exchange drawn by Dr Everett in favor Thos J. Randolph Esq^e is herewith returned, for want of form, & a <u>correct</u> one accompanying it for his signature—You will observe the amount of <u>Sterling</u> money drawn for, should be expressed in the <u>body</u> of the bill, in writing, just preceding the value given in currency here for it, which should also be expressed, as in the one now returned—beside this, <u>three</u> bills are expressed to be drawn, & only two are sent—all that are drawn should be together when sold—The bill should likewise have been drawn in favor of the Shipper here (Ed^d Anderson & Co) to be by them endorsed, who will then be followed by the agent of Messrs: Maury & Latham in this city, (Robert Pollard & Son) & which will give the bill such an undoubted character as to place it on the best footing as to sale—Its proper also that the bill should be drawn at <u>sight</u>, or one day after,[1] those at ten days being very uncommon, & also unsalable, on consulting with Ed^d Anderson & Co, who ship^d the Tobacco, & who know that the money has been in the hands of M & L. of Liverpool for six months, subject to D^r E's order, we have tho't it most proper to fill up the bills returned at one day[2]— According to this arrangement T. J. Randolph can endorse or not as he may please.—   I regret much that there should have been a difficulty in the sale the bill in question as you seem to be under necessity for the proceeds of it; not much delay however will arise, as you can speedily convey it to the D^r, get his signature, & return it to me, when a sale will be immediately effected, & your several requests complied with.—in the mean time, should your draft for $152.90. in favor Jacob W White appear, it shall be honored—

The blanks you enclose for the renewal your notes at the Farmers & U. S. Banks shall be attended to.—I find you are in an error as to the requisition[3] of the U. S. B.—It was, that an <u>additional</u> name to Mr Gibson's should be added as an endorser on your note, & that, that name might be Thomas J. Randolph—Knowing however that no great value is attached to the name just mentioned, (<u>between ourselves of course</u>) have no doubt I can get the note passed in its present shape—   No note can be discounted at any of the Banks in this City that has longer than sixty days to run, consequently your notes should always be written, "sixty days after date &C:";—

I have rec^d of Mr Gibson the small bundle of Books mentioned in yours, & will forward them by the first Waggoner to be relied on, care James Leitch Esq^e Charlottesville—
For the small purchases I from time to time make, & cash advanced for freight & charges on packages rec^d & forward backward & forward for you, I have heretofore been in the habit of presenting my account once a year, & receiving^4 pay^t from Mr Gibson, as directed by you in every case, & to avoid the trouble of calling for every little amount as it arises—12 Months has now elapsed since I have presented an ℁, which I did to=day, amounting to $56.31. & Mr G. says he has no funds to meet it; please say in your next whether I shall retain this sum out of the proceeds the sale of the Sterling Bill, as well as the several discounts on your notes about to fall due—say on the $8,250 for 64 days; $88—

 With great respect D^r sir
 Your Mo: Obd: Servt: BERNARD PEYTON

N.B. I send two blank notes merely as forms   B.P.

RC (MHi); endorsed by TJ as received 21 July 1820 and so recorded in SJL; with additional notations by TJ beneath endorsement pertaining to his reply to Peyton of 21 July: "Everett's bill error in notes 60.d. form F's bk retain the 56.31 & 88. G's endorsem^t funds in his hds." RC (ViU: TJP); address cover only; with PoC of TJ to Thomas Mann Randolph, 6 Jan. 1822, on verso; addressed (torn): "Mr Thomas Jef[. . .] M[. . .]"; postmarked Richmond, 17 July. Enclosures not found.

[1] Preceding four words interlined.
[2] Reworked from "at sight."
[3] Manuscript: "requistion."
[4] Superfluous colon editorially omitted.

From Peter S. Du Ponceau

DEAR SIR   Philad^a 18th July 1820
 I hope I shall not be considered intrusive in communicating to you the Substance of the answer I have just received from Mr Heckewelder to a Letter I wrote to him on the Subject of the <u>Nottoway</u> Indians. He thinks with me they are of the Iroquois, not of the Lenape family. He considers their name <u>Nottaway</u>, to be the Same with <u>Nadowési</u> or <u>Naudowessie</u> the denomination which the Chippeways (a branch of the Lenape) & the Northern Indians generally give to the Hurons or Wyandots, who are themselves an Iroquois tribe. He Says that in ancient times thro' Civil Wars among the Iroquois themselves, many of their people were dispersed, & fled to other tribes of Indians, who permitted them to live under their protection, & that the

Tuscaroras, who had Sought protection from the Lenape, were placed by them to the Southward, in what we now call North Carolina, having the Lenape between them & their persecutors. (Some may have Settled in Virginia), and that these Tuscaroras, or more properly <u>Tuscorawas</u>, after Some Years became formidable, & were excited by the parent stock to join them again & aid them in their Wars against the French, whence the Sixth Iroquois Nation in their Confederacy.

Mr Heckewelder believes as I do, that the Lenape were the principal people of Virginia, & that Powhatan, Pocohontas &c were of that stock. He Says Indian tradition & the Indian words brought to view by the Author of the History of Virginia confirm the fact.[1] But that the Nottoways were not of that stock, their language Sufficiently Shews.

Mr Heckewelder has given me the meaning of Several Indian Names existing in Virginia; all of the Delaware stock, which I beg leave to Subjoin

<u>Pocahontas</u> =   Del. Pokcha Hanne, the Stream between two ridges.

<u>Pohattan</u> =   to blow on something (the blower, probably the great Wizzard, Conjurations being performed by blowing) This explanation between parentheses is not M^r H's.

<u>Rappahannock</u>, <u>Lappa hanne</u>, the Stream again flowing, the river where the Water ebbs & flows (N.B.) The Southern Delawares had the Letter R where the Northern had the L.

<u>Lenno & Renno</u>, a Man.

Potomack—Peethammock, they are coming. (Many Indian names thus contain an affirmative Sentence)

Kentucky—Kenthuk—the turkies are flown off.

<u>Mattaponey</u>—<u>Mattach ponink</u>, the place where bad bread is eaten; <u>bad bread</u> with the local termination <u>ink</u>, corrupted by the English into <u>ey</u>, as frequently happens. <u>Mattach poan</u>*, means Simply <u>bad bread</u>.

<u>Chickahominy</u>—   <u>Chickamahoning</u>, the Turkey lick; the lick where the Turkies resort to.

<u>Tuckahoe</u>—<u>Tuckhanne</u>, the Stream which has large bends; Same with <u>Tunkhannah</u> or <u>Tunkhannock</u>.

<u>Tappahanock</u> =   Tuppēkhánnēk, the cold stream—Same name which we have corrupted into <u>Tippecanoe</u>.

<u>Manakin</u>—<u>Manachkink</u>—the Fort or enclosed place The English often drop the guttural <u>ch</u> in Indian names—almost always.

*Achpoan, in Delaware is <u>Bread</u>, in Mattachpoan, the <u>ach</u> is not duplicated.

Chappook—Chappichk; the place where medicinal plants grow

I have the honor to be with the greatest respect Sir   Your most obed^t hum^l serv^t PETER S, DU PONCEAU

P.S. If Mr Correa Should be with you when You receive this letter, I beg you will present to him my best respects, & my affectionate regards to his Nephew.—

P.S. I must acknowledge that I do not find much affinity between the words in the Nottoway Vocabulary & the Short one given by Carver of the Naudowessie language, (which appears to me to differ from the Wyandot or Huron); more So from the Nottaway; the[2] Numerals, in particular, are entirely different; I find more affinity between Carver's Naudowessies & the Assinipoctuk, whom we call assinipoils or Assiniboils—Yet all those languages have an Iroquois color not to be mistaken. The name Naudowessie, Nottaway, has probably been a generic Name among a number of Lenape Tribes, to distinguish those of the Iroquois Stock—More light is yet wanted on this Subject, Still there can be no doubt of the Nottoway's being an Iroquois idiom.   P.S.D

RC (DLC); at head of text: "Thomas Jefferson, Esqr"; endorsed by TJ as received 23 July 1820 and so recorded in SJL. FC (PPAmP: APS Historical and Literary Committee Letterbook); lacking first postscript and with author's footnote, worded slightly differently, added in Du Ponceau's hand.

Du Ponceau and John Heckewelder corresponded for several years about the languages spoken by various Indian tribes. Some of their earlier letters were printed in APS, *Transactions of the Historical & Literary Committee* 1 (1819; Poor, *Jefferson's Library*, 7 [no. 343]): 351–450. Heckewelder's ANSWER, dated Bethlehem, Pa., 15 July 1820, is in PPAmP: Heckewelder–Du Ponceau Letters. The AUTHOR OF THE HISTORY OF VIRGINIA is presumably John Smith, whose *The Generall Historie of Virginia, New-England, and the Summer Isles* (London, 1624; Sowerby, no. 461) contains a list of Indian words.

Elizabeth Trist reported to her grandson Nicholas P. Trist from Farmington on 31 July 1820 that José Corrêa da Serra had arrived at Monticello on 26 July 1820, three days after the receipt of this letter (RC in NcU: NPT). Corrêa da Serra's NEPHEW and traveling companion was actually his illegitimate son, Eduardo (Edouard; Edward) José Corrêa da Serra (Richard Beale Davis, *The Abbé Corrêa in America, 1812–1820: The Contributions of the Diplomat and Natural Philosopher to the Foundations of Our National Life* [1955; repr. 1993], 307n).

Jonathan CARVER included "A Short VOCABULARY of the Naudowessie Language" in his *Travels through the Interior Parts of North-America, in the Years 1766, 1767, and 1768* (London, 1778, and other eds.; Sowerby, no. 3994), 433–41.

[1] Du Ponceau here canceled "Therefore."

[2] Preceding seventeen words interlined.

From George L. Montgomery

Highly respected Sir, Petersburg July 18ᵗʰ 1820

Wishing to become a Student of your preparatory school, and being unacquainted with its situation, I presume on the liberty of addressing you on the subgect, to inform me of the course of study pursued, the annual expences, and when your next session commences, will be doing me a kindness that will greatly oblige—

your humble and obˡᵍ Seʳᵗ   GEORGE L. MONTGOMERY

RC (CSmH: JF); between dateline and salutation: "Mr Jefferson"; endorsed by TJ as a letter from "L." Montgomery received 27 July 1820 and so recorded in SJL.

The PREPARATORY SCHOOL was Gerard E. Stack's Charlottesville Academy.

From Benjamin Morgan

DEAR SIR   Philadᵃ July 18ᵗʰ 1820

Since writing you under date of the 12ᵗʰ Instant I have seen two Gentlemen just arrived from NO who Assure me that the Christian name of the Mʳ Bostwick who failed there[1] a few years ago was John and they further state that his failure was a disreputable one having left the country without dividing anything among his Creditors—

I am with much respect & esteem Your most O S—

BENJᴬ MORGAN

RC (MHi); between dateline and salutation: "Thomas Jefferson Esqʳ"; endorsed by TJ as received 23 July 1820 and so recorded in SJL.

NO: "New Orleans." O S: "Obedient Servant."

[1] Word interlined.

From Samuel Garland

SIR.   Lynchburg July 20. 1820.

I am in receipt of your favors of 30 June & 13ᵗʰ[1] inst, the last covering a draft upon Capt Peyton for $152.90 in favour of Mʳ White, and I hand you enclosed your note receipted

Anticipating the pleasure of seeing you shortly in Bedford I forbear commenting[2] upon the subject mentioned in your first letter, My instructions are general and preremptory and when I shall see you hope some araingements can be made satisfactory to both—

With sentiments of Respect. I remain Yr obt St   S GARLAND

RC (MHi); endorsed by TJ as received 27 July 1820 from "Garland <E> S." and so recorded in SJL. RC (MHi); address cover only; with PoC of TJ to Jonathan Thompson, 23 Dec. 1821, on verso; addressed: "Thomas Jefferson esqʳ Charlottesville"; franked; postmarked Lynchburg, 21 July. Enclosure not found.

[1] Reworked from "15ᵗʰ."
[2] Manuscript: "conmenting."

From Lafayette

MY DEAR FRIEND   La Grange July 20ʰ 1820

On my Long Wished Return to my farm and to a family Circle, it Becomes a first object for me to Let You Hear from Us, and to Entreat Some Lines Acquainting me With the State of your Health and personal Concerns. this packet is intrusted to mʳ frederick Jacquemont, the worthy Son of my intimate friend who in the times of the Republican Government Was at the Head of the direction for public instruction. it is the Second Voyage of this Young man to the U.S. on Commercial Business. He intends Going from Newyork to Haïtÿ. I gave Him a Letter of introduction to president Boyer who wrote to me Some months Ago in terms which entitle me to Hope my Recommendation Will Be acceptable.

The Great Work of general Enfranchisement to Which, you and I, my dear friend, Have devoted ourselves So many Years Ago, is progressing through innumerable obstacles of despotism, privilege, and Every kind of political, Sacerdotal, personal Aristocracy. But Never did those Ennemies So effectually defeat the Cause of freedom as when Under the Mask of popular Licentiousness, or the glittering Seductions of military glory, they Spread terror and Oppression, in Concert With the ignorance of an ill Educated population, and the folly of a misled patriotism. Yet Before our Half Century of Revolutionary times is over we Shall Have the Comfort to See the affairs of mankind in a good Way of improvement. The Late change in Spain Has Been Welcomed By the patriots of france, particularly at the tribune where the minister of foreign affairs Was obliged to disclaim any intention to oppose it. what Has Lately passed at Naples Will Receive a Sympathical Applause. there is also Sympathy Betwen the german and french nations, nay, among us and the Liberal part of the British Empire, However averse they Generally Are to mingle with an Extensive Common interest. in this European Contest Betwen Right and privilege, france Holds the Honor to Be a kind of political Head quarters for liberalism. much attention is paid to Her debates as if there Was an instinctive universal Sentiment that on Her Emancipation depends the Solidity of Every other Succès in the Cause of Europe. Yet when our Neighbours Have gained ground We found ourselves materially defeated, altho' the Strugle Has greatly advanced our moral maturity.

A great Leading feature in our Circumstances is that the french youth Being Remarkably more Enlightened than You Have known them, they Have Risen above the Spirit of faction, and Care Very little about dynasties, Generals, and even Secondary forms of Government. they are generally Republicans. Jacobinism and Bonapartism are to them objects of disgust. Some traces of the former You find Among Revolutionary Veterans; the other Still lives in the Hearts of military or administrative Companions of Napoleon. Both might be found in the ignorant mass. But there is Now at the Head of public opinion a Set of men Quite devoted to the Cause of liberty, and Behind them a Certain number of military and Civil Remnants of the Successive Systems Who Have Remained in or Return to the true principles, while that disposition is generally diffused Among our Young Generations. Hence my predilection for them, I may Be permitted to add, their friendship for me, Both of which are daily and Severely Reflected Upon By our Adversaries.

in this Situation of things, it Has pleased government, the Ultras and ministers, now United, the chief as Well as the other Members of the Roïal family, (duke d'orleans excepted) to enter oppenly in the Carrière[1] of Counter Revolution. liberty of the press, individual liberty Have Been Suspended. a most insolent bill of election Has Been introduced Which altho' Amended Still Leaves one forth of the Body of Electors, already So aristocratical, invested With the privilege of a peculiar College and of a double Vote. attempts of a Serious Nature Have Been made, an impeachement Has Been Announced against Some of us. the manifestation of public opinion Has Been Repress'd by the Sword. and while Every thing Seems to give our adversaries a momentary triumph, they Cannot But feel that there is more true danger impending on them than Upon the objects of their Animadversion.

the Jacobinical and terrorist times Had Crushed the nation and disgusted it. the directors altho' they Gave Some good institutions, Had nothing Expansive and truly liberal. the imperial Whirlwind Had Hurried away the Spirits and Judgment of the people. the two Restorations, intermixed With the Remarkable period of the Hundred days, Have put every thing and Every party Upon its truer and more proper ground; We are Recovering the Sentiments of 89, and meet them With the Acquirements of the past thirty Years. You know I am

Sanguine in My Expectations, But I do not think they Will, this time, Be greatly disappointed.

inclosed You Will find Some short Speeches of mine during this Session which Have Since Been printed. I do not Give them to You on Account of any intrinsic merit, But as a Specimen of our line of debate; I Send also a pamphlet of my Colleague Benjamin Constant Relating to a very strange Enterprise Upon our letters to one of our Constituents.

My family are With me at La Grange Excepting my Eldest Grand daughter Celestine maubourg, lately married to m. de Brigode, a member of our House; they are gone to their Very agreable Country Seat in flanders. I am Requested to present to You the Most affectionate Respects of our whole Colony. Be the kind interpriter of my Sentiments around You and think often of Your old, obliged, affectionate friend   LAFAYETTE

m. de tracy Has to Some degree Recovered the use of His Eyes. not So much as to Enable Him to pursue His publications. He now is in the Country near moulins.

RC (DLC); at foot of first page: "mr Jefferson"; endorsed by TJ as received 28 Sept. 1820 and so recorded in SJL. Enclosures not found.

On 24 Mar. 1820 Étienne Denis Pasquier, the French MINISTER OF FOREIGN AFFAIRS, spoke to the Chambre des Députés, stating of the recent political upheaval in Spain that "I heartily wish it may make the Spanish people happy; I wish it may in cementing on a new basis, the union of the throne and of the nation, give to public liberty, as well as to the rights of the crown, all desirable guarantees. . . . Let Spain then be free, great and happy with her King. We ought to

wish it. I wish and hope it. But let us be willing to acknowledge that the end which she is eager to attain is precisely the same which we have reached" (*City of Washington Gazette*, 19 May 1820).

The CHIEF of the French royal family was King Louis XVIII. The HUNDRED DAYS refers to the period in 1815 between Napoleon's return from exile on the island of Elba and his second abdication. Romain Joseph, baron de Brigode, and Lafayette both sat at this time in the Chambre des Députés (OUR HOUSE).

[1] Manuscript: "Carrier." The French word "carrière" means "career."

To Martin Dawson

DEAR SIR   Monticello July 21. 20.

Your favor of the 10th was recieved duly and I meant in one of my daily rides to have called and entered into verbal explanations in answer to it. but not having yet been able to go in that direction, I do now what I ought to have done sooner.   getting for my last year's flour but 3.D. a barrel I fell exactly one half short of meeting the engagements of the year. it has placed me in the most painful situation I have ever known, and I have not hesitated to resolv[e] on selling property, and mean to go on, as fast as I can sell at reasonable prices until I pay every dollar I owe on earth. this cannot be done but by such instalments as I shall be obliged to yield to. I give up all[1] expectation of relieving myself by crops, as quite visionary on the fall of produce now likely to be permanent. your store account I shall be abl[e] to pay in a few days. the two notes in your hands I can not fix to a certain day, but the reciepts of money I am entitled to count on from time to time, authorise me to say they shall not be long unpaid.   with respect to Bacon's money, the presumption of his death the law now considers as a certainty. when a man dies all his powers of attorney become null. his nearest relations will have to get an administration appointed[.][2] by the time this is done I shall probably be able to provide payment, and could I make it sooner (which I acknolege I could not) there is no person who by recieving it could give me a legal discharge. I salute you with friendship and respect.

Th: Jefferson

PoC (MHi); on verso of reused address cover of John Holmes to TJ, 19 June 1820; edge trimmed; damaged at seal, with seven words rewritten by TJ; at foot of text: "Mr Dawson"; endorsed by TJ.

Dawson's letter OF THE 10TH has not been found and is not recorded in SJL.

[1] TJ here canceled "idea."
[2] Punctuation faint.

To Charles Everette

Dear Sir Monticello July 21. 20.

On the preceding page you will see the extract of a letter from Capt Peyton explaining the want of form in the bill of exchange signed by yourself to Th: J. Randolph, and forwarded to Capt Peyton, & inclosed are the return^d bills, and others in correct form to be signed by you. my grandson being absent from the neighborhood, I send them by the bearer, in the hope of recieving them back by him, signed, that I may return them to cap^t Peyton by the mail of tomorrow morn^g

My grandson informed me you wished to recieve a copy of the Patent of the land at Pouncey's which you have purchased. I therefore inclose you an office copy, and a plat made by myself, and salute you with friendship and respect   Th: Jefferson

PoC (MHi); on verso of reused address cover of John Laval to TJ, 19 June 1820;

at foot of text: "Dr Charles Everett"; mistakenly endorsed by TJ as a letter of 21

June 1820, but correctly recorded in SJL. Enclosures: (1) extract, not found, from Bernard Peyton to TJ, 17 July 1820.

(2) enclosure to William G. Pendleton to TJ, 11 July 1820. Other enclosures not found.

From Charles Everette

D<small>R</small> S<small>IR</small>   Bellmont [21 July 1820]

A severe attack of cholera this morning scarcely enables to sign the bills you sent which I trust will prove satisfactory—

very respetfully yr ob st   C<small>HS</small> E<small>VERETTE</small>

RC (MHi); undated; addressed: "Thos Jefferson Esqr Monticello"; endorsed by TJ as a letter of 21 July 1820 received the day it was written and so recorded (without date of composition) in SJL. Enclosure: corrected bills of exchange, not found, enclosed in TJ to Everette, 21 July 1820.

To Bernard Peyton

D<small>EAR</small> S<small>IR</small>   Monticello July 21. 20.

I recieved this morning your favor of the 17th have got the correct bills signed by Dr Everett, now inclose them and hope they will get to hand before my draught in favor of White gets round to you. the 56.31 and 88 D. curtail must be retained out of the proceeds of the bill of Exchange: I had in mr G.'s hands at the last statement of our accounts but about 30.D. and he may have paid some little matters of small charges since & unknown to me, consequently he had not funds to meet your bill. I shall attend hereafter to the forms of Notes to the US. & Virga banks which you have been so kind as to send me, and I should be glad of a form of the Notes of the Farmer's bank, having never seen one.   on sending you the note to the US. bank endorse[d] by my grandson instead of mr Gibson, I gave him notice that I had relieved him from that endorsement, and should be unwilling to retract that, and I hope the bank will be satisfied with it as it is. I salute you with affectionate friendship   T<small>H</small>: J<small>EFFERSON</small>

PoC (MHi); on verso of reused address cover of George S. Gibson (for Patrick Gibson) to TJ, 21 June 1820; edge trimmed; at foot of text: "Capt B. Peyton"; endorsed by TJ. Not recorded in SJL. Enclosures: enclosures to Charles Everette to TJ, [21 July 1820].

From Bernard Peyton

DEAR SIR,   Rich'd 21 July 1820

I send by the stage under care a friend of mine, your bundle Books rec^d from Mr Gibson—They are directed to be left with Mr Ja^s Leitch Charlottesville, & hope they will reach you safely—

I understand from Governor Randolph that Mr Monroe is at present in Albemarle, should I be asking too much, or desiring you to depart from any rule of conduct you may have laid down for yourself, in requesting that you would mention to Mr Monroe[1] the subject of the appointment of a Post Master,[2] or Collecter for this City, whichever may be first vacated?—if I should, nothing believe me would be further from me than a desire that you would do so.—If you have no scruples, it might be of service to one who is already under many obligations to you—

From the loud & increasing complaints against the P.M. here, should not be surprised at his removal, particularly as these complaints are certainly <u>well</u> <u>founded</u>, it is therefore that I am the more solicitous to be in the view of the President in time, & thinking too you would probably prefer mentioning the subject in person, <u>confidentially</u> to him, to writing, if you think proper to interfere in the business at all,—which I beg you will not do, further than you have already done me this favor, if you feel the least delicacy on the subject from any cause, for I would not cause you one unpleasant feeling to possess the office— may I ask the favor of a reply, to this at your convenience? giving any information you may possess as to my prospects of success—

With sincere affection Yours Mo Truely   B. PEYTON

RC (MHi); endorsed by TJ as received 23 July 1820 and so recorded in SJL.

William Foushee was the POST MASTER of Richmond, while James Gibbon was customs collector (COLLECTER) there until he died in 1835. Foushee remained in office until his own death in 1824.

[1] Manuscript: "Monre."
[2] Manuscript: "Mastr."

From John B. Mitchell

SIR   Richmond July 22nd 1820

I have been informed that you want a person in the Situation of an Overseer—I am at presant out of a place And would be glad to make an engagement with you if It meets your approbation I can bring you Respectable Recommendations as to Probity &^a I have never been in the Situation of an Overseer But has conducted a large Farm on my own Acco^t in Europe I understand Acco^{ts} If you should want please write me what you would give a Year to a Man that would be capable of Filling the Situation—

Yours very Respectfully   JN^o B MITCHELL

P.S.. I will consider it a particeler favour by hearing from you as early as convenient and direct to me Richmond=   JBM

RC (MHi); postscript on address leaf; addressed: "Thomas Jefferson Esqr near Charlotesville V .. .. a"; stamped; postmarked Richmond, 24 July; endorsed by TJ as received 27 July 1820 and so recorded in SJL.

From Bernard Peyton

DEAR SIR,   Rich'd 24 July 1820

Your esteemed favor 21 current, covering the bills of exchange I forwarded you, was rec^d last evening, & I have this morning disposed of the same at par, which is the highest rate for Small bills: After deducting 1 $⅌$ C^t Commission, you have credit for $1059.45, out of which, agreeable to your request, I enclose herewith $225—will by this mail enclose $200 to Mr John Vaughan of Philadelphia, & when your draft for $152.90 is presented, it shall be paid—which will leave due you, after deducting my account of $56.31, & discounts $88.— $337.24 at your credit—

The United States Bank consented to receive your note endorsed by Thos J. Randolph Esqr without the additional name of P. Gibson, which enables you to keep your promise to him.

The notes for the Farmers & Virginia Banks are just the same exactly, save the difference in the <u>names</u> of the two Banks, as you will observe by the blank sent, a space is left before the word "Bank," in the body of the note, to be filled up with "Farmers", if it is intended for that Bank, or left, if it is for the other.

With great respect D^r sir
Your Mo Obd & Obliged Servt: BERNARD PEYTON

RC (MHi); endorsed by TJ as received 26 July 1820 and so recorded in SJL; additional notations by TJ beneath endorsement: "bill   1070.15

comm^n	10.70
cash	225.
Vaughan	200
White	152.90
Peyton	56.31

disc^{ts} E^{t}c   88.
balance   337.24"
                    1070.15."

RC (MHi); address cover only; with PoC of TJ to Frederick A. Mayo, 3 Jan. 1822, on verso; addressed: "Mr Thomas Jefferson Monticello Milton"; franked; postmarked Richmond, 24 July. Enclosure not found.

From William R. Swift

Winchester Vᵃ 25 July 1820

I take the liberty to trouble you Sir, with a letter for His Excʸ Mʳ Corria which, should he have left Monticello, the forwarding it will much oblige him and particularly

Sir, Your most obedient Servt   W: R: SWIFT

RC (MHi); dateline beneath signature; at foot of text: "To Thomas Jefferson Esq Monticello"; endorsed by TJ as received 2 Aug. 1820 and so recorded in SJL. Enclosure not found.

William Roberdeau Swift (1787–1833), merchant, was born in Alexandria. By 1804 he had relocated to Baltimore, where he worked in a countinghouse and sailed as supercargo on several sea voyages. A mercantile partner in his own right by 1815, Swift served, at the behest of José Corrêa da Serra, as Portugal's vice-consul in Baltimore in 1818 and as consul the following year. He supported John C. Calhoun politically prior to the 1824 presidential election and Andrew Jackson thereafter. By the mid-1820s Swift was dividing his time between New York City, where directories list him as a trader, 1826–31, and Washington, North Carolina, where he died (Roberdeau Buchanan, *Genealogy of the Roberdeau Family* [1876], 139–40; Harrison Ellery, *The Memoirs of Gen. Joseph Gardner Swift* [1890], 48, 216, genealogical appendix, p. 27; Jackson, *Papers,* 6:521–3; *Baltimore Price Current,* 1 July 1815; Léon Bourdon, *José Corrêa da Serra: Ambassadeur du Royaume-Uni de Portugal et Brésil a Washington, 1816–1820* [1975], 404–5, 462, 466; *Baltimore Patriot & Mercantile Advertiser,* 18 May, 1 June 1818; Washington *Daily National Intelligencer,* 6 Mar. 1819; Samuel Jackson, comp., *The Baltimore Directory, corrected up to June, 1819* [Baltimore, 1819]; *Longworth's New York Directory* [1826]: 460; [1831]: 615; gravestone inscription in Oakdale Cemetery, Washington, N.C.).

From Josiah Meigs

Washington City—

DEAR & RESPECTED FRIEND,   July 26, 1820.

I hope you will excuse the trouble I may perhaps occasion by this Letter.

A worthy friend of mine from Connecticutt wishes to be informed what is the proper mode of application for a Professorship in the University of Virginia—

With the great body of the People of the United States I am grateful to the Author of all good that he continues your life and health & usefulness—

I have frequently intended to pay my respects to you personally at Monticillo, but official business has hitherto prevented the gratification of my wishes—

Whereever I may be you will not doubt of my sincere esteem, respect and veneration—   JOSIAH MEIGS

RC (DLC); endorsed by TJ as received 4 Aug. 1820 and so recorded in SJL. RC (DLC); address cover only; with PoC of TJ to Levett Harris, 12 Dec. 1821, on verso; addressed: "Thomas Jefferson, Virginia"; franked; postmarked Washington, 28 July.

From John Clapper

Charlestown Jefferson County

GREAT SIR, [received 27 July 1820]

I may appear to take a liberty, which I ought not to do, but your liberality will countenance it, because addressed through patriotic motives, and a confidence in my capacity to be useful. As the superintendant of a great concern, including multifarious duties, may by his influence, or right appoint subordinate agents, I entreat that you will be so good as to give me some employment under you in the conduct of the central college of Virginia to its completion. I am a man of good education & will devote it in any way to the benefit of the work, & my own support. If you will be so kind as to let me know whether[1] there is any vacancy, I will forward the necessary recommendations

with great esteem Your [. . .] JOHN CLAPPER

RC (MHi); undated; one word illegible; endorsed by TJ as received 27 July. Recorded in SJL as received 27 July 1820.

John Clapper (ca. 1799–1834) may be the man of that name who attended Hampden-Sidney College around 1815. He apparently lived from at least 1816 in Jefferson County, Virginia (later West Virginia). Unsuccessful in his bid to ob-

tain employment through TJ, Clapper worked thereafter in that county as a physician (*General Catalogue of the Officers and Students of Hampden-Sidney College. Virginia. 1776–1906* [(1908)], 55; Charles Town *Farmer's Repository*, 3 July 1816; Charles Town *Virginia Free Press*, 9 Jan. 1834).

[1] Manuscript: "whethr."

To George Watterston

DEAR SIR Monticello July 27. 20.

When I recieved the favor of your visit two days ago, your companion mentioned your name, but my hearing is so slow that I did not catch it, and he did not happen to call you by your name in conversation afterwards: hence I had no suspicion, during your short stay, who you were. after your departure, recollecting you had said you resided at Washington, that you spoke with familiarity of the library of Congress, and particularly the part which had been mine, and putting these things together, I began to doubt that it was the person who had the care of that library, and with whom I had had correspondence[1] and riding the same day to the President's he confirmed my doubt. had I been fortunate enough to catch your name I should certainly have pressed for a longer continuance of the favor of your visit, and with my regrets for the loss of that, I pray you to accept my assurances of the pleasure it would have given me and of my esteem & respect.

TH: JEFFERSON

PoC (DLC); on verso of reused address cover of Rufus Woodward to TJ, 20 June 1820; endorsed by TJ: "Watterston George. July 27. 20." Mistakenly recorded in SJL as a letter of 21 July.

Watterston's COMPANION on his recent visit to Monticello was a Dr. Hamilton, probably United States naval surgeon Charles B. Hamilton (*City of Washington Gazette*, 8 July 1820; Callahan, *U.S. Navy*, 241). THE PRESIDENT'S: Highland, James Monroe's Albemarle County residence.

[1] Manuscript: "corrispondence."

From Frances Wright

SIR   Whitburn-Sunderland. July 27th 1820.

The very gratifying letter which you did me the honor to address to me in May last, has followed me from the States until it has reached me at this place in England.

I cannot resist the impulse of my heart which leads me to express to Mr Jefferson the pleasure that his letter has imparted to me. The approbation of such a mind as Mr Jefferson's does indeed make the heart of the poet proud;—and very proud does mine feel at this moment. It is a reward such as has been conveyed to me Sir, in your letter that more than balances against the chilling disappointments which fall on the ardent spirit in its first intercourse with the world, and which strengthens it to bear up against those rubs and discouragements which sometimes go nigh, not merely to dispel all its hopes and dreams, but to destroy its energy, and make it forego its efforts after usefulness, and its desire of honor.

Will you permit me Sir, this expression of my sentiments, and forgive me if I farther add—that mingled with the affection I feel for the young and free America, and the deep interest with which I regard her amazing progress in all that renders a nation important in its foreign relations, and happy in its internal arrangement, is the reverence I feel for the name of Mr Jefferson, to whose enlightened, active and disinterested patriotism his country owes much of its glory, its virtue and its happiness.

I am Sir, with sentiments of the highest respect
your most obliged and obedient servant   FRANCES WRIGHT

[144]

RC (CSmH: JF-BA); endorsed by TJ as received 29 Oct. 1820 and so recorded in SJL. RC (DLC); address cover only; with PoC of TJ to Thomas M. Hall, 12 Apr. 1821, on verso; addressed: "Thomas Jefferson Esqʳ Monticello State of Virginia U. S. of America"; franked; postmarked Washington, 26 Oct.

To James Bowling

SIR   Monticello July 28. 20.

I recieved last night only your favor of the 13ᵗʰ. it was the first notice I had of any difficulty in the settlemen[t] with your son. I shall be in Bedford within three weeks from this time and shall readily concur in an amicable arrangement of it: nor can I apprehend any difficulties between reasonable men, acting on just views, and with some spirit of conciliation and concession. should any arise however, good men mutually chosen will decide what is right and bring all to rights. I will give you notice on my arrival at Poplar Forest and in the mean time salute you with respect.   TH: JEFFERSON

PoC (MHi); on verso of reused address cover of John Laval to TJ, 1 Apr. 1820; edge trimmed; at foot of text: "Mʳ James Bowling senʳ"; endorsed by TJ.

James Bowling (1752–1836), soldier and farmer, was born in Saint Marys County, Maryland. Having moved by the outbreak of the Revolutionary War to Amherst County, Virginia, he enlisted there as a private in the autumn of 1775. During service of more than a year, Bowling saw action at the Battle of Great Bridge in December 1775 and at Norfolk shortly thereafter. Later in the conflict he helped guard British and Hessian prisoners of war in Albemarle County. Following the cessation of hostilities, Bowling returned permanently to Amherst County, where he owned ten slaves in 1810 and nineteen in 1830. He left an estate that included 606 acres of land and nine slaves, with his combined real and personal property worth just over $9,000 (National Society of the Daughters of the American Revolution, *DAR Patriot Index* [2003], 1:272; Vi: photocopies of Bowling pension papers; *The Pension Roll of 1835* [1835; indexed ed., 1992], 3:748; DNA: RG 29, CS, Amherst Co., 1810, 1830; *Lynchburg Virginian*, 24 Nov. 1836; Amherst Co. Will Book, 9:311–2).

Bowling's letter OF THE 13ᵀᴴ July 1820, not found, is recorded in SJL as received 27 July 1820 from "near Lynchbg." At this time TJ owed Bowling's SON Lewis Bowling $300 plus interest for his recent service as a Poplar Forest overseer (*MB*, 2:1378).

From Thomas B. Robertson

SIR   New Orleans July 28ᵗʰ 1820

I am frequently asked if I am acquainted with the situation of the Central College; if I know the course of education that will be pursued there, and the price of boarding and tuition.[1] Unfortunately I am ignorant of all these things. Can you give me the required information, concisely and in the way least troublesome to yourself. Several fathers of families are desirous of sending their sons to that institution, and it will be agreeable to me with reference both to my native and adopted State, to encourage intentions so complimentary to the one, and when carried into effect so productive of utility to the other.

Since I wrote to you last in answer to your letter of the day of May, I have been elected Governor of the State. The manner of my election has been more gratifying to me than the office itself. I was opposed by wealth, extensive family connexions, intrigue, and federalism, Bank Directors, priests, players & Yankee Merchants; I was accused of being from Virginia, and of hostility to Mr Monroe and Genl Jackson. I had nothing to offer but plain honesty & firm Republicanism. The <u>people</u>, the Country people took me up, and bestowed the appointment on me by an overwhelming majority.

There were four Candidates, Mr Derbigny, Mr Destrehan both of whom you have seen at Washington; and Abner L Duncan known to you probably by reputation.

Our Constitution requires that the two highest on the list shall be submitted to the General Assembly, which shall appoint one of them to the office of Governor. Judge Derbigny stands next to me, and it now remains to be seen whether he or myself will be preferred. My majority however is too great to render it probable that the popular choice will be disregarded. I received 1900 votes, that Gentleman 1100.

I consider myself elected and now feel in all its force the responsibility of such a situation—not that Government or the portion of it that will devolve upon me is extremely arduous. It has been surrounded by mystery & imagined difficulty, by disingenuity and cunning, and for bad purposes. But be this as it may, too much importance is attached to the Executive department every where, and in no State in the Union is this more the case unhappily, than in Louisiana. I wish then to turn the influence I shall possess to good account.

I wish above all things to aid in establishing a general and practicable system of Education. I consider information in the people as of the first necessity, and alone sufficient to preserve their liberties & to increase their prosperity. Governments generally point out the paths that lead to National strength & wealth and use both for its own purposes.[2] The strength of the nation they waste in wars of glory, its wealth in splendour and magnificence. Education will give strength, & point out the road to prosperity, better than governments can, & at the same time secure these advantages to those entitled to enjoy them.

I have no doubt of your having turned your attention deeply and frequently to this subject. Can you be of service to us in this respect? Can you give me your ideas of a plan of education suited to this state—I assure you, we always look towards you with a kind of filial regard. Louisiana acknowledges no individual, so eminently entitled to its gratitude as yourself. If however you find it inconvenient to comply with the request I make of you, I hope you will not undertake to do so, but excuse the liberty I have taken and accept the assurances of the high respect and sincerity with which

I am yo. ob. st.   THO[s] B ROBERTSON

RC (DLC); at foot of text: "Tho[s] Jefferson Esq Monticello"; endorsed by TJ as received 23 Aug. 1820 and so recorded in SJL.

Although the word PLAYERS was more often associated in the nineteenth century with actors and musicians, Robertson may have used it here to mean "gamblers" (*OED*).

[1] Manuscript: "tuitiion."
[2] Omitted period at right margin editorially supplied.

From Edmund Bacon

DEARE SIR.   July 29th 1820.
    some few days since M[r] Randolph and myself had some conversation on the subjec of my moove and it so happened that I informed him of my application to you to see if it could soot you in case that I could not so arrainge my affairs to get off in time whither I could be permitted to go on horse back myself and that your answer was Opposed to it unless a person of skill could be had during my absence M[r] Randolph said that he made no doubt but that arrangement could be affected without injury to you that I could get a man to attend to my business for my own wages whom would be satisfactory to you and that he would speak to you on the subjec he has informed me that he has done so and that your answer was that you had no Objection to the arraingment. the time has now arrived within a short time[1] when I must decide both as to your interest as well as my own whither I go or stay. I am almost certain that if I moove that I shall be compelled to leave a part of my debts to do that may accation me to have to return in a short time which will badly soot me and I am yet even undetermined whithe[r] to still proceed to moove or to ride out. but in whatever I do my sincere desire is for it to be as sootable to you as I can I am as I may say compelled to go in some way or to sustain injury both to myself and my brothers in Missouri

how would you like to take Mr Gilmer in my place he has offer[d] to do so for not a great deal above my own wages

If I ride out I dont expect that I shall want above $700 from you the balance you can keep if You chuse it untill next yeare If I shall decide to ride out the person that I get shall be such a one as Mr Randolph will no something off so as to not indanger you of sustaining injury. but I ask you sir to freely chuse whatever you like best and Just inform me according

    I am yours sincerly   E Bacon

RC (MHi); edge trimmed; addressed: "Mr Jefferson Monticello"; endorsed by TJ without date of receipt, with his additional notations beneath endorsement: "Gilmore in his place. 700.D."

TJ paid Bacon $700 "on account" on 9 Aug. 1820 (*MB*, 2:1366).

[1] Preceding two words interlined in place of "few days."

To John Wayles Eppes

Dear Sir   Monticello July 29. 20.

In my letter of June 30. I informed you I would write to Dr Cooper for information as to the state and expences of education at Columbia S.C. I will quote his answer in his own words. 'I am not fully prepared to answer your queries as to the expence of education at the S. Carolina college. but I have always understood it was very cheap, not exceeding 250.D. for the session of nine months. the particulars I do not know. boarding in college is I believe $3\frac{1}{2}$ D per week paid in advance. there is a tutor in Rhetoric and Metaphysics,[1] one in logic, & ethics, a classical tutor, a teacher of mathematics, natural philosophy & astronomy, who I believe will be mr Nulty, and a teacher of Chemistry. the principal, Dr Maxcy is dead[2] and I am in hopes mr Stephen Elliott of Charleston[3] will succeed him. if they send for a person from New England, as the fashion is, I shall be strongly inclined to resign. I greatly dislike this combination of character which promises little better than a mixture of cunning, sciolism, canting and bigotry.' so far Dr Cooper.

Mr Correa, who is now here, informs me that mr Elliott is the first character in the US. for botany & Natural history; and I have the best information that Nulty is next to Bowditch as a mathematician. here then is exactly what we want for Francis. Cooper for chemistry & geology, Nulty for nat. philos, astronomy, mathematics, Elliott for Botany & Nat. history, and a school of Rhetoric. there can be nothing equal to this in the US. it is believed that Stack will quit in October, and the Columbia session commences I believe in that month. and within a 12month from that time our university will open, if the legislature does what is expected. the society at Columbia is said to be not numerous, but polite, liberal and good; a mixture of Virginians and S. Carolinians. there is a teacher of languages, mathematics E^t come to this neighborhood and established half a dozen miles from here. he is from Edinburgh,[4] but as yet I know nothing of him. but Genl Cocke has established a Seminary at his house opposite New Canton, where he has a professor of classics, Richardson, said to be a good one, a teacher of Mathematics and a 3^d of Modern languages. there can be no doubt it will be correctly conducted under the General's controul, and I think it is probably the best and safest for young pupils, now in the state. it would probably be a desirable one for your younger sons.

One of the propositions in your letter of the 8th inst. is so exactly suited to my situation and feelings on the subject of the negroes for Francis, that I cannot hesitate a moment to accede to it. it is that which proposes to loan me the stock you mean to lay out in this way, to be paid for two years hence in negroes, without having moved them at all from their present settlements. in this way they will continue undisturbed where they always have been, without separation from their families, and pass with the ground they stand on, without being sensible of the transition from one master to another. the benefit of the intermediate loan too will be a present and great relief to me, from the pressure of debts which 2. or 3. years of short crops & short prices have accumulated, and for which the distress of the times occasions those to whom they are due to be very importunate. I accept it therefore willingly, and undertake that any sum [as 6000.D. for instance] with it's interest, shall be paid for two years hence in negroes from my Bedford estate, to be fairly chosen and valued by disinterested persons, of men, women & children in the usual proportions, excluding superannuation. I think this much better too for Francis. for were[5] they all to be present laborers, without young ones to come on in succession, he would be apt, as most of us would to look on that as his regular sum of labor and income, and fix his habitual expences by that standard, without considering that his standard would be lessening by the progressing ages and deaths of his laborers, leaving no successors to supply their places. and I have observed that young negroes from 12. or 13. years of age, and women also, are of real value in the farm, where there is abundance to be done of what they can do, and which otherwise would employ men. this arrangement has the further advantage that by two years hence property will have settled down to the value it is to hold hereafter; whereas value at this time is totally unsettled, and so much a matter of guess-work, that no two judgments fix in the same notch, and not often in sight of one another.

I will add an assurance that I shall carry into the execution of this transaction all the disinterested affection and anxiety for Francis, which you could yourself. your answer therefore may close this agreement finally on your part, as this letter is meant to do on mine; and if it is given immediately, it will reach me here before my departure for Bedford, which will be within a fortnight or a little over, and in that case I may probably take Millbrook in my way. Francis is here and in perfect health; Wayles is here also just relieved from a fever of some days. we all join in salutations to mrs Eppes and family and in affectionate respects to yourself.   TH: JEFFERSON

P.S. since writing this Francis tells me his brothers are but 6. or 8. years old. the Bremo Seminary recieves none under ten.

RC (ViU: TJP); brackets in original. PoC (ViU: TJP); first two pages only; at foot of first page: "J. W. Eppes."

WAYLES: John Wayles Baker.

[1] In extracting a passage from Thomas Cooper's letter of 12 July 1820, TJ here omitted "in my view very useless studies."

[2] Preceding two words altered in TJ's extract from Cooper's "died the day after I left Columbia."

[3] Preceding two words altered in TJ's extract from Cooper's "of the Charleston Bank."

[4] Manuscript: "Edingburgh."

[5] PoC ends here.

To Mathew Carey

DEAR SIR   Monticello July 31. 20.

Your favor of July 13. was recieved on the 21st inst. and I now inclose you 25.D. in bills of the bank of Virginia as none of the US. are to be had here. the surplus of 1.75 may cover the discount perhaps.

I presume you import from time to time books from England, and should be glad if on the first occasion you would write for a copy of Baxter's history of England for me. and if there be an 8vo edn of it, I should greatly prefer it. if none, I must be contented with the original 4to. I doubt whether it went to a 2^{d} edition, even the whigs of England[1] not bearing to see their bible, Hume, republicanised. octavo volumes suit my hand, and my shelves so much better than any other size, that if the Conversations in chemistry, mentioned below can be had from England in 8vo I would rather wait for their importation. if not, I would prefer the English edition 12mo that of Humphreys being bad print & coarse paper. if Sir J. Sinclair's book is not to be had with you it might be added to the importation. I salute you with great friendship & respect.   TH: JEFFERSON

Baxter's history of England.
Conversations in Chemistry.
Sr John Sinclairs Code of agriculture. this is the work which is in a single vol. thick 8vo and must be distinguished from a similar work in several volumes published some years ago and of which this is a condensed digest.

RC (PHi: Lea & Febiger Records); addressed: "Mr Matthew Carey Philadelphia"; franked; postmarked Charlottesville, 1 Aug.; endorsed by a representative of Mathew Carey & Son as received 4 Aug. and answered the following day. PoC (DLC); on verso of reused address cover of John H. Cocke to TJ, 12 Apr. 1820; edge trimmed; endorsed by TJ.

Sinclair's monograph, *The Code of Agriculture* (London, 1817), was a CON-

DENSED DIGEST of the ninety county surveys and other works published by the British Board of Agriculture since the 1790s (Heather Holmes, "Sir John Sinclair, the County Agricultural Surveys, and the Collection and Dissemination of Knowledge 1793–1817, with a Bibliography of the Surveys: Part 1," Edinburgh Bibliographical Society, *Journal* 7 [2012]: 29–70).

[1] Preceding two words interlined.

From David Isaacs

SIR   31st July 1820
    I sent you Six & $\frac{3}{4}$ ℔ of Tallow   D. ISAACS

RC (MHi); written on a small scrap; dateline at foot of text; at head of text: "Mr Jefferson"; endorsed by TJ without date of receipt, with his additional notation beneath endorsement: "Aug. 2. 20. p^d by Burwell."

TJ recorded payment on 2 Aug. 1820 of 1.12\frac{1}{2}$ to Isaacs for TALLOW (*MB*, 2:1366).

From Edmund Bacon

DEARE SIR.   [before 1 Aug. 1820]
    I send you a list of my own family. Mr Meeks's & Cardens with the age opposite each name

	age		
Edmund Bacon	35. years old	Edmund Meeks	28 years old
Ann Bacon	37 —	Mary Meeks	23 do

Fielding W Bacon	16
Thomas J Bacon	15.
William L Bacon	13

slaves

Betty	25 years old	
Meria	19 years do	
Ellen	10. do	
Lilly	9 do	} Females
Eadey	8.	
Martha	7	
Mary	1	

Thuston	4 years old	} Males
Reuben	7 do	

1 Male child	1 yare old
1 Female slave	20 do
Youen Carden	61 years old
his wife	58 do
William Carden	27 do
Sally Carden	23 do
Elizabeth Carden	21
Mary Carden	13
1 Female slave	12

RC (MHi); written on a small scrap; undated, but composed prior to TJ's summarizing of this information on 1 Aug. 1820 in census information on a detached sheet from his Farm Book in ViU:

TJP; endorsed by TJ: "Census" and "Census. 1820."

An image of the entry for TJ in the 1820 census return for Albemarle County is reproduced elsewhere in this volume.

To Bernard Peyton

DEAR SIR   Monticello Aug. 1. 20.

Your favors of July 21. & 24. have been recieved, the latter covering 225.D. and I shall immediately draw on you in favor of A. Garrett for 300. or 325.D. before the reciept of yours of the 21s[t]1 I had already[2] availed myself of the first good opportunity of speaking to the President on what is the subject of it. it was impossible to reply more frankly or more favorab[ly] than he did as to his earnest dispositions on that subject towards you. I could not ask a promise certainly, but he said that it should be as I pleased. he added that acting with responsibility between candidates, it would be necessary to furnish him with the best grounds of justification by as strong recommendations as could be obtained, whenever either event should happen. these should be from the resp[e]ctable merchants the gentlemen of the best standing of the place, and particularly[3] your brother officers of the late war; to be obtained at the moment when either event happens, and in the mean time to be as silent as the grave as to your views. no removal will probably take place. revolutionary whiggism and services are a strong ground of tenure. affectionately yours

TH: JEFFERSON

PoC (MHi); on verso of a reused address cover from Mark Langdon Hill to TJ; edge trimmed; mutilated at seal; at foot of text: "Capt Peyton"; endorsed by TJ.

On 2 Aug. 1820 TJ gave Alexander GARRETT an order on Peyton for $325, of which $250 was to pay the third installment of TJ's subscription to the University of Virginia (*MB*, 2:1366; Garrett's Account with the University of Virginia, 30 Sept. 1820, enclosure no. 1 in University of Virginia Board of Visitors Report to Literary Fund President and Directors, 2 Oct. 1820).

[1] Word faint.
[2] Manuscript: "alreeady."
[3] Manuscript: "particully."

From Constantine S. Rafinesque

RESPECTED SIR,   T. U. August 1, 1820

The attention of many of our enlightened writers, as well as historical antiquarian societies, has lately been directed towards the interesting investigation of the numberless and astonishing monuments of remote origin scattered through the western states.

Of the utmost simplicity of structure and materials, they afford, nevertheless, the greatest variety of forms and dimensions, with evident proofs of geometrical and astronomical knowledge, in the nation which erected them, and yet they evince every where that such a people must have been in one of the first stages of rude civilization.

The valuable tradition lately recorded by Mr. Heckenwelder, which ascribes them to the Alleghawian, a powerful nation or nations which once inhabited the extensive country extending from the Lakes to the Gulf of Mexico, and from the Alleghany Mountains to the Prairies of Louisiana, is quite likely to lead us at last, to the true path of remote historical knowledge, and all our future researches ought to be directed towards the illustration of this rational and probable tradition, rather than the comment of the manyfold absurd opinions heretofore advanced on the subject.

We have three different sources of information on this point, or three means of investigation, which ought to be consulted simultaneously and comparatively: the most interesting results are likely to flow from an attentive recurrence to them by a discriminating and philosophical mind; we may perhaps succeed, through those means, to restore, in part from total oblivion, the origin, achievements, attainments and history of that ancient nation, which preceded us and the hunting tribes on this fruitful soil, which was no doubt cultivated by them.

They are 1st. Records—2dly. Monuments—and 3rdly. Implements.[1]

I include among Records, all the historical and traditional knowledge which has reached us, respecting this people, and the neighbouring nations, such as the Floridans, Haytians, Cubans, Mexicans, &c. or their conquerors, the Lennapians and Mengweas. They are to be found in the travels and histories of the first discoverers and explorers of this continent, particularly those of the 15th and 16th centuries. There is no doubt that all those former nations belonged to a similar race, and did no more differ among themselves than the Swedes do now from the Spaniards. The Floridans particularly, appear to have been an identical nation with the Alleghawians, and might as well be called the southern Alleghawians. Of these southern tribes we happen to have an excellent account of 300 years standing, in Soto's expedition in Florida, which, leaving apart a few evident exaggerations, gives us an idea of the flourishing state of this nation, which was then as yet unconquered in the south. The account given us by Charleveix of the Natchez[2] nation, which was 200 years after, a remnant of it confirms the account of Soto.

Two new opinions have lately been emitted by Mr. John D. Clifford on the subject of their origin. 1. That all these nations (which he calls Mexicans) are of Hindoo origin. 2. That the Alleghawians were the ancestors of the Anahuacans, or real Mexican nations. Altho' he has made these opinions highly probable, they are, as yet, liable to some objections in the details: for instance, it does not appear that all the nations of Anahuac, or the Mexican regions, have come from the north-east, or from our Alleghawians, although some may.[3] The Antillan nations, Haytians, Cubans, &c. may perhaps claim an eastern origin, and have come easterly from Spain or Africa: although they were of a similar Hindoo race. It would be no wonder that this primitive race, which spread itself from Ireland to Japan, should have reached America by the two opposite quarters as the Europeans have lately done, since the Russians are establishing themselves on this continent from the west. Besides those Hindoo tribes, which came to America from the west, must have reached it gradually through the Polynesian Archipelago, and not direct as Mr. Clifford supposes. This last opinion (which is more probable) has been long ago assumed by Mr. Gebelin, and latterly by Dr. S. Mitchell; but he is, perhaps, mistaken when he endeavours to prove a total identity between the Peruvians, Mexicans and Alleghawians, with the actual Polynesian Islanders, which have been satisfactorily proved to be of Malay origin, that is to say, of another distinct and modern branch of the Hindoo race.

These conjectures, and many others which might be suggested, offer an immense field to our antiquarians and historians. I hope they will soon undertake to explore it, and elucidate the facts in all their proximate and remote consequences, comparing them accurately with all that we know already on analogous subjects. The writer who wishes to become eminently useful and correct, must be intimately acquainted with all the opinions already suggested, all the facts already stated, and all the materials already detected: he must select from their mass what is most certain and probable, without neglecting what may be less so, although yet highly valuable in a comparative or relative point of view, and from these various elements he must endeavour to trace a perspicuous and comprehensive survey of the early history of our continent, which will become thereby an interesting addition to the ancient history of mankind. Meantime all those who feel an interest in the pursuit of this knowledge ought to labour in collecting materials for such a future history.

This is what I have undertaken to do by beginning to survey accurately all the Alleghawian Monuments of Kentucky. The nucleus of the northern Alleghawian population appear to have been scattered near the rivers Ohio and Mississippi; but remains of its monuments are found all over the fertile parts of the western states, particularly near streams. The principal monuments of the state of Ohio have already been pretty well described; but those of Kentucky and many other states, have hardly been noticed, although they are equally interesting. I shall endeavour to supply this deficiency, and I now mean to describe to you several of them, which exist within a short compass in the neighbourhood of Mountsterling; I have lately surveyed them, and taken accurate plans of the whole, which I shall forward to the Antiquarian Society of Massachusetts.

But before I undertake their description, it will be proper to notice the third kind of information alluded to, or the Alleghawian Implements. These consist in a variety of idols, vases, pipes, hatchets, amulets, spears, arrows, shells, clothing, ornaments, &c. which are found every day through our country, and particularly near or within the monuments. Although one half of them are lost or broken by the discoverers, many find their way in our museums, where they are scattered promiscuously with the Lennapian Implements or modern Indian articles of clothing and ornament, of which they ought to be distinguished. An accurate knowledge of all the Alleghawian implements will enable their future historians to give us an insight into their private life, domestic arts, religious ceremonies, manner of fighting, clothing, &c. It is therefore very needful to collect all such implements, to preserve them with care and describe them properly.

A fourth kind of remains might perhaps be added, including mummies and bones, of which many have been found; which may serve to prove what kind of men, were the Alleghawians.

I call monuments,[4] all those remains of labour and art on a large scale, which stand on the soil or under it. They might be distinguished by their use into 1. Religious; 2. Civil; 3. Military; 4. Domestic; 5. Sepulchral, and 6. Miscellaneous Monuments: but as it is often difficult to distinguish at first the probable use of each monument, or as they may have been sometimes employed for two or several such purposes, it will be more convenient to distinguish them in the first instance by their structure, rather than their ultimate use, the knowledge of which, will result afterwards from our comparative researches.

They may therefore be classed into 1. Inclosures or Circumvallations. 2. Mounds. 3. Platforms or raised Areas. 4. Embankments. 5. Graves. 6. Miscellanies. Their materials are either earth, gravel, stone, mud or bricks baked in the sun.

The most remarkable monuments are the inclosures: their shape is very various, and of almost all the regular geometrical forms, or even quite irregular. They consist in their utmost perfection of 5 parts. 1. Parapet. 2. Ditch. 3. Gateway. 4. Area. 5 Mound, which are sometimes double or multiple, while they may occasionally be totally missing, except the ditch and area, by which they are essentially constituted. It is highly probable that when the shape is irregular, and there is no parapet or earthen wall, or when it is inside of the ditch, they have been forts or fortified towns and camps; but when the parapet is outward or double, and the shape regular, they must have been temples or palaces, places used for religious or civil purposes.

In my next letter I shall describe to you the monuments lately surveyed near Mountsterling.[5]

Meantime I remain, respectfully,
Your well wisher,   C. S. RAFINESQUE.
                                     Prof in Transylvania University.

Printed in Lexington *Kentucky Reporter*, 16 Aug. 1820, and *City of Washington Gazette*, 26 Aug. 1820; dateline at foot of text; at head of text (one word editorially corrected from "U.T."): "*THREE LETTERS* ON AMERICAN ANTIQUITIES, DIRECTED TO THE HONORABLE THOMAS JEFFERSON, *LATE PRESIDENT OF THE UNITED STATES. FIRST LETTER*. ON THE ALLEGHAWIAN RECORDS. TO THE HONORABLE THOMAS JEFFERSON, L.P. U.S." Not recorded in SJL and probably never received by TJ.

John Heckewelder (HECKENWELDER) discussed the Alligewi Indians and their conquest by the Lenni Lenape and a group of Iroquois in his "Account of the History, Manners, and Customs, of the Indian Nations, who once inhabited Pennsylvania and the neighbouring states" (APS, *Transactions of the Historical & Literary Committee* 1 [1819; Poor, *Jefferson's Library*, 7 (no. 343)]: 1–350, esp. 29–32). THE LAKES: the Great Lakes. The work on Hernando de Soto's EXPEDITION IN FLORIDA was probably Garcilaso de la Vega, *La Florida del Ynca* (Lisbon, 1605, and other eds.; Sowerby, no. 4084). Pierre François Xavier de Charlevoix (CHARLEVEIX) provided information about the Natchez Indians in his

Histoire et Description Generale de la Nouvelle France (Paris, 1744, and other eds.; Sowerby, no. 4004).

Between September 1819 and April 1820 JOHN D. CLIFFORD published eight articles on "Indian Antiquities in the Western Country" in vols. 1 and 2 of the *Western Review and Miscellaneous Magazine*. DR. S. MITCHELL: Samuel L. Mitchill. ANTIQUARIAN SOCIETY OF MASSACHUSETTS: the American Antiquarian Society.

[1] *Kentucky Reporter*: "Improvements." Correction noted in *Kentucky Reporter*, 23 Aug. 1820, immediately after Rafinesque's 7 Aug. 1820 letter to TJ.

[2] *Kentucky Reporter*: "Matches." Corrected as above.

[3] Omitted period editorially supplied.

[4] *Kentucky Reporter*: "monnments." *City of Washington Gazette*: "monuments."

[5] *Kentucky Reporter*: "Mounstterling."

From James Monroe

DEAR SIR   Highland Augt 2. 1820.

In addition to mr Gallatin's & mr Rush's letters which I promised last night to send you to day, I enclose a copy of the instructions given to mr Forbes appointed agent to S^o America, either Buenos Ayres, or Chili, to be decided, by a circumstance mentiond in them. as they explain in a general way, our relations with that country, and state some facts of an interesting nature, I have thought that it might be agreeable to you to see them. The instructions to Com: Perry, which are mentiond in those to m^r Forbes, & m^r Prevost, I should be glad to send you if I had them here as they wo^d give the whole view. You shall see them on some future occasion.

Yours with the greatest respect & regard   JAMES MONROE

RC (DLC); endorsed by TJ as received 2 Aug. 1820 and so recorded in SJL. Enclosure: John Quincy Adams to John M. Forbes, State Department, 5 July 1820, appointing Forbes as "agent for commerce and seamen for either of the provinces of Buenos Ayres or of Chili, in whichsoever of them Mr. J. B. Prevost shall not be. He is at this time at Buenos Ayres; but having, at one period, intimated to the President a preference to return to Chili, where he some time resided, it is thought due to him to leave the selection of his residence, after your arrival at Buenos Ayres, to himself"; lamenting the widespread and "atrocious acts of piracy" committed by foreign privateers with commissions from and operating out of these two places; revealing that in "the instructions to the late Commodore Perry . . . certain articles in the Buenos Ayrean privateering ordinance were pointed out, particularly liable to the production of these abuses, and which, being contrary to the established usages among civilized nations, it was hoped would have been revoked, or made to disappear from their otherwise unexceptionable code"; and commanding Forbes to execute the applicable portions of Perry's orders, prevent American seamen from enlisting on privateers in the region under his purview, maintain his own neutral stance, and forward to the United States government any relevant commercial and political information that comes to his attention (*ASP, Foreign Relations*, 4:820). Other enclosures not found.

[157]

From Samuel Smith (of Maryland)

D^R SIR   Baltimore 2 August 1820

The total ruin in which my private fortune is involved, and my inability for¹ want of Capital to pursue any probable means of support for my family induced me to give my Consent to become a Candidate for the Speakers Chair—The Views of N. Carolina who first mentioned the subject to me were bottomed on the Idea, that it would be unwise for the South to irritate the East by the Choice of a Speaker south of Potomack, and equally unwise to take a Speaker from among those who were active in favor of the Missouri question. they, therefore thought it advisable to fix on me, as from a State not obnoxious to either great division,—The Southern Candidate will be Mr Nelson, the Eastern Mr Taylor of N. York,—the division of the Southern Votes between Mr Nelson and me may give Mr Taylor a majority on the first Vote. if my number should be such as to induce my friends to withdraw my name the Contest will thus be between Mr Nelson and Mr Taylor, and will probably be in favor of the latter. it will thus be determined by Votes founded on the Missouri question.—If however the Contest should be between Mr Taylor and me,—and if I should be supported by Virginia there would be little doubt of my succeeding.—I know not any person who Could influence Mr Nelson, and I doubt much whether any ought to make the attempt, if any person could I presume Mr Madison might—I fear the Contest for Speaker between East and South will Call up the unpleasant question of Slavery and no Slavery again.

I have been a sincere supporter of the present Administration, because I have thought little wrong had been done, and because I thought the President meant to do right—Some expenditures had been commenced proper in themselves, but not Convenient in the present State of our Affairs—I believe they are postponed for a time when our finances will be in a better State

I have thought (perhaps vainly) that I Could render essential service in Spain. that nation was our best Customer formerly for flour, until it imposed a prohibitory duty.—To induce its removal will require more commercial knowledge than is usually sent on foreign missions—I know that Merchants have Scarcely² ever been sent by any nation to the Courts of Europe, but may not this be one of the prejudices of the World, if So—ought we not to be superior to them,— I however think it highly probable that the new Order of things in Spain may induce the President to continue Mr Forsyth. I have the honor to be

with the sincerest attachment
your most Obed^t serv^t

S. SMITH

RC (DLC); addressed: "Thomas Jefferson Monticello"; franked; postmarked Baltimore, 3 Aug.; endorsed by TJ as received 11 Aug. 1820 and so recorded in SJL. Enclosed in TJ to James Madison, 13 Aug. 1820.

The occupant of the SPEAKERS CHAIR in the United States House of Representatives received a per diem twice as large as that of an ordinary member (*U.S. Statutes at Large*, 3:404 [22 Jan. 1818]). The SOUTHERN CANDIDATE for the speakership was ultimately William Lowndes, of South Carolina, not Hugh Nelson, of Virginia. After twenty-two ballots, on 15 Nov. 1820 John W. Taylor (MR TAYLOR OF N. YORK) was elected Speaker, with

Smith finishing a distant third (*JHR*, 14:7; John S. Pancake, *Samuel Smith and the Politics of Business: 1752–1839* [1972], 155).

THE NEW ORDER OF THINGS: large-scale uprisings throughout Spain in the early months of 1820 had induced Ferdinand VII to restore the nation's 1812 constitution, which promoted the concept of popular sovereignty and restricted monarchical power through an elected parliament (Paul W. Schroeder, *Metternich's Diplomacy at Its Zenith, 1820–1823* [1962], 25–6).

[1] Manuscript: "fo," reworked from "to."
[2] Word interlined.

José Corrêa da Serra's Plan for a Botanical Garden

[by 4 Aug. 1820]

Plan of a Botanic garden for a public school
on the most useful, and Less[1] expensive plan.

Almost all the Botanic gardens seem rather destined to increase the catalogue of the species and genera of vegetables, than to furnish to students useful notions of the vegetable kingdom. They are filled with plants which though they may in future times turn useful, do not afford to the student any other information, but a bare name, and a few caracters to distinguish it from its neighbours very often as unmeaning as that plant itself. Such expensive gardens of mere curiosity, may be Left to the vanity of Nabobs or to the magnificence of Sovereigns. I am persuaded a greater profit with much Less expense could be obtained in a garden of a public school if the following plan was adopted.

1. In order that the knowledge of vegetables be a science, a clear idea must be given of vegetable anatomy and physiology. This only can furnish a solid and philosophical basis to Botany and agriculture. The Laws of the vitality of plants, their growth, decay, irritability, and excitability, power of external actions on them, must be taught and demonstrated, before teaching classification and nomenclature, which cannot be true if not grounded on this basis

2. A method must be taught of distinguishing plants, and getting acquainted with their species and genera. This method cannot be but artificial; that of Linné is good enough and easy. This part of botany may be justly called <u>the art of botany</u>, and though many persons, even professors take it for science, is at the bottom nothing more than an empty nomenclature and acquaintance with external forms of vegetables.

3.[2] The true science which is coeval with the French revolution does not consist only in distinguishing plants by their external forms but in grouping them by all the assemblage of organisation, in the different orders of affinity in which nature has distributed them. It is incredible what consequences this new study has had[3] in so short a time, on all the arts that depend from[4] the knowledge of vegetables

4. The Last and most useful part, is the knowledge of the use of vegetables, for food of man and beast, for medicine, for dying,[5] for building, for clothing, for ornament &[a]

5. There is also a sort of botanical erudition, about plants which have figured in history, for superstition, for civil usages, or that are mentioned by the great classical writers.

The plan proposed consists simply in this

That no plant be admitted in the garden, but such as are necessary to furnish samples for vegetable anatomy and physiological phenomena, or of the most important natural groupes, or which have economical or medical uses, or concur to the true intelligence of history and the great classical writers.

In this manner no plant would exist in the garden, about which the professor besides the name and the caracters, would not have also some valuable information to impart. It is evident, that at the end of a course of botany given on such plan by a competent professor, the students would have acquired more real knowledge, than if they had seen the external form, and Learned the names of ten times the number of plants requisite for such a course

Fifteen hundred plants at the utmost would be the necessary stock of a garden on this plan, and four acres of ground i estimate would be fully sufficient, even allowing to the plants that it would be useful to introduce in Virginia a much larger Lot than to the others, in order to obtain seeds to distribute through the country

I would add to these four acres, two more for a grove of trees, none of them of Virginia, but either from other states of the Union, or from other countries of temperate climates, that could grow here. This grove would require Little care and expense, and Leave the four acres unincumbered from trees, to the better culture of the other plants

MS (ViU: TJP); in Corrêa da Serra's hand; undated, but evidently composed prior to his final departure from Monticello in August 1820 (see TJ to William Short, 4 Aug. 1820); endorsed by TJ: "Botanical garden for the University Mr Corea's observations." Tr (ViU: Ellen W. Randolph Coolidge Correspondence); prepared after TJ's death in an unidentified hand; at head of text in Martha Jefferson Randolph's hand: "by Mr Correa de Serra"; addressed: "For Mrs Randolph, Care of Joseph C. Coolidge Esqe, Boston"; stamped; postmarked University of Virginia, 3 Nov. Enclosed in TJ to John P. Emmet, 27 Apr. 1826.

LINNÉ: Carolus Linnaeus (Carl von Linné).

[1] Tr: "least."
[2] Number not in Tr.
[3] Word interlined in place of "produced."
[4] Tr: "upon."
[5] MS: "diyng." Tr: "dying."

From John Hollins

DEAR SIR   Baltimore 4th August 1820

The Revd Mr Sparks, the bearer of this, being on his travels in your part of Virga and naturally feeling a desire to have an introduction to your worthy self—I have at the request of some of your friends, & my particular acquaintances, used the freedom to address you a few lines, introducing that Gentleman to your usual civilities & politeness=it is true I have no personal knowledge of Mr Sparks, but my good Sir, I am very well assured & am justified in saying, you will not regret the satisfaction, you will derive from the pleasure of his acquaintance, being a Gentleman of first rate abilities—   Mr S not having resided long in our City & being a native of the Eastern States, is my apology for not having a personal intimacy with him, but am sure that will not weigh to his disadvantage in your estimation

Very respectfy &c &c   JNo HOLLINS

RC (MHi); endorsed by TJ as received 19 Aug. 1820 and so recorded in SJL. RC (DLC); address cover only; with PoC of TJ to Hiram Haines, 8 Dec. 1821, on verso; addressed: "Thomas Jefferson Esqe Monticello By the Reverd Mr Sparks."

From Abner B. Hunt

REVD AND D— SIR   Lebanon Warren County Ohio Agt 4th 1820

It will no dout somewhat Surprise you when you cast your eyes blow and be hold their a strang signiture. but as surprising as it may be your goodness will not suffer you to cast it off without at least a slight reflection, particularly when you learn its contents.

Knowing it is the characteristic of great men not to be indifferent to the wants and necessities of those of an inferior grade, it is therefore most aged Sir, I thus attempt to intrude these lines upon you, to give you a short discription of the person who has assumed the liberty to address you. I will informe you I am a young man in low and indigent circumstanes, who has been unfortunate in business and on whom the oppression of the times has borne with great severity. My Father is an old man and has a large family to support and consiquently is not able to releave my necessities, I have been advised my friends to acquire an knowledge of the Law and have commenced the study, I therefore ask your charity for a small assistance in the way of furnishing me with a few Law books and that only. could your goodness procure for me and forward on to Cincinnati a small library of this discription of books, I trust I should feel ever greatfull, and I while you are sleeping in the caverns of the earth may reap the benifit of your kindness and think of those that once lived.

I must inform you my Father was three years in our revolutionary strugle and happy I am to say that ancient days record his servises and not withstanding he has received no pension

it was then he saw the immortal Jefferson and it was from him in my younger days I have learned in part your charactor

should I attempt to enumerate the various functions you have been call'd to discharge in the counsils of this mighty nation you might think I aimed at flattery but Sir—I cannot think of closing this without at least that I have some small knowledge of your charactor. I have beheld you legislating in states minester to foreign courts and also in the counsels of this great Nation, and to whom we are for ever bound for our indissoluble and hallowed Constitution upon which our great national superstructure is founded. and now you in your declining years can repose in peace and tranquility and behold the groing greatness of this vast and immesureable Empire, of which you have been so conspicuously instrumental in forming. you have now my aged Sir— almost terminated your mortal existance to leave this stage of tumult and take your flight to celestial region their to receive the reward due to the virtuous where you will meet your Brother the once mortal but now immortal Washington who their awaits your arrival

then no more will the person of Jefferson be seen or his voice heared. then memory alone will recount to us his mighty deeds and the latest posterity of the american people will be proud to mention his name as there country

Dear Sir In the high[t] Esteem and Regard I shall ever remain yours

ABNER B. HUNT

RC (MHi); at foot of text: "Thomas Jefferson"; endorsed by TJ as received 30 Aug. 1820 and so recorded in SJL.

From William Paxton

SIR,   Lexington. August 4th 1820.

Not long since when passing the Natural Bridge, I was solicited by Patrick Henry to write you on the subject of some tresspasses he Alledges are committing on your premises there, such as cutting timber &C. He is desireous to know If you purpose a visit to the Bridge this season, or If 'tis your wish that he should in your Absence endeavour to Asscertain the bounderies of your Original Grant, some difference of Opinion as to the lines of Adjoining lands appear to exist.   I went to the Bridge I think in April last for that purpose at Patrick's request, where I understood you expected to be, but nothing was done, the bad weather as we Supposed, or some Other cause prevented your crossing the mountain.

It is certainly to be regretted that the timber, no matter to whome belonging should have been destroyed so near the top of the Bridge.

Accept my Sincere regard   Wᴹ PAXTON

RC (MHi); endorsed by TJ as received 10 Aug. 1820 and so recorded in SJL. RC (MHi); address cover only; with PoC of TJ to Bernard Peyton, 3 Nov. 1821, on verso; addressed: "Thomas Jefferson esq. Monticello"; franked; postmarked Lexington, Va., 6 Aug.

William Paxton (ca. 1777–1853), farmer and public official, served Rockbridge County as a justice of the peace, 1807–27. He was county surveyor for many years prior to his resignation in 1831 and sheriff during the latter half of the 1830s. Paxton also represented Rockbridge County for two terms in the Virginia House of Delegates, 1816–18. He surveyed TJ's property at Natural Bridge in November 1821, sat for a time on the Virginia Board of Public Works, and superintended a great deal of local canal and road construction. Paxton owned seven slaves in 1830 and eleven a decade later, with the value of his real estate estimated at $10,000 in 1850 (William M. Paxton, *The Paxtons* [1903], 263; *Daughters of the American Revolution Magazine* 48 [1916]: 439; Oren F. Morton, *A History of Rockbridge County Virginia* [1920], 564–6; Leonard, *General Assembly*, 287, 291; *MB*, 2:1380, 1381; *JHD* [1820–21 sess.], 164 [6 Feb. 1821]; DNA: RG 29, CS, Rockbridge Co., 1830, 1850, Lexington, 1840; gravestone inscription in Paxton Family Cemetery, Mechanicsville, Rockbridge Co.).

The ORIGINAL GRANT from the Crown to TJ for the 157-acre Natural Bridge tract is dated 5 July 1774 (Vi: RG 4, Virginia Land Office Patent Book, 42:657–8).

To William Short

DEAR SIR   Monticello Aug. 4. 20.

I owe you a letter for your favor of June 29. which was recieved in due time, and there being no subject of the day of particular interest I will make this a supplement to mine of Apr. 13. my aim in that was to justify the character of Jesus against the fictions of his pseudo-followers which have exposed him to the inference of being an impostor,[1] for if we could believe that he really countenanced the follies, the falsehoods and the Charlatinisms which his biographers father on him, and admit the misconstructions, interpolations & theorisations of the fathers of the early, and fanatics of the latter ages, the conclusion would be irresistible by every sound mind, that he was an impostor. I give no credit to their falsifications of his actions & doctrines; and, to rescue his character, the postulate in my letter asked only what is granted in reading every other historian. when Livy or Siculus, for example, tell us things which coincide with our experience of the order of nature, we credit them on their word, and place their narrations among the records of credible history. but when they tell us of calves speaking, of statues sweating blood, and other things against the course of nature, we reject these as fables, not belonging to history. in like manner, when an historian, speaking of a character well known and established on satisfactory testimony imputes to it things incompatible with that character, we reject them without hesitation, and assent to that only of which we have better evidence. had Plutarch informed us that Caesar & Cicero passed their whole lives in religious exercises, and abstinence from the affairs of the world, we should reject what was so inconsistent with their established characters, still crediting what he relates in conformity with our ideas of them. so again, the superlative wisdom of Socrates is testified by all antiquity, and placed on ground not to be questioned. when therefore Plato puts into his mouth such fancies, such paralogisms[2] & sophisms as a schoolboy would be ashamed of, we conclude they were the whimsies of Plato's own foggy brain, and acquit Socrates of puerilities so unlike his character. (speaking of Plato I will add that no writer antient or modern has bewildered the world with more ignes fatui than this renowned philosopher, in Ethics, in Politics & Physics. in the latter, to specify a single example, compare his views of the animal economy, in his Timaeus, with those of mrs Bryan in her Conversations on chemistry, and weigh the science of the canonised philosopher against the good sense of the unassuming lady. but Plato's visions have furnished a basis for endless systems of mystical theology, and he is therefore all but adopted as a Christian saint.—it is surely time for men to think for themselves, and to throw off the authority of names so artificially magnified. but to return from this parenthesis, I say that) this free exercise of reason is all I ask for the vindication of the character of Jesus. we find in the writings of his biographers matter of two distinct descriptions. first a ground work of vulgar ignorance, of things impossible, of superstitions, fanaticisms, & fabrications. intermixed with these again are sub-

lime ideas of the supreme being, aphorisms and precepts of the purest morality & benevolence, sanctioned by a life of humility, innocence,
and simplicity of manners, neglect of riches, absence of worldly ambition & honors, with an eloquence and persuasiveness which have not
been surpassed. these could not be inventions of the grovelling authors who relate them. they are far beyond the powers of their feeble
minds. they shew that there was a character, the subject of their history, whose splendid conceptions were above all suspicion of being
interpolations from their hands. can we be at a loss in separating such
materials, & ascribing each to it's genuine author? the difference is
obvious to the eye and to the understanding, and we may read; as we
run, to each his part; and I will venture to affirm that he who, as I
have done, will undertake to winnow this grain from it's chaff, will
find it not to require a moment's consideration. the parts fall asunder
of themselves as would those of an image of metal & clay.

There are, I acknolege, passages not free from objection, which we
may with probability ascribe to Jesus himself; but claiming indulgence from the circumstances under which he acted. his object was
the reformation of some articles in the religion of the Jews, as taught
by Moses. that Seer had presented, for the object of their worship,
a being of terrific character, cruel, vindictive, capricious and unjust.
Jesus, taking for his type the best qualities of the human head and
heart, wisdom, justice, goodness, and adding to them power, ascribed
all of these, but in infinite perfection, to the supreme being, and
formed him really worthy of their adoration. Moses had either not
believed in a future state of existence, or had not thought it essential
to be explicitly taught to his people. Jesus inculcated that doctrine
with emphasis and precision. Moses had bound the Jews to many
idle ceremonies, mummeries & observances of no effect towards producing the social utilities which constitute the essence of virtue. Jesus
exposed their futility & insignificance. the one instilled into his people
the most anti-social spirit towards other nations; the other preached
philanthropy & universal charity and benevolence.   the office of
reformer of the superstitions of a nation is ever dangerous. Jesus had
to walk on the perilous confines of reason and religion: and a step to
right or left might place him within the gripe of the priests of the superstition, a bloodthirsty race, as cruel and remorseless as the being
whom they represented as the family god of Abraham, of Isaac & of
Jacob, and the local god of Israel. they were constantly laying snares
too to entangle him in the web of the law. he was justifiable therefore
in avoiding these by evasions, by sophisms, by misconstructions and
misapplications of scraps of the prophets, and in defending himself

with these their own weapons as sufficient, ad homines, at least. that Jesus did not mean to impose himself on mankind as the son of god physically speaking I have been convinced by the writings of men more learned than myself in that lore. but that he might conscientiously believe himself inspired from above, is very possible. the whole religion of the Jews, inculcated on him from his infancy, was founded in the belief of divine inspiration. the fumes of the most disordered imaginations were recorded in their religious code, as special communications of the deity; and as it could not but happen that, in the course of ages, events would now and then turn up to which some of these vague rhapsodies might be accomodated by the aid of allegories, figures, types, and other tricks upon words, they have not only preserved their credit with the Jews of all subsequent[3] times, but are the foundation of much of the religions of those who have schismatised from them. elevated by the enthusiasm of a warm and pure heart, conscious of the high strains of an eloquence which had not been taught him, he might readily mistake the coruscations of his own fine genius for inspirations of an higher order. this belief carried therefore no more personal imputation, than the belief of Socrates that himself was under the care and admonitions of a guardian daemon. and how many of our wisest men still believe in the reality of these inspirations, while perfectly sane on all other subjects. excusing therefore, on these considerations, those passages in the gospels which seem to bear marks of weakness in Jesus, ascribing to him what alone is consistent with the great and pure character of which the same writings furnish proofs, and to their proper authors their own trivialities and imbecilities, I think myself authorised to conclude the purity and distinction of his character in opposition to the impostures which those authors would fix upon him: and that the postulate of my former letter is no more than is granted in all other historical works.[4]

M. Correa is here on his farewell visit to us. he has been much pleased with the plan and progress of our University and has given some valuable hints for it's botanical branch. he goes to do, I hope, much good in his new country; the public instruction there, as I understand, being within the department destined for him. he is not without dissatisfaction, and reasonable dissatisfaction too with the piracies of Baltimore: but his justice and friendly dispositions will, I am sure, distinguish between the iniquities of that den of plunder and corruption, and the sound principles[5] of our country at large, and of our government especially. from many conversations with him I hope he sees, and will promote, in his new situation, the advantages of a cordial fraternisation among all the American nations, and the importance of their coalescing in an American system of policy, totally independant of, and unconnected with that of Europe. the day is not distant when we may formally require a meridian of partition thro' the ocean which separates the two hemispheres, on the hither side of which no European gun shall ever be heard, nor an American on the other: and when, during the rage of the eternal wars of Europe, the lion and the lamb, within our regions, shall lie down together in peace. the excess[6] of population in Europe, and want of room, render war, in their opinion, necessary to keep down that excess of numbers. here, room is abundant, population scanty, and peace the necessary means[7] for producing men, to whom the redundant soil is offering the means of life and happiness. the principles of society there and here then are radically different: and I hope no American patriot will ever lose sight of the essential policy of interdicting in the seas and territories of both Americas the ferocious and sanguinary contests of Europe. I wish to see this coalition begun. I am earnest for an agreement with the maritime powers of Europe assigning them the task[8] of keeping down the piracies of their seas and the cannibalisms of the African coast, and to us the suppression of the same enormities within our seas: and for this purpose I should rejoice to see the fleets of Brazil and the US. riding together, as brethren of the same family, and pursuing the same object.[9] and indeed it would be of happy augury to begin at once this concert of action here, on the invitation of either to the other government, while the way might be preparing for withdrawing our cruisers from Europe, and preventing naval collisions there which daily endanger our peace.[10]

Turning to another part of your letter, I do not think the obstacles insuperable which you state as opposed to your visit to us. from one of the persons mentioned, I never heard a sentiment but of esteem for you: and I am certain you would be recieved with kindness and cordiality. but still the call may be omitted without notice. the mountain lies between his residence and the mail road, and occludes the expectation of transient visits. I am equally[11] ignorant of any dispositions not substantially friendly to you in the other person. but the alibi there gives you ten free months in the year. but if the visit is to be but once in your life, I would suppress my impatience and consent it should be made a year or two hence. because, by that time our University will be compleated and in full action: and you would recieve the satisfaction, in the final adieu to your native state, of seeing that she would retain her equal standing in the sisterhood of our republics. however, come now, come then, or come when you please, your visit will give me the gratification I feel in every opportunity of proving to you the sincerity of my friendship and respect for you.

Tн: Jefferson

RC (ViW: TJP); addressed: "William Short esquire Philadelphia"; redirected in an unidentified hand to Shrewsbury, N.J.; franked; postmarked Milton, 11 Aug., New York, 16 Aug., and Philadelphia, 21 Aug.; endorsed by Short as received 23 Aug. 1820. PoC (DLC); edge trimmed, with parts of two words rewritten by TJ. Tr (DLC); extract in TJ's hand; at head of text: "Extract of a letter from Th: Jefferson to a friend dated Aug. 4. 20"; edge trimmed, with portion of one word rewritten by TJ. Tr enclosed in James Monroe to TJ, 23 Aug. 1820, and TJ to José Corrêa da Serra, 24 Oct. 1820.

SICULUS: Diodorus Siculus. Jane Haldimand Marcet's anonymously published *Conversations on Chemistry. in which the elements of that science are familiarly explained and illustrated by experiments* (London, 1806, and other eds.; Sowerby, no. 837; Poor, *Jefferson's Library*, 6 [no. 291]) is presented as a dialogue between two pupils and their teacher, "Mrs. B."

The authorship of the work was frequently misattributed to Margaret BRYAN (*ODNB*). THE LION AND THE LAMB references the Bible, Isaiah 11.6.

The Southwest Mountains lay between James Madison's RESIDENCE AND THE MAIL ROAD. The OTHER PERSON alluded to in Short's letter to TJ of 29 June 1820 was President James Monroe.

[1] RC: "impstor." PoC: "impostor."
[2] Preceding three words canceled by TJ in PoC and replaced with "paralogisms, such quibbles on words."
[3] Manuscript: "subsequnt."
[4] Tr begins here.
[5] Tr: "dispositions."
[6] Tr: "surplus."
[7] Tr: "state."
[8] Tr: "duty."
[9] Instead of preceding five words, Tr reads "& having the same interests."
[10] Tr ends here.
[11] RC: "eqally." PoC: "eqully."

From George Watterston

Dᴿ Sɪʀ,   City of Washington Augᵗ 4th 1820.

I have received your polite letter of the 27th ult; & in answer, beg leave to assure you that both Dʳ Hamilton & myself were more gratified, by the reception you gave us as strangers, than we should have been, had we had the honor of your acquaintance—The President, from whom we could have procured letters of introduction, informed us that you considered such passports unnecessary & that our reception would, he felt confident, be agreeable to us; nor were we disappointed—We called from a motive of respect & not from any vain curiosity: as travellers in your neighbourhood, we deemᵈ it our duty to call & to enjoy with you the pleasure of a few moments conversation—a pleasure which, I assure you, will be duly appreciated & long remembered—

I beg you to accept the small work which accompanies this: it was written by me some winters ago to amuse the tedium of confinement

& to give those at a distance some little knowledge of our most prominent & leading men—From the deleniations, it contains, of those you know—you will be enabled to judge of the correctness of the sketches of those with whom you are not acquainted—Should it contribute to the amusement of a solitary or a leisure hour, I shall deem it a small equivalent for the very high gratification I experienced in your society the day I had the honor to see you—I pray you to accept the assurances of my great respect & esteem—& am

yr ob^t serv^t   GEO, WATTERSON

RC (DLC); endorsed by TJ as received 11 Aug. 1820 and so recorded in SJL. RC (MHi); address cover only; with PoC of TJ to Thomas Mann Randolph, 4 Dec. 1821, on verso; addressed: "Thos Jefferson Esq^e Charlottesville Albemarle c^t Virg^a"; franked; postmarked Washington, 5 Aug. Enclosure: "A Foreigner" [Watterston], *Letters from Washington, on the Constitution and Laws; with Sketches of some of the prominent public characters of the United States. Written during the winter of 1817–18* (Washington, 1818; Poor, *Jefferson's Library*, 5 [no. 147]).

From Mathew Carey & Son

SIR   Philad. Aug. 5. 1820.

Your favour addressed to mr M.C. who is now absent on a trip to the North, came to hand Yesterday with Twenty five dollars enclosed.— The surplus of $1.75 is placed to your credit, as the disc^t off Virginia notes is but small.—

We shall order Baxter's Hume immediately from London—Of the Conversations on Chemistry there is no 8vo edition, but a much improved 12mo in 2 Vols. from w^h we have published an edit. which we send You by this mail. It is improved by the additions of Professor Cooper.—should you not like it you will please return it, & another shall be ordered from London.—We shall omit ordering sinclair's Code of Agriculture until we hear again from You. An edition has been published in this country, & is nearly sold out—It contains the matter of the English edit. with notes on the American system of Agriculture—Shall we send this copy, or order an English one?

We are, very respectfully Your obed ser^{ts}   M CAREY & SON

RC (MHi); in the hand of a representative of Mathew Carey & Son; dateline at foot of text; endorsed by TJ as received 13 Aug. 1820 from "Cary Matthew" and so recorded (with surname spelled correctly) in SJL. RC (MHi); address cover only; with PoC of TJ to Rejoice Newton, 8 Dec. 1821, on verso; addressed (in the hand of a different representative of the firm): "Thomas Jefferson Esqr Monticello V^a"; stamp canceled; franked; postmarked Philadelphia, 5 Aug.

From John Vaughan

Dᴿ SIR   Philad. 5 Aug. 1820

When my friend The Revᵈ Mʳ Jared Sparks (who is the Unitarian Minister at Baltimore) proposed going to the Vᵃ Springs for his health, I urged his paying a Visit to yourself, who had I knew always felt pleasure, in seeing literary men of Liberal & enlarged minds—He could not then flatter himself with being able to compass So extensive a tour & did not avail himself of my offer—By a letter this moment received he has hopes of accomplishing his wishes & I send this to Staunton to meet him—He is an eleve of Cambridge Uʸ: an Institution to which we are indebted for many Shining & Useful Characters—

The Unitarians are erecting a church at N York & are about attempting to Organise a Socʸ there, with some prospect of success—our friend Mʳ Law, offers a Lot a 500$—

I remain with great respect Your friend & sert

Jɴ Vᴀᴜɢʜᴀɴ

RC (MHi); between dateline and salutation: "Thomas Jefferson Vᵃ Monticello"; endorsed by TJ as received 19 Aug. 1820 and so recorded in SJL.

ELEVE OF CAMBRIDGE Uʸ: student educated at Harvard University in Cambridge, Massachusetts.

From Bernard Peyton

Dᴇᴀʀ Sɪʀ,   Rich'd 7 Augsᵗ 1820

I was duely favor'd with yours of the 1st: Inst: & am extremely thankful to you for your kind interfereance in my behalf with the President.

I shall as you suggest remain profoundly silent on this subject until it is necessary to act, when I have no doubt of obtaining such letters from the respectable part of the society here, of all professions, & of my brother Officers of the late War, as will be perfectly satisfactory to the department at Washington.

When the draft you speak of in favor A. Garrett for $300 or $325 appears, it shall be honored.

I set out in a few days on a Mercantile excurtion thro' the principal Northern & Eastern Cities as far as Boston & Salem; if I can by any means render you a service in any of those places or Washington, I shall be happy indeed to do so, & you have only to address your commands to me at Fredericksburg care Mʳ John Scott, in the neighbourhood of which place I shall remain some days with my family.

My object is to increase my business in the Commission line, finding it too small just now for the support of a growing family, & leave a profit to add to the Capital: —with this view, have procured letters to many of the most respectable merchants & Gentlemen in these Cities, & hope to derive some advantage from the trip.

My feelings of gratitude & obligation to you my dear sir will never cease to exist, & shall be glad of every occasion in my humble way of rendering myself useful to you.

> With great respect & sincere esteem
> Yours very Truely   B. Peyton

RC (MHi); endorsed by TJ as received 11 Aug. 1820 and so recorded in SJL. RC (DLC); address cover only; with PoC of TJ to John H. Cocke, 1 Dec. 1821, on verso; addressed: "Mr Thomas Jefferson Monticello Milton"; stamped; postmarked Richmond, 7 Aug.

From Constantine S. Rafinesque

RESPECTED SIR,   T. U. August 7th, 1820.

Within a few miles of Mountsterling, the county seat of Montgomery county, which lays 33 miles east from Lexington, there are a great number of earthen inclosures and mounds which I have lately visited & surveyed. Many of them are rapidly sinking under the plough, and some have even totally disappeared. This is more or less the case throughout the country, and it is therefore highly necessary that they should all be examined accurately before their partial or total destruction.

The monuments which I am going to describe, are 28 in number, and lay in 6 different groups, either compact or scattered.

I. Group. A compact group of monuments on the west side of Brush Creek, a branch of Slate Creek, 6 miles S. E. from Mountsterling, between Montgomery's farm, and a Methodist meeting-house, which has taken from them the name of Fort Meeting-house. They are on a fine level high ground, not far from the creek, and which has never been cultivated as yet: they are five in number.

No. 1. The nearest from the meeting-house towards the south is a square inclosure, 400 feet in circumference: each side is equal, 100 feet long, laying perfectly opposed to the four cardinal points. The parapet is 15 feet broad, 4 feet high over the inside ditch, and 2 over the ground. There is a gateway due east, in the middle of the eastern side. The central area is a small *oblong* square, greater length from east to west, 35 feet; breadth 25.

No. 2. Lays about 200 yards east from No. 1, and at nearly an equal distance from No. 3 and 4 forming with them the centre of a figure shaped like Y. It is a singular[1] elliptical mound, the length of which lays N. and S. with an appendage to the south. Circumference 270 feet, height 9 feet, top elliptical, 100 feet round with raised ends, and a small central rounded mound about one foot high, over which were laying, in a square form, some loose flat stones. A short appendage to the south connects it with a small circular mound, 100 feet round and 4 feet high.

No. 3 Lays N. E. from No. 2. It is a circular inclosure, 510 feet in circumference. Parapet 20 feet broad, 5 feet high over the ditch which lays inside. Gateway due east, 15 feet broad. Area perfectly square, 300 feet circular, or 78 feet on each side, which lay towards the cardinal points, raised 2 feet over the ditch. A small circular mound of 42 feet, and 1 high, on the western side of the area opposite to the gateway.

No. 4. An hexagonal inclosure, laying south of No. 3, and S. E. from No. 2. Sides equal, each 50 feet, one of which lays N. and another S. Whole circumference therefore 300 feet. Parapet 25 feet broad, 4 feet above the inside ditch. Gateway at the east corner 15 feet broad. Area square, sides equal, 40 feet long, laying towards the cardinal points, and raised 2 feet above the ditch.

No. 5. An oblong mound, laying south of No. 1. On the opposite side of Brush Creek. I have not measured it.

II Group. A scattered group immediately round the town of Mountsterling, on each side of Hinkston Creek. It contains 6 monuments.

No. 6. A simple inclosure, one mile east of Mountsterling, on Smart's farm, in a fine level high ground, on the east side of Hinkston Creek, between the Mud Lick road and the Salt Works road. It consists of a simple ditch without visible parapet. The form is a decagone nearly regular; but two sides appear to be somewhat smaller, or of 75 feet, while the 8 others are all of 125 feet. Total circumference 1150 feet. Ditch about 2 feet deep and 6 to 8 broad; but often obliterated. No gateways could be perceived; they may have been where the ditch is not easily seen. There are two small eccentric circular mounds in the inside towards the west. Largest 105 feet and 2 high. Smallest 50 feet and 1 high, nearer to the ditch. This has all the appearance of a very remote origin. It lays in the woods, and has never been ploughed.

No. 7. A circular mound, about 350 feet in circumference, and 20 feet high, laying half a mile N. W. of No. 1, on the east or right side of Hinkston Creek.

No. 8. A circular mound 400 feet in circumference, and 24 feet high, laying in the town of Mountsterling, to which it has given its name. it lays towards its S. E. extremity, north of Hinkston Creek, on its left side. They have dug in it on the side and the summit, and found in both instances bones mixed with the earth, after digging a couple of feet.

No. 9. A simple inclosure about one mile N. N. E. from town, round the hill on the west or left side of Hinkston Creek and the Flemingsburg road. It is a polygon,[2] but whether a regular or irregular one, is rather difficult to ascertain; I could not even trace the number of sides. It lays in an iron weed brake in woods; but the ground being on a slope, the rains have filled up the ditch in many parts; towards the west the ditch is yet 4 feet deep and 8 broad. I was told that it was much plainer about 20 years ago; a few years make, therefore, great alterations, even without the help of the plough. I have traced, however, the outlines, and reckoned the circumference at about 1500 feet.

No. 10. A circumvallation in Read's corn fields, about one mile N. N. W. of the town, near a small branch of Hinkston Creek. It has been ploughed up for many years, and has nearly disappeared; I could not trace its circumference, but it was very plain a few years ago.

No. 11. Singular mound, about one mile N. from town, near the Blue Lick road. It is of an oval shape; smallest end to the south, where it is lower and only 14 feet high, while it is 24 feet high to the north. Circumference 575 feet. Summit level inclined, 135 feet long, and 40 broad, with a circular concavity to the northern extremity.

III Group. Compact, on a level ground in the woods, about two miles north from Mountsterling, on Jameson's farm, and on the left of the Paris road. Sommerset Creek is half a mile off towards the west, and there are no springs in the immediate neighbourhood at present. It consists of five mounds.

No. 12. A large and singular circular mound 32 feet high, surrounded by a circular parapet and intermediate ditch, interrupted by four large level gateways, 50 feet broad, equal in size and distance, looking towards the N. E.—N. W.—S. E. and S. W. The four parts of the parapet are therefore opposed to the 4 cardinal points; whole circumference 800 feet, ditch 4 feet deep. Central mound about 500 feet round. Summit 120 feet round and somewhat concave.

No. 13. Similar mound, smaller, only 15 feet high, and 130 feet distant from No. 12, towards S. E. It has also 4 gateways, but they lay N.—E.—W. and S. W. and the northern one is much larger, and inclined in the shape of an ascent; breadth 40 feet, the others 30 feet. Circumference of the parapet 430 feet; ditch 3 feet deep. Summit small, somewhat concave.

No. 14 Simple mound, without ditch or parapet; 250 feet in circumference, and 10 feet high. It lays 80 feet S. W. of No. 13.

No. 15. A similar mound, laying 312 feet east of No. 13. It is 6 feet high, and 165 feet round.

No. 16. Another mound, 80 feet from No. 14, due east. It is 8 feet high and 200 feet in circumference.

IV. Group. Compact and remarkable by its size, high parapet, &c. although it lays in fields which have often been ploughed. It is situated on Johnson's farm 3 miles north of Mountsterling, on the right and east bank of Sommerset Creek, and on a high level hill. It contains an inclosure and 4 outward mounds.

No. 17. A large circumvallation, quite circular and 1150 feet round, with a high parapet, a deep inside ditch, a single gateway due east, & a central mound. Parapet 55 feet broad, 4 to 5 feet over the ground, and 8 to 12 over the ditch, inside slope 25 feet. Gateway 50 feet broad. Area 3 feet high over the ditch. Central mound 75 feet from the ditch, 206 feet in circumference and 3 feet high. The parapet and ditch were 15 feet high and deep, before the ground was ploughed. Many remains of pottery, fine pipe-heads, and several other implements have been found in ploughing the area.

No. 18. Large circular mound, 60 feet due north from No. 17, and united to it by a raised platform. It has two spurs, or oval inclined appendages to the north and west: the northern one is larger. Circumference with the spurs 800 feet, without 600. Height 25 feet, summit level with a small central concavity.

No. 19, 20 and 21. Three outward and unconnected mounds, laying irregularly to the S. E. of No 17. The largest, No. 19, lays easterly of No. 20. It is 220 feet round, and 5 feet high.

No. 20 lays in the middle and only 50 feet from No. 17. It is only 175 feet round and 3 high.

No. 21. The smallest and western, is near No. 20, and nearly south from No. 17. It is only 150 feet round and 2 high.

V Group. Is quite scattered, and contains 3 inclosures with two mounds, laying near Sommerset Creek, about 4 miles to the northward of Mountsterling.

No. 22. Square inclosure on John Higgins's farm, on the south and left side of Sommerset creek. Each side equal, 150 feet long, and laid towards the 4 cardinal points; gateway single, due east, 30 feet broad; area square, each side 90 feet long. The parapet, area and ditch are now only one foot high or deep, the ground having been repeatedly ploughed; they were 3 feet high and deep, when the ground was cleared.

No. 23. A circular inclosure, laying on James Higgins's farm, 300 yards[3] from No. 22, towards the N. W.; but on the opposite side of Sommerset Creek, in a corn field, and in the flat bottom of the valley. This is a singular instance, since nearly all the Alleghawian monuments are on high ground. The place is even sometimes overflowed at present, which, however, is owing to the bed of the creek having been raised of late by its alluvions. Circumference 800 feet; gateway S. E. directed towards No. 22. Parapet only one foot high, and often obsolete: it was 3 feet high before being ploughed; but it may easily be traced by the growth of corn on it, being much lower and poorer than inside and outside. This happens in all instances, the ground of the parapets having been made up by throwing on them different and often gravelly earth, taken from the ditch or some deep place.

No. 24. A large circular inclosure on Colonel Williams's farm, nearly a mile S. W. from No. 22, and near a branch of Sommerset Creek called Higgins's Branch. I did not visit it, because it was represented to me as laying in several fields which have been under cultivation for 20 or 30 years, and to be therefore very difficult to trace; but it is said to cover about 10 acres of ground, and to have been formerly very distinct.

No. 25. A mound on Moses Higgins's farm, S. E. of No. 22, and between Sommerset Creek (left bank) and Higgins's Branch. Circumference about 150, and 5 feet high.

No. 26. Another mound 160 round and 6 feet high, west of No. 22, about half a mile distant, and near Grass Lick Creek.

VI Group. A small one, consisting of an inclosure and a mound, situated on a high hill in John Wilson's farm, about 5 miles N. W. from Mountsterling, above the junction of Aaron's run and Grass Lick Creek, and on their left side near Duncan's mill, in a corn field.

No. 27. A circular inclosure, 1100 feet in circumference. Parapet 40 feet wide, 4 feet high over the ditch, 2 over the ground. Ditch 20 feet broad, and inside as usual. Gateway towards the S. E. The ditch was 6 or 8 feet deep formerly.

No. 28. A circular mound, joining No. 27, and laying to the N. E. Circumference 225 feet, height 5 feet at present; but it was much higher before being ploughed.

From the above descriptions, it may safely be surmised that each group of monuments belonged to a peculiar town, and that there were therefore 6 towns, within the same space of ground, where only one exist at present, whence it might be conceived that the Alleghawian[4] population was there sixfold the actual one.

From the rapid decay, or rather diminution of height in these monuments, even without the help of the plough, it is evident that they must all have been formerly much higher, with deeper ditches, &c.; therefore much more remarkable and difficult to raise.

Allow me, besides, to venture a few peculiar suggestions, respecting their ultimate use, which may be considered as probable hypothesis.

1. I conceive that each group was surrounded by a town, particularly the compact and complicated groups.

2. The circular inclosures with outward parapets, were probably temples dedicated to the sun, like those of the Natchez nation.

3. The square inclosures might have been the palaces of their kings or chiefs, who were called children of the sun, as in Peru, and among the Floridans, Natchez, &c. or perhaps the council houses, places of meeting for public purposes.

4. All the mounds are evidently barrows or sepulchral monuments, and natural appendages to temples, like our church yards are to our places of worship; but No. 12 and 13, by their peculiar inclosures and avenues, must have been the tombs of great kings, heroes, priests or queens, which may have been worshipped after death. Similar apotheosis were common among many ancient nations.

5. The use of Nos. 4 and 6, is more problematical; but must have been analogous, owing to the connection with mounds. Else No. 4 may have been used for civil purposes, and No. 6 for military ones, as likewise No. 9.

Hoping that these remarks, observations and details, may not prove entirely uninteresting to you, and the friends of historical knowledge,

I remain, respectfully, Your well wisher,

C. S. RAFINESQUE.
Prof. in Transylvania University.

Printed in Lexington *Kentucky Reporter*, 23 Aug. 1820; dateline at foot of text; at head of text: "*THREE LETTERS ON AMERICAN ANTIQUITIES*, DIRECTED TO THE HONORABLE THOMAS JEFFERSON, *LATE PRESIDENT OF THE UNITED STATES. SECOND LETTER.* DESCRIPTION OF THE ALLEGHAWIAN MONUMENTS, *In the neighbourhood of Mountsterling*, Montgomery county, Kentucky. TO THE HONORABLE THOMAS JEFFERSON, L.P. U.S."; with subjoined corrections to Rafinesque's letter to TJ of 1 Aug. 1820. Not recorded in SJL and probably never received by TJ.

[1]*Kentucky Reporter*: "sigular."
[2]*Kentucky Reporter*: "poligone."
[3]*Kentucky Reporter*: "yeards."
[4]*Kentucky Reporter*: "Allexhawian."

From John Vaughan

D^R SIR   Philad^a 7th Aug 1820

On 24 July, I procured from Mr Girard his Dfts on Lafitte & Co on your acco^t to my order viz

2353.$\frac{20}{}$ f^s endorsed by me to Thomas Appleton a 5$\frac{30}{}$ p

Doll^r   444—

1060 f^s endorsed to Joshua Dodge[1]   200—

on 28th I received[2] from Mr Peyton rem^e for this last sum—I have sent these Bills via France & England as no Vessel offerd direct—

I hope Mr Correa was fortunate enough to arrive before your Departure for Bedford.   I remain with great respect

Your friend   JN VAUGHAN

RC (MHi); endorsed by TJ as received 13 Aug. 1820 and so recorded in SJL. RC (MHi); address cover only; with PoC of TJ to Frederick W. Hatch, 8 Dec. 1821, on verso; addressed in a clerk's hand: "Thomas Jefferson Monticello V^a"; franked; postmarked Philadelphia, 8 Aug.

REM^E: "remittance."

[1] Surname interlined in an unidentified hand in place of "Dogde."
[2] Manuscript: "recived."

From Constantine S. Rafinesque

RESPECTED SIR,   T. U. August 10th, 1820.

I propose to describe in this last letter some remarkable remains of sculpture, &c. belonging to or performed by the Alleghawians, which have lately fallen under my notice. They consist in 16 specimens.

No. 1. Is the head of an Idol, about one inch in diameter. It is made of a soft white stone, a real pagodite or graphic Talc (Bildstein of the Germans) which may be easily carved with iron or flint tools. This head has never been connected with a body, since the lower part is entire. It is solid. The upper part is flattened and has a small hole, used probably to suspend it as an amulet. The hind part and the neck is covered with a yellow varnish, full of small pits. The face has the Indian countenance; the forehead is small, the eyes large, and transversal, the nose big, mouth small, chin round with a dimple: the ears are covered by the yellow varnish, which represents the hair or rather a cap. It was found in one of the mounds near Nashville, in Tennessee, and is deposited in the Lexington Museum.

No. 2. Is also a head, but it is made of baked clay and hollow inside, with 6 round clay-balls, and therefore used as a rattle. The clay is brown with the usual white specks. Size about[1] two inches. It has a very large round knob on the back of the head, and 3 smaller ones on the crown, the middle one of which is larger and oblong. Face as broad as long, with a very large nose extending to the middle knob. No forehead. Eyes rather obliqual, mouth small. Ears large and on a kind of knob. It was found also near Nashville in a mound. The surface is yet polished. The little balls of the inside are about the size of a pea and of a grey colour; it is singular how they have been inclosed within; it was by perforating the nape of the head that they were discovered, their rattling having attracted the attention.

No. 3. Another rattle of baked clay representing a bird's head, probably a crested parrot. Clay of a redish colour, with white angular specks as usual. Bill large, compressed, hardly crooked, eyes well formed, a large compressed crest on the tip of the head, neck compressed and closed. Inside hollow with clay balls. Found in the large Cemeteries of Augusta in Kentucky.

No. 4. A very fine large Pipe head representing a bird. The substance is of a beautiful heavy Talc or Bildstein, which has acquired a blackish varnish outside, but is inside of a pale greenish white with silvery specks: it is easily cut by iron and flint. The length is eight inches, height four, thickness two, weight several pounds. The head of the bird which fronts the inner side of the pipe, is very well sculpted, and represents the head of a bird of prey, probably a buzzard, the cera at the base of the bill is very well marked and raised; the bill is crooked, the lower mandible as well as the upper. The eyes are hollow, and must have been filled with something. The head, neck and body are somewhat squared, the chin has a remarkable angular depression. The body is small and out of proportion; but with the wings partly marked, and with a very large hollow tail, nearly vertical, forming the principal tube of the pipe; this tube is conical inside, with an oblong opening nearly two inches long; it communicates inside with the inner and horizontal tube which perforates the body, and comes out at the breast by a round opening one inch in diameter.[2] This is upon the whole a remarkable piece of sculpture, and must have been used as a great national Calumet. It was found in Clay county, Kentucky, on the ground and partly buried in it, by a hunter, whose dog was barking at the head of the bird (which appeared above ground) as if it had been a living bird.

No. 5. An elegant small pipe head of white graphic Talc or Bildstein. It has a beautiful polish and transparency like Alabaster, and some brown veins. It is nearly cylindrical and about two inches long. It is very highly carved and ornamented, and difficult to describe. The upper part is round with a flat border, indented on the sides. The outside represents a female face and breast merely drawn, with coarse features, &c. There is a broad belt with angular lines in the middle on the other sides, and below it a small one. The lower part is distinct, rounded horizontally with 4 angles and furrows, and a round opening inside, and there are two small rings beneath it, united together by the side. This beautiful implement was found 6 feet under ground in Ohio, in digging a mill race at the lower Sandusky falls.[3] The present Wyandot Indians on seeing it, thought that it was made by their ancestors, with sturgeon nose, which they had the art of hardening, and that the female figure represented their famous Queen *Crana*. This of course is only a fanciful tale.

No. 6. Another Pipe-head of a hard brown stone, and in the shape of a duck's bill. It is 3 inches long. The upper mandible is convex with some transversal notches, and two large round nostrils. The lower mandible has a large longitudinal depression. The sides of both are serrated as in the duck. The posterior opening is round conical without brim, while the upper one has a very large flat brim. The stone is a kind of homogenous freestone, which may be merely scratched by iron and flint; but not easily worked. I am ignorant where it was found.

No. 7. A plain globular Pipe-head, of a hard red sandstone, about one inch and one half in diameter, with two openings as usual, plain and conical, but with concentric furrows inside, the upper one large. The substance is homogenous and hardly scratched by iron or flint. It was found in ploughing the ground, in one of the circumvallations near Mountsterling described in my last.

No. 8. A plain cylindrical Pipe-head, in the shape of a small barrel and of a similar sandstone. It is flat beneath. Found in a mound in Kentucky.

No. 9. Is an amulet of a hard jasper; it is spindle shaped, about 3 inches long, with both ends pointed, and a large hole in the middle. The jasper is of a dark olive green with longitudinal blackish stripes. It cannot be scratched by iron nor steel. It was found in the graves near Augusta.

No. 10. Another Amulet found with the foregoing, and of the same stone. It bears a slight resemblance to a bird, being flat beneath, with a kind of head and tail. It is about 4 inches long, and might be suspended by 4 small holes, two at each end, communicating together.

No. 11. Is a beautiful War-Axe, or Tomahawk, of a very heavy and hard jasper, somewhat similar to that of No. 9; but is pale, and instead of blackish streaks, it has only brown linear specks. Length over one foot, handle cylindrical, tapering downwards, head semicircular small, about 2 inches broad, flattened, and with a sharp edge. It was found in Alabama, and when striken, sounds like basalt.

No. 12. Is the foot of an Idol, of a peculiar kind of redish and hard baked clay, without the usual white specks. Length 3 inches, inside hollow, no mark of toes; but the mark of a garment is apparent above. It has a fine shape and appears plainly to have been the left foot of an Idol. It was found in the ground at a spring, about two miles from Versailles, in Woodford[4] county, Kentucky. Several others were found at the same time, and many broken fragments; but it is singular that they were all feet and legs. The person who found them called them petrified mocasins. I was told that one of the largest was sent to you.

No. 13. A singular Disk, of a hard granitic grey stone, about 4 inches in diameter, circular with flattened edges, and a large circular depression on each side.

No. 14. Several iron rings or bracelets, about 3 inches in diameter, plain, round and thick. They were found on the wrists of some skeletons in the graves near Augusta in Kentucky. They are of course very rusty.

No. 15. Blue Beads, forming a Collar, found in the same place. They are nearly globular, with flattened sides, and perforated throughout. Size of a pea. Substance a hard bluish and semi opaque Agatic or Calcedonic stone.

No. 16. White Beads forming many Collars, found also at the same place and elsewhere. They are unequal cylindrical, about half an inch long, perforated lengthways, and of a white polished Calcedony or consimilar stone.

All these implements are deposited in the Museum collected at Lexington by the late Mr. John D. Clifford, except Nos. 2, 4 and 7, which are in my possession. I have drawn the whole and shall send the drawings to the Antiquarian Society of Massachusetts

Many inferences and results may be drawn from these descriptions—For instance.

1. That the arts of sculpting, carving, polishing and perforating (even hard) stones were known to the Alleghawians, which could only be done with iron tools, and in some instances, with tools of a harder nature, or by friction of harder stones.

2. That they knew iron, could work it, and forge it into bracelets, &c.

3. That they could mould clay and bake it: forming with it not only pots and vases; but figures, &c.

4. That they knew tobacco and cultivated it; also that they used Calumets as our modern Indians.

5. That they used Rattles, Amulets, Collars, Bracelets, Beads and other ornaments of Stone, Baked Clay or Metals.

6. That they used Tomahawks in war.

7. That they worshipped Idols, besides the Sun and the Moon, or used them as symbols.

8. That they knew the diversion of throwing rolling disks, as the Greeks, &c.

9. That they sometimes wore a head dress as in the figures Nos. 9 and 2.

10. And lastly, that they procured from a great distance, by trade exchanges, purchases or journeys, the articles wanted for the manufacture of their implements. Hardly any of the stones mentioned above are found in the Western States. The green Jasper and white Talc are very scarce stones, and I am even ignorant where they might have been drawn; unless they came from Asia. The Bildstein is only found in China, where it is used for the same purpose of sculpting images, idols and holy vases

All these facts are new links in our archeological knowledge, and evident proofs corroborating the accounts of Soto, and in support of the Hindoo origin of our ancient Alleghawees or Alleghawians. The extensive graves of Apes lately found in Missouri and Tennessee, show that some of these ancient nations worshipped them, as did many Asiatic and Mexican tribes, and brought them in countries where they are no longer found.

I shall conclude these remarks by removing a difficulty which I have lately seen stated. It has been doubted that our western waters could produce the quantity of Pearls mentioned to have been seen by Soto. Most of the numerous species of Bivalve shells living in our rivers, and called Muscles, (or *Unio*, by the naturalists) produce Pearls. I have seen several myself, and they may be made to produce them at pleasure by a peculiar operation in some circumstances. The Alleghawians had probably that art which is known in Asia.

Let us hope that some able hand will soon rescue from oblivion the scattered materials relating to these ancient nations, and furnish us with an interesting narrative of their history and manners, similar to the one lately furnished us by Mr. Heckenwelder, concerning the Lennape and Mengwee nations.

Meantime I consider that a translation of Soto's quixotic expedition into Florida, or rather our Western States, would be highly acceptable to the public. It is a fascinating narrative, and as entertaining as the conquest of Mexico.

I conclude by assuring you of my respectful esteem,

Your well wisher,   C. S. RAFINESQUE.

Prof. in Transylvania University.

Printed in Lexington *Kentucky Reporter*, 6 Sept. 1820; dateline at foot of text; at head of text: "*THREE LETTERS* ON AMERICAN ANTIQUITIES, DIRECTED TO THE HONORABLE THOMAS JEFFERSON, LATE PRESIDENT OF THE UNITED STATES. *THIRD LETTER*. ON SOME ALLEGHAWIAN IMPLEMENTS, &c. TO THE HONORABLE THOMAS JEFFERSON, L.P U.S." Not recorded in SJL and probably never received by TJ.

PAGODITE, or agalmatolite, is a soft mineral often used for carving decorative figurines (*OED*). Rafinesque's friend John D. Clifford operated the short-lived Museum of Natural and Antiquarian History (LEXINGTON MUSEUM) at the Lexington Athenaeum until his death early in May 1820 (Lexington *Western Moni-*

tor, 30 Aug. 1817; Lexington *Kentucky Reporter*, 10 May 1820; Rafinesque to TJ, 2 Feb. 1822).

CERA: "cere." CALCEDONIC and CALCEDONY are "chalcedonic" and "chalcedony," respectively. CONSIMILAR: "entirely similar; like" (*OED*). Rafinesque sent his drawing of the sixteen Alligewi Indian artifacts described above to the American Antiquarian Society (ANTIQUARIAN SOCIETY OF MASSACHUSETTS), which elected him to membership on 24 Aug. 1820 (*Proceedings of the American Antiquarian Society, 1812–1849* [1912], 153–4). MR. HECKENWELDER: John Heckewelder.

[1] Printed text: "a-about."
[2] Omitted period editorially supplied.
[3] Omitted period editorially supplied.
[4] Printed text: "Wooodford."

To David Gelston

DEAR SIR   Monticello Aug. 13. 20.

I am obliged to renew my annual tax on your goodness by asking the favor of your procuring a passage for the inclosed letters to their address. the commerce of New York, is so much more extensive than from any other port of the US. as to give it a great preference for the conveyance of foreign letters, and it is this circumstance which brings on you the present trouble for which I can offer but the poor tribute of my thankfulness, esteem, & respect.   TH: JEFFERSON

RC (Sotheby's, New York City, 2002); with notations by Gelston at foot of text: "letter for Tho[s] appleton consul Leghorn
"   " Josh[a] Dodge—   "   Marseilles"; addressed: "David Gelstone esquire New York"; franked; postmarked Charlottesville, 17 Aug.; endorsed by Gelston. FC (MHi); abstract in TJ's hand on verso of reused address cover to TJ, reading in

full: "Aug. 13. 20. Inclosed to D. Gelston my letters (duplicates) for Marseilles & Leghorn"; endorsed by TJ. Recorded in SJL with additional bracketed notation: "letters to Marseilles." Enclosures:
(1) TJ to Thomas Appleton, 13 July 1820.
(2) TJ to Eulalie Cathalan, 13 July 1820.
(3) TJ to Joshua Dodge, 13 July 1820.
(4) TJ to Julius Oliver, 13 July 1820.

To William Gray

DEAR SIR   Monticello Aug. 13. 20.

Altho' fortune has never so far befriended me as to procure me the advantage of a personal acquaintance with you, yet a harmony in political pursuits has not left us altogether strangers. on this unassuming ground I take the liberty of presenting to you a friend. Capt Bernard Peyton, a commission merchant of Richmond proposing a tour to the North, wishes particularly to have the benefit of being made known to you. he has been engaged in his present line five or six years, has acted in it with an integrity and punctuality which has procured him the unlimited confidence of all who have employed him, and their wishes for his success; of which indeed we cannot doubt if punctuality, prudence and faithful attention to business can ensure it. the unshaken solidity with which he past the late mercantile ordeal is of itself a title of credence to him; and to enlarge the field of his commission business is, I believe the object of his present journey.

any portion of civilities and attentions which you may be so kind as to shew him will be considered as a favor to myself; and begging here to place myself under the friendly recollection of mr Francis Grey I salute you with assurances of my high respect and esteem.

TH: JEFFERSON

PoC (DLC); on verso of reused address cover of John G. Robert (for Patrick Gibson) to TJ, 13 Apr. 1820; at foot of text: "Wm Gray esq."; endorsed by TJ. Enclosed in TJ to Henry A. S. Dearborn and TJ to Bernard Peyton, both 14 Aug. 1820.

William Gray (1750–1825), merchant and public official, was born in Lynn, Massachusetts. With his family he moved as a child to nearby Salem, where he trained as an apprentice and then entered the countinghouse of one of the town's most prominent merchants. Having gone into business for himself late in the 1770s, Gray owned several American privateers during the Revolutionary War. His fortunes continued to rise after hostilities ceased. With his vessels trading as far afield as China, India, and Russia, Gray employed hundreds of seamen and amassed an estate worth approximately $3 million by the first decade of the nineteenth century. He held local office in Salem during the mid-1780s and voted in favor of the new federal constitution at the Massachusetts ratification convention in 1788. Gray's support for the Embargo while a Federalist state senator, 1807–09, made him unpopular in Salem and led him to relocate permanently to Boston in the latter year. Switching his allegiance to the Republican party, he was the lieutenant governor of Massachusetts, 1810–12, and a staunch supporter of President James Madison's administration during the War of 1812. Gray later served as a delegate to the state's 1820 constitutional convention and as president of the Boston branch of the Second Bank of the United States, 1816–23. At his death he held assets valued in excess of $1 million. His son Francis C. Gray corresponded with TJ and visited him at Monticello in 1815, and another son, Horace Gray, saw TJ there five years later (*ANB*; *DAB*; *Doc. Hist. Ratification*, 6:1464, 1479; *Newburyport Herald*, 10 Apr. 1807; *Salem Gazette*, 12 Aug. 1808, 24 Feb. 1809; *Greenfield* [Mass.] *Gazette*, 5 June 1810; *The Boston Directory* [Boston, 1810], 89; Salem *Essex*

Register, 26 Feb. 1812, 7 Nov. 1825; *Boston Gazette*, 16 Dec. 1816; *Pittsfield* [Mass.] *Sun*, 20 Nov. 1823; Boston *Columbian Centinel*, 27 Apr. 1808, 18 Oct. 1820, 5 Nov. 1825).

To James Madison

DEAR SIR   Monticello Aug. 13. 20.

I recieved yesterday the inclosed letter proposing to me an interposition which my situation renders impracticable. the gentlemen of my family have manifested at times some opposition to mr Nelson's elections: which has produced an intermission of intercourse between the families: and altho' I never took the smallest part in it, and nothing but what is respectful has ever passed between mr Nelson and myself, yet I cannot but feel the ground too suspicious to venture on the experiment proposed. and indeed the thing is so delicate that I know not whether any ground, however cordial, could render it safe: but of this you will be the best judge as to yourself, for which purpose I inclose you the letter. I suppose myself it is impossible that a Virginian can be elected and that mr N's competition would only defeat Genl Smith's election and ensure a Northern and unfriendly choice.

Our buildings at the University go on so rapidly, and will exhibit such a state and prospect by the meeting of the legislature that no one seems to think it possible they should fail to enable us to open the institution the ensuing year. I salute mrs Madison & yourself with constant affection & respect.   TH: JEFFERSON

PoC (DLC); on verso of reused address cover of Charles Willson Peale to TJ, 10 Apr. 1820; at foot of text: "Mr Madison"; endorsed by TJ. Enclosure: Samuel Smith (of Maryland) to TJ, 2 Aug. 1820.

Madison's missing reply to TJ of 19 Aug. 1820, which presumably covered the return of the above enclosure, is recorded in SJL as received four days later from Montpellier.

To Josiah Meigs

DEAR SIR   Monticello Aug. 13. 20.

In answer to your enquiry as to the proper mode of^1 application for a Professorship in the University of Virginia? I can only say we are not yet advanced to the point where Professors will be wanting. our whole funds are applied to the comp[le]tion of our buildings, and when they will become liberated from that so as to enable us to employ Professors is quite uncertain.   I am very sensible of your kind and friendly expressions towards myself. the approbation of the good & wise is the balm of retiring life, and the supposition that we may not have lived in vain is it's richest consolation. should your convenience ever bring you into this quarter and to Monticello particularly, it would be a great gratification to have an opportunity of assuring you personally of my great esteem & respect.

TH: JEFFERSON

PoC (DLC); on verso of reused address cover of John Hollins to TJ, 14 Apr. 1820; one word faint; at foot of text: "Josiah Meigs esquire"; endorsed by TJ.

Tr (Mrs. Howard B. Field, Durham Center, Conn., 1944).

[1] Instead of preceding two words, Tr reads "of ap of."

To William Munford

DEAR SIR   Monticello Aug. 13. 20.

On the 30th Ult. I recieved from the President of the board of the Literary fund the copy, which altho not authenticated, he assured me was correct, of a resolution of the board in answer to my letter of May 1. agreeing to lend to the Visitors of the University of Virginia the further sum of 20,000.D. provided it be applied for on or before the 1st day of June then next ensuing. the date of my reciept of the notice of this resolution will explain the cause of our not having made the application before the day it required: but this I trust will be deemed of less importance as the President of the board assures me the treasurer informed him the sum would be more conveniently paid if not called for till October. as that will be in time for us I shall only say that it shall be called for then, or at any earlier day at which the board shall require it. but as it is made a condition in the resolution that a bond for payment of the interest and principal shall be executed in the same manner and form as the former bond for 40,000 and as I did not keep a copy of that bond, I must ask the favor of you to be so kind as to send me a copy whenever you shall notify the wish of the board that the money should be called for. be pleased to accept the assurance of my great esteem and respect.   TH: JEFFERSON

RC (Vi: RG 50, Office of the Second Auditor, Literary Fund, Letters Received); addressed: "William Munford esq Richmond"; franked; postmarked Charlottesville, 15 Aug.; endorsed by Munford. PoC (ViU: TJP); on verso of reused address cover of John Vaughan to TJ, 16 Apr. 1820; edge trimmed; mutilated at seal, with part of one word rewritten by TJ; endorsed by TJ, with his additional notation beneath endorsement: "Literary board."

Virginia governor Thomas Mann Randolph was, by virtue of his office, PRESIDENT OF THE BOARD OF THE LITERARY

FUND. The RESOLUTION OF THE BOARD is printed above at 1 May 1820. The TREASURER of Virginia was Jerman Baker. For the FORMER BOND, see the Resolution of the President and Directors of the Literary Fund, 25 Mar. 1820.

To Samuel Smith (of Maryland)

DEAR SIR   Monticello Aug. 13. 20.

If you have not heard from me since the lamentable cata[s]trophe which befell your mercantile house, it has not been from the want of a sincere sympathy with you: but because experience has taught me that time and silence are better anodynes to misfortune, than condolances which only serve to recall painful recollections to the mind. I should suppose there could hardly be a member who would not think the chair of the H. of R.[1] due to your past services. and could I be useful towards ensuring it by withdrawing the competition you mention, there would not be a moment's hesitation on my part. but the gentlemen of my family have sometimes been in opposition to mr Nelson's elections here: & altho' I have never taken the smallest part in that opposition, it has produced an entire intermission of intercourse between the famil[ie]s, & placed me perhaps in an attitude which, for aught I know, might render an intimation from me more injurious than useful. my friend mr Madison is on cordial terms with him, and I have written to him this day to see if he can do any thing.

That you might be valuably employed in our diplomatic line and particularly with the nations with which we have principal commerce cannot be doubted. but I do not know whether there is likelihood of any vacancy. mr Gallatin I know is expected to remain indefinitely. mr Rush I believe the same. and if mr Forsythe can obtain forgiveness from the Cortes for his rudeness to their royal government, I presume he will remain also. yet these employments are so illy paid & the consequen[t] changes so frequent that vacancies are always possible, and should the governmen[t] see with my eyes, there would be no hesitation in the choice of a successor. and I pray you to be assured that no one would be more gratified than myself by such a testimony of gratitude for your services rendered in all times of trial: and that my sentiments of friendship and respect continue constant and undiminished.   TH: JEFFERSON

PoC (DLC); on verso of a reused address cover from Arthur S. Brockenbrough to TJ; edge trimmed; mutilated at seal, with two words rewritten by TJ; at foot of text: "General Samuel Smith"; endorsed by TJ.

John Quincy Adams described the LAMENTABLE CATASTROPHE in his diary on 30 May 1819: "The House of Smith and Buchanan, which has been these thirty years one of the greatest commercial Establishments in the United States, broke last week, with a crash which staggered the whole City of Baltimore, and will extend, no one knows how far." While Adams did not assign blame to him, he added that in consequence of the event, Smith had reportedly "gone distracted" and been "confined dangerously ill in bed" (MHi: Adams Papers).

Several newspapers had recently reported that the American diplomat John Forsyth (FORSYTHE) had used "rude, ungentlemanly and impolitic language . . . at the court of Spain" (*Boston Daily Advertiser*, 22 Mar. 1820, and elsewhere).

[1] Preceding seven words interlined in place of "it."

To Mathew Carey & Son

MESS[RS] M. CARY & SON   Monticello Aug. 14. 20.

I recieved yesterday your favor of the 5th and by the preceding mail the Conversations in Chemistry had come to hand. I am quite content with the edition, as I shall be with the American edition of S[r] J. Sinclair's Code of agriculture. I had not before known that it had been reprinted in America. I wish that there may have been an 8[vo] edition of 'Baxter's history of England' published there: if not I must be contented with the 4[to]. order it to be well bound if you please, as I am attached to good bindings. I salute you with esteem & respect.

TH: JEFFERSON

RC (PHi: Lea & Febiger Records); addressed: "Mess[rs] M. Carey & son Philadelphia"; franked; postmarked Charlottesville, 17 Aug.; endorsed by a representative of the firm as received 20 Aug. 1820. FC (DLC); misdated abstract in TJ's hand on verso of reused address cover from Alexander Murray to TJ, 1 Jan. 1819, reading in full (edge trimmed): "Aug. 13. 20. wrote to M. Carey & son for American edn of S[r] J. Sinc[lair's] Code of Agriculture"; endorsed by TJ as a letter of 13 Aug. 1820 to Mathew Carey and so recorded in SJL.

To Thomas Cooper

DEAR SIR   Monticello Aug. 14. 20.

Yours of the 24th ult. was recieved in due time and I shall rejoice indeed if mr Elliot and mr Nulty are joined to you in the institution at Columbia, which now becomes of immediate interest to me. mr Stack has given notice to his first class that he shall dismiss them on the 10th of the next month, and his mathematical assistant also at the same time, being determined to take only small boys in future. my grandson Eppes is of his first class; and I have proposed to his father to send him to Columbia, rather than any where Northwardly. I am obliged therefore to ask of you by what day he ought to be there, so as to be at the commencement of what they call a session, and to be so good as to do this by the first mail, as I shall set out to Bedford within about a fortnight. he is so far advanced in Greek & Latin that he will be able to pursue them by himself hereafter; and being between 18. & 19 years of age he has no time to lose. I propose that he shall commence immediately with mathematics and Nat. Phil^y to be followed by Astronomy, chemistry, mineralogy, botany, Nat. history. it would be time lost for him to attend professors of ethics, metaphysics, Logic E^{t}c. the first of these may be as well acquired in the closet as from living lectures: and supposing the two last to mean the science of <u>mind</u>, the simple reading of Locke, Tracy, & Stewart, will give him as much in that branch as is <u>real</u> science. a relation of his (mr Baker) and class mate will go with him.

I hope and believe you are mistaken in supposing the reign of fanaticism to be on the advance. I think it certainly declining. it was first excited artificially by the sovereigns of Europe as an engine of opposition to Bonaparte and to France. it arose to a great height there, and became indeed a powerful engine[1] of loyalism, and of support to their governments. but that loyalism is giving way to very different dispositions, and it's prompter, fanaticism, is evanishing with it. in the meantime it had been[2] wafted across the Atlantic, and chiefly from England, with their other fashions. but it is here also on the wane. the ambitious sect of Presbyterians indeed, the Loyalists and Loyalists[3] of our country, spare no pains to keep it up. but their views of ascendancy over all other sects in the US. seem to excite alarm in all; & to unite them as against a common and threatening enemy. and altho the Unitarianism they impute to you is heterodoxy with all of them, I suspect the other sects will admit it to their alliance in order to strengthen the phalanx of opposition against the enterprises of their more aspiring antagonists. altho' spiritualism is most prevalent with all these sects, yet with none of them, I presume, is materialism declared heretical. mr Locke, on whose authority they often plume themselves, openly maintained the materialism of the soul; and charged with blasphemy those who denied that it was in the power of an almighty creator to endow with the faculty of thought any composition of matter he might think fit. the[4] fathers of the church of the three first centuries,[5] generally, if not universally were materialists, extending it even to the creator himself. nor indeed do I know exactly[6] in what age of the Christian church the heresy of spiritualism was introduced. Huet, in his commentaries on Origen, says 'Deus igitur, cui anima similis est, juxta Origenem, reapse corporalis est, sed graviorum tantum ratione corporum incorporeus.'[7] St Macarius speaking of angels says 'quamvis enim subtilia sint, tamen in substantia, forma, et figura, secundum tenuitatem naturae eorum corpora sunt tenuia, quemadmodum et hoc corpus in substantia sua crassum et solidum est.'[8] St Justin Martyr says expressly 'το θειον φαμεν ειναι αϛωματον, ουχ ότι εϛιν αϛωματον.'[9] Tertullian's words are, 'quid enim Deus nisi corpus?' and again 'quis autem negabit Deum esse corpus? etsi deus spiritus, spiritus etiam corpus est sui generis, in suâ effigie'.[10] and that the soul is matter he adduces the following tangible proof. 'in ipso ultimo voluptatis aestu, quo genitale virus expellitur, nonne aliquid de animâ sentimus exire?[']'[11] the holy father thus asserting, and, as it would seem, from his own feelings, that the sperm infused into the female matrix deposits there the matter and germ of both soul and body, conjunctim, of the new foetus. altho' I do not pretend to be familiar with these fathers, and give the preceding quotations at second hand, yet I learn from authors whom I respect, that not only those I have named, but S[t] Augustin, S[t] Basil, Lactantius, Tatian, Athenagoras and others[12] concurred in the materiality of the soul. our modern doctors would hardly venture or wish to condemn these fathers as hereti[cs,] the main pillars of their fabric resting on their shoulders.

In the consultations of the Visitors of the University on the subject of releasing you from your engagement with us, altho' one or two members seemed alarmed at this cry of 'fire' from the Presbyterian pulpits, yet the real ground of our decision was that our funds were in fact hypothecated for 5. or 6. years to redeem, the loan we had recently made: and altho' we hoped and trusted that the ensuing legislature would remit the debt and liberate our funds; yet it was not just, on this possibility, to stand in the way of your looking out for a more certain provision. the completing all our buildings for professors and students by the autumn of the ensuing year is now secured by sufficient contracts, and our confidence is most strong that neither the state nor their legislature will bear to see those buildings shut up for 5. or 6. years, when they have the money in hand, & actually appropriated to the object of education, which would open their doors at once for the reception of their sons, now waiting and calling aloud for that institution. the legislature meets on the 1st Monday of December, and before Christmas we shall know what are their intentions. if such as we expect, we shall then immediately take measures to engage our professors and bring them into place the ensuing autumn or early winter. my hope is that you will be able and willing to keep yourself uncommitted, to take your place among them about that time: and I can assure you there is not a voice among us which will not be cordially given for it. I think too I may add that if the Presbyterian opposition should not die by that time, it will be directed at once against the whole institution, and not amuse itself with nibbling at a single object. it did that before only because there was no other, and they might think it politic to mask their designs on the body of the fortress, under the feint of a battery against a single bastion. I will not despair then of the avail of your services in an establishment which I contemplate as the future bulwark of the human mind in this hemisphere. god bless you and preserve you multos años.

TH: JEFFERSON

PoC (DLC); edge trimmed; at foot of first page: "Doct^r Cooper."

Cooper's letter OF THE 24TH ULT. was actually dated 12 July 1820. Elizabeth Trist informed her grandson Nicholas P. Trist from Ridgway on 10 Sept. 1820 that Gerard E. STACK "has broke up his School and is going to Phila^d" and that Peter Laporte "who kept the Boarding House has gone off in debt" (RC in DLC: NPT). Thomas Ragland was the MATHEMATICAL ASSISTANT at Stack's Charlottesville Academy. EVANISHING: "vanishing; disappearing; dying out" (*OED*).

DEUS IGITUR, CUI . . . RATIONE CORPORUM INCORPOREUS: "God, therefore, like the soul, is, according to Origen, in fact corporeal, but, by reason of so much heavier bodies, incorporeal." QUAMVIS ENIM SUBTILIA . . . ET SOLIDUM EST: "For although they are of light texture, nevertheless in substance, form, and figure, their bodies are fine, according to the fineness of their nature, while this body too in its substance is thick and solid." το θειον φαμεν ειναι αςωματον, ουχ οτι εϚιν αςωματον: "We say that the divinity is without body, not because it is bodiless." QUID ENIM DEUS . . . IN SUÂ EFFIGIE: "'For what is God, except body?' and again 'Who, however, will deny that God is body? Although God is spirit, yet the spirit is body of its own nature, in its own image.'" IN IPSO ULTIMO . . . ANIMÂ SENTIMUS EXIRE?: "When, in the ultimate heat of pleasure, the genital liquid is expelled, do we not feel some of the soul issue forth?" For the sources of these quotes, see notes 7–11 below.

CONJUNCTIM: "conjointly." MULTOS AÑOS: "many years."

[1] Manuscript: "ingine."

[2] Manuscript: "bien."

[3] Thus in manuscript, with latter two words interlined in place of "in a double sense."

[4] TJ here canceled "antient."

[5] Preceding five words interlined.

[6] Word interlined. TJ here keyed a note with an asterisk reading (one word editorially corrected from "believi"; edge trimmed, with "ha" and "nc" supplied from earlier microfilm [DLC: TJ Papers, 218:38910], now missing in manuscript) "I believe by At[ha]nasius & the cou[ncil] of Nicaea."

[7] In right margin adjacent to this section, TJ wrote "Ocellus de d'Argens pa. 97" (Jean Baptiste de Boyer, marquis d'Argens, *Ocellus Lucanus en grec et en françois* [Utrecht, 1762; Poor, *Jefferson's Library*, 8 (no. 418)]), and "Enfield VI. 3" (William Enfield, *The History of Philosophy, from the earliest times to the beginning of the present century; drawn up from Brucker's Historia Critica Philosophiæ*, 2 vols. [London, 1791; Sowerby, no. 1337; Poor, *Jefferson's Library*, 9 (no. 518)]).

[8] In right margin adjacent to this section, TJ wrote "ib. 105" (correctly, p. 103).

[9] In left margin adjacent to this section, TJ wrote "Timaeus. 17" (Boyer, marquis d'Argens, *Timée de Locres en Grec et en François* [Berlin, 1763; Poor, *Jefferson's Library*, 8 (no. 419)]) and "Enfield. VI. 3."

[10] In left margin adjacent to this section, TJ wrote "18."

[11] In left margin adjacent to this section, TJ wrote "1. Hist. des Saints 2. c. 4. pa. 212–218." This work was Paul Henri Thiry, baron d'Holbach, *Tableau des Saints*, 2 vols. (London, 1770; Poor, *Jefferson's Library*, 9 [no. 478]).

[12] In left margin adjacent to this section, TJ wrote (edge chipped) "[Oc]ellus. 98."

To Henry A. S. Dearborn

DEAR SIR   Monticello Aug. 14. 20.

Capt Bernard Peyton, a commission merchant of Richmond, and particular friend of mine, being now on a tour to the North and East, informed me that he would have occasion to call on you, and that a letter lodged with you would be sure to get to his hands. on this ground I ask the favor of your care of the within. Capt Peyton served honorably as an officer in the last war, since which he has acted in the commission line, with a prudence, punctuality and fidelity which has procured him the affection and confidence of all who know him, and as far as these can be titles of credence, he merits it from all. any civilities you may be so kind as to render him will be acknoledged by me with thankfulness and with the assurance of my great esteem and respect.   TH: JEFFERSON

RC (TxDaHCL); addressed: "Henry A. S. Dearborne esquire Boston"; franked; postmarked Charlottesville, 17 Aug.; endorsed by Dearborn, in part, as "introducing B, Peyton of Richmond Virg^a." PoC (DLC); on verso of reused address cover of Fernagus De Gelone to TJ, 11 Apr. 1820; mutilated at seal; endorsed by TJ. Enclosure: TJ to Bernard Peyton, 14 Aug. 1820, and enclosure.

To James Leitch

Aug. 14. 20.

1. ℔ allspice
2. oz. nutmegs
2. oz. ginger
1. oz. cinnamon
1. oz. mace.   TH:J

RC (NcD-MC: Trent Collection); written on a small scrap; dateline beneath signature; at foot of text: "Mr James Leitch." Not recorded in SJL.

Leitch's records indicate that on this date TJ purchased by order

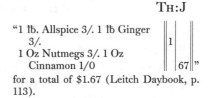

"1 ℔. Allspice 3/. 1 ℔ Ginger 3/.
1 Oz Nutmegs 3/. 1 Oz Cinnamon 1/0 | | 1 | 67 | "
for a total of $1.67 (Leitch Daybook, p. 113).

[191]

To Bernard Peyton

Th:J. to Capᵀ Peyton. Monticello Aug. 14. 20.

In a letter addressed to mr Dearborne I inclose this which covers the one to mr Gray which Jefferson told me would be acceptable to you.—about 20. years ago, mr Stewart of Boston drew my portrait, for which I then paid him 100.D. about 12. or 15. years ago he desired me to set for him again saying he did not like the former portrait & would rather draw another for me. I sat for him, and moreover yielded to his request to keep it until he could have an engraving from[1] it. that has been done long ago, but notwithstanding repeated applications he has never delivered either portrait. Genˡ Dearborne in the last instance undertook to try if he could obtain either, and I believe did obtain a promise thro mr Henry Dearborne, who can tell you the present state [of the?] negociation. perhaps your presence there and the conv[enience] of it's coming to me under your care may be a stimulus to mr Stewart to deliver it to you, in obtaining which I am sure mr Dearborne will lend his kind assistance. affectionate salutns.

PoC (MHi); on verso of reused address cover of otherwise unlocated letter from James Madison to TJ, 8 Apr. 1820 (addressed: "Mʳ Jefferson Monticello near Charlottesville Vᵃ"; franked; postmarked Orange Court House, 10 Apr. 1820; recorded in SJL as received 10 Apr. from Montpellier); dateline at foot of text; mutilated at seal; endorsed by TJ. Enclosure: TJ to William Gray, 13 Aug. 1820. Enclosed in TJ to Henry A. S. Dearborn, 14 Aug. 1820.

JEFFERSON was Thomas Jefferson Randolph, and MR STEWART was the artist Gilbert Stuart.

[1] Word interlined in place of "for."

From Andrew Smith

Sir Richmond 14ᵗʰ Augᵗ 1820

Since the receipt of your respected letter of 5ᵗʰ July 1819, I have not been favor'd with any communication from you, and therefore presume, that, owing to your long continued[1] indisposition last year, and your various avocations since the restoration of your health, it may have escaped your recollection, that a Small Sum of $68–78 has been a considerable time due to the Estate of the late firm of Smith & Riddle, for Glass ordered by them for your use—

Having been appointed Agent for the Trustees of said Estate, and likewise resumed the Agency of the Boston Glass House sometime ago, it is expected by both, that due attention has been paid by me to the settlement of all outstanding debts, I hope, Sir, this will be a sufficient apology for my now asking the favor of you to remit me the above Amount together with legal interest from the time of purchase, as is customary—

The Glass furnaces at Boston have been lately rendered more complete—and now in full operation—all orders executed thro' my Agency are delivered here at the Manufactory prices, and free of charge,

I am Sir—Respectfully   AND^W SMITH

RC (MHi); at foot of text: "Thos Jef-   [1] Manuscript: "continud."
ferson Esqr"; endorsed by TJ as received
21 Aug. 1820 and so recorded in SJL.

To John Adams

Monticello. Aug. 15. 20.

I am a great defaulter, my dear Sir, in our correspondence, but prostrate health rarely permits me to write; and, when it does, matters of business imperiously press their claims. I am getting better however, slowly, swelled legs being now the only serious symptom, and these, I believe, proceed from extreme debility. I can walk but little; but I ride 6. or 8. miles a day without fatigue; & within a few days, I shall endeavor to visit my other home, after a twelve month's absence from it. our University, 4. miles distant, gives me frequent exercise, and the oftener as I direct it's architecture. it's plan is unique, and it is becoming an object of curiosity for the traveller. I have lately had an opportunity of reading a critique on this institution in your North American Review of January last, having been not without anxiety to see what that able work would say of us: and I was relieved on finding in it much coincidence of opinion, and even, where criticisms were indulged, I found they would have been obviated had the developements of our plan been fuller. but these were restrained by the character of the paper reviewed, being merely a report of outlines, not a detailed treatise, & addressed to a legislative body, not to a learned academy. e.g. as an inducement to introduce the Anglo-Saxon into our plan, it was said that it would reward amply the <u>few weeks</u> of attention which alone would be requisite for it's attainment; leaving both term and degree under an indefinite expression, because I know that not much time is necessary to attain it to an useful degree, sufficient to give such instruction in the etymologies of our language as may satisfy ordinary students, while more time would be requisite for those who would propose to attain a critical knolege of it. in a letter which I had occasion to write to mr Crofts (who sent you, I believe, as well as myself, a copy of his treatise on the English & German languages, as preliminary to an Etymological dictionary he meditated) I went into explanations with him of an easy process for simplifying the study of the Anglo-Saxon, and lessening the terrors, & difficulties presented by it's rude Alphabet, & unformed orthography. but this is a subject beyond the bounds of a letter, as it was beyond the bounds of a Report to the legislature. mr Crofts died, I believe, before any progress was made in the work he had projected.

The reviewer expresses doubt, rather than decision, on our placing Military, and Naval architecture in the department of Pure Mathematics. Military architecture embraces fortification and field works, which with their bastions, curtains, hornworks, redoubts E[t]. are based on a technical combination of lines & angles. these are adapted to offence and defence, with and against the effects of bombs, balls, escalades E[t]c. but lines and angles make the sum of elementary geometry, a branch of Pure Mathematics: and the direction of the bombs, balls, and other projectiles, the necessary appendages of military works, altho' no part of their architecture, belong to the Conic sections, a branch of transcendental geometry. Diderot & Dalembert therefore, in their Arbor scientiae, have placed military architecture in the department of elementary geometry. Naval architecture teaches the best form and construction of vessels; for which best form it has recourse to the question of the Solid of least resistance, a problem of transcendental geometry. and it's appurtenant projectiles belong to the same branch, as in the preceding case. it is true that so far as respects the action of the water on the rudder and oars, and of the wind on the sails, it may be placed in the department of Mechanics, as Diderot & Dalembert[1] have done: but belonging quite as much to geometry, and allied in it's military character, to military architecture, it simplified our plan to place both under the same head. these views are so obvious that I am sure they would have required but a second thought to reconcile the reviewer to their <u>location</u> under the head of Pure Mathematics. for this word <u>location,</u> see Bailey Johnson, Sheridan, Walker E[t]c. but if Dictionaries are to be the Arbiters of language, in which of them shall we find <u>neologism</u>? no matter. it is a good word, well sounding, obvious, and expresses an idea which would otherwise require circumlocution. the Reviewer was justifiable therefore in using it; altho' he noted at the same time, as unauthoritative, <u>centrality</u>, <u>grade</u>, <u>sparse</u>; all which have been long used in common speech and writing. I am a friend to <u>neology</u>. it is the only way to give to a language copiousness & euphony. without it we should be still held to the vocabulary of Alfred or of Ulphilas; and held to their state of science also: for I am sure they had no words which could have conveyed the ideas of Oxigen, cotyledons, zoophytes, magnetism, electricity, hyaline, and thousands of others expressing ideas not then existing, nor of possible communication in the state of their language. What a language has the French become since the date of their revolution, by the free introduction of new words! the most copious and eloquent in the living world; and equal to the Greek, had not that been regularly modifiable almost ad infinitum. their rule was that whenever their language furnished or adopted a root, all it's branches, in every part of speech were legitimated by giving them their appropriate terminations. αδελφος. αδελφη, αδελφιδιον, αδελφοτης, αδελφιξις, αδελφιδους, αδελφικος, αδελφιζω, αδελφικως. and this should be the law of every language. thus, having adopted the adjective fraternal, it is a root, which should legitimate fraternity, fraternation, fraternisation, fraternism, to fraternate, fraternise, fraternally. and give the word neologism to our language, as a root, and it should give us it's fellow-substantives, neology, neologist, neologisation; it's adjectives neologous, neological, neologistical, it's verb neologise, & adverb neologically: Dictionaries are but the depositories of words already legitimated by usage. society is the work-shop in which new ones are elaborated. when an individual uses a new word, if illformed it is rejected in society, if well-formed, adopted, and, after due time, laid up in the depository of dictionaries. and if, in this process of sound neologisation, our transatlantic brethren shall not chuse to accompany us, we may furnish, after the Ionians, a second example of a colonial dialect improving on it's primitive.—but enough of criticism: let me turn to your puzzling letter of May 12. on matter, spirit, motion E'c. it's croud of scepticisms kept me from sleep. I read it, & laid it down: read it, and laid it down, again, and again: and to give rest to my mind, I was obliged to recur ultimately to my habitual anodyne, 'I feel: therefore I exist.' I feel bodies which are not myself: there are other existencies then. I call them matter. I feel them changing place. this gives me motion. where there is an absence of matter, I call it void, or nothing, or immaterial space. on the basis of sensation, of matter and motion, we may erect the fabric of all the certainties we can have or need. I can concieve thought to be an action of a particular organisation of matter, formed for that purpose by it's creator, as well as that attraction is an action of matter, or magnetism of loadstone. when he who denies to the Creator the power of endowing matter with the mode of action called thinking shall shew how he could endow the Sun with the mode of action called attraction, which reins the planets in the tract of their orbits, or how an absence of matter can have a will, and, by that will, put matter into motion, then the materialist may be lawfully required to explain the process by which matter exercises the faculty of thinking. when once we quit the basis of sensation all is in the wind. to talk of <u>immaterial</u> existences is to talk of <u>nothings</u>. to say that the human soul, angels, god, are immaterial, is to say they are <u>nothings</u>, or that there is no god, no angels, no soul. I cannot reason otherwise: but I believe I am supported in my creed of materialism by Locke, Tracy, & Stewart.[2] at what age of the[3] Christian church this heresy of <u>immaterialism</u>, this masked atheism crept in, I do not know. but a heresy it certainly is. Jesus taught nothing of it. he told us indeed that 'God is a spirit,' but he has not defined what a spirit is, nor said that it is not <u>matter</u>. and the antient fathers generally, if not universally, held it to be matter: light and thin indeed, an etheriel gas; but still matter.[4] Origen says 'Deus reapse corporalis est; sed graviorum tantum corporum ratione, incorporeus.' Tertullian 'quid enim deus nisi corpus?' and again 'quis negabit deum esse corpus? etsi deus spiritus, spiritus etiam corpus est, sui generis, in sua effigie.' St Justin Martyr 'το θειον φαμεν ειναι αϛωματον· ουκ ὁτι αϛωματον,—επειδη δε το μη κρατειϛθαι ὑπο τινος, του κρατειϛθαι τιμιωτερον εϛι, δια τουτο καλουμεν αυτον αϛωματον.' and St Macarius, speaking of angels says 'quamvis enim subtilia sint, tamen in substantiâ, formâ et figurâ, secundum tenuitatem naturae eorum, corpora sunt tenuia.' and St Austin, St Basil, Lactantius, Tatian, Athenagoras and others, with whose writings I pretend not a familiarity,[5] are said by those who are, to deliver the same doctrine. turn to your Ocellus d'Argens 97. 105. and to his Timaeus 17. for these quotations. in England these Immaterialists might have been burnt until the 29. Car. 2. when the writ de haeretico comburendo was abolished: and here until the revolution, that statute not having extended to us. all heresies being now done away with us, these schismatists are merely atheists, differing from the material Atheist only in their belief that 'nothing made something,' and from the material deist who believes that matter alone can operate on matter.   Rejecting all organs of information therefore but my senses, I rid myself of the Pyrrhonisms with which an indulgence in speculations hyperphysical and antiphysical so uselessly occupy and disquiet the mind. a single sense may indeed be sometimes decieved, but rarely: and never all our senses together, with their faculty of reasoning. they evidence realities; and there are enough of these for all the purposes of life, without plunging into the fathomless abyss of dreams & phantasms. I am satisfied, and sufficiently occupied with the things which are, without tormenting or troubling myself about those which may indeed be, but of which I have no evidence. I am sure that I really know many, many, things, and none more surely than that I love you with all my heart, and pray for the continuance of your life until you shall be tired of it yourself.

TH: JEFFERSON

RC (MHi: Adams Papers); at foot of first page: "M[r] Adams." PoC (DLC).

The CRITIQUE in the *North American Review and Miscellaneous Journal* 10 (new ser., 1) (1820): 115–37, was a lengthy review of the Rockfish Gap Report of the University of Virginia Commissioners of 4 Aug. 1818, which is printed above as document 5 in a group of documents on The Founding of the University of Virginia: Rockfish Gap Meeting of the University of Virginia Commissioners, 1–4 Aug. 1818. TJ's letter to Sir Herbert Croft (MR CROFTS) is dated 30 Oct. 1798 (*PTJ*, 30:568–71). HIS TREATISE is *A Letter, from Germany, to the Princess Royal of England; on the English and German languages* (Hamburg, 1797; Sowerby, no. 4840).

HORNWORKS are single-fronted fortifications, "the head of which consists of two demi-bastions connected by a curtain and joined to the main body of the work by two parallel wings" (*OED*). ARBOR SCIENTIAE ("Tree of Science"): editors Denis Diderot and Jean Le Rond d'Alembert presented a figurative system of human knowledge in the preface to the first volume of their *Encyclopédie, ou Dictionnaire Raisonné des Sciences, des Arts et des Métiers* (Paris, 1751–72; for a later ed. see Sowerby, no. 4890). Ulfilas (ULPHILAS) was a fourth-century bishop who translated the Bible into the Gothic language. αδελφος. αδελφη . . . αδελφιζω, αδελφικως: "brother, sister, little brother, brotherhood, brotherly affinity, nephew, brotherly [as adjective], to adopt as a brother, brotherly [as adverb]." The Ionic DIALECT of Greek, which was spoken mostly by colonists on the west coast of Asia Minor, is associated with the poetry of Homer, the early philosophy of the Ionian school, and the historian Herodotus. I FEEL: THEREFORE I EXIST is a variant of René Descartes's famous philosophic principle "Cogito, ergo sum" ("I think, therefore I am"). Jesus taught that GOD IS A SPIRIT in the Bible, John 4.24.

DEUS REAPSE CORPORALIS . . . CORPORUM RATIONE, INCORPOREUS: "God is in reality corporeal, but, by reason of so much heavier bodies, incorporeal." QUID ENIM DEUS . . . IN SUA EFFIGIE: "'For what is God, except body?' and again, 'Who will deny that God is body? Although God is spirit, yet the spirit is body of its own nature, in its own image.'" το θειον φαμεν . . . καλουμεν αυτον αςωματον: "We say that the divinity is without body, not because it is bodiless, but since the state of not being bounded by anything is a more honorable one than that of being bounded, for this reason we call him bodiless." QUAMVIS ENIM SUBTILIA . . . CORPORA SUNT TENUIA: "For although they are of light texture, nevertheless in substance, form, and figure, their bodies are fine, according to the fineness of their nature." For the source of these quotes, see note to TJ to Thomas Cooper, 14 Aug. 1820.

S[T] AUSTIN: Saint Augustine. 29. CAR. 2. was the twenty-ninth year of the reign of King Charles II of England, with the WRIT DE HAERETICO COMBURENDO ("on the burning of heretics") repealed in 1677 (David Loewenstein, *Treacherous Faith: The Specter of Heresy in Early Modern English Literature & Culture* [2013], 304).

[1] Manuscript: "Dalambert."
[2] PoC: "the Lockes, the Tracys, & the Stewarts."
[3] In PoC TJ here keyed a note with an asterisk reading "that of Athanasius and the Council of Nicaea anno 324."
[4] In left margin of PoC adjacent to following section, TJ wrote "Enfield VI. 3" and "ib."
[5] In right margin of PoC adjacent to this line, TJ wrote "Enfield X. 2."

Account of a Visit to Monticello and Montpellier by "W." (possibly George Watterston)

DEAR SIR: [before 15 Aug. 1820]

You request me to give you some account of my late excursion to Virginia.[1] I comply with the request, but am sorry to observe, that the time occupied in making it was too short to enable me to take those views of the country through which I passed that are necessary to render any description pleasing or satisfactory. The observations, however, I had the power to make, in my rapid journey, I submit to your examination, with a hope that they may be found not entirely destitute of interest. The appearance of this state, towards its eastern boundary, is not the most beautiful, or the most promising; the soil is generally poor, and but little attended to; it is composed of sand and clay, interspersed with granite, quartz, and schist, at least in the direction I took. As you approach the mountains, however, the prospect is more inviting, and you advance through a region of beauty and magnificence that never fails to charm and delight. The peculiar color of the soil (a red argillaceous earth) found every where among the south-west mountains, is indeed the only object that can detract from the pleasure the rich and variegated aspect of the country around you is calculated to produce: groves of the most stately trees; vales of the richest verdure; slopes beautified with golden grain; and mountains, "blue fading into mist," meet the eye on every eminence and through every vista you pass. "Ould Virginia" is not indeed now as it was in the time of the author from whom I make the following quotations:* "All over a naturall grove of oakes, pines, cedars, cipresse,[2] chesnut, laurell, sassafrass, *cherry*, and *plum trees*,[3] all of so delectable an aspect that the melanchollyest eye in the world cannot looke upon it without contentment, nor content himself without admiration." But there is still but a small portion of it in cultivation, compared with the magnitude of that which is yet in a state of rude and native wildness: and that which is cultivated has not been much improved by the industry of man or the lights which modern agriculture has afforded.

The tributary streams which flow into the Rappahannock and James rivers are very beautiful and very picturesque. It is to situations like these that the muses delight to resort; and the time may not be very distant when they will be celebrated in the "wood notes wild"

*Virginia, by E. W. Gent. 1650.

of some native bard, fired by the enthusiasm of genius, and roused by the beauties of nature that surround him. The mountain cataract and the meandering rivulet, whose current glides silently and smoothly between its banks, shaded by the embrowned foliage of the lofty forest tree and the humble but aromatic shrub, are apt to predispose the mind to that state of melancholy feeling which is not unfrequently the parent of poetical inspiration. In the elegant and poetical mythology of the Greeks, you will recollect that every stream had its god, and every fountain its nymph, and that the favorite haunts of the muses themselves were by the far-famed Hippocrene, the fountain of Helicon. It is along those streams, too, and through the forests which are near them, that the botanist delights to stroll. Every step is beguiled by some new object in the vegetable kingdom, or some old acquaintance to which his eye has before been familiarized. I regretted you were not with me, in the little rambles I took, to participate in the rich banquet that nature presented to my senses. Your botanical enthusiasm would have been gratified, and your knowledge enlarged, by the variety and beauty of the specimens occasionally to be met with among the "wilds and melancholy glooms" through which I wandered. The sumach is every where seen along the road; but I have often been surprised that the poet Moore should have selected, amidst the great variety of beautiful plants every where abounding in this country, this shrub—the *rhus coccineum* of the fields—to introduce into one of the finest lyrical effusions he wrote while in the United States:
"By the *shade* of yon *sumach*, whose red berry *dips*
In the gush of the fountain, how sweet to recline."
There is, you know, scarcely any plant less worthy a place in poetry than this, from its absolute want of any thing like beauty; and, as it is a shrub which, I believe, very rarely exceeds the height of six feet, it affords too little *shade* to repose under, and it never bends sufficiently to dip its berries in the gush of any fountain. But I am wandering.

I must now take you with me to the residence of the sage of Monticello, whom I felt it my duty to visit, and whom I could not pass by without paying my respects. The approach to his house was by a gradual ascent from the road which leads to Charlottesville. The friend who accompanied me was equally desirous to see the venerable patriarch, whose fame has been so widely extended, and whose patriotism and usefulness his country will never cease to remember. We ascended the eastern side of the mountain on which he resides, and it seemed as if we should never reach its summit, from its lofty but gradual elevation. The morning was beautiful; the sun beamed forth in all his majesty; the birds warbled sweetly around us; the air was pure, balmy, and elastic; and, when within sight of the house, we paused for some time to contemplate the sublime scene that burst upon our view. To the right, the eye ranged over an expanse of forty miles, and was limited by the verge of the horizon, which resembled that of the ocean; behind us, "Alps on Alps arose," and bounded the prospect; to the left could be seen the Sugar Loaf Mountain, in Maryland, a distance of 110 miles, and, not far below us, the village of Charlottesville and the University now building, with the rich and cultivated country around. Monticello, the name of Mr. Jefferson's dwelling, is situated on a conical hill, about 600 feet high. This modest title (in English, *little mountain*) was given to it to distinguish it from the more lofty elevations behind. "It was a debt," says a traveller who visited Mr. Jefferson about forty years ago,† "nature owed to a philosopher and a man of taste, that in his own possessions he should find a spot where he might better study and enjoy her;" and it would indeed seem that scarcely any region was better calculated for such a purpose than the one he has selected for his residence. The sublimity and grandeur of the objects of nature which surround him, the mountain scenery and elastic atmosphere he enjoys, must have had the effect of producing a corresponding elevation and greatness of soul; and "it should seem," to use the language of the traveller quoted, "as if Mr. Jefferson, from his youth, had placed his mind, as he has done his house, on an elevated situation, from which he might contemplate the universe." I saw near his house a great quantity of Scotch broom, (*spartium,*) ranged on either side of the road, a large field of elephantopos, and a great number of beautiful plants, resembling the Ixia, which I had not time to examine.

Mr. Jefferson is now near eighty years of age; his person is tall and stately; his countenance mild and agreeable; his step, though at so advanced an age, is firm and springy; and his whole appearance is that of a philosopher and a well-bred gentleman. I could perceive no marks of the imbecility of age in any thing he said or did; he indeed complained of the decay of his memory, but his memory seemed to be stored with the treasures of learning, and with all that was useful and agreeable. In his manner he is dignified without being haughty, and easy without being familiar. What he says has the weight of authority and the impressiveness of wisdom, and he never tires by detailing events that have passed, a propensity so common with those whose energies have been weakened by the decay of age. Mr. Jefferson's constitution has always been, as it still is, vigorous and healthy, and

† Chastelleux's Travels.

it is not likely, from the regularity and temperance he observes, and the exercise he takes, that he will be immediately sensible of that gradual waste of body and intellect which accompanies our progress to the grave from old age. He is now surrounded by his family, and seems to experience all that happiness that flows from a long life of usefulness and virtue; but, though abstracted from the cares and miseries of state, and buried in the shades of retirement, the same eagerness to be useful, & the same desire to promote the welfare of his country and his native state which always distinguished him, still accompanies him; and the attention he bestows, and the time he devotes to the Charlottesville University, evince his former vigor of mind, and display the native and prominent virtues of his heart. His house is an elegant octagonal building, with a large doric portico in front; the entrance, or hall, contains a considerable collection of curiosities in nature and art, such as statues, busts, paintings by Raphael, Reubens, Pouisson, &c., and many other curiosities of nature, more complete, interesting, and valuable, than can be found in any other private collection, perhaps, in the world. The conversation of Mr. Jefferson is replete with amusement and edification, and is never withheld by any feeling of reserve from those who desire it. It is a pity some of his relations or friends do not endeavor to form, from their close intimacy with him, an *ana*, for the gratification and instruction of those who survive him, and who must and will feel the deepest interest in all that concerns a man who has been so distinguished and useful in every walk of life.

Having visited this illustrious patriarch, we could not resist the inclination to call upon his friend, and the friend of his country, Mr. Madison. The natural scenery around this gentleman's residence is also rich and magnificent. The building is of brick, ornamented in front with a Roman portico, and opening, from a saloon behind, into a beautiful lawn, from which, through an artificial vista, you have a view of the range of mountains, called, from their appearance, the Blue Ridge. Groves of forest trees, extensive spots in cultivation, and the waving line of stupendous mountains, are constantly presented to the eye from this elegant retreat.

Montpelier, the residence of Mr. Madison, is about 25 miles from Monticello, situated in Orange county, so called from the Prince of Orange and about 5 miles from the Court House and the little village in which it stands. His farm is extensive and well improved; the soil, though of a deep orange, is[4] rich and productive; and he seems to want no convenience that might contribute to his comfort or add to his happiness.

It is amidst those isolated mountain habitations that the social affections of our nature become more durable and vigorous, because, being less liable to distraction, they are more concentrated. It is in situations like these that man feels the dignity of his nature, and the happiness of which he has been made susceptible. Nature spreads before him her beauties; masses of verdure surround him; his foot softly presses the green lawn that has been furnished as his carpet; his eye plays over the ever-varying landscape; his ear is regaled by the melody of the grove; and he breathes an air as pure as his heart, and as gentle as the current of his feelings.

Oh, rus! quando te aspiciam?

In such sequestered retirements the heart acquires a purity and innocence that nothing can destroy, and the happy inhabitant contemplates the objects around him with a pleasure that it would be difficult to describe. He beholds in the rising sun the grand epoch of creation, and sees in his descent, when he paints the clouds with a thousand colors, and gilds the summit of the trees that veil his retreat, the last scene of life, in which the projects of ambition and the pomp and trophies of greatness are "ingulphed in an abyss that never restores its prey."

We found Mr. Madison in good health, very cheerful, and very happy. His person, you know, is small, and his countenance grave; but it is soon illuminated when he enters into conversation, and the ease and fluency with which he speaks, gives to what he says a charm that cannot be resisted. His deportment has the same ease and dignity in private, as it had in public, life, and the former politeness of his manners, and hospitality of his heart, are still recognized and felt by all who have the happiness to visit him in his delightful retirement. In this retirement he devotes himself to the innocent pursuits of agriculture, and, like the patriarch of Monticello, he[5] seems to manifest a degree of delight at the idea of having honorably freed himself from the cares, the burdens, and the miseries of government. It is certainly a spectacle of no ordinary grandeur to see those who have revolved in the highest spheres of life sinking down into the bosom of society, without a sigh of regret, or an effort to "cast one longing, lingering look behind." The relinquishment of power is not often attended with the enjoyment of happiness. The splendor which surrounds the head of him who wields the destinies of a nation has been considered too alluring and attractive to be abandoned without reluctance and regret; but in the instances this country has furnished, it may be safely averred, that pleasure, rather than pain, has been felt by those who have yielded up the "rod of empire."

[202]

"It is seldom (says Gibbon) that minds long exercised in business, have formed any habits of conversing with themselves; and, in the loss of power, they principally regret the want of occupation." But, like Dioclesian, both Mr. Madison and Mr. Jefferson have preserved their taste for the most innocent, as well as natural pleasures, and their hours, like those of that Roman emperor in retirement, are sufficiently employed in reading, planting and cultivating their farms, to exclude the miseries of indolence, and the horrors of *ennui*. The residence of both Mr. Jefferson and Mr. Madison, is the residence of taste and elegance, and to both may be applied, with peculiar aptitude, the lines of the poet of nature;

"An elegant sufficiency—content,
Retirement, rural quiet, friendship, books,
Ease and alternate labor—useful life,
Progressive virtue, and approving Heaven."   W.

Printed in Washington *Daily National Intelligencer*, 15 Aug. 1820, Charlottesville *Central Gazette*, 25 Aug. 1820, and elsewhere; undated; with faint punctuation in *National Intelligencer* supplied from *Central Gazette*; at head of text: "MONTICELLO AND MONTPELIER."

Watterston's possible identity as "W." is inferred from his surname's initial and from his having briefly visited TJ at Monticello on 25 July 1820, accompanied by a Dr. Hamilton (TJ to Watterston, 27 July 1820; Watterston to TJ, 4 Aug. 1820). VIRGINIA, BY E. W. GENT. 1650 was Edward Williams, *Virginia: More especially the South part thereof, Richly and truly valued* (2d ed., London, 1650; Sowerby, no. 4008), quote on p. 1. WOOD NOTES WILD is from line 134 of John Milton's poem *L'Allegro*. WILDS AND MELANCHOLY GLOOMS appears in Regina Maria Roche, *The Monastery of St. Columb; or, the Atonement* (London, 1813), 1:17. BY THE SHADE OF YON SUMACH . . . HOW SWEET TO RECLINE is from lines 13–4 of "Ballad Stanzas," a short poem in Thomas Moore, *Epistles, Odes, and Other Poems* (4th ed., London, 1814), 2:108. ALPS ON ALPS AROSE is a variant of "Alps on Alps arise!" from Alexander Pope's *Essay on Criticism* (London, 1711), 15. The Marquis de CHASTELLEUX's quotes come from his *Travels in North America in the Years 1780, 1781 and 1782*

(Paris, 1786; English trans. London, 1787; Sowerby, nos. 4021, 4023), 2:41, 46. REUBENS and POUISSON were the painters Peter Paul Rubens and Nicolas Poussin, respectively. OH, RUS! QUANDO TE ASPICIAM? ("o rus, quando ego te aspiciam!"): "O rural home: when shall I behold you!" (Horace, *Satires*, 2.6.60, in Fairclough, *Horace: Satires, Epistles and Ars Poetica*, 214–5).

INGULPHED IN AN ABYSS THAT NEVER RESTORES ITS PREY, with most of the paragraph preceding it, is a free translation from Ferdinand Marie Bayard's *Voyage dans l'intérieur des États-Unis, a Bath, Winchester, dans La Vallée de Shenandoha, etc. etc. etc. Pendant l'Été de 1791* (Paris, 1797), 32–3, quote on p. 33. CAST ONE LONGING, LINGERING LOOK BEHIND and ROD OF EMPIRE are from lines 88 and 47, respectively, of Thomas Gray's "Elegy Written in a Country Churchyard" (Roger Lonsdale, ed., *The Poems of Thomas Gray, William Collins, Oliver Goldsmith* [1969], 126, 133).

The passage concerning MINDS LONG EXERCISED IN BUSINESS is from Edward Gibbon, *The History of the Decline and Fall of the Roman Empire* (London, 1776–88; Sowerby, no. 101), 1:394. AN ELEGANT SUFFICIENCY . . . AND APPROVING HEAVEN is from lines 1157–60 of the poem "Spring" in James Thomson's *The Seasons* (London, 1744, and other eds.; Sowerby, no. 4392), 49.

[1] Omitted period editorially supplied.

[2] Wiliams, *Virginia*, here adds "Mulberry."

[3] Wiliams, *Virginia*, here adds "and Vines."

[4] *National Intelligencer*: "orange,is." *Central Gazette*: "orange, is."

[5] *National Intelligencer*: "Monticello,he." *Central Gazette*: "Monticello, he."

From Louis H. Girardin

DEAR AND RESPECTED SIR,   Hermitage, Aug[t] 16th 1820.

I ought long since to have thanked You for your very friendly attention in informing me of the appearance of a translation of Botta by M[r] G. A. Otis. I ought, above all, immediately upon receiving that information, to have replaced in Your hands the two vol[s] of the italian work, so obligingly lent me, as it was natural enough to suppose that You would wish to compare the copy with the original. The thousand and one insect vexations which have, of late especially, buzzed about my ears, have prevented me, in spite of my better intent, from sooner fulfilling that duty. I have relapsed into the worst of my <u>péchés d'habitude</u>, procrastination; and I now have, as on many a former occasion, to claim Your characteristic indulgence and forbearance.

Luckily as it happens, the inconceivable drudgery of multiplied classes, first in Staunton, and afterwards here, together with the numberless interruptions of a farm upon an humble scale, with bad servants, and a roguish manager, have rendered my progress in the translation of Botta's work extremely slow. The anticipation of M[r] G. A. Otis frustrates, therefore, no sanguine hope, defeats no promising scheme of mine. Indeed, I rejoice at his having put the American Public in possession of so valuable a record of national history. For my part, insulated as I am from publishers, printers, and booksellers, who, of right, should be the mere agents of authors, but who, as the often inverted course of things will have it, have become their task-masters, and according to the dictates of individual interest, shew themselves either their patrons or their enemies, their benefactors or their tyrants, even if my translation had been completed in due time, I should, I presume, have had to struggle with, perhaps, insurmountable difficulties for the successful publication and diffusion of it. I judge so, at least, from what has happened in respect to my ill-fated vol[e] of the "Continuation"—wretchedly printed—reluctantly circulated—as yet scantily remunerated by the Proprietors—and not even honoured with the notice of professional critics. The Editor of the Portfolio had, indeed, asked me to supply him with certain data respecting my work. I know such things to be pretty customary between authors and

reviewers, but I really am not sufficiently stocked with unblushing assurance and overweening vanity to review, and, of course, to eulogize
my own production. I prepared for him, however, naked outlines, and
pointed out such passages as I deemed calculated to produce a favourable impression. Among these was my narrative of the arrival and
reception of Dr Franklin in France. Soon after an oblique blow was,
I thought, inflicted on me in the Portfolio vol. VIII, oct^r 1819, n° IV,
page 315.[1] In a review of Franklin's correspondence, the Dr is there
illiberally abused for his expressions of partiality to the french nation—
that nation itself for frivolity, debasement, thraldom—and its government for profligacy, tyranny, hypocrisy, depravity &c. . . . I am not
sure that the passage issued from the pen of the Editor, Mr J. E. Hall,
who, jointly with Mr Duponceau, has procured for me, on the ground
of the "Continuation," the unexpected and surely unmerited honour of
being appointed a member of the American philosophical Society—
but whether it was his own production, or that of a Collaborator, I
was not pleased with it, and the intended review rested there. The
whole passage is disgusting in the extreme. No man of the least experience in politics can possibly mistake the leading motives of the
French Court in affording aid to the American States. Yet, there might
exist, and there actually existed, what I mentioned in the "Continuation," national enthusiasm. Besides, where is the philosophy,[2] and the
policy, too, of ungenerously depressing the human character, which,
heaven knows, is low enough of itself? Further, did it become Dr
Franklin, either as the ambassador of a country so efficiently assisted
by France, or as a private man loaded with courtesies, friendship, and
admiration, to express scorn, contempt, a condemnatory judgment,
and what not? Dr Franklin, it seems, spoke well both of the government and of the People of France, both in his official and in his private letters.—Our Anglomanes acrimoniously censure him for it. They
almost stultify him on that account. Indeed and in truth! it would
have done great honour to the Dr to have held one language openly,
and another secretly! They impeach his judgment—very well! let
him rather have erred in that way, than in point of veracity and consistency. An Augur, says Cicero, can scarcely look at another Augur
without laughing. It may be so, at times, with Politicians. Yet, there
is a decorum both in public and in private life with which I am sure
that Dr Franklin was too well acquainted to have practised the duplicity which the Reviewer is astonished not to find in any part of his
correspondence. He even goes so far as to suspect that the Publisher
of that correspondence has withheld from the Public eye those expressions of contempt &c for the french government and nation to which

[205]

I have above alluded. Be this as it may, I shall never regret having ascribed something to national sympathy and enthusiasm, in that case. The truth is that our Anglomanes would be delighted in finding even the flowers in Franklin's <u>parterre</u> infected with the venom of their own minds; and I am inclined to think that Mr Hall is not altogether free from the sin of Anglomany.

Notwithstanding so many causes of despondency, I would delight in revising and finishing the "History of Virginia," and in publishing, in a better form, the whole of my own task under the title of "History of Virginia during, and since, the Revolution." This, however, requires data, many of them, I fear, unattainable. The copy-right must be ceded to me by the Proprietors, which they once seemed inclined to do, in lieu of that part of the stipulated compensation yet due me; I must become possessed of leisure and other means to collect further documents, and to mould them into a clear, animated, interesting narrative. Your friendly wish that I should devote my attention to that object—similar wishes expressed by Mr Duponceau, and other <u>Literati</u>, are stimulants which must necessarily act on my mind with considerable force. Unfortunately my situation is far from being favourable to the prosecution of any literary design. Except the recovery of my health [an important advantage, it is true!] every thing is here contrary to my interest, my repose, my comfort. I shall not weary and disgust You with the details of the petty miseries attached to this situation. Suffice it to say that, although a tolerably good algebraist, I have mistaken <u>minus</u> for <u>plus</u>. No matter in what point of view, I consider this solitude—intellectually, morally, physically—I cannot (so great and So radical the evil is) draw out of it a single atom of good. I sink part of my little capital every year, and still I am incessantly at work. The worst is the fatal influence of this climate on the feeble and delicate constitution of a sister-in-law, who, for 8 years, has devoted her whole time and attention to my motherless children, and to myself. I see her with anguish daily declining, and withering in the keen breezes of this mountain air. Another deep source of tribulation is the want of means for the improvement of my Daughters in <u>Music</u> and <u>drawing</u>. Nature has gifted them with happy dispositions, and I can instruct them myself in the substantial branches; but I wish to fit them for the task of Female Teachers (the best legacy which I think I can leave to them) and it is not my intention that they should stop at mediocrity. Half-talents and accomplishments are not worth attainment. These two last circumstances especially—the bad health of my sister, in this climate, and under this drudgery, and the education of my daughters, are considerations which overbalance in my mind the censure and reflections of the world on my fickleness, inconsistency &c—. I must remove to a more favourable theatre. The times are highly unfavourable for renting my little farm, and selling my stock &c—&c—, but I have committed the error, and I must expiate it—Too happy, if I can only preserve, in another place, my restored health!

Some of the Trustees of the Baltimore College have thought of me as Principal of that Institution, which they are anxious to revive, and to place on the high ground of liberality and usefulness. But, independently of the want of funds in that Establishment, a circumstance which allows the Trustees to offer to the Principal merely the use of large, commodious, and handsome buildings for himself and for the school, together with their personal influence among the Parents and Guardians of the Youth of Baltimore, I am informed by Dr T. Watkins, who is extremely friendly to me, that the Board of Electors chiefly consists of bigoted Sectarians, wedded to particular men, as well as to particular doctrines—that, among 37 Trustees, not more than 4 or 5 have received even the rudiments of Education, and that it is probable they would be ever ready to commit any absurdity, however gross, in the management of a literary institution—that, although the first article of their charter denounces, in the strongest terms, both political and religious intolerance, the object of a majority of them, it is apprehended, is to establish both.—I learn from another Gentleman that a Dr Barry, an Episcopalian minister, and the spoiled child of fortune and of his sect, though not desirous to take an active share in the labours of Juvenile instruction, ardently aspires to the title of Praeses Baltimoriensis Collegii, and to the honour of conferring degrees &c. Connected with the clerical and literary ambition of this Gentleman, a scene of intrigue is developed which has astonished and almost petrified a poor Recluse like myself.—Dr Watkins has for many Years nobly struggled against the fatal propensities of the Trustees and others, and, in the present case, he has prevented a hurried and almost clandestine election of Barry—But I augur ill of so much partiality, bigotry, and illiberality—Indeed, I know too little, as yet, of the specific duties of the situation, of its probable emoluments &c—to make up my own mind on the subject. I have, however, placed in the power and discretion of Dr Watkins, a declaration that I would act, if appointed. What the result has been, or is likely to be, I have not yet been informed.

In Scotland, Professor Leslie maintained, on the occasion of his appointment to the Professorship[3] of Mathematics in the University of Edinburgh, a glorious and successful struggle with a Presbyterian

[207]

opponent, and, indeed, with the whole <u>Kirk</u>. Judge Cooper, who is loudly threatened by the champions of the same sect in this part of Virginia, will, I trust, if he ever comes to Charlottesville, enjoy a similar triumph.—But I am not armed with the panoply of science and merit of either Leslie or Cooper. I do not, therefore, entertain any sanguine hope of success in respect to that situation; nor, indeed, am I anxiously desirous to obtain it, except inasmuch as it would afford great facilities for the education of my Daughters in the ornamental branches (Baltimore abounding in good teachers of music and drawing) and a climate more propitious to the health of my sister.

This mania of placing Academies, Colleges, Universities &c—in the hands of men professionally disposed to propagate opinions rather than truths, will, I apprehend, ultimately prove injurious, if not to the liberties, at least, to the liberal spirit of the Country. Look at Hampden and Sidney, at the Lexington-college &c—&c! Condorcet in a <u>mémoire</u> which I have some where in my little collection, and Dugald Stewart in his "Short statement of facts relative to Leslie," have luminously and forcibly developed the evils arising from this adherence to the old <u>monacal</u> system. Unfortunately, we possess few of those liberal, intelligent, and patriotic minds that have courage, power, and ascendency enough to oppose and counteract with efficiency this highly pernicious gravitation. I have told the Persons concerned that I would always be ready to inculcate sound fundamental principles in religion, morals, and politics, but that I could do no more. I wish for a task purely literary.

Mr B. Fuller, who is a <u>good</u> man, and the best Euclidian, I ever knew, is (between us) very much inclined to try with me an Academy at Richmond. The Staunton establishment has dwindled to 22 Pupils, and this worthy Professor does not receive enough to support his family. His colleague, a clergyman of the Episcopal church, would be in a still worse predicament, having a more numerous family to maintain, were it not for his parish, or parishes. Mr Fuller is the Gentleman whom I once mentioned to You with respect to a Book-store in Charlottesville. I am now at liberty to name him, and I again take the liberty to recommend him to Your good offices, should any prospect ever present itself to his advantage.—This plan of a Joint establishment at Richmond requires maturing. I will make enquiries of my friends there, and not commit Mr Fuller with the Staunton-Gentlemen, until positive data are obtained.

For myself, I am conscious that I can act only in three Situations— that of Teacher, of Librarian, of Editor. The last would be most to my taste; but the times are peculiarly hard. In my <u>dreams</u>, I have sometimes thought of a Quarterly publication in the latin language, with the motto, <u>Pro orbe, et per orbem</u>. It would be a miscellany containing the essence of that information which our Gazettes afford respecting truly important subjects connected with the literature, the arts, commerce, agriculture, politics &c—of the United-States. The latin language is understood by men of Education in all countries, and by addressing the <u>Prospectus</u> to foreign ministers, consuls &c—I might probably obtain adequate support; and although I foresee many difficulties in respect to the multiplicity of modern ideas to be expressed in an ancient idiom, still I am sanguine enough to think that I could conquer them. In[4] conjunction with that q^{ly} publication, I would edit a french paper for mere matters of fact, and intitule it, <u>Le Narrateur</u>.—also, a weekly, or semi-weekly Journal, in English.—But these probably are mere <u>chateaux en Espagne</u>.

A narrative of <u>Burr's conspiracy</u>, after the manner of Sallust, or the Abbé de St Real, in his <u>Conjuration de Venise</u>, has sometimes appeared to me a subject favourable to historical enterprize. Perhaps, however, the time has not yet come for the successful execution of such a design.

Pardon me, Dear and respected Sir, for this prolix letter, and, I fear, unpardonable obtrusion upon Your time and repose. I can not well account to myself for having been betrayed into it, for I did not, at first, intend such details. Your indulgent philosophy will easily excuse the schemes of one in my situation, especially when those schemes originate in such motives. My little resources are here wasting away— my humble abilities utterly neutralized—the health of my sister visibly suffering—and the object for the attainment of which alone I still feel enthusiastic ardour, the education of my Daughters, necessarily, insurmountably deficient. In the failure of some earlier establishment, I mean to locate them and their aunt, for the winter, in Richmond, and myself to look about, for some suitable scene. Experience has too well taught me the errors of precipitancy, to permit me to relapse into them.

Once more, Dear and respected Sir, forgive my confidential effusions, and believe in my sincere gratitude, veneration, and friendship.

L. H. GIRARDIN

P.S.

I have prepared, and mean soon to publish, "<u>a System of demonstrated arithmetic</u>," an humble, but, I am sure, useful work. I have always found Youth deplorably deficient in that fundamental branch.— The 2 vol^s of Botta accompany this.

[209]

RC (DLC); ellipsis and brackets in original; pages numbered by Girardin; endorsed by TJ as received 23 Aug. 1820 and so recorded in SJL. Enclosure: Carlo Botta, *Storia della Guerra dell' Independenza degli Stati Uniti D'America* (Paris, 1809; Sowerby, no. 509; Poor, *Jefferson's Library*, 4 [no. 134]), vols. 1–2.

PÉCHÉS D'HABITUDE: "habitual sins." The ILL-FATED VOL[E] OF THE "CONTINUATION" was the fourth and final volume of John Daly Burk, Skelton Jones, and Girardin's *History of Virginia, from its First Settlement to the Present Day* (Petersburg, 1804–16; Sowerby, no. 464; Poor, *Jefferson's Library*, 4 [no. 127]). FRANKLIN'S CORRESPONDENCE was William Temple Franklin, ed., *The Private Correspondence of Benjamin Franklin, LL.D. F.R.S. &c.* (London, 1817). The AMERICAN PHILOSOPHICAL SOCIETY elected Girardin to membership on 15 Jan. 1819 (APS, Minutes [MS in PPAmP]).

ANGLOMANES were "partisans or advocates of English (or British) interests

in North America" (*OED*). CICERO wrote in *De Natura Deorum*, 1.71, that "Mirabile videtur quod non rideat haruspex cum haruspicem viderit" ("It is thought surprising that an augur can see an augur without smiling") (*Cicero. De Natura Deorum, Academica*, trans. Harris Rackham, Loeb Classical Library [1933; rev. ed., 1951], 68–9). Girardin's SISTER-IN-LAW was Frances Catherine Cole.

PRAESES BALTIMORIENSIS COLLEGII: "President of Baltimore College." The LEXINGTON-COLLEGE was Washington College (later Washington and Lee University). CONDORCET published five works *Sur l'instruction publique* early in the 1790s. Bartholomew Fuller's COLLEAGUE at the academy in Staunton was James G. Waddell. PRO ORBE, ET PER ORBEM: "For the world, and through the world." LE NARRATEUR: "The Narrator."

[1] Manuscript: "page 815."
[2] Manuscript: "philisophy."
[3] Manuscript: "Professorhip."
[4] Manuscript: "I."

From John Wayles Eppes

DEAR SIR, Mill Brook August 19th 1820.

Your letter of the 29th of July was received by the last mail—I am highly gratified at the prospect held out in it of our seeing you here— I shall feel great pleasure in accomodating you with a loan of 4000 dollars in the mode you propose—In the present uncertain condition of Bank stock it will be better for me to dispose of the stock and loan you the money—I would not wish a cent more or less than the fair selling price of the stock & disposing of the stock and loaning the money will probably be the readiest mode of rendering the contract satisfactory to each of us. I have written by this mail to M[r] Cheves whose situation gives him the best means of knowing the real value of the stock & who will I know aid me in disposing of it at a fair price. As soon as the stock can be disposed of I will write to you and you can have the money either immediately afterwards or at the end of the year according as the one or other arrangement may best answer your purposes—In the event of your taking the 4000 dollars I shall calculate on receiving the interest annually, & the principal in Negroes at the end of two years—in the mode you propose.

I am much obliged to you for the information on the subject of the Columbia college—I have always admired the character of Cooper & I consider Francis particularly fortunate in having the prospect of being placed in a situation, where all the departments of science essential for him at present are filled by professors the first in their several branches—Whatever may happen Francis will be able to finish his Education there—And although I hope every thing from the Legislature of Virginia, I have my fears that even the favorite child (the[1] University) may (as[2] is but too common) find its parent more liberal in every thing than money—

Francis considers the rout from Monticello by Buckingham court house the nearest and best—Since you were here last some additional difficulties have been presented on the rout from Canton. From Buckingham Court house by M[r] Bollings and Capt[n] Evans's is the best rout—Francis can inform you as returned on that rout—

Our crops are uncommonly fine at present—From the 25th of June to the 27th of July we had not a drop of Rain—Since that time we have had almost continued Rains—

Present me affectionately to the family & accept yourself my best wishes.

With every sentiment of respect & affection I am yours.

JNO: W: EPPES

RC (ViU: TJP); endorsed by TJ as received 25 Aug. 1820 and so recorded in SJL.

COLUMBIA COLLEGE was South Carolina College (later the University of South Carolina). CANTON was New Canton in Buckingham County.

[1] Misplaced opening parenthesis in front of "that" editorially moved in front of this word.

[2] Omitted opening parenthesis editorially supplied.

From William W. Hening

SIR,   Richmond August 19. 1820.

Having resumed the publication of the Statutes at Large, under the patronage of the legislature, I beg permission to manifest my gratitude for the aid you have afforded, by presenting you with a copy, elegantly bound, as far as the work is yet published, which is to Vol. 6. inclusive. The 7th volume is printed, but not yet bound. The subsequent volumes shall be bound uniformly with those now sent. The 8th volume will terminate the laws under the colonial government, and embrace all those in your 5th Volume of the sessions acts;

after which I shall send it on to the librarian of congress, as I have already done with M.S. **D**, which I received from Mr Randolph, but which you satisfied me belonged to your library.

In order to commence the laws of the Revolution with a volume, I have found it necessary to make the 7th & 8th volumes considerably larger than either of the former.—

Indeed my anxiety to complete the work is so great, that I would submit to no small sacrifice to effect it. I could very easily publish <u>four</u> volumes a year; but as the law now stands, I can only be paid for <u>one</u>, in each year; and the expenses are so great, that I cannot furnish capital to remain so long inactive.—Had it not been for the peculiar state of the treasury, I should have made an effort last session to get the law so amended, as to authorise payment for each volume, as it was published

I am resp^y Yr^s   W^M W: HENING

RC (DLC); endorsed by TJ as received 25 Aug. 1820 and so recorded in SJL. Enclosure: Hening, vols. 1–6.

Five years previously TJ had asked Hening to forward his 5TH VOLUME OF THE SESSIONS ACTS to George Watterston, the LIBRARIAN OF CONGRESS (TJ to Hening, 11 Mar. 1815; Hening to TJ, 15 Mar. 1815). For the circuitous travels of M.S. D, which Edmund Randolph had borrowed from TJ's library during the 1780s, see TJ to Hening, 25 Apr. 1815. AS THE LAW NOW STANDS: the 5 Feb. 1808 "Act authorising William Waller Hening to Publish an Edition of certain Laws of this Commonwealth, and for other purposes," provided that no "more than one volume of the said edition . . . be paid for out of the treasury in any one year" (*Acts of Assembly* [1807–08 sess.], 24).

From James Monroe

DEAR SIR   aug 19. 1820.

A man of whom I heard you speak lately, as a gardener,[1] to whom you had rented some land below me, called with mr Price, some days since, to rent, a piece of my land, on my saw mill stream. Finding that he was the person of whom you spoke, I observ'd that unless, I knew, that you consider'd him at liberty, to treat with another, I could have nothing to say to him. He promised to produce that evidence. To day he called again, & on my asking for it, he observd, that as I had given him no promise, he might by relinquishing his [hope?][2] with you, lose both objects. I told him that I would communicate with you myself, after which I would give him an answer. as he professes to be a gardener you may wish to retain him. If you do, I can easily give him an answer, that will be satisfactory to him, which I shall most willingly do, in complyance with your desire.

The Emperor of Russia has instructed his ministers, at all the European courts, to make known his disapprobation, of the movment in

Spain, which he calls a <u>suite</u> of the French revolution. The reply given at St Petersburg, to the spanis[h][3] not[e] announcing the reestablishment of the constitution of 1812. is decidedly to that effect. In terms very distinct, tho' sufficiently kind, he regrets the want of firmness & energy in the king of Spain, which he seems to anticipate will be productive of much mischief.

with great respect & regard yours   JAMES MONROE

RC (DLC); dateline at foot of text; edge torn; mistakenly endorsed by TJ as a letter of 20 Aug. 1820 written at "Highlands."

The MAN OF WHOM Monroe had heard TJ SPEAK LATELY was William Bain. SUITE in this sense means a "sequel, result" (*OED*).

The REPLY issued by the Russian government in the spring of 1820 in response to Ferdinand VII's acceptance of the liberal Spanish constitution of 1812 was published widely in the United States: "Constantly animated by the desire of seeing the prosperity of the state and the glory of the Sovereign maintaining themselves and flourishing together in Spain, his Majesty the Emperor could not, without profound affliction, learn the events which have occasioned the official note . . . nothing can justify the aggressions which deliver up the destinies of the country to a violent crisis. Too often have similar disorders announced days of sor-

row for empires. . . . Institutions which emanate from thrones are conservatory; but if they spring amidst troubles, they only engender a new chaos. In declaring his conviction on this point, the Emperor only speaks according to the lessons of experience. . . . It now belongs to the Government of the Peninsula to judge whether institutions imposed by one of those violent acts (the fatal patrimony of the revolution against which Spain had struggled with so much honor) can realize the benefits which both the worlds expect from the wisdom of his most Catholic Majesty, and the patriotism of his councils," with Spain's future actions to "determine the nature of the relations which his Imperial Majesty will preserve with the Spanish Government" (*American Beacon and Norfolk & Portsmouth Daily Advertiser*, 16 Sept. 1820, and elsewhere).

[1] Manuscript: "garderner."
[2] Word illegible.
[3] Word interlined.

From John Sanderson

SIR,   Philad^a Augst 19th 1820

I have taken the liberty of addressing to you the title page, & some specimens of a work I have just put to press in Philad^a—A copy of which I shall convey to you, entire, as the numbers or half vol^s are completed. The first will be published in a few weeks, & the others successively, at entervals of six months. The whole will probably be contained in ten no^s—

I wished very much to consult you on the subject of this publication before the present time, & especially to request from you some notice of Mr Geo. Wythe; but from the respect which I felt was due to that repose so long sacrificed to the interests of others, I abstained from it. On a nearer view, however, of the difficulty, the importance &

sacredness of the task I have undertaken; I now venture to solicit your attention & advice.—I might have addressd you on this subject through the intervention of one of your friends, but have chosen rather to rely upon the usual benevolence with which you have at all times patronized the literary[1] attempts of your countrymen, for my recommendation.—

I am at present collecting whatever incidents are within my reach of the life of M[r] Hancock, whose biography with the Introduction is designed for the first number. In describing the character of those to whom we are indebted for the best of all human blessings, I feel urged by my warmest inclinations as[2] well as interests to use no expressions unworthy of them; I need not, therefore, declare to you the gratitude I should owe to your kindness for any information, (& particularly of M[r] Hancock) that may promote interests of an undertaking, for which I feel at present[3] the most anxious & religious solicitude.

With great respect, I have the honor to be, Sir, <u>Your Most Obt. Svt.</u>

JOHN SANDERSON

RC (DLC); between dateline and salutation and repeated adjacent to closing: "Thos. Jefferson Esq[r]"; endorsed by TJ as received 23 Aug. 1820 and so recorded in SJL.

John Sanderson (ca. 1783–1844), educator and author, was born near Carlisle, Pennsylvania, and schooled privately by tutors. Although he moved to Philadelphia during the first decade of the nineteenth century in order to study law, by 1811 he had joined John T. Carré in a pedagogical partnership that would last until at least 1822. When Sanderson was not teaching classics, the English language, and French literature, he wrote prolifically for both newspapers and periodicals. In addition, between 1820 and 1822 he edited and saw into print the first two volumes of the *Biography of the Signers to the Declaration of Independence*, a project that was completed by others later that decade and totaled nine volumes (Philadelphia, 1820–27; Poor, *Jefferson's Library*, 5 [no. 152]). Sanderson took a break from teaching in 1835 and went on a year-long trip to France. Drawing on this sojourn, he produced *Sketches of Paris: in Familiar Letters to His Friends* (1838), which went through several editions over the next decade under the variant title of *The American in Paris*. After his return

from Europe, Sanderson was elected to the American Philosophical Society in 1840 and taught Greek, Latin, English, and belles lettres at the Central High School of Philadelphia from the same year until his death in that city (*DAB*; Peter S. Du Ponceau to TJ, 3 Jan. 1821; *Clermont Seminary. . . . Disciplinary Rules to be strictly observed in Said Seminary* [Philadelphia, 1811]; *Baltimore Patriot & Mercantile Advertiser*, 8 Sept. 1817; *The Philadelphia Directory and Register, for 1822* [Philadelphia, 1822]; Robert Desilver, *The Philadelphia Index, or Directory, for 1823* [(Philadelphia, 1823)]; *Desilver's Philadelphia Directory and Stranger's Guide, 1830* [1830], 168; APS, Minutes, 17 July 1840 [MS in PPAmP]; Franklin Spencer Edmonds, *History of the Central High School of Philadelphia* [1902], 53–4; Philadelphia *North American and Daily Advertiser*, 6 Apr. 1844; gravestone inscription in Presbyterian Cemetery, Pottsville, Pa.).

Sanderson's profiles of George WYTHE and John HANCOCK appeared in the second and first volumes, respectively, of the *Biography of the Signers*.

[1] Manuscript: "literay."
[2] Manuscript: "&."
[3] Manuscript: "presnt."

Jared Sparks's Account of a Visit to Monticello

[19–20 Aug. 1820]

But one of the greatest curiosities I met with was Thomas Jefferson. Whether you will call this a natural or an artificial curiosity, I am puzzled to know. At all events, I went to see him at the exhibition-house at Monticello, up a long hill, which is almost daily trod by many a weary pilgrim's foot. I was very kindly received and politely treated; and I think there are very few persons who would not feel inclined to say at once, that this is no common man. He bears the marks of age, but his mind is vigorous, excursive, and quick. His college is no less curious than himself. It consists of twelve large buildings, and many smaller ones, and together they form incomparably the most beautiful specimens of architecture in this country.

Printed in Herbert B. Adams, *The Life and Writings of Jared Sparks* (1893), 1:173, and there described as an extract of a letter from Sparks to Ann Gillam Storrow, dated Baltimore, 10 Oct. 1820; timing of Sparks's visit deduced from his delivery to Monticello on 19 Aug. 1820 of letters of introduction from John Hollins of 4 Aug. and John Vaughan of 5 Aug. 1820, and his note of 20 Aug. 1820 accepting TJ's invitation to dinner.

A portrait of Sparks is reproduced elsewhere in this volume.

From Jared Sparks

Charlottesville Aug. 20.

Mr. Sparks accepts with pleasure Mr. Jefferson's invitation to dinner at 3 oclock. His friend and travelling companion, Mr. Steell of Baltimore will accompany him.

RC (NNPM); partially dated; dateline at foot of text; addressed: "Thomas Jefferson. Esqr. Montecello"; endorsed by TJ as a letter of 20 Aug. 1820.

From Thomas Cooper

DEAR SIR   Aug. 21. 1820

I thank you for your friendly letter. I hope to go by land to Carolina & to be there, about the middle of Octr. Mrs Cooper takes my family by sea in November.

I think if Messrs Eppes & Baker are at Columbia by the beginning of the second week of Octr it will be quite soon enough. Nulty cannot be elected till the meeting of the Trustees, when the Legislature meet. They[1] (Mess. E & B.)[2] will not gain much during the interval from the present mathematical tutor.

We have had about 50 Cases of malignant or yellow fever in this city: but it is local or endemic: in no case & in no sense epidemic or even sporadic. It has been communicated from its habitat to Persons, but not in any instance that I know of, from Person to Person. One case only has occurred within the last 2 days.

I remain with all kindness, and sincere respect

Dear sir Your friend and Servant   Thomas Cooper

RC (MHi); endorsed by TJ as received 26 Aug. 1820 from Philadelphia and so recorded in SJL. RC (MHi); address cover only; with PoC of TJ to Bernard Peyton, [3] Oct. 1821, on verso; addressed: "Thomas Jefferson Esq Montecello Virginia"; franked; postmarked Philadelphia, 21 Aug.

Hugh McMillan was the PRESENT MATHEMATICAL TUTOR at South Carolina College (later the University of South Carolina) (Maximilian LaBorde, *History of the South Carolina College* [1874], 528).

[1] Manuscript: "Thiy."
[2] Parenthetical phrase interlined.

From David Gelston

Dear Sir,   New York August 21st 1820—

It gave me much pleasure this morning, to receive your letter of the 13th from which I infer you enjoy good health—the two letters enclosed will be forwarded the very first good opportunity, which will probably offer in a few days.—

I also this morning received by the Comet, from Havre, a letter from Mr Beasley, enclosing bill of lading for a bale of books for you, which I shall ship to Richmond by the first good conveyance, after I have the means of ascertaining the duty, probably the invoice may be forwarded to you—

with very great respect & esteem,—I am; Dear Sir, your obedient servant,   David Gelston

RC (MHi); at foot of text: "Thomas Jefferson Esquire"; endorsed by TJ as received 25 Aug. 1820, but recorded in SJL as received a day later.

On 22 Aug. 1820 Gelston paid Griswolds & Coates, the New York firm that owned the *Comet*, two dollars for transporting A BALE OF BOOKS for TJ from Le Havre plus twenty cents for primage ("a charge to cover the cost of loading or unloading a ship" [*OED*]) (MS receipt in MHi; written in an unidentified hand on a small scrap; with notation at foot of text indicating that W. Hall Jr. had received payment on behalf of Griswolds & Coates).

From James Maxwell

Philadelphia August 23rd 1820
Your subscription to the "Analectic Magazine"[1] being due, according to the terms in June, I beg leave to remind you of the same and to request that a remittance of the amount $6.00 May be made by Mail or Otherwise

Very respectfully your &c &c   JAS MAXWELL

RC (MHi); addressed: "Thomas Jefferson Esqr Monticello Virga"; stamp canceled; franked; postmarked Philadelphia, 23 Aug.; endorsed by TJ as received 30 Aug. 1820 (with his additional notation: "6") and so recorded (with additional bracketed notation: "analect. mag.") in SJL.

James Maxwell (b. ca. 1788), printer and bookseller, plied his trade in Philadelphia from 1810 until 1831. During this period he printed, among other works, the *Analectic Magazine*, 1815–20, and inexpensive editions of Sir Walter Scott's novels. Maxwell relocated by 1832 to Louisville, Kentucky, where he still resided in 1844. He owned two slaves in 1840 (DNA: RG 29, CS, Pa., Philadelphia, 1810–30, Ky., Louisville, 1840; James

Robinson, *The Philadelphia Directory, for 1810* [(Philadelphia, 1810)], 191; Edward Whitely, *The Philadelphia Directory and Register, for 1820* [(Philadelphia, 1820)]; Philadelphia *Poulson's American Daily Advertiser*, 1 Jan. 1820; Philadelphia *National Gazette and Literary Register*, 17 June, 22 Nov. 1820; *Desilver's Philadelphia Directory, and Strangers' Guide. 1831* [1831], 142; William Prescott, *The Prescott Memorial: or a Genealogical Memoir of the Prescott Families in America* [1870], 111; *The Louisville Directory, for the year 1832* [1832], 54; *Haldeman's Picture of Louisville, Directory and Business Advertiser, for 1844–1845* [1844], 297).

[1] Omitted closing quotation mark editorially supplied.

From James Monroe

DEAR SIR   Augt 23. 1820.
I return you the extract which you were so kind as to give me the perusal of, with an assurance of my thorough conviction that it cannot fail to have a good effect. The sentiments expressd in favor of an American interest & policy, extended in the first instance to the preservation of order, along our coast, & in our seas, are sound, and will in all probability ripen into a system, at no distant period. The destiny however of this western world depends on the continued prosperity & success of this portion of it. If the European, has more wisdom & energy, than the African, or Asiatick, I am satisfied that the citizens of this Republick, have in like proportion, more, & for the same causes, than the inhabitants of any other portion of this hemisphere, not excepting those, or their descendants, who emigrated from other countries, than that, from which we took our origin.

The only danger attending a close connection with Portugal, or rather[1] Brazil, is that which I suggested to you yesterday. Our union at this time against pirates, would be represented, by some, as an union, against the Colonies, since unfortunately all the piracies, if not connivd at by them, as I verily believe they are not, proceed from that quarter. Portugal would of course turn it to her account in that way, using it as an instrument to prop her up against a revol[u]tionary movment, which must overwhel[m] her with the others. The project of such an union will produce, as I presume, a good effect with the present gov^t of Brazil, but it can never take effect with any but the revolutionary gov^ts, of S° America.

very respectfully & affectionately yours   JAMES MONROE

RC (DLC); edge torn; endorsed by TJ as received 23 Aug. 1820 and so recorded (with the additional notation: "High-lands") in SJL. Enclosure: extract from TJ to William Short, 4 Aug. 1820.

[1] Manuscript: "tather."

To Henry Orne

Monticello Aug. 25. 20.

I thank you, Sir, for the pamphlet you were so good as to send me, with your letter of July 12. and still more for the kindness towards myself with which you have been pleased to express yourself. if I have been[1] able to be of any use to my fellow citizens, it is amply remunerated by such assurances of their satisfaction & approbation. for their long continuance in the spirit of freedom I have no fear[.] for their continuance in union and love of one another I do sincerely pray. to yourself I tender the assurances of my esteem and respect.

TH: JEFFERSON

PoC (MHi); on verso of reused address cover to TJ; edge trimmed; at foot of text: "Mr Henry Orne"; endorsed by TJ.

[1] Manuscript: "bein."

To Louis H. Girardin

DEAR SIR   Monticello Aug. 26. 20.

Your favor of the 16th with the 2. vols of Botta are safely recieved, and I am much pleased to learn that you still contemplate the completion of your history of Virginia. the sale of the 1st vol. was undoubtedly damped by the wretched style of paper and print in which it was published: and I cannot but believe that, with more attention to this, the entire work compleated would ultimately remunerate the cost and labor of the work.

if the misfortunes of Baltimore have not too much reduced the means of education, I should suppose the situation proposed to you there would be tempting both as to honor & emolument. I shall be happy to hear if you find it so. mr Fuller's views of a bookstore in Charlottesville have not been anticipated by any other. but as yet it would be premature. the grammar school there will shortly I think break up; and the epoch of opening our university is still quite uncertain.

I observe your inclination to print a quarterly paper in Latin. I very much doubt it's success. periodical papers are generally taken up for light reading, which would not be the character of a Latin paper. men of science would probably read it for the novelty: but these are few, and so scattered over the whole surface of the union, that their subscriptions could never be collected. but be this or whatever other the pursuit you adopt, with my sincere wishes for your success, accept the assurance of my great esteem & respect.   TH JEFFERSON

RC (PPAmP: Thomas Jefferson Papers); with internal address and signature added separately to RC and PoC; addressed: "Mʳ L. H. Girardin Hermitage near Staunton"; franked; postmarked Charlottesville, 29 Aug. PoC (MHi); on verso of portion of a reused address cover from Fernagus De Gelone to TJ; edge trimmed; endorsed by TJ.

To Charles Willson Peale

DEAR SIR   Monticello Aug. 26. 20.

I ought sooner to have thanked you for your sketch of the Court of death, which we have all contemplated with great approbation of the composition and design. it presents to the eye more morality than many written volumes, and with impressions much more durable and indelible. I have been sensible that the scriptural paintings in the Catholic churches produce deeper impressions on the people generally than they recieve from reading the books themselves. with much more good to others,[1] I hope mr Rembrandt Peale will recieve for himself not only the future fame he is destined to acquire, but immediate and just compensation and comfort for the present: for I sincerely wish prosperity and happiness to you and all yours.

TH: JEFFERSON

PoC (DLC); at foot of text: "C. W. Peale esq."; endorsed by TJ. Printed in New York *National Advocate*, 19 Dec. 1820, and elsewhere.

[1] Preceding clause attached to previous sentence in *National Advocate*.

To Thomas B. Robertson

Your favor of July 28. was recieved two days ago, and I sincerely congratulate you on the high testimony given by your fellow citizens of their sense of your merit, which I hope has been confirmed by the legislature. I rejoice in it the more as education, I believe, has been too much neglected by your native citizens, and it's ameliorating effects will not be lost on some of their new-comers. this subject I observe as of the first importance, has attracted your first attentions: and my views of it, which you ask, will be best explained by the Report I inclose you, of what has been proposed here. your other enquiries I can answer conjecturally only. our institution was at first proposed merely as a local one, founded on private subscriptions of about 50,000.D. under the name of the Central college. the legislatu[re] afterwards adopted it for their University, and endowed it wit[h] 15,000.D. a year. at the close of the last year, we had expended about 70. or 80.M.D. on the buildings; and the legislature authorised us to borrow 60,000.D. more on the hypothecation of our annuity. with this aid we have made contracts which will ensure the completion of all the buildings for the accomodation of the Professors & student[s] by the autumn of the next year. if we are left to repay the loan from our own funds, the buildings will be shut up for five years. but we think with confidence that the legislature,[1] at their next session will not only take the debt of our buildings off ou[r] hands, but add a sum of 40.M.D. necessary to build our library. in this case our annuity will be liberated on the 1st day of January next, and will enable us to take immediate measures for engaging professors, which we hope to do, & to have them in place by autumn or winter of the next year. being determined to accept of no Professor who is not of the first order of science in his line, we shall have to procure most of them from the other side of the Atlantic, where we must acknolege they are far ahead of us in science. by sending thither a competent agent; and engaging for him the advice and aid, of characters on the spot, on whose zeal and knolege of the ground, we know we can count, we have no doubt of being inabled to open an institution, inferior certainly to none in America, and such as may command European respect. with regard to expences they will be moderate. board in our neighborhood is about 10.D. a month exclusive of fire, candles, washing and bedding. tuition fees will be high, say probably from 30. to 50.D. a year to each professor attended, supposing them not more than two at a time. but this is only what is talked of, but not fixed. we shall be gratified if our

Southern and Western brethren should find a convenience in this establishment, and none of them will be recieved with more cordial welcome than our friends from the state of Orleans: who possess my warmest wishes for their general prosperity and my special congratulations that, by your election, they have taken the first step towards entering on the path of science. to yourself I tender sincere [sentime]nts of friendship & respect. TH: JEFFERSON

PoC (DLC); edge trimmed; mutilated at seal, with two words rewritten by TJ; at foot of first page: "T. B. Robertson esq."; endorsed by TJ. Enclosure: *Proceedings and Report of the Commissioners for the University of Virginia. Presented Decem-* *ber 8, 1818* (Richmond, 1818; Poor, *Jefferson's Library*, 6 [no. 233]).

STATE OF ORLEANS: Louisiana.

[1] Manuscript: "legislatiure."

From Samuel Smith (of Maryland)

Dᴿ SIR   Baltimore 26. Aug. 1820

I have had the honor to receive your very friendly letter, and I pray you to accept my sincere thanks for your good wishes.—My health since my last has been declining. my mind naturally active, & heretofore kept Constantly employed, is left for want of occupation to prey on itself.—and the consequence must be serious.—I was in a similar State when I went last Winter to Congress—from which I was relieved by the incessant labour incident to my situation as Chairman of the Ways & Means—

I take it for granted that Mʳ Forsyth will remain some time longer at Madrid, and I hope he may be able to induce Spain to relieve our flour from the present prohibitory duty. a similar duty exists in Portugal. the loss of those two markets, (which we formerly supplied) is very severely felt by our farmers. the fact is, there are no longer any substantive Markets for our flour, and the nominal price is $4.50 without demand.—France is now the best market, but our late law levying a tonnage duty of $18 on French ships deterrs the ships of the U.S. from adventuring to French Ports.—England will not want our Grain, yet Flour actually goes to Liverpool & is transported thence to all the W. Indies.—the loss of double transport is paid by our farmers.

Mʳ Rush will remain in Engᵈ until he shall be elected Governor of Pennsᵃ when Findlay's time has expired, that attempt is contemplated.—In the mean time he lives in retirement out of the City.—Mʳ Gallatin[1] consented reluctantly to remain another year for the purpose of completing a Commercial treaty. he will leave France next May. I should doubt whether the salary & Outfit[2] would meet the expenses of that Court longer than two years—I would be glad to have it, but I have some Idea, that the mission will be filled by a Gentleman in whom a deep interest is felt, and if So, I would not on any Account interfere— I am D sir

your friend sincerely & truly   S. SMITH

RC (DLC); endorsed by TJ as received 1 Sept. 1820 and so recorded in SJL. RC (DLC); address cover only; with PoC of TJ to Benjamin A. Gould, 25 Sept. [1821], on verso; addressed: "Thomas Jefferson Monticello near Charlotteville V^a"; stamped; postmarked Baltimore, 26 Aug.

The LATE LAW was the 15 May 1820 "Act to impose a new tonnage duty on French ships and vessels" (*U.S. Statutes at Large*, 3:605).

[1] Smith here canceled "agreed."
[2] Preceding two words interlined.

To Thomas Cooper

DEAR SIR   Monticello Aug. 27.[1] 20.

I recieved yesterday your favor of the 21. and am glad to learn that you will return to Columbia by land; in which case I hope you will take this in your way, and to prevent disappointment I must state to you my movements.

Sep.   6. I shall set out to Poplar Forest.
        24. I shall be at home.
Oct.   4. the Visitors of the University meet.
        11. I shall return to Poplar Forest to stay till winter.

as you propose to be at Columbia about the middle of October, it will bring you here in the interval of my being at home, and if your movements require it I can without inconvenience delay my departure of Oct. 11. to any later time.

You mention that mr Nulty cannot be appointed until the trustees meet. when will that be?   my grandson & his relation have been lately told that Columbia is pestiferously unhealthy, that it is on a peninsul nearly surrounded by the river and it's low grounds. as I had ever understood it to be in a hilly, healthy country, I give no ear to this information: but to satisfy mr Eppes (the father) I will thank you for information; and if put into the mail immediately, it may get here before my departure. I salute you with constant friendship and respect.   TH: JEFFERSON

PoC (DLC); at foot of text: "Doct^r Cooper"; endorsed by TJ.

[1] Reworked from "20."

To John Wayles Eppes

DEAR SIR   Monticello Aug. 27. 20

Yours of the 19th was received on the 25th. what it proposes on the subject of the stock is perfectly agreeable to me; but I shall be glad to recieve the proceeds as soon as they can be had, that I may the sooner relieve myself from the applications of those to whom it is destined, and them from the want of it.

Our court is Monday sennight (Sep. 4.) and I see nothing to prevent my setting out the 2d day after to Poplar Forest, and shall certainly go viâ Millbrook where I presume we may be about the 7th or 8th. ever & affectionately your's   TH: JEFFERSON

PoC (MHi); on verso of portion of reused address cover of Caesar A. Rodney to TJ, 19 Dec. 1819; at foot of text: "J. W. Eppes esq."; endorsed by TJ.

To David Gelston

DEAR SIR   Monticello Aug. 27. 20.

I recieved last night your favor of the 21st and at the same time an invoice of the books from Debure, cost[1] 180. ƒ charges 11–50 making 191–50 ƒ which invoice I now inclose you with a request of it's return, with notice of the duties and charges for which I shall be your debtor. the sum being too small to be remitted by a draught, I will inclose it in a bank bill with an allowance for their discount at N. York. I shall be thankful to you to forward the books to Richmond either to mr Gibson, or to Capt Bernard Peyton, who, during the long illness of mr Gibson, has done business for me occasionally. I salute you with great esteem and respect.   TH: JEFFERSON

RC (Grace Floyd Delafield Robinson, Greenport, N.Y., 1947); addressed: "David Gelston esq. New York"; franked; postmarked Charlottesville, 29 Aug.; endorsed by Gelston, with his additional notation at foot of text: "sep 1—pd 5\frac{55}{100}$

" pd fret— 2.20 7\frac{75}{100}$." PoC (MHi);

on verso of portion of reused address cover; mutilated at seal; endorsed by TJ. Enclosure: enclosure to de Bure Frères to TJ, 26 June 1820.

[1]RC: "cost <19>," with number not canceled in PoC.

To Henry Guegan

SIR   Monticello Aug. 27. 20.

I recieved from mr Negrin, a watchmaker settled lately in the neighboring village of Charlottesville, a 4ᵗᵒ printed leaf entitled 'Catalogue of Latin and Greek books,' which he says are to be sold at your foreign bookstore in Baltimore. among these I observe the following noted with their prices.

pa. 2. col. 1. Persoon Synopsis plantarum 2. v. 12ᵐᵒ 3.D.

   col. 2. Thesauri lenguae Groecae 5. v. fol. vel. bound. 28 D. if
    this is Stephani Thesaurus linguae Graecae I will take it.
    Vossii Etymologicon. fol. bound. 4.D.
    Xenophontis. 5. 8ᵛᵒ 3.50. if this be of all the works of
    Xenophon, I will take it.

there is a Longinus Gr. & E. 12ᵐᵒ translated in Baltimore & printed there which if you will add to the above I shall be obliged to you. I will either pay the amount to mr Negrin, or remit it to you by mail as you shall direct. pack the books very securely if you please and send them by water to Richmond addressed to me to the care of mr Gibson merchᵗ of that place, which will be the same as if delivered to myself. I shall be from home from the 6ᵗʰ to the 24ᵗʰ of the next month which I mention to account to you for any delay in my answer which may happen: and I [sa]lute you with respect.   TH JEFFERSON.

PoC (MHi); on verso of reused address cover to TJ; two lines rewritten by TJ due to polygraph misalignment; damaged at seal, with three words rewritten by TJ; at foot of text: "M. Henry Guigam"; endorsed by TJ as a letter to "Guigan Henry" and so recorded in SJL.

Henry Guegan (Louis Henri Guégan) (ca. 1793–1842), bookseller and educator, was a native of Guémené, in the French region of Brittany. He served in Napoleon's army for several years, and he wrote and in 1818 published in Paris two short works on tachygraphy, or shorthand. Guegan immigrated to the United States in January 1819 and settled in Baltimore shortly thereafter. By early in 1820 he had established a "FOREIGN BOOKSTORE" in that city, with a satellite operation on Pennsylvania Avenue in Washington, D.C. Guegan moved permanently within a year or two to the nation's capital, where he sold books, engravings, stationery, and some food items until around 1825. By that point he had embarked on a career as a teacher of the French language, taking private students and teaching at various schools in Alexandria, Georgetown, and Washington from 1823 until at least 1838. To aid him in his educational endeavors, he authored *A Compendious and Easy Grammar for Teaching and Learning the French Language*, which was printed in Washington in 1831 (DNA: RG 21, NPM; René Havette, *Bibliographie de la Sténographie Française* [1906], 93; Washington *Daily National Intelligencer*, 18 Mar. 1820, 6 Apr. 1821, 9 Apr., 11 Oct., 9 Dec. 1823, 19 Mar. 1825, 27 Aug. 1827, 7 Oct. 1829, 23 Apr. 1832, 6 Apr. 1835, 3 Dec. 1838, 8 Oct. 1842).

VEL.: "vellum."

To Thomas Ewell

Dear Sir   Monticello Aug. 28. 20.

Your letter of the 7th came to hand on the 14th and I kept up the one it inclosed until I could have a favorable opportunity of presenting it to the President. on delivering it, I took occasion to go into such explanations as I thought might do you justice, and manifest my own views and wishes. I found him in the best dispositions towards yourself; but cautious, as was proper, not to commit himself where other interests & opinions ought also to be attended to. yet so far as these may not justly overweigh predispositions in your favor, I think you may count on his friendly will. I learn with real regret the situation to which you have been reduced by unfavorable incidents, and shall be sincerely gratified by success in the resources to which your views are now turned; being with sincere esteem and respect

Your friend and serv[t]   TH: JEFFERSON

PoC (DLC); at foot of text: "D[r] Thomas Ewell"; endorsed by TJ. Ewell's letter OF THE 7TH, not found, is recorded in SJL as received 14 Aug. 1820 from Washington. The ONE IT IN-CLOSED is also missing.

From Francis Adrian Van der Kemp

Dear and respected Sir.   Montezillo 28 Aug. 1820

Confident, that it Shall be gratifying to you, to receive an answer on your favour of July 9—written under the hospitable roof of our honoured friend, I indulge in the pleasure of Sending you a few lines. My inducement to this was So much the greater, as I found mr. Adams enjoying a large Share of health in body and mind—the latter equal, the former far Superior, than what he enjoyd Seven years past,—the trembling of his hands excepted. His Steps are yet firm, more So than mine—his conversation is animated—So that he is listened to with marked attention by his Surrounding friends—and he Seems to forget that he is 85—otherwise his memory is yet great, So that I heard him detail with exactness minutiæ with which I had been partially acquainted for forty years. It did give my friend a Sensible pleasure, when I communicated to Him, how he was remembered in your last Letter. and he hoped, I Should answer it from Montezillo—

His partiality towards me continues to procure me the affectionate regards of many, whom otherwise I must have passed unnoticed when I am warned by their renewed[1] attentions not to indulge too much in feelings, by which I might become elated and then even it might in part be excusable, or deemed So at least, when known—that a Jefferson and Adams took Such a warm interest in my health and happiness—

Have you Seen the publications of michael Majo from the Vatican Library—Fronto—Cicero de Rep—the lost Books &c—Some of these are arrived at Boston—or rather I ought to Say Cambridge—I flatter myself with the prospect that our travelling, learned and wealthy Americans Shall obtain a full Share in the discoveries—yet to be made in the immense Libraries in Italy and Germany—and delightful Sensations would be created, if returning with these treasures to Columbia's Strand—these blessings were from here Scattered over Europe.

But I hear preparations for breakfast—I ought not to prolong my intrusion, only you will, I know it, permit me the earnest Solicitation, for your continued remembrance—while I assure that I remain with unabated respect

Your obliged—   FR. ADR. VANDER KEMP

RC (DLC); dateline at foot of text; endorsed by TJ as received 6 Sept. 1820 and so recorded in SJL.

The Vatican librarian Angelo Mai (Maio) (MICHAEL MAJO) is best known for his discovery and publication of a num-

ber of classical texts, including the letters of the Roman lawyer and grammarian Marcus Cornelius FRONTO and Cicero's *De Re Publica* (DE REP).

[1] Manuscript: "rnewed."

From Daniel Humphreys

SIR,   Portsmouth NH. August 30th 1820

Permit me to tender to your acceptance the enclosed short piece; not as being worth your acceptance, but as a small token of <u>a respect, neither small, nor of a late date.</u>

The attempt originated from the following question.

Is it not practicable to abridge the labour of men of Study, who commit much to writing for their own after inspection; and may not this be done without any heavy tax on the memory?

Having been deterred by the apparent labour, from learning a shorthand, and afterward having partially learned, & practised <u>more</u> than one sort, and discontinued them; after some efforts, I fell upon the one I have the honour to present to you, & have used it for some time.

If it may be considered as affording a <u>proper opportunity</u> of testifying <u>a respect where due</u>, one valuable purpose <u>at least</u>, will be attained. I have the Honor to be

with much regard & best wishes Your obed[t] Hum[e] Ser[vt]

DAN[L] HUMPHREYS

[226]

RC (DLC); endorsed by TJ as received 24 Sept. 1820 and so recorded in SJL. RC (DLC); address cover only; with PoC of TJ to William Wallace, 19 Aug. 1821, on verso; addressed: "The Honourable Mʳ Jefferson late President of the United States of America at his Seat Monticello"; franked; postmarked Portsmouth, N.H., 31 Aug.

Daniel Humphreys (1740–1827), attorney and elder brother of the soldier and diplomat David Humphreys, was born in Derby, Connecticut. He graduated from Yale College (later Yale University) in 1757 and was admitted to the bar at New Haven a few years later. Although Humphreys moved in 1770 to Portsmouth, New Hampshire, he spent most of the Revolutionary War in New Haven teaching grammar and literature. At the end of the conflict he returned to Portsmouth, where he reestablished his legal practice. Humphreys served as United States district attorney for New Hampshire, 1804–27. He was described a decade prior to his death as "poor" and entirely dependent for support "on the

emoluments of that office." An early and lifelong convert to Sandemanianism, a sect that opposed any connection between church and state and advocated a return to primitive Christianity, Humphreys issued a number of works on religion. He also published *The Compendious American Grammar, or Grammatical Institutes in Verse* (Portsmouth, 1792). Humphreys died in Portsmouth (Samuel Orcutt and Ambrose Beardsley, *The History of the Old Town of Derby, Connecticut, 1642–1880* [1880], 735–6; Dexter, *Yale Biographies*, 2:471–4; *Catalogue of the Officers and Graduates of Yale University . . . 1701–1910* [1910], 64; DNA: RG 29, CS, N.H., Portsmouth, 1790–1810; *PTJ*, 43:355n, 506, 680; *JEP*, 1:471, 473, 3:234, 248, 353, 358 [12, 20 Nov. 1804, 15 Jan., 26 Feb. 1821, 8, 20 Jan. 1824]; William Plumer to James Monroe, 11 Dec. 1818 [DNA: RG 59, LAR, 1817–25]; Portsmouth *New-Hampshire Gazette*, 2 Oct. 1827).

The ENCLOSED SHORT PIECE on a new form of SHORTHAND has not been found and does not seem to have been published.

From Thomas Cooper

Dᴿ SIR   Aug. 31. 1820

When I can be at Monticello I cannot yet determine. I attend to your movements. I write to say, that Columbia is situated on a Sand bank. One mile from the River, & 200 feet above it. I believe it to be as healthy, as any place in the Union, if I can judge from what I have seen of the place, & the uniform testimony of its most respectable Inhabitants.

The situation impressed me with the common opinion concerning it, or I wᵈ never have consented to remove my family there.

I believe you may rely on this general accᵗ of the place. With affectionate esteem

I remain   Dear sir Yʳ friend   THOˢ COOPER

RC (MHi); endorsed by TJ as received 24 (reworked from 20) Sept. 1820 from Philadelphia and so recorded in SJL. RC (DLC); address cover only; with PoC of TJ to James Hamilton (1786–

1857), 9 Sept. 1821, on verso; addressed: "Thomas Jefferson Esq Montecello Virginia"; franked; postmarked Philadelphia, 31 Aug.

To John Sanderson

Monticello Aug. 31. 20.

Your letter of the 19th was recieved in due time, and I wish it were in my power to furnish you more fully, than in the inclosed paper, with materials for the biography of George Wythe. but I possess none in writing, am very distant from the place of his birth and early life, and know not a single person in that quarter from whom enquiry could be made with the expectation of collecting any thing material. add to this that feeble health disables me almost from writing, and entirely from the labor of going into difficult research. I became acquainted with mr Wythe when he was about 35. years of age. he directed my studies in the law, led me into business, and continued until death my most affectionate friend. a close intimacy with him during that period of forty odd years, the most important of his life, enables me to state it's leading facts, which being of my own knolege, I vouch their truth. of what precedes that period I speak from hearsay only, in which there may be error, but of little account, as the character of the facts will themselves manifest. in the epoch of his birth I may err a little, stating that from the recollection of a particular incident, the date of which, within a year or two, I do not distinctly remember. these scanty outlines you will be able I hope, to fill up from other information, and they may serve you sometimes as landmarks to distinguish truth from error, in what you hear from others. the exalted virtue of the man will also be a polar star to guide you in all matters which may touch that element of his character. but on that you will recieve imputation from no man; for, as far as I knew, he never had an enemy.[1]

Little as I am able to contribute to the just reputation of this excellent man, it is the act of my life most gratifying to my heart: & leaves me only to regret that a waining memory can do no more.

Of mr Hancock I can say nothing, having known him only as in the chair of Congress. having myself been the youngest man, but one, in that body, the disparity of age prevented any particular intimacy. but of him there can be no difficulty in obtaining full information in the North.

I salute you, Sir, with sentiments of great respect.

Th: Jefferson

RC (ICN: Thomas Jefferson Letters); addressed: "M[r] John Sanderson Philadelphia"; franked; postmarked Charlottesville, 5 Sept.; endorsed by Joseph M. Sanderson. PoC (DLC); edge trimmed. Enclosure: TJ's Notes for a Biography of George Wythe, [ca. 31 Aug. 1820].

Edward Rutledge (1749–1800) was the only ONE in the Second Continental Congress younger than TJ during his tenure, 1775–76 (*ANB*).

[1] Omitted period supplied from PoC.

Notes for a Biography of George Wythe

[ca. 31 Aug. 1820]

Notes for the biography of George Wythe.

George Wythe was born about the year 1727. or 1728. of a respectable family in the county of Elizabeth city on the shores of the Chesapeak.

he inherited from his father a fortune sufficient for independance & ease.

he had not the benefit of a regular education in the schools, but acquired a good one of himself, and without assistance; insomuch as to become the best Latin and Greek scholar in the state. it is said that while reading the Greek testament his mother held an English one to aid him in rendering the Greek text conformably with that. he also acquired by his own reading a good knolege of Mathematics, of natural and moral philosophy.

he engaged in the study of the law under the direction of a mr Lewis of that profession, and went early to the bar of the General court, then occupied by men of great ability, learning & dignity in their profession.

he soon became eminent among them, and, in process of time, the first at the bar, taking into consideration his superior learning, correct elocution, and logical style of reasoning. for in pleading he never indulged himself with an useless or declamatory thought or word; and became as distinguished by correctness and purity of conduct in his profession, as he was by his industry & fidelity to those who employed him.

he was early elected to the House of representatives, then called the House of Burgesses, and continued in it until the revolution.   on the first dawn of that, instead of higgling on halfway principles, as others did who feared to follow their reason, he took his stand on the solid ground that the only link of political union between us and Great Britain was the identity of our Executive; that that nation and it's parliament had no more authority over us than we had over them, and that we were co-ordinate nations with Great Britain and Hanover.

in 1774. he was a member of a Committee of the H. of Burgesses, appointed to prepare a Petition to the king, Memorial to the H. of Lords, and a Remonstrance to the H. of Commons, on the subject of the proposed stamp act. he was made draughtsman[1] of the last, and following his own principles, he so far overwent the timid hesitations of his colleagues that his draught was subjected by them to material modifications. and, when the famous resolutions of mr Henry, in 1775. were proposed, it was not on any difference of principle that they were opposed by Wythe, Randolph, Pendleton, Nicholas, Bland and other worthies, who had long been the habitual leaders of the House; but because those papers of the preceding session had already expressed the same sentiments and assertions of right, and that an answer to them was yet to be expected.

In Aug. 1775. he was appointed a member of Congress, and in 1776. signed the Declaration of Independance, of which he had, in debate, been an eminent supporter. and subsequently in the same year he was appointed, by the legislature of Virginia, one of a Committee to revise the laws of the state, as well of British, as of colonial enactment, and to prepare bills for reenacting them with such alterations as the change in the form and principles of the[2] government, and other circumstances required: and of this work he executed the period commencing with the revolution in England, and ending with the establishment of the new government here;[3] excepting the Acts for regulating descents, for religious freedom, and for proportioning crimes & punishments.

In 1777. he was chosen Speaker of the H. of Delegates, being of distinguished learning in Parliamentary law and proceedings; and towards the end of the same year he was appointed one of the three Chancellors to whom that department of the Judiciary was confided, on the first organisation of the new government. on a subsequent change of the form of that court, he was appointed sole Chancellor in which office he continued to act until his death which happened in June 1806. about the 78th or 79th year of his age.

M[r] Wythe had been twice married, first, I believe to a daughter of the mr Lewis, with whom he had studied law: and afterwards to a miss Taliaferro, of a wealthy and respectable family, in the neighborhood of Williamsburg, by neither of whom did he leave issue.

No man ever left behind him a character more venerated than G. Wythe.

his virtue was of the purest tint; his integrity inflexible, and his justice exact; of warm patriotism, and, devoted as he was to liberty, and the natural and equal rights of men, he might truly be called the Cato of his country, without the avarice of the Roman; for a more disinterested person never lived. temperance and regularity in all his habits gave him general good health, and his unaffected modesty and suavity of manners endeared him to every one.

he was of easy elocution, his language chaste, methodical in the arrangement of his matter, learned and logical in the use of it, and of great urbanity in debate. not quick of apprehension, but with a little time profound in penetration, and sound in conclusion. in his philosophy he was firm, and neither troubling, nor perhaps trusting any one with his religious creed, he left to the world the conclusion that that religion must be good which could produce a life of such exemplary virtue

his stature was of the middle size, well formed and proportioned and the features of his face manly, comely and engaging.   Such was George Wythe, the honor of his own, and model of future times.

MS (ICN: Thomas Jefferson Letters); entirely in TJ's hand; undated. PoC (DLC: TJ Papers, 218:38933–4); edge chipped. Enclosed in TJ to John Sanderson, 31 Aug. 1820.

George Wythe (ca. 1726–1806), attorney, educator, public official, and signer of the Declaration of Independence, was probably born in Elizabeth City County. Largely self-educated, he was admitted to practice in the county courts in 1746. Wythe moved within a few years to Williamsburg, where he rose to prominence within both the legal profession and colonial politics. He held a seat in the Virginia House of Burgesses, 1754–55 and 1758–68, and was clerk of the House, 1768–76. Wythe mentored TJ while the latter was a student at the College of William and Mary early in the 1760s, and the two men remained close thereafter. During the Revolutionary War he supported independence as a member of the Second Continental Congress, 1775–76, undertook, along with TJ and Edmund Pendleton, the task of revising the laws of Virginia, and was Speaker of the House of Delegates, 1777–78. In the latter year Wythe was elected a judge of Virginia's High Court of Chancery, a position he retained until his death. A delegate who served only briefly at the 1787 constitutional convention in Philadelphia, he voted in favor of the new federal constitution at his state's ratification convention the following year. After serving as professor of law at William and Mary for a decade, Wythe relocated by 1791 to Richmond, where he continued to take students. He died there, having apparently been poisoned by his grandnephew George Wythe Sweeney, the principal beneficiary of his will. Sweeney was never prosecuted for his actions because the key testimony of Lydia Broadnax was inadmissible under state law due to her status as a free woman of color. However, Wythe lingered long enough to disinherit him. In codicils to his will Wythe left TJ his library and some silver from which TJ had commemorative cups made (*ANB*; *DAB*; Imogene E. Brown, *American Aristides: A Biography of George Wythe* [1975]; John Sanderson and others, eds., *Biography of the Signers to the Declaration of Independence* [Philadelphia, 1820–27; Poor, *Jefferson's Library*, 5 (no. 152)], 2:155–80; Leonard, *General Assembly*; Bernard Schwartz, Barbara Wilcie Kern, and Richard B. Bernstein, eds., *Th: Jefferson and Bolling v. Bolling: Law and the Legal Profession in Pre-Revolutionary America* [1997]; *William and Mary Provisional List*, 50; *Doc. Hist. Ratification*, vols. 8–10; Julian P. Boyd and W. Edwin Hemphill, *The Murder of George Wythe: Two Essays* [1955]; Richmond *Enquirer*, 10 June 1806; gravestone inscription in Saint John's Episcopal churchyard, Richmond; TJ to John Le Tellier, 27 Mar. 1810).

Zachary LEWIS was Wythe's father-in-law, but Wythe actually studied law under Stephen Dewey. OUR EXECUTIVE: George III, king of Great Britain. The PETITION, MEMORIAL, and REMONSTRANCE of the House of Burgesses protesting the proposed Stamp Act dated from 1764, not 1774. Patrick Henry's FAMOUS RESOLUTIONS on the same subject passed in 1765, not 1775.

The REVOLUTION IN ENGLAND was the so-called "Glorious Revolution" of 1688, which resulted in the ouster of the Catholic James II and accession to the throne of his Protestant son-in-law and daughter,

William III and Mary II. TJ had himself drafted the Virginia ACTS FOR REGULATING DESCENTS, FOR RELIGIOUS FREEDOM, AND FOR PROPORTIONING CRIMES & PUNISHMENTS (*PTJ*, 2:391–3, 492–507, 545–53).

[1] Manuscript: "draughstman."
[2] Preceding four words interlined in place of "of."
[3] Word interlined.

To Jerman Baker

DEAR SIR   Monticello Sep. 1. 20.

It may be of service to the Visitors of the University to possess a statement of the quota of taxes payable into the treasury by the several counties respectively. that being the ratio[1] of the distribution of their portions of the literary fund to the primary schools we may have occasion to make use of it. I presume you possess such a statement, and therefore ask the favor of you to furnish me with a copy.

Wayles is perfectly recovered. he sets out for Richmond on Tuesday, and will be able to inform you of the grounds on which I recommend to mr Eppes that Francis should go to Columbia.[2] with my affectionate respects to mrs Baker I salute you with great friendship.

                                                                    TH: JEFFERSON

PoC (DLC); on verso of reused address cover of John Vaughan to TJ, 22 Mar. 1820; at foot of text: "Jerman Baker esq."; endorsed by TJ.

[1] Word interlined in place of "basis."
[2] Preceding two words interlined in place of "there."

From James Clarke

DEAR SIR   powhatan county, Sept[r] 1st 1818 [1820]

By the advice, and persuation of several Gentlemen who are anxious to get an Odometer like mine, I have at length concluded to take a pattent, and establish a manufactory of them.

As you have had one of them in use many years, I'll thank you for your opinion of them, as to accuracy, Simplicity, and durability; whether it incommodes, or disfigures a carriage. And, whether you believe the plan to be original, or whether you ever saw, or heard of one in Europe or America upon the same plan, previous to the adoption of mine—And be pleased Sir, to accept the highest respect, and veneration of your obed[t] Serv[t]   JAMES CLARKE

RC (DLC: TJ Papers, 213:38078); evidently misdated; endorsed by TJ as a letter of 1 Sept. 1820 received three days later and so recorded in SJL.

From William J. Coffee

New, York Sep^t 1–1820

Hon^{BL} & Respected Sir   n° 501—Greenwich St

I arrived in New York on the 18 of July much fatigued with a Journey of 1203 miles by Land, that is from Monticello to Canada & from Canada to N. York Via—Albany, and as Soon as I was recoverd from a slight Indisposition owing to the Heat of the season, I search out the proper person for the Information you wished to have as related to your Engine,

At N° 293 Pearl, St. New, York lives a man by the name of Able. W. Hardenbrook maker of fire[1] Engins, His Prices for Hose are as follows,

For Hose or Leaders as they are Called here[2] of 3¾ hinchs from out to out of the diameter $1—that is 8 shillings this City money, for Hose of One hinch & ¾ diameter which[3] I should suppose is the Size you Should have, Price 50 Cents that is ℔ Foot, & for the Suckers or Suction Pipes Price 3$ ℔ Foot,—it will take for one City Engine from 3-to 400 Feet but the Common Lenth of Leaders for a House Engine is 100 Feet. If there should be anny thing more that I can do for m^r Jefferson, in this City before I Leave it which I think will Probable be soon I should be very Proud to receive your Commands,

I am Dear Sir With much Esteem & Respect You Ob^t & He—S &—&—   W. J. Coffee

I now sir have[4] to Solicite a favor which I know You will Immidiateley grant, it is to beg your goodness to send one of your Servants to make Every necessary Inquiries for my Case of Paintings, which your kindness sent to milton on the morning I Left Monticello, it was to be in the Care of m^r Ficth I think the Tavern keeper names is, & was to have[5] being sent from milton on the next day morning to Richmond, as it has not yet com to hand I am fearfull it may be Lost, but If it is not[6] being I rest much satisfied that you will caus your People to do all that Can be don to recover it,

RC (DLC: TJ Papers, 218:38938); evidently misdated, based on unlikely speed of transmission; adjacent to signature: "to Thos Jefferson Es^r"; at foot of first page (one word editorially corrected): "Please to turn ove[r]" for postscript on verso; endorsed by TJ as a letter of "Sep. 1.?" received 2 Sept. 1820 and so recorded in SJL.

MR Ficth: William D. Fitch.

[1] Manuscript: "frire."
[2] Manuscript: "her."
[3] Manuscript: "whih."
[4] Manuscript: "hav."
[5] Manuscript: "hav."
[6] Manuscript: "no."

From Thomas Cooper

DEAR SIR   1 Sep. 1820.

I wrote hastily yesterday for fear of losing the post. But as I believe I am in time to day, I write to say that I think there is nothing to be apprehended at Columbia in point of health. There is no swamp, no stagnant water near it; the mist of the River grounds, has never been known to cross the main street; and during the three last years, it has not only been healthy, but singularly so. This year has furnished no exception to its general character so far as I know. We have yellow fever in and near Water Street in this City, and about a case a day on the average, since the bulletins of the board of Health have appeared. It may spread, but no alarm prevails as yet, among men of usual information.

I send you to day, my article on Weights & Measures in the new edition of Willichs domestic Encyclopædia, which will out in about a month. Knowing the interest you have taken in this question, I thought it would amuse you.

Accept my respectful good wishes.   THOMAS COOPER

RC (MHi); endorsed by TJ as received 6 Sept. 1820 from Philadelphia and so recorded in SJL. RC (DLC); address cover only; with PoC of TJ to Benjamin L. Lear, 25 Sept. 1821, on verso; addressed: "Thomas Jefferson Esq Montecello"; franked; postmarked Philadelphia, 1 Sept.

Cooper published his piece on WEIGHTS & MEASURES in Anthony F. M. Willich, *The Domestic Encyclopedia: or A Dictionary of Facts and Useful Knowledge. chiefly applicable to Rural and Domestic Economy* (2d American ed., Philadelphia, 1821; ed. Cooper), 3:458–71. In this article Cooper engaged directly with TJ's 1790 Report on Weights and Measures (*PTJ*, 16:602–75): "Mr. JEFFERSON, then secretary of state for the United States . . . seems not to have been fully aware of what the French philosophers were at that time about to execute, and he therefore objects to a degree of the meridian as a standard, owing to the uncertainty in the measurement of it. That objection I apprehend, since the experiments of MECHAIN and DELAMBRE in France and Major MUDGE in England; and particularly considering the wonderful accuracy of the verification of a base on Hounslow Heath by Messrs. WILLIAMS, DALBY, and MUDGE some years before is now without weight. Mr. JEFFERSON next proceeds to the objects to which a second pendulum is liable, but upon the whole prefers it. His computation is formed on the calculation of Sir ISAAC NEWTON, that a second pendulum in the lat. of London is 39.1682 inches, but Mr. GRAHAM by more accurate experiments, made it 39.128. Taking the pendulum as the standard, Mr. JEFFERSON proposes it shall be divided into a certain number of equal parts, and applies them to the several denominations already in use of length, capacity, and weight. Should this plan not be approved, he proposes another, further removed from the present denomination, and in itself more complete. I refer for this to his very able memoir upon the subject" (p. 465; footnotes omitted; two commas editorially altered to decimal points). In the second instance here, "objects" is an obsolete variant of "objections" or "hindrances" (*OED*).

To Jacob De La Motta

Monticello Sep. 1. 20.

Th: Jefferson returns his thanks to Doct^r de la Motta for the eloquent discourse on the Consecration of the Synagogue of Savannah which he has been so kind as to send him.   it excites in him the gratifying reflection that his own country has been the first to prove to the world two truths, the most salutary to human society, that man can govern himself, and that religious freedom is the most effectual anodyne against religious dissension: the maxim of civil government being reversed in that of religion, where it's true form is 'divided we stand, united we fall.' he is happy in the restoration, of the Jews particularly, to their social rights, & hopes they will be seen taking their seats on the benches of science, as preparatory to their doing the same at the board of government. he salutes Dr de la Motta with sentiments of great respect.

PoC (DLC).

Jacob De La Motta (1789–1845), physician, was born in Savannah, Georgia, but soon moved with his family to Charleston, South Carolina. After receiving a medical degree from the University of Pennsylvania in 1810, he was elected to the Medical Society of South Carolina and began work as an attending physician at the Charleston Dispensary. Following service as a surgeon in the United States Army, 1812–14, De La Motta practiced medicine in New York City for four years. He returned first to Savannah, 1818–23, and then to Charleston, where he reestablished a private practice, operated an apothecary shop, and was active in local politics, philanthropy, freemasonry, and the Jewish community. De La Motta served as secretary to the state medical society for a decade and to the Literary and Philosophical Society of South Carolina, 1832–40. President William Henry Harrison appointed him receiver of public money for the Charleston district early in 1841. De La Motta's publications included articles on botany, silkworms, and the causes of mortality among visitors to Savannah. He owned five slaves in 1830 and four a decade later. Having suffered a series of strokes late in life, De La Motta died in Charleston (Thomas J. Tobias, "The Many-Sided Dr. De La

Motta," *American Jewish Historical Quarterly* 52 [1963]: 200–19; Will J. Maxwell, comp., *General Alumni Catalogue of the University of Pennsylvania* [1917], 570; *Charleston Courier*, 3 July 1810; Charleston *City Gazette and Commercial Daily Advertiser*, 31 July 1810, 13 May 1824; Heitman, *U.S. Army*, 1:365; Charleston *Southern Patriot*, 20 Aug. 1832, 18 May 1840, 22 Feb. 1845; Baltimore *Niles' National Register*, 3 Apr. 1841; DNA: RG 29, CS, S.C., Charleston, 1830, 1840; *Occident and American Jewish Advocate* 3 [1845]: 59–60; gravestone inscription in Coming Street Cemetery, Charleston).

De La Motta enclosed his ELOQUENT *Discourse, delivered at the Consecration of the Synagogue, of the Hebrew Congregation, Mikva Israel, in the city of Savannah, Georgia. On Friday, the 10 of Ab, 5580; corresponding with the 21st of July, 1820* (Savannah, 1820; Poor, *Jefferson's Library*, 10 [no. 545]), in a missing letter to TJ of 7 Aug. 1820, which is recorded in SJL as received 30 Aug. from Savannah. The author also sent a copy to James Madison on 7 Aug. 1820 (Madison, *Papers, Retirement Ser.*, 2:80–1).

The MAXIM OF CIVIL GOVERNMENT, "united we stand, divided we fall," can be traced to both Aesop's fable of the lion and the bulls and the Bible (Matthew 12.25; Mark 3.25; Luke 11.17).

From Peter F. Fritez

RESPECTED SIR, Philadª Sept. 1. 1820.

By the request of Dʳ Cooper, I have the honour to enclose to you, two halfsheets of the 2ᵈ American edition of Willich's "Domestic Encyclopedia," edited by him, and now nearly ready for publication by Mr. Ab. Small, of this city. PETER F. FRITEZ.

RC (MHi); addressed: "Thos. Jefferson, Esqʳ Monticello, (Vir.)"; endorsed by TJ as received 6 Sept. 1820 and so recorded in SJL. Enclosure: Anthony F. M. Willich, *The Domestic Encyclopedia: or A Dictionary of Facts and Useful Knowledge. chiefly applicable to Rural and Domestic Economy* (2d American ed., Philadelphia, 1821; ed. Thomas Cooper), portion of vol. 3, not found, but including pp. 458–71 (see Cooper to TJ, 1 Sept. 1820, and note).

Peter F. Fritez (ca. 1787–1829), printer, worked in that capacity in Philadelphia from around 1810 until at least 1824. He served thereafter as a prison inspector, 1825–27, and as a deputy sheriff, notary public, and justice of the peace. Fritez was also a sergeant in the militia during the War of 1812, a longtime member of the Philadelphia Typographical Society, secretary of the local Democratic-Republican society, 1819–20, and a supporter of An-

drew Jackson's presidential candidacy in 1828. He died in Philadelphia (Philadelphia *Press*, 3 Nov. 1810; *Census Directory For 1811* [Philadelphia, 1811], 116; Daniel Bowen, *A History of Philadelphia* [1839], 42; Philadelphia *Franklin Gazette*, 26 July, 3 Nov. 1819, 20 Mar. 1820; Robert Desilver, *The Philadelphia Directory, for 1824* [Philadelphia, (1824)]; Thomas Wilson, ed., *The Philadelphia Directory and Stranger's Guide, for 1825* [Philadelphia, 1825], 54; *The Eighth Annual Report of the Inspectors of The Philadelphia County Prison* [1855], 53–4; Washington, Pa., *Examiner, And Farmers' and Mechanics' Repository*, 26 Jan. 1828; *Philadelphia Directory and Stranger's Guide, 1829* [1829], 67; Philadelphia *Poulson's American Daily Advertiser*, 20 Oct. 1829).

HALFSHEETS of paper, in printing, are cut and set up in the press so that all the pages of a single signature fit on one of them (*OED*).

To Henry Guegan

SIR Monticello Sep. 1. 20.

I wrote to you on the 27ᵗʰ ult. on the subject of some books I had seen noted on a loose leaf accompanying your catalogu[e of] books for sale. I have since observed on the same leaf two othe[rs]

Patres Graeci. 21. vols. 8ᵛᵒ 45. D

Patres Latini. 13. vols 8ᵛᵒ 28.D.

being unacquainted with these editions, will you be so good as to take the trouble to describe them to me in the following partic[ulars?]
of what particular fathers do they contain the works?
are there translations to the Greek volumes?
are there notes, and by whom?
when & where were they printed?

what is the binding & condition of the volumes?

on recieving information of these particulars, I shall b[e] able to decide whether it will suit me to take them.

I salute you with sentiments of respect. Th: Jefferson

PoC (MHi); on verso of reused address cover to TJ; mutilated at seal and edge trimmed, with five words rewritten by TJ; at foot of text (faint): "M. Hen[r]y Guigan"; endorsed by TJ.

Patres graeci: Franz Oberthür, ed., *Opera Omnia Sanctorum Patrum Græcorum: Græce et Latine*, 21 vols. (Würzburg, 1777–94). Patres latini: Oberthür, ed., *Opera Omnia Sanctorum Patrum Latinorum*, 13 vols. (Würzburg, 1780–91).

Michele Raggi and Giacomo Raggi to Thomas Jefferson and John H. Cocke

Ilustrissimi Signori Tomaso
Jefferson e Ge^LE Cock— [received 1 Sept. 1820]

Li loro Servi Michele e Giacomo Raggi esebisconsi per fare un Acomodo di fargli tre proggetti, che loro Sig^ri potranno apprendersi a quello che gli senbrerà piu Aproposito ⅌ il loro Avantaggio.

P^mo Che il Súnomato Michele prontamente si porterà nel piu Vicino Porto D'Europa a prendere sua moglie a proprie Spese e Carico de Viaggi, sempre che gli rinovino il Contrato per Anni cinque; e nel medemo intervallo di tempo potranno far Venire li marmi di Filladelppia, o D'Italia Come meglio gli piacerà a lor Sig^ri giache li Sudetti Raggi non possono piu lavorare di queste pietre pregiudicandoli la loro Salute.

Se^do Sentendo che lor Sig^ri Avrebero piacere di Aver questi lavori in Marmo di Carrara ⅌ Aver Miglior lavoro, e piu presto Eseguito, Si Esebiscono li Sottoscritti Raggi di Andare a farli, e ristringersi li Corinti Grandi per

il prezzo di Taleri quatro cento Cadauno dico T^li 400–

e li Ionici al prezzo di Taleri cento sesanta Cadauno. 160

e di Darglieli in Livorno ben finiti ed incassatti al tempo che lor Sig^ri desidererano, e se gli piacerà faremo anche gli altri corinti che gli daremo il prezzo quando ci daranno la misura, potendoli Assicurare che non potrano aver da Alcuno l'avantaggio che noi gli potremo fare facendo noi questo lavoro con le nostre bracie e di qualche parente, e poi lor Sig^ri anno di gia Conosciuto la fatica dificoltà, e richezza di lavoro, che ciè in detti Capittelli, e cosi potrano regolarci, e Conoscere che si siamo messi in un discretissimo prezzo.

3^{zo} Non piacendo a lor Sig^{ri} di fissare in nesuno dei sudetti proggetti gli proponghiamo di portarsi noi a fare questo lavoro a Carrara a loro Conto e lavorare come fossimo sotto a loro Ochi ✿ la sola pensione pecuniaria che abiamo presentemente, e su la detta somma dovremo pensar noi al nostro nudrimento Assicurandoli di fare tutto il loro interesse tanto ✿ la Spesa dei Marmi come delle altre spese necessarie per il detto lavoro, e non Mancandoli a lor Sig^{ri} mezi di Sapere se tireremo ad ogni loro interesse, si rasegniamo ala loro Volontà dichiarandoci delle loro Signo^e Ilmi Um^{mi} devmi Servitori

MICHELE RAGGI
GIACOMO RAGGI

MOST ILLUSTRIOUS GENTLEMEN THOMAS
JEFFERSON AND GENERAL COCKE— [received 1 Sept. 1820]

Your servants Michele and Giacomo Raggi hereby offer three compromise proposals, from which you may choose the one that seems most advantageous to you.

First. That the abovementioned Michele go immediately to the nearest European port in order to bring his wife here with him at his own expense, provided that his contract be renewed for five years and that, at the same time, the marble blocks be brought from either Philadelphia or Italy, as you prefer, because the aforesaid Raggis can no longer work these stones without endangering their health.

Second. Having heard that you would like to have this work done in Carrara marble, because working with it is better and faster, the undersigned Raggis offer to carry it out and cut the large Corinthian capitals for the price of four hundred talers each, that is T^{rs} 400— and the Ionic capitals for the price of one hundred and sixty talers each. 160

and to give them to you in Leghorn, finished well and boxed up, whenever you wish. In addition, if you like, we will also make the other Corinthian capitals, for which we will quote you the price once you have provided us with the measurements. We can assure you that no one else will give you a better deal than we can offer by doing the work with our own hands and the aid of a few of our relatives. You know very well, moreover, the fatigue, difficulty, and expense of the work entailed by these capitals, and thus you will be able to ascertain and understand that we have offered you a very fair price.

Third. If you do not wish to accept either of the aforesaid proposals, we offer to carry out this work on your behalf in Carrara, to do it as if we were under your eyes for no more than our current monetary compensation, and, out of this sum, to arrange for our own meals. We assure you that we will do everything in your best interest with regard to the cost of the marble and the other expenses arising out of this work, and as you gentlemen have many ways of knowing whether we are, at all times, promoting your interests, we submit

ourselves to your will, declaring that we are,   Most illustrious gentlemen, your very humble, devoted servants   MICHELE RAGGI
      GIACOMO RAGGI

RC (ViU: TJP); in Michele Raggi's hand, signed by him and Giacomo Raggi; undated; addressed: "Alli Signori Tomaso Jefferson e Generale Cock Sopra Intendenti del Coleggio di Virginia" ("To Messrs. Thomas Jefferson and General Cocke Superintendents of the College of Virginia"); endorsed by TJ as received 1 Sept. 1820, with his additional notations beneath endorsement: "articles dated Feb. 17. 1819. arrived at Charlottesville June 30. 19." Translation by Dr. Jonathan T. Hine.

To George Watterston

SIR   Monticello Sep. 1. 20.

Having lately met with a very full catalogue of books relating to America, I have supposed it could not be better placed than in your hands for the use of the library committee with whom I presume it is a primary object to obtain every thing of that description. by taking the trouble to mark on this catalogue those you possess, (which make a great part of those most valuable),[1] the unpossessed will be obvious. I think however that in the catalogue of authorities stated in Robertson's America there must be several important works omitted in this and which I could never get. a standing instruction to the Minister in Madrid might in time procure them.

I send you herewith a thin MS. vol. marked **A.** being the 1st vol. of the MS. laws of Virginia, belonging to your library. you will find it entered in the catalogue of 1815. pa. 73. N° 191. it was one of those I had lent to mr Hening, who has printed it's contents in his 1st vol. of the Statutes at large pa. 122. E^{t}c and I never doubted it had been returned to you & was in the library. how it happened otherwise how it got into the hands of a private gentleman in W^{ms} burg and from his into those of a gentleman in of[2] the Western states, is to me unknown. but this last gentleman, seeing the endorsement in my hand writing, judging thence it might be mine, & having occasion to pass thro' this neighborhood lately, brought it with him and returned it to me. I am happy that chances so favorable and extraordinary have enabled me to place it in it's proper home. mr Hening informs me he has returned you the vol. **D.** of the same collection. I salute you with great esteem & respect   TH: JEFFERSON

PoC (DLC); on verso of reused address cover of Thomas Cooper to TJ, 21 Mar. 1820; at foot of text: "Mr Watterston"; endorsed by TJ. Enclosure: Manuscript A, a part of TJ's collection of Virginia statutes that he had sold to the nation in 1815 (DLC: TJ Papers, ser. 8; Sowerby, no. 1822). Other enclosure not found.

The congressional Joint LIBRARY COMMITTEE worked with Watterston to direct the operations of the Library of Congress. The current United States MINISTER IN MADRID was John Forsyth. The PRIVATE GENTLEMAN in Williamsburg was Littleton W. Tazewell, while the individual from a WESTERN state was George Croghan.

[1] Omitted closing parenthesis editorially supplied.
[2] Thus in manuscript.

From David Gelston

DEAR SIR,   New York Sep: 2[d] 1820—
I am now favored with your letter of the 27th ult: with the invoice of the books.—the invoice I now return,
The amount of duties is 5\frac{55}{}$ I have paid freight 2\frac{20}{100}$—
The first good opportunity to Richmond I shall ship the books, and drop you a line at the time, and give you the name of the Vessel and the Captain.—
with great truth & esteem I am, Dear Sir, sincerely your's
DAVID GELSTON

paid duties   5.55
   " fre[t]   2.20 7\frac{75}{100}$

RC (MHi); endorsed by TJ as received 24 Sept. 1820 and so recorded in SJL. RC (MHi); address cover only; with PoC of TJ to Smith Thompson, 19 Aug. 1821, on verso; addressed: "Thomas Jefferson Esquire Monticello"; franked; postmarked New York, 2 Sept. Enclosure: enclosure to TJ to Gelston, 27 Aug. 1820.

To William W. Hening

DEAR SIR   Monticello Sep. 3. 20.
I thank you for the handsome set of your Statutes at large which you have been so kind as to send me.
For your satisfaction I will mention that in my letter to you of Apr. 8. 15. I stated that you had not returned me the MS. laws of 1623/4. marked **A.** and I add with pleasure that it is now recieved, after the strangest circuit possible, and unknown, I dare say, to yourself, in 1810. it seems, Col[o] Croghan found it in possession of mr Lyttleton Tazewell of Williamsburg among some neglected papers, and carried it into the Western country. on examining it there, for the first time, and observing an endorsement in my handwriting [as described in your 1st vol. pa. 121.] he conjectured it might be mine, took care of it,

& having occasion lately to come to Virginia, and to pass through this neighborhood, he left it for me with a friend, and I have recieved and returned it to the librarian of Congress.

I am glad to learn from you that the MS. volume **D.** has been sent also to the librarian. with respect to this volume, I refer you to my letter of Apr. 25. 15. for it's true history. in that however I omitted to state the date of the laws it contained, to wit, from 1642/3 Mar. 2. to 1661/2 Mar. 23. which you will find confirmed by the list annexed to my letter of Jan. 16. 1795. printed by mr Wythe, and in my Catalogue pa. 73. printed by Congress. this renders erroneous therefore your caption of all the laws quoted from that volume, to wit, from your 1st volume pa. 238. to Vol. 2d pa. 149–162. it never was the property of mr Edmund Randolph, nor ever in his hands, until 1784. when he borrowed it out of my library with the other MS. volumes, and omitted to return it with the others. it was a part of Peyton Randolph's library which I purchased at his death, as stated in that letter, bookcases and all as they stood. this error is of little other consequence than inasmuch as a correct account of the regular transmission of this volume, with the others of it's suite, from Sr John Randolph, with his library, to Peyton Randolph his eldest son, and from his possession at his death, to mine, would by this specific deduction, strengthen confidence in it's authenticity, and in the literal exactitude which constitutes much of the value of such a collection as yours. you however are the best judge whether such an error is worth a note in your next volume. I rejoice much to learn that the public patronage will enable you to finish your whole work in two more volumes. I shall consider it the most useful work we possess of the antiquities of our country. Accept the assurance of my great respect and esteem.

TH: JEFFERSON

PoC (DLC); brackets in original; at foot of first page: "Wm W. Henning esq."

The LIBRARIAN OF CONGRESS was George Watterston. TJ enclosed his "Statement of the Laws of Virginia" (THE LIST ANNEXED) in a letter to George Wythe of 16 Jan. 1796, not 1795 (*PTJ*, 28:583–91). TJ's CATALOGUE . . . PRINTED BY CONGRESS was the *Catalogue of the Library of the United States. To Which is Annexed, A Copious Index, Alphabetically Arranged* (Washington, 1815). In 1796 TJ stated that he had acquired manuscript **D** of Virginia's early statutes from the estate of Richard Bland rather than in his purchase of PEYTON RANDOLPH'S LIBRARY (*PTJ*, 28:586; Sowerby, no. 1825).

From Gerard E. Stack

Sɪʀ,   Charlottesville Septʳ 3. 1820.

Enclosed I return you fifteen dollars of the forty which you enclosed for the tuition of J. M. Randolph.[1] He returned to the Academy about the first day of April last; and from that time to the present, his tuition fees amount to twenty five dollars which I retain in full for all pecuniary demands on you.

Yours respectfully.   G. E. Sᴛᴀᴄᴋ.

RC (MHi); addressed: "To Thomas Jefferson Esqʳ"; endorsed by TJ, in part, as a "reciept for 25.D."

[1] Manuscript: "Randolp."

From Jerman Baker

Dᴿ Sɪʀ,   Treasury Office 4 Sepʳ 1820

Yours of the 2ⁿᵈ Insᵗ was received this morning, & it affords me much pleasure to have it in my power forthwith to furnish you with the document you desired; I wish the Visitors of the University may be enabled to devise any means by which they may prevail in the Legislature to increase the annual appropriation to the object of their care—

Permit me my dear Sir, at the moment when my Son is about to take leave of yourself & family to tender in behalf of my Wife & self our grateful acknowledgements for the very friendly & affectionate attentions which he has so lavishly received while under your Roof; of which I trust he will never prove himself unworthy.

Present our affectionate regards to Mʳˢ R & the young Ladies & accept the assurance of my great respect & esteem.   Yʳˢ

Jᴇʀᴍᴀɴ Bᴀᴋᴇʀ

RC (MHi); endorsed by TJ as received 6 Sept. 1820 from Richmond and so recorded in SJL.

TJ's letter to Baker ᴏꜰ ᴛʜᴇ 2ᴺᴰ ɪɴsᵀ was actually dated 1 Sept. 1820.

The enclosed ᴅᴏᴄᴜᴍᴇɴᴛ ʏᴏᴜ ᴅᴇꜱɪʀᴇᴅ may have been "A Statement shewing the amount of Taxes on lands, Slaves, horses, carriages, licenses to merchants, pedlars, exhibitors of shows, ordinary keepers, keepers of houses of private entertainment, law process seals of Courts, Notarial seals, and on tobacco shipped also the amount of militia fines, payable in each of the great districts of Virginia," broken down by district and county, with the district west of the Allegheny Mountains paying $35,076.30, nearly 9 percent of the total; that between the Blue Ridge and Allegheny Mountains paying $70,336.95, nearly 15 percent; the district between the Blue Ridge and the Tidewater paying $190,725.44, nearly 40 percent; and that below the Tidewater paying $179,570.11, roughly 37.5 percent (MS in ViU: TJP; in an unidentified hand; undated, but "made up from the Taxes &ᶜ payable in 1821").

ᴍʳˢ ʀ: Martha Jefferson Randolph.

To James Clarke

DEAR SIR   Monticello Sep. 5. 20.

I have duly recieved your favor of the 1st instant requesting my opinion of the merits of your Odometer, which I shall give with pleasure and satisfaction having had it in use for 13. years. I think it as simple as we can expect such a machine to be, having only three toothed wheels, entirely accurate inconsiderable in weight and volume, and of convenient application to the carriage. with respect to it's originality, I can only say I have known no Odometer either in Europe or America, resembling it in any degree, or at all to be compared with it, in all it's characters and merit taken together. I continue still to use it, finding great satisfaction in having miles announced by the bell as by milestones on the road. with this testimony whic[h] I render as a duty, I pray you to accept the assurance of my great esteem and respect.   TH: JEFFERSON

PoC (DLC); on verso of reused address cover of otherwise unlocated letter from a Mr. Roscoe to TJ, 22 Mar. 1820 (addressed: "To his Excellency Thomas Jefferson Monticello Virginia"; franked; postmarked Boston, 22 Mar.; recorded in SJL as a letter of that date received 30 Mar. 1820 from "Roscoe. publisher of poems. Boston"); mutilated at seal, with one word rewritten by TJ; at foot of text: "Colo James Clarke"; endorsed by TJ.

To John H. Cocke

DEAR SIR   Monticello Sep. 5. 20.

We have a difficulty with our Italian Sculptors which I need your aid and advice to get over. the wife of the elder one refuses to come to America, & that of the younger could not come alone. this has thrown the younger man into great despondency. he had just married when he left Italy, and has had a child born since he came away. he has sprained his wrist also so that he will not be able to work this month or two. in this state of body, and homesick, & love-sick mind, he will be of no use to us. he makes 3. propositions. 1. to go home, bring back his wife and engage with us for 5. years. 2. to go home and furnish our capitals of marble at Leghorn, Corinthian at 400.D. Ionic at 200.D. apiece. 3. to go home and make them there on wages and on our account. I like none of them, as I am confident Appleton will furnish them cheaper, and I may get his answer in 2. or 3. months. I sketch my own proposition in form of a letter to mr Brockenbrough, but will join you in that or any other you like better. I therefore send you a blank, signed in which you will write what you think best and send it to mr Brockenbrough. I set out to Bedford the day after tomorrow, and should have gone by your house to consult with you on this subject, but I learn that your house is crammed full of your friends, and cannot think of adding the inconvenience of my caravan. I get mr Brockenbrough therefore to send an express with this as the sooner the Raggis can go, the better for us, and most agreeable to them. affectionately yours   TH: JEFFERSON

RC (ViU: TJP); addressed: "General John H. Cocke Bremo"; endorsed by Cocke. PoC (DLC); on verso of reused address cover of otherwise unlocated letter from Bernard Peyton to TJ, 30 Mar. 1820 (see note to TJ to Peyton, 11 Apr.

1820); mutilated at seal; endorsed by TJ. Enclosures: (1) Dft of Cocke and TJ to Arthur S. Brockenbrough, 7 Sept. 1820. (2) blank sheet signed by TJ to be used for RC of same.

To Andrew Smith

SIR   Monticello Sep. 5. 20.

I duly recieved your favor of Aug. 14 and can assure you, Sir, that I have never been unmindful of the debt to you which ought so long ago to have been paid, but the Catastrophe of the last year took no one by surprise more than myself. my expences of the preceding year had been on the usual scale, & such as the usual prices of produce would have fully met. I got but half price, say $3\frac{1}{8}$ D. clear, for my flour. this left me in default for one half my current expences. difficult and disadvantageous as was the sale of property, & impossible for ready money, I sold immediately. the proceeds are now becoming due, and I have deferred answering your letter to this day, expecting to have recieved the amount, of your debt at least at our court yesterday. but I was disappointed.

I set out to my place in Bedford tomorrow where I have a very confident assurance that there is some money in hand waiting for me, and shall return the last of the month when I shall certainly remit my debt and interest to you. I assure you, Sir, I have suffered greatly in mind for this delay, and have been very sensible and thankful for your kind forbearance, which shall not be abused by a moments' delay after the first money I can recieve. I pray you to accept the assurance of my great esteem & respect.   TH: JEFFERSON

PoC (MHi); on verso of reused address cover of otherwise unlocated letter from LeRoy, Bayard & Company to TJ, 23 Mar. 1820 (see note to TJ to LeRoy, Ba-

yard & Company, 15 Mar. 1820); at foot of text: "Mr Andrew Smith"; mistakenly endorsed by TJ as a letter of 5 Sept. 1821, but correctly recorded in SJL.

TJ expected soon to receive further PROCEEDS from his sale of Pouncey's tract in Albemarle County to Charles Everette (*MB*, 2:1365, 1369).

To William J. Coffee

DEAR SIR   Monticello Sep. 6. 20.
I recieve your's of the 1st just as I am setting out for Bedford. I sent a servant instantly to Milton and he brings me the inclosed answer. I have written to Capt Bernard Peyton requesting him to explain either to you or myself, so that enquiry may be made for the box. in great hurry I salute you with friendly esteem and respect.

TH: JEFFERSON

PoC (MHi); on verso of reused address cover of otherwise unlocated letter from John Laval to TJ, 29 Mar. 1820 (see note to Laval to TJ, 1 Apr. 1820); at foot of text: "Mr Coffee"; endorsed by TJ as a letter to "W. F." Coffee and so recorded in SJL. Enclosure not found.

From Thomas Ewell

Washington 6th septr 1820
The continuation Good sir, of your kindness—shewn by your last letter—does truly render my feelings unspeakable. Great indeed has been the service you have often rendered me: more than all the world together; more than you can have been aware of. When in trouble I apply to you: my troubles have been the signal of abandonment, by the mass of others: and still more galling—the time for their confederation to encrease difficulties, in order to rise by the spoil of falling fortunes. Would to god I could requite to you or to yr descendants what I have received: or that I might be more worthy of such a benefactor.   Indeed I have been greatly pained at this last begging for your interposition: you would have pitied my feelings if you could have witnessed their agitation. It was the result of a hard and very hard reduction of fortune—commanding irresistably that I should leave no effort untried to entreat that I may receive employment.

my object in now writing to you, is to satisfy you that my misfortunes have arisen from circumstances—which but few if any, could foresee. From the spirit, given to my first exertions—by your patronage I freely speculated: established manufactories, reclaimed farms & marshes; and I made more money than I believed I or my children

[245]

would ever want. After success—impatience in idleness, eagerness to be acting—urged me to go on. The belief in affluence—begat want of caution: facility in giving credit: too after relieving unworthy applicants: so that one loss to another so fast succeeded: efforts to retrieve blunders, adding to the downfal, with such rapidity—that almost before I was conscious—all my clear gainings—were encumbered. Debts contracted while money was in circulation had to be paid, when scarcely any could be had. The whole system of accomodation—of mutual confidence seemed at once to be converted into the spirit of seeing which in the community could do the "other the most harm": at least so with our stockjobbers & money dealers of the Towns. The result has been in my loss of more than an hundred thousand doll^s; besides unemployment in a profession which properly followed, never fails yielding a maintenance.   Because you may have heard what Mr Madison here heard—the reverse of the Truth, respecting the late poor and most good Mr Hamilton & myself—I add this particular case of my loss of ten thousand dollars: to shew you that I could not as reported—have arrested him who was my friend: and that in the days of my success—I was to him no common Friend. Besides his note I enclose to you of $7200 I advanced him $1,000 to pay his expences to return to Charleston: He was arrested by all the vile sycophants to whom he was indebted—and I only could he procure for Bail & in every case have paid his debts. The unhappy gentleman in his last letter—to me—wrote that he was old enough to be my Father—but that I had been a Father to him! Please return the note. The debts exceeding 2000 dolls I have paid for him are on record: & yet malice has represented me as his persecutor!!

As proved in memorials to Congress—my allowances for the manufacture of Powder were settled by W. Jones—rejected by Yankee Crowninshield, because I told him what he was!—so that I had to sell the Contract to the late Dr Ott for 5,000 Doll^s who sold it to D. Bussard for 10,000 Dolls who rec'd on its completion 16,800 Dolls from the navy: leaving me a loser thus of ten thousand more: besides as much more I shall ever believe, some navy agents swindled me of. From this I have learnt the lesson,—"never again to provoke the meanest Foe."

I send for your perusal—a project for a Hospital in this place. I hope it will succeed—so that I may return to the poor—what you have done for me.

I never more at heart prayed to our Creator than I do—that when you are "gathered to y^r Fathers"—you may be the happiest of the happy.   Thos Ewell

RC (DLC); endorsed by TJ as received 24 Sept. 1820 and so recorded in SJL. RC (DLC); address cover only; with PoC of TJ to Patrick Gibson, 19 Aug. [1821], on verso; addressed: "Thomas Jefferson Esqʳ Former President U.S. Charloottes'ville Vᵃⁿ"; franked; postmarked Washington, 6 Sept. Enclosure: note from Paul Hamilton for $7,200, not found.

In his annual message to Congress of 3 Dec. 1805, TJ expressed hopes that European belligerent nations would deal justly with the neutral United States, but added that "should any nation decieve itself by false calculations, and disappoint that expectation, we must join in the unprofitable contest, of trying which party can do the OTHER THE MOST HARM" (DLC).

Medicine was the PROFESSION WHICH PROPERLY FOLLOWED, NEVER FAILS YIELDING A MAINTENANCE. NEVER AGAIN TO PROVOKE THE MEANEST FOE apparently alludes to Aesop's fable of the bull and the mouse.

The PROJECT FOR A HOSPITAL was probably a copy of the printed circular and prospectus that Ewell sent James Madison around this time. The circular, which is dated Washington, September 1820, and concludes with Ewell's printed signature, reads "SIR: I take the liberty of directing this to you, to ask your encouragement of an establishment designed to promote medical science, by the means of relieving the diseased poor around us. There is not in our country a population equal to that of this city and Georgetown, (exceeding twenty thousand,) which has not some medical institution for the relief of the sick. In addition to the number of poor common to such a population, there are many more arising from the resort of strangers to the seat of government. It is not to be denied, that many cases of severe suffering, even of death, have occurred, from the want of an Hospital in Washington.

Although anxious to make this establishment, I am not unconscious that many philanthropists believe that hospitals have done more harm than good. But the fact is, that the injuries have proceeded from those who planned them. Splendid buildings have been erected, chiefly to display the vanity of the founders. It appears always to have been forgotten that the best means of relieving the sick is to accommodate them in the manner to which they have been accustomed. Instead, therefore, of a large house, of crowded rooms, generating and diffusing the foulest atmosphere, there should have been small and detached buildings, such as the inhabitants of hospitals are accustomed to at their homes. It is from this view that I propose to establish the Columbia Hospital, on some square convenient to the City and Georgetown, which shall be selected by the majority of the contributors.

The regulations of the establishment will be such as are believed to be unexceptionable. Its government and use of funds are to be conducted exclusively by the clergymen of the county, who will monthly meet for the management. The medical department will be as exclusively under the direction of the regularly qualified physicians of the City and Georgetown; and every clergyman, physician, and contributor to the Hospital, shall have the right of ordering the admission of any sick person deemed a proper object.

In order to add to the utility of this institution, a part of it will be assigned for a lying-in-hospital, where women will be instructed in the duties they should perform to each other in child-bed; a school from which much good may be expected.

Should you approve of this establishment, I hope you will be pleased to request the gentlemen of your particular acquaintance to join in the subscription, and to return this to me as soon as convenient. Respectfully, your obedient servant."

The undated prospectus, on the verso of the circular, is entitled "COLUMBIA HOSPITAL" and promises to give the "OUTLINES *Of the Institution designed, in the least expensive and most expeditious way.*" It reads "*First.* To relieve the poor who are sick and have no accommodations at home.

Second. To administer medicines to those requiring, and unable to pay for them at their houses.

Third. To promote Medical Science by making the practice public; so as to lessen the impositions of pretenders to great skill among the unknowing part of society.

ARTICLE I. The Board of Management of the Institution, governing exclusively, excepting in the Medical Department, to consist of all the Clergymen, and of all the Members of the Corporations of Washington and Georgetown, to meet and regulate as they shall, by a majority, determine.

ARTICLE II. The Medical Department to be exclusively under the direction of the regularly qualified physicians of the two corporations, restricted to the republican rule, of letting each, in succession, share in the duties of the Hospital, and the practice as dispensary physicians; every physician having the right to witness the practice of each other at the hours of prescription.

ARTICLE III. All persons connected with the management, and all contributors, shall have the right of sending such patients to the Hospital as they may deem worthy objects; excepting that the owners of slaves shall pay as much as the cost of their accommodation.

ARTICLE IV. The Hospital to be seated convenient to Georgetown and Washington; to consist of small buildings, of the plainest kind, detached from each other to prevent the propagation of infectious diseases, and maniacs from being made more mad by hearing each other's cries; each house not to contain more than six or eight persons, excepting a centre building for the resident officers, an apothecary shop, and a room for teaching women the duties they should perform to each other in child-bed, or for other purposes of lecturing.

THE subscribers agree to pay the sums annexed to our names, for the establishment of the Columbia Hospital, one half in six months, the remainder in one year: provided, the Mayors of Washington and Georgetown shall certify that the amount is due for the materials and building of houses designed for the use of the sick, according to the plan stated above" (DLC: Madison Collection, Rare Book and Special Collections Division; circular printed in Madison, *Papers, Retirement Ser.*, 2:99–100; prospectus printed in Washington *Daily National Intelligencer*, 6 Sept. 1820, and elsewhere).

A variant of the phrase GATHERED TO Yᴿ FATHERS appears in the Bible (Judges 2.10).

To Patrick Gibson

DEAR SIR   Monticello Sep. 6. 20.

I set out for Poplar forest tomorrow to be back [on the] 24ᵗʰ and think it safe to send you my note for the Virginia bank lest it should be wanting. the others endorsed by my grandson go to Capᵗ Peyton his agent. I shall recieve a sum of money, in Bedford which I am told is in hand for me and ready of which I [s]hall take care to remit you what will cover my discounts, and besides that I leave orders if there should come a rain making the river boatable to send off some flour. I do not certainly know the day of renewal, but I believe it is in October. I salute you with affectionate esteem & respect

TH: JEFFERSON

PoC (DLC); on verso of a reused address cover from Alexander Garrett to TJ; two words faint and a third partially obscured by TJ's enhancement; at foot of text: "Mʳ Gibson"; endorsed by TJ. Recorded in SJL with additional notation: "notes of renewal." Enclosure not found.

A missing letter of 13 Sept. 1820 from TJ to his GRANDSON Thomas Jefferson Randolph is recorded in SJL.

To Bernard Peyton, with Jefferson's Note

DEAR SIR   Monticello Sep. 6. 20.

I set off for Poplar forest tomorrow to be back on the 24.th and think it safe to send you my notes for the farmers and US. banks, lest they should be wanting. I shall recieve in Bedford a sum of money which will enable me to remit you the discounts and also the curtailment of 500.D. which you were so kind as to give me timely notice of. besides this I leave directions if a rain should sufficiently raise our river to send off a sufficiency of flour as a double resource. I do not certainly know the day of renewal, but I believe it is in October. I salute you with great friendship and respect.   TH: JEFFERSON

[*Note by TJ at foot of text:*]
P.S. ab^t Coffee's box

PoC (MHi); on verso of reused address cover of George Evans to TJ, 29 Mar. 1820; adjacent to signature: "Capt Bernard Peyton"; endorsed by TJ. Recorded in SJL with additional notation: "notes of renewal." Enclosures not found.

From Charles Pinckney

DEAR SIR.—   Charleston September 6th 1820

It is a great while since I have written you for which I feel regret & some shame, as I ought to have considered it in some degree my duty to have frequently enquired how you do & to have requested the pleasure to hear from you—it was very seriously my intention at the close of the late session of Congress to have endeavoured to visit both yourself & Mr Madison—but the great length of the Session & the fear of losing my passage home by water in a Ship then ready to sail from Philadelphia prevented & obliged me to go on there immediately after the adjourment.—

I have lately written Mr Madison but as is reported he is about to go to Europe on a visit he will not recieve it.—I had the pleasure to hear from some gentlemen in Congress You were well & perfectly recovered from the severe indisposition You had some time before suffered under.—my friend & connection Colonel Alston told me he had seen you among the mountains of Virginia the year before travelling in quest of health & shewed me a letter you had written him since by which I had the satisfaction to hear you had greatly benefited by the excursion

As Mr Madison by his going to Europe will not probably recieve my letter I shall not have the pleasure of hearing from him.—it was very much my wish to know your & his opinions on the subject which now agitates the Union although not so much as the Missouri yet still in a degree very much to destroy the harmony that ought ever to prevail in a government like this—I mean the Tariff Question—this favour I ask as I am obliged to go once more very reluctantly to that dreadfully cold & bleak place Washington & shall have to give opinions & votes on it if I live as my constituents in Charleston are meeting to express their abhorrence of it—by the by what do you think of these gentry at the northward on their Missouri & Tariff & other questions of that sort—You see how Mr King has come out on the former & is expected to do so on the latter at the next session—If not inconvenient I will thank you to give to me your opinions on the Tariff Question as I believe They have been misrepresented in Congress—not with a view that I should say any thing about them, as any thing which comes from you to me on that or any subject that may come before Congress shall be considered by me always as <u>sacredly confidential</u> unless you should express a wish to the contrary—I will thank you also for Your Opinions as to Spain & the Course to be pursued with her—I fear the Cortes will not advise or consent to ratify the Treaty.—if not what shall be done?—shall we occupy Florida or take any other course—please favour me with your opinions on this fully if convenient or at leisure to do so.—it is the last session in which I expect ever to be in Congress & must from the nature of the 2 Questions as they affect the Southern States say something upon them, & should be happy to find my opinions in unison with yours[1]—I congratulate you on the increase & rise of our Country in every thing which can make it great free & of course happy since I saw you—this I knew would always be & soon the case & used to tell them so in Europe—but they never would believe it—they always had the idea, to use Cevallos's expression, that We were a People in the Woods & that as soon as We increased in numbers We would separate into small confederacies & therefore used to think very little about us[2]—unfortunately Graham who you sent me as Secretary had got the same Notions into his head & all that I could do I could never persuade him to the contrary.—In the Affair of the Deposit at New Orleans I never saw any one more astonished than he was when late one Evening I brought him home the Kings order to open it, as he was convinced they never would do it & did not care a farthing about what we said to them

Although I have in a great degree made up my own opinions on both the Questions I mention yet as I am always open to conviction I wish very much to have yours, as if coinciding with me, as I expect

& hope, they may tend to strengthen me in them & give me new lights on them, or if differing, may give me such a View of them as may convince me I am wrong & induce me to give them further consideration.—As I suppose You take both Niles's Register & the National Intellegencer[3] You there saw my opinions at length on the Missouri Question & particularly on the importance of the State Governments & how much their increase would tend to strengthen & give permanency to our Union[4]—I hope they will not trouble us any more on this subject although I should not be surprised if they attempted it when the Constitution of Missouri comes to be laid before Congress—

I was surprised to see so great a number of very young men in Congress & to find so great a proportion of the older members had like myself determined to decline a reelection—my constituents wished me very much to be a candidate for reelection & I should have been reelected without an opponent—but the Trouble of going there—the long absence from my home & friends—the constant confinement—crowds of company & above all the dreadfully rigorous climate where the thermometer is sometimes 6 to 8 degrees below zero & 40. degrees colder than it is in Charleston make it not only prudent but indispensable to decline it—of the 230[5] Members now in Congress there are only 4 or 5 who were there when I was last there in 1801— General Smith—.[6] Mr Macon . . Mr Dana Mr Randolph & probably Mr Otis—of the Members who signed the declaration of[7] Independence, I found only 4 are alive—but what is still more extraordinary there are only six who signed the Constitution so long afterwards & of these three are from the "unhealthy" South Carolina—General Pinckney Pierce Butler & myself—You have seen no doubt the newly published Journals of that body & I hear that Mr Madison is soon to publish an account of their proceedings with all the Speeches from his notes—is it so?—Lowndes mentioned something about it the other day but he did not know distinctly or positively.—

In writing to Mr Madison lately[8] I told him it was 33 Years since we had seen each other & alluded to the great changes that had taken place since—& that in my opinion one of the worst to us was that we were so much older, for I cannot but think in spite of all that Divines & Philosophers may tell us that Old Age is not the most comfortable state in the World—I dare say You remember what I wrote him that Doctor Franklin used to frequently wish "he could live his life over— that it had been a very good world to him & his life a succesful one"— I have heard him say so at his own Table more than once—if the age of any one, can be comfortable to him it must be yours & living as You do on the mountains, with your temperate habits & mountain air & water I do not see why You should not live as long & as comfortably as Cornaro did—I remember You once wrote me some opinions, if not wishes rather contrary to these but it is so long agoe You had not the experience You have now & which I hope has given you reasons to alter them—

I will thank you to be so good as to let me hear from you as soon as convenient—I hope to be able to leave this if nothing should happen to prevent it about the middle of October for Philadelphia on my way to Congress—in the interim please direct Your letter to me in Charleston—With affectionate regard & best Wishes remain Dear Sir
Yours Truly   CHARLES PINCKNEY

RC (DLC); ellipsis in original; endorsed by TJ as received 24 Sept. 1820 and so recorded in SJL. Tr (ViU: TJP); extract in Nicholas P. Trist's hand, with his note at foot of text made at a separate sitting: "The letter from T.J. of Sep. 30 is in answer to that from which these extracts are made."

The LATE SESSION OF CONGRESS ran from 6 Dec. 1819 until 15 May 1820 (*JHR*, 13:3, 550). The 2 Sept. 1820 letter that Pinckney had LATELY WRITTEN from Charleston to former president James Madison contained this postscript: "When you see Mr Jefferson please Remember me very affectionately to him—as his name was very repeatedly mentioned in Congress as favourable to the Tarif & manufacturers, I intend to write to him on it as Newton was the only Virginian who voted for it" (Madison, *Papers, Retirement Ser.*, 2:95–8).

During the summer of 1820 some American newspapers announced that Madison was not just ABOUT TO GO TO EUROPE but had actually arrived in Ireland. The reports, however, often contained a disclaimer that correctly cast doubt on the story's accuracy: "Mr. Madison, we suspect, is quietly cultivating his farm in Virginia. It is *possible*, that some impudent pretender has assumed his name, for the purpose of attracting a little more attention than is bestowed upon ordinary travellers; but it is more *probable* that the editor, and the London editors who have copied the paragraph, have been hoaxed"

(New York *Commercial Advertiser*, 24 Aug. 1820, and elsewhere).

The TREATY was the 1819 Adams-Onís Treaty between the United States and Spain. Pinckney would have heard the EXPRESSION by Pedro Cevallos (Ceballos) Guerra, the Spanish secretary of state, during his diplomatic service in that country. The AFFAIR OF THE DEPOSIT at New Orleans refers to Spain's October 1802 closure of that port to American goods. King Charles IV ordered the ban lifted the following spring (Madison, *Papers, Sec. of State Ser.*, 4:469–71).

Pinckney spoke to the United States House of Representatives about THE MISSOURI QUESTION on 14 Feb. 1820 (Washington *Daily National Intelligencer*, 23, 24 June 1820; Baltimore *Niles' Weekly Register*, 15 July 1820). The four surviving signers of the DECLARATION OF INDEPENDENCE at this time were John Adams, Charles Carroll (of Carrollton), William Floyd, and TJ. In addition to the three South Carolinians listed by Pinckney, five people WHO SIGNED THE CONSTITUTION were still alive: Jonathan Dayton, William Few, Jared Ingersoll, Rufus King, and James Madison.

Benjamin Franklin wrote Catharine Greene on 2 Mar. 1789 of his willingness to LIVE HIS LIFE OVER: "Hitherto this long Life has been tolerably happy, (God grant it may so continue to the End) so that if I were allow'd to live it over again, I should make no Objection, only wishing for Leave to do, what Authors do in a second Edition of their Works, correct

some of my Errata" (PPAmP: Miscellaneous Franklin Collections). TJ expressed
SOME OPINIONS of a negative nature
about his own descent into old age in a 3
Sept. 1816 letter to Pinckney.

[1] Tr begins here.
[2] Tr ends here.

[3] Tr begins here.
[4] Tr ends here.
[5] Reworked from "200."
[6] Pinckney here canceled "Mr King."
[7] Preceding three words interlined.
[8] Word interlined in place of "the other
day."

From Joel Yancey

DEAR SIR   Bedford 6th September 1820

I have been anxiously expecting you at the P. Forest for some time
past, or should have written you sooner, Since Mr Randolph was here
it has been reported that he had taken the management of your Estate
here for the ensuing year, and that he intended to send up Overseers,
indeed he mentioned to me himself when he was here last, that something of the kind was talked of between you and himself, I wish to
know the fact, as it is getting late in the season to get good overseers
and you can,t do without, and as it is my duty should you desire it to
engage them for you—   Our crop of Tob^o will be short, owing
to the Scarcity of plants, the first time I ever fail^d in plants,[1] some of
my most industrious nieghbors fail^d entirely and I am satisfied,[2] there
will not be more than $\frac{1}{2}$ crops To^{bo} in this part of the country, and
yours is as promising as any, with the hay that can be spared I think
it will be equal to a full crop, should they go on with the turnpike
road, every pound of hay will be wanted and taken from the meadow
at a 6/– ℔^{ct} and I think you can spare 30 or 40 ton—the crop of
Wheat is only tolerable, the Ridge & Tomahawk fields were both in
wheat, and they are too much exhausted for any thing, too much of
our labour here every year, has been wasted upon poor land, our crop
of corn is abundant, you have not had a better crop in 15 years I dare
say and a fine crop of Oats, the bill of sawing is compleated long
since, & appears to be pretty well seasoned, I will thank you to write
me as soon as convenient whether any change in the dispositions of
your affairs here has, or likely to take place next year, In the mean
time you may rely on my best exertions for your interest and my best
wishes for your happiness.   JOEL YANCEY

RC (MHi); addressed: "Mr Thomas
Jefferson Monticello"; franked; postmarked Lynchburg, 8 Sept.; endorsed by
TJ as received 24 Sept. 1820 and so recorded in SJL.

[1] Preceding two words interlined in
place of "before."
[2] Manuscript: "satisfieed."

From John H. Cocke

DEAR SIR,   Bremo Sept: 7. 1820
I think your proposals to the Raggis reasonable and more liberal
than they cou'd have expected—and for the interest of the University, by far more eligible, than any of their own propositions:—I
have therefore copied your proposals, over your signature, and added
my own in the form of a letter to Mr Brockenbrough—You will receive it herewith.

I am sorry that you have declined calling upon me on your way to
Bedford—the consideration urging you to it, is the effect of mistaken
information—A short time ago, we had many friends with us, but at
present we have very few—if therefore, you still mean to visit M^r
Eppes, I hope, you will resume your original intention of taking this
in your route.—

I am, Sir, with highest respect & Esteem
Yours   JOHN H. COCKE

RC (CSmH: JF); endorsed by TJ as received 25 Sept. 1820 and so recorded in SJL.
Enclosure: Cocke and TJ to Arthur S. Brockenbrough, 7 Sept. 1820.

John H. Cocke and Thomas Jefferson
to Arthur S. Brockenbrough

SIR,   Sept: 7. 1820
We the subscribers, acting as a committee of superintendance under
the authority of the Visitors of the University of Virginia have consider'd the proposals of Michael and Giacomo Raggi Sculptors, that
we shou'd relinquish their obligation to continue longer in the service
of the University & permit them to return to Italy under certain other
stipulations: and we do not think we should be justifiable in acceding
to either of the stipulations they propose as substitutes to the original
Contract.

But willing to indulge their strong desire to return to their families
we agree to relinquish their future services to pay up their wages to
the day of discontinuing them, they relinquishing all further wages,
and the expences of their journey & voyage back. They will doubtless
think it just that as we have borne the extra expence of their voyage[1]
coming, & have received about[2] 14 months labour only of the one &
12 months of the other, they should bear the extra expence of their return on their withdrawing 18 months labour of the one & 20. months

of the other still due under the original contract. If they consent to this you are authorised to carry it into execution forthwith.

JOHN H. COCKE
TH: JEFFERSON

RC (ViU: TJP-PP); in Cocke's hand, signed by Cocke and TJ; at head of text in Cocke's hand: "Mr Arthur S. Brockenbrough"; endorsed by Brockenbrough, in part, as "Respecting contract with the Raggis" and "cont: to dischar Raggi." Dft (ViU: TJP); written entirely in TJ's hand on a small scrap; undated and unsigned. Not recorded in SJL. Enclosed in

TJ to Cocke, 5 Sept., and Cocke to TJ, 7 Sept. 1820.

A letter from TJ to Brockenbrough of 6 Sept. 1820, not found, is recorded in SJL with additional notation: "acc^ts."

[1] Dft here adds "& journey."
[2] Word interlined in Dft.

From Thomas Cooper

D^R SIR   sep. 8. 1820 Philad^a

Mr Vaughan cut the inclosed out of a Carolina Paper that came here yesterday. I suppose it must have been of date about the last of last month.

I understand there have been no cases of sickness but among the irish who work on the Canal. I am with great respect

D^r sir Yr obliged friend & servant   THOMAS COOPER

RC (MHi); endorsed by TJ as received 24 Sept. 1820 and so recorded in SJL. Enclosure: clipping, pasted at foot of text, from the *Charleston Courier*, 26 Aug. 1820, which reads "HEALTH OF COLUMBIA.—The citizens of Columbia continue to enjoy uninterrupted good

health. But two or three inhabitants of the place have died during the summer, and perhaps as many strangers; and at present our physicians are the most idle men in town." The *Courier* credited this article to the 22 Aug. 1820 issue of the *Columbia Telescope*.

From William Charles Jarvis

HON^D SIR   Pittsfield September. 8. 1820

I take the liberty of transmitting to you a copy of a book, which has employed a few of my leisure hours, and I beg you to do me the honour to accept it. I do not however present it to you, under a beleif that it is worthy of your perusal; I merely offer it as a testimony[1] of that respect & esteem which I have invariably entertained for your private & public character. Should, however, the sentiments & veiws developed by it, be in any measure worthy of your approbation it will be the greatest satisfaction to me.—

As I am altogather unknown to you you will permit me to remark, that I am the nephew of the late Doctor Charles Jarvis of Boston, in which place I formerly resided. You will allow me to add my fervent wishes, that the evening of your days may be as serene & happy as the most enlightened phylosophy, & the gratitude of a nation, can render it=

I am

With the highest respect Your very Ob^t Ser^t

WILLIAM, CHARLES. JARVIS

RC (MHi); endorsed by TJ as received 24 Sept. 1820 and so recorded in SJL. RC (DLC); address cover only; with PoC of TJ to Theodorus Bailey, 9 Sept. 1821, on verso; addressed: "Hon^l Thomas Jefferson Montecello Verginia"; franked; postmarked Pittsfield, Mass., 9 Sept. Enclosure: Jarvis, *The Republican; or, A Series of Essays on the Principles and Policy of Free States. having a particular reference to the United States of America and the Individual States* (Pittsfield, 1820; Poor, *Jefferson's Library*, 11 [no. 653]).

William Charles Jarvis (1782–1836), attorney and public official, was born in Boston. Having been trained in the law, he received an honorary master's degree from Williams College in 1811 and settled in Pittsfield by the following year. Jarvis established a legal practice there, served as secretary of the Berkshire Agricultural Society, was a founder and director of the Pittsfield Mutual Fire Insurance Company, and ran unsuccessfully for the United States House of Representatives in 1822. A member of the Massachusetts House of Representatives in 1821–25, 1826–28, and 1830–31, he was its Speaker for four terms, 1823–25 and 1826–28. After moving back to the Boston area in 1825, Jarvis was a director of the state penitentiary, a state senator in 1828–29

and, briefly, a federal customs inspector before his removal from office early in Andrew Jackson's presidency. Apparently upset at being defrauded of some property, he killed himself with a pistol in Weathersfield, Vermont. Jarvis left real estate and personal property worth $1,786 (*General Catalogue of the Officers and Graduates of Williams College* [1920], 185; Pittsfield *Sun*, 20 June 1812; *Pittsfield Sun*, 3 Aug. 1815, 17 Mar., 5 May 1819, 8 May 1822, 18 Sept. 1828, 3 Dec. 1829; *Resolves of the General Court of the Commonwealth of Massachusetts* [Boston, 1824], 339, 501; Henry D. Coolidge and James W. Kimball, *A Manual for the Use of the General Court for 1921* [1921], 260; *Independent Chronicle & Boston Patriot*, 30 Oct. 1822, 7 May 1825; Worcester *National Ægis*, 4 Jan. 1826; *Salem Gazette*, 24 June 1828; Jackson, *Papers*, 7:552–6; Lenox *Berkshire Journal*, 13 May 1830; DNA: RG 29, CS, Mass., Woburn, 1830; *New-Bedford Mercury*, 14 Oct. 1836; gravestone inscription in Weathersfield Bow Cemetery; Middlesex Co., Mass., Probate Court Records, case no. 12515).

Jarvis also sent the enclosed book to John Adams with a brief 17 Feb. 1821 covering letter (MHi: Adams Papers).

^{1} Manuscript: "testmony."

From Alexander Garrett

D^R SIR   Charlottesville 9th September 1820

Before you left home, I examined the state of the funds of the University at the command of the Bursar, and thought them sufficient to meet the usual drafts, untill your return but contrary to my expectation, the drafts for the current week have been unusually heavy. I have therefore enclosed you a check on the Farmers bank of Virginia for five thousand dollars, the remainder of the deposit there which please approve and forward me by the return of the mail, I have left my signature blank to avoid accidants.

Very Respect^y Your Mo. Ob^t S^t   ALEX: GARRETT

RC (CSmH: JF); endorsed by TJ as received 15 Sept. 1820 and so recorded in SJL. Enclosure not found.

From Henry Guegan

MONSIEUR,   Baltimore, 9 Septembre, 1820.

Je n'ai reçu qu'aujourd'hui l'honneur de vos missives datées 27 Aout et 3 Septembre en vous répondant de suite, je m'empresse de reparer un retard causé par mon absence de Baltimore.

Conformément aux dispositions de votre honorée du 27, je vous adresserai:

Stephani Thesaurus linguae Groecae 5 vol. fol. vel. Bound.

je ne pensais pas qu'un de mes catalogues Grecs et Latins vous parviendrait sans que l'erreur typographique de 28 D. au lieu de 38 ne fut relevée le prix de cet ouvrage étant de 300 francs à Paris je ne puis sans trop grande perte le placer à moins de—$38 c'est-à dire presqu'au deux tiers de sa valeur. je vous l'expedierai persuadé que le mérite de ce livre fera qu'il vous conviendra encore à ce prix.

Vous recevrez également,

Vossius Etymologicon Linguæ Latinæ f° Bound   4

Longinus in Greek, with the English translation, printed in Baltimore. 1810. price   1 50

je n'ai plus à ma disposition Persoon synopsis plantarum et Xenophon Edition de Leipsic complète en 5 vol. in—18, sans notes, ni version latine, mais je ne tarderai pas à recevoir de nouveau ces deux ouvrages.

Je prendrai la liberté de joindre à l'envoi un catalogue des livres Grecs et latins les plus rares (avec prix) imprimés en Allemagne et en france et qui se trouvent à la librairie de paris avec laquelle je Suis en relation directe; j'y joindrai aussi, une liste complette des classiques qui forment ma collection actuelle.

quant au paiement, il se fera à votre plaisir après la reception et la vérification des livres, qui non seulement devront vous arriver en Bon état, mais encore être conformes à ceux Stipulés dans votre demande.

Voici les titres exacts demandés par votre lettre du 1er Septembre pour vous fixer sur les Editions <u>Patres Græci</u>, <u>Patres Latini</u>.

<u>Patrum sanctorum Grœcorum</u> Opera polemica; A. Justini, (S.) Clementis Alexandrini (S.) Origenis; ad Edition. Parisiensis. recusa, grœce et latine; ed. Oberthür. Wirceburg. 1777— —1794. 21 vol. in 8° 45 D./

Patrum (ss.) Latinorum Opera omnia; ed. Oberthür. Wirceburg. 1780. 13 vol. in 8° 28 D./

Cette collection renferme:

Q. Septimii florentis <u>Tertulliani</u> opera omnia	2 vol.
<u>S. Cœcilii Cypriani</u> Opera omnia (acced. varia variorum opera) <u>M. minucii felicis Octavius</u>	2.—
<u>Arnobii Afri adversus</u> Gentes libri VII; et <u>Julii firmicii</u> materni de Errore profanarum Religionum libellus.	1.—
<u>Lucii Cæcilii firmiani Lactantii</u> Opera omnia	2.—
<u>S. Hilarii</u> Opera omnia	4.—
<u>S. Optati Afri</u> de Schismate Donatistarum[1] libri VII et alia huc pertinentia vetera monumenta.	2.—
	13.

Les deux ouvrages Mentionnés ci-dessus sont Brochés une reliure Soignée couterait ici 50 cents par Volume

N'ayant pas encore assez l'habitude d'Ecrire en Anglais, J'ose compter, Monsieur, Sur votre indulgence pour me pardonner d'avoir employé la langue de mon Pays, <u>avec la certitude qu'elle vous est familière.</u>

J'ai l'honneur d'Etre avec le plus profond respect,

De votre Excellence, le très humble et très obéissant Serviteur

HENRY GUEGAN

EDITORS' TRANSLATION

SIR,   Baltimore, 9 September, 1820.

I have only today had the honor of receiving your letters dated 27 August and 3 September. I hasten to make up for the delay caused by my absence from Baltimore by replying to you at once.

In accordance with the provisions of your honored letter of the 27th, I will send you:

Stephani Thesaurus Linguae Graecae 5 vol. fol. vel. Bound.

I did not think that one of my Greek and Latin catalogues would reach you before the typographical error of $28, instead of $38, was corrected. As this book costs 300 francs in Paris, I cannot, without suffering too great a loss, sell it for less than $38, which is hardly two-thirds of its value. Convinced that this book's merit will make it agreeable to you even at this price, I will send it to you.

You will also receive,

Vossius Etymologicon Linguæ Latinæ f° Bound   4

Longinus in Greek, with the English translation, printed in Baltimore. 1810. price   1.50

I no longer have at my disposal <u>Persoon Synopsis Plantarum</u> or <u>Xeno-phon</u>, either the complete 5-volume Leipzig edition in 18mo, without notes, or the Latin version, but before long I will receive these two works again.

I will take the liberty of adding to the package a catalogue of the rarest Greek and Latin books (including prices) printed in Germany and France that are to be found in the Paris bookstore with which I am in direct contact. I will also enclose a complete list of the classical works making up my current collection.

Regarding payment, you may do so at your pleasure after receiving and looking over the books, which should reach you not only in good condition, but also matching the ones stipulated in your order.

Here are the exact titles of the editions of the <u>Patres Græci</u> and <u>Patres Latini</u> requested in your letter of 1 September.

<u>Patrum Sanctorum Græcorum</u> Opera Polemica; A. Justini, (S.) Clementis Alexandrini (S.) Origenis; ad Edition. Parisiensis. Recusa, Græce et Latine; ed. Oberthür. Wirceburg. 1777— —1794. 21 vol. in 8° 45 D./

Patrum (ss.) Latinorum Opera Omnia; ed. Oberthür. Wirceburg. 1780. 13 vol. in 8° 28 D./

This collection includes:

<u>Q. Septimii Florentis Tertulliani</u> Opera Omnia	2 vol.
<u>S. Cæcilii Cypriani</u> Opera Omnia (acced. varia variorum opera)	
M. minucii Felicis Octavius	2.—
<u>Arnobii Afri</u> Adversus Gentes Libri VII; and <u>Julii Firmicii</u>	
Materni de Errore Profanarum Religionum Libellus.	1.—
<u>Lucii Cæcilii Firmiani Lactantii</u> Opera Omnia	2.—
<u>S. Hilarii</u> Opera Omnia	4.
<u>S. Optati Afri</u> de Schismate Donatistarum libri VII et alia huc	
pertinentia vetera monumenta.	2.—
	13.

The two works mentioned above are stitched in paper. A good binding here would cost fifty cents per volume

Not yet having acquired the habit of writing in English, I dare to rely on your indulgence, Sir, to forgive me for having used the language of my coun-try, <u>with the certainty of your familiarity with it.</u>

I have the honor to be with the most profound respect,
Your Excellency's most humble and very obedient servant

HENRY GUEGAN

RC (MHi); addressed: "His Excellency Th,, Jefferson Monticello"; franked; inconsistently postmarked Baltimore, 8 Sept.; endorsed by TJ as received 24 Sept. 1820 and so recorded in SJL. Translation by Dr. Genevieve Moene.

TJ's letter to Guegan of 3 SEPTEMBRE was actually dated 1 Sept. 1820.

VEL.: vellum. For the PATRES GRÆCI and PATRES LATINI, see TJ to Guegan, 1 Sept. 1820, and note. ACCED. VARIA VARIORUM OPERA: "with works by various individuals." ET ALIA HUC PERTINENTIA VETERA MONUMENTA: "and other old and related written memorials."

[1] Manuscript: "Donastitorum."

From William W. Hening

SIR,   Richmond Sept. 9. 1820

I am just favored with your letter of the 3rd of this month.

How the M.S. volume A. should have found its way to Williamsburg, is to me perfectly incomprehensible. I rejoice that it is regained.

I was so well sa[tis]fied, from your letter of April 25 1815, that the M.S. D. was your property, that I did not hesitate to give it the destination you requested. At the same time I explained the reasons for its detention, after the other volumes had been forwarded. The caption prefixed to the laws, taken from that Volume, was warrantd by the information which I then possessed.—I am now sensible that it was erroneous.—I shall make a note to that effect, in the preface to the next volume I publish; and whenever the early volumes may be republished, I shall mark it, in its proper place

The 7th Volume of the Statutes at Large having been completed, I send you a volume, bound in elegant calf, to match the set I last sent you, also one in ordinary binding to complete the former set; the 4th 5th & 6th volumes of which were left with Mr Gibson, to be forwarded to you.

As soon as I shall have finished the printing of the 3rd edition of[1] the Virginia Justice, which will probably be in three weeks, I shall put the 8th Volume of the Statutes at Large to press.—This will terminate the laws under the Colonial government. It has occurred to me, that between the acts of 1773, and the Ordinances of Convention of 1775, the chasm might be filled up to great advantage, with papers, marking the rise and progress of those troubles, which led to the revolution.—On this subject I should be greatly indebted for your advice and assistance.

In your letter of Apr. 8. '15, you observe that you have still a volume of ancient records, not in your catalogue, which might furnish matter for a valuable supplementary appendix, when the work shall have been brought down to the revolution. If you would point out the mode in which I could have access to it, as well as furnish some hints, as to the best use to which it could be converted, I should be much delighted.

I should be gratified, indeed, if my labours could be brought to a close, with two more volumes.—But, after the publication of the 8th they will just commence with the Ordinances of Convention, & Laws of the revolution,—a very interesting period to the people of Virginia.—I have determined, however, to make my volumes larger, keeping within a convenient[2] size, so as to effect my great object as early as possible.—My original prospectus contemplated the bringing down the laws to the revisal of 1792. Perhaps it may be found expedient to come down to a later period.

I am resp[y] yr[s]   W[M] W: HENING

RC (DLC); hole in manuscript; endorsed by TJ as received 24 Sept. 1820 and so recorded in SJL. Enclosure: two copies of Hening, vol. 7.

[1] Preceding five words interlined.
[2] Manuscript: "convenent."

From Peter S. Du Ponceau

DEAR SIR   Philad[a] 12th Sep[r] 1820

The Vocabulary of the Nottoway language which you have had the goodness to send to me, has only encreased my thirst for more. There are, you Say, yet in Virginia remnants of the Mattaponey & Pamunkey Tribes—If vocabularies of those could be obtained, it might lead to interesting results. The Nottoways, I have no doubt, were the ancient Tuscaroras, who the two others were, remains to be discovered. The principal Indian population must have been Delaware or Algonkin—Yet there were other Savage nations, particularly the Hurons or Wyandots. For in Burkes History of Virginia, we find mention made of an Indian Idol called <u>Oki</u>; now <u>Oki</u> in Wyandot means a "<u>Spirit</u>," & the word is found in no other Indian language that I know of.

It appears to me that the Algonkins or Delawares inhabited all the Country between Canada & Carolina, the Iroquois had their Chief Settlements on the great Lakes, yet, like the Modern New Englanders, they were found every where; their alliance with the English gave them a Superiority & ascendancy over the rest, to which their numbers did not entitle them. If thr[o]' some of your inquisitive Country men, other Vocabularies of the Virginia Indian languages could be obtained, I think it might lead to interesting Conclusions.

I regret that Professor Wilson did not ask for the true national name of your Nottaways, for <u>Nottaway</u>, it seems, or Naudowassie, is a Name which the Algonkins gave to other Nations differing from themselves, much as the Turks call all the Europeans <u>Franks</u> & as we call all the Mahometans Turks—The name of the Nottaways <u>in</u> <u>Nottaway</u>, Seems yet to be known.

Mr Pickering, of Salem, has made a Communication to the American Academy of Boston, in which he proposes an uniform Orthography for Indian Words. I have the honor of enclosing a Copy of it for your Acceptance.

I have the honor to be With the highest Veneration & respect Sir Your most obedient humble servant   PETER S, DU PONCEAU

RC (DLC); edge chipped; at head of text: "Thomas Jefferson, Esqr"; endorsed by TJ as received 24 Sept. 1820 and so recorded in SJL. FC (PPAmP: APS Historical and Literary Committee Letterbook). Enclosure: John Pickering, *An* *Essay on a Uniform Orthography for the* *Indian Languages of North America, as* *published in the Memoirs of the American* *Academy of Arts and Sciences* (Cambridge, Mass., 1820), or an earlier printing of this work.

From Patrick Gibson

SIR   Richmond 12 Septr 1820

I have recd your favor of the 6th Inst inclosing your note for $1378. for the renewal of one in the V^a Bk due <u>this day</u>—in my letter of the 17 July I informed you that this note had then been reduced to $1307. and as it must now be renewed for $1240. of course the note you inclosed will not answer the purpose but having still the one last sent, in blank, I am enabled to accomplish it.—the next renewal in November will be for $1180.—Annexed is a statement of your acct balanced by $262.72 in my favor

Yours respectfully   (signed) PATRICK GIBSON

RC (DLC); entirely in a clerk's hand; between dateline and salutation: "Thomas Jefferson Esqre"; enclosure on verso; endorsed by TJ as received 3 Oct. 1820 and so recorded in SJL; with notation by TJ at foot of verso: "1378:1307:1240:1180: 71   67   60."

Account with Patrick Gibson

[ca. 12 Sept. 1820]

Account Sales of 19 Bbls flour & One Hhd Tobacco for Th: Jefferson

1820

May 1	Recd for 1 Hhd Tobacco Shockoe				
	TJ 1710.160.1550. Refused @ $5.10				$79.05
June 21	Recd of Robt Pollard for 13 bbls S:fine flour @ 4\frac{1}{8}$.			$53.63	
22	" " John Bell for 5 bbls Fine flour @ $3.$\frac{3}{4}$			18.75	
23	" " Cash for 1 S:fine Cond bbl		4.	76.38	
	Charges				155.43
	Toll on 19 Bbls Flour $1.98 d° on 1. Hhd Tob° 42¢	$2.40			
	dray° on 2 Hhds 40¢ Insp^n on 1 Hhd 50¢	90	$3.30		
	Insp^n on 19 Bbls 38¢. Coop^e 38¢ Storage $2.38	3.14			
	Commission on $155.43 @ 2$\frac{1}{2}$ pr Ct	3.89	7.33	10.63[1]	
				144.80[2]	

MS (DLC: TJ Papers, 218:38949); undated; on verso of and in same clerk's hand as covering letter.

S:FINE: "superfine."

[1] The correct sums are 7.03 and 10.33.
[2] The correct sum is 145.10.

Extract from Ellen W. Randolph (Coolidge) to Martha Jefferson Randolph

Poplar Forest. Sept. 13th 1820

We have reached our journey's end my dear Mother, in safety, not without some disagreable adventures, such as being confined one whole day by the rain—at <u>Flood's tavern</u>.[1] we left Uncle Eppes's before sun-rise monday—the morning was lowering, and it was dropping rain before we set out, but you know Grand-papa—he was morally certain we should have "a cool agreable cloudy day for our journey, so preferable to travelling through the hot sun"[2]—about nine o clock it began to rain violently; we were exposed two hours and a half, untill at half after eleven oclock we were glad to take shelter in the filthiest of all filthy places, and remain untill the next morning when we were enabled to continue our journey—it is impossible to describe, the horrors which we witnessed at Floods—and I do not believe that in any civilized country such another spesimen could be given of the degree of degradati[on] to which man may be reduced by dirt—these people have been growing worse and worse, untill it has become absolute pollution to breathe the same air with them—I believe a Hottentot would turn away with loathing—add to this the old woman has fallen into her dotage, and both the old and the young are eternally scolding, and their discordant screaming voices, drove me from corner to corner of the filthy sewer they inhabit—there was literally no rest for the "soles of our feet",[3] and we should all have preferred travelling through the rain, had it not been for Burwell & the drivers—Grandpapa has born the journey pretty well, but to day one of his legs on which the bandage had slipped is a good deal swelled and even blistered. I am afraid he is beginning to get too old for these long journeys, in all weathers and with such uncomfortable fixtures. I look forward with alarm to almost[4] the whole of autumn past,[5] at a distance from his family, his physician and the comforts of his home.

I found the harpsichord in a very bad state, the sound-board split for 12 or 14 inches, the strings almost all gone, many of the keys swelled so that when pressed down they do not rise again, and the steel part of the different stops so much rusted that several of them refuse to obey the hand. the music is mouldy, and some of it dropping to pieces—the instrument itself & the books lay in a cellar, I think Mrs Eppes told me six or seven years. Francis and myself turned over the books together; we found the name of Maria Jefferson, & the initials of M. E. written in Aunt Maria's own hand in a great many different places; some of the songs, too were evidently copied by herself. I have almost entirely[6] forgotten her, but these were so many mute memorials;

RC (ViU: Coolidge Correspondence); extract, consisting of opening of letter; edge trimmed; signed with the initials "E.W.R." on concluding page above two postscripts; addressed: "Mrs T. M. Randolph Monticello Charlottesville Post Office Albemarle," with additional notation: "Lewis"; stamped; postmarked New London, 14 Sept.; endorsed by Martha Jefferson Randolph. In the unextracted portion of this letter, Randolph reflects on how different things would have been if her aunt Maria Jefferson Eppes had lived; describes John Wayles Eppes's second wife, Martha B. Eppes, as "very amiable" and "an excellent manager both of her children, and her household affairs"; remarks that the Eppes offspring are "the very best I ever saw, and the boys as good and as clean as the girls"; expresses her love for her mother and siblings and for her sister "Virginia in particular"; states that she will write her sister Cornelia shortly "about her Bedford acquaintances"; requests that Aunt Virginia Randolph Cary be informed that her ring is safe and that at Mill Brook an old beau of hers inquired about her so minutely as to make Randolph think that "neither time, nor absence, nor <u>marriage</u>, had produced the usual effect"; and reveals that their party will "almost certainly" be back at Monticello for dinner on 24 Sept. 1820.

Accompanied by his granddaughters Ellen W. Randolph (Coolidge) and Mary J. Randolph, TJ set out for his Bedford County estate on 7 Sept. 1820, spent 8–11 Sept. at Mill Brook (UNCLE EPPES'S), was obliged to TAKE SHELTER one night at Henry Flood's Ordinary, arrived at Poplar Forest on 12 Sept. 1820, and got back to Monticello twelve days later (Elizabeth Trist to Nicholas P. Trist,

9 Oct. 1820 [RC in DLC: NPT]; *MB*, 2:1367–8).

In this context a HOTTENTOT is a "person of inferior intellect or culture" or "an uncivilized or ignorant person" (*OED*). Variants of the phrase NO REST for the SOLES OF OUR FEET appear in the Bible (Genesis 8.9; Deuteronomy 28.65). TJ's PHYSICIAN was Thomas G. Watkins. An image of a similar HARPSICHORD is reproduced elsewhere in this volume.

[1] Omitted period at right margin editorially supplied.
[2] Omitted closing quotation mark editorially supplied.
[3] Reworked from "sole of my foot."
[4] Word interlined.
[5] Reworked from "whole fall past here."
[6] Word interlined.

From David Gelston

DEAR SIR,   New York September 15th 1820.

I have this day shipped the small <u>bale</u> of books, bill of lading enclosed,

I wish them safe to hand, and am, with great affection and esteem,

Dear Sir, your obedient servant,   DAVID GELSTON

RC (MHi); endorsed by TJ as received 24 Sept. 1820 and so recorded in SJL; with TJ's notation adjacent to endorsement: "7.75." RC (MHi); address cover only; with PoC of TJ to Joel Yancey, 18 Aug. 1821, on verso; addressed: "Thomas Jefferson Esquire Monticello"; franked; postmarked New York, 16 Sept.; redirected in an unidentified hand above postmark: "Fwd From Monticello Sullivan County New York." Enclosure not found.

From Samuel Thurber

HONR[D] SIR,   Providence R.I. 15th Sep[t] 1820

Six years have almost expired since I rec[d] your much esteemed reply to my request, I have often red it, then paused with gratitude for the fatherly admonition; About that time the Cotton, as well as all other business began to require new calculations, the fortunate circumstance of a general peace, caused such an overturning as confounded all speculation, Cotton Mills stopping, Owners failing, such estates selling at several hun[d] [P]r C[t] loss to the owners, On that business was my princeple dependence, Such circumstances checked my intention and caused me to call on my family to double our diligence and to attend to riged oeconomy, all ware agreed, HEAVEN, hath favr^d us, all have been blest with health, all have managed to general satisfaction none complain, consequently we have not lestned our property, altho I presume it would not bring more than half so many dollars[1] as it might have done about the time I wrote you, The business is now good; But by no means so lucrative as to admit of waste or neglect, it is such however as will admit an industerious careful company (if not too numerous) a comfortable support, Was all business as that now is by some carefully attended to, the people would in my opinion be much more happy than they are; Government hath done enough for that branch, more would according to my understanding reather injure than benefit even the Manufacturers themselves, by causeing them to become inattentive; Since I have become located as I am, I feel anxious for an additional fav^r that is, a Meeting House in my neighberhood, not that I expect to gain HEAVEN, by climbing a sectary's steeple, but believeing that nothing hath a better tendency to moralize a people, than to have at hand a convenant place where to attend and hear true republican preaching; While museing on the subject, something seems to whisper in my ear; Inform your friend Jefferson, let him know the subject on which you are contemplateing, the impulsion is such that I am induced to transmit a copy of our proposed constitution, to which we should be highly gratefyed by having a portion of your wisdom and benovelence annexed,[2] preveous to applying for an act of incorperation;—Be pleased to accept my most fervent desires for the continuance

of your health, strength and prosperity,   SAM^L THURBER

A number of the inhabetants in the Northerly part of the town of Providence, are desirous for errecting a house wherein to meet for the worship of Almighty GOD, but are unable of themselves to do it; and are not all agreed in their religious opinions; They are however all agreed that every man has a right to his own opinion and to put his own construction on the words of holy writ, and have agreed on the following as the foundation of their society; that those of whom donations are soliceted may know that they ask not aid to support bigotry, but to enlarge that charity which "envieth not and is not easily provoked,"

1st   As a majority of those engaged in the errection of said house are of the Baptist[3] perswasion, the said house when erected shall be a Baptist meeting house,

2nd   That to become a member of said Society or the Church which may meet in said house for worship, no subscription to any Creed, articles of faith or Covenent shall be required, nor shall any person be required to make any other confession of faith than a belief in the scriptures of the Old and New Testament; Every member shall also have the right to give that meaning to the words of Scripture, which shall accord with his own understanding of truth,

3rd   Exclusions from the Church shall be had for immoral conduct, and for a denial of the faith stated in the second article, but for no other cause,

4th   No person shall be permitted to preach in said house who does not sustain a good moral Charictor; nor shall any Stranger be permitted to preach in said house, unless he produces satisfactory testimonials[4] of his charictor and standing;

5th   Any preacher, sustaining the charictor or produceing the testimonials above mentioned, shall at the request of any three members of said society, have a right to preach in said house at any time when the same shall not be ocupied by the society's preacher and is not preveously engaged, Provided however that there shall be no meeting in said house for worship by candl light, unless by consent of a majority of the society,

6th   The property and exclusive controle of said house shall be in the owners of the pews,[5] and such others as may have subscribed twenty Dollars towards erecting said house; Each owner of a pew and such subscriber to have one Vote and such and such onley to be members of the society,

7th   There shall be one pew on each side of the pulpit for such white persons as are hard of hearing, also suitable seats in the Galery for Strangers and a place shall be assigned for people of collour,

8th   A majority of the pew holders, shall have a right to order all necessary repairs to said house, and to assess the expence of the same, on the pews according to a standing valuation thereof, they shall also have a right to make assessments on said pews for the payment of any contracts which they may make appertaining to the institution, the pews to be answerable for all such assessments,[6]

9th   The care of the house, and the management of the affairs of the society, shall be in a Committee of five to be anually appointed by the society and to whom application shall be made for the ocupancy of said house for any purpose other than worship, and for any preacher other than the regular preacher of the society,

Thus we have for the present concluded   S T

NB. considering who and what we are, we have met with tolerable incouragement having the promise of something more than 300 Federal Dollars,

NB, Mr Eddy hath been roughly handled for his vote in Congress on the Mossouri question, nothing hath been left undone to prevent his reelection, there are some doubts wheather scattering votes will not prevent it, he could not have succeeded had the vote been taken ten days before it was, his opposers began a little too soon, every day gave new light to the people, every day was so in his fav^r that I have no doubt but that if the vote was now to be taken he would gain a large majority,   S T

Between the 1st & 12th Ins^t the weather was so hot and the air (being mostly from the SW) so dense that it generated a contagion in a thick part of our town, several ware taken off[7] suddenly, others are now convalescent, happely on the 12th we had a brisk gale with a little rain from the South, which in the after part of the day changed with violence into the N,W, from thence it came cool and the air pure, I have since heard of but two new cases—

RC (RHi); addressed: "Thomas Jefferson Esqr Virginia"; stamped; postmarked Providence, 18 Sept.; endorsed by TJ as received 28 Sept. 1820 and so recorded in SJL.

The Fourth Baptist Society of Providence received its ACT OF INCORPERATION from the Rhode Island legislature later in 1820. It held its first meeting in May 1821 and dedicated its new meetinghouse in August 1822 (William R. Staples, *Annals of the Town of Providence* [1843], 471–2). The biblical phrases that charity ENVIETH NOT and IS NOT EASILY PROVOKED are in 1 Corinthians 13.4–5. Although he was sharply criticized for supporting the admission of Missouri into the Union as a slave state, Samuel EDDY continued to represent Rhode Island in Congress until 1825 (*JHR*, esp. 13:276 [2 Mar. 1820]; *Biog. Dir. Cong.*).

[1] Manuscript: "dollers."
[2] Word interlined.
[3] Manuscript: "Babtist."
[4] Manuscript: "testimorials."
[5] Manuscript: "pewes."
[6] Manuscript: "assesments."
[7] Manuscript: "of."

To John H. Cocke

DEAR SIR   Poplar Forest Sep. 16. 20

It this moment occurs to me that on presenting, with our annual report, the accounts of the Bursar and Proctor we ought to be able to state that they have been examined, vouched and passed. you were so kind on behalf of the board, as to undertake this task. would it be practicable for you to do this before our meeting?   I hope you will do us the favor to[1] dine at Monticello the day before meeting as our other brethren are requested to do also. it is a great convenience to have the afternoon and evening to talk over our business at leisure, to make up our minds on it, and go to the University the next day pro formâ only. I salute you with sincere friendship and respect.

TH: JEFFERSON

RC (ViU: TJP); addressed: "Genl John H. Cocke Bremo near New Canton"; franked; postmarked Lynchburg, 18 Sept.; endorsed by Cocke. PoC (DLC); on verso of reused address cover of John Adams to TJ, 28 July 1819; endorsed by TJ.

The ANNUAL REPORT was the 2 Oct. 1820 University of Virginia Board of Visi-

tors Report to Literary Fund President and Directors. The ACCOUNTS of Alexander Garrett as University of Virginia BURSAR and of Arthur S. Brockenbrough as PROCTOR are printed as enclosures to that document.

[1] Manuscript: "to to."

To Alexander Garrett

DEAR SIR   Poplar Forest. Sep. 16. 20.

Your letter of the 9th did not come to hand until yesterday (Friday) and the Charlottesville mail had left Lynchburg the evening before. as the next mail will not reach you until the evening of Saturday next, and I shall be at home to dinner the next day I have thought it safer to carry your blank myself than to trust it by mail. it will be equally ready for the Richmond mail of Tuesday.

The exact sums due on each of the 3 past instalments, & which will be due on the 4th will enter into the body of the report we have to make. as time will press I wish I could find your & the Proctor's accounts at Monticello on my arrival there. affectionately yours

TH: JEFFERSON

PoC (MHi); on verso of reused address cover of Wilson Cary Nicholas to TJ, 17 Aug. 1819; at foot of text: "M[r] Garrett"; mistakenly endorsed by TJ as a letter of

13 Sept. 1820, but correctly recorded in SJL.

For the REPORT and ACCOUNTS, see note to preceding document.

From Thomas Newton

DEAR SIR.   Norfolk Sep[b] 16th 1820

M[r] Everard Hall a respectable Citizen of Princess Anne County— will do himself the pleasure of presenting this to you. He is on a tour through the Western Country. In taking his direction by your Seat, he is solicitous to stop for a moment—and make his respects to you.— they will be sincere—and likewise expressive of his gratitude for your public services—your zealous devotion to your Country's good. Pardon me for this liberty.

I remain with great respect and veneration. Yr: Obt: Servt:

THO: NEWTON

RC (MoSHi: TJC-BC); endorsed by TJ as received 6 Oct. 1820 "by mr Hall" and so recorded in SJL. RC (MoSHi: TJC-BC); address cover only; with PoC of TJ to John A. Wharton, 13 May 1821, on verso; addressed: "Thomas Jefferson esq: Abemarle County V.a."

To Bernard Peyton, with Jefferson's Note

DEAR SIR   Poplar Forest Sep. 16. 20.

In the 1st week of Oct. perhaps on the 3d or 4th day mr Eppes will deposit with his agent in Richmond, 500.D. subject to my order. this is intended to meet the curtailment of October of which you were so kind as to give me timely notice. at the same time perhaps, or if not, then certainly in all that month he will deposit 3500.D. more in like manner. for these sums I shall send you an order on his agent as soon as I shall know his name.

I am here in a leaky house, which cannot be remedied but by sheet iron & tin. I have no funds at present in Richmond, but I presume you can purchase these articles for me on a little credit, which can be paid from the deposit before mentioned. will you then be so good as to procure me a box of tin, and 24. sheets of iron not less than 5. feet long but as much longer as can be had. the breadth to be any where from 12. to 18 I. I shall be at Monticello by the 24th and shall send off my waggon to this place about the 3d or 4th of Oct, and as that will be my quickest & surest conveyance I must pray you to send the iron and tin immediately by some Augusta waggon, to be lodged with James Leitch in Charlve who will pay the carriage, and drop me a line to Monticello that I may know what to depend on. I shall set out again for this place on the 7th of Oct. to continue here till December.[1] I have ordered 100. bar. of flour to be sent to mr Gibson from the Shadwell mills on the first rain which shall make our river boatable. affectionly yours   TH: JEFFERSON

[*Note by TJ at foot of text:*]
P.S. added for books from N.Y.

PoC (MHi); adjacent to signature: "Capt Peyton"; endorsed by TJ.

John Wayles Eppes's AGENT IN RICHMOND was George Perkins. Peyton gave

TJ TIMELY NOTICE of the upcoming $500 curtail on his note with the Farmers' Bank of Virginia in a letter dated 1 June 1820.

[1] Reworked from "Oct."

To Thomas Mann Randolph

DEAR SIR   Poplar Forest. Sep. 16. 20.

In a letter of the 13th ult. to the Secretary of the board of the Literary fund I stated to him that whenever it should be the wish of the board to close the contract for the loan of 20,000.D. to the Visitors of the University of Virginia I would execute the necessary bond on his sending me a copy of it. the Visitors are to meet on the 2[d] of October, and if it would suit the convenience of the board, it would be desirable for the visitors, in the annual report which they are then to address to you, to be laid before the legislature, to be able to state in their report that the whole of the loan has been effected. I shall be at Monticello on the 24th instant ready to recieve the pleasure of the board on this subject. I salute you with affectionate friendship and respect.

TH: JEFFERSON

RC (DLC); addressed: "His Excellency Thomas Mann Randolph Governor of Virginia Richmond"; franked; postmarked Lynchburg, 18 Sept.; endorsed by Randolph as received 28 Sept. 1820. PoC (ViU: TJP); on verso of reused address cover of Peter Poinsot to TJ, 6 June 1819; torn at seal, with one word rewritten by TJ; endorsed by TJ.

From Tobias Watkins

SIR,   Baltimore 16[h] Sept[r] 1820

The Trustees of Baltimore College have received an application for the place of Principal to that institution, from Mr. L. H. Gerardin of Virginia, who has referred us, among other distinguished personages, to you, as being acquainted with his character and pretensions.

As I have been the channel of Mr. Gerardin's application to the Board of Trustees, they have requested me to solicit from you, such information concerning him, as it may be in your power to give. An anxious desire to resuscitate our long dormant College, could alone have induced the Board or myself, to take the liberty of troubling you on this occasion. Your favourable report of Mr. G. will ensure his immediate election.

With sentiments of unfeigned respect and veneration

I have the honor to be Sir Yr. Ob[t] H[l] Sv[t]   T, WATKINS.

RC (CSmH: JF-BA); endorsed by TJ as received 24 Sept. 1820 and so recorded in SJL. RC (DLC); address cover only; with PoC of TJ to Nathaniel Macon, 19 Aug. 1821, on verso; addressed: "Thomas Jefferson Monticello Virginia"; franked; postmarked Baltimore, 16 Sept.

Tobias Watkins (1780–1855), physician, public official, and author, was born in Anne Arundel County, Maryland. He graduated in 1798 from Saint John's College, Annapolis, and was an assistant surgeon in the United States Navy, 1799–1801. After completing medical studies in Philadelphia in 1802, Watkins settled briefly in Havre de Grace, Maryland. He then relocated to Baltimore, where in addition to his medical practice he edited several medical and literary journals, helped write a history of the American Revolution, translated a monograph by Luis de Onís on the negotiations leading up to the 1819 Adams-Onís Treaty between the United States and Spain, and assisted in the revival of Baltimore College. Watkins served as an army surgeon during the War of 1812 and as an assistant surgeon general, 1818–21. He was also a prominent Freemason. By 1822 Watkins moved permanently to Washington, D.C. Appointed fourth auditor of the United States Treasury in 1824, he was imprisoned for fraud and embezzlement five years later. Following his release in 1833, Watkins resumed his medical practice and worked as an educator (James Grant Wilson and John Fiske, eds., *Appletons' Cyclopædia of American Biography* [1887–89], 6:388; Howard A. Kelly and Walter L. Burrage, *American Medical Biographies* [1920], 1205; *Triennial Catalogue of St. John's College* [1858], 17; Callahan, *U.S. Navy*, 571; Heitman, *U.S. Army*, 1:1008; Watkins to James Madison, 31 May 1815 [DNA: RG 107, LRSW]; Frank Luther Mott, *A History of American Magazines* [1930–38; repr. 1970], 1:293–6; Judah Delano, *The Washington Directory* [Washington, 1822], 80; Washington *Daily National Intelligencer*, 5 May, 15 Aug. 1829, 22 Apr. 1833, 15 Nov. 1855; Anthony Reintzel, comp., *The Washington Directory, and Governmental Register, for 1843* [1843], 94; DNA: RG 29, CS, Washington, D.C., 1840, 1850).

From Jared Sparks

Sir,   Baltimore, Sept. 18. 1820.

I hope you will pardon the liberty I take in sending you a work, which I have lately published, and which accompanies this note. I know not whether the sentiments advanced in it agree in any respect with yours; but should you have leisure & inclination to look it over, I trust you will not be displeased with its manner & spirit. You will at least be ready to countenance any fair and liberal discussions of topics, which have a bearing on the interests of society, and which have long engaged the attention of wise and good men.

I was sorry not to find, in the library of Congress, Ledyard's Book, which you were so kind as to mention to me. The librarian thought it could never have been there. I may find it perhaps in Connecticut among some of the family. I have taken pains to procure from England materials for a life of Ledyard. I shall spare no exertions to obtain the letters, which he wrote to you. Should any thing occur to your mind, which may give interest to the subject, in addition to what is contained in those letters, & in your[1] Life of Lewis, you will confer a particular favour by making me acquainted with it.

With sentiments of high respect and esteem, your humble Sevt—

JARED SPARKS.

RC (DLC); between dateline and salutation: "Thomas Jefferson, Montecello"; endorsed by TJ as received 31 Oct. 1820 and so recorded in SJL. FC (Lb in MH: Sparks Collection); with parenthetical note at foot of text identifying the enclosure and stating that "I lately saw Mr. Jefferson at Monticello, where I talked with him about Ledyard." Enclosure: Sparks, *Letters on the Ministry, Ritual, and Doctrines of the Protestant Episcopal Church, addressed to the Rev. Wm. E. Wyatt, D.D.* (Baltimore, 1820; Poor, *Jefferson's Library*, 9 [no. 530]).

The LIBRARIAN of Congress, George Watterston, mistakenly suggested that John Ledyard, *A Journal of Captain Cook's last Voyage to the Pacific Ocean, and in quest of a North-West Passage, between Asia & America* (Hartford, 1783; Sowerby, no. 3940), COULD NEVER HAVE BEEN in the collection. It was in fact among the books TJ sold to the nation in 1815 (*Catalogue of the Library of the United States. To Which is Annexed, A Copious Index, Alphabetically Arranged* [Washington, 1815], 120). For the LIFE OF LEWIS, see TJ to Paul Allen, 18 Aug. 1813.

[1] RC: "you." FC: "your."

To Samuel Garland

DEAR SIR   Poplar Forest Se[p.] 20. 20.

Altho I am to return to this place again within three weeks, and then to remain here till December, yet not having had the pleasure of seeing you while here I think it a duty to say something as to my expectations of discharging my debt to mr Millar. I have already made sales[1] [o]f some property and expect to recieve a part of the money in all October, which will enable me to pay you 800. or 1000.Ď. then: and in the spring, say in all May & June 1500.D. more; and the balance, I hope, within a twelve month from that time. if I should be able to make a further sale of some land in this county I may accomplish the whole sooner. the difficulties of collecting money, so well known to yourself and that they are likely to continue some time, may produce some delay to me also: but nothing shall be spared on my part to prevent it, nor shall I one moment lose sight of this object. accept the assurance of my great esteem & respect.   TH: JEFFERSON

PoC (MHi); on verso of reused address cover to TJ; two words faint; at foot of text: "M^r <E> S. Garland"; endorsed by TJ.

MR MILLAR: Boyd Miller. TJ had recently sold the 400-acre Pouncey's tract in Albemarle County to Charles Everette. He received his second installment from the purchaser in two parts, on 9 Aug. and 19 OCTOBER 1820 (*MB*, 2:1366, 1369).

[1] Manuscript: "salas," with word misspelled by TJ while enhancing faint text.

From Cesario Bias

Your letter of the 16ᵗʰ Inst to B. Peyton was yesterday received. The iron and tin, you wished sent up, have been to day procured and forwarded to Mʳ Leitch: the iron, (the longest I could get) is $5\frac{1}{2}$ feet. And was got on a credit of 60 days, the tin was a very saleable article and could not be got on a credit of any definite period; the seller said he would settle it with Mʳ Peyton on his return. Copies of the bills are herewith sent you.— Your note for $3000 to be renewed at the Farmers Bank on the 4ᵗʰ of Oct. will be attended to. the curtailment of $500 of which you speak will have to be met; it is hoped Mʳ Eppes will make the deposit by that time as it might be of some inconvenience to advance the sum, even for a few days; funds being low at present. The package of Books which you mention as having arrived at Richᵈ Mʳ Gibson says has not come to hand as yet—Your request shall be attended to—so soon as the Books arrive.

Yours Respectfully   Cesario Bias

Capt B. Peyton,

Boᵗ of Haxall Brothers & Cᵒ

21ˢᵗ Sept.   24 Sᵗˢ Sheet Iron wᵍ 258ᵗᵇ at 15¢ $38.70.

═══

B. Peyton

Boᵗ of Robert Gordon

21ˢᵗ Sept.

1 Box Tin $14—

═══

RC (MHi); in a clerk's hand, signed by Bias; with postscript in same clerk's hand on verso; endorsed by TJ as a letter from Bernard Peyton "by Cesario Bias" received 24 Sept. 1820 and so recorded in SJL. RC (DLC); address cover only; with PoC of TJ to Frederick W. Hatch, 9 Sept. 1821, on verso; addressed in same clerk's hand: "Mʳ Thomas Jefferson Monticello"; franked; postmarked Richmond, 21 Sept.

Cesario Bias (d. 1866), businessman and farmer, was born in Venice, Italy, and immigrated while young to the United States. He worked as a clerk for Bernard Peyton in Richmond, 1820–22, visited TJ at Monticello in the latter year, and then apparently moved to the Shenandoah Valley. By 1830 Bias had settled in Shelby County, Tennessee, where he was a successful merchant, insurance agent, and bank president, and an active parishioner in Memphis's First Presbyterian Church. He returned to Virginia by the middle of the 1850s and purchased Red Sweet Springs in Alleghany County. Bias operated a hotel and bath there and served as the community's postmaster. In 1860, shortly before he sold his business interests and retired to a farm in Charlotte County, he owned ten slaves, real estate worth $100,000, and personal property valued at $27,000. Late in 1865 Bias relocated to Richmond, where he died after a brief illness (Frances Beal Smith

Hodges, *The Genealogy of the Beale Family, 1399–1956* [1956], 104–5; Bias [for Peyton] to TJ, 9 Apr. 1822; Peyton to TJ, 29 Apr. 1822; Tennessee Genealogical Society, *"Ansearchin'" News* 16 [1969]: 121; DNA: RG 29, CS, Rockbridge Co., 1830, Tenn., Shelby Co., 1840, 1850, Va., Alleghany Co., 1860, 1860 slave schedules; *Register of Officers and Agents, Civil, Military, and Naval, in the Service of the United States* [1855], 147; Richmond *Daily Dispatch*, 28 June 1866; gravestone inscription in Warm Springs Cemetery, Warm Springs).

To Francis Eppes

DEAR FRANCIS   Poplar Forest Sep. 21. 20

I leave at Flood's with this letter a packet containing 3. small volumes of my petit format library containing several tragedies of Euripides, some of Sophocles and one[1] of Aeschylus. the 1st you will find easy, the 2d tolerably so; the last incomprehensible in his flights among the clouds. his text has come to us so mutilated & defective and has been so much plaistered with amendments by his commentators that it can scarcely be called his.

I inclose you our measured distances expressed in miles and cents. we leave this tomorrow morning and shall be at Monticello the next night. from thence you shall hear from me about the end of the 1st week of October. by that time I shall either see Doctr Cooper, or know that I shall not see him. I was decieved in the weather the day we left Millbrook.[2] we past thro' 2. hours of very heavy rain, and got to Flood's at 11. aclock where we staid the day. we did not suffer ourselves but the servants got very wet. present our cordial love to the family. ever & affectionately yours   TH: JEFFERSON

RC (DLC); addressed: "Mr Francis Eppes Mill brook near Raine's tavern"; franked; postmarked Flood's, 22 Sept. PoC (MHi); on verso of reused address cover of Thomas Ewell to TJ, 10 Aug. 1819; endorsed by TJ.

This letter and the books for Eppes were probably left at the post office AT FLOOD'S in Buckingham County in the care of its postmaster, Thomas H. Flood (Axelson, *Virginia Postmasters*, 30). The TRAGEDIES came from TJ's petit-format classical library at Poplar Forest (Leavitt, *Poplar Forest*, 38–9 [no. 647]).

[1] Word interlined.
[2] Manuscript: "Milbrook."

Thomas Jefferson's Notes on Distances between Monticello and Poplar Forest

[ca. 21 Sept. 1820]

Mont°	
Carter's bridge	10.37
Warren ferry	12.35
Raleigh	16.44
Buck. C.H	1.72
Len. Bol's	9.22
Millbrook	6.86
	56.96.
Hendrick's	2.16
new store	6.66
Flood's	15.00
Hunter's	10.44
Chilton's	12.17
Pop. For:	12.15
	58.58

MS (DLC: TJ Papers, 218:38957); written in TJ's hand on verso of a small scrap, attached with wax to covering letter, containing a portion of a note by the Charlottesville merchant John B. Benson: "J. B. Benson pres[ents his?] Compliments to Tho[. . .]"; undated.

CARTER'S BRIDGE was located in Albemarle County on the Hardware River roughly ten miles south of Monticello (Woods, *Albemarle*, 71–2). The RALEIGH was an ordinary situated just west of Buckingham Court House (BUCK. C.H) (*MB*, 2:1161n). LEN. BOL's was the home of Lenaeus (Linnaeus) Bolling in Buckingham County.

From Joel K. Mead

DEAR SIR,   Washington City 25th Septr. 1820

Permit me so far to intrude upon your leisure as to request a few moments of your attention to a project I have in contemplation. I will not take up your time with apoligies or preface, nor weary your attention with a dull enumeration of the advantages I may think it calculated to produce, or the credit it may do us for benevolence or philanthropy. If it possesses any merit you will readily perceive it. My object is to solicit a frank expression of your opinion on its practicability, and such remarks as you may be pleased to make.

A society is about to be formed, or rather I ought to say, I am about to endeavour to form one for the purpose of founding a seminary, or University, for the instruction of indigent young men, of native talents and genius, in the higher branches of literature, the Arts and sciences; to be selected from any and every part of the nation where they may be discovered. But preparatory to any exertion in this respect I am desirous to obtain the opinion of a few gentlemen of liberal minds, eminent for their knowledge and wisdom; and who are above the influence of passion or prejudice.

My plan, should it be thought,[1] advisable, is simply this; in the first place for a few respectable individuals to form themselves into a society (which may hereafter [be][2] increased) then apply to congress for an act of incorporation, and petition that body for a grant of previledge to raise a sum of money by lottery to enable them[3] to carry into effect their object, say 30.000$ pr ann. for ten years. If this be granted, and I see no reason why it should not be, I feel confident that that sum may be raised every year untill it be completed. Which would enable the society, in a few years to lay a permanent foundation, and put into successful opperation, an institution, which, at no very distant day would vie with any in this country, and in time with any in the world. An institution which may be expected to do great credit to[4] the literary character of our country—promote the general defusion of knowledge, and thereby strengthen the bonds of our political union, and rescue from sloth and vice talents capable of great usefulness, which otherwise would be lost to the commonwealth.

But to show my views as far as I have matured them, I will suppose the society organized, with a grant to raise 30.000$ per Ann. for 10 years. This would be sufficient to commence and mature an institution which could be made, under a proper direction, to support itself without further pecuniary aid, by purchasing in the first place, say 40.000 acres of the public lands, which may be had of first quality at the minimum price ($1.25) this would take $50,000. Suppose the lands be located at some proper point in the west, Ohio, Indiania, Illenoise, or Missouri, for example, which, I think advisible on account of the cheapness of living and the future advantage to be realized by the rise in property as the country becomes settled. At the end of the second year we may suppose there will be 60.000$ in hand, a sum sufficient to pay for 40,000 Acres of land and send out under a proper superintendant, at least 30 labourers and support and pay them for one year, to begin a settlement. These 30 laborers, healthy active white young men, enough of whom may be obtained from the north & east for about 100$ pr ann. would be able, if I am correctly informed, to clear in ordinary lands, from 20 to 30 Acres each in the year, or altogether from 600 to 900 Acres. but I will suppose only 400, and cultivate a sufficient quantity to supply themselves in the second year with provisions. This would enable the society to prosecute their settlement[5] at reduced expenses and to commence at least a part of the contemplated buildings. The annual income of 30,000$ would put at the disposal of the society at the end of the fourth year, 60,000$ more, or in all 120,000$ a sum sufficient to effect the clearing and cultivation of at least 1000 acres of land, and erect the necessary buildings for the accommodation of as many pupils as may be supposed to be had in that time, so that I do not think it unreasonable to suppose, before the ten years shall have expired, an institution may grow up in what is now a desert wild, adiquate to support and educate from 200 to 500. pupils continually

Of the 40.000 acres purchased, I would have 4 or 5000 reserved, to be cultivated by the society, for the support of the institution, in provisions, clothing &c, the remainder to be surveyed into lots of 250 or 300 acres each, and every other one leased permanently to good settlers; who should be allowed 5 or 7 years for improvement rent free, after that to pay an annual rent. By this means 50 or 60 families might be settled in the compass[6] of a few miles in extent, whose labours and improvements would greatly enhance the value of the reserved lots, and which might be made in a few years very productive. These remarks are made, as you will perceive, without calculating upon any aid from any other source than the lotteries. But I do not think it unreasonable to suppose that Congress would afford some aid when the institution should get into successful opperation, by the grant of lands, or in some other way. Besides, if the society be so organized to admit an unlimited number of members, each of whom should pay an annual contribution, a considerable revenue would be raised in this way. To insure success it seems to me it is only necessary that a good beginning be made.

The above remarks will be sufficient to communicate a general view of my ideas on this subject. I am aware that some objections may be urged, but I see none which I should deem sufficient to forbid its prosecution. Among other things I know it will be urged that to insure success it ought to be directed by a competent person, who would identify his own interest with that of the institution, and devote himself to its promotion. To this I hope I may be permitted to reply, that my situation will enable me, and my inclination strongly prompts me to devote the remainder of my life to this object. Being a bachelor, and having arrived at what is termed the maredian of life, I feel the full fource of the doctrin taught by one of the Ancient philosophers, I think Pythagoras, "that every useless man is a dead man." He directed that when any of his deciples became weary of studying to make themselves useful to others they should be regarded as <u>dead</u> and have tombs erected to them with suitable inscriptions as warnings to others. Tired of living any longer in death, I know of nothing of which I am capable, that will better intitle me to a place among the living than the devotion of my efforts to the advancement of an institution of the kind above proposed.

Whilst I crave your indulgence for the plain uncourtly style of this note, I beg leave to tender to you my best wishes for the long continuance of your life and health.   JOEL K. MEAD

RC (DLC); endorsed by TJ as received 28 Sept. 1820 and so recorded (mistakenly dated 15 Sept.) in SJL. RC (MHi); address cover only; with PoC of TJ to William Barret, 17 Aug. 1821, on verso; addressed: "Thomas Jefferson Monticello Vᵃ"; franked; postmarked Washington, 26 Sept.

Joel Keeler Mead (ca. 1792–1840), journalist and lottery operator, edited and published the Washington *National Register*, a weekly "Political, Scientific, and Literary Journal," from 1816 to 1818. Apparently unsuccessful in his attempt to establish a charitable society and seminary, he relocated permanently by 1822 to New Orleans, where in 1824 he coedited the daily *Mercantile Advertiser, and Evening Recorder*. Mead operated a lottery office from at least 1828 until 1840. Shortly after his death his net worth was estimated at almost $38,000, including one slave (Washington *National Register*, 2 Mar. 1816; *New-York Columbian*, 16 Mar. 1818; Georgetown *National Messenger*, 29 July 1818; John Adems Paxton, *The New-Orleans Directory and Register* [New Orleans, 1822], 34; Paxton, *A Supplement to the New-Orleans Directory of the Last Year* [New Orleans, 1824]; Little Rock *Arkansas Gazette*, 11 May 1824;

New-Orleans Argus, 21 June 1828; S. E. Percy & Company, *The New-Orleans Directory* [1832], 123; New Orleans *Daily Picayune*, 21 Mar. 1840; L-Ar: Vital Records Indices; LN: Estate Inventories of Orleans Parish Civil Courts, 1803–77).

An eighteenth-century French classicist reported that when any of Pythagoras's disciples lost interest in trying TO MAKE THEMSELVES USEFUL TO OTHERS "all the others regarded him as a dead Person, made his Obsequies, and rais'd him a Tomb, to shew, that if a Man, after having enter'd into the Ways of Wisdom, turns aside and forsakes them, 'tis in vain for him to believe himself living, he is dead" (André Dacier, *The Life of Pythagoras, with his Symbols and Golden Verses. Together with the Life of Hierocles, and his Commentaries upon the Verses* [London, 1707], 26).

Mead addressed a similar letter to James Madison on 12 Oct. 1820 (Madison, *Papers, Retirement Ser.*, 2:128–30).

¹Manuscript: "though."
²Omitted word editorially supplied.
³Manuscript: "then."
⁴Manuscript: "to to."
⁵Manuscript: "settement."
⁶Word interlined in place of "space."

From Samuel Walkup

DEAR SIR,   Natural Bridge, 25 Septr. 1820

I was appointed, with others to view a way for a road from the "Red mill to Gilmore's Mill on James' river by the way of the Natural Bridge." And as the proposed road will goe through a part of your land I have been requested to know whether you will give your approbation to its being established. It is proposed that the "road leave the great road at the Natural Bridge Tavern, thence passing Barclay's & Waskey's land to your line & Ocheltree's & running nearly with said lines to the small house on your land near the Natural Bridge." The other persons interested, agreeing to the establishment, the court, directed that your consent should be applied for[.] This road is considered of public utility, and would be as good a way for a road as is common in this country. From your knowledge of the proposed way through your land I am satisfied you would not consider it an injury to you: it is therefore hoped your consent will be granted. If so, please signify the same to me at Post-Office in Lexington

Very respectfully your Hmb^{le} serv^t   SAM^L WALKUP

RC (MHi); edge trimmed; endorsed by TJ as received 29 Sept. 1820 and so recorded in SJL. RC (DLC); address cover only; with PoC of TJ to Archibald Thweatt, 13 May [1821], on verso; addressed: "Th: Jefferson Esq. Monticello"; franked; postmarked Natural Bridge, 27 Sept.

Samuel Walkup (ca. 1783–1852), farmer and public official, may have been the man of that name who published the *Virginia Religious Magazine* in 1804 and a Lexington newspaper, first known as the *Virginia Telegraphe, and Rockbridge Courier*, and continued under variant titles, 1803–04 and 1806–08. Walkup owned seven slaves in 1820, thirteen twenty years later, and fifteen in 1850. In addition to raising crops, he was a Rockbridge County revenue commissioner, 1839–47. Walkup owned real estate worth $1,000 in 1850 and personal property valued shortly after his death at almost $6,500 (Oren F. Morton, *A History of Rockbridge County Virginia* [1920], 217; Brigham, *American Newspapers*, 2:1119; Lexington *Virginia Telegraphe*, 23 Aug. 1806, 3 Feb. 1808; DNA: RG 29, CS, Lexington, 1820, 1840, Rockbridge Co., 1850, 1850 slave schedules; Rockbridge Co. Will Book, 8:153, 9:14, 282, 392, 10:348, 12:167–8; epitaph in High Bridge Presbyterian Church Cemetery, Natural Bridge).

From Jesse Wharton

DEAR SIR.   Nashville Tennessee Sepr 25th 1820

The subject upon which I wish information, is of such an interesting nature to me, that it will serve as an apology for troubling you so often. I mean the education of the rising generation. No man in the nation, I am well convinced, has had it more at heart and few have done more than yourself, in support of literary institutions; and in exciting among the people a spirit of acquiring useful knowledge— To the point—I have a son and a nephew, both about 16 or 17 years old, they have become pritty well acquainted with the latin & Greek Languages; and I have a wish to take them to some one of the various collidges in these united states; but am a little at a loss to which. If the seminary near Charlottesville will be in complete operation in the spring, I propose bringing them there, particularly if you can recommend the institution. It is located in my native county, and on the very spot where I studied law; and altho I have resided in this state for about 23 years, still feel some little partiality for my native state, and the manners of its citizens.   If that institution will not be in operation by that time, I would be very much oblidged by having your opinion, to what seminary you would advise the sending my children.

I have the honor to be With great respect Y^r friend & ob^t Servt

J. WHARTON

RC (MoSHi: TJC-BC); endorsed by TJ as received 19 Oct. 1820 and so recorded in SJL. RC (MHi); address cover only; with PoC of TJ to John Vaughan, 20 Apr. 1821, on verso; addressed: "Tho. Jefferson Esquire Montecello V^a"; stamped; postmarked Nashville, 27 Sept.

The SON and NEPHEW mentioned above were probably John Overton Wharton and Dabney Miller Wharton, respectively.

From Jerman Baker

D^R SIR,   Richmond 26 Sepr 1820

I received a letter from my friend Co^l Burton of North Carolina a few days since in which he requests me to inform you that he had directed a Cask of very superior Scuppernon Wine to be sent you, by way of Norfolk to this place; It will be brought up in the Steam Boat from Norfolk, with one for me, any Directions that you may give about it shall be particularly attended to.

May I my dear Sir, ask you to have the goodness to enclose me a letter of introduction for my Son Wayles to Judge Cooper of Columbia; Notwithstanding my fears of the climate & the expense I think I Shall indulge him in accompanying his Cousin Francis, particularly as it is so highly recommended by you. If it would not be trespassing too much on your goodness, I should be much gratified if you would give the outlines of the course of study you would recommend him to pursue—

Was the document sent you not long since shewing the amount of Revenue paid by the several Counties such as you wished. There is no table yet made out of the amount paid agreable to the last assessment of the Lands, when it is a copy shall be forwarded if you wish it.

Be pleased to present our affectionate regards to Mrs Randolph & family and accept the assurances of my

Great respect & esteem   JERMAN BAKER

[281]

RC (MHi); endorsed by TJ as received 5 Oct. 1820 and so recorded in SJL. RC (MHi); address cover only; with PoC of TJ to Bernard Peyton, 18 May 1821, on verso; addressed: "Thomas Jefferson es-quire Monticello"; franked; postmarked Richmond, 28 Sept.

COUSIN FRANCIS: Francis Eppes.

Robert Mitchell to Joel Yancey

DEAR SIR   Sep[t] 26=1820

M Turner will hand you Mr Jefferson[s] ⅗, which you will be pleased to collect while down, as I am in extreame want of the money

As to the $50 spoaken of, it will not be an offset against this claime, as the debt is not due to M Jefferson, but to a subscription—I trust M Jefferson will not claime it as an offset—

Respectfully   RO. MITCHELL

RC (ViU: TJP-ER); dateline at foot of text; addressed: "Joel Yancy Esqr Present"; endorsed by TJ: "Mitchell W[m] & Rob[t] Sep. 26. 20."

The $50 SPOAKEN OF was an installment due from Mitchell's brother William Mitchell on his subscription of $200 to Central College in 1817 (Master List of Subscribers to Central College, [after 7 May 1817], document 5 in a group of documents on The Founding of the University of Virginia: Central College, 1816–1819, printed at 5 May 1817; Robert Mitchell to Yancey, 29 Dec. 1819).

From Michele Raggi

STIMATISSIMO SIG[R] JEFFERSON
CHARLOTTESVILLE   Washington 26. 7bre 1820—

Non potendo piu Sofrire il Cativo tratamento della nudritura che mi inviava il suo diretore dl. Coleggio, e vedendo che lei non si prendeva alcuna premura ℔ far venire dei marmi aciò io potessi finire il tempo dl mio Contrato, come avrei fatto se questa sua pietra non avesse rovinato il mio stomaco assieme alla pecora che mi mandava ℔ mangiare il d[to] Sig[r] diretore, che la sol vista di detta vivanda mi stomacava, lei sà bene che il mio Contrato diceva di eser alogiato e nurito a seconda della mia Professione; ne tanpoco ignora come sonno tratati gli Artisti in Italia e Francia! la convenienza il dovere, e Giustizia Vole che io sia sodisfato almeno del viaggio giache lei non mià procurato la materia da lavorare non avendo li mezi di darmi li marmi come spiega il mio ben servito che mi fece il suo diretore del Coleggio ℔ conseguenza senza che io vadi a mover una giusta causa potrà rimetermi qui in questa Capitalle la

Somma di Doleri trecento, che la Detta somma mi apartiene fra le
spese di Viaggio ed il mio tenpo di circa tre mesi che ci vorà ℔
rimetermi in grembo della mia famiglia, dove lei mi à levato, non
dubito, che sia lei che li Signori rivisori suoi Confratelli abino
nesuna dificoltà di rimetermi la dᵗᵃ Soma considerando il levare un
artista della Sua patria a 5000. Miglie distante, e che il dᵗᵒ Artista
à soferto di tutto, e che, e stato tanto prudente di non far nesun ri-
corso ateso l'atacamemento che aveva alla di lei ℔sona pensi Sigʳᵉ,
che la sola sua fama mi fece venire in America, e che ò rovinato il
mio interesse e la mia Salute, e che ritorno a casa mia forse con un
bracio inservibille ℔ guadagnarmi il pane, se lei mi avesse dato la
Comissione dei capittelli Corinti come Ionici da eseguiglieli in Carrara di Marmo sarebbe stato un affare da acomodarci, e avantagioso
℔ lei facendomi passare il denaro in Livorno dal Sigʳ Appleton nel
Ato che gli consegnavo il detto lavoro, ma di ritornare a casa mia
con delle mosche in mano, non lo vole ne il dovere, ne la giustizia,
Se poi lei desiderase che io finisca il mio tempo dei anni tre non
avrò nesuna dificolta di farli li suoi lavori di questa pietra di Washington e di lavorarli qui al Canpidoglio dove lei non li manchera
modi di avere un agente di questi stessi che servono la medesima
fabrica, e senza avere il fastidio di pensare al mio nurimento e Alogio
mi passerà Mile doleri al Anno diˡᵒ 1000. la minima pensione che à
l'infimo de miei patrioti e che credo di meritare anche io, la prego
dunque Sigʳ Jefferson di non metermi in mezo di una Strada considerando che il solo suo nome e la mia buona opinione mi fece
venire al suo Servizio e che non gli farebbe onore che io andassi a
ripetere in Livorno dal Sigʳ Appleton quello che mi è dovutto In
America Atendo dunque un suo riscontro assieme alla sudᵗᵃ Somma
oltre che mi è dovuta gliene sarò grato, o pure una decisione dl
lavoro da farsi in Carrara ò in quel modo che piu li piacera pregandolo di solecitare un favorevole riscontro giache sono qui in sù le
spese e sono stato fin ora malato ateso li strapazi e mal vivere che ò
fato Costì mi racomando alla di lei bontà e giustizia dichiarandomi
di lei Sigᵃ Ilmo

Devmo Obmo Servitore   Michele Raggi Scultore

P.S.

la Sopra Scrita avrà la bontà di dirigermela dalla Vedova Franzoni e
potra se li piace rispondermi in Francese

MOST ESTEEMED MR. JEFFERSON
CHARLOTTESVILLE   Washington 26. September 1820—
No longer able to stand the fare supplied to me by the proctor of the college
and inasmuch as you were not hastening to have the marble brought to me,
I cannot complete my contracted time, as I would have done if your stone,
along with the mutton the proctor sent me to eat, had not ruined my stomach. The mere sight of this meat nauseates me. You know well that my
contract stipulated that I was to be lodged and fed as befits my profession.
Nor are you ignorant as to how artists are treated in Italy and France!
Expediency, duty, and justice demand that I at least be compensated for
my journey home, because you could not procure suitable marble for me
to work with, as is explained in the dismissal letter that the proctor of the
college gave me. To prevent a justifiable lawsuit, therefore, you should pay
me in this capital city the sum of three hundred dollars. That amount belongs to me and is needed, among other things, to defray the cost of my
travel and the roughly three months it will take me to return to the bosom
of my family, whence you detached me. I believe that you and your colleagues will have no difficulty paying me this sum, considering the removal
of an artist from his homeland 5,000 miles away, that the said artist has
suffered greatly, and that his attachment to you caused him to file no complaints. Consider, Sir, that your reputation alone induced me to come to
America, that I harmed my interests and health by doing so, and that I am
likely to return home with an arm so unusable as to leave me unfit to earn
my daily bread. If you had given me the commission for the Corinthian
capitals that are to be executed, like the Ionic, in Carrara marble, we could
have come to an agreement. It would have been advantageous for you to
have Mr. Appleton pay me in Leghorn on the delivery to him of my work.
I return home instead nearly penniless, which neither duty nor justice au-
thorizes. If you desire, in the end, for me to complete my three-year contract, I will have no difficulty working with Washington stone here in the
capital, where you can hire an agent from among those who do the same
sort of work and without having to bother with my food and lodging. You
would only need to pay me one thousand dollars a year, which is the mini-
mum given to my least-skilled compatriots and which, in addition, I believe I deserve. I implore you, Mr. Jefferson, not to cast me into the street,
considering that only your name and my high opinion of you made me
enter your service and that it would do you no credit if I returned to Leghorn and told Mr. Appleton that I am owed money in America. I therefore
await your reply, accompanied by the aforesaid sum as well as any other
amount due me, for which I will be grateful, or for a decision regarding the
work to be done either in Carrara or in any other way that better pleases
you. I pray you to send me a favorable reply in haste, because my expenses
here have been mounting and I have been ill until just now due to the
hardships and poor living conditions I was forced to endure. I commend
myself to your goodness and justice, declaring myself to be, most illustrious Sir
Your most devoted and obedient servant
                                        MICHELE RAGGI Sculptor

P.S.
Please address your letter to me at the residence of the widow Franzoni. You may, if you like, answer me in French

RC (ViU: TJP); addressed: "M[r] To[s] Jefferson Monticello Charlottesville Virginia"; endorsed by TJ as received 5 Oct. 1820 and so recorded in SJL. Translation by Dr. Jonathan T. Hine.

From James Breckinridge

DEAR SIR   Fincastle Sep. 28th 1820
I must beg you to excuse me for not attending the board of Visitors on Monday next. I am so much afflicted with a pain in the back that the journey, even in a carriage, would be attended with great inconvenience. I will endeavour to visit [the][1] University on my way to the assembly when I hope to have the pleasure of seeing you.
Yours with sincere friendship & esteem

JAMES BRECKINRIDGE

RC (CSmH: JF); endorsed by TJ as received 3 Oct. 1820 and so recorded in SJL. RC (MHi); address cover only; with PoC of TJ to Louis H. Girardin, 17 Aug. 1821, on verso; addressed: "M[r] Thomas Jefferson Monticello Albemarle C[o]"; stamped; postmarked Fincastle, 30 Sept. 1820.

[1]Manuscript: "to visit to."

To Thomas Ewell

DEAR SIR   Monticello Sep. 28. 20.
On my return after an absence of three weeks from home, I found here your favor of the 6th inst. I concur with you entirely in favor of hospitals, and think the religion of a place more justly tested by the number of it's hospitals than of it's churches.
I return you the Note inclosed in your letter, and sincerely sympathise with[1] misfortunes, which the evils of the times have suffered few of us to escape. great errors in political economy have led us to a catastrophe, so general and so severe as, in a course of 77. years of life, I have never before witnessed. a general revolution of property is the unhappy consequence. this too has befallen many too much enfeebled by age in body and mind ever to repair their losses. it is a happiness in your case that you are young & healthy, have a great deal of life before you, with vigor of body and mind. these I hope will enable you to start anew, and run yet a long & prosperous race. I trust you will do it, and opposing firmness of mind to the assaults of fortune,

look steadily forward to the means of acquiring competence and comfort. with my sincere prayers for your success in this career accept assurances of my friendly respect & attachment

TH: JEFFERSON

PoC (DLC); on verso of reused address cover of Elihu F. Marshall to TJ, 17 Feb. 1820; at foot of text: "Dʳ Thoˢ Ewell"; endorsed by TJ. Enclosure: enclosure to Ewell to TJ, 6 Sept. 1820.

¹ TJ here canceled "your."

To William W. Hening

Monticello Sep. 28. 20.

I recieve with many thanks, Sir, the two copies of the 7ᵗʰ volume of your valuable work, and am anxious to see it's completio[n.] when done, I shall gladly resign to you for publication the 4. vols of MS. state papers which I possess. their titles and marks are

A. letters, proclamns, petitions in 1622. 23. & Correspondence 1625.
⟨42⟩ Transactions in council & assembly, their petition & his majesty's answer

B.⟨9⟩ Orders from Feb. 1622. to Nov. 1627.

C. 32. A. { Foreign business & Inquisitions from 1665. to 1676.
Transactions of the Council from Dec. 9. 1698. to May 28. 1700.

In these will be found things of a very interesting nature, & particularly the official correspondence of the Governor & Council with the government of England during the interesting period of the Revolution, shewing truly the views and principles on which that nation acted in it's government of the colonies. it would have furnished some good matter for mr Walsh's able Appeal on that subject, and parts of it would certainly be in general demand over the US. Accept the assurance of my friendly esteem and respect.　　TH: JEFFERSON

PoC (DLC); on verso of a reused address cover from Thomas Mann Randolph to TJ; edge trimmed; at foot of text: "Wᵐ W. Hening esq."; endorsed by TJ.

The Library of Congress acquired these volumes of Virginia STATE PAPERS from TJ's estate shortly after his death. They are now in DLC: TJ Papers, ser. 8 (Poor, *Jefferson's Library*, 4 [no. 122]; *Catalogue of the Library of Congress* [1830], 167).

To Daniel Humphreys

Monticello Sep. 28. 20.

I thank you, Sir, for your MS. on Stenography. past the use of such things at present, I have nevertheless paid attention to the principles of your plan, and think them well judged. the adaptation of elementary marks to elementary sounds and the omission of useless letters form a solid basis on which whatever is further wanting may be erected with a little practice. accident threw Shelton's tachygraphy into my way when young, and I practised it thro' life. altho it had serious defects, I have not looked into any other with fewer. the simplicity of yours admits I think of improvement which may render it preferable to any other. I pray you to accept my respectful salutations.

Th: Jefferson

PoC (DLC); on James Madison to TJ, [ca. 20 Mar. 1820], which reads in full: "The enclosed found among the papers of J. Madison" (addressed: "Mr Jefferson Monticello near Charlottesville Virgª"; stamped; postmarked Orange Court House, 20 Mar. 1820; endorsed by TJ as covering Madison to TJ, 7 Jan. 1808 [DLC: Madison Papers], which was received 9 Jan. 1808 from the State Department and concerned "lots Etc" in New Orleans); adjacent to signature: "Mr Daniel Humphreys Portsmouth"; endorsed by TJ.

To William Charles Jarvis

Monticello Sep. 28. 20.

I thank you, Sir, for the copy of your Republican which you have been so kind as to send me; and I should have acknoleged it sooner, but that I am just returned home after a long absence. I have not yet had time to read it seriously: but in looking over it cursorily I see much in it to approve: and shall be glad if it shall lead our youth to the practice of thinking on such subjects & for themselves[.] that it will have this tendency may be expected, and for that reason I feel an urgency to note what I deem an error in it, the more requiring notice as your opinion is strengthened by that of many others. you seem in pages 84. & 148. to consider the judges as the ultimate arbiters of all constitutional questions: a very dangerous doctrine indee[d] and one which would place us under the despotism of an Oligarchy. our judges are as honest as other men, and not more so. they have, with others, the same passions for party, for power, and the privileges of their corps. their maxim is 'boni judicis est ampliare jurisdictionem,' and their power the more dangerous as they are in office for life, and not responsible, as the other functionaries are, to the elective controul.

the constitution has erected no such single tribunal knowing that, to whatever hands confided, with the corruptions of time & party it's members would become despots. it has more wisely[1] made all the departmen[ts] co-equal and co-sovereign within themselves. if the legislature fails to pass laws for a census, for paying the judges & other officers of government, for establishing a militia, for naturalisation, as prescribed by the constitution, or if they fail to meet in Congress, the judges cannot issue their Mandamus to them. if the President fails to supply the place of a judge, to appoint other civil or military officers, to issue requisite commissions, the judges cannot force him. they can issue their Mandamus or distringas to no Executive or Legislative officer to enforce the fulfilment of their official duties, any more than the President or legislature may issue orders to the judges or their officers. betrayed by English example, & unaware, as it should seem, of the controul of our constitution in this particular, they have at times over-stepped their limit by undertaking to command executive officers in the discharge of their executive duties. but the constitution, in keeping the three departments distinct & independant, restrains the authority of the judges to judiciary organs, as it does the executive & legislative, to executive and legislative organs. the judges certainly have more frequent occasion to act on constitutional questions, because the laws of meum & tuum, and of criminal action, forming the great mass of the system of law, constitute their particular department. when the legislative or executive functionaries act unconstitutionally, they are responsible to the people in their elective capacity. the exemption of the judges from that is quite dangerous enough. I know no safe depository of the ultimate powers of the society, but the people themselves: and if we think them not enlightened enough to exercise their controul with a wholsome discretion, the remedy is, not to take it from them, but to inform their discretion by education. this is the true corrective of abuses of constitutional power.   Pardon me, Sir, for this difference of opinion. my personal interest in such questions is entirely extinct; but not my wishes for the longest possible continuance of our government on it's pure principles. if the three powers maintain their mutual independance on each other, it may last long: but not so if either can assume the authorities of the other. I ask your candid reconsideration of this subject, and am sufficiently sure you will form a candid conclusion. Accept the assurance of my great respect.   TH: JEFFERSON

PoC (DLC); edge trimmed; ink stained, with obscured text rewritten by TJ; at foot of first page: "Mr Jarvis." Printed as a letter of 20 Sept. 1820 in Stockbridge,

Mass., *Berkshire Star*, 8 Nov. 1821, and as a letter of 20 Sept. 1821 in *Richmond Enquirer*, 20 Nov. 1821, and elsewhere.

Jarvis's *Republican; or, A Series of Essays on the Principles and Policy of Free States. having a particular reference to the United States of America and the Individual States* (Pittsfield, Mass., 1820; Poor, *Jefferson's Library*, 11 [no. 653]) contains the following passages on PAGES 84. & 148, respectively: "In drawing this conclusion, we are naturally led to contemplate the importance of the Judicial authority, established by our constitutions, in its operation as a check upon any unconstitutional exercise of power, by any other branches of the government. Fundamental laws would be useless, and worse than useless, if they might be disregarded or neglected, in the administration of the government: it is therefore within the authority, delegated to our judicial tribunals, to refuse to give effect to any unconstitutional laws or ordinances. The judicial authority, thus constituted, operates continually, to keep the administration of government true to its fundamental laws, and original principles" and "a departure from the true intent and meaning of the laws . . . will necessarily occur, in every country, where the judges are dependent upon the sovereign, or people; and no guard can be interposed against their recurrence, so effectual, as the complete independence of judges during good behaviour."

BONI JUDICIS EST AMPLIARE JURISDICTIONEM: "It is the role of a good judge to enlarge (or use liberally) his jurisdiction (or remedial authority)."

DISTRINGAS: "A writ ordering a sheriff to distrain a defendant's property to compel the defendant to perform an obligation" (*Black's Law Dictionary*).

[1] Preceding two words interlined.

To James Leitch

Sep. 28. 20.

4. wash basons & pitchers.
$\frac{1}{2}$ doz. chamber pots.
1. ℔ pepper

TH:J.

RC (ViU: TJP); written on a small scrap; dateline beneath signature; at foot of text: "Mr Leitch." Not recorded in SJL.

Leitch's records indicate that on this date TJ purchased by order "82 ℔. Bar Iron 6ᵈ, 1 ℔ Pepper 3/. ‖ 7 | 33 ‖

2 Basons & Ewers 10/6. 2
  do Liverpool China do
  15/.
6 Liverpool China Chamber
  pots 6/9

‖ 8 | 50 ‖
‖ 6 | 75 ‖"

for a total of $22.58 (Leitch Daybook, p. 134).

To Tobias Watkins

SIR   Monticello Sep. 28. 20.
    I have duly recieved your favor of the 16th on the application of mr Girardin for the place of Principal in your College, and wish it were in my power to give as particular information as the objects of the

College would require. during the two or three years that mr Girardin resided in this neighborhood, we were in habits of frequent & friendly intercourse, which gave me the sort of opportunity which neighborly visits afford, of judging of his merits. I found him a person of superior understanding; and, as far as could be judged from ordinary conversation, a well educated one. some Latin compositions published by him, proved him an excellent Latinist; and I have been led, from conversations, to believe him a Greek scholar also, and that he has a familiar knolege of the Mathematical sciences: but to what particular extent I cannot say, having never presumed to question him on them so minutely as to know the exact measure of his proficiency. but this the trustees will of course ascertain in such way as they shall think sufficient. he is perfectly sober & correct in his morals and deportment, and liberal & enlarged in his views. indeed his history of Virginia affords in itself sufficient matter for the trustees to judge for themselves of the capacities of his mind. mr John Patterson of your city, having been well acquainted in this neighborhood, can probably give you further information respecting mr Girardin's general character, and to him I would beg leave to refer you in aid of my information. I pray you to accep[t] the assurance of my best wishes for the prosperity of your college and of my high respect to yourself

TH: J[E]FF[ER]SON

PoC (CSmH: JF); on verso of reused address cover to TJ; closing and signature faint; at foot of text: "Mr Watkins"; endorsed by TJ.

An example of the LATIN COMPOSITIONS PUBLISHED by Louis H. Girardin is *De Monomachia, sive Duello. Hoc in Monomachiam, sive Duellum, Poema, Comitiis Americanis, Devoto, Humilique Animo Lines, on Duelling. Addressed to the Legislative Assemblies of America* (Richmond, 1810; Poor, *Jefferson's Library*, 12 [no. 725]; TJ's copy in DLC: Rare Book and Special Collections).

To Charles Pinckney

DEAR SIR   Monticello Sep. 30. 20.

An absence of some time from home has occasioned me to be thus late in acknoleging the reciept of your favor of the 6th and I see in it with pleasure evidences of your continued health & application to business. it is now, I believe, about 20. years since I had the pleasure of seeing you, and we are apt, in such cases, to lose sight of time, and to concieve that our friends remain stationary at the same point of health and vigour as when we last saw them. so I percieve by your letter you think with respect to myself. but 20. years added to 57.

make quite a different man. to threescore and seventeen add two years of prostrate health, and you have the old, infirm, and nerveless body I now am, unable to write but with pain, and unwilling to think without necessity. in this state I leave the world and it's affairs to the young and energetic, and resign myself to their care, of whom I have endeavored to take care when young. I read but one newspaper, & that of my own state, and more for it's advertisements than it's news. I have not read a speech in Congress for some years. I have heard indeed of the questions of the Tariff & Missouri, and formed primâ facie opinions on them, but without investigation. as to the Tariff, I should say put down all banks, admit none but a metallic circulation; that will take it's proper level with the like circulation in other countries, & then our manufacturers may work in fair competition with those of other countries: and the import duties which the government may lay for the purposes of revenue will so far place them above equal competition.[1] the Missouri question is a meer[2] party trick. the leaders of federalism defeated in their schemes of obtaining power by rallying partisans to the principle of monarchism, a principle of personal, not of local division, have changed their tack, and thrown out another barrel[3] to the whale. they are taking advantage of the virtuous feelings of the people to effect a division of parties by a geographical line. they expect that this will ensure them, on local principles, the majority they could never obtain on principles of federalism. but they are still[4] putting their shoulder to the wrong wheel. they are wasting Jeremiads on the miseries of slavery as if we were advocates for it. sincerity in their declamations should direct their efforts to the true point of difficulty, and unite their councils with ours in devising some reasonable and practicable plan of getting rid of it. some of these leaders, if they could attain the power they ambition, would rather use it to keep the union together. but others have ever had in view it's separation. if they push it to that, they will find the line of separation very different from their 36.° of latitude: and as manufacturing and navigating states, they will have quarrelled with their bread & butter; and I fear not that after a little trial, they will think better of it, and return to the embraces of their natural and best friends. but this scheme of party I leave to those who are to live under it's consequences. we who have gone before have performed an honest duty, by putting in the power of our successors a state of happiness which no nation ever before had within their choice. if that choice is to throw it away, the dead will have neither the power nor the right to controul them. I must hope nevertheless that the mass of our honest and well meaning brethren of the other states will discover the use which designing leaders are making of their best feelings, & will see the precipice to which they are led, before they take the fatal leap. God grant it,[5] and to you health & happiness 　　　　　　　　　　TH: JEFFERSON

PoC (DLC); on reused address cover to TJ; at foot of first page: "Mr Pinckney." Tr (ViU: TJP); extract in Nicholas P. Trist's hand.

The *Richmond Enquirer* was the ONE NEWSPAPER that TJ read at this time. THROWN OUT ANOTHER BARREL TO THE WHALE: "That Sea-men have a Custom when they meet a *Whale*, to fling him out an empty *Tub*, by way of Amusement, to divert him from laying violent Hands upon the Ship" ([Jonathan Swift], *A Tale of a Tub. Written for the Universal Improvement of Mankind* [London, 1704], 14).

[1] Tr begins here.
[2] Tr: "mere."
[3] PoC: "barre." Tr: "barrel."
[4] Word interlined.
[5] Tr ends here.

From Thomas Cooper

DEAR SIR 　　　　　　　　　　October 1. 1820 Philadelphia

I find it impossible to be with you so early as the 11th of this month, I will therefore defer my visit, to <u>Poplar forest</u>, which will not be out of my way from Richmond to Columbia.

I send you and Mr Madison to day a pamphlet which I know not how to account for not having been Sent before.

The contest so disgraceful to the Democracy of this state, whether Mr Findlay whose character is so suspicious, or Mr Heister, who is so decidedly and notoriously, a miser, and blockhead, shall be the Governor, will be settled in favour of the latter. I think it the least of two evils; but we have in this state, a strange predilection for ignorance and vulgarity in our popular favourites. I wish it were otherwise. Education is sadly retrograde here.

Adieu. I will <u>endeavour</u> to be at Poplar forest in the third week of October. Consider me always as being with great esteem, your faithful friend. 　　　　　　　　　　THOMAS COOPER

M. Correa, is not yet gone: I suppose he will stay here a week longer.

RC (MHi); endorsed by TJ as received 7 Oct. 1820 and so recorded in SJL. RC (MHi); address cover only; with PoC of TJ to Joseph Gilmore, 12 May 1821, on verso; addressed: "Thomas Jefferson Esq Montecello Virginia"; stamp canceled; franked; postmarked Philadelphia, 1 Oct.

The PAMPHLET for TJ and James Madison has not been identified. MR HEISTER: Joseph Hiester.

To David Gelston

DEAR SIR   Monticello Oct. 1. 20.

On my return home after some absence I found here your favors of Sep. 2 & 15.[1] stating the amount of freight & duties on my books at 7.75 D   Having no medium of remittance but in the bills of our banks I inclose 8.D. presuming they are negociable with you, and that the fractional surplus may cover their discount at market. I salute you with continued friendship & respect.   TH: JEFFERSON

RC (William Doyle Galleries, Inc., New York City, sale 16BP02, 22 Nov. 2016, lot 129); at foot of text: "David Gelston esq." PoC (MHi); on verso of reused address cover of otherwise unlocated letter from Mathew Carey to TJ, [30] Mar. 1820 (see note to TJ to Carey, 13 Mar. 1820); endorsed by TJ. Recorded in SJL with additional bracketed notation: "8.D."

[1] Reworked from "favor of Sep. 15."

To James Maxwell

SIR   Monticello Oct. 1. 20.

I find here your letter of Aug. 23. on my return home af[t]er an absence of several weeks, which must apologize for this delay of it's acknolegement. Having no medium in which my subscription for the Analectic magazine for the last year can be remitted but the bills of our state banks, I now inclose you 6.D. in their notes. observing that Peter Cottom is your agent at Richmond it will be more convenient to me in future to give him a standing order on my agent in that place to pay him the annual price on his application, which I shall take care to do. Accept my respectful salutations.   TH: JEFFER[SON]

PoC (MHi); on verso of reused address cover of Henry Dearborn to TJ, 3 Mar. 1820; one word faint; signature torn at seal; at foot of text: "Mr James Maxwell"; endorsed by TJ. Mistakenly recorded in SJL in the column for letters received under 6 Oct. 1820, with additional bracketed notation: "6.D. for analect. magazine."

MY AGENT: Bernard Peyton.

From James Maxwell

Philadelphia October 1st 1820

In August I forwarded a letter reminding you that according to the terms your subscription to the Analectic Magazine was due in June; presuming that it has not reached you I now address you on the same subject requesting a remittance of the amount $ by mail or otherwise

Very respectfully Yours: &c &c   JAS MAXWELL

RC (MHi); addressed: "Thomas Jefferson Esqr Monticello Virginia"; stamp canceled; franked; postmarked Philadelphia, 2 Oct.; endorsed by TJ as received 16 Oct. 1820 and so recorded in SJL.

From Caesar A. Rodney

Wilmington

HONORED REVERED & DEAR SIR,   Octob. 1st 1820.

I lamented extremely that my time, did not allow me to stay longer with the best of friends, on my late visit to Monticello. I had intended to leave home the last of June, instead of July, but was unfortunately prevented by an attack of Lumbago, which confined me to my house for a month nearly. This delay, made the period of my departure approach near the commencement of our Court of Chancery which began on the 19th of august, and compelled me, most reluctantly to leave so soon[1] your hospitable mansion. For as I am dependent on my profession for my daily bread I am necessarily obliged to devote my attention to it. If health permits I hope next summer to repeat my visit and indeed if it were in my power, I would make an annual pilgrimage to Monticello, to visit my second father.

I have spoken to Mr Alrich about your wool-carding machine & he says he will take great pleasure in putting it in complete order, whenever you may send it on. He is a very ingenious man, & has been a decided friend in gloomy times[.] He is among the most intelligent of our numerous Republican Quakers, in this place.

The Maldonado Pumpkin seed shall be selected from some of the best melons & shall be sent as soon as they are fit; and indeed any thing of the kind in my power. Did you ever see any of the Paraguay Tea of S. America? Shall I send you a sample, by mail, as your frank will allow me to do it?

Let me recommend to you for employment, as a carpenter at your University, Mr Samuel Askew, of this place. He is a most excellent workman & has long been a master carpenter here. He has always done my work & all the public buildings at this place. In these dull times he is willing to go to Virginia & to work as low as one dollar & fifty cents per day, in hopes that he will soon recommend himself to something better. In addition to this, he has been politically faithful in the worst of times. I am sure you would be pleased with him, & I should be much gratified if he could be usefully employed.

Remember me particularly to M^r & M^s Randolph & all your family.

With every sentiment of respect gratitude & affection I remain Dr Sir

Yours Most Truly   C. A. RODNEY

P.S. as soon as I can get possession of Governor MKean's letter, relative to the conduct of my uncle Cæsar on the question of Independence I will transmit a copy without delay. I enclose you a letter for Mr Coles from our old friend A. H. Rowan of Ireland lately transmitted to me. I do not know where to direct it to him, agreeably to Mr Rowan's request, & I am very anxious it should reach him in safety.   C.A.R.

RC (DLC); edge chipped; endorsed by TJ as received 7 Oct. 1820 and so recorded in SJL. Enclosure not found.

PARAGUAY TEA, in this context, is the dried or roasted leaves of the South American maté plant (*OED*).

[1] Preceding two words interlined.

Cost Estimates for University of Virginia Board of Visitors

[by 2 Oct. 1820]

Notes for the consideration of the Visitors.[1]

This Report proposes to the Legislature: qu. 1820.?
1. to cancel the loan authorised & transform it into an
   approprian of   60,000.
2. to relieve the present annuity from the further[2] charge
   of buildings   45,000[3]
3. to appropriate of the Literary fund for building the
   Library   40,000
                                                     ‾‾‾‾‾‾‾
                                                     145,000[4]

4. to enlarge the annuity to the full establmt of the law.
   [say to 30,000.]

A general idea of the application of a revenue of
30,000.D.

	D
9. Professors @ 2000.D. each	18,000
1. d° of Modern languages	1,000.
Books, suppose 600. vols a year @ 10.D.	6,000
Philosoph[l] Chemical & astronomical instruments	1,000
Bursar & Proctor	1,500.
Laborers and servants	1,000
Botanic garden, grounds, repairs, contingencies	1,500[5]
	30,000

A general idea of the application of a revenue of
15,000.D.

*6. professors. towit of	Antient languages	2,000
	Modern languages	1,000
	Mathematics.	2,000
	Natural Philosophy, chemistry, mineralogy	2,000
	Botany, Zoology	2,000
	Law.	1,000
Books, say 150. vols. a year @ 10.D.		1,500.
Philosoph. Chemical & Astronomical instruments		500.
Bursar & Proctor		1,500.
Laborers and servants		750.
Botanic garden, grounds, repairs, contingencies		750
		15,000.

In both cases there will be a supplementory[6] fund of rents viz.

5. hotels at half rent, say of about 5. p[r]cent on their cost	1,000.
100. Dormitories @ 20.D. each [i.e. 10.D. a head on each student] to be reserved for additional dormitories, or for a saving fund	2,000.
	3,000.[7]

*omitting 1. Anatomy & Medecine
2. Govmt, polit. econ.
    L. nature & nations
    History
3. Ideology, gen[l] grammar
    Ethics. Rhetoric
    Belles Letters. fine arts

MS (ViU: TJP); entirely in TJ's hand; undated, but presumably composed prior to the 2 Oct. 1820 meeting of the Board of Visitors; brackets in original; endorsed by TJ: "Estimates."

The REPORT was the University of Virginia Board of Visitors Report to Literary Fund President and Directors, 2 Oct. 1820. The LAW was "An act for establishing an University," which the Virginia General Assembly approved on 25 Jan. 1819 (*Acts of Assembly* [1818–19 sess.], 15–8; TJ's Bill to Establish a University, printed above at 19 Nov. 1818). L. NATURE: "Law of nature."

[1] Preceding seven words in left margin at head of text.

[2] Word interlined.
[3] Reworked from "30,000."
[4] Reworked from "130,000."
[5] Reworked from "2,500."
[6] Word interlined.
[7] Remaining text is in left margin adjacent to asterisk to which it is keyed.

Minutes of University of Virginia Board of Visitors

At a meeting of the Visitors of the University of Virginia, at the sd University, on monday 2[d] of Oct[r] 1820, present Thomas Jefferson, James Madison, Robert B. Taylor, John H. Cocke, and Joseph C. Cabell;

The Board proceeded to the consideration of the Annual Report, and not having time to go through with the same, adjourned to tuesday 3[d] October.

At an adjourned meeting of the Visitors of the University of Virginia, held on 3[d] October 1820, present Thomas Jefferson, James Madison, Robert B. Taylor, John H. Cocke and Joseph C. Cabell;

The Board approved the arrangement made by the Committee of Superintendence relative to the annulment of the contract with Doctor Thomas Cooper.

Resolved, that[1] From & after the first day of October 1820, the compensation to the[2] Bursar of the University for his services,[3] shall be at the rate of one per cent on the amount of disbursements.

Resolved, that Joseph C. Cabell be & he is hereby desired & authorized to examine and verify the accounts of the preceding year, not already examined and verified.

Resolved, That the Committee of Superintendence be authorized to enter into negociations, with the following persons,[4] with the view of engaging them as Professors of the University,

viz: M[r] Bowditch of Salem

and M[r] Tichenor of Boston.

Resolved, That in the negociations with M[r] Bowditch & M[r] Tichenor, the committee be authorized to offer the[5] compensation hereinafter specified—

[297]

viz: 1. Apartment.[6]
    2. A Salary of $2000 per annum.
    3. A fee of $10– for each student engaged to attend the Lectures of the Professor.
    4. If the aggregate amount of the Salary and of the fees of tuition, should fall short of $2500, in either the first, second, or third year, the deficiency to be paid out of the funds of the University.[7]

The following report was agreed to
[*The report that follows at this point is printed as the next document.*]
and the board adjourned without day.   Th: JEFFERSON Rector

MS (ViU: TJP-VMTJ); in Joseph C. Cabell's hand, with report, conclusion, and signature by TJ. Tr (ViU: TJP-VMJCC). Tr (ViU: TJP-VMJHC). Tr (ViU: TJP-VMJB).

TJ and John H. Cocke comprised the COMMITTEE OF SUPERINTENDENCE, while Alexander Garrett was the BURSAR OF THE UNIVERSITY. MR TICHENOR: George Ticknor. WITHOUT DAY: "sine die."

[1] Word interlined in place of "for the year commencing."
[2] Cabell here canceled "Proctor."
[3] Preceding three words not in VMJHC Tr.
[4] Preceding four words interlined.
[5] Cabell here canceled "advant."
[6] MS: "Apartments." Trs: "Apartment."
[7] Remainder of MS in TJ's hand.

University of Virginia Board of Visitors Report to Literary Fund President and Directors

To the President and Directors of the Literary fund.

In obedience to the Act of the General assembly of Virginia requiring that the Rector and Visitors of the University of Virginia should make report annually to the President & Directors of the Literary fund (to be laid before the Legislature at their next succeeding session) embracing a full account of the disbursements, the funds on hand, & a general statement of the condition of the said University, the said[1] Visitors make the following Report.

The General assembly, at their last session of 1819.20. having passed an Act authorising the sd Visitors, for the purpose of finishing the buildings of the University, to borrow the sum of 60,000.D. and to pledge, for repayment of the sd sum & interest, any part of the annual appropriation of 15,000.D. heretofore made by law, the board of Visitors, at their semi-annual meeting of April last, proceeded to the consideration of the sd act, and of the authorities therein permitted to them. they were of opinion, in the first place, that it would be most expedient to compleat all the buildings necessary for the accomodation of the Professors & Students, before opening the Institution, as the Maintenance of that, when opened, by absorbing all it's funds, would leave nothing to compleat what might yet be requisite for the full establishment called for by law.

On view of the accounts rendered by the Bursar & Proctor they found that with the aid of the loan authorised (if the commencement of it's instalments for repaiment could be suspended four years) and of their annuity during the same time, they might accomplish the whole of the buildings of accomodation for the Professors & Students according to the estimates, heretofore made, of their probable cost, of which the following statement presents a summary view.

		D
1820. Apr.	The existing debts are	10,000.
	To compleat the 7. pavilions and 31. Dormitories on hand	18,000.
	To build three more pavilions & 24. Dormitories to compleat the lawn	27,600.
	To build 3. Hotels & 25. Dormitories, compleating the East back street	19,000.[2]
1821.[3]	To build 2. Hotels & Proctor's house, & 25. Dormitories compleating the West back street	19,000
		93,600

Means.		D
1820. April.	Loan from the Literary fund.	40,000.
1821. Jan. 1.	Annuity of 15,000.D. – 2,400. int. of 40,000.D	12,600.
	Additional loan of	20,000.
1822. Jan. 1.	Annuity of 15,000.D. – 3600. int. of 60,000.	11,400.[4]
1823. Jan. 1.	Annuity of 15,000.D. – 3600. int. of 60,000	11,400.
		95,400.

They therefore proceeded to negotiate a loan of 40,000.D. from the President and Directors of the Literary fund, reimbursable by five instalments of 14,244.D. a year beginning on the __ day of April 1824: and afterwards a second loan of 20,000.D. reimbursable by like[5] instalments, commencing from the day when the others should end.

[299]

On this view of their resources, the Board proceeded to authorise their Proctor to enter into contracts for the completion of the buildings already begun, and for the erection of those still wanting, so as to provide, in the whole, ten Pavilions for the Professors required by law, five Hotels for dieting the Students, and a sixth for the use of the Proctor, with an hundred and four Dormitories, sufficient for lodging 208. students: and they instructed him to make, in his contracts, effectual provision that the whole shall be compleated in the autumn of the ensuing year 1821. at that time therefore the buildings of accomodation for the Professors and students are expected to be all ready for their reception; and the institution might then be opened, but that the remaining engagements for the buildings, and the reimbursement of the sums borrowed from the Literary fund, will require the whole revenue of the University for seven years to come, that is to say until the __ day of April 1828.

In the statement of the expenditures and means of the University it will be percieved that we have not taken the private subscriptions into account. of these 2079.D. 33. cents of the 1st instalment, 3914.13 D. of the 2d & 8217.09 D. of the 3d are still due: and the last, amounting to 10,666.50 D. will become due on the 1st day of April next. but of these some loss will be occasioned by the distresses of the times; and the residue, from the same cause, will be so tardy and uncertain[6] in the times of it's receipt, that the Visitors have not thought it safe to found on it any stipulations requiring punctuality in their fulfilment. they have thought it more advisable to reserve it as a supplementary and[7] contingent fund, to aid the general revenue, as it shall be recieved, and to meet casualties unforeseen, errors of estimate, & expences other than those of meer building.

In the Report of the Commissioners who met at Rockfish-gap on the 1st day of August 1818. it was stated that 'a building of somewhat more size, in the middle of the grounds, may be called for in time, in which may be rooms for religious worship, under such impartial regulations as the Visitors shall prescribe, for public examinations, for a Library, for the schools of Music, drawing & other associated purposes.'[8] the expences of this building are not embraced in the estimates herein before stated. it's cost will probably be of about 40,000. Dollars, and it's want will be felt as soon as the University shall open. but this building is beyond the reach of the present funds. nor are these indeed adequate to the maintenance of the institution on the full scale enacted by the legislature. that body, aware that Professors of desirable eminence could not be expected to relinquish the situations in which they might be found, for others, new, untried and unknown, without a certainty of adequate compensation, confided to the discretion of the Visitors the salaries which should be stipulated to the Professors first employed. but the annuity heretofore appropriated to the maintenance of the University cannot furnish sufficient inducement to ten Professors, of high degree each in his respective line of science. and yet to employ inferior persons, would be to stand where we are in science, unavailed of the higher advances already made elsewhere, and of the advantages contemplated by the statute under which we act.[9] if the legislature shall be of opinion that the annuity already apportioned to the establishment and maintenance of an institution for instruction in all the useful sciences, is it's proper part of the whole fund, the Visitors will faithfully see that it shall be punctually applied to the remaining engagements for the buildings and to[10] the reimbursement[11] of the extra sum lately recieved from the general fund: that during the term[12] of it's exclusive application to these objects[13] due care shall be taken to preserve the buildings erected from ruin or injury, and at the end of that term, they will provide for opening the institution in the partial degree to which it's present annuity shall be adequate.   If, on the other hand, the legislature shall be of opinion that the sums so advanced in the name of a loan, from the general fund of education were legitimately applicable to the purposes of an University, that it's early commencement will promote the public good, by offering to our youth, now ready and waiting for it an early and near[14] resource for instruction, and by arresting the heavy[15] tribute we are annually[16] paying to other states and countries for the article of education, and shall think proper to[17] liberate the present[18] annuity from it's engagements, the[19] Visitors trust it will be in their power, by the autumn of the ensuing year 1821. to engage and bring into place that portion of the Professors designated by the law, to which the present annuity may be found competent; or, by the same epoch, to carry into full execution the whole objects of the law, if an enlargement be made of it's participation in the general fund adequate to the full establishment contemplated by the law.

The accounts of reciepts, disbursements, and funds on hand[20] for the year ending with the present date, as rendered by the Bursar and Proctor of the University, are given with this Report, as is required by law.   TH: JEFFERSON, Rector

October 2. 1820.

MS (Vi: RG 79, House of Delegates, Speaker, Executive Communications); in TJ's hand; docketed in an unidentified hand: "B. Decr 5th 1820." MS (ViU: TJP-VMTJ); in TJ's hand; dated 3 Oct. 1820; embedded in MS of preceding document. Dft (ViU: TJP); fragment in TJ's hand consisting of one page with a slip pasted to it; dated 2 Oct. 1820. Tr (ViU: TJP-VMJCC); dated 3 Oct. 1820; embedded in Tr of preceding document. Tr (ViU: TJP-VMJHC); dated and embedded as in above Tr. Tr (ViU: TJP-VMJB); dated and embedded as in above Trs. Printed in *Report and Documents for 1820*, 5–9, *Richmond Enquirer*, 9 Dec. 1820, and elsewhere. Enclosed in TJ's missing letter to Thomas Mann Randolph of 20 Nov. 1820 (see note to TJ to Randolph, 20 Nov. 1820).

A provision of the 25 Jan. 1819 "Act for establishing an University" required the University of Virginia Board of Visitors to REPORT ANNUALLY (*Acts of Assembly* [1818–19 sess.], 15–8, esp. p. 17). The structure intended by TJ to serve as the PROCTOR'S HOUSE became Hotel E, and the BUILDING OF SOMEWHAT MORE SIZE became the Rotunda.

[1] VMJCC Tr here adds "Rector and."

[2] In ViU MS, below and to the left of this figure, TJ interlined the intermediate sum of "74,600."

[3] Year not in Trs.

[4] In ViU MS, below and to the left of this figure, TJ interlined the intermediate sum of "84,000."

[5] Trs here add "annual."

[6] Dft starts here.

[7] Preceding two words interlined in Dft.

[8] Dft ends here.

[9] Dft resumes here, preceded by text canceled by TJ (edge trimmed): "The Visitors, as in duty bound, thus present for the consideration of the legislature all the material facts on which their wisdom will have to act. the ample fund which has been provided by the care of their predecessors, & appropriated exclusively to the object of education, renders unnecessary all calls on our fellow citizens for further contributions from them[.] of the three grades of education defined in the Report of the Commissioners before referred to, the Middle one may probably be left with safety to the numerous private schools academies and other seminaries already existing and hereafter to arise. these being distributed over the whole face of the state, placed within convenient distances from all it's members, and needing little advance of capital, may be properly insti-

tuted & maintained, at the expence of those who profit immediately by them and the emulation of rival establmts may with them supply responsibility to the public authorities. but the lowest, and the highest grades need the fostering care of the state at large: and between these the Visitors are far from wishing an undue proportion of the funds provided for them to be appropriated to either to the injury of the other. they are <*aware*> sensible of the importance of the Primary schools, and that the people at large, the ultimate depositories of the public rights & liberties, to be qualified to guard them, and to exercise all the functions of good & useful citizens, must be instructed by competent education. but they are also aware that, for their good government, for the management of the public interests, and for the advancement of those arts and sciences which render industry more productive, and give to a state that increase of power which is the fruit of knolege, a higher establishment is equally necessary. and this requiring preparations and advances far beyond the faculties of private individuals, needs also the fostering care and aid of the public, without which it will not exist. the due partition therefore of the funds provided for these objects is the present concern, and is the proper office of those who preside over the interests and well being of our country."

[10] Preceding eight words interlined in Dft.

[11] Word interlined in Dft in place of "replacement."

[12] Word interlined in place of "seven years."

[13] Preceding two words interlined in Dft in place of "that reimbursement."

[14] Preceding two words interlined in Dft.

[15] Word interlined in place of "great and annual."

[16] Word interlined in Dft in place of "now."

[17] In Dft TJ here canceled "remit the loans &."

[18] Word interlined in Dft in place of "existing."

[19] Preceding thirteen words interlined in Vi MS, with all but the last word also interlined in Dft.

[20] Preceding five words interlined in place of "and expenditures."

Alexander Garrett's Account with the University of Virginia

The University of Virginia — in account with Alexander Garrett — Bursar

Dr 1820				In account		Cr 1820		
April	1	To Expences to Richmond in Febuary last omitted $		25	00	April 1	By Ballance reported in the Treasury this date $	645 20
	2	" ditto this date		20	00		" James Lindsay 3d Instalment his subscription	25
		" Luther M George	Draft	16	95	3	" Isaac A Coles ditto ditto	50
		" Daniel Coleclaser for Wiley Harris	"	42	50	4	" John Coles ditto ditto	125
	4	" John C Ragland for Jno. Bishop	"	40	00		" John H Cocke ditto ditto	250
	8	" John Rucker	"	45	82	13	" Check approved on Farmers Bank of Virginia	15,000
		" Henry Marr	"	46	37	May 9.	" Charles A Scott 3d Installment his subscription	125
	10	" John Priddy	"	7	59			
		" James Leitch for Johnson Rowe	"	15		19	" Reubin Maury ditto ditto	25
		" James Brown	"	16	37	22	" Check approved on Bank of Virginia	10,000
	11.	" Jesse Lewis	"	135	88	June 5	" Martin Thacker 3d Installment his subscription	15
	13	" John Vaughan for Tho. Cooper	"	750		July 3	" John Harris 2d & 3d ditto	500
		" James Leitch	"	551	31			
		" Henry Watkins blank ledger	"	7		19	" Check on Bank of Virginia approved by Tho. Jefferson	10,000
	17	" John Pollock for Thomas Garth	"	40		Aug 2	" Thomas Jefferson 3d Installment his subscription	250
		" James Leitch	"	61	97	4	" A S Brockenbrough- for James Madison 3d Installment	250
		" Stephen Bowles	"	1	43		" same for Hall Nielson 1 & 2d ditto	15
		" Joseph Pitt	"	168	15		" same for Edmund Anderson 2d ditto	50
	18	" Henry Chiles for A. Thorn	"	46			" same for Geo. Divers 3d ditto	250
		" George Tool for Jno. Gormon	"	11	72		" same for Chs Harper 3d ditto	50
		" William Watson for A. Garrison	"	81	07		" same for Micajah Woods part 3d ditto	31
		" William Philips	"	1000				
		" ditto for Curtis Carter	"	1200				
		" Bramham & Jones	"	46	66			
		" ditto for J Bishop	"	7	50			
		" ditto for Jno. Mayo	"	10	83			

Dr   **The University of Virginia**   **In account with**   **Alexander Garrett Bursar**   **Cr**

Date	The University of Virginia	for	In account with	Alexander Garrett Bursar	Cr
	" ditto	for ditto	28	" same for James Dinsmore 3d ditto	50
	" Negroe Nelson	for ditto	7	" same for Henry Chiles 3d ditto	25
19.	" Willis Garth		55	" same for Henry Lee 1 & 2d ditto	100
21.	" Edward Callard	for John Gormon	26 04	" same for Tucker Coles 3d ditto	125
	" ditto	for John Dowell	4 58	" same for Robert Gentrys 3d ditto	
	" Jesse Henlow	for Jno. M. Perry	46 15		25
	" Negroe Willis		5	" same for C Wertenbaker 3d ditto	6 25
	" John H Craven		28 16	" same for John Pollock 3d ditto	50
	" Nelson Barksdale		383 89	" same for Wm Garth 3d ditto	
	" ditto		90 33	part	17
	" Benjamin Austin	for F. Birckhead[1]	40	" same for Jesse Lewis 3d ditto	25
22	" John Rodes		437 38	" same for Wm Brent jr 2nd ditto	25
	" Reubin Sandridge		5	7. " William C. Rives 3d ditto	50
	" William D. Merewether		64 13	8. " William F. Gordon 3d ditto	50
	" John M. Perry		1.500	9. " Thomas E Randolph 2d ditto	50
	" Negroe Milly		4	24 " David Isaacs 3d Installment his subscription	50
24.	" John T Bishop		29 25	Sep 4 " Daniel M Raily 2d Installment his subscription	25
	" John Gormon		75		
	" James Campbell		77	25 " Check on Farmers Bank of Virginia approved	
	" ditto	for Jos. Cowden	87 50	by Tho Jefferson	5.000
	" C. P. & J H McKennie		69	" A S Brockenbrough for Wm Garths 3d Instl his	
	" John E. Mitchell[2]		66 03	subscription	20 50
	" John Winn & Co		235 08	" same for N H. Lewis 2d & 3d ditto	150
	" Lucy Brockenbrough for ASB		31	" same for M. Cary 1 & 2d ditto	50
25	" W. Hudson		57 54	" same for W J Cary 2d ditto	50
	" ditto		5 15	" same for Geo Holeman 1 & 2d ditto	100
	" John M Perry		338 90		
27	" George W. Spooner		200		
28	" James Leitch		629 89		
	" Thomas W Gooch	for Daniel Davis	30 95		

Date		Name		Amount
29	"	Robert Gentry		10
	"	ditto		49
May 1	"	William Bowen		37 60
	"	William H Merewether		197 28
	"	Randolph & Coleclaser		19 33
	"	Frances Mellot		16 67
	"	Ambrose Flanagan		106 57
	"	James Black		8 40
	"	John Dudley		45
	"	David Owens		169 48
	"	J H. Timberlake		75 11
	"	Thomas Ritchie		2 50
	"	William Watson	for G Garth	35
	"	Robert Lindsay		19 83
	"	ditto		10 08
	"	Richard Ware		500
	"	Joseph Pitt		30
	"	John Fretwell		30
	"	M Raggi		60
2	"	Edward Callard		23 23
	"	A Hertane[3]		5 50
	"	William D. Merewether		12 18
	"	John Pittman	for Jno H Wood	8 50
	"	John W. Mayo		15
3	"	John Porterfield		92 90
5	"	John M. Perry		665 66
6	"	J Dold		59 28
	"	J E. Mitchell[4]		98 90
	"	Michael Graham		10 67
8	"	Ambrose Flannagan		55
9	"	James Dinsmore	for Opie Norris	50 50
10	"	John Moore	for Wm Payne	5
	"	John M. Perry		845 04

	Name		In account with	
11	" John Rodes	"	53	86
	" A S Brocken-brough			
	ditto	for Richard Ware	60	
	ditto	for T B. Conway	110	
	ditto	for Salary	300	
	ditto	for Jno Vanlew & Co	318	72
12	" ditto	for T B Conway	75	
	" Tyler Clift	for George Milleway	15	
	" John H Craven		16	25
	" Henry McCormick		28	14
13	" I. Raphail	for J. Dowell	4	
	" ditto	for W. Barnett	4	66
15	" James Dinsmore	part	1500	
	" ditto		22	15
	" Henry Stone	for James Stone	87	90
	" Fanny Barnett		3	75
	" Edward Callard		14	88
16	" Ira Harris	for Robert McCullock	90	73
	" ditto	for ditto	26	57
	" ditto	for ditto	65	86
	" John Vowles	for ditto	50	
	" William Pitt	for Joseph Pitt	51	92
17	" Joel Wolfe	for A S. Brockenbrough	15	
	" Negroe	for L. M. George	13	34
	" David Isaacs	for Jno. M. Perry	201	40
	" Nicholas Bizett	for Edward Callard	30	

	Name	For		Amount
18	" Lewis Baily		"	8
19	" V W southall	for Nelson Barksdale	"	100
	" Reubin Maury		"	87 96
	" George Leonard		"	13 50
22	" R Sandridge			5
	" James McDonnell		"	26 55
23	" John Winn	for Jno M Perry	"	605 64
	" John M Perry		"	350
	" Negroe		"	12
	" David Isaacs	for L M George	"	4
24	" William Bowen	for negroe Milly	"	27 25
	" John Dowell		"	21 84½
27	" David Owens	for Thomas Gardner	"	73 20
29	" Walker Timberlake		"	400
	" I Raphail	for E Callard	"	14 67
	" ditto	for J Herren	"	13 80
	" ditto	for F. Barnett	"	6 25
	" ditto	for D. Smith	"	12 50
	" ditto	for W. Payne		4
	" James Dinsmore	Ballance	"	500
	" John Cullin		"	10
30	" Samuel Leitch jr	for Jno. Lee	"	5 25
	" James McCullock	for Robert McCullock		
31	" Benjamin Austin	for Z. Baily	"	39 25
	" Samuel Leitch jr	for Curtis Carter	"	33 65
June 1.	" Thomas Divers	for G Garth	"	25
	" Joseph Waltman[5]	for J Antrim	"	100
3	" Robert Piggot	for Jno. M Perry	"	150
	" E Huffman		"	1000
	" George Rupple		"	5
	" ditto		"	82 50
			"	68 38

The University of Virginia

In account with

Alexander Garrett Bursar

	" John Nielson		400
	" Negroe		2
4	" Henry Sprouce		33 33
5	" John R Campbell		177 04
	" Robert Lindsay		45 25
	" ditto		178 18
	" David Owens		124 50
	" William Garth		6 48
	" N. G Rogers		75
	" A S Brocken-brough	for Ed Lowber	500
	" James Magruder		155
	" A. Flanagan		199 62
6	" Thomas Draffen		30
	" Nelson Barksdale		11 06[6]
	" ditto		400
	" Robert McCullock		137 02
	" A H. Brooks		51
7.	" John H Craven		17 46
9.	" Ira Harris	for Jno Pollock	11 62
	" I Raphail	for M Lahay	4 50
	" ditto	for W. Barnett	4 50
	" ditto	for Lewis Baily	10
	" John Pillson	for A C. McWilliams	8 25
10	" Robert Harper	for J T. Bishop	13 75
13	" William Bowen		58 50
	" ditto	for M. Dobb	10
	" John Gormon	for Jos: Cowden	213 23
	" John W Mayo		19 34
15	" Samuel Leitch	for Jno. Callum	10
	" ditto	for Ed. Callard	25

	Name	For		$	¢
	" Willis D. Garth		"	41	85
19	" William Garth		"	25	
	" George Tool	for John Gormon	"	17	
21	" William Banks	for Wᵐ Clopton	"	6	
	" John Winn	for N Thacker	"	13	83
	" ditto	for N H. Lewis	"	49	08
22	" Casper Coiner	for Jos: Pitt	"	53	90
	" N Roberts	for Geo. Coiner	"	47	76
	" John Rodes		"	365	23
	" I Raphail	for Jno Carter	"	25	
	" ditto	for Jos: Gilmer	"	16	
	" Gasper Coiner		"		50
23	" John M Perry		"	600	
	" Samuel Leitch jr for Robert McCullock		"	70	06
	" I Raphail	for C. [Onon?][7]	"	5	
	" M. Dobb		"	7	50
	" Wᵐ B	for Ed. Callard	"	12	56
24	" John Cullin		"	20	80
	" Dinsmore & Perry		"	1000	
26	" G. Raggi		"	4	
	" Wᵐ Priddy		"	4	86
	" Sam		"	7	50
27	" Joseph Antrim		"	200	
	" Garland Garth		"	109	85
July 3	" David Owens		"	114	38
	" John M Perry	for Richard Ware	"	18	25
	" Samuel Leitch	for Wᵐ B Philips	"	100	
	" Thomas Priddy		"	33	27
5	" Francis Modeana		"	15	50
6	" Milly a Negroe		"	8	
8	" Joel Yancey		"	21	
	" Wᵐ Pitt	for Jos: Pitt	"	42	

Dr	The University of Virginia		In account with	Alexander Garrett Bursar	Cr
	" Dabney C. Garth	for G Garth	81 25		
7	" I Raphail	for D Smith	17 50		
10	" Solomon Ballew[8]	for Jno Bishop	12		
	" John W. Davis	for Geo W Spooner	200		
	" Dabney C. Garth	for Johnson Rowe	5		
	" John Vowles		50		
14	" Lucy Brockenbrough		51 39		
15	" John Cullin		20		
17	" Abraham Hawley		50		
18	" Z Bailey		15 41		
	" John Gormon		140		
19	" Samuel McAffee	for Richard Ware	14		
20	" Bramham & Jones		10		
	" James Leitch	for E Huffman	100		
	" A. Leitch	for John Nelson	75 90		
	" ditto	for L Meade	94 65		
	" ditto	for Tho. Leason	95		
	" ditto	for Aaron Cross	75 08		
21	" James Oldham	for James Megaw	500		
22	" John Herren		9 25		
	" Wm Pitt	for Jos: Pitt	56 33		
	" Reubin Maury		76 01		
	" J P. Shepperd	for Robert McCullock	184 16		
26	" V W southall	for Wm Payne	10		
29	" John W Davis	for David Fowler	21		
	" W. Priddy	for Thomas Priddy	8 25		
	" ditto	for ditto	16 16		

	Name	For		Amount	
31	" I Raphail	for David Owens	"	47	33
	same	for same	"	46	14
	same	for Jno. M. Perry	"	7	75
	same	for Jno. Pile	"	10	16
	same	for Sarah Morland	"	2	66
	same	for Hembro. Pendleton	"	22	31
	same	for Jos: Antrim	"	33	18
	same	for Z. Bailey	"	19	52
	same	for John Carter	"	25	
	same	for Tho Jackson	"	13	92
	same	for Randolph	"	1	87½
	same	for Robert Gentry	"	67	89
	same	for same	"	30	24
	same	for Alfred Wren	"	283	66
	same	for Mr Irvine	"	29	61
	James Toley		"	136	40
	Benjamin Moore			12	
	Francis Cockes	for Loury & Black	"	25	
	John E Mitchell		"	56	25
1	" John W Davis	for Jno. M. Perry		20	
	same	for J Herren	"	51	50
	William B. Philips		"	52	40
	Curtis Carter		"	46	50
	John Gormon		"	10	30
2	" John Pollock		"	137	17
	Naiman Roberts		"	27	68
4	" A S. Brocken-brough	for Andrew Jameson	"	$2:25.	
	same	for Bernard Peyton	"	25:07	
	same	for M Raggi	"	50.	

Aug^t

Dr	The University of Virginia		In account with	Alexander Garrett Bursar	Cr
" same	for Jesse Lewis	" 25.			
" same	for Tho. Bunch	" 14:34			
" same	for Richard Ware	" 108.76			
" same	for Jno. M. Perry	" 220.			
" same	for F. Mellet	" 5.			
" same	for Wᵐ Selkirk	" 3:62½			
" same	for Jno. T. Bishop	" 50.			
" same	for M. Woods	" 31.			
" same	for James Dinsmore	" 50:			
" same	for Jos. Pitt pʳ H Chiles	" 25:			
" A S Brocken-brough	for A B Hawkins	" 4:00			
" Same	for Curtis Carter	" 25:00			
" Same	for A Jameson	" 19.00			
" Same	for M. Raggi	" 25:00			
" Same	for Jno. Mᶜ Perry	" 50.00			
" Same	for Wᵐ Garth	" 17.00			
" Same	for Jno Pollock	" 50.00			
" Same	for Robert Gentry	" 25.00			
" Same		" 63.34			
" Same	for Jno Vanlew & Co	" 205:86	1094 24½		
5 " C C C. Owen		"	700		
" Wᵐ Pitt	for Jos: Pitt	"	22 92		
" M W. Maury	for Jno M. Perry	"	218 75		
7 " Abraham Johnston		"	53 25		
" Isaac W. Durrett		"	10		
" Nˡ H. Lewis		"	31 50		
" Walker Timberlake		"	137 97		
			270		

	Name		Note	Amount
8	" I Raphail	for John Pile	"	9 25
	" Same	for Jno. Smith	"	6
	" same	for Ed. Callard	"	10
	" same	for Elijah Huffman		
	" same	for John M Perry	"	5
	" same	for Reuben Wayt	"	10
	" same	for Jos: Antrim	"	15
	" same	for Wᵐ & Dab. Mooney	"	79
	" Richard E Johnson		"	6 75
	" James Brown		"	4
	" John W. Davis	for Jno. M. Perry	"	27 95
	" Robert McᶜCullock			600
9	" Opie Norris	for Jno. M. Perry	"	108
	" N. Roberts			100
	" John W Davis	for A Hawley	"	43 85
	" David Isaacs	for C C Owen	"	38 65
	" same	for Jno Cullin		10
	" same	for Sam. Goodman		10
11	" John Rodes		"	10 59
	" Thomas Abner		"	64 68
	" Abner Hawkins	for A B Thorn	"	54
	" John W Davis	for Curtis Carter		69
	" I Raphail	for Jos: Taylor	"	40
	" same	for Jos: Pitt	"	77 36
	" same	for Allen W Hawkins		25
	" same	for Francis B Dyer	"	5 75
12	" R Burton	for A B Thorn	"	163 06
	" Wᵐ Pitt	for Jos: Pitt	"	96 43
				112 47

Date	Name	For	Amount
	" David Smith		10 50
	" Wm D. Merewether		45 08
14	" Saml Leitch		75 86
	" A H. Jameson	for Jno Fretwell	342
	" Garland Garth	for A H Brooks	77 86
21	" John W. Davis	for Jno. M. Perry	1000
	" A S Brockenbrough		150
	" same	for Jno Carter	25
	" Bramham & Jones		
	" Robert Brooks	for Tho. Bunch	18 15
22	"	for Wm B. Philips	19 60
	" William Watson	for Johnson Rowe	24
	" John Pollock	for Alfred Wren	46 25
23	" John E Mitchell		24 58
	" Lewis Baily		25
24	" Thomas Draffen	for Crenshaw Fretwell	50
	" David Isaacs	for Joseph Pitt	30
	" same	for John Carter	50
	" same	for J Herren	2 25
	" John Koiner	for M Beck	5 62
	" same	for Wm & D. Mooney	5
25	" Wm A. Bibb		250
	" John Cullin	for Wm B Philips	100
	" John M Perry	for A B. Thorne Ball.	118
28	" George Ruper		19 85
	" Bramham & Jones	for James Stone	27 96
29	" David Owens		110 27
	" same		59 40

		" Andrew McKee	for R E Johnson	"	19	83
		" Negroe Sam		"	2	
		" Edward Callard		"	25	
		" P. Myers		"	11	56
		" Daniel Coleclaser		"	10	
	31	" W & D. Mooney		"	10	37½
		" Clerk of Albemarle his Ticketts 1817.				
		'18 & '19		"	8	85
Sept	4	" Philip Watts	for Wm Humphrey	"	95	69
		" Willis D. Garth		"	18	05
		" Thomas Amonet		"	10	
		" John M. Perry		"	212	79
		" Robert Brooks	for Wm B Philips	"	19	60
		" Christian Wertenbaker		"	31	12½
		" same		"	15	
		" James Dowell		"	13	65
		" Robert Wood	for C Fretwell	"	94	81
	5	" I Raphail	for Jno Carter	"	50	
		" same	for Robert Gentry	"	65	50
		" same	for Curtis Carter	"	50	
		" same	for same	"	50	
		" same	for George Ruple	"	16	50
		" same	for Jos: Antrim	"	6	44
		" same	for A P. Perryman	"	20	
		" same	for Jno Williams	"	6	66
		" same	for Jno Phile	"	4	20
		" John M. Perry	for Crenshaw Fretwell	"	62	06
		" Wm Huntington	for Mary Garner	"	10	
		" Opie Norris	for Jno. Rogers	"	105	
		" Jno. W. Davis	for Wm Garth	"	23	14

Dr	The University of Virginia		In account with	Alexander Garrett Bursar	Cr
6	" Jno Herren	for N Barksdale	300		
	" John Hutchenson	"	52		
7	" John W Davis	for N Barksdale	68 03		
	" Samuel Leitch	for Lyman Pecks	6		
	same	for John Cullin	30		
	" Barnett Cola	for McDermot	9 50		
8	" M. Raggi	"	293 60		
	" Joseph Pitt	"	119 16		
	" J Hollins	"	10		
	" J Dold	"	63 35		
	same	"	116 65		
	" John M. Perry	"	200		
	" William Garth	"	20 50		
	" N. H. Lewis	"	150		
18	" Lucy Brockenbrough	"	61 50		
	" Angus M Key		40		
	" John M Perry	"	44		
	" A S. Brockenbrough	"	23 76		
	" Joseph Antrim	"	31 55		
	" John Gormon	"	21		
	" Richard Ware	"	41 89½		
	" John Herren	"	23 13		
	" Anthony P. Peryman	"	25 93		
	" John Carter	"	26 46		
	" John M. Perry	"	93 18		

			^{s} 43.699	95

25	" Alexander Garrett for R. Ware & J^s Oldham	"	87	50
	" Alexander Garrett	"	125	
	" Nicholas H. Lewis	"	144	53
	" William D. Merewether	"	70	
	" Nathan Herren	"	20	
	" John Gorman	"	30	
	" M. Mooney	"	5	
	" John Carter	"	25	
	" Thomas Bunch	"	22	65
28	" A H. Brooks	"	389	36
	" Robert Gentry	"	77	30
	" John Gorman	"	7	31
	" Sarah Moorland	"	4	34
	" John Campbell	"	40	
	" P. Eades	"	9	34
	" E Huffman	"	3	25
	" R. Sandridge	"	2	50
	" John M. Perry	"	12	50
	" Hastings Colier	"	87	89
	" Joseph Antrim	"	37	87
	" John M Perry	"	30	
	" James Wedderfield	"	10	
30	" Ballance remaining in the Treasury this date	"	3963	48
			^{s} 43.699	95

The foregoing is an account of the reciepts and disbursements of money by the Bursar of the University[9] of Virginia, from the first day of April one thousand eight hundred and twenty, to the thirtyeth day of September one thousand eight hundred and twenty (inclusive) shewing a ballance remaining in the Treasury[10] on the last mentioned date of Three thousand nine hundred and Sixty three dollars forty eight cents, All of which is respectfully reported to the Rector & Visitors of the University of Virginia this 30th day of September 1820—   ALEX: GARRETT Bursar

MS (Vi: RG 79, House of Delegates, Speaker, Executive Communications); in Garrett's hand; with page numbers, internal headings, and running totals at breaks of pages editorially omitted; docketed by Garrett as "Report Bursar University Virginia From 1st April 1820 to 30th Sept. 1820" and, in an unidentified hand, "Examined." Printed in *Report and Documents for 1820*, 14–33.

WILLIAM BOWEN: William Boin. AARON CROSS: Aaron Cress. JAMES TOLEY: James Foley. ANGUS M KEY: Angus McKay (MKay). JAMES WEDDERFIELD: James W. Widderfield.

[1] *Report and Documents*: "F. Buckhead."
[2] *Report and Documents*: "John G. Mitchell."
[3] *Report and Documents*: "A. Herlane."
[4] *Report and Documents*: "J. G. Mitchell."
[5] *Report and Documents*: "Joseph Wallman."
[6] *Report and Documents*: "4 06."
[7] Name illegible. *Report and Documents*: "C. Onnen."
[8] *Report and Documents*: "Solomon Ballno."
[9] Manuscript: "Uneversity."
[10] Manuscript: "Treasuary."

II

Arthur S. Brockenbrough's Statement of Expenditures by the University of Virginia

A Statement of the application of the Funds of the University of Virginia, showing how much has been paid to each undertaker of work and for what purposes, and to other individuals on acc[t] of the buildings and other expences, from the 1st day of October 1819 to the 30th day of September 1820—

	$	Ct	$	C[ts]
This sum paid to John M Perry on acc[t] of the last payment for the 48¾ Acres of Land & improvement		3 615.90		
To J. M. Perry on acc[t] of the brick work of Pav: N° 3 & 7 Dormitories executed in 1819		2 990.54		
To the same on acc[t] of[1] work on Pavilion N° 4 West and 16 dormitories, including plastering & Bill of lumber, and the brick-work of Pavilion 4 East with 8 dormitories & the brick & wood work of Hotel B with 9 dormitories, lumber included[2]		8.598.75	15.205	19
To this sum paid to James Dinsmore on acc[t] of Carpenter & Joiners work on Pav: N° 2 West and Pav: N° 4 East & eight dormitories including lumber & other articles			5 314	15

[318]

To Dinsmore & Perry, for Carpenters & Joiners work and lumber for Pavilion N° 3 West and six dormitories		1 544	11
To Richard Ware for brick work in Pav: 1 and 2 East & four dormitories	3 891.72		
" same for Carpenter & Joiners work & lumber for Pavilions 1, 2 and 3 & 13 dormitories	6 503.77	10.395	49
To Carter & Phillips for am^t of their brick work last year in Pav^s N° 1 & 5.^{3} & five dormitories &c		3.506	75
To James Oldham on acc^t of Carpenters & Joiners work on Pavilion N° 1 West with four dormitories and Hotel A. with nine dormitories & lumber		2 919	99
To A. Thorn for stone foundation for Columns to Pavilion N° 1 West		86	50^4
To George W. Spooner on acc^t Carpenters work on Pavilion N° 5 West and on Hotel C with 10 dormitories and lumber		2 084	57
To John Nelson for work & lumber for Pavilion N° 5 West & Pavilion N° 5 East with seven dormitories	1 486.57		
To Peter Myers for brick work in Pavilion N° 5 West	11.56	1 498	13
To William B Phillips on account of brick work the present year^5		898	71
To Curtis Carter on acc^t of his contract for brick work the present year^6		926	79
To Nelson Barksdale for lumber for the buildings	800.00		
same for the hire of Negroes for 1819	1 101.00		
same for a Horse for the use of the Institution	65.00	1 966	00
To Michele & Giacomo Raggi on acc^t wages as Sculptors board washing &c	1 294.24		
" Giacomo Raggi on acc^t wages	70.	1 364	24
To Joseph Cowden & James Campbell stone cutters	314.50		
To John Gorman on acc^t of stone work	679.06	993	56^7
To John Cullen & others for quarrying stone for Bases, Caps, door sills, steps &c		269	25^8
To Thos B. Conway for free Stone		75	
To Joseph Antrim for Plastering	681.69		
To Edward Lowber for Painting and Glazing	598.25		
To A. H. Brooks, for covering Pavilions 1 and 5 West and 1 and 2 East with Tin & pipes^9 N° 2 West	798.47	2 078	41
To James Leitch for sundries furnished for the buildings including, Glass, Tin, hardware &c in^{10} 1818 and 1819	1 332.73		
To Brockenbrough & Harvie for Nails	282.96		
To John Van Lew & Co for Tin, hardware &c	1 360.76		
To D. W. & C Warwick for sundries	37.00	3 013	45

To Elijah Huffman for boring & laying water pipes	242.53		
" Lewis Bailey for ditching for water pipes	25.50		
" William Boin & others for do do	85.67	353	70
To John Herron for Wages as overseer	106.00		
" Jesse Lewis blacksmith work	160.88		
To this paid for provision for laborers & overseer	797.83		
" this sum paid for the hire of laborers, waggonage and other unavoidable expences	1 620.26	2 684	97
To A. S. Brockenbrough on acc^t services[11]	1 604 85		
" Alex Garrett on acc^t services	375.00	1 979	85
Total amount paid out[12] from 1 Oct: 19 to 30th Sep^t 1820		$ 59.158	81

An Estimate of what will probably be required to complete the buildings now on hand and two other Hotels, a Proctors house and twenty eight dormitories to complete the range on the Western Street—

	$	C^{ts}
Agreeable to our estimate on the 1st Oct 1819 we required to complete the buildings then contracted for the sum of	38.898	25
For 3 other Pavilions now building 18.000		
" 3 Hotels or boarding houses do 9.000.		
45 Dormitories do 18.000		
	45,000	00
For 2 Hotels & a Proctors House on the west street with 28 dormitories[13] 20.200		
	$ 104.098	25
To which may be added on account of stone work diging & removing earth and other unavoidable[14] expences at least 25 pCent	26.024	56
	$ 130.122	81
From which deduct the sums paid to the several undertakers of the buildings & others as p^r the foregoing acc^t—since Oct: 1st 1819	59,158	81
	$ 70.964	00
Funds required to meet the above balance $		
This sum unappropriated of the sum borrowed of the Literary fund[15] 20.000		
The State donation of 1821 after paying 2.400 Ds interest for money borrowed[16] 12.600		
Balance required to complete the buildings 38.364	70,964	

From the foregoing estimate it will be seen that the sum of $38.364 will be wanting to complete the buildings contemplated for the accommodation of the Professors & students at the University of Virginia, the sum wanting is enlarged by adding to our former estimate a Proctors house and ten Dormitories which are required to make the Ranges on the East & West streets equal—In my estimate of October 1st 1819 the cost of the buildings alone was brought into the calculation, to make good what has been paid out for land and a variety of unforeseen[17] contingent expences I have added 25 p^{r}cent on the estimate of October 1ˢᵗ 1819 which I am confident will be sufficient to complete the aforesaid buildings—the foregoing statements are respectfully submited to the board of Visitors by thier obᵗ Humbˡᵉ Sevᵗ

A. S. BROCKENBROUGH Proctor

University Sept: 30ʰ 1820

MS (Vi: RG 79, House of Delegates, Speaker, Executive Communications); entirely in Brockenbrough's hand; with internal running totals at breaks of pages and small check marks adjacent to some entries editorially omitted; docketed in an unidentified hand. FC (DLC); entirely in Brockenbrough's hand. Printed in *Report and Documents for 1820*, 10–3. MS probably also enclosed in either Brockenbrough's letter to TJ of 30 Sept. or that of 2 Oct. 1820, neither found, with the former inconsistently recorded in SJL as received 28 Sept. 1820 from the University of Virginia and the latter recorded as received on the day it was written. FC enclosed in Brockenbrough to TJ, 7 Nov. 1820.

PAV: Nº 3 was later redesignated as Pavilion V. PAVILION Nº 4 WEST and PAVILION 4 EAST became pavilions VII and VIII, respectively, while HOTEL B became Hotel D and PAV: Nº 2 WEST became Pavilion III. Richard Ware worked on PAVILIONS 1, 2 AND 3, which were renamed as pavilions II, IV, and VI. Curtis Carter and William B. Phillips did the brickwork on PAVˢ Nº 1 & 5, with the latter later redesignated as Pavilion IX. HOTEL A and HOTEL C became hotels B and F, respectively. PAVILION Nº 5 EAST is Pavilion X.

[1] FC here adds "carpenters."
[2] Preceding two words not in FC.
[3] FC here adds "West."
[4] In FC the preceding two amounts are rendered in the left column, with the subtotal "3.006 49" in the right.
[5] FC here adds "in pavilion Nº 5 East and Hotel C."
[6] Instead of preceding four words, FC reads "in Pavilion Nº 3 East & Hotel A."
[7] Subtotal not in FC.
[8] In FC this amount is rendered in the left column, with the subtotal "1262 81" in the right.
[9] Instead of this word, FC reads "tin pipes for."
[10] Instead of preceding six words, FC reads "in the year."
[11] FC: "salary."
[12] Instead of this word, FC reads "to Undertakers & others."
[13] FC here adds "yet to be put up."
[14] MS: "inavoidable." FC: "unavoidable."
[15] In FC this entry reads "This Balance of the $60.000 loan."
[16] In FC this entry reads "The Annuity of 15.000. $ deduct 2.400 Int: on the 40.000 borrowed."
[17] MS: "unforesen." FC: "unforeseen."

From Joseph C. Cabell

DEAR SIR,   Charlottesville 3ᵈ Oct: 1820

I neglected to bring with me Mʳ Garrett's account, which I am instructed to examine & verify; and beg the favor of you to send it by the Bearer. I wish to compare it with the account in the Bursar's Books from which it was copied; at the same time that I check the latter by the vouchers. Perhaps I shall be induced to take the account home, in order to examine the additions at my leisure.

I am, Dʳ Sir, faithfully yours   JOSEPH C. CABELL

RC (ViU: TJP-PC); endorsed by TJ as received the day it was written and so recorded in SJL.

University of Virginia bursar Alexander GARRETT'S ACCOUNT is printed above as the first enclosure to the University of Virginia Board of Visitors Report to Literary Fund President and Directors, 2 Oct. 1820.

Notes on Thomas Cooper and the University of Virginia

[ca. 3 Oct. 1820]

Extract from a letter of Sep. 19. 1817. from Dr Cooper to Th: Jefferson

'I calculate that in a course of Philosophical & Chemical lectures at Philadelphia the expences would be 300.D. for articles quæ ipso usu consumantur. it would cost about 100.D. in Charlottesville.'

Extract from the Journals of the Visitors 1817. Oct. 8.

'Certain letters from Dr T. Cooper to Th Jefferson dated Sep. 17. & 19. being communicated to the B. of Visitors E^{t}c. Resolved E^{t}c.'[1]

'3.[2] That the expence in articles consumed necessarily in a course of chemical lectures shall be paid by the College.'

———

At a meeting of the Visitors E^{t}c. Mar. 29. 1819.

Dr Cooper confirmed in his appointment, E^{t}c

'Resolved that until he shall have 50. students in Chemistry, the expence in articles consumed necessarily in the courses of Chemical lectures be defrayed by the University; not exceeding 250:D. in any course.'[3]

———

At a meeting E^{t}c. 1820. Oct. 3. the contract with Dr Cooper is annulled.

[Note at the meeting Mar 29. 19. the established tuition fee to the Professor[4] is 'for instruction in any or all the branches of science which constitute his department.'[5]

———

MS (DLC: TJ Papers, 211:37647); on verso of reused address cover to TJ; entirely in TJ's hand; undated; unmatched bracket in original; endorsed by TJ: "Chemical contribns Extracts from Journals."

The University of Virginia Board of Visitors MEETING E^{T}C. 1820. OCT. 3 began on the previous day, at which date its minutes are printed.

[1] Omitted closing quotation mark editorially supplied.

[2] TJ added the number of the resolution passed on 8 Oct. 1817 by the Central College Board of Visitors beneath the opening quotation mark.

³ Omitted closing quotation mark editorially supplied.
⁴ Preceding three words interlined.

⁵ Omitted closing quotation mark editorially supplied.

To Peter Cardelli

SIR   Monticello Oct. 4. 20.

I understand you have taken the busts in plaister of the President of the US. and of mr Madison of the size of the life and have to request the favor of you to send me a copy of each. as they are to stand en suite of those of Gen¹ Washington & Dʳ Franklin which perhaps you may have noted in our tea-room and these are of a brick-dust color, I should be glad that those you send me should be of the same color. address them, well packed in a box or boxes, if you please, to Capᵗ Bernard Peyton of Richmond, sending them by water, and drop me a line at the same time noting their cost and it shall be remitted to you. I salute you [with] great esteem & respect.

TH: JEFFERSON

PoC (MHi); on verso of reused address cover to TJ; mutilated at seal, with one word rewritten by TJ; at foot of text: "Mʳ Cardelli"; endorsed by TJ.

From Henry Clark

DEAR SIR   Lynchburg Ocbʳ 4ᵗʰ 1820

Having hear from a source which seems to be entitled to credit that it is your intention to Lease your Poplar Forist Estate I avail myself of the first opportunity of declareing my wish to take the Lease, provided your Terms be such as will enable me to do so—

As I have no reasons to beleeve you will know any thing of me, I refer you to Capt Wᵐ Irvine Capt James Martin or Mʳ Joel Yancy Your present Agent—I am Son of Bowling Clark—formerly your agent upon these Estates

You will oblige me very much Sir by letting me know your Terms as early as possible should you be disposed to make me your tenant   Most Respectfaly

You Ob Serᵗ   HENRY CLARK

RC (MHi); endorsed by TJ as received 16 Oct. 1820 and so recorded in SJL. RC (MHi); address cover only; with PoC of TJ to Robert R. Glinn & Company, 10 May 1821, on verso; addressed: "Thomas Jefferson Esqure Monticello"; stamped; postmarked Lovingston, 13 Oct.

Henry Clark (1792–1834), the eldest son of former Poplar Forest overseer Bowling

Clark, worked as a manufacturer in Lynchburg in 1820. He moved thereafter to an 800-acre plantation in Bedford County left to him by his father. Clark owned fourteen slaves in 1830. Shortly after his death his personal property was valued at nearly $250 (Clark Family Bible Record [Vi]; Campbell Co. Will Book, 4:138; DNA: RG 29, CS, Lynchburg, 1820, Bedford Co., 1830; Bedford Co. Will Book, 8:366–7).

From Donald Fraser

VENERABLE SIR—   New York Oct[r] 4th 1820

I beg leave to present for the honor of Your perusal, a copy of a Prospectus of a work of mine nearly ready for Press.

I have written a Sketch concerning <u>Your self</u> & the former Presidents, which Shall appear in the body of my work; Perhaps You might desire to See it, previous to its appearance in Print.

I trust, that I have done justice to Your Superior talents & Merit.

Perhaps, You may think proper to take a couple of copies.

I have the honor to be, with great respect, Sir, Your humble Servant   DONALD FRASER SEN[R]

RC (MHi); dateline between closing and signature; endorsed by TJ as received 11 Oct. 1820 and so recorded in SJL. Enclosure: second enclosure to Fraser to TJ, 4 Feb. 1820.

To John S. Skinner

SIR   Monticello Oct. 4. 20.

When I had the pleasure of seeing you here, you asked for a letter from mr Calvin Jones to mr Burton on the subject of the Scupernon wine, and supposing I had recieved it from mr Burton I searched my alphabetical files under his name, and not finding it, I concluded I no longer had it. on a visit since that to mr Eppes he informed me that it was himself who had sent it to me. on my return, examining my files under his name, I found and now inclose it to you. I will ask the favor of a copy of it when you shall have printed it, and I salute you with great respect.   TH: JEFFERSON

RC (DLC: TJ Papers, ser. 9); at foot of text: "M[r] Skinner"; with signed note (edge trimmed) from Robert Gilmer, 7 May 183[ ], reading "This letter was given to me by M[r] Skinner, the Editor of the American Farmer, in 1829." PoC (MHi); on verso of a reused address cover from Thomas Mann Randolph to TJ; at foot of text: "M[r] John S. Skinner"; endorsed by TJ. Enclosure: Calvin Jones to Hutchins G. Burton, [before 28 Apr. 1817] (printed as a letter of 17 June 1817 in *American Farmer* 3 [1822]: 332–3). This document, which was originally enclosed in John Wayles Eppes to TJ, 28 Apr. 1817, was located after print publication of that volume, has been added digitally, and will appear in the concluding supplement to the print edition.

Skinner gave TJ THE PLEASURE OF SEEING him when he visited Monticello on 6 Sept. 1820 bearing an introductory letter from Tench Coxe (see note to TJ to Coxe, 13 Oct. 1820). Skinner recalled many years later that "Mr. Jefferson was going next day to his estate in Bedford, but was very civil, and as always highly entertaining and instructive, but not very exemplary in his dieting or drinking on that occasion; for we well remember, that in following his recommendation and example in *eating millet*, (then the one in his constant succession of hobbies,) and in *mixing our* wine too, at his instance, the consequence was what might have been expected—an intestine commotion in the abdominal regions . . . One agricultural or horticultural fact we remember to have heard from Mr. Jefferson. We were speaking of the influence of soils, climates, and manures on plants, when he said that a large income of some one whom he knew in Europe, from a *Port wine* estate, had been ruined by the application to it of fresh, unsuitable stable manure" (*The Plough, the Loom, and the Anvil* 3 [1851]: 491–2). Closer to the time of his visit, Skinner reported hearing from TJ that José Corrêa da Serra, "one of the most learned botanists" of his day, had "remarked to him that in his rambles over the Monticello estate, he had discovered a greater variety of individuals of the vegetable family than are to be found in all England" (*American Farmer* 2 [1821]: 401).

From Fernagus De Gelone

SIR.   New York Octob. 5. 1820.

I thank you much for your polite & encouraging letters. Nothing can be more conducive to my perseverance in procuring to America all The means of amelioration which I ardently wish to communicate, not certainly from a sense of interest. Brought up in Military Schools and Watched afterwards by rigid Parents, I got acquainted with the practical Science of Men, on the same plan on which Berthier (the Prince of Neufchatel) his father, his Brothers and The <u>Leturcq</u> were educated. The plan stands not so much upon reading as it does upon demonstration. Thus Mathematics, Architecture, The Cutting of Matter, in any shape, as from Joinery, & Carpenting; Melting, forging, Surveying, The construction of Canals, roads and bridges, are reduced to plain rules. Language also is Submitted to the same Mathematical principles, from The different powers of the human organs.— at last, The course embraces the grand Military evolutions of frederic The 2^{ond}, folard, Guibert & Jomini. And The arrangement is so simple, that almost any number may be taught together: it is Lalande's, Lancaster's,[1] Pestalozzi's, Bell's System, which is now followed thro' all Europe.

I was lately invited to publish a Method on those principles. Books never suffice to convince; and a Man who introduces any thing new, labours under The disadvantage of not Judged at once.

I may after few weeks publish a Sketch of The plan, and in the case, I Shall be very happy to Send you a copy.

I remain most respectfully

Sir. Your most humble obedient Servant

FERNAGUS DE GELONE

RC (MHi); endorsed by TJ as received 11 Oct. 1820 and so recorded in SJL. RC (MHi); address cover only; with PoC of TJ to Bernard Peyton, 11 May 1821, on verso; addressed: "Thomas Jefferson. Esqr

Monticelo—Milton. Virg^a"; franked; post-marked New York, 5 Oct.

[1] Manuscript: "Lancaster,'s."

From Bernard Peyton

MY DEAR SIR,   Rich"d 5 October 1820

I should have done myself this pleasure by the last Mail, but finding on my arrival Mr Eppes had not reached Town & not having sufficient time to execute your order for the Harpsichord strings determined to defer it until to=day.

Mr Eppes has still not arrived, & as I had no blank of yours for the Farmers Bank of $2,500 instead of $3,000, was obliged to offer the note without the curtail, but addressed a note to the Directors expressing my readiness to pay $500 on ¾ of that note agreeable to their former requisition if they would receive it, & allow you a Credit on the back of the note for it—they preferred however to discount the note for the full amount of $3,000, giving you another sixty days to pay the curtail, when you will bear in mind that a note for $2,500 is to be sent instead of $3,000: the discount I have paid.

I had the good fortune to engage the services of Mr Stoddart, the Celebrated Piano maker late from Europe, now in this City, thro' the agency of Miss Gibbon, in selecting the strings for your Harpsichord, which I send herewith, & altho' this City does not afford a complete set for any instrument, yet Mr S. hopes those sent will be made to answer, they are the best to be had here.   I hope they may reach you safely, but they are so much more weighty than I antisipated, that I shall feel uneasy until I hear of their arrival.

Your Box of Books from Mr Gelston of N. York reached me on Monday, & yesterday I forwarded them by a trusty Augusta Waggoner to Charlottesville, care of James Leitch Esqr, & wish them safe to hand, as well as the Tin & Sheet Iron before sent.

You desired me to apprise you of the falling due of your $2,250 note at the U.S. Bank, it will be on the 15/18th of this month:—that of $3,000 at the same Bank, on the 19/22 Nov^r: & that of $3,000 at the Farmers Bank on the 4/7 Decem^r—If you fill up the <u>dates</u> of the notes, recollect it should always be on the <u>last</u> day of grace—

When Mr Eppes comes to Town you shall be apprised of it, his agent here is George Perkins Esq^e

With sincere affection D^r sir

Yours very Truely   B. Peyton

Tobacco $ 4½ @ 9
Flour   " 4 @ 4⅛
Wheat   75¢
Corn $ 2

RC (MHi); endorsed by TJ as received 19 Oct. 1820 and so recorded in SJL. RC (MHi); address cover only; with PoC of TJ to Andrew Smith, 20 Apr. 1821, on verso; addressed: "Mr Thomas Jefferson Monticello Milton"; franked; postmarked Richmond, 5 Oct.

MR Stoddart was possibly the William Stodart who partnered with William Dubois late in 1821 to operate a music store on Broadway in New York City (Martha Novak Clinkscale, *Makers of the Piano* [1993–99], 2:360; *New-York Evening Post*, 7 Nov. 1821; *Longworth's New York Directory* [1822], 174).

To Samuel Walkup

Sir   Monticello. Oct. 5. 20.

I have duly recieved your favor of Sep. 25. informing [me] it is proposed to establish a road thro my lands at the Natural bridge which, you observe, will be a convenience to the public and no injury to me. being a stranger to the grounds, I place myself under the guardianship of the court, who weighing reasonably the public and private interest, will, I am sure, do what is right and I shall acquiesce in it. accept the assurance of my great respect.

Th: Jefferson

PoC (MHi); on verso of a reused address cover from Thomas Mann Randolph to TJ; one faint word supplied from Tr; at foot of text: "Mr Samuel Walkup"; endorsed by TJ. Tr of RC (Rice M. Youell, Richmond, 1950); typescript; addressed: "Mr. Samuel Walkup near Lexington. Rockbridge Va."; franked.

To Jerman Baker

D[E]AR SIR   Monticello Oct. 6. 20.

Your favor of Sep. 26. came to hand yesterday only. I had before mentioned Wayles in a letter to Dr Cooper so as to engage his friendly attentions to him, and I now inclose you a letter to him to be handed personally. in that I have expressed my views of the most profitable course for him according to your request; and if you approve of it, perhaps Wayles might do well to take a copy of that part for his government. I am sure he will find in Dr Cooper a most useful friend and Mentor. on a suggestion unfavorable to the healthiness of Columbia, I wrote to Dr Cooper, enquiring particularly into it's character in that respect. he gives me the strongest assurances and proofs of it's being perfectly healthy; and indeed we may be assured of it ourselves from it's being in a hilly country, and selected, for it's salubrity by the legislature for the place of their sessions. I believe therefore there is nothing to be feared on that account; and if our ensuing legislature give us the aid we trust they will, our institution here may be opened the next fall, so that coming home for his autumnal vacation he may come here instead of returning to Columbia.

If the Scuppernon wine you announce to me from mr Burton is delivered to Capt Peyton, he knows so well all our boatmen, that he will be able to forward it by a safe hand, and he will pay for me any expences which may have attended it.—the document on the taxes which you were so kind as to send me was exactly what I wanted: but should a new one be formed I shall be glad of a copy. our family join me in affectionate salutations to mrs Baker & yourself.

TH: JEFFERSON

PoC (MHi); on verso of reused address cover to TJ; salutation faint; mutilated at seal, with one word partially rewritten by TJ; at foot of text: "Jerman Baker esq."; endorsed by TJ. Enclosure: TJ to Thomas Cooper, 6 Oct. 1820.

To Thomas Cooper

DEAR SIR   Monticello Oct. 6. 20.

This will be handed you by mr John Wayles Baker son of the Treasurer of this state, and a connection of mine whom, in a former letter, I mentioned to you with my grandson Francis Eppes, presuming they would go together to the College of Columbia. you will find him a youth of excellent dispositions and orderly conduct, and well worthy of any patronage and good offices you may be so kind as to extend to him. indeed at such a distance from his natural guardians and advisers, you will lay them as well as myself under tender obligations by giving him your friendly and salutary advice on all occasions on which you may think it may be useful to him. I am not sufficiently acquainted with his proficiency in the languages to judge whether he may at once enter on the sciences; but this you can learn from himself, and whenever you think him so, we would wish him to enter on the Mathematics & Chemistry; and that these should be followed by Astronomy, Natural philosophy, Natural history, & botany: for I suppose him to attend two schools at a time, and to keep up & improve his knolege of the languages by reading at spare hours. I tender you my affectionate and respectful salutations.   TH: JEFFERSON

PoC (DLC); on verso of a reused address cover from Thomas Mann Randolph to TJ; at foot of text: "Dr Thomas Cooper"; endorsed by TJ. Enclosed in TJ to Jerman Baker, 6 Oct. 1820.

COLLEGE OF COLUMBIA: South Carolina College (later the University of South Carolina).

To Francis Eppes

DEAR FRANCIS.   Monticello Oct. 6. 20.

Your letter of the 28th came to hand yesterday, and, as I suppose you are now about leaving Richmond for Columbia, this letter will be addressed to the latter place. I consider you as having made such proficiency in Latin & Greek that on your arrival at Columbia you may at once commence the study of the sciences: and as you may well attend two professors at once, I advise you to enter immediately with those of Mathematics & Chemistry. after these go on to Astronomy, Nat^l philosophy, Nat^l history & Botany. I say nothing of mineralogy or Geology, because I presume they will be comprehended in the Chemical course. nor shall I say any thing of other branches of science, but that you should lose no time on them until the accomplishment of those above named, before which time we shall have opportunities of further advising together. I hope you will be permitted to enter at once into a course of mathematics, which will itself take up all that is useful in Euclid, and that you will not be required to go formally thro' the usual books of that Geometer. that would be a waste of time which you have not to spare, and if you cannot enter the Mathematical school without it, do not enter it at all, but engage in the other sciences above mentioned. your Latin & Greek should be kept up assiduously by reading at spare hours: and, discontinuing the desultory reading of the schools, I would advise you to undertake a regular course of history & poetry in both languages. in Greek, go first thro' the Cyropaedia, and then read Herodotus, Thucydides, Xenophon's Hellenics & Anabasis, Arrian's Alexander, & Plutarch's lives, for prose reading: Homer's Iliad & Odyssey, Euripides, Sophocles in poetry, & Demosthenes in Oratory; alternating prose & verse as most agreeable to yourself. in Latin read Livy, Caesar, Sallust Tacitus, Cicero's Philosophics, and some of his Orations, in prose; and Virgil, Ovid's Metamorphoses, Horace, Terence & Juvenal for poetry. after all these, you will find still many of secondary grade to employ future years, and especially those of old age and retirement. let me hear from you as soon as you shall have taken your stand in College, and give me a general view of the courses pursued there, and from time to time afterwards advise me of your progress. I will certainly write to you occasionally, but you will not expect it very frequently, as you know how slowly & painfully my stiffened wrist now permits me to write, & how much I am oppressed by a general and revolting correspondence, wearing me down with incessant labor, instead of leaving me to the tranquil happiness with which reading and lighter occupations would fill pleasantly what remains to me of life.   I had written to Dr Cooper that I should leave Monticello for Poplar Forest about the 11th of this month. he informs me he cannot be here so soon as that but will call on me at Poplar Forest in the 3^d week of the month. Adieu, my dear Francis. consider how little time is left you, and how much you have to attain in it, and that every moment you lose of it is lost for ever. be assured that no one living is more anxious than myself to see you become a virtuous and useful citizen, worthy of the trusts of your country and wise enough to conduct them advantageously, nor any one more affectionately yours.

Th: Jefferson

RC (DLC). PoC (CSmH: JF); on re-used address cover to TJ; edge trimmed; at foot of first page: "Francis Eppes"; endorsed by TJ.

Eppes's letter to TJ OF THE 28TH Sept. 1820 has not been found (address cover only in DLC; with PoC of TJ to Patrick Gibson, 18 May 1821, on verso; addressed: "Thomas Jefferson Esqr Monticello near Charlottesville Albermarle"; stamped; postmarked Raines Tavern, 30 Sept.; recorded in SJL as received 5 Oct. 1820 from Mill Brook).

From Michele Raggi

Sig^r Tomaso Jefferson

Stimatissimo   Washington 6. 8bre. 1820.

Losingandomi da un giorno al altro di avere un riscontro della mia
scrito la, mi ritrovo tutore in questa Capitale ad atendere li di lei
pregiatissimi Carateri, e nel tenpo istesso il mio pensiere mi asicura
che lei vorà consolarmi con rimetermi almeno li denari del viaggio
giache non atendo altro, ℔ poi subito rimetermi nella mia patria, e
senza una di lei Asistenza non sò come potrò [. . .] il mio viaggio,
avendo di già speso una buona porzione del denaro che avevo e
secondo li miei calcoli non e possibile poss[. . .]sier suficienti li denari che mi restono ℔ rinpatriarmi; al presente mi ritrovo in buona
salute, ma mi è costato di medicine, e medici, la prego di oservare
in qual Stato mi ritrovo, e a chi nella Caggione, non sò qual di-
manda farci ℔ rimediare a cosi gran male qualunque sia la somma,
che lei mi rimeterà io ne sarò contento e gli farò una quietanza,
purche basti da potermi rinpatriare, qualunque sarà la proposizione
che lei mi farà io l'aceterò purche non resti in mezo di una strada;
il mi Bracio e guarito ℔fetamente dunque non manca che da lei se
mi vuole assistere, potrebbe farmi finire il mio tenpo dl Contrato
con lavorare qui in Washington in questo Canpidoglio al medesimo
prezo che lei mi passara al suo Coleggio, e a seconda dl mio Contrato, la prego sig^r Jeffirson di osservare in qual stagione mi con-
viene traversare l'oceano, e in qual modo cioè a dire senza li mezi
necessari se non è una di lei asistenza, e rifleti che fù il suo sol nome
che mi fece venire in America mi racomando dunque a la di lei
bontà e asistenza che gliene sarò grato fino al ultimo giorno di mia
vita come pure la prego di un suo onorevole ed avantaggioso riscontro, che altro non atendo ℔ determinarmi è ad una pronta
partenza o a quanto lei mi ordinerà, essendo io qui senza inpiego
[. . .] considerare che non facio che spender denaro ed anoiarmi del
ozio, mi racomando di nuovo che mi rispondi a posta corente che
appena ricevutto la sua letera assieme a quel denaro che vora rimetermi io partiro subito ℔ la Nuova Iorck ℔ colà inbarcarmi ò ℔
Inghiltera o ℔ Francia facio dunque nell[a] di lei bonta ansioso di
un suo riscontro mi Confermo di lei

Sig^{ria} Ilma Devmo. Obmo Servitore   Michele Raggi

[331]

EDITORS' TRANSLATION

MOST ESTEEMED
MR. THOMAS JEFFERSON   Washington 6. October 1820.
Hoping to receive any day now an answer to my letter, I find myself still in
this capital city awaiting a specimen of your highly regarded handwriting.
At the same time, my thoughts assure me that you will ease my distress
by sending me, at the least, the money for my voyage, and I expect nothing else, so that I may return to my homeland at once. Without your assistance, I do not know how I will be able to [. . .] my journey, as I have
already spent a large portion of the money I had and, according to my
calculations, no longer have enough to repatriate myself. I am once again
in good health, but the doctors and medicine were expensive. Behold, if
you would, my situation and what caused it. I do not know what to ask for
in order to remedy such a great evil. I will be happy with, and give you a
receipt for, whatever you choose to send me, so long as it is enough to allow
me to return home. To keep myself off the streets I will accept whatever
proposal you make. My arm has healed perfectly, so that you might assist
me in many ways if you so desire. You could allow me to fulfill my contracted time by working here in this capital city of Washington for the same
amount you paid me at your college and in accordance with my contract. I
implore you, Mr. Jefferson, to tell me both the most convenient season for
my ocean crossing and how I can do it without the necessary means, that
is, if you do not help me. Reflect on the fact that your name alone induced
me to come to America. I commend myself, therefore, to your kindness and
assistance, for which I will be grateful until the last day of my life. I beg
you, in addition, for an honorable and favorable reply, which is all I need
either to settle on a prompt time of departure or learn your other instructions. Being unemployed here, it might be said that all I do is spend money
and live in bored idleness. Again, please answer me by the return of the
post. Once I receive your letter, together with what money you are pleased
to send me, I will leave immediately for New York and embark there for
England or France. Relying on your goodness and anxious for your reply,
therefore, I confirm myself
Most illustrious Sir, your most devoted and obedient servant
                                                    MICHELE RAGGI

RC (DLC); mutilated and edge chipped; endorsed by TJ as received 11 Oct. 1820 and so recorded in SJL. RC (DLC); address cover only; with PoC of TJ to James Barbour, 11 May 1821, on verso; addressed: "M͏ʳ Tomas Jefferson a Monticello Charlottesville Virginia"; franked and postmarked. Translation by Dr. Jonathan T. Hine.

From Francis Clark

DEAR SIR.   Fredericksburg 7ᵗʰ Ocᵗ 1820
I have not the honour of a personal acquaintance with you, but perhaps the <u>object</u> of my communication, will sanction the <u>liberty</u> I have taken.

I have ever felt from the earliest period that I recollect, an unconqurable thirst for literary acquirements, but my pecuniary resources have been so contracted, that I never have been able to procure leisure sufficient, for the pursuit of any <u>regular</u> Course of Study; Nor have I had it in my powir to acquire any thing more than a tolerable english education.   At present, I am engaged in the merchantile business, and as I am pretty well pleased with it, (as a means of support) Shall probably continue to pursue it. but while I am in this way provided with <u>food</u> for the <u>body</u>, I am unwilling to neglect the acquisition of that <u>interlectual</u> <u>food</u> which Sustains the <u>Soul</u>, and which I believe is the Only Source of Solid happiness.

My business, is of Such a nature as to demand my undivided attention during the <u>day</u>, but the <u>nights</u> I am anxious to devote to some profitable Course of Study;—and my Object now, is to beg the favour of you, to Sugest to me that method which you think will prove most beneficial to One situated as I am. In doing which you will Confer an Obligation that will ever be had in gratefull remembrance by

Yr Mst. Obᵗ Hbˡ Servᵗ   FRANCIS CLARK

RC (MHi); between dateline and salutation: "Thomas Jefferson Esqr"; endorsed by TJ as a letter of 9 Oct. 1820 received seven days later and so recorded in SJL.

From John Wayles Eppes

DEAR SIR,   Richmond october 7. 1820.
The unpromising appearance of the weather prevented my leaving home until the third instant—I have this day lodged with Mʳ Peyton five hundred dollars for you—I have also sold my United States stock at 103—If therefore you will take my house on your way to Bedford I shall be ready to conclude our contract and give you a check for the balance of the 4000 dollars—

I shall be at home on Tuesday or Wednesday next—Wednesday most probably—Francis came down with me and will take the Stage on Monday for Columbia—

Present my respects and friendly wishes to the family.

Yours sincerely   JNO: W: EPPES

[333]

RC (MHi); endorsed by TJ as received 12 Oct. 1820 and so recorded in SJL. RC (NHi: Thomas Jefferson Papers); address cover only; with PoC of TJ to John Taylor, 10 May 1821, on verso; addressed: "Thomas Jefferson Esqʳ Near Charlottes-ville"; stamped; postmarked Richmond, 9 Oct.

Eppes's HOUSE was located at his Mill Brook estate in Buckingham County.

From Alexander Garrett

Sunday morning [8 Oct. 1820]

Alex Garrett sends Mr Jefferson the Govenors letter recieved last night, a copy of my account & report will be ready by tomorrow. Mr Brockenbrough will have his ready by tuesday.

RC (DLC: TJ Papers, 220:39260); with PoC of TJ to James Gibbon, 12 Apr. 1821, on verso; partially dated at foot of text. RC (MHi); address cover only; with PoC of TJ to Bernard Peyton, 11 Apr. 1821, on verso; addressed: "Mr. Jefferson Monticello." Recorded in SJL as a letter of 8 Oct. 1820 received that day from Charlottesville.

The GOVENORS LETTER was probably Thomas Mann Randolph to TJ, 5 Oct. 1820 (see TJ to Randolph, 8 Oct. 1820, and note). Garrett's ACCOUNT & REPORT as bursar and that of University of Virginia proctor Arthur S. BROCKENBROUGH, both dated 30 Sept. 1820, are printed above as enclosures to the University of Virginia Board of Visitors Report to Literary Fund President and Directors, 2 Oct. 1820.

From Francis W. Gilmer

DEAR SIR.   Richmond. Octr. 8ᵗʰ 1820

one of the last injunctions of our excellent & ever to be cherished friend Mr Corrêa, was, that I should send a small quantity of the ashes of Salsola kali to Dʳ Cooper, that he might learn whether it contain as much Soda when growing remote from the sea, as when contiguous to it. The season being rather far advanced for a fair experiment even when I returned to Richmond, I lost little time in preparing the ashes. I have been able however to think of no opportunity for conveying them to Dʳ C. so safe, as that afforded by your grand-son who goes to Columbia; may I therefore ask of you the favor to forward it by him. Your esteem for Mr. Correa, as well as your love of the Sciences, I am sure will interest you in the experiment.

with great and sincere esteem your friend &c

F. W. GILMER.

RC (MoSHi: Gilmer Papers); endorsed by TJ as received 11 Oct. 1820 and so recorded (mistakenly dated 9 Oct.) in SJL.

SALSOLA KALI is commonly known as Russian thistle or saltwort. Francis Eppes, TJ's GRAND-SON, was about to matriculate at South Carolina College (later the University of South Carolina) in Columbia.

To Michele Raggi

SIR   Monticello Oct. 8. 20.

Your letter of Sep. 26. did not come to hand until the 5th instant and the necessity of enquiring into some facts, not within my own knolege before I could answer it, must apologise for the delay of answer.

On the 19th of Feb. 1819. yourself and your relation Giacomo Raggi entered into a Notarial contract in Leghorn, with mr Appleton, acting in my name, on behalf of the University of Virginia, to come to Virginia, and continue in our service as Sculptor for the term of three years from that date, we paying the expences of your voyage hither, finding you lodging and diet while here, paying you 526. Dollars a year, during the three years, and the expences of your voyage back. 400.D. were advanced to you at Leghorn, to wit, 200. to each, your expences by sea and land to this place were paid; and when afterwards you both became desirous that your wives should come to you, we remitted to mr Appleton 400.D. the sum you desired, to enable them to come. they declined coming. yourself became uneasy & desponding, declared you could not continue here according to your contract, without your wife, and solicited to be discharged from your obligation. in pure commiseration of your feelings, it was yielded to, & the Proctor was instructed to arrange with you the conditions of dissolving the contract and to settle and pay whatever was your due. one half of your term having now elapsed, it was agreed that the expences of your coming and wages to that date should be at our charge, but that those for your return should be your own, as the retirement from the fulfilment of your engagements for the latter half of your term, was your own act, and not our wish. on the settlement of your account with the Proctor, the balance of 293.D. 60 cents was agreed to be due, and were paid you, as appears by a receipt signed by your own hand and now lying before me in these words. 'University of Virginia Sep. 9. 1820. Recieved of A. S. Brockenbrough Proctor of the University of Virginia a draught on the bursar of the same for two hundred & ninety three dollars 60. cents, being the balance in full for my wages as Sculptor; and I do hereby relinquish all further claim for wages and expences of my journey & voyage back to Italy, in consideration of my being permitted to withdraw my obligation to continue three years in the service of Thomas Jefferson esq. as Agent for the said University of Virginia; or on him individually. witness my hand the day & year above written. Michele Raggi.'

By the account settled between yourself and the Proctor, it appeared that your travelling expences and wages had cost us 919.D. 68. cents, exclusive of board & lodging during the 15. months you were here. for this you know, we have nothing to shew but a single Ionic capitel, and an unfinished Corinthian. this proceeded chiefly from the insufficiency of the stone of the neighboring quarry we had counted on, and the delay occasioned by having to send 80. miles to another. this misfortune was ours, and was increased by that of the sprain of your wrist disabling you from work, and it is mentioned, not to throw any blame on you, but to shew that notwithstanding a contract so losing to us, we gave up the remaining portion of it which might have lessened our loss, merely to indulge the feelings and uneasiness under which we saw you.　　As to your lodging, it was in as decent and comfortable a room as I would wish to lodge in myself. so far I have spoken of my own knolege.　　On the subject of diet, I learn from others that, in the beginning, it was furnished you from a French boarding house of your own choice. from this you withdrew, of your own choice also, and boarded with the Proctor himself, sharing the same fare with himself, which was that of the respectable families of the neighborhood, plentiful, wholsome, & decent, in the style of our country, and such as the best artists here are used to, and contented with. your uncle & companion, Giacomo Raggi, is so far satisfied with it, and with the treatment he has recieved in common with you, that altho' he was offered permission to return with you, he chose to abide by the obligations and benefits of his contract, and continues his services with perfect contentment. I am conscious of having myself ever treated you with just respect, and the character of the Proctor, the most unassuming and accomodating man in the world, is a sufficient assurance of the same on his part.　　On a review therefore, Sir, of this case, and a just attention to your own formal & voluntary engagements, I am persuaded you will see that it is a very plain one and not at all justifying the complaining style of your letter. you will surely be sensible that all the claims of justice, of indulgence, and of liberality have been fulfilled on our part, and that the desponding and unhappy state of your mind, while here, proceeded from the constitutional and moral affections resulting from your own temperament and the incidents acting on it, and not from anything depending on those in our employ—but if this correspondence is to proceed further, I must pray you to direct it to the Proctor, within whose duties it lies, and not within mine. and the rather as I leave this place within a few days, to be absent until December. Your offers to make our capitals at Washington on terms much higher than we were entitled to, if we had chosen to hold you to your contract, do not suit us. With every wish for your safe return and happy meeting with your family & friends, I salute you with a friendly and respectful Adieu. TH: JEFFERSON

PoC (DLC); on reused address cover to TJ; at foot of first page: "Mr Michael Raggi"; endorsed by TJ. FC (DLC); in Hore Browse Trist's hand, with signature and internal address by TJ.

Thomas Appleton formalized the NO-TARIAL CONTRACT with Michele Raggi and Giacomo Raggi on 17, not 19 Feb. 1819. It is printed above as an enclosure to Appleton to TJ, 25 Feb. 1819.

The ACCOUNT WITH THE PROCTOR, Arthur S. Brockenbrough, lists payments made to the Raggis between 17 Feb. 1819 and 25 July 1820 totaling $1,252.16, or $626.08 each; determines that as of 8 Sept. 1820 Michele Raggi's wages amounted to $819.68 and that his expenses, totaling $100, consist of $30 spent in Leghorn, $24 for sea stores, $26.50 in travel expenses from Baltimore, $7.50 for "the expence of boarding selves & finding Spirit &c & cash p^d for looking Glasses," and $12 for "tools furnished"; and concludes that the departing sculptor is due a balance of $293.60 (MS in ViU: PP; in Brockenbrough's hand; undated). A separate listing of Michele Raggi's wages and expenses due from the University and dating between 17 Feb. 1819 and 8 Sept. 1820 gives a higher total of $1,390.56, with additional items not in the account

described above consisting of $22.20 for "loss in exchange on money advanced him in Leghorn," $140 for "Passage Money," $9 for "Expences in Baltimore," $205.07 for "Boarding" and "washing" in Charlottesville, and $102.11 for "Extra: Expences for Spirits, candles, sugar bed clothing & other necessaries" (MS in ViU: TJP; in Brockenbrough's hand, signed by him as proctor, and with his notation on verso: "M. Raggis expences"; endorsed by TJ: "Raggi Michael. bill of his wages E^{t}c.").

The manuscript RECEIPT of Michele Raggi has a subjoined promissory note, also of 9 Sept. 1820, which states that, since a credit given to Michele Raggi of $54 for his one-half share of "expences in Leghorn & laying in sea stores" has not been approved by Brockenbrough due to a lack of supporting vouchers, Giacomo Raggi agrees "to pay or return" this sum "if the claim will not be admited by Thos Jefferson & Genl J. H. Cocke acting as a committee of superintendence" (MS in ViU: PP; in Brockenbrough's hand, with receipt signed by Michele Raggi and note signed by Giacomo Raggi; endorsed by Brockenbrough, in part, as "Acc^t Sept 9th 1820 M. & G. Raggi with University– V^a" and "$293.60").

To Thomas Mann Randolph

DEAR SIR   Monticello Oct. 8. 20.

Yours of the 5th was recieved yesterday, and having carefully perused the Report of Feb. 14. 20. and the other papers, I now return them according to your request. I have marked with a pencil in the 4th page of the Report two items which, if I understand them, may I hope be disposable in favor of the University, to wit,

Amount of arrears to schools not drawn in 1818. 40,632.20
Surplus disposable revenue for 1820. 43,230

Mr Garrett called on me yesterday to inform me that the 40,000 D. of the preceding loan are exhausted, and demands now pressing hardly on him: and requesting that I would sollicit from your board an immediate attention to the supplementory loan of 20,000.D I must therefore ask the favor of you to consider the letter of Sep. 16. as meant to urge the attention of the board to this sollicitation. if mr Munford will be so good as to send me a bond prepared for execution, I will immediately sign, seal & return it, and give to mr Garrett the authorities necessary to avail himself of it. it may be directed to me at this place, unless you should have heard of my departure for Bedford, in which case it may go to Lynchburg direct.

Mr Nicholas is still at Tufton and much worse. Doctors Watkins and Kain are now in consultation on him. all here are well, and we hope to set out for Poplar Forest about the 16th or 17th James, I think, is losing precious time which can never be recovered. your necessary absences rendering your close attention to him and the other boys impossible, I wish you would consign to me the cost and care of their education. I will send them to any schools you shall prefer, and direct any course you may desire. and I will guard them from idle intervals, during which they are not merely stationary but retrograde in their acquirements. at present I know no better disposition of James and Ben than with Carr at George Gilmer's; and if I could have your permission I would place James there before I go to Bedford. it would be a great comfort to have them qualified to get their livings under whatever misfortunes may befall them in life. but all this I leave to you with the assurances of my affectionate attachment and respect

Th: Jefferson

RC (DLC); addressed: "His Excellency Governor Randolph Richmond"; franked; postmarked Milton, 10 Oct.; endorsed by Randolph as received 12 Oct. 1820. PoC (MHi); on verso of reused address cover to TJ; edge trimmed; endorsed by TJ. Enclosure: Report of the President and Directors of the Literary Fund, 14 Feb. 1820 (printed in *JHD* [1819–20 sess.], 182–4). Other enclosures not found.

Randolph's letter to TJ OF THE 5TH, not found, is recorded in SJL as received 7 Oct. 1820 from Richmond.

Despite the efforts of doctors Thomas G. Watkins and Andrew Kean (KAIN), Wil-son Cary Nicholas died at Tufton two days later, on 10 Oct. 1820 (*Richmond Compiler* and *Richmond Enquirer*, both 17 Oct. 1820). Elizabeth Trist informed her grandson Nicholas P. Trist from Farmington on 1 Nov. 1820 that Nicholas's death had been "a very unexpected event to the family tho they had every reason to expect that he wou'd not live many months he expired setting in his chair just after he got up and dress'd in the morning he died without a struggle or a groan, at Jefferson Randolphs and was buried at Monticello I am told that Jefferson R was extremely effected at his funeral" (RC in NcU: NPT).

From an Unidentified Correspondent, with Closing by "Thomas Dissatisfaction"

DEAR BROTHER   Chapel Hill Octr 8th 1820

I am once more seated to perform a duty which unintentionly has been delayed too long. But, as I have your promise to answer me when I write, no circumstance shall prevent my enjoying that pleasure. Altho we are seperated by an immense tract of country yet there still exists a tie between us, which will forever make the situation of the one more or less interesting to the other of us; the disparity of our ages I know necessarily breaks off that familiarity & intimacy which is common to brothers nearer the same age. As I am not able to give you a fanciful idea of this little village or work upon your imagination in any great degree by a discription of my situation in it, I hope you will excuse a plain statement of facts concerning them. Chapel Hill is a small village in the county of Orange with a population of nearly 500 inhabitants including the students of the university, Its situation is rather hilly, which gives it something of a romantic appearance. The buildings are of wood, (with few exceptions) and quite ordinary.[1] The inhabitants generally are poor, tho they by their industry & exertions support a plain neatness, which would cause strangers to judge them in a tolerable state of independence. The adjacent country is tolerably fertile and produces in abundance the articles of corn & wheat. Here you may be surprised, when I tell you that by the exertions of one man a university was established at this place. Genl Davie who was once minister from the US. to France or Russia one, (I do not exactly recollect which) while in the legislature of this state procured the passage of a bill making this establishment. The legislature afterwards gave him the power to locate the university wherever he chose.[2] he

Accordingly Placed it at this damned village, with the[3] best curses of the Students for Such location. I am your

Enemy   THOMAS DISSATISFACTION

P.S

I am great friend of your political tenets & am really sorry you could not give better advice to Genl Davie.   T D.

RC (MHi); written in two unidentified hands, with portion by "Thomas Dissatisfaction" probably added to an incomplete, unrelated missive to an unknown recipient; endorsed by TJ as an anonymous letter received 27 Oct. 1820, with additional notation "insane," and so recorded in SJL.

William Richardson Davie, the founder of the University of North Carolina, introduced the 1789 bill chartering the institution, oversaw its early construction and endowment, and was responsible for selecting the school's location, first faculty, and curriculum. He later served as MINISTER plenipotentiary to France in 1799–1800, during which time he helped negotiate an end to the Quasi-War between that country and the United States (*ANB*; William S. Powell, ed., *Dictionary* *of North Carolina Biography* [1979–96], 2:28–9).

[1] Omitted period at right margin editorially supplied.
[2] Remainder in hand of "Thomas Dissatisfaction."
[3] Manuscript: "the the."

From Peter S. Du Ponceau

DEAR SIR   Philadelphia, 9. Oct. 1820

I take the liberty of introducing to you in the person of M[r] L. C. Vanuxem, the bearer hereof, a young American, who to a mind formed by nature for the Philosophical Sciences, unites the advantages of a regular Scientific education in the best Schools & under the best professors abroad. He is lately returned from Paris where he was three Years engaged exclusively in the Study of Chemistry & Mineralogy. When his father sent him thither, he had already acquired considerable knowledge in the latter Science by his own unaided efforts, & young as he was at that time, he was an useful & active Member of our Academy of Natural Sciences. I have no doubt that he will distinguish himself in the Career into which he has been thrown by the irresistible bent of his genius, & I have thought that such a Character was deserving of your high patronage.

I have the honor to be with the greatest respect

Sir   Your most obed[t] humble serv[t]

PETER S, DU PONCEAU

RC (DLC); endorsed by TJ as received 17 Oct. 1820 and so recorded (with additional bracketed notation: "by mr Vanuxem") in SJL. RC (MHi); address cover only; with PoC of TJ to Bernard Peyton, 10 May 1821, on verso; addressed: "Thomas Jefferson, Esq Monticello" by "Mr Vanuxem."

Lardner Clark Vanuxem (1792–1848), geologist, educator, and son of the merchant James Vanuxem, was born in Philadelphia. He became a member of the Academy of Natural Sciences of Philadelphia in 1815 and, after studying for several years in his father's native France, graduated from the École des mines in Paris in 1819. Vanuxem visited Monticello with Thomas Cooper in 1820 and joined him the following year at South Carolina College (later the University of South Carolina) as professor of geology and mineralogy. He remained at the school until 1827, after which he served as a consultant for a gold mine in Mexico and undertook geologic fieldwork in Kentucky, New York, Ohio, Tennessee, and Virginia. In 1830 Vanuxem established his permanent residence on a farm just outside of Bristol, Pennsylvania. Best known for introducing stratigraphic paleontology into the United States, he worked for the New York geological survey, 1836–41, and published his findings in an 1842 monograph entitled *Geology of New-York. Part III. Comprising the Survey of the Third Geological District.* In 1822 Vanuxem was elected to the American Philosophical Society, and in 1840 he helped to establish the Association of American Geologists and Naturalists, which became, a few years later, the American Association for the Advancement of Science (*ANB*; *DAB*; *DSB*; United States Geological Survey, *Bulletin* 746 [1923]: 1045–6; *Act of Incorporation and By-Laws of the Academy of Natural Sciences of Philadelphia* [1857],

28; Hore Browse Trist to Nicholas P. Trist, 23 Oct. 1820 [RC in DLC: NPT]; Maximilian LaBorde, *History of the South Carolina College* [1874], 527; middle name given in Du Ponceau to James Madison, 23 Mar. 1821 [Madison, *Papers, Retirement Ser.*, 2:285]; APS, Minutes, 18 Oct. 1822 [MS in PPAmP]; DNA: RG 29, CS, Pa., Bristol, 1830, 1840; Philadelphia *North American and United States Gazette*, 24 Feb. 1848; gravestone inscription in Saint James the Greater Episcopal Churchyard, Bristol).

From Bernard Peyton

DEAR SIR,   Rich'd 9 October 1820

Mʳ Eppes reached Town on Friday last, & on saturday handed me five hundred $500 Dollars for your ⅜, which is at your credit, & will be held subject to your order—

Hoping the articles sent by the last mail may have reached you safely, remain—

With sincere regard Dʳ sir

Yours very Truely   BERNARD PEYTON

RC (MHi); endorsed by TJ as received 11 Oct. 1820 and so recorded in SJL. RC (DLC); address cover only; with PoC of TJ to Josiah Meigs, 12 May 1821, on verso; addressed: "Mʳ Thomas Jefferson Monticello Milton"; franked; postmarked Richmond, 9 Oct.

To Caesar A. Rodney

DEAR SIR   Monticello Oct. 9. 20.

Your's of the 1ˢᵗ is recieved, and I note your recommendation of mr Askew, to whom I should be glad to be useful, as well on account of your recommendation as of his merit. but our work has been done entirely by undertakers, bricklayers at 10.D. a thousand, & house carpenters at the Philada prices. so that we have nothing to do with the daily laborers, or any body but the Undertaker. I wish mr Askew had come on in time to undertake a part; but I believe that every part of the work remaining to be done is already engaged and to be finished within 12. months from this time.

Your Maldonado pumpkin will be very acceptable.   I regretted much your short stay with us: but if a hope could be entertained of a repetition, and especially of what you call an annual pilgrimage, it would be well indeed. at the end of a long journey, one loves to talk over the occurrences of the road, and especially with those who were fellow travellers. you and I have travelled gloomy days together. yet we never despaired of the Commonwealth, and, by perseverance, happily got thro'. I see still a breaker ahead, which fills me with horror. but I hope that prudence & moderation, a regard for our own happiness, and especially for the cause of reformation thro' the world, will induce a spirit of accomodation, and save our country, and the world entire from the calamity threatened. we are the world's last hope; and it's loss will be on our heads. god bless you and preserve you multos años.   TH: JEFFERSON

RC (TxDaHCL); at foot of text: "Caesar A. Rodney esq." PoC (DLC); on verso of reused address cover of William F. Gray to TJ, 6 May 1820; endorsed by TJ.

MULTOS AÑOS: "many years."

From Thomas Appleton

DEAR SIR   Leghorn 10th October 1820—
Your favor of the 13th of July & postscriptum of the 30th reach'd me on the 4th of the present month.—A few days previous, I receiv'd, by duplicates, mr Vaughan's letters, containing a bill on Paris, for Two thousand three hundred & fifty three francs.[1] 20 cts, which when negotiated, deducting brokerage & postage, left 436– Dollars, which I have paid mde Pini & now inclose you their receipt for—444:44 Doll—the expences they insisted on paying, and which is correct.—I translated to them, all you wish'd, in relation to the delay; and they desire me to say to you, that even should the capital, not be convenient for you to remit, even in[2] a couple of years, they will wait with great pleasure; and again to repeat to you, the infinite obligations, they have receiv'd from your hands.—
for everything in relation to the wives of the Raggi's, I must refer you to my letter of 2nd of June; in which I mention'd, that the four hundred dollars, had been paid to them in equal parts; the determination of the elder, not to leave her native country, and the numerous obstacles to the departure of the younger, with her infant-child, unaccompanied by some protecting friend.—
I lose no time, as you percieve by the date of my letter, to reply, as I n[ow] do, to your questions in relation to the capitals for the columns.—
You mention, the corinthian capitals to be similar to Palladio, book.

1—plate 26—now the edition I possess, this plate contains the edifice of Counts francesco e fratelli Tiene; the order is composite.[3]—your's, I presume is a different edition.—this is not material, I shall[4] reply specifically.—they will cost deliver'd here from Carrara, & well cas'd, the following prices.—to wit.—

	English inches	Dollars
a corinthian capital for a column, diminish'd diameter	$20\frac{8}{10}$	110—[5]
a ditto d° " " "	$25\frac{2}{10}$	180.—[6]
an Ionic capital " " "	$26\frac{1}{8}$	55.—[7]
a ditto " " " "	$26\frac{1}{2}$	60.—[8]

You desire, also, to know the time requir'd, to deliver them in Leghorn; but you have omitted to mention the <u>number</u> of capitals wanted.—supposing, however, that your order should be for[9] twenty capitals, half corinthian & the remainder Ionic.—they could be deliver'd here, in <u>five</u> months, from the receipt of your order to procure them—the freight to the U: States from hence, of marble-works in cases, & which I have frequently sent, will cost—Sixteen dollars, the ton measure of 40 cubic feet.[10]—You may rest assur'd, shou'd you confide to me the order, that the work will be perform'd by the most skilfull hands, & they will be cas'd in the Strongest boxes; as they are accustom'd to transport the finest workmanship, to every part of Europe.—The best mode of remittance, is by the way of London; and the man in whom I have the most confidence, indeed, he is unexceptionable for solidity & prudence, is Samuel Williams, N° 13. Finsbury Square London.—shou'd you approve this mode, the bill should be bought by your correspondent, say at Phil[a] remitted to s[d] Williams to collect, & hold the amount to my order.[11]—I have, in the hands of mess[rs] Snowden & Wagner, merchants of Philadelphia, several marble busts, larger than life, of Washington, copied from my original Gesso, by Ceracchi.—of Cristo[r] Columbus, & Amerigo[12] Vespuccio, copied from original paintings, in the gallery of Florence; they may be seen on application to the above-merchants, and may be had at very moderate prices, if they should be useful in ornamenting your edifices.—when you shall have determin'd the diameter of the columns for the Pantheon, the capitals & pilastres, can be sent to you, before it will be necessary to place them; by comparing those you may require, with the prices herewith, it will be easy to judge, nearly the cost.—I send this letter, by duplicates, in order to insure its safe delivery to you.[13]—I have also in the hands of the abovemention'd Snowden & Wagner 4. or 5 Statuary marble chimney pieces of <u>exquisite</u>

workmanship—two, I think, are sculptur'd with the Goddess Ceres, accompanied by all the emblems of agriculture, in releivo—the others represent Bacchus, with his emblems on the frontispiece & columns, agreeably to mythology.—no Superior workmanship has ever been sent from Italy—they would ornament the most noble palace; I presume, they could be bought, for <u>about</u>[14] 200– Dollars each—at mess[r] Snowden & Wagner.—I have mention'd this, because, I thought it probable, you might have occasion for such, in Some of the superior Saloons, of your edifices.[15]—on the 6th ins[t] the neapolitan troops under Gen[l] Pepe, enter'd, by capitulation, the city of Palermo.—The government of naples progress with energy & wisdom; and the patriotism of the people, is, perhaps, equal to 1775 in our country—The regular troops have all been withdrawn from the interior, and plac'd on the frontiers—the provinces are left to the guard of some hundred thousand well arm'd Guarillos; while the capital has a national guard of nearly fifty thousand men.—The Emp[r] of austria, hitherto, confines his army within his italian States; those who believe his counsels guided by wisdom & prudence, judge he will not invade the neapolitan territory.—

Accept Sir, the renew'd expressions of my unfeign'd esteem & respect   TH: APPLETON

RC (DLC); edge chipped; endorsed by TJ as received 6 Feb. 1821 but recorded in SJL as received a month later. RC (MHi); address cover only; with PoC of TJ to Francis Eppes, 12 June 1822, on verso; addressed: "To Thomas Jefferson esq—Monticello—Virginia"; franked; stamped "SHIP"; postmarked Boston, 24 Feb. Dupl (DLC); with RC of Appleton to TJ, 2 Nov. 1820, subjoined; at head of text: "Duplicate." FC (Lb in DNA: RG 84, CRL); in Appleton's hand; adjacent to salutation: "Sent by Orlanda—20. Oct[r] for Boston. duplicate by Ship Eliza ann. for new York. 24. nov[r]"; at foot of text: "mem[o] mention'd the Surrender of Palermo— & that no late occurence indicates the aggression of the austrians into the neapolitan territory." FC (Lb in NNGL); in Appleton's hand; incomplete and canceled, consisting of dateline, salutation, and first paragraph. Tr (ViU: TJP); extract in TJ's hand; at head of text: "Extract of a letter from Tho[s] Appleton (Consul of the US. at Leghorn) dated Oct. 10. 20." Enclosure: receipt from Elisabetta Mazzei Pini and Andrea Pini to TJ, Leghorn, 10 Oct. 1820, indicating that from TJ through Apple-

ton they had received 444 pesos duros and 44 cents, "un Anno di frutti del Capitale che si trova nelle mani del detto Sig[e] Jeffersen Resultato della vendita fatta in Richmond dello stabile appartenente al defunto mio Padre Filippo Mazzei" ("the interest for one year on the capital in the hands of the said Mr. Jefferson resulting from the sale in Richmond of the building belonging to my deceased father, Philip Mazzei") and that the sum was received in cash (MS in DLC, in an unidentified hand, with sums filled in a different hand, signed by Elisabetta Mazzei Pini and Andrea Pini; Dupl in DLC, written and signed as above; translation by Dr. Jonathan T. Hine).

COUNTS FRANCESCO E FRATELLI TIENE were Count Francesco Trissino and the Thiene brothers, Marcantonio and Adriano. GUARILLOS: "guerrillas." The ITALIAN STATES controlled by Francis I of Austria were the northern provinces of Lombardy and Venetia.

[1] RC: "frances." Dupl and FC: "francs."
[2] Dupl and FC: "under."

[3] TJ here noted above the line "Pallad. B. II. pl. IX. XLVIII."

[4] Extract begins here with "to your questions relating to the Capitels for the columns I."

[5] To left of this line in extract TJ wrote "Nº IV. E" [Pavilion VIII].

[6] To left of this line in extract TJ wrote "II. W" [Pavilion III].

[7] To left of this line in extract TJ wrote "III. W." [Pavilion V].

[8] To left of this line in extract TJ wrote "I. E." [Pavilion II]. Extract ends here.

[9] Extract resumes here with "as to time, suppose you order."

[10] TJ here noted above the line "or .40 C the Cub. foot. a capitel of 25.I. diam contains ab^t 6. cub. f. = 2.40."

[11] Extract ends here.

[12] RC: "Amrigo." Dupl and FC: "Amerigo."

[13] Sentence not in Dupl.

[14] Dupl: "little more than."

[15] Dupl and FC end here with closing and signature.

From José Corrêa da Serra

DEAR SIR.   Philadelphia 11. October. 1820.

I cannot Let go Judge Cooper to Monticello, without once more before i Leave your country expressing to you my strong attachment to you, of which you shall have constant proofs as Long as i Live.

He will inform you of the things, which i promised to write to you—as he is thoroughly informed of them. I respect your person and your repose too highly, to wish to meddle you in the Least in this dirty affair. I am resolved to Let things have their course, and time will insensibly bring on the proper reaction and due retribution. If in the end it proves an unprofitable and ruinous trade, Let the parties now concerned bewail the consequences, of which they themselves are the manufacturers.

Mr Vanhuxem of Philadelphia accompanies Judge Cooper. He is one of the most thriving among the many proselites of science, which the nursery established by Mr Maclure in this city has already afforded. Some of them and Mr Vanhuxem amongst the others have gone to Paris at the fountain head of natural sciences, and with great profit. Multa ferunt anni venientes commoda secum. I can add also, multa recedentes adimunt, because i see with pain that the beautiful and novel caracter which you had imprinted on your nation is fast wearing away. Posterity will discriminate easily what belonged to your mind, and what was natural to the soil, which is productive of rank weeds, rather smothering the fine crop.[1] I know you well enough to suppose that though your historical caracter will certainly appear brighter, you may feel flattered from what i am saying.

My most cordial souvenirs to Colonel Randolph, and my respects to his Lady and family.

Most attached faithful friend and serv^t

JOSEPH CORRÈA DE SERRA

RC (DLC: TJ Papers, 218:38992); endorsed by TJ as received 17 Oct. 1820 and so recorded in SJL. RC (MHi); address cover only; with PoC of TJ to Frederick A. Mayo, 11 May 1821, on verso; addressed: "T. Jefferson Esq Late President of the U.S. Monticello."

Mᴿ VANHUXEM: Lardner C. Vanuxem. MULTA FERUNT ANNI VENIENTES COMMODA SECUM ("Many blessings do the advancing years bring with them") and MULTA RECEDENTES ADIMUNT ("many, as they retire, they take away") are from Horace, *Ars Poetica*, 175–6 (Fairclough, *Horace: Satires, Epistles and Ars Poetica*, 464–5). SOUVENIRS: "regards; remembrances."

[1] Omitted period at right margin editorially supplied.

From Joseph Delaplaine

DEAR SIR,   Philadᵃ October 11. 1820

At the request of the author, I have the honour of transmitting to you, for your kind acceptance, a volume of poetry, for your good opinion of which; I know he would feel much gratified.

An elementary book for the use of schools, new in its design & arrangement, will be issued from the press by the same author, in a few months, at which time I shall have the pleasure of sending to you a copy.

With very high regard,

I am, dear sir your most obedᵗ st.   JOSEPH DELAPLAINE

RC (DLC); addressed: "His Excellency Thomas Jefferson <*Montpel*> Monticello Vᵃ"; endorsed by TJ as received 20 Oct. 1820 and so recorded in SJL. Enclosure: Charles Mead, *Mississippian Scenery; A Poem, descriptive of the interior of North America* (Philadelphia, 1819).

On this date Delaplaine sent a similar letter and enclosure to James Madison (Madison, *Papers, Retirement Ser.*, 2:127).

From John Vaughan

Dᴿ SIR   Philad. Oct. 11. 1820

My young friend M Lardner Vanuxem accompanies M Cooper, & will also be mentioned to you by M Correa—It would seem a work of supererrogation to add my recommendation[1] to theirs—But having for a Series of years been his fathers friend, & long known his own devotion to Scientific pursuits, I must be permitted to add my testimony. He has past some years in france in adding to his acquiremts in Chemistry & Mineralogy which he means at a future day Professionally to make useful to his Country; he accompanies D Cooper, & will be his assistant in his Lectures at Columbia & make a part of his family—He will thus add to his Stock of knowledge & familiarise himself with the best method of communicating it to others

I remain aff[e] Yours &ca   JN VAUGHAN

RC (MHi); at head of text: "Thomas Jefferson Monticello"; endorsed by TJ as received 17 Oct. 1820 and so recorded (with additional bracketed notation: "by mr Vanuxem") in SJL.

[1] Manuscript: "recommendatin."

From Thomas Mann Randolph

DEAR SIR,   Richmond Oct. 12. 1820

I received your letter with the papers of the Literary Board again at 10 A.M. today. Hoping to hear from home I sent to the P. office yesterday evening, but they would not open the Mail untill a late hour today, as the Messenger of the Executive reported to me when he returned.

The Bond you desire is inclosed, M[r] Munford having this instant waited on me with it. The Blank being filled with October 1st may appear strange. The Directors[1] contemplated in the spring to make a farther payment on that day in full of their Loan to the University, and M[r] M. and myself concluded it to be safest to insert the day which had been spoken of. When M[r] Munford put into my hands the Resolution on this subject which I gave you, I was much surprized that I had no recollection of the occurrence. In fact there never was such a Resolution upon the Journal, or ever adopted, and instantly rescinded. I had moved the subject, from zeal, which inclined me to keep the remainder of the Loan constantly in view of the Board. That resolution was sketched by M[r] M. in consequence, and the [1][st] day of June some how got into it instead of 1st October. but it was never even proposed to the Board, the first general agreement with the University being quite sufficient.

I expect to leave this on Saturday for Albemarle the public business admitting of my absence for part of a Week at this time. I must come away again by the 18[th][2] inst.

your most obed[t] St.   TH M RANDOLPH

RC (ViU: TJP); one number illegible; endorsed by TJ as received 16 Oct. 1820 and so recorded in SJL. RC (DLC); address cover only; with PoC of TJ to David Hosack, 11 May 1821, on verso; addressed: "Thomas Jefferson Esq[r] Mon- ticello"; franked; postmarked Richmond, 12 Oct. Enclosure not found.

[1] Manuscript: "Diretors."
[2] Reworked from "17th."

To Tench Coxe

DEAR SIR   Monticello Oct. 13. 20.

Your favor of Aug. 4. was handed to me by mr Skinner whom I recieved with great pleasure, as well on account of his merit, as of your recommendation. I valued it the more as it has furnished me an occasion to renew recollections of our antient friendship, and to assure you that time has neither weaned nor weakened it with me. we were fellow laborers indeed in times not to be forgotten. a stiffened wrist, the effect of age on an antient dislocation, makes writing now a slow & painful operation and disables me for regular correspondence. but while embarrassing the expression, it does not diminish the feeling of former cordialities, and I pray you to accept the assurance of the faithful remembrance of mine with yourself.   TH: JEFFERSON

PoC (DLC); at foot of text: "Tenche Coxe esq."; endorsed by TJ.

Tench Coxe (1755–1824), merchant, public official, and political economist, was born in Philadelphia. Between the age of six and the year 1771 he attended the academy division, and possibly briefly the college division, of the Philadelphia College and Academy (later the University of Pennsylvania). In 1772 Coxe entered business on his own before becoming a partner in his father's mercantile firm four years later. During the American Revolution he remained ostensibly neutral, but he went to British-occupied New York City in 1776 and returned to Philadelphia in the wake of the British army the following year. This led to an accusation of treason. After his case was dismissed in 1778, Coxe resumed commercial activities in his native city. During the 1780s he participated in western land speculations that eventually established his family's fortunes. Influential in debates on political economy and a promoter of domestic manufactures, Coxe attended the 1786 Annapolis convention to consider reforming the American government, supported the new United States Constitution in a number of pamphlets, and was appointed late in 1788 to represent Pennsylvania during the last months of the Confederation Congress. In 1790 he became the assistant secretary of the trea-

sury, and two years later he was made commissioner of the revenue. Coxe joined the American Philosophical Society in 1796 and subsequently served as one of its counsellors. He eventually became dissatisfied with Alexander Hamilton's economic program, and on being removed from the Treasury Department in 1797, Coxe became one of the most influential writers supporting the Republican party. In 1803 TJ appointed him purveyor of public supplies, a position he held until it was abolished in 1812. Coxe then returned permanently to Philadelphia, where he unsuccessfully sought various federal appointments and continued to write on a wide variety of subjects (*ANB*; *DAB*; Jacob E. Cooke, *Tench Coxe and the Early Republic* [1978]; PHi: Coxe Family Papers; Harold C. Syrett and others, eds., *The Papers of Alexander Hamilton* [1961–87], esp. 26:519–22; *PTJ*, esp. 19:122–7; Sowerby, nos. 3422, 3622–32; *JEP*, 1:124, 453, 455, 2:242, 243, 456, 497 [8 May 1792, 11, 15 Nov. 1803, 1, 3 Apr. 1812, 18 Jan., 18 Feb. 1814]; APS, Minutes, 15 Jan. 1796, 5 Jan. 1797 [MS in PPAmP]; Madison, *Papers, Retirement Ser.*, esp. 2:142–3, 152, 155–6; Philadelphia *Aurora General Advertiser*, 17 July 1824).

Coxe's letter to TJ OF AUG. 4, not found, is recorded in SJL as received 6 Sept. 1820 from Philadelphia, with additional bracketed notation: "by mr Skinner."

[348]

Jared Sparks by Rembrandt Peale

Harpsichord

Theater Advertisement

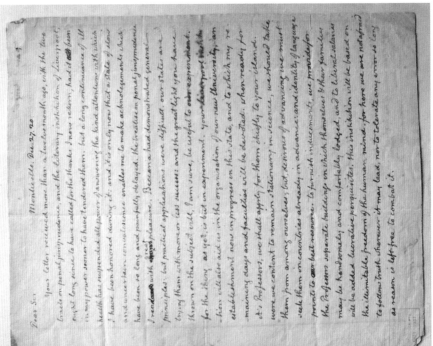

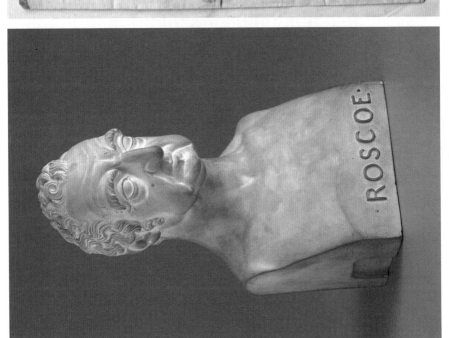

Bust of William Roscoe

"the illimitable freedom of the human mind":
Thomas Jefferson to William Roscoe, 27 December 1820

St. Ann's Parish, Albemarle County.

NAMES OF HEADS OF FAMILIES.																						
Thomas Jefferson																						
Thomas J. Randolph																						
Charles Harris																						
Nancy H. King																						
William King																						
Joseph Schutt																						
Nancy Wair																						
Mary Timberson																						
N. Timberson (Allen)																						
Th. Jackson																						
J. John Nimie?																						

1820 United States Census

Notes for the biography of George Wythe.

Jefferson's Notes for a Biography of George Wythe (first and last pages)

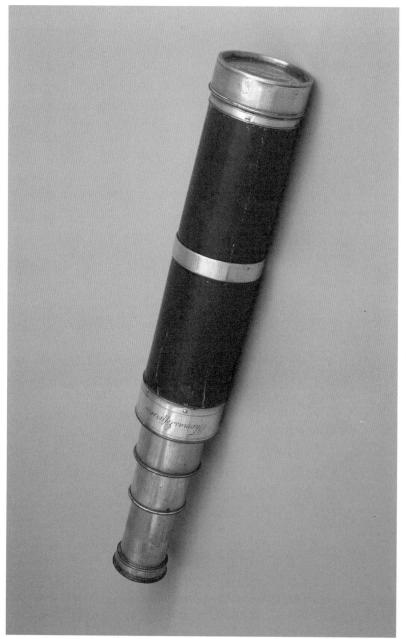

Hand Telescope

José Corrêa da Serra by Rembrandt Peale

Monticello's North Square Room

To John Wayles Eppes, with Eppes's Note

DEAR SIR   Monticello Oct. 13. 20.

Your favor of the 7th came to hand yesterday. my journey to Bedford is of necessity postponed indefinitely by the circumstance of 3. of my carriage horses being recently taken with the disease called the sore tongue, which I am told will require 10. days for cure and leave them so emaciated as not to be able to take the road for some time. this will bring on cold weather which will oblige us to hurry thro' our journey by the most direct route. I therefore send a sober and trusty servant by whom I must request you to send the check proposed in your letter. I annex a reciept for it, and obligation for the negroes, interest E'c according to what has past between us. if I am mistaken in any circumstances, or if there is any defect of form or substance in the paper, I will renew it with such corrections as shall be satisfactory to you. the bearer is charged with special care of your letter as containing a paper of great consequence to me, and not to trust it to any pocket, but to sew it inside of his waistcoat, & not to pull that off at night.

Francis had informed me he should go with you to Richmond and proceed thence to Columbia, and requested me to write to him there. I have done so, advising him as to his course, and the letter will be there by the time he arrives. Dr Cooper writes me he will be here the next week, and I shall take care to engage his best offices & patronage to Francis. we are all well here and salute yourself & family with affectionate attachment and respect.   TH: JEFFERSON

[*Note by Eppes at foot of text:*]

Richmond oct. 7. paid Bernard Peyton by directions from Thos Jefferson	500. dollars.
oct. 15th delivered to his servant Gilly a check on the Bank of Virginia for	} 3.500.
These two payments amount in the contract annexed	4.000 as stated

RC (CSmH: JF); on a sheet folded to form four pages, with letter on p. 1, p. 2 blank, enclosure on p. 3, and TJ's endorsement on p. 4; adjacent to signature: "John W. Eppes esq."; additional notation by TJ beneath endorsement: "with my bond."

On this day TJ paid Gill Gillette (GILLY) one dollar for his "exp. to Mr. Eppes's," and Gillette returned thirty-one cents in change on 19 Oct. 1820 (*MB*, 2:1368, 1369).

ENCLOSURE

Receipt and Bond to John Wayles Eppes

I Thomas Jefferson of Albemarle acknolege that I have recieved of John W. Eppes of Buckingham checks on the bank of   for the sum of four thousand Dollars in consideration whereof I oblige myself to deliver to him, on or before the twenty fifth day of December eighteen hundred & twenty two such and so many of my slaves now residing on my lands in Bedford as shall be equal in value to the sd sum of 4000. Dollars, to be designated and valued by persons mutually chosen by us, they observing, in their designation, as to age and sex, what they shall deem an usual proportion of age and sex, or what shall be the actual proportion among the body of slaves from which they are to be taken, whichever proportion the sd John W. Eppes shall prefer, such designation to include none superannuated. and I farther covenant to pay to the sd John W. in the mean time lawful interest on the said sum of 4000. Dollars on the 25th day of December annually from this date until the delivery of the said slaves; to which several obligations I bind myself my heirs executors and administrators, as Witness my hand and seal[1] this 13th day of October one thousand eight hundred and twenty.

TH: JEFF[ERSON]

Witness
H B TRIST

MS (CSmH: JF); in TJ's hand, signed by TJ and Hore Browse Trist; torn at foot of text with loss of seal and part of

TJ's signature, presumably to cancel the bond; conjoined with covering letter.

[1] Preceding two words interlined.

From Simon Harris

State of New Hampsher—
Hon & Dear Sir—   Bridgwater October 14th 1820
Althow I never had the pleasurer of Seeing you, yet I take the liberty to writing a few lines to you hoping you will not be ofended—when you was first elected President of the U— States I trust no man within the U, S. was more highly pleased then my Self, I called my first born son after you was elected, Thomas Jefferson Harris he is now almost 19 years of age is a bright Boy, and as your property is immence, when you dispose of your property I hope you will remember him, I always ment to have brought him up to Learning but my property is not Sufficient, having ben too liberal in helping Poor people out of Debt have lost considerable property, I have ben informed you have no very near relatives hope you will give him a Small plantation or give me one and I will give him my farm and will come and assist you

in your age and Stay up your hands as the Children of Israel Stayed up the hands of Moses—

I am now at the City of Washington on busness and am likely to get through on monday next Shall leave the City for home as soon as possable other wise I ment to have Called on you had time prmitted— hope you will use the freedom to rite to me on the Subject, to recive a comunication from you would be received[1] with grate Satisfaction— This from your very obedent & humble Serviant—

SIMON HARRIS—

RC (MHi); at foot of text: "Hon Thomas Jefferson late President of the United States"; endorsed by TJ as received 19 Oct. 1820 and so recorded in SJL.

Simon Harris (ca. 1770–1821), public official, was born in Bridgewater, Grafton County, New Hampshire. He served as the town's tax collector, 1793–97 and 1800–02, as mail carrier, 1807–09 and 1817–20, and as deputy sheriff, 1807–18. Harris congratulated TJ on his election in 1802 and unsuccessfully asked him in 1805 for a federal appointment in Louisiana. He represented Bridgewater in the New Hampshire General Court, 1811–12, 1816, and 1818, and he served as the town treasurer in 1819. Harris owned a store in nearby Grafton in 1816. He died in

Bridgewater (Richard W. Musgrove, *History of the Town of Bristol, Grafton County, New Hampshire* [1904], 1:139, 249–50, 500–2, 509, 2:224; *PTJ*, 36:378–9; Harris to TJ, 16 Aug. 1805 [DNA: RG 59, LAR, 1801–09]; *Concord Gazette*, 1 Sept. 1807; Concord *New-Hampshire Patriot*, 12 Sept. 1809, 8 Oct. 1816; Concord *New-Hampshire Patriot & State Gazette*, 29 Jan., 23 Apr. 1821; gravestone inscription in Green Grove Cemetery, Ashland, N.H.).

During their biblical battle with Amalek, the Israelites could only succeed as long as Moses kept "the rod of God" raised in the air, and so when he tired, Aaron and Hur STAYED UP his hands (Exodus 17.8–12).

[1] Manuscript: "reived."

To Isaiah Thomas

Monticello Oct. 14. 20.

Th: Jefferson presents his thanks to mr Thomas for the copy of the Archaeologia Americana which he has been so kind as to send him, and his congratulations on the proof this volume affords that the American Antiquarian society will deserve well of their country. it is truly pleasing to hope that, by their attentions, the monuments of the character and condition of the people who preceded us in the occupation of this great country will be rescued from oblivion before they will have entirely disappeared. he prays for their success, and would gladly take a part in their labors, but nature had limited the term of his services to an earlier day. he salutes mr Thomas with great esteem & respect.

RC (MWA: Thomas Papers); dateline at foot of text. PoC (MHi); on verso of reused address cover of Samuel Adams Wells to TJ, 2 June 1819; mutilated at seal, with one word rewritten by TJ; endorsed by TJ.

Isaiah Thomas (1749–1831), printer and publisher, was born in Boston. At the age of six he was apprenticed to a Boston printer, with whom he remained until 1765. Thomas afterward worked successively in printing offices in Halifax, Nova Scotia; Portsmouth, New Hampshire; Boston; and Charleston, South Carolina. He returned to Boston in 1770 and partnered with his former employer to publish the *Massachusetts Spy*, which Thomas purchased outright three months later and continued alone. He used this newspaper to promote American independence and was active in the Sons of Liberty before being forced to move his printing operation in 1775 to Worcester when British forces occupied Boston. Thomas soon resumed publication of the *Massachusetts Spy* in Worcester and continued it, leasing it to others between 1776 and 1778, until he passed it to his son in 1801. After the Revolutionary War ended Thomas commenced publishing and selling books on a large scale, and he also expanded the geographical range of his printing and bookselling operations to Boston, Newburyport, and Brookfield, Massachusetts; Walpole, New Hampshire; Baltimore; and Albany, all of which were managed by partners, many of whom had previous experience as Thomas's apprentices. With his associates he published more titles than any other contemporary American, including the *Massachusetts Magazine*, almanacs, works using a Greek typeface, musical scores, numerous books for children, and what has been called the first American novel, *The Power of Sympathy: or, the Triumph of Nature*, 2 vols. (Boston, 1789), attributed to William Hill Brown. Having achieved great financial success, Thomas retired from business in 1802. After he used his extensive private library to write *The History of Printing in America*, 2 vols. (Worcester, 1810), he was elected to most of the learned societies in the United States, including the American Philosophical Society in 1816. Thomas founded the American Antiquarian Society in 1812 and served as its president until his death in Worcester, with the bequest of his library forming the core of that institution's collections (*ANB*; *DAB*; MWA: Thomas Papers; Clifford K. Shipton, *Isaiah Thomas: Printer, Patriot and Philanthropist, 1749–1831* [1948]; Benjamin Thomas Hill, ed., *The Diary of Isaiah Thomas, 1805–1828*, 2 vols. [1909]; Thomas, *History of Printing in America*, esp. 1:368–85, 401–4; Brigham, *American Newspapers*; APS, Minutes, 18 Oct. 1816 [MS in PPAmP]; Washington *Daily National Intelligencer*, 11 Apr. 1831).

No letter from Thomas covering the American Antiquarian Society's *Archæologia Americana: Transactions and Collections* 1 (1820; Poor, *Jefferson's Library*, 4 [no. 115]) is recorded in SJL, and none has been found. Around this time he also sent this work to James Madison (Madison, *Papers, Retirement Ser.*, 2:127–8).

To Joel Yancey

DEAR SIR   Monticello Oct. 14. 20.

We should have been now about setting off for Poplar Forest, but for the accident of 3 of my carriage horses being recently taken with the disease called the sore tongue. I am told that the cure of this will require 10. days and will leave them so emaciated as to require time to make them able to take the road. the time of my setting out depends therefore on this uncertainty. mrs Randolph will accompany me. John Hemings & his people will go about the same time. I will thank you to procure a couple of barrels of fine family flour. I am in hopes you will not let the chance slip of selling the spare hay at the market price, whatever that may be. by extending our timothy grounds we may make that article a great resource. I salute you with friendship and esteem.   Th: Jefferson

P.S. this unexpected delay of my journey and return home will render it quite too late for mr Hepburn to begin his works, which I must therefore postpone to March. of this I pray you to inform him that he may not be in suspence & uncertainty.

PoC (MHi); on verso of reused address cover of Bernard Peyton to TJ, 31 May 1819; between signature and postscript: "Mr Yancey"; endorsed by TJ.

A missing letter of 23 Mar. 1821 from TJ to Alexander HEPBURN is recorded in SJL.

From William Charles Jarvis

Pittsfeeld Octr 16. 1820.

Yours of the 20th Ult^o I have received, and the pleasure it gave me is by no means diminished by the objection you make to what seems to be the opinion expressed in pages 84 & 148 of the Republican. I acknowlidge, that there is too much ground for the inference you have drawn, in regard to those parts of the book; but I have a satisfaction in saying, that I have exposed myself to your judicious criticism much more from an unguarded mode of expression, than from any difference of opinion between us, in relation to the subject upon which you have remarked.

I have never thought that the Judicial power had any superiority or preeminence over, any branches of the Legislature, or the supreme executive; nor have I considered that power as competent in all cases[1] to control the doings of the legislative or executive departments of government.   My idea simply is, that the Judicial authority <u>tends</u> to keep the administration of government true to its fundamental principles, by <u>refusing</u> to give effect to unconstitutional laws, when the rights of citizens, litigating, depend upon laws, the constitutionality of which is questioned. As for instance,: if I am on trial for an offence created by an unconstitutional law, or if my property is taken away from me under colour of a like law, the Judges are bound, I apprehend, to "<u>refuse to give effect</u>" to such laws, or else my liberty and rights are rather nominal, than real,   In the exercise of this sort of control, however, great candour is necessary, on the part of the judges; they never ought to be rash in questioning the doings of the Legislative and executive branches of the government.

I feel much flattered by the concluding line of your letter, in which you are pleased to[2] ask my candid reconsideration of the subject, which I have been remarking upon; adding your belief, that I shall come to a candid conclusion,   In reply, particularly, to this, I have much satisfaction in saying to you, that if I could recall the present edition, I should make such an alteration in pages 84 & 148, as would exclude the inference, which now presents itself to the reader=

If after further consideration of the book you find other parts of it exceptionable, you would confer a particular favour, in suggesting them to me, with the most perfect freedom, I am by, no means, too well informed not to need further instruction; and I know of no person better able to impart instruction than yourself.=

Your letter would have received from me a more early reply, had not absence from home on professional business prevented an earlier answer.=   Accept the assurance of my most sincere respect & esteem—   WILLIAM. C. JARVIS

RC (MHi); addressed: "Hon: Thomas Jefferson—Monticello.—Virginia"; redirected in an unidentified hand to "near Lynchburg"; franked; postmarked Pittsfield, Mass., 4 Nov.; endorsed by TJ as received 28 Nov. 1820 and so recorded in SJL.

TJ's letter to Jarvis was dated 28 Sept. 1820, not THE 20TH ULT°.

[1] Preceding three words interlined.
[2] Jarvis here canceled "say."

To William Munford

SIR   Monticello Oct. 17. 20.

I have this day duly executed, and now inclose the bond you were so kind as to prepare & forward me for the 20,000 D. now proposed to be borrowed of the Literary fund by the Visitors of the University. and I have executed it as I found it prepared, requiring that the interest should commence on the 1st day of the present month. it is a question however which it is my duty to refer to the justice of the[1] President and directors whether the interest should commence before the money is placed under the order of the University? I must observe at [this] same time that the sooner this is done the more desirable on our part, as the Proctor informs me that the necessities of his workmen render the final order for the money very urgent.

I tender you the assurance of my great esteem & respect.

                                              TH: JEFFERSON

PoC (CSmH: JF); on verso of reused address cover of Robert I. Evans to TJ, 3 June 1819; one word illegible; at foot of text: "Wᵐ Munford esq."; endorsed by TJ. Enclosure: enclosure to Thomas Mann Randolph to TJ, 12 Oct. 1820.

[1] Preceding three words interlined.

To Henry Clark

Sɪʀ   Monticello Oct. 18. 20.

Your favor of Oct. 4. is recieved. you have been quite misinformed[1] as to my having any intention to lease my possessions in Bedford. nothing would induce me to put my negroes out of my own protection. from the good opinion I entertained of your father I should have as willingly listened to proposals from yourself as from any body, had I the intentions you supposed. I tender you the assurance of my respect.   Tʜ: Jᴇꜰꜰᴇʀꜱᴏɴ

PoC (MHi); on verso of reused address cover of John Quincy Adams to TJ, 24 May 1819; at foot of text: "Mʳ Henry Clark"; endorsed by TJ.

[1] First syllable reworked from "un."

From Constantine S. Rafinesque

Rᴇꜱᴘᴇᴄᴛᴇᴅ Sɪʀ—   Lexington Kʸ 18ᵗʰ Octʳ 1820

I lately took the liberty to address you three Letters on American or rather Alleghawee Antiquities, which were published in the Kentucky Reporter

I now transmit you Prospectus of a new literary undertaking, with some details of its future contents, (in a number of the Reporter). I will be the principal Editor of this Journal, to which many eminent Individuals will contribute. We solicit your patronage, and hope to deserve it.

I sent you the first number of my Annals of Nature last Spring. I hope that it was duly received.

If you should answer me, please to let me know something about the prospects of the Central University of Virginia.

Believe me Sir! respectfully and sincerely

Your Sᵗ & wellwisher   Pʀᴏꜰ ʀ C S. RᴀꜰɪɴᴇꜱQᴜᴇ

PS. Having observed last Spring the beautiful Plant called <u>Jeffersonia binata,</u> I have made two discoveries relating to it. 1. That the flowers smell like Jonquil

2. That the Stamina are opposed to the petals, and the plant belongs therefore to the natural order of Berberides.

RC (MHi); addressed: "Hon^bl Thomas Jefferson Late Pres^t of the Un. St. Monticello near Charlotteville Virginia"; stamped; postmarked Lexington, 23 Oct.; endorsed by TJ as received 5 Nov. 1820 and so recorded in SJL. Enclosure: prospectus for the Lexington *Western Minerva, or American Annals of Knowledge and Literature*, announcing that this quarterly literary and scientific journal will include "original tracts and essays on all subjects," particularly the "Statistics, Geography, Geology, Antiquities, Civil and Natural History of the Western States," exclude "Local politics and sectarian controversies," but admit "political science and metaphysical disquisitions"; that it will be published for a $2 annual subscription by Thomas Smith beginning in January 1821; and concluding with a lengthy list of essays to appear in its first numbers (printed in Lexington *Kentucky Reporter*, 18 Oct. 1820).

JEFFERSONIA BINATA is an older name for *Jeffersonia diphylla*, or twinleaf (Betts, *Garden Book*, 173). The family of Berberidaceae (BERBERIDES) includes twinleaf (*Hortus Third*, 156).

From Arthur S. Brockenbrough

DEAR SIR,   October 19^h 1820

I must beg leave to suggest some few alterations[1] in the arcade in front of Hotel **A** without altering the height of the building, as the Span of the arch is 6 feet and the arches in front of the adjoining dormitories are only 5. F 4 I it requires 4 inches more height for the arcade in front of the Hotel than those in front of the dormitories,[2] I think it will look better to let the entablature of the dormitories[3] finish against the arcade of Hotel **A** as it does at Hotel **B** and let the arcade of Hotel **A** rise as at Hotel **B**—the entablature to rest on the Key stone which is 14 inches high the arch in the flank walls I think should be of the same span of those of the front as a view of the whole can be taken at once from the road—It will certainly be better [to][4] raise the windows 24 or 30 inches above the floor of Hotel **A**. as the back windows will otherwise be very near the ground in consiquence of the rise in the ground—I have sent you the plan of Hotel **A** that you may see the alterations I propose making as Mr Oldham has not yet taken it off you will please return it after an examination, the work of the Hotel is now progressing, it will therefore be important to deside on it immediately—the same difficulty presents itself at Hotel **C** the arches there are 6 ft wide & 5 f^t 4 in front of the dormitories, as the entablature cannot be raised[5] at that Hotel would it not be better to reduce the width of the arches to 5 feet 4 inches as in front of the dormitories,[6] you will please let me hear from you by the return of the boy or early in the morning as the work is progressing[7] fast—On Saturday

I propose going to Richmond, to purchase a tinman for the use of this institution, and also a parcel of tin which has been offered me, & to procure clothing for our laborers, any business that I can transact for you I will attend to with pleasure   most respectfully

Sir your Ob[t] sev[t]   A. S. BROCKENBROUGH

P.S.

> I must ask the favor of you to let me see my last report, I believe I have made some small errors, which if corrected I hope will not make any difference as to the report of the Visitors

A.S.B—

RC (ViU: TJP-PP); endorsed by TJ as received the day it was written from the University of Virginia and so recorded in SJL.

HOTEL A, HOTEL B, and HOTEL C were later redesignated B, D, and F, respectively.

[1] Manuscript: "altrations."
[2] Manuscript: "dormitores."
[3] Manuscript: "dormitores."
[4] Omitted word editorially supplied.
[5] Manuscript: "rased."
[6] Manuscript: "dormitores."
[7] Manuscript: "progrssing."

From David McClure

DEAR SIR,   Philad[a] October 19th 1820

Some time since I took the liberty to forward you a description of a plotting table. I have concluded to present it to the public and the pamphlet I forward you contains a sufficient description by which to make, and apply the same.

The pamphlet you will perceive is my report on a late survey of a section of the River Delaware, and contains some original matter which I would be happy to have your Sentiments on. With sincere respects

I am your Obt sert   DAVID MCLURE

RC (MoSHi: TJC-BC); endorsed by TJ as a letter from "M[c]lure David" received 27 Oct. 1820 and so recorded in SJL. RC (MHi); address cover only; with PoC of TJ to Joshua Dodge, 19 Apr. 1821, on recto and verso; addressed: "Thomas Jefferson Esq[r] Monte=Cello"; franked; postmarked Philadelphia, 19 Oct. Enclosure: McClure, *Report of the Survey of a Section of the River Delaware, from one mile below Chester, to Richmond, above Philadelphia* (Philadelphia, 1820).

To Craven Peyton

DEAR SIR   Monticello Oct. 19. 20.

I avail myself of the first moment it has been in my power to commence the repaiment of the sum with which you were so kind as to
accomodate me by sending you an order on Capt Peyton for 500.D.
as much as I am indebted to you for your friendly forbearance, I am
afraid to name dates for further payments. the spring will be the earliest, at which I shall be able to pay the half or the whole of the balance, according as the price of our produce shall enable me. I pray
you to be assured that I have no payment more at heart, and that I will
not delay it one moment beyond my ability. as a proof the means of
sending you this order were not recieved by me till last night. believe
me to be ever & affectionately yours   TH: JEFFERSON

RC (G. G. Imbert, Paris, 1950); addressed: "Craven Peyton esq. Monteagle";
with notation by Peyton at foot of text:
"1820
Octr 19   1500
    Int.
3^Y & 8^M." PoC (MHi); on verso of a reused address cover from Martin Dawson
to TJ; endorsed by TJ. Enclosure not
found.

For the letter from John Wayles Eppes
to TJ received LAST NIGHT, see TJ to
Eppes, 22 Oct. 1820, and note.

From Craven Peyton

DEAR SIR   Monteagle Octr 19. 20.

I am favoured with Yours of today inclosing a Draft On Capt Bernerd Peyton of Richm^d for Five hundred Dollars at sight, to be placed
to Your Credit with me, I was spoken to by Your Amiable Grand
Son, several months past, asking[1] my indulgence, On the debt due
from You, untill I might want it; I informed him; I had made Arrangements for its use, On the 25 Decr Next & the Undarstanding
was he wou^d go into Bank rathar then a disappointment shou^d take
place, I was to endorse for him. I feal confident there is no Man live-
ing who feals more for Your ease & happiness then, I do & will see
You soon On the subject.

with the greatest Respect and Esteem   C. PEYTON

RC (MHi); endorsed by TJ as received
19 Oct. 1820 and so recorded in SJL.
TJ's GRAND SON was Thomas Jefferson Randolph.

[1] Manuscript: "aking."

To Andrew Smith

Sir   Monticello Oct. 19. 20.

I avail myself of the first moment it has been in my power to inclose you an order for the 68 D–78 which has been due to you so long, with interest from June 18th 1819. the date of the account. I will not repeat the explanations of my letter of Sep. 5. but am not the less sensible of my own delinquency nor of your indulgence, with which assurance be pleased to accept that of great esteem and respect.

                                                   Th: Jefferson

PoC (MHi); on verso of reused address cover of John Laval to TJ, 28 May 1819; adjacent to signature: "M[r] Andrew Smith"; with notation by TJ at foot of

text: D

"debt   68.78

16. mo. int. 5.42

74.20"; endorsed by TJ. Enclosed order on Bernard Peyton not found (*MB*, 2:1369).

From Tobias Watkins

Dear Sir,   Baltimore 19th October 1820

As it may afford you some gratification to know the result of your representations concerning Mr. Gerardin, I have taken the liberty to intrude on you once more, to say, that that Gentleman has been unanimously elected by our Board of Trustees, Principal of Baltimore College. Permit me to use this opportunity to thank you for your polite and prompt reply to my letter, and to renew to you the expression of my devoted respect & veneration.   T. Watkins.

RC (CSmH: JF); endorsed by TJ as received 27 Oct. 1820 and so recorded in SJL. RC (DLC); address cover only; with PoC of TJ to Robert Greenway, 17

Apr. 1821, on verso; addressed: "Thomas Jefferson Monticello"; franked; postmarked Baltimore, 20 Oct.

To Arthur S. Brockenbrough

Th:J. to mr Brockenborough.   Oct. 20. 20.

I think the raising the windows above the floor will be proper for the reason you mention. with respect to the arches & entablature of Hotel **A.** there would be 3. modes of doing it. 1. to make the arches of the width of those of the dormitories. but this would make the piers too heavy. 2. to raise the entablature[1] as you propose, the[2] objection to which is the breaking the line of the entablature. 3. to lower the arches of the hotel by making them semioval, to wit [4].I.[3] lower[4] than the semicircle would be. [n]ot [be]ing certain that I comprehend exactly your difficulty I leave the 2. last modes to yourself, having a better opinion myself of the 3[d]. your decision on this will perhaps determine you whether to let the entabl. of the dormitories finish against the flank of **A.**

I approve of enlarging the flank arches to the width of those in front to give a better view of the internal range. I wish you may buy the tinner it will save great expence at first and be ready for repairs. money will be on hand as soon as the Literary board can have a meeting. friendly salutations

PoC (DLC); on verso of a reused address cover from Brockenbrough to TJ; mutilated at seal, with one word rewritten by TJ; dateline at foot of text; endorsed by TJ.

[1] Word interlined in place of "cornice."
[2] Manuscript: "th."
[3] Number illegible.
[4] Word interlined in place of "less."

Thomas Cooper's Order on Alexander Garrett

SIR   Oct[r] 20. 1820

Please to pay to my order, at the Bank of Virginia in Richmond, on the first day of January 1821, Seven hundred and fifty dollars, being the remaining portion of the sum of fifteen hundred dollars, allowed me as Professor, by the Visitors of the University of Virginia at Charlottesville.

I am sir Your humble Servant   THOMAS COOPER MD

MS (ViU: TJP-PP); in Cooper's hand, with notations in other hands as indicated; at foot of text in Cooper's hand: "To Alexander Garrett Esq[r] Treasurer of the University of Virginia"; with signed notes, by TJ as rector adjacent to closing and signature ("this shall be paid"), and by Garrett as bursar perpendicularly across middle of page ("Accepted"); endorsed in two unidentified hands and signed by Cooper on verso; signed notation beneath Cooper's signature on verso by Henry Kuhl (cashier of the Farmers' & Mechanics' Bank of Philadelphia) asking that Manuel Eyre (a director of the Second Bank of the United States) pay William Dandridge (cashier of the Bank of Virginia).

Around this time Cooper wrote Garrett that he had drawn for the $750 "with the approbation of M[r] Jefferson" (RC in ViU: PP; undated; endorsed in at least two unidentified hands, in part, as "p[d] 18th Nov[r] 1820").

To Richard Rush

In your favor of May 3. which I have now to acknolege, you so kindly proffered your attentions to any little matters I might have on that side of the water, that I take the liberty of availing myself of this proof of your goodness so far as to request you to put the inclosed catalogue into the hands of some <u>honest</u> bookseller of London who will procure and forward the books to me, with care and good faith. they should be packed in a cheap trunk, and not put on ship-board until April, as they would be liable to damage on a winter passage. I ask an <u>honest</u> correspondent in that line, because when we begin to import for the library of our University, we shall need one worthy of entire confidence.

I send this letter open to my correspondent in Richmond, Capt Bernard Peyton, with a request that he will put into it a bill of exchange on London of 40.£ sterling, which of course therefore I cannot describe to you by naming drawer and drawee. he will also forward, by other conveyances, the duplicate and 3.plicate as usual. this sum would more than cover the cost of the books written for, according to their prices stated in printed catalogues. but as books have risen with other things in price, I have enlarged the printed amount by about 15. percent to cover any rise. still should it be insufficient, the bookseller is requested to dock the Catalogue to the amount of the remittance.

I have no news to give you: for I have none but from the newspapers, and believing little of that myself, it would be an unworthy present to my friends. but the important news lies now on your side of the Atlantic. England, in throes from a trifle, as it would seem, but that trifle the symptom of an irremediable disease proceeding from a long course of exhaustion by efforts and burthens beyond her natural strength; France agonising between royalists and constitutionalists; the other states of Europe pressing on to revolution & the rights of man, and the colossal powers of Russia and Austria marshalled against them. these are more than specks of hurricane in the horison of the world. you, who are young may live to see it's issue. the beginning only is for my time.[1]   Nor is our side of the water entirely untroubled. the boisterous sea of liberty is never without a wave. a hideous evil, the magnitude of which is seen, and at a distance only, by the one party, and more sorely felt and sincerely deplored by the other, from the difficulty of the cure, divides us at this moment too angrily. the attempt by one party to prohibit willing states from sharing the evil, is thought by the other to render desperate, by accumulation the hope of it's final eradication. if a little time however is given to both parties to cool, and to dispel their visionary fears, they will see that concurring in sentiment as to the evil, moral and political, the duty and interest of both is to concur also in devising[2] a practicable process of cure. should time not be given, and the schism be pushed to separation, it will be for a short term only. two or three years trial will bring them back, like quarelling[3] lovers, to renewed embraces, and increased affection. the experiment of separation would soon prove to both that they had mutually miscalculated their best interests. and even were the parties in Congress to secede in a passion, the soberer people would call a Convention and cement again the severance attempted by the insanity of their functionaries. with this consoling view, my greatest grief would be for the fatal effect of such an event on the hopes and happiness of the world. we exist, and are quoted, as standing proofs that a government, so modelled as to rest continually on the will of the whole society, is a practicable government. were we to break to pieces, it would damp the hopes and the efforts of the good, and give triumph to those of the bad thro' the whole enslaved world. as members therefore of the universal society of mankind, and standing in high and responsible relation with them, it is our sacred duty to suppress passion among ourselves, and not to blast the confidence we have inspired of proof that a government of reason is better than one of force.[4]—this letter is not of facts but of opinions as you will observe: and altho the converse is generally the most acceptable, I do not know that, in your situation, the opinions of your countrymen may not be as desirable to be known to you as facts. they constitute indeed moral facts as important as physical ones to the attention of the public functionary.   Wishing you a long career to the services you may render your country, and that it may be a career of happiness and prosperity to yourself, I salute you with affectionate[5] attachment and respect.   TH: JEFFERSON

P.S. Richmond or Norfolk would be the most convenient ports to send my books to; and I presume there are always at London ships bound to one of those ports.

RC (PHi: Gratz Collection); postscript added separately to RC and PoC; endorsed by Rush, with his subjoined notation: "Encloses a catalogue of books to be supplied by an honest bookseller; his good directions in this respect. His glance at the threatening aspect of the political horizon in Europe; only the beginning of which it will be for him to see. He alludes to trouble on our side of the water also; and after the remark that 'the boisterous sea of liberty is never without a wave,' has anxious but hopeful reflections on the slavery question growing out of the angry Missouri dispute. His kind words towards me in the conclusion." PoC (DLC); at foot of first page: "Richard Rush esquire." Tr (ViU: TJP); extract in Nicholas P. Trist's hand. Enclosure: TJ's List of Books to be Acquired in London, 21 Oct. 1820. Enclosed in TJ to Bernard Peyton, 21 Oct. 1820.

The incident TJ described as A TRIFLE was probably the popular furor in England over the parliamentary investigation of Queen Caroline (see TJ to William Ros-coe, 27 Dec. 1820, and note). The HIDEOUS EVIL was slavery.

[1] Tr begins here.
[2] Tr: "divining."
[3] Word interlined.
[4] Tr ends here.
[5] Manuscript: "affectioionate."

To James Leitch

DEAR SIR   Monticello Oct. 21. 20.

I inclose you an order on Capt Bernard Peyton for 533.D. of which I would wish 500.D. to be credited on my bond, and the balance 33.D. to be placed in our current account to reimburse the 33.D. on my order of Apr. 15. in favor of Josiah Leake. I assure you I have not before had that sum in my hands at any moment when urgent calls have not required it from me.   I believe you settle the annual accounts of your customers in September. I shall be glad to recieve mine as soon as convenient, for altho' I cannot pay it till my produce is all down in the spring, yet it is advantageous to know it's amount to prevent other engagements.

I am not able to name specific times as to the discharge of my bond, but I shall certainly do it by such instalments as my means will enable me. the desire of doing this induces me to curtail my expences as much as I can; and particularly, in consideration that groceries are cash purchases by the merchant I have withdrawn that pressure on you, and dealt for them with mr Raphael. accept the assurance of my constant friendship and respect.   TH: JEFFERSON

PoC (MHi); on verso of reused address cover of Wilson Cary Nicholas to TJ, 1 June 1819; at foot of text: "Mr James Leitch"; endorsed by TJ. Enclosure not found.

Leitch's records indicate that he received TJ's "draft on Bernard Peyton" on 24 Oct. 1820 (Leitch Daybook, p. 147).

List of Books to be Acquired in London

Grammatica Anglo-Saxonica ex Hickesiano Thesauro excerpta.
Institutiones grammaticae Anglo-Saxonicae et Moeso-Gothica Hickesii
Vocabularium Anglo-Saxonicum à Benson.
The Saxon Heptateuch by Thwaites.

Spelman's Anglo-Saxon Psalter.

Marshal's Saxon gospels. 4to Dordrecht. 1665.

Parker's edition of Walsingham's history with the Aelfridi annales Asseri Menevensis in Latin but expressed in Anglo-Saxon types. fol. Lond. 1574. see Nicholson's library 119.

Bede's Ecclesiastical history with Alfred's paraphrase Anglo-Sax. by Wheeloc.

Bede's history of the church of England translated by Stapleton.

Gibson's Saxon Chronicle.

Spelman's life of Alfred, Saxon, with Walker's translation.

Elstob's English-Saxon Homily.

Alfred's Anglo-Saxon Boethius by Rawlinson.

Wilkins's Leges Anglo-Saxonicae.

Wotton's view of Hickes's Thesaurus by Shelton.

Cooperi Thesaurus linguae Romanae et Britannicae.

The Universal History. the antient part only in 20. vols. 8vo

Clarke's Bibliotheca legum. the last edition.

Owen's Geoponics. Eng. 2. v. 8vo

Bass's Gr. & Eng. Lexicon. 18mo 1820. see Quarterly catalogue Edinb. Review N° 66.

Hone's Apocryphal New testament. Ludgate hill. Lond. 1820.

Whateley on gardening. an edition with prints.

for

TH: JEFFERSON
Oct. 21. 20.

MS (ViU: TJP); entirely in TJ's hand. Enclosed in TJ to Richard Rush, 20 Oct. 1820, and TJ to Bernard Peyton, 21 Oct. 1820.

To Bernard Peyton

DEAR SIR   Monticello Oct. 21. 20.

Having occasion for some books from London, the inclosed letter requests my friend mr Rush our Minister there to engage some bookseller to furnish them. I state to him that you will be so good as to put into my letter a bill of exchange of £40. sterl, and that you will forward 2plic^s & 3plic. by other conveyances. I leave the letter open for your perusal and request you to put a copy of such a bill into it, then to seal the letter and forward it by some safe vessel. pray use your best attentions that the bill be a good one. affectionate salutations.

TH: JEFFERSON

PoC (MHi); on verso of reused address cover to TJ; at foot of text: "Capt B. Peyton"; endorsed by TJ. Enclosures: (1) TJ to Richard Rush, 20 Oct. 1820.

(2) TJ's List of Books to be Acquired in London, 21 Oct. 1820.

2PLIC^s & 3PLIC: "duplicates and triplicates."

To John Wayles Eppes

DEAR SIR   Monticello Oct. 22. 20.

Your favor of the 16th was safely recieved with the check on the bank of Virginia for 3500.D. inclosed. the expression in the reciept I sent you of 2[1] checks on the bank E^{t}c for 4000.D. will I think comprehend with sufficient certainty the deposit of 500 D. as well as the check of 3500. I did not know at the time whether the 500.D. had been paid in cash, or by a check, but thought it indifferent. if you think otherwise however I shall be ready to change it.

The continued illness of all my carriage horses and of my riding horse renders desperate my journey to Bedford till cold weather, possibly December, when none of the family will acompany me. we think therefore it is better to bring the harpsichord here where my daughter with Jon Hemings can put it into order & string it at their leisure, and have it ready to go to Bedford by the waggon at Christmas when she goes there empty to bring down our por[k]. I therefore send her to Millbrook for the instrument express. Doctor Cooper was 3. or 4. days with us, & returned yesterday to Richmond to proceed by the stage to Columbia. he has promised me faithfully to be the Mentor of Francis and I am sure he will faithfully perform it. we all join in saluting mrs Eppes & yourself & family with affection & respect.

TH: JEFFERSON

PoC (MHi); on verso of reused address cover of John Adams to TJ, 27 May 1819; mutilated at seal, with one word rewritten by TJ; at foot of text: "J. W. Eppes esq."; endorsed by TJ.

Eppes's 16 Oct. 1820 FAVOR to TJ, not found, is recorded in SJL as received 18 Oct. 1820.

Elizabeth Trist said of the abortive JOURNEY that "most of the family were to have gone to poplar Forest. and M^{rs}

Randolph was only to Stay to put the Harpsicord in tune and Return and then the carriage was to convey Virgina and my self to Bedford" (Trist to Emma Walker Gilmer [Breckinridge], Farmington, 26 Oct. 1820 [RC in ViU: FWG]).

A missing letter from Eppes to TJ of 25 Oct. 1820 is recorded in SJL as received two days later from Mill Brook.

[1] Number interlined.

To Bernard Peyton

DEAR SIR   Monticello Oct. 23. 20.

My draughts on you have been as follows

		D
Sep. 30. in favor of Joel Wolfe		100.
Oct. 13. Taxes Albemarle.		197.21
d° Bedford.		175.
19. in favor of Craven Peyton		500.
	Th: J. Randolph.	106.
	Andrew Smith ab^t	74.20
21.	James Leitch.	533.
	Joel Wolfe.	200
23.	Martin Dawson.	339.52
		2224.93[1]

tomorrow I shall draw in favor of Alexr Garrett for 210. something more or less, and of John Watson somewhere about 70.

The harpsichord strings came safe, but the letter of Oct. 5. loitered somewhere till the 19th. I see a Franklin Almanac advertised at the[2] Franklin office, opposite the Market. will you be so good as to send me 2. copies by mail? I expect you have recieved a small package of books for me from Guigam: Baltimore. be so good as to forward them by a waggon to James Leitch. mr Baker informed me he should recieve soon a cask of Scuppernon wine for me, which I desired him to deliver to you, & I pray you to send by the boats of Johnson, Gilmore or any other boatman whom you know to be trusty. God bless you.

TH: JEFFERSON

PoC (MHi); on verso of reused address cover of Lydia Broadnax to TJ, 2 June 1819; at foot of text: "Capt. Peyton"; endorsed by TJ. Not recorded in SJL.

TJ drew on Peyton for his BEDFORD taxes for $175 on 21 Sept. 1820 although he noted that the amount "shd. be 157.95" (MB, 2:1367). His records indicate that the payment to Thomas Jefferson RANDOLPH was "in full of 1000.D. borrowed for me from   Carr ante for repayment of which he recd. for me from Charles Everett 929.85 (ante July 13.) which with the 1000.D. ante Aug. 9. compleated Everett's payment of 1929.85. and the 106.D. now paid to Th:J.R. pays principal & int. in full of the 1000.D. he borrowed for me of   Carr" (MB, 2:1369).

The payment to MARTIN DAWSON covered an order on TJ by Edmund Meeks for $174.47 including interest, TJ's note to Peter Laporte for $50.45 including interest, Youen Carden's order on TJ for $8 in favor of John Ormond, a payment to Dr. Thomas G. Watkins on TJ's behalf of $60, and TJ's store account with Dawson through 31 July 1820 totaling $46.60 (MB, 2:1369). GUIGAM: Henry Guegan.

[1] Reworked from "2234.93."
[2] Manuscript: "the the."

From Bernard Peyton

DEAR SIR,   Rich'd 23ᵈ Octobʳ 1820

I am in recᵗ this morning your esteemed favor covering J. W.
Eppes's draft on the Virgᵃ Bank for thirty five hundred $3,500 dol-
lars payable to my order, which is drawn & at your credit, & will be
paid to your orders as fast as called for—   In the last three or
four days have paid several small drafts of yours to various persons—

I have met with the half of a delightful double Gloucester cheese,
which I have had carefully put up for you, & only wait to forward it,
to be informed whether it shall go to Monticello or Poplar Forrest—I
beg you will accept it, & am sorry I could not obtain the whole—

You did not mention in your last whether the Harpsichord strings
had reached you safely, & whether they would answer.

With great respect & regard Dʳ sir

Yours very Truely   B. PEYTON

RC (MHi); endorsed by TJ as received   TJ's letter to Peyton COVERING J. W.
29 Oct. 1820 and so recorded in SJL.   EPPES'S DRAFT has not been found and is
                                        not recorded in SJL.

To José Corrêa da Serra

Monticello Oct. 24. [20.]

Your kind letter, dear Sir, of Oct. 11. was handed to me by Dʳ Cooper, and was the first correction of an erroneous belief that you had
long since left our shores. such had been Colᵒ Randolph's opinion,
and his had governed mine. I recieved your Adieu with feelings of
sincere regret, at the loss we were to sustain, and particularly of those
friendly visits by which you had made me so happy. I shall feel too the
want of your counsel and approbation in what we are doing and have
yet to do in our University, the last of my mortal cares, and the last
service I can render my country. but turning from myself, throwing
egoism behind me, and looking to your happiness, it is a duty and
consolation of friendship to consider that that may be promoted by
your return to your own country. there I hope you will recieve the
honors and rewards you merit, and which may make the rest of your
life easy and happy. there too you will render precious services by
promoting the science of your country, and blessing it's future generations with the advantages that bestows. nor even there shall we lose
all the benefits of your friendship: for this motive as well as the love

[367]

of your own[1] country will be an incitement to promote that intimate harmony between our two nations which is so much the interest of both. nothing is so important as that America shall separate herself from the systems of Europe, & establish one of her own. our circumstances, our pursuits, our interests are distinct & the principles of our policy should be so also. all entanglements with that quarter of the globe should be avoided if we mean that peace & justice shall be the polar stars of the American societies.   I had written a letter to a friend while you were here, in a part of which these sentiments were expressed and I had made an extract from it to put into your hands, as containing my creed on that subject. you had left us however in the morning earlier than I had been aware. still I inclose it to you because it would be a leading principle with me, had I longer to live. during six & thirty years that I have been in situations to attend to the conduct and characters of foreign nations, I have found the government of Portugal the most just, inoffensive and unambitious of any one with which we had concern, without a single exception. I am sure this is the character of ours also. two such nations can never wish to quarrel with each other. subordinate officers may be negligent, may have their passions & partialities, & be criminally remiss in preventing the enterprises of the lawless banditti who are to be found in every seaport of every country. the late pyratical depredations which your commerce has suffered as well as ours, & that of other nations seem to have been committed by renegado rovers of several nations, French, English, American which they as well as we have not been careful enough to suppress. I hope our Congress now about to meet will strengthen the measures of suppression. of their disposition to do it there can be no doubt; for all men of moral principle must be shocked at these atrocities. I had repeated conversations on this subject with the President while at his seat in this neighborhood. no man can abhor these enormities more deeply. I trust it will not have been in the power of abandoned rovers, nor yet of negligent functionaries to disturb the harmony of two nations, so much disposed to mutual friendship, and interested in it. to this, my dear friend, you can be mainly instrumental, and I know your patriotism & philanthropy too well to doubt your best efforts to cement us. in these I pray for your success, and that heaven may long preserve you in health and prosperity to do all the good to mankind to which your enlightened and benevolent mind disposes you. of the continuance of my affectionate friendship with that of my life and of it's fervent wishes for your happiness, accept my sincere assurance.   Th: Jefferson

PoC (DLC); dateline faint; mutilated, with one word rewritten by TJ; at foot of first page: "Mr Correa." Not recorded in SJL. Enclosure: extract from TJ to William Short, 4 Aug. 1820.

¹Word added in margin.

From Pascal Etienne Meinadier

SIR,   Salem, Massachusetts, oct. 24. 1820

In the year 1819 I had the honour to address a letter to you requesting your friendly aid in enabling me to pursue with effect my just demands against Isaac Cushing, my former partner, who carried off a large amount of property; and I had the honour of an answer from you on the 31ˢᵗ August of that year. I have lately heard of the death of Cushing by the enclosed advertisement dated at Huntsville, Alabama Aug. 16ᵗʰ 1820; & I have in consequence published in various newspapers the Notice which is in the enclosed paper, to which I take the liberty of calling your attention, in the hope that it may lead to something that may be advantageous to me. May I now take the liberty, Sir, as a friendless stranger in this country, and ignorant upon whom I can rely, to beg the favour of your good offices (or by means of some of your friends) in furnishing me with a letter of introduction to some professional or other confidential person in Huntsville or its vicinity to whom I could apply for assistance in my affairs. I am fully sensible of the justness of your remark to me, that the state of your health & other circumstances do not permit you to lend me the aid of personal services; & be assured, Sir, that nothing but my peculiar situation in a foreign country would induce me to make the request which I now do: I will also add, that it is not my intention to occasion you any further trouble than the present in a case in which you can take no other interest than that which one of your benevolence will always entertain.

I have the honour to be Sir, with the highest respect your most obed^t & humble serv^t   MEINADIER L'AINÉ

RC (DLC); in an unidentified hand, signed by Meinadier; dateline at foot of text; endorsed by TJ as received 5 Nov. 1820 and so recorded in SJL.

Several newspapers printed a letter of AUG. 16ᵀᴴ 1820 received from Huntsville, Alabama, announcing the death four days earlier of a mysterious man who arrived in Huntsville in November 1819 and went by the name of James Cochran, but who was discovered to be Isaac Cushing when his papers were posthumously examined (New-York Evening Post, 11 Sept. 1820, and elsewhere). The Salem Essex Register, likely enclosed here, reprinted the letter on 16 Sept. 1820 and added an explanation, also reprinted elsewhere, that Cushing had partnered with Meinadier in Marseille but had then stolen a ship and property belonging to him, and that Meinadier, who came to the United States in search of Cushing, "received by the above notice, the first information of the hiding place and fate of his partner, and will proceed immediately to Alabama to secure the property left by Cushing at Huntsville." In a published NOTICE, also enclosed here, after noting that Cushing had sailed from Marseille on 30 May 1817 as supercargo on the ship *Braque*, Meinadier requested "all persons who have knowledge of any property in the possession of said Cushing, or of any other person for his use, at this time or at any other time since the said 30th May, 1817, or of any papers or documents relative thereto, to which the subscriber is thus entitled, to give him information thereof accordingly" (*Essex Register*, 11 Oct. 1820, and elsewhere).

From Andrew Smith

SIR   Richmond 24th October 1820

I yesterday was favor'd with your respected Letter dated the 19th Inst, enclosing your Draft for $68–78 on Captn Bernard Peyton, which was promptly paid, together with interest from the 18th of June 1819, say $5–57 in all $74–32. for which be pleased to accept my thanks—

I believe I already informed you of my having resumed the Agency of the Boston Glass Manufactory, in my Individual capacity, and should be happy to receive your farther orders for any other articles, besides Window Glass—

I beg leave to mention, that I have lately received the Agency of an Iron Compy in Pennsylvania, from whose furnace is produced a better quality than any other in the U States—or imported—universally declared so by all who have tried it, and from which the Armory at Harpers Ferry is supply'd for the manufacture of Muskets &c.— should you require supplies of this Article for your Estates, I may with safety recommend it, and shall be pleased to furnish you   I am Respectfully   ANDW SMITH

RC (MHi); endorsed by TJ as received 29 Oct. 1820 and so recorded in SJL. RC (DLC); address cover only; with PoC of TJ to Thomas Appleton, 16 Apr. 1821 (second letter), on recto and verso; addressed: "Thomas Jefferson Esqr Monticello Albemarle County Virginia"; franked; postmarked Richmond, 24 Oct.

From William Short

DEAR SIR   Philada Oct: 25. 1820

I could hardly have thought it possible that a letter from you could have remained in my hands unacknowleged so long, as I find your last to be, which I have now before me. It is of the 4th of August last, but was not recieved by me until the 23ᵈ. I was then on the sea shore, whither I had fled from the heats of Philadelphia, in pursuit of cool air—As this is a retired part of the state of N. Jersey, the post is unfrequent & irregular, & thus it was that your letter was so long on its way to me. Very soon after its reciept I left the sea shore for Schooley's mountain, & after a short stay there I returned towards the City waiting in the neighborhood until the fever should so far cease as to admit of my entering it. During all this time I find that I wrote not a letter that I was not under the immediate necessity of writing. The consequence is that on my return here I find such a number to be answered as deterred me for some time from entering on the duty. But with respect to yours, my inclination is at least equal to my duty—And I therefore always take up my pen to address you with a pleasure equal to that which I felt in my early days. This sentiment at least in my heart I can truly say time has not been able to weaken—although I could not say it of many others.

I thank you most sincerely for the continuation of the subject in your last letter. It is one that I have occupied myself about less than most persons; because I felt <u>in limine</u> that I could not attain that degree of conviction; less than which never satisfies me. I had a fellow student when at College who took precisely the contrary line, & ever occupied himself in the pursuit of an object, which I saw he was as far from attaining as I was—The only difference was that he had taken a great deal of useless labor, which I had saved, & could therefore bestow on other more attainable matters. It was this circumstance probably which has operated on me to prevent my engaging in such researches.

The explanation which you have been so good as to give me, shews much research on your part—& to me is perfectly satisfactory. I cannot say how much I am obliged to you for it. I have read over both your last letter & its predecessor several times—& always with increased satisfaction. And it will be probably all I shall ever read on the subject.

My endeavour has been from the time of my earliest recollection to do what was right, or what appeared to me to be so—& this really not with any view to a reward in another world. I had no merit in this; for I certainly should have felt uneasy here if I had acted otherwise. Those who are placed in easy and competent situations in this life will naturally act in this way. It is the ill treated—the suffering & distressed who may have need of some greater check than their own sense of what is right. A man for instance, who labors all the day & who cannot with this procure bread for a starving family. It is to such a man that I give credit for his good actions—And I am always at a loss to say what is his motive to them—Some say it is the fear of the Devil—& that a Devil is necessary if it were only for this class of men—But it seems to me when the punishment is so distant, & the relief to present sufferings, so much wanted at the moment, this alone cannot suffice to explain the conduct of the distressed man, if that conduct be honest. However I leave such subjects to themselves as beyond my ken, & confine myself to act well myself as far as in my power, & this for my own satisfaction.

M. Correa is here, & I believe on the eve of his departure, although he seems to make a mystery of the time. He is not without some apprehension, I believe, of the Baltimore patriotic pirates. I should look forward indeed with great satisfaction to the consummation you contemplate—that of an American system as contradistinguished from the European—if I could flatter myself with the hope of it. Correa may carry back favorable sentiments with respect to us at large, but certainly he does not as to the administration. Nor do I see how he could inspire his Government with any confidence, as to our entering on any general anti-piratical system for the Americas generally, when we cannot, or if we can, will not take effectual measures for suppressing under the immediate eye of Government (for they cannot but see the Pirates at Baltimore) the equipments which are there going on. Although to us there is a talisman in the word Patriot which makes it sacred when assumed even by a Pirate, yet I do not believe it has the same virtue with Correa or with his Government. I hope when Monroe's election shall be over, as he probably will not look to another, that he will endeavour to excite Congress to take up this subject in good earnest.

I am very much obliged to you for what you said on the two obstacles, or rather objections, to my making the visit which I have long had much at heart. I did not suppose any active hostility on their part—nor that they had expressed any sentiment unfavorable to me. I was certain they did more justice to my known sentiments towards you than to have expressed such in your presence. Yet I have not been satisfied with their manner—& my philosophy leads me always to keep out of view of objects of dissatisfaction. Neither of them could have conferred any favor on me—for most certainly (although many would not believe this) there is nothing in the power of either of them that I would accept. One of them, the first in order, had it perfectly in his power to have saved my amour propre blessé, as he knew—& this without any inconvenience to himself. However he was then in his true honeymoon, & probably his only one, & therefore could not think of such trifles—And I certainly forgive him & wish never to see him from the motive abovementioned, but at the same time, am not so much dissatisfied, that I would have the appearance of avoiding him.

I regret now very much having not passed the last summer or the present season in this excursion—the summer & fall are the only parts of the year in which it is agreeable to travel—Indeed as to myself I find travelling disagreeable here in all seasons. I have increased in bulk & still more in indolence, & the revolution in the pecuniary affairs of this country has prepared for me a great deal of travelling each year, which I fear will be indispensable. This enigma requires a solution. I have been led on very good ground & on just calculation as I supposed, to convert the greater part of my property (which was in stock, the only kind of property suitable to a bachelor) into mortgages in the state of New-York. The law of mortgages was considered better in that State than in this, & the legal interest was 7. instead of 6. p^{ct}. the property mortgaged was new land, which was settling & of course, as stated to me, increasing in value. This was the case for some years, & the interest was therefore regularly paid then—but this was before our late war—some of these mortgages were prior to my late voyage to Europe. Since then several of the mortgagers have failed in consequence of the times, the interest has of course remained unpaid, & when the mortgage was foreclosed I have been obliged in every instance to purchase the land, as it was struck off for much less than the amount of my debt. I have thus became a large landholder in different & distant parts of the State of New-York, & shall probably be under the necessity of making frequent journies thither.

This is inflicted perhaps as a punishment (& a very severe punishment it is) for my want of confidence in the funds of my country. And to this, I must plead guilty. I had been but a short time here after my first return eighteen years ago, before I convinced myself that this country would be engaged in a war before the termination of the then existing war in Europe. In this I was right—but I was perfectly mistaken in the consequence which I drew from it, viz. that the war would destroy the funds of this country. It was this mistake wch made me as soon as I could effect it, convert my stock into N. York mortgages, w^{ch}, for my misfortune, have become unproductive land—I consider this land as deferred stock—& ultimately, that is when I am dead & gone, it will produce much more than the money it has cost—To me it will produce only trouble & travelling.—My paper obliges me to end—otherwise I sh^d take up much more of your time—As it is, I will however add that I am as ever, dear sir, yours affectionately

W Short

RC (MHi); endorsed by TJ as received 5 Nov. 1820 and so recorded in SJL.

AMOUR PROPRE BLESSÉ: "wounded self-esteem."

To Jesse Wharton

S<small>IR</small>   Monticello Oct. 25. 20.

Your favor of Sep. 25. is just now recieved, and to answer it will require some explanation. our legislature, at their last session authorised the Visitors of the University to borrow money to finish the buildings, pledging the public annuity of 15,000.D. settled on it for the repayment of the loan. money was accordingly borrowed and the buildings will be compleated by this time twelvemonth. if the annuity is to redeem the debt, it will take seven years, during which time the buildings will be locked up. if however the legislature liberate us from the debt, measures will immediately on such liberation, be taken to have all the Professors in place by the time the buildings are done, and to open the institution the 1st of February twelvemonth. this will be known to the public[1] by the proceedings of the legislature the ensuing winter.

In answer to your 2^{d} question as to the best of the existing [se]minaries, I must answer that also hypothetically. Dr Cooper is appointed a Professor of Chemistry E^{t}c at Columbia college. it is expected that at the next meeting of their trustees, mr Nulty one of the best Mathematicians in the US. will be appointed to that professorship, and mr Elliot President with the department of botany & Natural history. if these appointments take place it will be the best seminary within my knolege, because no other will possess three such men. in this expectation I have recently[2] sent my own grandson there, to remain till our University is opened. with this imperfect information, be pleased to accept the assurance of my great esteem & respect

T<small>H</small>: J[<small>EFFERSO</small>]N

PoC (MoSHi: TJC-BC); on verso of reused address cover of John J. Boyd (for LeRoy, Bayard & Company) to TJ, 14 June 1819; mutilated at seal; signature faint; at foot of text: "Mr Wharton"; endorsed by TJ. Not recorded in SJL.

C<small>OLUMBIA</small> C<small>OLLEGE</small>: South Carolina College (later the University of South Carolina). TJ's G<small>RANDSON</small> was Francis Eppes.

[1] Preceding three words interlined.
[2] Reworked from "sent."

From Martin Dawson

DEAR SIR   Milton 26ᵗʰ October 1820:
   Mr Edmund Meeks hath drawn on you in my favour for eighteen
Dollars Thirty five cents payable 1ˢᵗ Janʸ next Please to write me—
whether I may put the same to your Accoᵗ or not   With Esteem
   Yo. Ob. Hu. Serᵛ   MARTIN DAWSON

$18.35

RC (ViU: TJP-ER); addressed: TJ accepted this order the following
"Thomas Jefferson esqʳᵉ } Monticello";   day (*MB*, 2:1370).
endorsed by TJ: "Meek Edmᵈ 18.35 to
M. Dawson."

From Bernard Peyton

DEAR SIR,   Rich'd 26 October 1820
   I was favor'd last evening with your two esteemed favors of the
21st: & 23ᵈ Inst: the latter addressed to "Capt: Craven Peyton";
expecting tho' it was a mistake, ventured to open it:—the former
covered one addressed to R. Rush Esqʳ now in London, which will be
sealed & forwarded by the fast sailing Ship Virginia Capt: Fisher in
a day or two, for Liverpool direct, & before sealing, will put in a Bill
drawn by Joseph Marx of this City on his correspondent in London
for £40,[1] which is undoubted:—& will by other conveyances forward
duplicates & triplicates of the same—
I hand under cover herewith two Franklin Almanacks for 1821[2] which
I wish safe to hand.
   The Box of Books you speak of from Baltimore I have not heard of,
when they reach me, no time shall be lost in dispatching them to
James Leitch Charlottesville:—As also the Cask of Scuppernon Wine,
which Mʳ Baker spoke to me about some time since—it has not yet
reached Richmond.
   The several drafts you enumerate having drawn on me, have gener-
ally been presented & paid, the balance shall be honored on demand.
   Learning by the return of the Governor that you are not likely
to leave Monticello soon, I send by a trusty Waggoner to=day, care
J. Leitch, the half cheese I spoke of in my last, which I hope will turn
out good, & reach you safely—the freight on it I have paid.
   Finding letters uncertain in reaching Milton, will for the future, if
agreeable to you, address to Charlottesville—
   With sincere regard Dʳ sir
   Yours very Truely   BERNARD PEYTON

[375]

RC (MHi); endorsed by TJ as received 29 Oct. 1820 and so recorded in SJL. RC: left half of address cover only (MHi), with PoC of TJ to Peyton, 16 Apr. 1821, on verso; right half of address cover only (DLC), with PoC of TJ to Samuel Williams, 16 Apr. 1821, on verso; addressed: "Mʳ Thomas Jefferson Monticello near Charlottesville"; franked; postmarked Richmond, 26 Oct. Enclosure: two copies of publisher Nathan Pollard's *The Franklin Almanack, calculated on a new and improved plan for the Year of our Lord, 1821* (Richmond, [1820]).

The GOVERNOR was Thomas Mann Randolph.

[1] Reworked from "$40."
[2] Reworked from "1820."

To Bernard Peyton

DEAR SIR   Monticello Oct. 28.[1] 20

Since mine of the 23ᵈ I have drawn as follows in favor of Alexr Garrett 217.29 and John Watson—72.76 and I have still two more to make, to wit for Joel Wolfe from 100. to 150.D. and in favor of E. Garland for 800.D.

Will you be so good as to send by the boats about 15 or 20. gallons of linseed oil. as it is apt to leak in a cask you will judge whether it is better or not to have it in jugs. I must also get you to send me stuff for the boulting cloth of a country mill, to wit 2. yds of N° 3. 4 yds of N° 5[2] and 6 yds of N° 7. I presume it is to be had in Richmond and if a good judge can be got to chuse it perhaps it may be well. this had better come by a trusty waggoner to mr Lietch. I expect to set out for Bedford on the 8ᵗʰ of Nov. and shall make a considerable stay there. affectionately yours.   TH: JEFFERSON

PoC (MHi); on verso of reused address cover to TJ; two numbers rewritten by TJ for clarity; at foot of text: "Capᵗ Peyton"; endorsed by TJ.

TJ recorded drawing on Peyton for $217.29 in favor of Alexander GARRETT on 24 Oct. 1820. This payment covered a $50.67 balance of TJ's assumpsit for Peter Laporte and the Central College–University of Virginia subscription installments of Joel Yancey, John Rogers, and Hugh Holmes of $50, $50.62, and $60, respectively. TJ's 27 Oct. 1820 draft on Peyton in favor of JOHN WATSON for $72.76 paid for Youen Carden's order on TJ for $59.38, plus an additional $2 in interest, and TJ's store account of $11.38 (*MB*, 2:1370). E. GARLAND: Samuel Garland.

[1] Reworked from "20."
[2] Reworked from "6."

From Michele Raggi

Sig^R Jefferson Stimatissimo   New York 28. 8bre. 1820—

Si puol persuadere Sig^{re}, che se mi fosse stato bene spiegata la ricevutta che lei qui mi a rimesso copia nella pregiatissima sua letera, non avrei avutto coraggio di ricercare il giusto viaggio; lei ben sà che io non lego l'inglese; ℞ conseguenza quando il Sig^r Brochenbord scrisse la ricevutta, aciò io mi firmassi, lo pregai prima di metere il mio nome, che avrei desiderato mi fosse spiegata in Francese, come in fatti il Sud^{eto} Sig^r Brochenbord, mi diede la detta ricevutta con tutta garbateza, e M'indico anche da chi dovevo andare a Charlottesville, ed io non mancai di farlo, e quei Sig^{ri} che mi tradussero qusta ricevutta non mi interpetrorono come mie stata interpetrata qui dalla di lei copia cosi fù che messi il mio nome, e ℞ conseguenza io sono restato inganato, essendo ℞ ò lei un uomo giusto come non ne dubito credo non sarà possibile potrà condiscendere ad una cosa cosi ingiusta che non mi sia pagato il Viaggio almeno. Lei ben sà che son venuto in America ℞ servirlo, e lavorare nella mia professione in marmo, e che se il suo lavoro non e stato molto avanzato, e stata la sol colpa che non mi à procurato la materia che ci vuole ℞ fare li lavori di mia professione, e che la Pietra che à procurato, e stata al ordine d'incominciare, a, metermi in lavoro, dopo 7. Mesi che ero arivato, e cativa pietra; Lei sà bene che nel medesimo tenpo che atendevo la materia ℞ metermi in lavoro, e che stavo da un giorno al altro ad Aspetare, che spontaneamente mi messi a fare li dissegni dei Capitelli ℞ farli un avantaggio, e non ℞ mia obbligazione; giache non era mia ispezione essendo venutto io in America ℞ lavorare il marmo, e non ℞ disegnare, Essendo l'ispezione di fare li disegni di una fabrica del Architetto ò Diretore, ℞ conseguenza in giustizia mi dovrebbe pagare anche li disegni ed io non ci avevo cercato niente, ma giache vedo che mi viene negato il dovuto mi Viaggio, mi pagherà duecento Pezi di Spagna ℞ li dissegni che questi me li rimeterà in Livorno a Posta corente giache ò dovuto pigliare del denaro inprestito da dei miei patrioti, che dovrò ristituire ai loro parenti arivato in Italia. Lei ben sà che sono venuto in America Con molte promesse del Sig^r Appleton, cioè che mi avrebero fatto venire Mia meglie a spese loro ℞ il viaggio, e non di doverlo pagare io, e che io sarei stato arivato in America lei mi avrebbe acresciuta la mia penssione, e come dovevo esser tratatto, che passerò soto silenzio la maniera che ero nurito giache lei e stato male informato sù di ciò, e se l'altro Raggi non a lasciato il suo inpiego le sue circostanze non lo ℞ metevano, e poi la questione non, e di fare dei paragoni che non ciè la convenienza; Io devo solo da lei dirigermi, e cercare giustizia, e non da Altri essendo venuto in America ℞ lei, e senza il di lei nome non sarei venuto, la scusi dunque o signore se non mi dirigo al suo diretore. Lei sa ancora che io in America non ò guadagnato in alcun modo, e che il solo mio scopo era ♑ servir lei e che non o cercato di fare nesun altro comercio, e ♑ ciò mi prendi in considerazione e cerchi di protegere la giustizia di rimetermi in Livorno duecento doleri al piu presto che io partiro domani ♑ Gibiltera ♑ poi andare in Livorno dove atendero con ansieta un suo avantagioso riscontro che potrà dirigere al Sig^r Appleton che da Esso riceverò il denaro e risposta che lei mi graziera ofrindole senpre li miei Servizi, e se volese fare qualche cosa in Marmo lei fà che sto in Italia e potra indirizarmi le letere in Livorno ♑ Carrara, che saro a servirlo in tutto quello che mi comanderà pregandolo la di lei protezione, e Mi Confermo di lei Sig^{ria}

Umo Devmo Servo   MICHELE RAGGI

MOST ESTEEMED MR. JEFFERSON   New York 28. October 1820—

You may rest assured, Sir, that if the receipt, a copy of which you sent me in your highly esteemed letter, had been fully explained to me, I would not have had the courage to request full payment for my voyage. As you well know, I cannot read the English language. Consequently, when Mr. Brockenbrough wrote out the receipt for me to sign, I asked him, before putting my name to it, to have it explained to me in French. In fact, the aforementioned Mr. Brockenbrough was very kind when he gave me the said receipt and even recommended to whom I should go in Charlottesville in order to get it translated, which I did not fail to do. Those gentlemen did not interpret the receipt in the same way as your copy has been explained to me here. This is how I came to sign it. I was, therefore, misled. I believe, however, that as an undoubtedly just man, it would be impossible for you to consent to such an injustice as failing to pay for my journey, at least. You know very well that I came to America to serve you and to practice my profession in marble, and that if your work is not very far advanced, it is only because you have not procured the material I needed to do my job. The stone you did obtain, furthermore, which was only ready for me to begin working seven months after my arrival, was bad. As you well know, while I was awaiting the material necessary for me to start working, I began, of my own accord, to make drawings of the capitals for your benefit, and not because it was part of my job. Since this was not my responsibility, I having come to America to work in marble, not to draw, and the latter being the responsibility of either an architect or the proctor, you should also, in all fairness, pay me for the drawings. I would have asked nothing for them, but as I am being denied the travel money due me, I ask that you pay me two hundred Spanish pesos for them and send this amount by the return of the post, because I had to borrow money from my compatriots and must repay it to their relations once I arrive in Italy. You know very well that I came to America with many promises from Mr. Appleton: that my wife was to travel here at your expense so that I would not have to pay for her trip, that on my arrival in America you would increase my salary, and that I should and would be well-treated. I will keep silent about how I was fed, as you were poorly informed of this, and if the other Raggi has not left his position, it is because circumstances prevented him from doing so. This is no time for inapt comparisons. I must turn for justice to you, not others, as I came to America because of you. If not for your reputation, I would not have come. For this reason, Sir, please excuse me if I choose not to deal with your proctor. You know that I did not profit in any way by coming to America, that my sole purpose was to serve you, and that I did business with no one else. Please consider my case, therefore, and safeguard justice by sending two hundred dollars to Leghorn as soon as possible. I depart tomorrow for Leghorn by way of Gibraltar and will anxiously await your favorable answer, which you may send through Mr. Appleton. I will receive the money and the answer with which you favor me from him. I am always at your service and, if you want something done in marble, know that I am in Italy, that you may send your letters to Carrara via Leghorn, and that I will be ready to serve you in any way you wish. Begging for your protection, I affirm that I am your lordship's

Very humble and devoted servant   MICHELE RAGGI

RC (DLC); addressed: "Mʳ Tomas Jefferson monticello Charlottesville Virginia"; franked; postmarked New York, 30 Oct.; endorsed by TJ as received 5 Nov. 1820 and so recorded in SJL. Translation by Dr. Jonathan T. Hine.

To Joel Yancey, with Jefferson's Note

DEAR SIR   Monticello Oct. 28. 20.

In my letter of the 14ᵗʰ I mentioned the circumstance of the illness of my horses which was likely to delay my visit to Poplar Forest. three of them are nearly well and the others begin to mend. I hope we may by high feeding get them able to take the road in 12. or 14. days, and I shall do it the moment they seem able. my hope is to set out about the 8ᵗʰ of Nov. the advance of the cold weather will prevent my daughter from going.   John Hemings and his gang will go about the same time. as the season will be getting cold so fast as to require us to[1] do every thing we can to hasten repairing the roof of the house, I must pray you to have 500 or 1000. chesnut shingles got and ready drawn for it. they must be of the [le]ngth of those we used before, & are not to be rounded. I presume you can get some workman there to do it immediately. [I][2] salute you with affectionate friendship & respect.   TH: JEFFERSON

[Note by TJ at foot of text:]
added P.S. for the harpsichord strings

PoC (MHi); on verso of a reused address cover from John Adams to TJ; mutilated at seal; adjacent to signature: "Mʳ Yancey"; endorsed by TJ.

[1] Preceding three words interlined.
[2] Word faint.

From Nathaniel Bowditch

SIR   Salem Octr. 30 1820

I have forwarded a few papers just printed in the 4th Vol. of the Memoirs of the Academy, with the request that you would do me the honor to accept them

It gives me great pleasure to hear that your health is better than it was a few months since & I pray that it may long continue so.

With great respect & Esteem I remain Sir, your obedient & humb ser[t]   NATH[L] BOWDITCH

RC (MHi); endorsed by TJ as received 28 Nov. 1820 and so recorded in SJL. RC: left half of address cover only (MHi), with Dft of TJ to Bernard Peyton, 25 May 1822, on verso; right half of address cover only (MHi), with Dft of TJ to Archibald Robertson, 25 May 1822, on verso; addressed: "The Honorable Thomas Jefferson late President of the United States Monticello"; franked; postmarked Salem, 1 Nov.

The second part of the 4TH VOL. of the *Memoirs* of the American Academy of Arts and Sciences (1818–20) contained five articles contributed by Bowditch: "On the Meteor which passed over Wilmington in the state of Delaware, Nov. 21, 1819" (pp. 295–305); "Occultation of Spica by the Moon, observed at Salem" (p. 306); "On a mistake which exists in the calculation of Mr. Poisson relative to the distribution of the electrical matter upon the surfaces of two globes: in vol. 12 of the 'Mémoires de la classe des sciences mathématiques et physiques de l'Institut Impérial de France'" (pp. 307–8); "On the Orbit of the Comet of 1819. By Alexander M. Fisher . . . Communicated in a letter to the Hon. Nathaniel Bowditch" (pp. 309–16); and "Elements of the Comet of 1819" (pp. 317–8).

From John H. Rice

Richmond 30th Octr 1820

Allow me, Sir, to offer thro' you to the Library of the University of Virginia, a copy of the new edition of Smith's History. It is a small donation, indeed, but a token of deep interest felt by the donor in the prosperity of that institution. May it become an honour and a blessing to our native state, and a model for the literary establishments of others.

Pardon me, a stranger, for adding my most earnest wishes that the last period of your life may be as distinguished for tranquility & happiness, as the former part has been for honourable activity in the service of our country.

With much respect I am &[c]   JOHN H. RICE

RC (CSmH: JF); endorsed by TJ as received 26 Dec. 1820 and so recorded in SJL. RC (DLC); address cover only; with PoC of TJ to John H. Cocke, 9 Apr. 1821, on verso; addressed: "Thomas Jefferson Esqr. Montecello" by "D[r] Carr."

The NEW EDITION was John Smith, *The Trve Travels, Adventvres and Obser-vations of Captaine Iohn Smith, in Eu-rope, Asia, Africke, and America*, 2 vols. (Richmond, 1819), the second volume of which contained *The Generall Historie of Virginia, New-England, and the Summer Iles*. The copy sent to TJ is in ViU.

From Francis Eppes

DR GRAND-PAPA   Columbia Oct^{br} 31st—20

I waited untill this time (before writing) that I might be able to give a more satisfactory, and circumstantial account, of the course and regulations of this institution, which are pretty nearly the same as those of the northern colleges, differing only in two points. in the first place the course here is neither as full nor as comprehensive a one as that of Cambridge, secondly the discipline is more lax and consequently better adapted, to the feelings & habits of the Southern Students. this latter circumstance too is somewhat surprising as the Faculty themselves (with the exception of Dr Cooper) are Clergy-men. the objection too to their course is obviated by the consideration of a college library the free use of which is permitted to the Students. they have four classes and to the Studies of each one year is allotted, so that the Lowest takes four years to graduate; in it Græca Minora, virgils Æneid, & Arithmetic are the studies, those of the next in grade are, the 1st part of the 1st vol. of Græca majora, Horace, Algebra as far as cubick equations, Geography. &^c. those of the Junior are Blairs <u>Lectures</u>, Watts^s Logick, Kames^s elements of Criticism, Paleys moral Philosophy, <u>cubick</u> equations, <u>Geometry</u>, <u>Trigonometry</u> &^c. Hutton alone is used, his demonstrations are much shorter than Simpsons. the Senior year <u>Logarithms</u>, conick sections & Fluxions, Cavallo's Natural Philosophy Butlers Analogy of Religion, Chemistry.[1] no one is allowed the privilege of entering as student, without pursuing this course, unless he does under the Title of Honorary, which besides being an unusual is moreover a disadvantageous standing. I have therefore entered as a regular student, and am a candidate for the Junior class, whose examination comes on in two weeks. after it is over I will write again & perhaps may be enabled then, to give you more Satisfactory information concerning the elections of a President & Professor of Mathematics. the only objection to Elliot who is talked of as President is his not being a minister of the Gospel, this too is urged as a very weighty one. Wallace whose merits you are better informed of than I, and who was formerly a Professor in the George-town College, is a candidate for the Mathematical chair, it is said however that Judge De Saussure, one of the Trustees and a man of great influence is opposed to him. what the result of these conjectures may be, it is impossible for me to say, I can only add that I hope they will terminate in the election of those whose abilities may confer a lasting advantage and prosperity on this institution. D[r] Cooper is very much beloved by the Students here and is in fact one of the most popular Professors that they have ever had. I find that this place is very healthy, a young man from the neighbourhood of Poplar-Forest, (who is the only Virginian in college except myself) stayed here the whole summer without experiencing the slightest inconvenience. Wayles has not arrived though I expect him daily. present me affectionately to Aunt Randolph and Family, I often think of the happy moments spent in your Society the happiest perhaps of my Life.

I remain Your affectionate Grandson   FR: EPPES.

RC (MHi); endorsed by TJ as received 28 Nov. 1820 and so recorded in SJL.

The college at CAMBRIDGE was Harvard University. GRÆCA MINORA and GRÆCA MAJORA: Andrew Dalzel, Ἀνάλεκτα Ἑλληνικὰ Ἥσσονα. sive Collectanea Græca Minora (1st American ed., Cambridge, Mass., 1804), and his Ἀνάλεκτα Ἑλληνικὰ Μείζονα sive Collectanea Græca

Majora, 2 vols. (1st American ed., Cambridge, Mass., 1808). WAYLES: John Wayles Baker.

[1] In margin adjacent to preceding section, TJ inserted the numbers 1 through 4 to delineate the subjects taught in each of the four years of instruction at South Carolina College (later the University of South Carolina).

From Thomas W. Maury

DEAR SIR.   Charlottesville 31st October. 1820

My relation William Maury of Liverpool will be here in a few days[1] on his way (thro the States of Kentucky, Tennessee, Alabama & Mississippi) to New-Orleans. I have lately received a letter from him, in which he requested me to ask the favor of you to give him letters to a few of the distinguished men in those states. Should you find it convenient to do so, be good enough to send the letters to me, to the care of M[r] James Leitch of this place.

respectfully y[r] mo: ob[t]   TH: W. MAURY

RC (DLC); endorsed by TJ as received 1 Nov. 1820 and so recorded in SJL.

[1] Preceding four words interlined.

From Thomas Appleton

Leghorn 2nd November 1820—

The tranquility of Sicily is restored, by the Surrender of Palermo to the neapolitan arms; the low populace have been disarm'd, & the factious leaders have been Sent to Naples.—The attitude of the Kingdom of Naples, is imposing in the highest degree—the Capital has a well-organiz'd national guard of 30,000—men, commanded by tried & experienc'd officers—the provinces are guarded by two or three hundred thousand guarillos, Similar to those of Spain during the invasion of the french; while an army of 120,000—regulars guard the frontiers.—the government progress with persevering dignity & energy, while the innumerable defiles, present infinite obstacles to a foreign invasion. Should the Emp^r of Austria, who discovers great irritation, put his foot on the roman territory, it will be as certainly invaded by the Neapolitans, who have declared to His Holiness, they shall not respect it any longer, than it is respected by the Emperor of Austria; and the enthousiasm of the Romans, is in no wise inferior to the Neapolitans: indeed, they have already discover'd the greatest impatience of the Slavery they now endure.—In a very recent reply of the Neapolitans, to the notes of the Emp^r to the German States, it appears, that King Murat had been prevented giving a constitution to his Subjects, by[1] the Emperor of Austria; and that in the tour of the latter, the last year, through Italy, he drew from all the Sovereigns of Italy, a promise, that they should not give constitutions, of any description, to the Subjects of their Several States.—The great question, which now occupies all Italy is: will the Emperor confine his views, Solely to the preservation of his italian States; or will he invade the neapolitan territory, in the hope of destroying the free government they have adopted? the opinion of all judicious men is, that he will adopt the former, knowing as they well do, the infinite obstacles to accomplish the latter, guarded by innumerable defiles in all the avenues, and by a million of determin'd men.—but, Sir, in giving you the opinion of the most judicious, it is no other, than the path, he ought to pursue, for the preservation of what he now holds; experience, however, teaches us, that implicit reliance should not be plac'd on Sovereigns adopting the wisest measures; and many, among the best inform'd, of the numerous obstacles to his Success in Offensive warfare, yet reflecting on the passion and irritation of the austrian cabinet, from the moment they learnt the revolution of Naples; and the ardent wish the Emperor discover'd, when last in Italy, to form a confederacy, of which, he propos'd himself, as chief & in which he was frustrated; these considerations may induce him, to hearken rather to the fallacious Suggestions of agrandizing his power in Italy, than to the wise result of calm deliberation.—in short, Sir, should he adopt offensive measures, he will, by a strange fatality, act in perfect conformity, to what he would be advis'd, were his council compos'd of the most liberal and patriotic italians, who wish the establishment of liberal constitutions, throughout the whole extent of Italy.   24 Nov^{r2} 1820.—I left my letter open to this day, & to the moment of departure of the vessel, to add, if possible, some conclusive acts of the assembly of the Sovereigns at Tropaw, in relation to Italy; but to the present time, they are envellop'd in mystery & obscurity—no event has, hitherto, occurr'd, which can throw any light, on their future[3] purposes; nor any one in Naples, to diminish the hopes and expectations of good men.—Accept, Sir, the renewal of

my invariable respect & esteem   Th: Appleton

inclos'd is a duplicate rec^t of mad: Pini—

RC (DLC); subjoined to Dupl of Appleton to TJ, 10 Oct. 1820; endorsed by TJ as a letter of "Nov. 2. & 24. 20" received 15 Apr. 1821 and so recorded in SJL. RC (MHi); address cover only; with PoC of TJ to Bernard Peyton, 6 July 1821, on verso; addressed: "For Thomas Jefferson, esq—Monticello—Virginia U: S. America"; stamped "SHIP"; franked; postmarked New York, 10 Apr. FC (Lb in DNA: RG 84, CRL); in Appleton's hand; at head of text: "The following was written with the duplicate of my letter of 10th Octr 1820"; at foot of text: "Sent by Eliza Ann. Golden for N-York & inclos'd duplicate rec^t of mad: Pini." Enclosure: Dupl of enclosure to Appleton to TJ, 10 Oct. 1820.

GUARILLOS: "guerrillas." HIS HOLINESS was Pope Pius VII. The ITALIAN STATES under Austrian control at this time were the northern provinces of Lombardy and Venetia.

Delegations led by Emperor Francis I of Austria, Emperor Alexander I of Rus-

sia, and the crown prince of Prussia (subsequently King Frederick William IV) met at Troppau (TROPAW) (later Opava, Czech Republic) in the autumn of 1820 to discuss the revolution in Bourbon-ruled southern Italy. The resulting Troppau Protocol declared that states whose governments or constitutions had been changed significantly as a result of revolutionary upheaval ceased to be members of the alliance. If they posed a threat, either directly or indirectly, to their neighbors, then the allies bound themselves to use all means, including force, to restore the old order (Paul W. Schroeder, *Metternich's Diplomacy at Its Zenith, 1820–1823* [1962], 60, 80–1).

[1] FC: "through the intervention of."
[2] Remainder of text in FC reads "I added in Substance, that no event had to that time occur'd to give any clearer view of the purposes of the Emp^r nor any in Naples to lessen the hopes & expectations of all good men—I am &^{c} T.A."
[3] Word interlined.

Isaac Briggs's Account of
a Visit to Monticello

My dear Wife
and children,   Richmond Vᵃ 11 mo. 21. 1820.

In my last letter to you, dated on the 7, I brought down to my arrival at Monticello the narative of the incidents of my journey. I will now continue the subject.

11 mo. 2—fifth day of the week, I reached Monticello about 4 o'clock afternoon. On entering the great hall I saw sitting just within the door a stranger; supposing him to be a member of the family, I asked him, "Is Thomas Jefferson at home?" he answered, "I believe he is—I am a stranger, on my way to the southward, and have called on purpose to see him—I have no one to introduce me—are you acquainted with him?"—I am—thou wilt not find him difficult of access, said I; for the man seemed under considerable embarrassment. I enquired if he had announced his being in waiting. He said he had, and in a few minutes the dear, venerable old man entered the hall. I instantly met him, took his offered hand and with warmth of feeling said, "my friend Jefferson! how art thou?" with equal cordiality he returned my salute; and then turning to the stranger saluted him, and asked us both to walk in and take a glass of wine with him. We followed him into the dining room, where were seated about a table his sister Marks, and three or four of his grand daughters, fine looking young women; Thomas Jefferson took his seat at the table, and placed me on his right hand and the stranger on his left; then turning to me, with a pleasant smile, he said—"Why, Mʳ Briggs, you have grown young again."

In a short time the stranger took his leave, saying that he had parted from his company on purpose to make his respects at Monticello, and must join them again that evening in Charlottesville. As soon as he had departed, Thomas Jefferson said, "Mʳ Briggs, who is that gentleman?" I answered, "I do not know—he is quite a stranger to me."—"I thought he came with you." "No; I found him in the hall, when I first arrived."

I told Thomas Jefferson I proposed to spend the next day with him and the day following to pursue my journey to Richmond, and that I wished to see the University of Virginia. He replied with quickness, "you <u>must</u> see it—I had intended to go there, the day after tomorrow, but it will be as well for me to go tomorrow, and you must ride with me."

In the course of the evening I communicated to him the remembrance of my wife and of my daughter Mary; he seemed highly gratified, and in an affectionate manner enquired after the health of my family particularly of Mary. I delivered to him Thomas Moore's message—"his Respects"—and that he had continually regretted, since it happened, that he did not visit him, when, in the course of his duties as Engineer in 1818, he passed within one mile of Monticello. "I blamed Mr Moore," said he—"Where is he now?"—At his home in Maryland.—"Is he well?"—He is well. About 8 o'clock, after a very friendly, social and agreeable evening so far, he rose from his seat and said to me, "I feel that I am an old man, and it is proper for me to retire early to bed, you will excuse me and choose your own time." I remained with his daughter and her daughters, the wife and daughters of Thomas M. Randolph, Governor of Virginia, till about 10 o'clock, when I retired for the night.

11 mo. 3—Sixth day of the week. This morning after breakfast, Thomas Jefferson and I rode to see the University of Virginia. It is situated about 4 miles from Monticello. The operations of tuition have not yet commenced, nor are the buildings finished, but the work is in active progress, and so far advanced, as to exhibit, to one acquainted with these things, a very good idea of the design, scope and probable fruits of the institution. It consists of three rows of buildings, each row a thousand feet long and having two fronts. The plan of it was furnished by Thomas Jefferson—it is going on, under his special superintendence and direction—it occupies a great portion of his time; his personal attendance is frequent and unremitted—it seems to be his favorite employment and the solace of his declining years. His 77th year finds him strong, active and in full possession of a sound mind. He rides a <u>trotting</u> horse and sits on him <u>as straight as a young man</u>. Compared with him, Madison, although ten years younger, looks like—a little old man. Returning to Monticello from the University of Virginia (which promises to be the greatest and most extensive establishment of the kind in the United States) we had much conversation. Among other political points, that which has been called the Missouri-question stood prominent. He said that nothing had happend since the revolution, which gave him so much anxiety and so many disquieting fears for the safety and happiness of his country. "I fear," said he, "that much mischief has been done already—but if they carry matters to extremities again at the approaching session of Congress, nothing short of Almighty power can save us. The Union will be broken. All the horrors of civil wars, embittered by local jealousies and mutual recriminations, will ensue. Bloodshed, rapine and

cruelty, will soon roam at large, will desolate our once happy land and turn the fruitful field into a howling wilderness. Out of such a state of things will naturally grow a war of extermination toward the African in our land. Instead of improving the condition of this poor, afflicted, degraded race, terminating, in the ordering of wisdom, in equal liberty and the enjoyment of equal rights (in which direction public opinion is advancing with rapid strides) the course pursued, by those who make high professions of humanity and of friendship for them, would involve them as well as us in certain destruction. I believe there are many, very many, who are quite honest in their humane views and feelings toward this people, lending their efforts, with an amiable but misguided zeal, to those leaders—those master-spirits, who raise the whirlwind and direct the storm,—who are not honest, who wear humanity as a mask, whose aim is power, and who 'would wade through slaughter to a throne and shut the gates of mercy on mankind.'"[1] "I have considered the United States as owing to the world an example, and that this is their solemn duty—a steady, peaceful example of morality and happiness in society at large, of moderation and wisdom in government, and of civil and religious liberty—an example, which, by its mild and steady light, would be far more powerful than the sword, in correcting abuses—in teaching mankind that they can, if they will, govern themselves, and in relieving them from the oppressions of king-craft and priestcraft. But if our Union be broken, this duty will be sacrificed—this bright example will be lost—it will be worse than lost. The predictions of our enemies will be fulfilled, in the estimation of the world, that we were not wise enough for self government. It would be said that the fullest and fairest experiment had been made—and had failed; and the chains of despotism would be rivetted more firmly than ever." This is the substance; I do not pretend to recollect, exactly, although I believe very nearly, his words, for his manner was impressive. I told him, my anxiety had also been very great, on the same subject, and very much in the same way.

On another point, he enquired—"Mr Briggs, did Congress ever allow you compensation for exploring and locating a Post road from Washington to New Orleans?"—No; the utmost they could be brought to do, was to balance my accounts.—"Did they not avail the public of your labors—did they not use the road?"—O yes, they adopted the road, and it is still used, nearly as I reported it.—"Well, I think, the refusal to compensate you for that service, is one of the most disgraceful things Congress have ever done."

After our return to Monticello, he left me in the hall, or drawing room, for a few minutes, and went into another room. Coming to me again, with something in his hand, he said, "Will your daughter, Mary, accept of this as a memorial of me?"—I replied, "She will most thankfully. Thou hast not, in the world, a more enthusiastic admirer than she is."

A company of visitors, male and female, collected in the drawing room, before dinner. My friend Jefferson introduced me to each one, in the manner following—"Mr Briggs, the Engineer, who is to shew us how to navigate across the mountains."

After dinner the company departed, and I spent the afternoon and evening in the delightful society of Thomas Jefferson, his sister ____ Marks, his daughter Martha Randolph, her daughters, Ellen, Cornelia, Virginia, Mary, and Septimia, & Browse Trist, the son of a former acquaintance of mine in New Orleans. Thomas Jefferson, as usual, retired about 8; and I continued until 10, chatting with Martha Randolph and her highly polished and highly instructed daughters. It seems to be a matter of equal facility with them to write or converse, in French, Spanish, Italian, or their mother tongue.

11 mo. 4—Seventh day of the week. After breakfast, I asked for my horse, and for a description of the road to Richmond. Thomas Jefferson rose to take leave of me, and, in a manne[r] which left no doubt of sincerity, said—"I am sorry you cannot stay with us another day." I had like to have forgotten to mention, that, in conversation last evening, Thomas Jefferson, recounting over past events, dwelt with apparent satisfaction on his intimate acquaintance with Thomas Pleasants of Goochland.—This was uncle Thomas Pleasants, cousin Deborah Stabler's father. About 9 o'clock, I departed from Monticello; after sunset, I arrived at Hayden's 35 miles; and the next evening (11 mo 5—first day) in Richmond 45 miles more. From Monticello to Richmond, 80 miles.

RC (MdHi: Briggs-Stabler Papers); extract, consisting of opening two-and-a-half pages of letter; mutilated; signed "Isaac Briggs" on last page; addressed: "Hannah Briggs, Sharon, near Sandy Spring, Maryland"; stamped; postmarked Richmond, 22 Nov.; endorsed in two unidentified hands. The unextracted conclusion to this letter is a note to his daughter Mary Briggs in which the elder Briggs complains of her delay in posting her most recent letter to him; notes that a promised letter from an acquaintance had not accompanied it; hopes for the full recovery of another correspondent; expresses amusement at his daughter's "philosophical disquisition on the question, whether curiosity be a male or female fault, exclusively one or the other—or whether it be common to both sexes—or if it be more commonly found in one sex than in the other, which has the larger share—to which I will add a fourth branch, whether it be a fault at all, if confined within reasonable limits"; informs her, so as to assuage her own curiosity, that the present from TJ "is his portrait, of small size, but an excellent likeness"; professes his love "to every branch of the family"; and asks that she write him punctually.

In his LAST LETTER to his wife and their children, dated Richmond, 7 Nov. 1820, Briggs described his visit more succinctly: "11 mo. 2—Fifth day of the week. This morning after breakfast, I left Montpelier and in the evening, about 4 o'clock, I arrived at Monticello, 28 miles— and (the way I came) 150 miles from Sharon. I found my dear, and venerable friend Thomas Jefferson in fine health. He expressed much pleasure in seeing me. I staid here on 5ᵗʰ day night, all sixth day, and seventh day morning till after breakfast, and when about to depart he expressed his sorrow that I could not stay longer. But my time at Monticello, was so very interesting that I cannot do justice to it, in this letter, I must reserve it for another. I am in possession of a present, from Thomas Jefferson to my Mary, but I cannot trust it to any messenger but myself; she must therefore wait till she sees me. In the mean time, she must guard herself against idolizing, even this good old man" (RC in MdHi: Briggs-Stabler Papers).

At the time of Briggs's visit, work had not yet commenced on the West Range, the fourth and last of the ROWS OF BUILD-INGS that TJ designed for the University of Virginia. WADE THROUGH SLAUGH-TER TO A THRONE AND SHUT THE GATES OF MERCY ON MANKIND quotes Thomas

Gray's "Elegy Written in a Country Churchyard," lines 67–8 (Roger Lonsdale, ed., *The Poems of Thomas Gray, William Collins, Oliver Goldsmith* [1969], 129–30). HAYDEN'S: "Haden's."

In 1822 Briggs evidently visited Monticello again. He wrote his wife, Hannah Briggs, from Richmond on 9 July of that year that he had been urged "to take a trip to the mountains for a week or two. Governor Randolph strongly and affectionately presses me to make a visit, for 8 or 10 days, to Monticello—he says the mountain air would be of great service to me, and that the old gentleman (meaning Thomas Jefferson) would be delighted to see me. I have consented to yield to this advice, and to accept this invitation. I propose to leave Richmond for Monticello on tomorrow-week, the 17ᵗʰ and to return here about the end of the month." Briggs added that while he was at Monticello a letter could be sent to him postage free under cover of one addressed to TJ (RC in MdHi: Briggs-Stabler Papers).

[1] Double quotation marks editorially altered to single, followed by editorially supplied closing double quotation mark.

From Bernard Peyton

DEAR SIR   Rich'd 2ᵈ Novʳ 1820

Your esteemed favor 28ᵗʰ ulto: did not[1] reach me until this morning—

When the additional drafts you speak of having drawn on me appear, they shall be honored, as have all that have yet been presented.

The first Boat for Milton shall carry you the Oil written for in Jugs—Casks never failing to leak with Oil for the first five or six months, however tight they may be made: The Bolting Cloth I have had selected of excellent quality by the Flour Inspector of this city, of the numbers you[2] directed, & will either forward it to Charlottesville care Mʳ Leitch, or will get the favor of Mʳ T. E. Randolph now in this City to take it up, of which you shall be advised.

I had a letter this morning from Genˡ H. A. S. Dearbourn of Boston in which he desires me to say to you that he has Mʳ Stewarts promise to deliver him your picture in ten days to be forwarded, & if he does not receive it in that time, he will continue to importune him unceasingly until he does procure it, which done, he will send it on to you as soon as possible—

I procured from Mr Marx a bill of exchange on London for £40 in favor R. Rush Esq^e at par; the first of which was ford^d several days ago in your letter to him[3] by the Virginia, & the duplicate shall go by the next vessel, which will be in a few days, all of which I hope is satisfactory—

Yours very Truely   B. Peyton

RC (MHi); endorsed by TJ as received 4 Nov. 1820 and so recorded in SJL. RC (MHi); address cover only; with PoC of TJ to David Hosack, 20 Apr. 1821, on verso; addressed: "Mr Thomas Jefferson Monticello near Charlottesville"; franked; postmarked Richmond, 2 Nov.

M^R stewarts: Gilbert Stuart's.

[1] Word added in margin.
[2] Manuscript: "your."
[3] Preceding five words interlined.

From James Publius

Respected Sir   Columbia So— Ca— Nov 2th 1820

A youth now addresses you, who has experienced the severest misfortunes—Not yet twenty years of age, turned on the wide world for support and protection, to whom shall I look, but to Jefferson. Do not beleive for a moment that any of the dissipations of youth are the causes of my misfortune—nor is it ill directed ambition to which man so often falls a prey—The causes of my misfortune's were beyond human foresight, and consequently could not be guarded against—I am now placed in such a situation that it is impossible for me to pursue my literary pursuits without your aid—I only ask from you $100— And for God sake grant my request or I am ruined. Remember that youthful ambition is easily damped, and also remember that when once the flame is outed it is hard to rekindle. Write me immediatly and for god sake refuse me not.   James Publius—

RC (MHi); at foot of text: "Columbia South Carolina"; endorsed by TJ as received 21 Nov. 1820 and so recorded in SJL.

From Archibald Robertson

DEAR SIR   Lynchburg 2ⁿᵈ Novʳ 1820

Allow me to introduce to your acquaintance the bearer Mr Read who expects to pass through your neighbourhood: any attention shewn him will oblige

Your Mo ob Sᵗ   A. ROBERTSON

RC (MHi); addressed: "Thomas Jefferson Esqʳ Monticello" by "Mr Read"; endorsed by TJ as received 7 Nov. 1820 and so recorded (with additional notation: "by mr Reed") in SJL.

Landon Cabell Read (b. 1803), merchant, was a native of Charlotte County. In the autumn of 1820 he visited Natural Bridge, Monticello, and Montpellier on a tour with his family tutor, Nathaniel Helme. In 1831 Read was a partner in a Richmond commission business, and from 1833 until at least 1839 he partnered with Pierce Bayly in a dry-goods firm.

He was still in Richmond in 1843 (Alice Read, *The Reads and Their Relatives* [1930], 296, 304–5; Madison, *Papers, Retirement Ser.*, 2:139; Helme's Account of a Visit to Monticello, [7 Nov. 1820]; canceled bond of 15 Mar. 1831 from Read to an unidentified recipient [ViHi: Hannah Family Papers]; *Richmond Enquirer*, 30 Sept. 1831, 19 Feb. 1835, 21 Sept. 1838; *Daily Richmond Whig & Public Advertiser*, 27 Dec. 1833; Read to John Sims, 9 July 1839 [ViHi: Bailey Family Papers]; *Manual for the members of the First Presbyterian Church, in Richmond, Va.* [1843], 12).

To John Brown (1757–1837)

DEAR SIR   Monticello Nov. 3. 20.

The son of the only class-mate I now have living proposes to visit your state, and naturally wishes to be made known to it's principal worthies. his father mr James Maury & myself were boys together at the school of the grandfather in this neighborhood.   with the present gentleman I am not personally acquainted; but all who are, speak well of him. and I think nothing, not good, could have come from such a father. shew him then, my friend, such civilities as shall be not inconvenient to you, and make him sensible that my recommendation is not a matter of indifference with you. that you may have health, happiness & long life are the prayers of your affectionate friend.

                                                      TH: JEFFERSON

PoC (MHi); on verso of reused address cover of William Sampson to TJ, 10 June 1819; at foot of text: "John Brown esq."; endorsed by TJ. Enclosed in TJ to William Maury, 3 Nov. 1820.

John Brown (1757–1837), attorney and public official, was born in Staunton and attended his father's school, which would

later become Liberty Hall Academy (and eventually Washington and Lee University). He enrolled at the College of New Jersey (later Princeton University), probably shortly before classes were suspended late in 1776 due to the American Revolution, during which Brown evidently served as an army private. He continued his education at the College of William and

Mary, 1778–80, studied law under George Wythe, and spent time in Albemarle County with access to TJ's library. In about 1783 Brown moved to Kentucky and practiced law, first in Danville and then in Frankfort. He represented the Kentucky district in the Senate of Virginia, 1784–88, and in the Confederation Congress, 1787–88, and he supported the new federal constitution. As a leading proponent both of Kentucky statehood and of the free navigation of the Mississippi River, Brown conferred in 1788 with Diego de Gardoqui, the Spanish chargé d'affaires, in discussions that drew criticism and accusations of trying to separate Kentucky from the United States in an alleged "Spanish Conspiracy." Nevertheless, Brown was elected from Virginia to the United States Congress, 1789–92, and he represented the new state of Kentucky in the United States Senate, 1792–1805, allying himself with TJ and James Madison and serving as president pro tempore, 1803–04. Losing his bid for a third term, Brown returned permanently to Liberty Hall, his home in Frankfort, where he again practiced law, entertained Aaron Burr when the latter visited the city in 1805, and served as a director of the Bank of Kentucky (*ANB*; *DAB*; *Princetonians, 1776–1783*, pp. 217–23; *William and Mary Provisional List*, 9; Leonard, *General Assembly*; *PTJ*, esp. 13:211–3, 19:xxxiii–xxxiv, 469–74; *Doc. Hist. Ratification*, 10:1579–80, 16:404; Washington *Globe*, 9 Sept. 1837).

To Samuel Brown

DEAR SIR   Monticello Nov. 3. 20.

The bearer of this is the son of mr James Maury an antient class-mate of mine, & the only one now living. I am not personally acquainted with this gentleman; but I love the father, and cannot be indifferent to the wishes of the son to be made known to the good of your state which he is about to visit. I commit him therefore to your kind attentions & good offices, and, from what all say of him, I am sure you will find them not misplaced. I am gratified in this act by the double consideration of serving one friend, and indulging recollections of another, to whom, with wishes for every blessing of health life & prosperity I present my affectionate and respectful salutations.

TH: JEFFERSON

RC (ViU: TJP); addressed: "Doct^r Samuel Brown Kentucky." PoC (DLC); on verso of reused address cover of John Barnes to TJ, 2 June 1819; mistakenly endorsed by TJ as a letter of 4 Nov. 1820, but correctly recorded in SJL. Enclosed in TJ to William Maury, 3 Nov. 1820.

To William Maury

DEAR SIR   Monticello Nov. 3. 20.

Mr Thos W. Maury informs me you are about visiting Kentucky, and wish to be made known to some of the characters of worth in that state. I do myself the pleasure therefore of inclosing you letters to two friends of antient date, to whom I am sure my recommendations will not be indifferent. I have formerly known, but less intimately, some other gentlemen of that state, while in public life. but long retired from that, I know not now who of them are living, or who removed to other states.

I sincerely regretted my accidental absence when you did me the favor to call at the Poplar Forest. I should have been much gratified in an opportunity of expressing to you, in person, the affectionate friendship I retain for your father, and the pleasure I recieve from every occasion [of] manifesting it to him, or his. I endeavored to repair my loss by sending to Lynchburg an invitation for a repetition of your visit, but you had left the place. I expect to set out for that neighborhood on Wednesday next, and if you should recieve this before that time, I hope you will do me the favor of a visit to Monticello: and in every event be assured of my great & friendly esteem & respect.

TH: JEFFERSON

PoC (DLC); on verso of reused address cover of William Eustis to TJ, 24 May 1819; torn at seal; at foot of text: "Mr Maury"; mistakenly endorsed by TJ as a letter of 4 Nov. 1820, but correctly recorded in SJL. Enclosures: (1) TJ to John Brown (1757–1837), 3 Nov. 1820. (2) TJ to Samuel Brown, 3 Nov. 1820.

To Henry Guegan

SIR   Monticello Nov. 4. 20.

The box of books came to hand yesterday, safely and in good order, and I shall immediately write to Capt Bernard Peyton, my correspondent in Richmond, to remit you the sum of 43 D–50 C, as in this inland situation we have no course of Exchange but thro' Richmond. I was gratified by the Catalogue of classical books, as it makes known to me some editions which I had not before known of. I presume you have no more of it than stated in your printed catalogue. I find the Patres Graeci & Romani to contain but a part of the Corpus patrum, and too dear for the present difficult times. I salute you with esteem & respect.

TH: JEFFERSON

PoC (MHi); on verso of reused address cover to TJ; at foot of text: "Mr Henry Guegan"; endorsed by TJ. Mistakenly recorded in SJL as a letter of 3 Nov. 1820.

To Jared Sparks

SIR   Monticello Nov. 4. 20.

Your favor of Sep. 18. is just recieved, with the book accompanying it. it's delay was owing to that of the box of books from mr Guegan, in which it was packed. being just setting out on a journey I have time only to look over the summary of contents. in this I see nothing in which I am likely to differ materially from you. I hold the precepts of Jesus, as delivered by himself, to be the most pure, benevolent, and sublime which have ever been preached to man. I adhere to the principles of the first age; and consider all subsequent innovations as corruptions of his religion, having no foundation in what came from him. the metaphisical insanities of Athanasius, of Loyola, & of Calvin, are to my understanding, mere relapses into polytheism, differing from paganism only by being more unintelligible.[1] the religion of Jesus is founded on the Unity of God, and this principle chiefly, gave it triumph over the rabble of heathen gods then acknoleged. thinking men of all nations rallied readily to the doctrine of one only god, and embraced it with the pure morals which Jesus inculcated. if the freedom of religion, guaranteed to us by law <u>in theory</u>, can ever rise <u>in practice</u> under the overbearing inquisition of public opinion, truth will prevail over fanaticism, and the genuine doctrines of Jesus, so long perverted by his pseudo-priests, will again be restored to their original purity. this reformation will advance with the other improvements of the human mind but too late for me to witness it.   Accept my thanks for your book, in which I shall read with pleasure your developements of the subject, and with them the assurance of my high respect.

TH: JEFFERSON

RC (MH); addressed: "The rev^d Jared Sparks Baltimore"; franked; postmarked Charlottesville, 7 Nov.; endorsed by Sparks. PoC (DLC). Mistakenly recorded in SJL as a letter of 3 Nov. 1820.

[1] Manuscript: "unintelligble."

From Thomas G. Watkins

DEAR SIR,   Glenmore Novr 5. 1820.

I have made this year a small experiment of the probable advantage of raising the mangel Wurtzel of the germans in our part of the country—It is the Disette of the French—scarcity root of the English—Beta altissima of Botanists. Those I send you are not quite the largest I have—one with the leaves weighed 10¾ ℔s without—8 ℔s—I intend to report my experiment to the agricultural society with much exactness as to facts and calculation, & think I shall shew that few articles more valuable for stock &^{c} can be raised among us—if you think it worth while, the largest four sent you, can be buried in a hole under a conical top like turnips, & preserved to bear seed next spring.[1] they shou'd be carefully set far away from the common beet, as they wou'd most probably amalgamate with these—The smaller ones sent I shou'd be thankful if the ladies at Monticello, wou'd give a fair trial, as to their esculent qualities—they may require more boiling than the common beet, as they are of a stouter texture

I am with the greatest respect
& affect^n y^r Obd^t Servt T G WATKINS

RC (MHi); dateline at foot of text; addressed: "Mr Jefferson Monticello"; endorsed by TJ as a letter of 6 Nov. 1820 received the following day.

Watkins gave his REPORT on the cultivation of mangel-wurzel in a letter dated Glenmore, 11 Nov. 1820, addressed to Peter Minor, secretary of the Agricultural Society of Albemarle, and printed in the *American Farmer* 2 (1820): 300. The letter was read at the society's 7 May 1821 meeting (True, "Agricultural Society," 293).

[1] Omitted period at right margin editorially supplied.

From David Higginbotham

DEAR SIR.   Morven 6th Novr 1820.

I Shall have to Pay my Overser Mr Moon on the 15th In^t his Sallery for his last years Servises, if you can with any convenience Pay me by that time the am^t of your small note to me for corn as under I shall be very thankfull   I am your mo^t Obt[1]

DAVID HIGGINBOTHAM

Note due 20th Mar 1820 $150.90
In^t to 6th Novr 1820.   5.50
                         $156.40

RC (MHi); addressed: "Thomas Jefferson Esq Monticello"; endorsed by TJ as received 6 Nov. 1820 and so recorded in SJL. FC (Lb in ViU: Higginbotham Manuscripts); in Higginbotham's hand.

[1] Preceding two words not in FC.

To Constantine S. Rafinesque

SIR   Monticello Nov. 6.

Your favor of Oct. 18. was recieved yesterday. the three letters on Alleganian antiquities have not yet come to hand. for the 1st n° of your annals of nature I have still to thank you. they have not been before acknoleged because the inexorable laws of old age and ill health have withdrawn me from the labors of the writing table to which I am no longer competent. writing is become slow, laborious and painful. the Western Minerva will doubtless be valuable, and give useful exercise to the talents of our Western brethren, whom I rejoice to see advancing in the career of science.

Our University, after which you enquire, will have all it's buildings compleated by this time twelvemonth. but to accomplish this we have contracted a debt which if not taken off our hands by our legislature, will require for it's redemption several years of our funds, and so long leave us without the means of employing professors, so that the epoch of opening it hangs on that dilemma, as does the question whether I shall live to see it. with sincere prayers for the progress of science in every part of our country I tender you my friendly and respectful salutations.   TH: JEFFERSON

PoC (MHi); on verso of reused address cover to TJ; partially dated; at foot of text: "Mr Rafinesque"; endorsed by TJ as a letter of 6 Nov. 1820 and so recorded in SJL.

Bond for a Literary Fund Loan to the University of Virginia

Know all men by these presents, that we Thomas Jefferson, Rector, and James Breckenridge, James Madison, Joseph C. Cabell, John H. Cocke, Chapman Johnson, and Robert B. Taylor, Visitors of the University of Virginia, are held and firmly bound to the President and Directors of the Literary Fund, in the sum of forty thousand dollars, to the payment whereof, well and truly to be made, we bind ourselves and our Successors, to the said President and Directors and their successors, firmly by these presents, sealed with the common seal of the said Rector and Visitors, this 7th day of November in the year one thousand eight hundred and twenty.—

The Condition of the above obligation is such, that whereas the President and Directors of the Literary Fund have this day loaned to the Rector and Visitors of the University of Virginia, the sum of twenty thousand dollars, for the purpose of completing the buildings thereof, upon the following terms, covenants and agreements, viz, that the lawful interest on the said sum shall be annually paid, and the principal be redeemed in five equal annual payments, that the first installment of said principal shall be paid at the expiration of four years from the date of the loan, and that the annual appropriation made by law to the said University, be legally pledged to the said President and Directors, for the punctual payment of the annual interest and redemption of the principal in manner aforesaid: now therefore if the said Rector and Visitors of the University of Virginia, and their successors, shall faithfully pay to the President and Directors of the Literary Fund and their successors, annually on the tenth day of November, the lawful interest on the said sum of twenty thousand dollars, for four years from this date, and annually thereafter the lawful interest on so much of the said sum as shall then be bearing interest, until the whole of said principal shall have been paid; and also shall faithfully pay the said principal sum of twenty thousand dollars, in five equal annual payments, commencing as aforesaid, applying to the purpose of making the said payments of interest and principal, in manner aforesaid, the sums of money appropriated by law to the use or for the benefit of the University of Virginia; or so much thereof as may be requisite, which sums of money so appropriated in each year, so far as requisite for the purpose, are hereby pledged and set apart by the said Rector and Visitors, to be applied by the President and Directors of the Literary Fund to the payments of said interest and principal sum of twenty thousand dollars, borrowed as aforesaid, and to no other uses or objects until the said payments shall have been made, then the above obligation shall be void, otherwise shall remain in full force and virtue.—

Signed, sealed and delivered ⎫ TH. JEFFERSON, (seal)
in the presence of us ⎭ Rector.

 H. B. TRIST—

LANDON C. READ.—

Tr (Vi: RG 27, Virginia Literary Fund Minute Book); in William Munford's hand; with meeting minutes signed by Thomas Mann Randolph as president of the Literary Fund and countersigned by Munford as clerk; at head of text in Munford's hand: "At a Meeting of the President & Directors of the Literary Fund, held at the Capitol in the Treasury Office at half after two o'clock in the afternoon of Saturday, November 11th 1820.— Pres- ent the Governor, Lieutenant Governor, and Treasurer.— [i.e., Thomas Mann Randolph, Peter V. Daniel, and Jerman Baker] The President laid before the Board a Bond executed by the Corporation of the University of Virginia to the Corporation of the Literary Fund in the terms following"; at foot of text in Munford's hand: "The said Bond was approved by the Board, and ordered to be kept by the Clerk:—whereupon, Resolved, that the loan of twenty thousand dollars therein mentioned, be made by the President and Directors of the Literary Fund to the Rector and Visitors of the University of Virginia upon the terms expressed in the said Bond; and that the Auditor of public Accounts [i.e., James E. Heath] be directed to issue a Warrant on the Treasury, in favour of Alexander Garrett Bursar of the said University for the said sum of twenty thousand dollars.— And then the Board adjourned."

From Arthur S. Brockenbrough

DEAR SIR,   Nov: 7ᵗʰ 1820

Enclosed you will find my duplicate report in the first report I had made an error in the addition, it should have been $ 59.158.81. instead of $ 49.158.81 in consiquence of that error I have varied the form of report, but making the balance required to complete the buildings nearly the same, I hope it will make no difference in the report made by the visitors you will find I have layed on 25 p Cent on the former estimate which I am confident will not be too much from the uneaveness of the ground our brick work is much more expensive than I calculated & the stone work was not taken into the estimate and a variety of other expences have occured not before calculated on—I am Sir respectfully your Obᵗ Sevᵗ   A. S. BROCKENBROUGH

RC (CSmH: JF); dateline at foot of text; addressed (torn): "[. . .]rson Esqʳ Monticello"; endorsed by TJ as received 7 Nov. 1820 and so recorded in SJL. Enclosure: FC of Brockenbrough's Statement of Expenditures by the University of Virginia, 30 Sept. 1820, enclosure no. 2 in University of Virginia Board of Visitors Report to Literary Fund President and Directors, 2 Oct. 1820.

Nathaniel Helme's Account of a Visit to Monticello

[7 Nov. 1820]

The next day we visited the venerable *Sage of Monticello*. We took a winding path, which conducted us to the summit of the mount, where we found Mr. JEFFERSON in the enjoyment of health. As you have been repeatedly apprised of the commanding and delightful view from the summit of Monticello, of the grandeur and magnificence which surround this illustrious character, of the great collection of curiosities in his possession, and of the elegance of his museum, a recapitulation of particulars on my part will be both superfluous and unnecessary. Mr. Jefferson's stature is tall and very erect; his step remarkably quick and active; his manners easy, graceful and polite; his mental powers, instead of being impaired by age, retain their native strength and energy; in fine, in his whole deportment are discoverable the characteristic traits of the sage, the patriot, and the gentleman. Mr. Jefferson in his dress, which was a grey coat, grey pantaloons and red vest, adheres very much to the old-fashioned style. We accepted his polite invitation to dine with him; we arose from table about sunset; the servant then brought our horses, and having shaken hands with the venerable man, we descended the mount.

Printed in *Providence* [R.I.] *Patriot*, 2 Dec. 1820, and elsewhere; undated extract, consisting of penultimate paragraph; at head of text: "INTERESTING SKETCHES. *Extract of a letter from a Rhode-Islander, now residing in Virginia, to a gentleman in this town, dated November 14, 1820*"; with date of Helme's visit to Monticello confirmed by SJL entry recording delivery of introductory letters "by mr Helm" at that place on 7 Nov. 1820 (David Howell to TJ, 1 Sept. 1819; James Fenner to TJ, 19 Oct. 1819). In the remainder of the newspaper extract, Helme describes his travels "of about three hundred and twenty miles" that included departing 31 Oct. and staying 1 Nov. in Lynchburg, passing Poplar Forest, and visiting Natural Bridge and its neighboring saltpeter cave; traveling to Charlottesville by way of Lexington, Fair-field, Greenville, Waynesboro, and Rockfish Gap; visiting the University of Virginia, "which is on a very extensive scale" and "consists of four rows of buildings, which, when completed, are designed to be 900 feet in length, or indeed, agreeably to the present plan, they can be elongated at pleasure; there is an interval of ground between each row of about 250 feet in breadth; the buildings, which are six pavilions in each row, connected together by dormitories, are 40 feet deep; the situation is healthy, and commands a fine view of the adjacent country and of Monticello"; and, after leaving Monticello and visiting James Madison at Montpellier, departing 10 Nov. 1820.

Landon C. Read accompanied Helme when they VISITED TJ (Archibald Robertson to TJ, 2 Nov. 1820).

To David Higginbotham

DEAR SIR   Monticello Nov 7. 20.

I recieved yesterday your letter of that date. I have not as yet got a single barrel of flour to market, nor does the present state of the river admit it. I leave injunctions here to omit no opportunity of sending it down, and you may be assured that the corn debt which you were so kind as to let lie over the last year shall be among the earliest to be paid by the present crop. I salute you with friendship & respect.

TH: JEFFERSON

PoC (MHi); on verso of reused address cover of Thomas O'Connor to TJ, 11 June 1819; at foot of text: "Mr Higgenbotham."

To Robert Patterson

DEAR SIR   Monticello Nov. 7. 20.

This letter will be handed to you by mr H. B. Trist, son of a gentleman of the same name a native of Philadelphia whom I think you must have known when young. he was the grandson of mrs House long & well known in that city.   he goes to your University for the benefit of your Mathematical instruction in the first place, and to attend some other branches of science. he has been an inmate with us at Monticello occasionally for a year or two, so that I can say on my own knolege that a more diligent student or a more correct & well disposed youth I have never known; and possessing an excellent genius. being young he may need the counsel of a friend, and your's, whenever he may need, he will recieve with thankfulness, and my thanks will be added to his.

I salute you always with friendship and respect.

TH: JEFFERSON

RC (ViU: TJP); addressed: "Doctor Robert Patterson Philadelphia. favored by Mʳ Trist." PoC (MHi); on verso of reused address cover of John Laval to TJ, 24 June 1819; endorsed by TJ. Recorded in SJL as conveyed "by H. B. Trist."

In a letter to his brother Nicholas P. Trist, dated Charlottesville, 3 Aug. 1820, Hore Browse Trist reported that Gerard E. Stack had written to Patterson at the UNIVERSITY of Pennsylvania on his behalf, "requesting to know whether I could enter the Junior class (the Second) at the same time giving him an account of the progress I had made in the usual studies. Mʳ P. replied in the affirmative, stating that the session began in September. the certainty of being able to enter the junior class is another inducement to my going to Philadelphia, as I could certainly get a degree of B.A in two years." Trist went on to say that he planned to devote some time to "reading Bezouts Algebra & reviewing the six books of E. [i.e., Euclid] although Mr Jefferson thinks them of no use" (RC in DLC: NPT).

Having determined to attend the University of Pennsylvania, based in part on the advice of William A. Burwell, Trist wrote to his brother again from Monti-

cello on 11 Nov. 1820, stating that Burwell was to give him letters of introduction to friends in Philadelphia and that while TJ "gave me one to Mʳ Patterson he could recollect no other person." He added that TJ "left us to day for Poplar Forest accompanied by Miss E. & miss V. [Ellen W. Randolph (Coolidge) and Virginia J. Randolph (Trist)] they expect to remain until Christmas" (RC in DLC: NPT).

After receiving a letter dated 20 Jan. 1821 from her grandson Hore Browse Trist in Philadelphia, Elizabeth Trist passed on the news that "he was invited by Mʳ Patterson to spend the evening with him where he met with a Party of 30 Gentlemen the literati of Phild." She also remarked that "we have experienced very severe weather have had nine snows which kept possession of the ground till within a day or two and we are threatend with more Virginia wrote me that the Thermometer was as low as five at the Mountain, some days the weather has been very cold than become moderate the Severest cold we have had commenced on the evening of the 24ᵗʰ Janʸ and Continued till the 26ᵗʰ," and she reported that "a son of Wilson Nicholas is going to establish him self on the Red River and I understand that Jefferson Randolph intends embark on that scheme but I am certain that neither his Grand Father or Mother will ever consent to his going to reside there" (Elizabeth Trist to Nicholas P. Trist, Farmington, 9 Feb. 1820 [1821] [RC in NcU: NPT]).

To Bernard Peyton

DEAR SIR   Monticello Nov. 7. 20

Yours[1] of the 2ᵈ has been recieved as also the books and boulting cloth. I drew on you yesterday in favor of Wolfe & Raphael for 180.D. and must ask the favor of you to remit for me to Henri Guegan bookseller at the foreign bookstore Baltimore 43. D 50 C I have now but one draught more to make on my present funds in your hands. that is the heavy one in favor of mr Garland of Lynchburg. my endeavor will be to leave the curtailment of 500.D. in your hands, either by docking Garland's draught, or by getting down flour. I set out for Bedford tomorrow and leave injunctions with Jefferson to take advantage of the very first swell of the river to get down a hundred [or] two barrels of flour, or as much as possible by the last day of this month. much pressed with preparation for my departure I must here close with my affectionate salutations.   TH: JEFFERSON

PoC (MHi); on verso of reused address cover of Wilson Cary Nicholas to TJ, 28 June 1819; one word illegible; at foot of text: "Capt Peyton"; endorsed by TJ.

JEFFERSON: Thomas Jefferson Randolph.

[1] Manuscript: "Your."

From Patrick Gibson

SIR   Richmond 8ᵗʰ Novʳ 1820.

Your note in the Virgᵃ bank for $1240.—falls due on the 14ᵗʰ Insᵗ before which time I hope to receive one from you for renewal say for $1180. as advised in mine of the 12ᵗʰ Septʳ: no flour or remittance has yet been received   With much respect & esteem

I am Your obᵗ Servᵗ   PATRICK GIBSON

RC (DLC); between dateline and salutation: "Thomas Jefferson Esqʳᵉ"; endorsed by TJ as received 28 Nov. 1820 and so recorded in SJL.

From Milton W. Rouse

HONOURED SIR,   Paris, November 8th 1820—

Long have I meditated upon the propriety and probable result of thus intruding upon your attention; but, knowing him whom I now address to be the friend of science and confiding in his willingness to afford every possible assistance to those who are in pursuit of wisdom, I shall proceed without dull apologies to lay before him my famishd heart divested of that glossy covering which prosperity would perhaps have thrown over it, and arrayed in the humble garb of simplicity and truth.—

Blessed in early youth with a kind and affectionate Father who took pleasure in beholding the[1] improvement of the infantile mind's of his children, I was favoured with as good an education as could be acquired at a common school, receiving instruction perhaps 3 month every year untill I arrived at the age of 16 years. At the age of 17, not satisfied with the occupation of a farmer, and in order to be better able to procure a livelihood, I persuaded my Father to place me under the instruction of a house carpenter.

I advanced rapidly in acquiring a knowledge of my trade, and should have been contented with my situation could I have been reconciled to a life of ignorance and[2] vice. But, when I became acquainted with the deplorable ignorance in which I must ever remain, & the despicable debauchery of the generality of those with whom my employment compelled me to associate, my soul shuddered at the prospect before me.

I had formerly been favoured with the conversation and advice of a sensible Father and had enjoyed in some measure the advantages of a circulating library; but now deprived at once of every means of cultivating my mind and of gratifying my desire for reading, constantly urged by my dissolute companions[3] to join with them in their vicious practices, hated & abused for my inflexibility, treated like a slave by all about me, I soon became disgusted and discontented with my situation. A constant witness of the ignorance and viciousness of my associates, my love of wisdom and virtue increased; and an habitual acquaintance with Slavery made Liberty more sweet than ever. When my companions were wasting the evening hours in vice and folly, I retired to some solitary place, where I gave full vent to the anguish of my overflowing soul. O ye stars! how often have ye witnessed my midnight lamentations[4] and in pity for my distress, shed sweet ambrosial tears! and thou pale Moon, didst paler turn and veil thyself behind the sable clouds, astonish'd at the sight! All nature groan'd!

distress'd that one solitary being should be compelled by poverty to languish in ignorance while thousands who scorned wisdom were wallowing in wealth, a mere fraction of which, if applied to the cultivation of his mind would ease his burdened soul, and produce more benefit to mankind than millions expended in luxury and dissipation. But midnight lamentations was not the only effect of my ardent desire for knowledge. I applied myself with redubled diligence to acquire a knowledge of my trade, hoping that I should one day be in a condition to gratify in some measure my apparantly insatiable appetite for learning: But alass, how vain are all human calculations! My mind, in the vehemency of desire, soaring on the wings of delightful imagination far above all difficulties under which she laboured, fondly looked forward to that happy day when she should behold fair Science in all her native lustre & glory; but pale disease hurled her from her ecstatick height to the lowest gulph of keen[5] despair. Too intense application to my employment, aided perhaps by the melancholy state of my mind, soon occasioned the decline of my health. Ill health obliged me to quit my employment after having laboured with persevering industry 1 year & 8 months. During this time I had witnessed the height of ignorance & vice, drunk to the very dregs of the cup of adversity, and my mind, receiving from every trial, additional strength and energy, steadily pursued the sole object of her desires, founding her whole happiness on the hope of one day acquiring an education that should enable her to search the depths of nature and diffuse instruction around her.

Fully sensible of my own weakness I despaired of ever being a useful member of society unless enlightened by the rays of learning.

Such was then the situation of my mind, & its propensity for learning and usefulness has to this day increased. I have made every exertion in my power to acquire the desired object, but without success. The 20th year of my life is just closed & my hungry[6] mind is still famishing in the prison of ignorance. Fair learning, heav'n's choisest gift, deny'd, nature, for me, wears not a single smile. Language is too poor to describe the feelings of my heart, and my imbecile pen but poorly employs poor language in the description. Entirely destitute of the means of acquiring an education, without a friend to assist me, & unknown to the world, to whom shall I apply for patronage but to the Venerable Friend of Science? I ask not for silver, but for instruction.[7] I ask not for gold, but for wisdom. O aid me to acquire the desired object!

I long to measure the length, the breadth, the height, & the depth of Learning! Why am I restrained? Because I am destitute of base metal? yes, base it is when compared with fair science; but when it is the only means by which Fair science can be attained it is more precious than even life itself—O that I could be permited to place one foot on the lowest step that ascends the hill of Science!

Venerable Sir, So great is my desire for Learning, and so utterly incapable am I of gratifying that desire without assistance, that I must languish out a tedious life of ignorance in a country where a liberal education can be acquired for 10 or 1200$. or I must beg for assistance. In this situation, what shall I choose? What, but petition for assistance to the Friends of Science? and who so proper to receive my petition as he whom I now address? I have used every other honourable means in my power to acquire the desired object, and now resort to this last strong hope of success,—and shall this be less honorable than its predecessors? Is it dishonourable for a son of poverty ardently to desire learning and usefulness? Is it dishonourable for him to crave assistance from his fellow citizens? I trust not—

Grant me assistance and my life shall be devoted to the cause of Liberty and Science.

If you can in any manner whatever afford me assistance I humbly request you to notify me speedily; and if you cannot assist me do Sir, inform me without delay, that I may be released from my anxiety and resign myself an unwilling slave to ignorance. If the will of Heaven is that the latter be my fate I shall still pursue Learning with my eyes although restrained by poverty from embracing her—

Father of Liberty & Science, May Heaven guide and protect you through a long and happy life and at last[8] bring your grey heirs with honour and peace to the grave.

Ever respectfully & obediently your's. MILTON W. ROUSE.

P.S. Be pleased Sir, to direct to Milton W Rouse, Paris Hill, Oneida County State of New York.

RC (MHi); addressed: "Hon. Thomas Jefferson, Monticello, State of Virginia"; redirected in an unidentified hand to "Lynchburg, Poplar Forest"; stamp canceled; franked; postmarked Utica, 12 Nov., and Milton, 2 Dec.; endorsed by TJ as received 5 Dec. 1820 and so recorded in SJL.

[1] Manuscript: "the the."
[2] Manuscript: "a."
[3] Manuscript: "compamions."
[4] Manuscript: "lamentotions."
[5] Word interlined.
[6] Word interlined.
[7] Omitted period at right margin editorially supplied.
[8] Preceding two words interlined.

To Thomas Mann Randolph

Sir   Monticello Nov. 9. 1820.

The Rector & Visitors of the University of Virginia, at their last semiannual meeting of Oct. 2. having agreed to a Report of the conditio[n] of that institution, it's disbursements and funds, as required by law, I now inclose it, with the accounts of the Bursar & Proctor. some difference will be found between the Proctor's account, & the general view presented in the Report of the board, which it is my duty to explain.

After the separation of the board, it occurred to the Proctor that the account he had last rendered, & on view of which their Report was formed, might, in some of it's articles, be made more specific & correct. it was given to him therefore, & that now inclosed was returned in it's stead. by the last article of this it might be understood that the buildings, whose completion was contemplated in the Report, would require an additional sum of 38,364.D. to compleat them. but this apparent excess proceeds chiefly from the circumstance that the annuities of 1822. & 23. are not entered in this account, as they are in the general statement made in the Report[.] this lessens the apparent difference by 30,000.D. leaving a real one of 8,364.D. only: and this the Proctor properly accounts for by observing that the former estimates comprehended buildings only, omitting the cost of 200. acres of land, and several other contingent expences not then foreseen.[1] we are now so near the end of our work, as to leave little room for future errors of estimate. the building requisite for a Library however is not included in this estimate.

It will readily occur that these observations cannot have had the sanction of the visitors, because the circumstance producing them arose after their separation. I have the honor to be with the highest consideration

Sir Your most obedient & most humble serv[t]

Th: Jefferson

RC (CSmH: JF); edge chipped, with missing text supplied from Dft; endorsed by Randolph, in part, as "to P. & Directors of Literary Fund." Dft (ViU: TJP); at foot of text: "Governor Randolph"; endorsed by TJ, with his additional notation beneath endorsement: "with Report of Visitors." FC (ViU: TJP); in Virginia J. Randolph (Trist)'s hand, initialed by TJ. Not recorded in SJL. Enclosures: University of Virginia Board of Visitors Report to Literary Fund President and Directors, 2 Oct. 1820, and enclosures. Enclosed in TJ to Joseph C. Cabell, 25 Dec. 1820.

[1] In Dft TJ here canceled "with this correction it will be found that the whole cost of the establishment, lands, buildings, & all other expenditures included, will, when compleated, have amounted to about 162,364.D. and."

From Tench Coxe

Philadelphia Nov. 11. 1820.

You are one of the last persons to whom it is necessary to observe how comfortable are the exchanges of the heart among those, who are united in principles at once virtuous and vital. I feel all that belong to such circumstances in the perusal of your letter of the 13th ult°. It is true that I aspired to be the fellow laboror (juvenile and modest) with superior men. I have been amply repaid by my belief that I helped to save our country, and its cause from menaced evils, and to promote its interests and dishonored fame at home and abroad. Amidst the injuries I have sustained from the weakness, avarice & jealousies of false or infirm brethren, and from opponents, who suffered in their conflicts with our friends and myself, I have never ceased to devote more than my leisure hours to the public interests political, moral & œconomical. In the volume of Murray & Co's Phil^a edition of Reess London Cyclopædia, which contains the "U. States" you will see my views of our country of the 4th July 1818. It was meant to insinuate and record many things in the light we have viewed them from 1774 to 1818. The enquiry, which it contains into the national character of the people of the United states was intended as a little summary of "Vindiciæ Americanæ." I think its enthusiasm, which I confess as a weakness on subjects of the heart, would gratify you in one of your calmest moods of moral philosophy.

I am now meditating "a manual of agriculture." Our family has been concerned in the landed interests of this country about 150 years. I have a love of its soil not only natural, but hereditary. This is one of my apologies for presuming treat of subject that many may suppose I have not observed from the time of my readings of Virgils Georgics, in our grammar School. But I have indulged myself with success on the cotton, on the vine, which to us Pennsylvanians are not indigenous, and I hope to compile and compose a better manual than we yet have for the rising generation of cultivators and for the uninstructed, unreflecting, and unsystemazied part of the practical and adult. There is another reason. I abandoned my profession in the year 1790, because I deemed it improper in me and unfavorable to our young reformed government that I as a public officer, possessed of political information & secrets & with many opportunities of influence, should be engaged in commerce. I am therefore without a profession, and entirely out of office, with a family of eight unmarried children all above 20. I some times receive a compensation for those services with my pen which I always gave to the public & the press, without price in our[1] time. If 1 or 200 copies were presented to me by a liberal printer, I gave them to eminent men, and public libraries to circulate their contents.

At the moment of receiving your letter I was meditating an application, from necessity, to M[r] Monroe. A law of last Session vacates all the offices throughout the Union, of certain descriptions, which have been held by the incumbents four years or more. M[r] Monroe[2] has overcome the old rivals (Mess[rs] G. & DeW. C.)[3] of yourself, M[r] Madison & himself in our Penns[a] election & extensively elsewhere. I have requested his consideration for some vacancy & particularly for one held by a person who has no claims upon the country civil or military; revolutionary or subsequent, but owes his appointment only to a connexion with a gentleman, once in office, & who has so conducted our first pecuniary institution as to make a fortune of 40,000 D[rs] and to ruin the energy & credit of our bank at home and abroad. That or some other appointment I wish for my old age, for my family, for sufferings in mind, person, estate and every thing pertaining to comfort, and for the duties I trust I am prepared to perform and the volunteer services I should be in the old habit of rendering. The office is one which I once asked, and which M[r] Madison gave me, but the war destroyed its emoluments. The naval office of this port is that I mean, or any other. If the remembrance and consideration of all you have known me to suffer and execute appear to justify an <u>early</u> interposition, in an emergent case, (with M[r] Madisons cooperation) by letters to the President, & members of the Senate it would relieve me from a scene of distress past, present & imminent which I should be pained to narrate. As the transmission of this letter to M[r] Madison by you would save time, and enable him to act, I authorize its communication. Any office would be equal to me, but the 2[d] in the customs, the Nav. offe, in which my mercantile and œconomical practice & vending would be of most value to my country, I would prefer to the 1st or any other.

I have just finished a series of papers for the national intelligencer under the signature of "<u>Greene</u>" upon the subject of the Northern temper & conduct upon the subject of the Missouri question and too hasty emancipation. I feel, to the bottom of my soul, the danger of political, religious & moral fanaticism on that subject. We have had no such topic of just apprehension since the settlement of Independence. I have endeavoured to infuse into the consideration of it as much as possible of truth not considered, and of reason, obscured by passion, prejudice and criminal intrigue.

My letter, too long for your convenience, I hasten to close: but will not promise that I will refrain from others concerning the public interests. I could say much now of wonderful Spain, of Naples, of Portugal and of the extension of the representative principle, and the decline of military and ecclesiastical despotisms. But I respectfully postpone.

I have the honor to be with perfect respect and attachment dear Sir y^r faithful friend & servant. TENCH COXE

RC (DLC); at foot of text: "Mr Jefferson"; endorsed by TJ as received 28 Nov. 1820 and so recorded in SJL. Enclosed in TJ to James Madison, 29 Nov. 1820, and Madison to TJ, 10 Dec. 1820.

The American edition of Abraham Rees, ed., *The Cyclopædia; or, Universal Dictionary of Arts, Sciences, and Literature* (Philadelphia, [1805–25?]), included Coxe's lengthy entry on the United States in VOLUME 39 (Coxe to James Madison, 2 Feb. 1819 [Madison, *Papers, Retirement Ser.*, 1:405–7]). At its LAST SESSION, on 15 May 1820 Congress passed an "Act to limit the term of office of certain officers therein named, and for other purposes" (*U.S. Statutes at Large*, 3:582).

G. & DEW. C.: George Clinton and DeWitt Clinton. In 1813 William Jones, who was then the secretary of the navy and later the president of the Second Bank of the United States, successfully recommended the selection of his CONNEXION and mercantile partner Samuel Clarke to be naval officer at the port of Philadelphia. Around the same time, Coxe turned down James Madison's offer of the same post due to its inadequate EMOLUMENTS (Madison, *Papers, Pres. Ser.*, 7:25, 37–8). A piece signed by "GREENE" appeared in the Washington *Daily National Intelligencer* on 13 Nov. 1820.

[1] Word interlined in place of "my."
[2] Manuscript: "Monroes."
[3] Parenthetical phrase interlined.

From Thomas Ewell

DEAR SIR, Washington 13th nov 1820

The letter you last favoured me with, found me on a sick bed with a bilious fever from which I am now slowly recovering. Your kindness in giving me the consolation of better times arising from vigour of mind & body—I duly appreciated; but felt anew the impracticability of making any efforts, without receiving some spring or countenance from those in influence and power. I am tied down to this spot by encumbered & unproductive property: which with proper management will become valuable. But in the mean time for want of employment am suffering the severest pains myself and my family the greatest deprivations: such indeed that I would not state to you.

The question has been long debated in my mind, whether it was better to encounter in silence the evils under which I labour, or be guilty of the indelicacy of further appealing to you. The troubling of you, was decided in my view, by the torture I have particularly felt at having to take my children from School from inability to meet their expenditures.

There are hundreds almost monthly getting employment here: and it is not to be disguised that these offices are bestowed in consequence of the efforts of Friends: generally, the most urgent, the most successful. In The days of M^r madison's administration, both in the navy & War Dept^s at pleasure I often procured for others, higher commissions than that I seek—restoration to the navy or surgeon in the army.

With more pain than your benevolence would have me encounter: acting from a sense of duty to my family I proceed to beg that you would wave your aversion to interference with your successors & give me a direct recommendation to the President or whom you please—conditioned on my not retaining the office one day if perfect satisfaction be not rendered by me.   The service that you will bestow on me you cannot fully estimate, without reference to the fact—that here every body depends on the Gov^t and a little of its patronage or countenance, is a passport to far better emoluments & standing.

May god grant all you wish!—   THOMAS EWELL

RC (DLC); endorsed by TJ as received 28 Nov. 1820 and so recorded in SJL.

To Samuel Garland

SIR   Pop. For. Nov. 15. 20.
    I had expected that on my arrival here I should be able to give you an order on Richmond for 800.D. but I find that my funds there at present will meet 600.D. only, for which sum I now inclose you an order on Capt. B. Peyton: and I will give a further order for 200. Dollars before I leave this place, say in December. I salute you with great esteem & respect.   TH: JEFFERSON

PoC (MHi); at foot of text: "Mr Saml Garland"; endorsed by TJ; with apparently unrelated "$36.60" in an unidentified hand on verso. Enclosure not found.

To Patrick Gibson

[DE]AR SIR   Poplar Forest. Nov. 15. 20.
    I was so much engaged for some time before I left Monticello that it quite escaped me that my note in the Virginia bank must be near it's term of renewal: and the failure occurs to me here where I have not your letter to remind me either of date or sum. thinking it must be over a thousand dollars I inclose you a note with a blank for the odd hundreds as well as for the date.   by my last account rendered I

percieved that you were upwards of 200.D. in advance for me. this happens at the unlucky season when our river i[s] generally in default. but I left in charge with my grandson to avail himself of the first tide to send you a boatload or two of flour, which I hope he will be able soon to do. with every wish for the reestablishment of your health I salute you with constant friendship and respect.

TH: JEFFERSON

PoC (DLC); on verso of reused address cover to TJ; salutation trimmed and one word faint; at foot of text: "Mr Gibson"; endorsed by TJ. Enclosure not found.

MY GRANDSON: Thomas Jefferson Randolph.

From Francis W. Gilmer

DEAR SIR.   Richmond. 15th Nov. 1820

I have this moment received the farewell of Mr. Corrêa to Virginia, to you, and to us all. I cannot so well acquit myself of the obligation his kindness has laid me under, as by inclosing his letter to you. I who know the sincerity of the sentiments it contains, can appreciate its worth. Read it, and be good enough to return it at your leisure.

with the highest respect & esteem &c your friend & Ser^t

F. W. GILMER

RC (MoSHi: Gilmer Papers); at foot of text: "Thomas Jefferson Esqr"; endorsed by TJ as received 28 Nov. 1820 and so recorded in SJL.

E N C L O S U R E

José Corrêa da Serra to Francis W. Gilmer

DEAR SIR AND FRIEND.   New York 9th November. 1820.

To morrow in the Albion packet i sail for England, and from thence in January i will sail for the Brazil, where i will be in the beginning of March. It is impossible to me to Leave this continent without once more turning my eyes to Virginia, to you and Monticello. I Leave you my representative in that State, and near the persons who attach me to it, and i doubt not of your acceptance of this charge. Mr Jefferson, Col. Randolph and his excellent Lady and family, the family i am the most attached to in all America, will receive my adieus from you. Do not forget also that pure and virtuous soul at Montpellier and his Lady. You will i hope Live Long my dear friend, and you will every day more and more see with your eyes, what difference exists between the two philosophical Presidents, and the whole future contingent series of chiefs of your union. You know the rest of my acquaintances in your noble State, and the degrees of consideration i have for each, and you will distribute my souvenirs in proportion.

At my return in Philadelphia i found a Letter from your brother in Law M[r] Minor of Ridgeway dated the 5th of July, to inform me as secr[y] of the Agric. Soc[y][1] that they had been so good as to elect me one of their body, and that they would be glad of receiving some communication from me. I found at the same time as many orders to execute and dispatches to answer, with plenty of troublesome trifles to expedite, and i am now ashamed to write; i beg you will be my Letter, and you can tell him, that i will send better proofs than compliments, of the price i attach to their kindness. I was in Virginia so Long after the Lette[r] that chuse just the moment of my departure, in order to arrive in Philadelphia, and could have personally answered if i had known it.

Glory yourself in being a Virginian, and remember all my discourses about the[m.] It is the Lot i would have wished for me if i was a North American, being a South American i am glad to be a Brazilian, and you shall hear of wha[t] i do for my country if i Live.

<u>Cras ingens iterabimus æquor.</u> but every where, you will find me constantly and steadily

Your faithful and sincere friend   JOSEPH CORRÈA DE SERRA

RC (ViU: FWG); edge trimmed; at head of text: "Frank. W. Gilmer Esq."; endorsed by Gilmer. Also enclosed in TJ to Gilmer, 29 Nov. 1820.

The Agricultural Society of Albemarle (AGRIC. SOC[Y]) elected Corrêa da Serra an honorary member on 8 May 1820 (True,

"Agricultural Society," 288). CRAS INGENS ITERABIMUS ÆQUOR: "Tomorrow we shall set out once more over the boundless sea" (Horace, *Odes*, 1.7.32, in *Horace: Odes and Epodes*, trans. Niall Rudd, Loeb Classical Library [2004], 38–9).

[1] Preceding six words interlined.

From James Monroe

DEAR SIR   Washington Novr 15. 1820

You will receive herewith a copy of the message, in which I have endeavour'd without looking at the old governments of Europe, to place our own, in such prominent circumstances, as seem'd to require attention from me, at this time, in such a light, as to shew a striking contrast between them. The amount of the debt paid off since the war, is, I presume, greater, than has been generally supposed, and the actual state of the treasury much better.

Soon after I left Albemarle, I made a visit here from Loudoun. M[r] Correa had been here, seen Mr Adams, & gone to the neighbourhood of Phil[a], to remain till he could enter the city, secure against the fever of the season. Mr Adams told me that he had shewn great moderation, in conferring on the subject of his note, demanding the institution of a board for the liquidation of claims, for property taken from Portughuese subjects, by Artigan privateers, charging two of our judges with having disgrac'd their commissions &[c]. I saw at once that his tone had been changed, by his communications with you, having made his demand under excitment, & without a knowledge of the subject. He had promised M[r] Adams to send him a comm[u]nication in the spirit of his former note, as soon as he enterd Phil[a]. I waited some time for it, but none arriving, and fearing that his demand might be the foundation of a similar one, on the part of Spain, as a sett off, against our claims admitted by two treaties, I requested him to write Mr Correa an answer to his former letter, declaring his demand to be inadmissible, unjust in itself, & unwarranted by the usage of all nations, & to request also the names of the judges whom he had denouncd in such unqualified & strong terms, as of the officers said to have servd on board Artigan privateers. A letter to this effect, was written, in the most mild & conciliatory terms; but he gave no answer to it. I suspect his intention has been to transfer this affair to the person left by him as chargé, and that we may probably hear from him on it.

very respectfully & sincerely your friend   JAMES MONROE

RC (DLC); edge chipped; endorsed by TJ as received 28 Nov. 1820 and so recorded in SJL. FC (DLC: Monroe Papers); in an unidentified hand, with emendations by Monroe; endorsed by Monroe. Enclosure: *Message from the President of the United States to both Houses of Congress, at the Commencement of the Second Session of the Sixteenth Congress. November 15, 1820* (Washington, 1820), stating that "I see much cause to rejoice in the felicity of our situation" (quote on p. 2); noting the ill effects of European events on the United States economy and outlining the country's current relations with Spain, Great Britain and its colonies, France, and South America; discussing public revenue and debt; describing recent progress in constructing coastal fortifications; reporting on trade regulations with American Indians intended to bring about "the great purpose of their civilization" (quote on p. 8); and approving of recent improvements in overseas commerce facilitated by the presence of American naval vessels.

In HIS NOTE to Secretary of State John Quincy Adams of 16 July 1820, José Corrêa da Serra listed nineteen Portuguese ships captured BY ARTIGAN PRIVA-TEERS, with a total value of $616,158. These vessels claimed to serve the Uruguayan revolutionary José Gervasio Artigas, but Corrêa da Serra complained that they were fitted out in United States ports and manned by American seamen. He wrote again on 26 Aug. 1820 regarding judges he believed had DISGRAC'D THEIR COMMISSIONS from the United States. At Monroe's behest Adams wrote Corrêa da Serra from Washington on 30 Sept. 1820 DECLARING HIS DEMAND TO BE INADMISSIBLE as indicated above but requesting documentation for his complaints and assuring him that if they "shall be found to contain evidence upon which any officer, civil or military, of the United States or any of their citizens can be called to answer for his conduct as injurious to any subject of Portugal, every measure shall be taken to which the Executive is competent to secure full justice and satisfaction to your Sovereign and his nation" (all printed in Léon Bourdon, *José Corrêa da Serra: Ambassadeur du Royaume-Uni de Portugal et Brésil a Washington, 1816–1820* [1975], 564–5, 578–9, 594–5).

The Portuguese CHARGÉ d'affaires was José Amado Grehon.

To Bernard Peyton

DEAR SIR   Poplar Forest[1] Nov. 15. 20

I had promised Samuel Garland to give him on my arrival here an order for 800.D. but, anxious to leave in your hands 500.D. for the curtail expected, I have this day drawn on you in his favor for 600.D. only, promising him the othe[r] 200 before I leave this place. by that time I hope Jefferson will have sent you on my account one or two boatloads[2] of flour, which I have charged him to do as soon as the river admits. ever and affectionately yours   TH: JEFFERSON

PoC (MHi); on verso of a reused sheet in an unidentified hand reading only "<Lynchburg> Sept"; edge trimmed; at foot of text: "Capt B. Peyton"; endorsed by TJ.

A missing letter of this date from TJ to Thomas JEFFERSON Randolph is recorded in SJL and is described in TJ's

financial records as enclosing "to Th:J.R. my notes of 3000. & 2250. bk. US. and 2500. Farm.'s bk. to be indorsed by him and forwarded to B. Peyton for renewal" (MB, 2:1371).

[1] Preceding two words reworked from "Monticello."

[2] Manuscript: "boatsloads."

From Joseph Wheaton

ILLUSTRIOUS SIR   Washington City Nov[r] 16. 1820

I approach your exalted character with great diffidence; but contemplating as I often do your labours, and how much good those labours have bestowed on the present & will on future Generations, (our decendants), I the more, admire and adore that Providence which continues your invaluable life to So long a period; an example and blessing to the present age—that I may be permitted to evince to you, that as a member of that number who has thrown into the scale, his might to raise our beloved country to the proud eminence on which it stands, please to examine the enclosed appeal.—

That I have done all in my power to promote the prosperity of this nation, I pray you to accept this assurance—.

with the homage of my heart & with the most profound respect.
I am Great Sir your Obe[dt] Serv[t]   JOSEPH WHEATON

RC (MHi); adjacent to closing: "Tho[s] Jefferson Esq[r]"; endorsed by TJ as received 25 Dec. 1820 and so recorded in SJL.

The ENCLOSED APPEAL was likely Wheaton, Appeal of Joseph Wheaton, late

deputy quarter master general and major of cavalry, to the Senate and House of Representatives of the United States of America (District of Columbia, 1820). In a 20 Oct. 1821 letter to James Madison, Wheaton presumably referenced the same publication: "Last autumn I had the honor to enclose to your address, my pamphlet, 'an appeal to Congress from the decision of the accounting officers of the War Department for compensation while detained by their orders in the Settlement of my public accounts, and for Extra Services'" (Madison, *Papers, Retirement Ser.*, 2:412–3).

On 15 Nov. 1820 Wheaton sent the publication enclosed here to John Adams (MHi: Adams Papers).

Receipt from Samuel Garland

Rec[dl] Lynchburg Nov 18th 1820 of M[r] Thomas Jefferson a draft on Capt B Peyton for Six hundred Dollars, in part payment of his bond to A Robertson & C[o] in my hands for collection as the atty in fact of B, Miller for whose benefit it is—   S, GARLAND

MS (MHi); in Garland's hand; addressed: "M[r] Jefferson Pop: Forest Bedford"; endorsed by TJ.

[1] Manuscript: "Rev[d]."

Jane Battles to Ann Carrington Cabell, with Postscript to Thomas Jefferson

DEAR MADAM   Lower Sandusky N[ov] 19th 1820
I embrace this opportunity to Inform you that I am well and am In hopes that these few lines will find you and famely enjoying the Same Blessing please to[1] assist me In geting my pay from the United States I have Been In their Service Considerable time Since I Saw you I went through Kentuckey by the way of the falls of the Ohio river from thence on to wabash river near the boundry line. and was there when Governer Jenings made the treaty with the Indians In the fall of 1818. please to exert your Self to assist me In geting my pay from the United States In money or lands. I have Friends In this Country who will assist me In takeing Care of my pay Should I get It. please to remember me to Doc[t] George Cavils Lady and family Co[l] Samuel Cavils Lady and famely at Soldiers Joy I remain your Frind and Humble Servant &[c]   JANE BATTLES

M[r] Thomas Jefferson
    Sir please to forward this letter to M[rs] William Cavil at Union Hill In Nelson County[2] and In So doing[3] you will Ob[l] your Humble Servant &c   JANE BATTLES

RC (MHi); between dateline and salutation: "M[rs] William Cavill"; endorsed by TJ as a letter to himself received 12 Dec. 1820 and so recorded in SJL.

Ann (Nancy) Carrington Cabell (1760–1838), the most likely addressee of this letter, was born in Charlotte County. She married William Cabell (1759–1822) in 1780 and thereafter resided in the portion of Amherst County that became Nelson County in 1807. Of the Cabells' fourteen children, eleven reached adulthood (Alexander Brown, *The Cabells and their Kin*, 2d ed., rev. [1939; repr. 1994], 207, 209, 219, 221–2, 227; Virginia Genealogical Society, *Quarterly* 13 [1975]: 66–8; *Lynchburg Virginian*, 16 Apr. 1838).

In October 1818 Indiana governor Jonathan Jennings (JENINGS) was at Saint Marys, Ohio, representing the federal government in the negotiation of land-purchase treaties with the Potawatomi, Wea, Delaware, and Miami Indians (*ASP, Indian Affairs*, 2:168–70).

Sarah Syme Cabell, the wife of Samuel J. Cabell (1756–1818), of SOLDIERS JOY, died in 1814. Ann Carrington Cabell and her husband moved into his parents' UNION HILL estate about five years after the death of his father, William Cabell (1730–98). His mother, Margaret Jordan Cabell, lived out her widowhood with them at Union Hill until her death in 1812 (Brown, *Cabells and their Kin*, 81, 83, 132, 139, 191, 204–5, 219). Having apparently been out of contact with the Cabell family for several years, Battles could also have intended this letter for Margaret Jordan Cabell.

[1] Battles here canceled "recollect that you promised to."
[2] Preceding three words interlined.
[3] Manuscript: "doimg."

From James Lyle (1798–1850)

D[r] sir   Richmond 20th Novr 1820

The subject of my letter will I hope be a sufficient apology for my addressing you—From the books of my Grandfather James Lyle, Geo:[1] Kipen & Co, & Henderson M[c]Call & Co, I find that there are some unsettled accounts with you; Statements of which will be handed to you by Mister T: Saunders, who is autherised by me to make a settlement—I am fully persuaded from your letters to my Grandfather, that there will be no difficulty thrown in the way to retard a final adjustment of accounts—Should money be as scarce with you, as it is with farmers nearer this City, a payment of the debt will probably put you to some little inconvenience, to avoid which, your bonds for the amounts will be satisfactory until, a payment is more suitable to your Convenience—with great respect

Your Obt: Srvt: JAMES LYLE admr &c with
the will annexed of Jas Lyle Sr decd

RC (MHi); between dateline and salutation: "Thos: Jefferson Esq[r]"; endorsed by TJ as received 4 Dec. 1820 and so recorded in SJL.

James Lyle (1798–1850), planter, was born in Chesterfield County. He attended the College of William and Mary, 1815–16. Lyle lived in Richmond until at least

1830, then moved permanently to Whitby, his ancestral plantation in Chesterfield County. He owned nine slaves in 1820 and about seventy slaves as part of personal property worth $31,000 at his death (G. Brown Goode, *Virginia Cousins: A Study of the Ancestry and Posterity of John Goode of Whitby* [1887], 118–9, 229; *William and Mary Provisional List*,

26; DNA: RG 29, CS, Richmond, 1820, 1830, Chesterfield Co., 1840, 1850 slave schedules; *Richmond Whig and Public Advertiser*, 18 June 1850; Chesterfield Co. Will Book, 19:2–3, 88–95).

Tarlton SAUNDERS became Lyle's stepfather when his mother, Sally Bland Goode Lyle, remarried after the death in 1806 of his namesake father (Goode, *Virginia Cousins*, 119). An *administrator de bonis*

non cum testamento annexo (ADMR &C WITH THE WILL ANNEXED) is "An administrator appointed by the court to administer the decedent's goods that were not administered by an earlier administrator or executor" when there was a will (*Richmond Enquirer*, 6 July 1821; *Black's Law Dictionary*).

[1] Manuscript: "Goo."

From Bernard Peyton

DEAR SIR,   Rich'd 20 Novr 1820

I am favor'd this morning with yours of the 15th: Inst: & observe contents—

Your draft favor Mr Garland for $600 shall be paid on demand—all the others of which you have apprised me, have been presented & paid:—and a few days ago, by a Milton Boat, forwarded the 18 Gallons Linseed oil you wrote for in a former letter, in 6 three Gallon Jugs, which I hope will reach Monticello safely.

By direction of Governor Randolph paid a few days since $10 for a Book of Prints of American Scenery from Matthew Carey & Son of Philadelphia for you,[1] which Book is still with me to wait your directions—Governor R. at the same time desired me to give notice to Mr Carey that both you & himself would withdraw your subscriptions to this work, which I accordingly did—they did not I fancy at-all equal his & your expectations.—

I have heard of no Flour from shadwell for you yet, altho' all the Milton Boats have been, & are now down—I presume it may soon be expected—the article is very dull sale indeed just now at $3⅝ @ 3¾— Tobacco $4½ @ 9—Wheat 67 @ 70¢—

With sincere regard D^r sir
Yours very Truely   B: PEYTON

RC (MHi); endorsed by TJ as received 28 Nov. 1820 and so recorded in SJL.

The BOOK OF PRINTS was the first part of *Picturesque Views of American Scenery* (Philadelphia, 1820–21), published in three numbers by Mathew Carey & Son, which contained aquatint prints by Joshua Shaw engraved by John Hill.

[1] Preceding two words interlined.

To Thomas Mann Randolph

Dear Sir   Poplar Forest Nov. 20. 20.

I write this separate letter, and endorse it as <u>private</u>, to prevent it's being opened by others in your absence. the object of it is to mention the importance which has been suggested to me of procuring a board of the Literary fund, before the meeting of the Legislature, and of laying the Report of the Visitors before the latter body on the 2ᵈ day of their session if possible. it is believed that if presented before the croud of other business comes in, they will act on it immediately, and before opportunities will have been obtained for caballing, circulating false rumors, and other maneuvres by the enemies of the institution. your zeal for the institution assures us of your efforts to give the Report this advantage: and I hope Governor Clinton's display of the gigantic exertions of N. York for the education of it's citizens will stimulate lagging members to wipe off the reproach of our neglect of it.

I need not write you news from Monticello, which you recieve more directly. the girls here are both well and pursuing their studies with undisturbed industry. they owe this much to the deaths and sickness in our neighborhood. I salute you with affectionate attachment and respect.

                                                        Th: Jefferson

RC (THi, on deposit T: Tennessee Miscellaneous Files); addressed: "Governor Randolph Richmond" and "Private"; franked; postmarked Lynchburg, 24 Nov.; endorsed by Randolph as received 26 Nov. 1820. PoC (MHi); on verso of a reused address cover from R. Pollard to TJ; endorsed by TJ.

This letter was separate from another of this date from TJ to Randolph, not found, recorded in SJL with TJ's notation that it concerned the "report of Visitors." On 5 Dec. 1820, the day after the Virginia legislative session opened, Randolph wrote as president of the Literary Fund to Linn Banks, the Speaker of the House of Delegates, enclosing the University of Virginia Board of Visitors Report to Literary Fund President and Directors, 2 Oct. 1820, "with the proper accompanying Documents," to be "laid before the Legislature" (RC in Vi: RG 79,

House of Delegates, Speaker, Executive Communications; docketed by William Munford as clerk of the House of Delegates: "250 Copies of this, and of the Report of the Rector & Visitors of the University, with the accompanying documents, to be printed <u>immediately</u>, in the Pamphlet form"; printed in *Report and Documents for 1820*, 3).

New York governor DeWitt Clinton reported on his state's "highly liberal" support for education in a speech to the state legislature on 7 Nov. 1820, noting that "perhaps the whole appropriation for the promotion of education, may be estimated at two millions and a half of dollars" (*Journal of the Senate of the State of New-York: at their Forty-Fourth Session* [Albany, 1820], 8; *Richmond Enquirer*, 14 Nov. 1820). the girls who traveled to Poplar Forest with TJ were his granddaughters Ellen W. Randolph (Coolidge) and Virginia J. Randolph (Trist).

From Edmund Bacon

DEARE SIR.   Monticello November. 21ˢᵗ 1820.

I send you a line informing you that Mr Meeks is not disposed to remaine with us the ensueing Yeare. he has not given me the information himself but his wife informed my family that he intended going away. what proves the thing to me I saw a cart at his house loading with his cabage yesterday I inquired whare they was carrying them to the reply was to the place that he was to live at the next yeare. I consider it necessary to inform you that if you chuse to imploy a workman that you may have time to furnish yourself

We are ingaged sawing barrill timber. Meeks is now frameing the safety gate but Mʳ Colclasor says they cannot stop to put it down. Meeks had quit on recieving this information but I considerd it most proper on our parts to have the gate ready made and if the Miller will not suffer us to stop the water only a day or two to put down the work that if any accident should happen it would not be our faults. I tharefore presed the Job on

Mʳˢ Randolph lift Monticello yesterday on a viset to Richmond. the balance of the family is all well

With sincere respect your Ob. St.   E: BACON

RC (ViU: TJP-ER); at foot of text: "Mr Jefferson"; addressed (torn): "[. . .] poplar forest. Lynchburgh"; endorsed by TJ as received 28 Nov. 1820 and so recorded in SJL.

A letter to TJ from Bacon of 14 Nov. 1820, not found, is recorded in SJL as received 21 Nov. 1820 from Monticello.

To Edmund Bacon

[Poplar Forest, 22 Nov. 1820. SJL entry reads "Ned & Wormly. garden, lawn & grove. roads." Letter not found.]

Joshua Dodge's Invoice of Items Shipped to Thomas Jefferson

Invoice of Sundries shipped by Joshua Dodge of Marseilles on board the Brig Union of Marblehead Capᵗ Simon T. Williams bound to the United States, consigned, by order & for account of Thomas Jefferson Esqʳ of Monticello, Virginia, to the Collector of the first Port, not South of the chesapeak, the said Brig arrives at.

TJ#1	One Case containing 50 B^lles White Wine			
	de Limoux at ƒ2.50	F^cs 125.—		
	Custom house & other petty charges	" 2.25		
		F^cs 127.25		
	Disc^t 2%	" 2.55.	F^cs 124.70.
TJ#1	one Case containing			
	℔¹ 57 Macaroni first Q^y at ƒ35%	F 19.95		
	Case	" 1.50.	" 21.45
TJ#2.	One Case containing			
	6 double Bottles anchovies	ƒ 14.40		
	Case	" —.60.	15.—
TJ#3/4	Two Cases containing			
	each 12 Bottles Virgin oil all at	" 50.—		
TJ 5/7	Three Cases containing each 48 B^lles			
	Bergasse Red Wine of 1815.			
	144 Bottles at ƒ1	ƒ 144.—		
	Custom house charges &c	" 3.60		
		ƒ 147.60		
	Disco^t 2%	" 2.90	144.70
			F^cs 355 85	
	Charges			
	Export duty on Macaroni & oil	F 3.19.		
	Shipping charges, Porterage &^c	" 5.66	8 85
			F^cs 364.70	

To the debit of Thomas Jefferson Esqr of Monticello Virginia
Errors & Omissions Excepted
Marseilles 22 Novr 1820.   Josh^a Dodge

MS (MHi); in a clerk's hand, signed by Dodge; with signed and embossed attestation by Isaac Story, deputy collector at Marblehead, Mass., on verso: "I Certify that the within is the Original Invoice presented on entry"; calculations by TJ

at foot of verso: "5.33|364.70|.68.
    319 9
    44 80";
endorsed by TJ: "Dodge Joshua. Invoice of articles rec^d June 1821."

¹ Preceding this symbol TJ added ".065 p^r ℔."

From Thomas Ritchie

Richmond, Novr 23, 1820.

T Ritchie, in his own name & that of the Author, requests Mr Jefferson's Acceptance of this Book.—T.R. trusts he will read it— and, if perfectly agreeable to Mr J. hopes, that at his leisure he will give his opinion of it. It were desirable that Mr J. would permit that opinion, if favorable, to go out to the Public—but, <u>that</u> must rest with himself.

With best respects, &c &c. in haste,

RC (MHi); dateline at foot of text; endorsed by TJ as received 19 Dec. 1820 and so recorded in SJL. Enclosure: John Taylor, *Construction Construed, and Con-* *stitutions Vindicated* (Richmond: Shepherd & Pollard, 1820; Poor, *Jefferson's Library*, 11 [no. 652]).

From Destutt de Tracy

Monsieur   Ce 24 9bre 1820.

Il y a precisement aujourdhui deux ans que vous avez pris la peine de m'ecrire une lettre bien aimable—et qui a excité toute ma reconnaissance. elle m'est arrivée le 13 janvier 1819 avec la traduction de mon Economie Politique, et qui lui fait tant d'honneur puisque vous avez Daigné y donner vos Soins. Je Suis confus de la peine que cela vous a causé, et je voudrai bien pouvoir me flatter que mon faible ecrit fut digne de tant de bontés et meritat les eloges que vous lui prodiguez dans la lettre à Mr Milligan que vous avez mise en tete du volume

Ces marques de votre bienveillance, Monsieur, ne S'effaceront jamais de mon cœur; mais ce Sont les dernières que j'aye reçues de vous, et depuis que vous m'honorez de votre correspondance je n'ai jamais été Si longtems Sans recevoir de vos nouvelles j'en Serais tourmenté Si, heureusement Messieurs Gallatin, Barnett et Lafayette ne m'assuraient que vous vous portez bien et que votre Santé qui avait été ebranlée est maintenant en assez bon etat. J'espere que vous ne doutez pas du Soin avec lequel je m'en informe.

Il me reste une inquietude qui n'est rien en comparaison de celle là, mais qui pourtant me tient fort à cœur. je crains que vous n'ayez pas reçu mes lettres et mes livres. je Serais bien faché que vous me crussiez capable d'une telle[1] negligence. cependant j'ai eu l'honneur de vous ecrire au Mois de Mars 1819 et même je me rappelle que dans cette lettre en vous faisant tous les remercimens que je vous devais je vous marquais mon regret de voir que Mr Milligan dans Son Prospectus affirmat que je n'avais pas osé publier dans ma patrie ce traité d'economie politique et je m'affligeai que dans votre pays on crut que chez nous la presse fut beaucoup moins libre qu'elle ne l'est reellement; et à ce Sujet je vous disais que dès l'année 1818 mon commentaire Sur l'esprit des Lois qui est bien autrement hardi avait été imprimé à Liege et entrait librement en france et que j'avais eu l'honneur de vous ecrire en vous l'envoyant. depuis dans l'hiver 1819

un libraire de Paris a fait Sans mon aveu et à mon insçu une reim-
pression de l'edition de Liège et l'a vendue publiquement ces deux
editions etant inexactes et Sans nom d'auteur je me suis determiné
à en faire une troisième en juillet 1819 en y mettant mon nom et en y
ajoutant un petit ecrit Sur cette question: Quels Sont les moyens de
fonder la morale d'un peuple? ouvrage que j'avais fait autrefois pour
la classe des Sciences morales et politiques de l'institut du tems de la
republique française. Comme je tenais à ce que ce dernier ouvrage fut
connu de vous j'ai eu l'honneur de vous ecrire en vous envoyant ce
volume, et ayant Su quelques tems après que le navire par lequel M^r
Barnett vous l'avait expedié S'etait perdu je vous l'ai renvoyé de nouveau. je ne Sais, Monsieur, Si tout cela vous Sera parvenu. Si cela est
perdu il n'y a pas grand mal, mais ce dont je ne me consolerais pas
c'est que l'expression de ma reconnaissance ne fut pas arrivée jusqu'a
vous et que vous pussiez douter un moment des Sentimens d'attache-
ment et de respect que je vous ai voués.   TRACY

P.S. Je voudrais, Monsieur, que le Sincère hommage que je vous
rends à la tête de l'edition du Commentaire Sur l'esprit des Lois à
laquelle j'ai mis mon nom, fut placé à la tête de la traduction Si l'on
en fait jamais quelque nouvelle edition. il Sera à la tête de celle que
l'on en fait actuellement dans la capitale de la vieille Angleterre en
depit des amis de Ses vieilles institutions. Ces defenseurs interessés
des prejugés et des abus ne Sont pas moins ennemies de mes principes economiques que de mes principes politiques et philosophiques
parce qu'en effet les uns Sont intimement liés avec les autres. Pour
complaire à ces Messieurs Mr Malthus dans Son dernier ouvrage vient
de dementir presque tout ce qu'il avait ecrit jusqu'a present, afin de
bien prouver que les gens qui ne font rien Sont de tous les hommes
les plus utiles, et que les pauvres diables qui meurent de faim Sont
très heureux de voir multiplier à coté d'eux les millionnaires. Mr Sismondi en vrai Genevois flatteur des anglais n'a pas manqué d'adopter
ces lumineuses decouvertes. voilà, Monsieur, les progrès que nous
faisons dans le nord de notre Europe pendant que le midi S'evertue à
Conquerir la Liberté et la verité qu'il aime et qu'il cherche Sans les
connaitre. au reste je Serais ingrat de dire du mal de ces nouvelles nations qui cherchent à Se former car elles me traitent très bien. je Suis
deja traduit en Italien et en Espagnol et on m'enseigne en Portugal.
    Je reviens, Monsieur, au desir que je vous exprimais tout à l'heure
Sur la manifestation de mon respect pour votre personne. je vous prie
d'y avoir egard car c'est pour ainsi dire, une disposition testamen-
taire. J'ai manqué mourir cet automne, et tout m'avertit que je n'irai

pas loin. au reste je suis bien degouté du Spectacle de ce monde où les hommes, je ne dis pas comme vous, mais qui vous ressemblent un peu, Sont trop rares, et où les malfaisans fourmillent.

SIR   24 November 1820.

Exactly two years ago today you took the trouble of writing me a very kind letter that made me extremely grateful. It reached me on 13 January 1819, along with the translation of my *Treatise on Political Economy*, which you have highly honored by deigning to attend to it. I am embarrassed by the trouble it has caused you, and I very much wish that I could flatter myself that my feeble writing is worthy of such kindness and deserves the compliments you lavished on it in the letter to Mr. Milligan you placed at the head of the volume

Although these marks of kindness, Sir, will never be erased from my heart, they are the last I have received from you, and ever since you began to honor me with your correspondence, I have never been so long without receiving news from you. This would torment me if Messrs. Gallatin, Barnet, and Lafayette had not fortunately assured me that you are well and that your health, which had been shaken, is now rather good. I hope that you do not doubt the care I take to inform myself about it.

An apprehension remains, which, while nothing in comparison with the above, is nevertheless close to my heart. I fear that you have not received my letters and books. I would be very upset if you thought me capable of such negligence. However, I had the honor of writing to you in the month of March 1819, and I even remember that in that letter, while giving you all due thanks, I expressed my regret at seeing that Mr. Milligan in his prospectus had stated that I dared not publish this *Treatise on Political Economy* in my native land. I was also upset that in your country people might believe that our press is much less free than it is. On this subject, I informed you that since 1818 my much bolder *Commentaire sur l'Esprit des Lois de Montesquieu*, which was printed in Liège, has entered France freely, and that I had had the honor of writing to you about it when I sent it to you. Then, in the winter of 1819, a bookseller in Paris reprinted the Liège edition without my knowledge or permission and sold it to the public. As these two editions are inaccurate and lack the author's name, I decided to issue a third edition in July 1819, with my name attached and including a short piece asking: What are the means to establish the morality of a people? I had written it during the time of the French Republic for the Institut de France's section on moral and political sciences. As I very much wished you to know this work, I had the honor of enclosing it to you. Having learned shortly thereafter that the ship in which Mr. Barnet dispatched this volume to you had been lost, I sent it to you again. I do not know, Sir, if all of this has reached you. If it is lost, there is no great harm, but I would be inconsolable if the expression of my gratitude did not reach you or if you doubted for a second the feelings of attachment and respect I have devoted to you.   TRACY

P.S. Sir, I want my sincere tribute to you, added at the head of the edition of the *Commentaire sur l'Esprit des Lois de Montesquieu* to which I have attached my name, to be placed also at the beginning of the translation, if another edition is ever issued. It will appear at the head of the one currently in press in the capital of old England in spite of the friends of its old institutions. These defenders of prejudice and abuse are no less the enemies of my economic as of my political and philosophical principles, because, in effect, the first is intimately connected with the other two. To please these gentlemen, Mr. Malthus, in his recent book, denied almost everything he had written up to the present day, so as to prove that the people who do nothing are the most useful of men and that the poor devils dying of hunger are quite happy to see millionaires multiply all around them. Mr. Sismondi, who, as a true Genevan, flatters the English, did not fail to embrace these enlightening discoveries. This, Sir, is the progress we are making in northern Europe, while in the South they struggle to win the liberty and truth that they love and seek despite knowing nothing about them. But it would be ungrateful for me to speak ill of these new nations while they try to shape themselves, because they treat me very well. I am already translated into Italian and Spanish, and I am taught in Portugal.

I return, Sir, to my earlier wish regarding my respect for you. I ask you to take it into consideration, because it is, in a manner of speaking, a bequest. I almost died this past autumn, and everything warns me that I have not long to go. I am, moreover, quite disgusted by the spectacle of this world, where men, I do not mean men exactly like you but ones who resemble you even a little, are all too rare, and evildoers abound.

RC (DLC); in an unidentified hand, signed by Destutt de Tracy; endorsed by TJ as received 8 Mar. 1821 from Paris and so recorded in SJL. Probably enclosed in a letter from Destutt de Tracy to Isaac Cox Barnet, dated only "Ce Mardi" ("This Tuesday"), which reads: "M^r De Tracy fait mille Complimens à M^r I Barnett. il a l'honneur de lui envoyer ci joint une lettre pour Mr Jefferson. il le lui a permis; & il prend la Liberté de la lui Recommander, Car il est bien affligé d'etre Si longtems sans avoir de nouvelles de Cet excellent homme" ("Mr. de Tracy extends a thousand compliments to Mr. I. Barnet. He has the honor of sending him the enclosed letter for Mr. Jefferson. Mr. Barnet having allowed him to do so, he takes the liberty of recommending it to him, because he is distressed at having received no news of that excellent man for so long") (RC in MHi; in the same unidentified hand; partially dated at foot of text, with possibly archival notation in pencil beneath dateline: "5 Dec^re 1820"). Translation by Dr. Genevieve Moene.

Destutt de Tracy included his SINCÈRE HOMMAGE in an advertisement at the beginning of his 1819 Paris edition of the *Commentaire sur l'Esprit des Lois de Montesquieu*, which reads "Cet ouvrage existe depuis plus de douze ans. Je l'avais écrit pour M. Jefferson, l'homme des deux mondes que je respecte le plus, et, s'il le jugeait à propos, pour les Etats-Unis de l'Amérique du nord, où en effet il a été imprimé en 1811" ("This work has existed for more than twelve years. I wrote it for Mr. Jefferson, the man of the two worlds I respect the most and, if he thought fit, for the United States of North America, where indeed it was printed in 1811").

The latest work by Thomas Robert MALTHUS was *Principles of Political Economy, considered with a view to their practical Application* (London, 1820).

[1] Manuscript: "tellre."

From John Sanderson

Sir,   Philad[a] Nov. 24th 1820.
I have addressed to you, by the Post Office, the first No. of the
Biography. &c.—which I beg the favour of you to accept, with my
grateful acknowledgements of your kind attention to my former letter. The hurry with which this vol. has been urged into the world, to
meet the conveniences of printers & publishers, has left me no time
for elaborate research, or for studying the graces of composition; & I
doubt whether, even with competent abilities, it could have been rendered, in the midst of the many obstacles that have been opposed to
the execution of it, worthy of your approbation.—The succeeding
numbers, with the assistance I have been promised, will perhaps appear with fewer imperfections; & being yet in the spring of life, I may
live long enough to render the whole work, by the corrections that
future experience may enable me to make, more equal to the importance & dignity of the subject.
    With great respct, I remain Your Obt. Svt.—
                                            JOHN SANDERSON,

RC (DLC); between dateline and salutation: "To thos. Jefferson Esq[r]"; endorsed
by TJ as a letter from "Saunderson John" received 12 Dec. 1820 and so recorded in
SJL.

From Joshua Dodge

Respected Sir,   Marseilles 25 Nov[r] 1820
I have been favored with your esteemed favor of 13 July last with
a note of sundry articles you wish me to procure & forward to you,
consigned to the Collector of the Port to which the Vessel bearer of
them is bound, I thank you Sincerely for having afforded me this
opportunity of being useful, as nothing can be more gratifying to me
than to Shew the warm & respectful attachment I Shall ever entertain
for you. Your enclosures were carefully delivered.
    You have enclosed bill of lading of what I have been able to procure
from the best sources & which I have Shipped on board the Union
Cap[t] Williams & consigned to the Collector of the first Port (not
South of the Chesapeak) the Said Brig may arrive at, I send to the
Collector the Invoice amounting to 364. Frs. 70 c which I have passed
to your debit. The price of the Clarette de Limoux having risen to 50
Sous & M[r] Chevalier, who informs me that he has only about one
hundred bottles left in his Store, having refused to let me have it at

the last price of 40 Sous, I have limited my purchase to fifty Bottles. The 150 bottles of Ledanon I have requested Mrs Priscilla Cathalan Of Nismes to procure & forward Same to me. she has informed me that Mr Tourneysen who had effected the last purchase would attend immediately to my Commission.

The Cask Rivesaltes ordered of Mr Durand arrived just in time to be Shipped on the Union, but I have not yet received an account of its Cost. I regret much that the 150 bottles Ledanon have not reached me in time for this Vessel, but I hope to receive them soon & you may rely on my zealously attending to their earliest Shipment. John Vaughan Esqr of Philadelphia has remitted to me for your account under date of 25 July a bill of 1060 frs at 60 days sight on Messrs James Lafitte & Co of Paris which I have negotiated & the net Proceeds of which I have credited your account. Our trade here is in a complete State of Stagnation since the measures lately enforced—notwithstanding the obstacles I have met from Some of the authorities here, I have succeeded in preventing any of our Vessels from coming in & they are now, I am confident, Sufficiently warned to avoid the Snare, Such Cargoes as were destined for this Port have proceeded to Nice where part has been Sold & the remainder Shipped for this place in French Vessels, thereby enjoying the benifit of a lesser Consumption duty. thus the measure of the French Government has not been injurious to any but themselves & this place Suffers from it in a much greater proportion than most French Ports as Our American Vessels now supply Piemont & the Levant, which formerly took their Supplies from the Entrepot of Marseilles. The Union is one of the Vessels that went to Nice from whence She has come round here in ballast to load. I sincerely wish matters may soon be arranged on the equitable grounds So properly insisted on by our Government. This letter and the Invoice of your Supplies (which I have Sent to the Collector in order to enable him to do the needful at the Custom house) will be sent you by him. If you are Satisfied with my endeavours to fulfil your wishes, may I request as a token of your satisfaction that you will on all occassions, where I can be of use, command my Services. for being occupied in any thing that relates to a person So justly intitled to love & veneration, is the most pleasing task to which I can devote my exertions.

I remain with the greatest respect
Your most Obed^t Servt   JOSH^A DODGE

RC (MHi); at foot of text: "To Thomas Jefferson Esqr Monticello, Virginia"; en-   dorsed by TJ as received 7 May 1821 and so recorded in SJL. Enclosure not found.

Enclosed in Joseph Wilson to TJ, 23 Apr. 1821, not found (see note to TJ to Wilson, 10 May 1821).

MEASURES LATELY ENFORCED: in retaliation for a 15 May 1820 United States "Act to impose a new tonnage duty on French ships and vessels," French authorities passed their own ordinance on 26 July of that year levying additional duties on American vessels arriving in French ports (*U.S. Statutes at Large*, 3:605; *American Beacon and Norfolk & Portsmouth Daily Advertiser*, 16 Sept. 1820).

From D. Mariano

HON^BLE SIR,   Washington city, 26th of Nov. 1820.

I had the honour of writing to you from Lexington K^y, and requesting your patronage in order of obtaining a birth in your University:— since that time having constantly applied myself to the study of the English language I dare to think myself more entitled to it, and now renew my request. Among the languages which I know those which I think myself qualified to teach are the Latin, Italian and French— even the Spanish could be reckaned among them, though being out of practice I do not speak it fluently.—As a scholar I refer to some specimens which you may probably have read in those numbers of a literary journal, which I had the honour of forwarding to you from Kentucky, and more particularly to Mr Holley, whose friendship and estimation are a subject of pride to me; as a Gentleman to Mr Monroe, and Mr Adams, whose kindness I daily experience—Should there be any probability of my being employed in your University, will you be so good, Sir, as to let me know which would be my duties, and what the salary and advantages annexed to[1] them.—

I hope, Sir, you will forgive this mine intrusion on your time, and permit me to subscribe myself most respectfully,

Your obedient Servant   D. MARIANO

RC (ViU: TJP); endorsed by TJ as a letter from "Mariana D." received 12 Dec. 1820 and so recorded in SJL.

[1] Manuscript: "to to."

From Joseph Milligan

                                        Georgetown
ESTEEMED & RESPECTED FRIEND   November 27th 1820

By this days mail I have sent you a copy of Ricardos Political Economy which please have the goodness to give a place in your library

It is long since we have exchanged letters but I am the debtor

The Bookselling part of my business has passed into other hands since the 1st of June 1819. At that time my business was drawn to a crissis by having to pay Endorsements. I then declined the selling part, of my business in favour of a young man who had been with me from a boy he is now doing as much in that way as I ever did and his attention to business has secured to him all my old customers

I have so far waded through my difficulties as to be confident that I feel the firm ground once more and the water not more than knee deep My difficulties were never brot on by a miscalculation in Bookselling or publishing therfore I am mustering my little matters all together (as I have made terms with my creditors) to resume the publishing and disposing of books by subscription and to the booksellers of respectable standing and leave Mr James Thomas (the young man who called on you about two years ago with Tracy) to carry on the retail bookselling in my old stand for his own profit

I find that there is not a[1] single copy of your notes on Virginia amongst the booksellers so with your permission I propose to print an Octavo edition on a fine paper from the original edition if I can procure one; but I know of none except the copy that is in the library of Congress— Could you tell me where I can procure a copy

I expect to have business at Richmond this Winter if so I will either go or return by Monticello and will then bring the little account with me that you requested to have furnished about 18 Months ago

I called on The President the 22nd inst: he wants me to do a considerable Job of bookbinding for him I enquired of him after your health which I am happy to hear is on the mend

Our old & mutual friend John Barnes is[2] in good health his family now consists of himself (his old housekeeper Mrs Ratcliff) his Grandson & two Granddaughters the whole of which seem comfortable and happy

With the best wishes for your health & happiness

I am dear friend   yours with respect

JOSEPH MILLIGAN

Kindly remember my respects to Mrs Randolph and all the family

J:M

RC (DLC); at foot of first page: "over"; endorsed by TJ as received 12 Dec. 1820 and so recorded in SJL. RC (DLC); address cover only; with PoC of TJ to Joseph Echols, 23 May 1822, on verso; addressed: "Thomas Jefferson Esqr Monticello Milton (virginia)"; franked; postmarked Georgetown, 30 Nov.

[1] Manuscript: "as."
[2] Manuscript: "is is."

To Joseph C. Cabell

I sent in due time the Report of the Visitors to the Governor, with a request that he would endeavor to convene the Literary board in time to lay it before the legislature on the 2^d day of their session. it was inclosed in a letter which will explain itself to you. if delivered before the croud of other business presses on them, they may act on it immediately, and before there will have been time for unfriendly combinations and maneuvres by the enemies of the institution.   I inclose you now a paper presenting some views which may be useful to you in conversations, to rebut exaggerated estimates of what our institution is to cost, and reproaches of deceptive estimates. 162.364.D. will be about[1] the cost of the whole establishment when compleated. not an office at Washington has cost less. the single building of the Courthouse of Henrico has cost nearly that: and the massive walls of the millions of bricks of W^m & Mary could not be now built for a greater sum.

Surely Governor Clinton's display of the gigantic efforts of N. York towards the education of their citizens will stimulate the pride, as well as the patriotism of our legislature, to look to the reputation & safety of their own country, to rescue it from the degradation of becoming the Barbary of the union, and of falling into the ranks of our own negroes. to that condition it is fast sinking. we shall be, in the hands of the other states what our indigenous predecessors were when invaded by the science & arts of Europe. the mass of education in Virginia, before the revolution, placed her with the foremost of her sister colonies. what is her education now? where is it? the little we have we import, like beggars, from other states; or import their beggars to bestow on us their miserable crumbs. and what is wanting to restore us to our station among our confederates? not more money from the people. enough has been raised by them, and appropriated to this very object. it is that it should be employed understandingly, and for their greatest good. that good requires that, while they are instructed in general, competently to the common businesses of life, others should employ their genius with necessary information, to the useful arts, to inventions for saving labor and increasing our comforts, to nourishing our health, to civil government, military science E^t.

Would it not have a good effect for the friends of the University to take the lead in proposing and effectuating a practicable scheme of elementary schools? to assume the character of the friends, rather than the opponents of that object? the present plan has appropriated to the primary schools 45,000.D. for 3. years, making 135,000.D. I should be glad to know if this sum has educated 135. poor children? I doubt it much. and if it has, they have cost us 1000.D. apiece for what might have been done with 30.D. supposing the literary revenue to be 60,000.D. I think it demonstrable that this sum equally divided between the two objects, would amply suffice for both.   100. counties, divided into about 12 wards each, on an average, and a school in each ward of perhaps 10. children, would be 1200. schools, distributed proportionably over the surface of the state. the inhabitants of each ward, meeting together (as when they work on the roads) building good log houses for their school and teacher, and contributing for his provisions rations of pork, beef & corn in the proportion each of his other taxes, would thus lodge and feed him without feeling it, and those of them who are able, paying for the tuition of their own children, would leave no call on the publick fund but for the tuition fee of here and there an accidental pauper, who would still be fed & lodged with his parents. suppose this fee 10.D. and 300.D. apportioned to a county on an average (more or less duly proportioned) would there be 30. such paupers for every county? I think not. the truth is that the want of common education with us is not from our poverty, but from the want of an orderly system. more money is now paid for the education of a part, than would be paid for that of the whole if systematically arranged. 6000. common schools in New York, 50. pupils in each, 300,000 in all; 160.000.D. annually paid to the masters; 40. established academies, with 2218. pupils, and 5. Colleges with 718. students, to which last classes of[2] institutions 720,000.D. have been given, and the whole appropriations for education estimated at $2\frac{1}{2}$ millions of Dollars! what a pigmy to this[3] is Virginia become! with a population all but equal to that of New York! and whence this difference? from the difference their rulers set on the value of knolege, and the prosperity it produces. but still, if a pigmy, let her do what a pigmy may do. if among 50. children in each of the 6000. schools of N. York there are only paupers enough to employ 25.D. of public money to each school, surely among the 10. children of each of our 1200. schools, the same sum of 25.D. to each school will teach it's paupers (5 times as much as to the same numbers in N.Y.) and will amount for the whole to 30,000.D. a year, the one half only of our Literary revenue.

Do then, dear Sir, think of this, and engage our friends to take in hand the whole subject. it will reconcile the friends of the elementary schools, (and none is more warmly so than myself)[4] lighten the difficulties of the University; and promote in every order of men the degree of instruction proportioned to their condition, and to their views in life. it will combine with the mass of our force, a wise direction of it, which will ensure to our country it's future prosperity and safety. I had formerly thought that Visitors for the schools might be chosen by the county, and charged to provide teachers for every ward & to superintend them. I now think it would be better for every ward to chuse it's own resident visitor whose business it would be to keep a teacher in the ward, to superintend the school, and to call meetings of the ward for all purposes relating to it. their accounts to be settled, and wards laid off by the courts. I think ward elections better for many reasons, one of which is sufficient, that it will keep elementary education out of the hands of fanaticising preachers, who in county elections would be universally chosen, and the predominant sect of the county would possess itself of all it's schools.

A wrist stiffened by an antient accident, now more so by the effect of age, renders writing a slow and irksome operation with me. I cannot therefore present these views, by separate letters, to each of our Colleagues in the Legislature: but must pray you to communicate them to mr Johnson and Genl Breckenridge, & to request them to consider this as equally meant for them. mr Gordon being the local representative of the University, and among it's most zealous friends would be a more useful second to General Breckenridge in the House of Delegates, by a free communication of what concerns the University, with which he has had little opportunity of becoming acquainted. so also would it be as to mr Rives,[5] who would be a friendly advocate.   Accept the assurances of my constant and affectionate esteem & respect.   TH: JEFFERSON

RC (ViU: TJP); at foot of first page: "Mr Cabell"; endorsed by Cabell. FC (DLC: TJ Papers, 218:39015, 39047); in the hands of Virginia J. Randolph (Trist) and Ellen W. Randolph (Coolidge), with emendations, closing, and signature by TJ. Enclosure: TJ's Estimate of University of Virginia Building Costs, [ca. 28 Nov. 1820].

TJ outlined what he FORMERLY THOUGHT about the selection of visitors for elementary schools in his Bill for Establishing Elementary Schools, [ca. 9 Sept. 1817], and his Bill for Establishing a System of Public Education, [ca. 24 Oct. 1817].

[1] Word interlined.
[2] Portion of FC in Virginia J. Randolph (Trist)'s hand ends here.
[3] Preceding two words interlined.
[4] Parenthetical phrase interlined.
[5] RC: "Rieves." FC: "Rives."

Estimate of University of Virginia Building Costs

[ca. 28 Nov. 1820]

A general view of what the lands, buildings & all other expenditures for the University will have cost, when compleated, estimated from the monies actually recieved, & what the Proctor states as further necessary.

		D
Recieved of the Subscriptions about		19,000
Loan from the Literary fund		60,000
Annuities of 1819.20.		30,000
	109,000	
to be recieved, the annuity of 1821. included in Proct's estimate		15,000
further necessary to compleat the Pavil^s Hotels & Dorm^s by d^o		38,364
Probable actual cost of whole establmt (exclus. of Library)[1]		162,364.

Estimates heretofore made.

	D
10. Pavilions for accomodn of Professors @ 6000.D. each	60,000.
6. Hotels for dieting the Students @ 3500.D. each	21,000
104. Dormitories @ 350.D. each	36,400.
200. a^s of lands & buildings purchased, may be stated as worth	10,000
covering with tin, instead of shingles, levelling grounds & streets bringing water in pipes & numerous other contingencies, say	10,000
Excess of actual cost above the estimates (about 18.[2] p. cent)	24,964
	162,364.

To liberate the funds of the University and to open it in 1821. with only 6. professors, will require

1. a remission of the loan of 60,000.D.
2. a supplementory sum to liberate the annuities of 1821.2.3.   45,000.
3. to make good the deficit estimated by the Proctor   8,364
4. an additional sum for the building of the Library   40,000
5. and to establish & maintain 10. Professorships an equal partition of the literary fund between the University & elementary schools will be necessary, say 30,000. a year to each.

A building for an Observatory not having been mentioned in the Rockfish Report, is not brought into view here. it will cost about 10.

or 12,000.D. and may be accomplished by the balance of subscription money not taken into account in the Report of 1820. and by the rents for the Hotels & Dormitories.

MS (ViU: TJP); entirely in TJ's hand; undated; final paragraph added separately to MS and PoC; endorsed by Joseph C. Cabell: "Statement by Mr Jefferson of the probable cost of the buildings of the University of Virginia, exclusive of the Library-House"; with additional notations by Cabell beneath endorsement giving the cost of constructing the entire campus, including the library, as $202,364, and listing the types and numbers of the various structures making up the university. PoC (DLC: TJ Papers, 218:39045). Enclosed in TJ to Cabell, 28 Nov. 1820.

[1] Omitted closing parenthesis editorially supplied.
[2] Superfluous opening parenthesis preceding this number editorially omitted.

To Edmund Bacon

DEAR SIR   Pop. For. Nov. 29. 20

Your's of the 21st came to hand yesterday.[1] you have done right in having the safety gate finished, and at any moment when the convenience of the great mill shall admit, it should be laid down, as we know not when a fresh may put us into danger. should mr Meeks be gone, get mr Gilmore to direct it, and indeed I would at any rate rather have it done under his direction. I must get you to look out for a successor to Meeks, and engage him on the best terms you can. in the mean time employ James & Beverly in dressing timber for the coopers under your own superintendance. I salute you with my best wishes.   TH: JEFFERSON

PoC (MHi); on verso of reused address cover of John G. Robert (for Patrick Gibson) to TJ, 16 Aug. 1819; at foot of text: "Mr Bacon"; endorsed by TJ.

[1] Omitted period at right margin editorially supplied.

To Francis W. Gilmer

Poplar Forest Nov. 29. 20.

I thank you, dear Sir, for the communication of mr Correa's letter, affectionate to us all, which I now return. no foreigner, I believe, has ever carried with him more, or more sincere regrets of the friends he has left behind. as he embraced in his affections our country generally, I hope his kind recollections will efface the little dissatisfactions he felt with our government before they can have any effect on the amities of the two countries. I think the events in Portugal, and possibly the effects of their example on Brazil, may yet disturb his purposes, & perhaps his destinies. while our duties oblige us to wish well to these revolutionary movements, they do not forbid our prayers for their favorable effects on his fortunes: and certainly in spirit he must go with them. ever & affectionately yours.   TH: JEFFERSON

RC (ViU: TJP); at foot of text: "Mr Gilmer"; endorsed by Gilmer. PoC (DLC); on verso of reused address cover to TJ; endorsed by TJ. Enclosure: enclosure to Gilmer to TJ, 15 Nov. 1820.

The recent EVENTS IN PORTUGAL came to be known as the Liberal Revolution,

during which revolutionaries demanded the return of the Portuguese court from Brazil, the end of absolutist rule, and the establishment of a constitutional monarchy, all of which took place over the next two years.

To James Madison

DEAR SIR   Poplar Forest Nov. 29. 20.

The inclosed letter from our antient friend Tenche Coxe came unfortunately to Monticello after I had left it and has had a dilatory passage to this place where I recieved it yesterday and obey it's injunction of immediate transmission to you. we should have recognised[1] the stile even without a signature, and altho so written as to be much of it indecypherable. this is a sample of the effects we may expect from the late mischievous law vacating every 4. years nearly all the executive offices of the government. it saps the constitutional and salutary functions of the President, and introduces a principle of intrigue & corruption, which will soon leaven the mass, not only of Senators, but of citizens. it is more baneful than the attempt which failed in the beginning of the government to make all officers irremovable but with the consent of the Senate. this places every 4. years all appointments under their power, and even obliges them to act on every one nominatim. it will keep in constant excitement all the hungry cormorants for office, render them, as well as those in place, sycophants to their Senators, engage these in eternal intrigue to turn out one and put in another, in cabals to swap work, and make of them, what all executive directories become, mere sinks of corruption & faction. this must have been one of the midnight signatures of the President, when he had not time to consider, or even to read the law: and the more fatal as being irrepealable but with the consent of the Senate, which will never be obtained.

F. Gilmer has communicated to me mr Correa's letter to him of Adieux to his friends here, among whom he names most affectionately mrs Madison and yourself. no foreigner I believe has ever carried with him more friendly regrets.[2] he was to sail the next day (Nov. 10.) in the British packet for England, & thence take his passage in Jan. for Brazil. his present views are of course liable to be affected by the events of Portugal, & the possible effects of their example on Brazil.   I expect to return to Monticello about the middle of the ensuing month and salute you with constant affection and respect.

TH: JEFFERSON

RC (DLC: Madison Papers, Rives Collection). PoC (DLC); edge trimmed; at foot of first page: "M͏ʳ Madison." Enclosure: Tench Coxe to TJ, 11 Nov. 1820.

In congressional debates culminating in the 27 July 1789 "Act for establishing an Executive Department, to be denominated the Department of Foreign Affairs," then-congressman Madison proposed a clause on 19 May giving the president sole power to remove secretaries of executive departments. Proposals to require that removals have THE CONSENT OF THE SENATE were discussed at length, but Madison's idea eventually prevailed (*U.S. Statutes at Large*, 1:28–9; Linda Grant De Pauw and others, eds., *Documentary History of the First Federal Congress* [1972–2017], vols. 10–11; Madison, *Papers, Congress. Ser.*, 12:55–7). NOMINATIM: "particularly; expressly" (*OED*).

[1] Word interlined in place of "known."
[2] Omitted period at right margin editorially supplied.

To Charles Vest

Poplar Forest Nov. 29. 20.

   Th: Jefferson salutes mr Vest with friendship and respect and there being no person now at Monticello to see to the weekly transmission of his mails to this place, he asks the favor of mr Vest[1] to do him that kind office, sending weekly by the Lynchburg mail all <u>letters</u>, the <u>Enquirers</u>, and <u>Niles's Registers</u> directed to him, and to retain all other newspapers pamphlets, books, or other packets of size, till he hears from him again

PoC (Corporation for Jefferson's Poplar Forest, on deposit ViU: TJP); on verso of portion of reused address cover of John Binns to TJ, 27 July 1819; dateline at foot of text; endorsed by TJ as a letter to "Vest Charles" and so recorded in SJL.

Charles Vest (d. 1828), merchant, postmaster, and tanner, was active in Albemarle County by 1809, when TJ noted that he had closed his grocery and "become a writer in a merchant's counting house." Vest served as postmaster at Mil-ton, 1811–24. He sold TJ a mule in 1812, and several times between 1813 and 1822 TJ paid him for tanning and leather or for stage carriage of books. In 1824 Vest and Nimrod Bramham leased TJ's Shadwell manufacturing mill. Vest moved to Randolph, Tipton County, Tennessee, in the spring of 1828 and worked there as a merchant before he died of a fever later that year (TJ to Abraham Bradley, 7 Sept. 1809; Axelson, *Virginia Postmasters*, 5; *MB*; Charlottesville *Virginia Advocate*, 22 Nov. 1828; Albemarle Co. Will Book, 9:348).

On this date TJ also sent an almost identically worded letter to John Winn, the Charlottesville postmaster (PoC in MHi; on verso of portion of reused address cover to TJ; dateline at foot of text; endorsed by TJ as a letter to "Winn John" and so recorded in SJL).

[1] Manuscript: "mr Winn."

From Lebbeus Chapman

SIR   New York 30 Nov[r] 1820

Enclosed you will receive my Work on interest which I have taken the liberty to send for your perusal when at leisure. I am now preparing a work on interest which will consist of nearly 400 Quarto pages, with the calculations all made at 6 p[r] c[t] p[r] Annum on all sums from $1– to $400. then by 50[s] to $2000.. then by 100[s] to $3000.. & then by 1000[s] to[1] $10.000.. from 1 to 365 days. Every day to Correspond with the page & on the same sums from 1 to 12 Months. in addition a Table Commencing at $10.000 progressing by 1000 to $100.000.. & then by 10.000 to $1.000.000.. with the interest together with the Fractions calculated thereon for one day at 5 & at 6 p[r] c[t] p[r] Annum.   If on Examination you find my principle of calculation Correct & should deem such a Work Worthy of Public patronage, will you have the goodness to Signify the same in a Letter to my address and allow me the honour of adding your name to the List of my Subscribers.

I am very respectfully dear sir your obed[t] Humble Servant

LEBBEUS CHAPMAN

RC (DLC); at foot of text: "Hon Tho[s] Jefferson"; endorsed by TJ as received 12 Dec. 1820 and so recorded in SJL. Enclosure: Chapman, *Tables of Interest and Discount, calculated on the only true principle of 365 Days to the Year; and compared with the erroneous method now in use* (New York, 1820).

Lebbeus Chapman (1785–1864), merchant and accountant, was born in Middlesex County, Connecticut. By 1808 he was partner in a New York City mercantile firm, and he was listed in that city's directories successively as grocer, 1809–10, merchant, 1811–16, auctioneer, 1817–18, accountant, 1822, and secretary of insurance companies, 1825–34 and 1842–47. Chapman lived in Jersey City, New Jersey, in the mid-1840s before moving in about 1848 to Brooklyn. He died in

Westchester County, New York (Frederick W. Chapman, *The Chapman Family: or the Descendants of Robert Chapman* [1854], 220–2; New York *Mercantile Advertiser*, 14 Sept. 1808; New York *National Advocate*, 25 Feb. 1817; *Longworth's New York Directory* [1809]: 130; [1810]: 136; [1811]: 52; [(1816)]: 154; [(1817)]: 145; [1818]: 79; [1822]: 118; [1825]: 36, 115; [1834]: 52, 186; [1842]: 145; *The New-York City and Co-Partnership Directory, for 1843 & 1844* [(1843)], 67; *Doggett's New-York City Directory, for 1847 & 1848* [(1847)], 84; *Doggett's New York City Directory . . . 1848–1849* [(1848)], 85; *New York Herald*, 9 Jan. 1864; gravestone inscription in Green-Wood Cemetery, Brooklyn).

On this day Chapman sent the enclosed work to John Adams with a nearly identical letter (MHi: Adams Papers).

Chapman soon published *Chapman's Tables of Interest, calculated according to equitable and legal principles, at the rate of six per cent. per annum; showing the interest of any sum, from one cent to ten thousand dollars, from one day to three hundred and sixty-five days, from one to* *twelve months, and from two to thirteen years. With several other useful tables, explanations, &c. The whole comprising nearly one hundred and eighty thousand calculations* (New York, 1821).

[1] Manuscript: "to to."

From Bernard Peyton

DEAR SIR,   Rich'd 4 Decem[r] 1820

Your draft favor M[r] Garland for $600 has been presented & paid some time since, & I will on Wednesday next pay $500 towards your $3,000 note due at the Farmers Bank on that day, being the am[t] of curtail called for by them on that note.   on Friday last rec[d] from Jefferson Randolph three Blank notes for the renewal your several notes under my management, which are in time, & shall be duely attended to: in his letter he mentioned that none of your Flour had then been shipped, but would dispatch it on the first rise of the water in the River, which the present thaw will afford, so that I presume it may be expected in a few days: The article is still declining, & now dull sale at 3\frac{9}{16}$—Wheat 67¢, Tobacco old 4\frac{3}{4}$ @ 9$\frac{1}{2}$, new 3\frac{3}{4}$ @ 7—

It affords me pleasure to inform you that the Gen[l] Court have decided, (in which they had the concurrence of the Jury), that there was no defalcation in the Treasury during the year 1819, (which year alone I am surety) & that consequently the securities of that year are free from responsibility:—the Commonwealth's Council have appealed from this decision to the Court of Appeals, where I hope we have still less to fear—   With sincere regard D[r] sir

Yours very Truely   BERNARD PEYTON

RC (MHi); endorsed by TJ as received 8 Dec. 1820 and so recorded in SJL.

Peyton was a SURETY for the former Virginia treasurer John Preston (*Richmond Enquirer*, 1 Dec. 1820, 3 July 1821).

From Michele Raggi

STIMATISSIMO SIG^R TOMASO JEFFERSON   Gibiltera
A MONTICELLO VIRGINIA   4. Xbre 1820—

Dalla mia Scritale di New york avra inteso che M'inbarcai in detta Cità ℔ questo porto di Gibiltera il qual passaggio l'abiamo fatto felicemente in trenta Giorni asieme à tre altri passegieri Americani che vengono in Italia ℔ loro divertimento, e ℔ vedere le antichità di Roma Napoli ed altre città questi l'i ò ritrovati bravissimi giovani dai qualli ò ricevutto delle grandi fineze nel bastimento, essendo io stato Senpre malato si sono prestati come veri frattelli questi sono tutti 3. di Boston io son disposto a fare il medesimo ℔ loro se potrò avere il piacere di rincontrarli in Toscana dove mi anno promesso di Passarci, mà la prima l'oro gita e di andare à Messina avendo di Già fissato il passaggio Fin da New york col Medesimo Bastimento che sia portali qui, di là verano a Napoli, ed entrerano nel continente d'Italia.

La prego Sig^r Jefferson di rimetermi in Livorno li duecento daleri o sia Pezi di Spagna, ò a titolo dei disegni come ci Scrissi di New york ò a titolo del mio dovuto mi Viaggio Sperò che avrà in consideralzione li grandi Strapazi e disastri che ò avuto, e che non Sarebbe giustizia oltre di ritornare a casa mia senza un Soldo di dovere fare anche dei debiti, Se poi lei vuole come ci esposi anche in Scrito costi, Sono Senpre pronto anche a ritornare con Mia Moglie purche mi faci un Contrato nuovo ℔ anni quatro, e lei non avrà da pensare che à un sol viaggio ℔ me solo e li altri viaggi e spese ℔ mia moglie sarà tutto a mio carico, e ℔ il nudrimento mi passerà quello che paga ℔ il Mangiare e Bere ed inbiancare, ed io penserò a tutto così nella buona Stagione io partirei con mia moglie e figlio ed avrei tenpo in questo Inverno di poterli fare abozare li Capitilli di Marmo in Carrara, che non gli costereberò nepure quanto la pietra e potrà avere un lavoro Stabile e ben lavorato, lei mi dice nella Sua che ricevei a Washington che se stavo a finire il mio tenpo gli potevo fare del Avantaggio nel lavoro; Si assicuri Signore che non era possibille di poter far piu avantaggio di quello che ciò fato in quei mesi che sono stato al Coleggio essendo questa una pietra inpraticabile ℔ lavori di Scoltura ornativa Se poi non vuole fissare un nuovo contrato, mi mandi la comissionne almeno di farci li quatro Corinti in Carrara, e ℔ fargli vedere che lo voglio Servire a pochissimo guadagno me li pagherà Solo trecento cinquanta doleri, e ce li darò ben finiti ed incassati in Livorno, e me li farà pagare al ato della consegna al Sig^r Console Appleton col qualle pote andar di concerto, e cosi allora non ci saraño piu questioni, ne di viaggi, ne d'altro, che io non gli prentendero piu niente, e gli farò cezione di tutto. Se poi non vuole conbinare ne in una maniera, ne nel altra, la prego di farmi passare li duecento Taleri che mi sono dovutti ℔ giustizia dovere, e Umanità. Se gli dissi che non ero bene costi nella maniera del nudrimento, e cativo Caffe, non erà ℔ intacare l'onestà e galantomismo del Sig\[r] Brockenbrog anzi lo Stimo credo anche io un gran galantuomo, ma la maniera di vivere non era come siamo soefatti noi Italiani, ed io avendo uno Stomaco molto debole se fossi restato anche qualche mese costi ci avrei lasciato la Vita sicuramente frà la povere della pietra e il nudrimento, credo benissimo che il Sig\[r] Brockenbrog le pi volte non avrà Saputo nepure quello che mi mandavano da mangiare avendo costi l'uso di affidare tutto alli Neri, la prego dunque di Salutarmi il d\[to] Sig\[r] Brockenbrog come tutti di Sua rispetabil famiglia, come rispetosamente facio con lei e tutti li suoi confrattelli augurandoli tutte le felicità e Salute come il Suo cuore desidera confermandomi di Vra Signoria Ilmo.   Umo devmo Servitore

MICHELE RAGGI

EDITORS' TRANSLATION

MOST ESTEEMED MR. THOMAS JEFFERSON   Gibraltar
AT MONTICELLO VIRGINIA   4. December 1820—
From what I wrote you from New York you will have surmised that I embarked in that city for the port of Gibraltar. I made the voyage with good fortune in thirty days, together with three American passengers who are going to Italy for pleasure and to see the antiquities of Rome, Naples, and other cities. I found them to be excellent young men, and they treated me with great kindness while on board. I was sick the whole time, and they assisted me like real brothers. All three of them are from Boston. I would like to repay them if I have the pleasure of seeing them again in Tuscany, where they have promised to spend some time. Having arranged in New York to travel to Messina in the same vessel that brought them here, however, their first excursion is to that place. From thence they will enter mainland Italy at Naples.

As I wrote you from New York, I beg you, Mr. Jefferson, to send to Leghorn two hundred dollars, or Spanish pesos, for my drawings or for the travel expenses owed to me. I hope that you will consider the great hardships and disasters I have suffered and that in addition to those it would not be fair if I returned home penniless and further in debt. Later, if you wish, I can always return to America with my wife, as will be explained below, provided that you give me a new four-year contract. You need only pay for my trip, as my wife's expenses will be my own responsibility. For board, you will have to give me enough for my food, drink, and laundry. I will ponder all this before departing with my wife and son after the weather improves.

This winter I will have time to rough out the marble capitals in Carrara and thus provide you with a solid, well-executed job that will cost you less than the stone itself. You say in the letter I received in Washington that if I had stayed and finished my contractual time, I would have made more progress in my work. Rest assured, Sir, that it was impossible for me to do any more than I had already done in the months I spent at the college, because the stone was unsuitable for ornamental sculpture work. If you do not wish to make a new contract, at least send me the commission to make the four Corinthian capitals at Carrara. To show that I am willing to serve you for very little gain, you will only have to pay me three hundred and fifty dollars for them. I will deliver the capitals to Leghorn, finished well and boxed up, and you can pay me when I give them to Mr. Consul Appleton, who acts in concert with you. In this way there would be no more questions, either of traveling or anything else; I would claim nothing more; and I would waive everything you still owe me. If, in the end, you decide not to make an agreement, please arrange to send the two hundred talers due me, so that justice and humanity will be served. When I told you that I did not fare well in America in terms of food and that the coffee was bad, I was not attacking Mr. Brockenbrough's honesty and integrity. On the contrary, I respect him and consider him to be a fine gentleman. We Italians, however, are not used to that way of life, and because of my exceedingly weak stomach, the stone dust and poor food would surely have cost me my life if I had remained there even a few months more. I truly believe that most of the time Mr. Brockenbrough did not even know what was being sent to me to eat, because the custom there is to entrust all of that to the blacks. I implore you, therefore, to give my regards to the said Mr. Brockenbrough and his estimable family, as I respectfully do to you and your compatriots, wishing you all the happiness and good health that your heart desires and confirming myself, most illustrious lordship   Your most humble and devoted servant   MICHELE RAGGI

RC (DLC); endorsed by TJ as received 10 Apr. 1821 and so recorded in SJL. Translation by Dr. Jonathan T. Hine.

From Edward Wiatt

SIR,   Cumberland, m^d Decem^r 4. 1820.

The known benevolence of your character renders apology for this address scarcely necessary.

I am anxious to make some enquiries respecting the Virginia University about to be established at Charlottesville, and, as I am personally unknown to any person from whom to expect it, I have taken the liberty of troubling you to inform me.

About what time is it expected the course of Education will commence?

What will probably be the annual cost of Tuition, board &C?

My motive for this inquiry is, that I have a Brother whom I am anxious to place in a suitable situation to acquire a good Education and various considerations make the scite of the Virginia University preferable to any other.

The opportunities to vice and immorality in our Cities are always numerous and alluring and my Brother is of that tender age when the propensities to indulge in evil habits are strongest.

Moreover, the present political state of the Northern and Eastern Sections of the Union is to my mind not a little objectionable. If therefore there is a reasonable prospect of the University of my native state going into early operation I will delay and place my Brother there.

Your reply will be duly estimated.

Permit me to add my unaffected wishes that the evening of your life may be as happy as the preceding part was distinguished and useful.

I am, Sir, your ob^t Servt EDWARD WIATT

RC (CSmH: JF); endorsed by TJ as received 31 Dec. 1820 and so recorded in SJL. RC (DLC); address cover only; with PoC of TJ to John H. Cocke, 1 Apr. 1821, on verso; addressed: "Thomas Jefferson, Esq Monticello Albemarle County," and redirected successively in unidentified hands to Lynchburg and Monticello; franked; postmarked Cumberland, 4 Dec., Milton, 10 Dec., and Lynchburg, 29 Dec.

Edward Wiatt, public official, was a native of Virginia who served as deputy postmaster of Winchester in 1816. He was appointed postmaster of Cumberland, Maryland, late in 1819 and removed early the following year. The 1820 Cumberland census lists Wiatt with three slaves, and he represented Allegany County for one term in the Maryland House of Delegates, 1821–22. Wiatt returned to Winchester by 1825 and proposed moving west the following year (*A Register of Officers and Agents, Civil, Military, and Naval, in the service of the United States, On the thirtieth day of September, 1816* [Washington, 1816], 71; Scharf, *Western Maryland*, 2:1339; Wiatt to James Monroe, 23 Jan. 1820 [DNA: RG 59, MLR]; DNA: RG 29, CS, Md., Cumberland, 1820; Edward C. Papenfuse and others, eds., *An Historical List of Public Officials of Maryland* [1990–], 1:129; Wiatt to Henry Clay, 14 Oct. 1826 [DNA: RG 59, LAR, 1825–29]).

From George Alexander Otis

SIR,   Philadelphia 5th Decem 1820

I have the honour to address to you the Second volume of my translation; which I have laboured with all the industry and care I am capable of, and Should deem myself amply rewarded if it is so fortunate as to find acceptance with the highest authority in my Country.

The President Adams is so good as to wish me well and success to my labours; but he complains that in the first Volume, there is "too manifest a disposition to bestow the laurels on the Southern States, which ought to decorate the brows[1] of the northern." As for myself, I feel no interest but for truth; considering the American nation as a whole, I as much participate in and Sympathize with the reputation and the glory which irradiates the South, as in that which gleams in the east. "I will mention an instance, continues the same gentleman, which you may attribute, if you please, to my vanity. The Speeches of Richard Henry Lee, and John Dickinson upon the question of Independence are gross impositions on mankind. I encourage however the propagation of the work upon all occasions, though it appears to me too much like Davila's History of the civil wars in France, which although it may compare as a composition with Livy, Thucydides or Sallust, and although it professes a wonderful impartiality, yet is as manifestly an apology for Catharine de Medicis and the Cardinal de Lorraine, as Hume's History of England is for the Stuarts. It is a tedious thing for me to read three Volumes, but if my life is spared and strength remains, I will read them, and then if I can in conscience, will retract all that I have Said about them."[2]==I ask pardon for taking the liberty of thus intimating the opposition which is likely to be made to my success in New England; as an apology for which, I have nothing to offer but the kind interest which you were pleased to express in the general tone of your letter for the interests of my enterprise; which I have no hope of any other recompense for executing than that of the approbation of those I most revere. Except indeed it should induce Mr Monroe[3] to appoint me to Some office such as my talents fit me for, and which I have already mentioned to him, and was heard with encouragement. I have lost an independent fortune within a few years by misfortune. My character is acknowledged by every one Spotless. If you find it in your noble breast to further my views, it cannot add to the veneration I already bear you, but it will to my happiness and Success.

The last volume is in press and will be published next month. I must frankly declare that I think this work calculated to do much good; and that if I had not undertaken it I know of no person in the United S. that would have done it. In all probability, fifty years might have elapsed before it would have been translated. I therefore feel that I have deserved well of my country.

I remain with that profound respect which I cannot but feel, and with a sense of real obligation, sir, Your most faithful And obedient Servant   GEORGE ALEXANDER OTIS.

RC (DLC); between dateline and salutation: "Honorable Thomas Jefferson"; endorsed by TJ as received 20 Dec. 1820, but recorded in SJL as received a day later. Enclosure: Botta, *History of the War*, vol. 2.

On this day Otis sent the same enclosure in letters to John Adams, John Quincy Adams, and James Madison (MHi: Adams Papers; Madison, *Papers, Retirement Ser.*, 2:168).

Former PRESIDENT John Adams wrote to Otis about his translation of Botta in a letter of 3 Aug. 1820 (Lb in MHi: Adams Papers).

[1] Manuscript: "braws." Adams to Otis, 3 Aug. 1820: "brows."
[2] Superfluous internal quotation marks in preceding four sentences editorially omitted.
[3] Manuscript: "Manroe."

From Alexander Garrett

DEAR SIR   Charlottesville 7th December 1820

On the 13th ult. the Literary[1] board deposited in the Bank of Virginia $20.000. for the use of the University, $10.000. of which you will recollect you check'd for in my favor as Bursar that sum I had passed to my credit and since my return home from Richmond the drafts on me being very heavy I have disbursed the whole and yet left some amount considerable unpaid,   I have therefore now enclosed you a check for the remaining $10,000 which please approve and return me by the return mail,

I am Dr Sir. Your mo Obt St   ALEX: GARRETT

RC (CSmH: JF); endorsed by TJ as received 12 Dec. 1820 and so recorded in SJL. Enclosure not found.

[1] Manuscript: "Litary."

To Archibald Robertson

DEAR SIR   Poplar Forest. Dec. 7. 20.

I believe it is your practice to settle the annual accounts of your customers about the month of Septemb[er.] I will thank you for the copy of mine for the last year, a[s] soon as convenient. it will be convenient for me to have it under view as soon as may be in preparing arrangement[s] for the paiment of monies the ensuing spring. I have it much at heart henceforward[1] to pay my merchant's account regul[arly] every spring. and altho it is a most inauspicious ye[ar] to begin such a course, the wheat of the last year having been mostly eaten for want of corn, and what is left not being likely to bring, clear of carriage, more than 2. or 3/. yet I must try to effect it. or as nearly as possible.

Will you come and take a dinner with two o[r] three neighbors on Sunday? it is long since you hav[e] done us that favor. I inclose a 30.D. bill with a reques[t] to send me smaller bills in exchange for it. accept the assurance of my friendly esteem & respect.

Th: Jefferson

PoC (MHi); on verso of reused address cover of Benjamin W. Crowninshield to TJ, 18 Aug. 1819; text lost at right margin due to polygraph misalignment, with three words rewritten by TJ; at foot of text: "Mr Robertson"; endorsed by TJ; with Dft of TJ to Robertson, 16 Nov. 1821, beneath endorsement.

A missing letter from Robertson to TJ of 7 Dec. 1820 is recorded in SJL as received the next day from Lynchburg.

[1] Manuscript: "hencefoward."

From John Wayles Baker

Dear sir   Columbia Decr 8th 1820

I arrived here on the 10th of Nov. but defer'd writing you until after the examination that I might give you some account of my studies. I have enter'd the Sophomore class in which are read Horaces Satires and Art of Poetry together with Collectanea Græca majora we also study Geography and Huttons mathematics as far as Cubic equations. this comprises the whole of the Sophomore studies. The college consists of two large buildings in which the students lodge, and three other brick houses divided into two tenements each for the accommodation of the Professors, who have fix'd salaries paid by the Legislature. the tuition fees which amount to forty dollars for nine months are appropriated to the repairs of the college &c &c. this institution has been in some confusion for a considerable space of time caused by the death of the late president Dr Maxy. The board of Trustees met on monday last when mr Elliott was elected president and mr Wallace professor of mathematics. it is not yet ascertained whether Wallace will accept the appointment as he was only elected for one year. mr Elliott is in town at this time but will not take his seat for some weeks. Any advice from you respecting my studies or on any other subject would be gratifying to my Father & be consider'd by me as a distinguish'd mark of your favour. Permit me to tender my sincere acknowledgements and unaffected gratitude to you and every individual of your aimiable family for the many friendly attentions I received while an inmate at Monticello—   Yours with sincere esteem & respect.

J W Baker

RC (MHi); endorsed by TJ as received 22 Dec. 1820 and so recorded in SJL. RC (DLC); address cover only; with PoC of TJ to James Monroe, 8 Apr. 1821, on verso; addressed: "Thomas Jefferson Esquire Monticello near Charlottesville Virginia"; franked; postmarked Columbia, 9 Dec.

For the COLLECTANEA GRÆCA MAJORA, see note to Francis Eppes to TJ, 31 Oct. 1820.

To William Steptoe

Dec. 8. 20.

Th: Jefferson asks the favor of Dr Steptoe to dine with him the day after tomorrow (Sunday.)

RC (Corporation for Jefferson's Poplar Forest, on deposit ViU: TJP); dateline at foot of text; addressed: "Dr Steptoe." Not recorded in SJL.

From Edmund Bacon

DEARE SIR.   Monticello December 9th 1820—

Yours by last weeks mail came to hand I shall certainly be on the serch for a workman and to imploy him on the best terms in my power.

I have not yet been able to get off any flour. the rent wheat was deliverd so long after that which was deliverd by others in the mill that it seems to give them the right to their flour first indeed thare is only a few hundred bushels of the rent wheat[1] yet deliverd nearly all the crop at Lego is yet in the field

I am now geting out my wheat which was stacked at Tufton the loss commited on it by the stock of that place is considirable we have experienc'd a very hard spell of wheather for the last 10 days. we had a plenty of Ice on the 2nd Instant and a bundance of snow which enable'd me to fill both houses I have a very good prospect of geting off a hundred or two barrills in a day or so. I shall attend properly to geting it down as spedily as possoble.

with sincere respect your Ob. St.   E: BACON

RC (MHi); at foot of text: "Mr Jefferson"; addressed (torn): "[. . .] [Je]ff[erson] bedford County Poplar Forest. Lynchburgh"; endorsed by TJ as received 12 Dec. 1820 and so recorded in SJL.

BOTH HOUSES: by 1817 TJ had two icehouses, one at Monticello used for storing snow and another on the Rivanna River for storing ice (Betts, *Garden Book*, 565, 566n).

[1] Preceding four words interlined.

From Patrick Gibson

SIR   Richmond 9ᵗʰ Decʳ 1820.

Your favor of the 15ᵗʰ Ultᵒ inclosing a blank note was received in the due course of mail, but too late to renew your note in bank due the 14ᵗʰ for which I had to substitute another in the meantime—Flour has fallen below anything I have ever yet known, and from the great anxiety shown by the Holders to sell, there is every appearance of its being still lower it is now offering at 3½$ and no purchasers, and even at this price, neither the Northern nor European markets hold out any encouragement to speculators—Wheat 60 Cents—I have not yet received any of your flour—With much respect

 I am Sir Your obᵗ Servᵗ   PATRICK GIBSON

RC (DLC); between dateline and salutation: "Thomas Jefferson Esqʳᵉ"; endorsed by TJ as received 31 Dec. 1820 and so recorded in SJL.

From Francis W. Gilmer

DEAR SIR.   Richmond Decʳ 10ᵗʰ 1820

I inclose you a little treatise which I wrote in Albemarle during my summer's visit; on what is growing every day to be an important question in jurisprudence & politics. The notions of Bentham are every day becoming more popular in Virginia, and it is time the other side should be heard.

I do not know your opinions on the subject, nor do I hope to edify you at all on the matter; I send you the pamphlet in testimony of

 my great respect & regard   F. W. GILMER

RC (MoSHi: Gilmer Papers); at foot of text: "Mr Jefferson"; endorsed by TJ as received 21 Dec. 1820 and so recorded in SJL. Enclosure: [Gilmer], *A Vindication of the laws, limiting the rate of interest on loans; from the objections of Jeremy* *Bentham, and the Edinburgh Reviewers* (Richmond, 1820; Poor, *Jefferson's Library*, 11 [no. 676]; TJ's copy in ViU, inscribed "To Thomas Jefferson esqʳ with the compliments & respects of F. W. Gilmer").

From James Madison

DEAR SIR   Montpellier¹ Decʳ 10. 1820

Yours of Novʳ 29. came to hand a few days ago. The letter from T.C.² is returned. I had one from him lately on the same subject; and in consequence reminded the President of his political career; dropping at the same time a few lines in his favor to our Senator Mr Barbour. I sincerely wish something proper in itself could be done for him. He needs it and deserves it.

The law terminating appointments at periods of four years is pregnant with mischiefs such as you describe. It overlooks the important distinction between repealing or modifying the office, and displacing the officer. The former is a Legislative, the latter an Executive function. And even the former, if done with a view of re-establishing the office and letting in a new appointment, would be an indirect violation of the Theory & policy of the Constitution. If the principle of the late Statute be a sound one, nothing is necessary but to limit appointments held during pleasure, to a single year, or the next meeting of Congress, in order to make the pleasure of the Senate a tenure of office, instead of that of the President alone. If the error be not soon corrected, the task will be very difficult: for it is of a nature to take a deep root.

On application thro' Mr Stephenson, I have obtained from the Legislative files at Richmond, a Copy of Col: Bland's letter to you, for which I gave you the trouble of a search last fall. The letter being a public, not a private one, was sent to the Legislature, according to the intention of the writer. It contains what I expected to find in it; a proof that I differed from him on the question of ceding the Mississippi to Spain in 1780.

This will wait for your return from Poplar forest; accompanied I hope with evidence of the good effects of the trip on your health.

Affectionately & truly yours   JAMES MADISON

RC (DLC: Madison Papers); at foot of text: "Mr Jefferson"; endorsed by TJ as received 22 Dec. 1820 and so recorded in SJL. FC (DLC: Madison Papers, Rives Collection); written in Madison's hand on verso of reused address cover to him; lacks closing; endorsed by Madison. Enclosure: enclosure to TJ to Madison, 29 Nov. 1820.

Having received his own letter from Tench Coxe (T.C.) dated 12 Nov. 1820, Madison wrote letters of recommenda-

tion IN HIS FAVOR to James Monroe and James Barbour on 19 and 25 Nov. 1820, respectively (Madison, *Papers, Retirement Ser.*, 2:142–3, 151–3, 155–6). On 3 Dec. 1820 Andrew Stevenson (STEPHENSON) sent Madison the 22 Nov. 1780 letter from Theodorick Bland to TJ (Madison, *Papers, Retirement Ser.*, 2:165–6; *PTJ*, 4:136–8).

[1] Word not in FC.
[2] FC: "T. Coxe."

From Elijah Griffiths

DEAR SIR,   Philadelphia December 11—1820

Your much esteemed favour dated May 15—20: was duly received. It gives me great satisfaction to believe, that I have been thought worthy to be enroled, amongst the number of your friends. The period of our former acquaintance has often recured to my mind with pleasing reflections; and the then portentous state of our national affairs, has since in happier times, greatly increased my confidence in the permanency of our republican system. It is very certain that the misguided, or venal, friends of that system alone can seriously injure it, in the minds of the people. This has been exemplified in the case of our late Governor; the cause has been seriously affected by the executive & Legislative branches of the government,[1] which at our late election, led to considerable changes with a view to reformation, but the practical effects of these changes are yet to be realised.

I am sensible that your situation must have been rendered unpleasant & painful, from many[2] soliciting your recommendation to their applications for offices from the President.

I have often desired to see your face once more, & that clause in your letter, which says, "I greet with good will my declining health &c" has awakened sensations in my mind, that I shall not attempt to describe. Having a young family to provide for, & a business more laborious than profitable, & increasingly so of late, has confined me pretty closely at home; otherwise I might have had the pleasure of paying you a visit at your peaceful retirement. In addition to the above, at the close of the late war I perchased & improved a property here, on which I have yet to pay $5000 or $6000, the change in business & value of property, has rendered this very burthensome. These circumstances, together with my being unknown to the President & members of the administration; will be accepted as an appology for my troubling you, to interest yourself in my behalf, & also for my applying for an appointment under the Government. I have anticipated much difficulty in obtaining this appointment, from the powerful & prompt interest, that is waiting to be put into opiration, the moment the Bankrupt Law passes, which it is expected to do, in some shape or other, this session.

I feel some hopes that the Misouri question will be gotten rid of, to make room for better business, by the national Legislature. It cannot however be concealed, that there is a plan matureing, to bring into power, an old party under a new name, viz: <u>Enemies</u> of <u>Slavery</u>,[3] for this old party had so wasted by disappointment, grief & despair, that it would have expired through a want of vitality, if some accession of strength could not be acquired, by exciting prejudices predicated upon Geographical & fortuitous distinctions. <u>Slavery</u> will now be the bell, on which the changes will be rung, to bring these new champions of <u>freedom</u> into power: but great will be the disappointment of these new patriots, if the next[4] candidate for the Presidential chair, should be selected by the Democratic party from any state north of Maryland. Indeed I think this would be the true policy of the party at the next Presidential election, I know the friends of the New-York candidate fear it.

I am probably calling your attention from sweet retirement to the unpleasant scenes of party & ambitious strife.

I hope your season has been like ours, which has been the most abundant in agricultural products, that I remember of.

On the subject of Banking, I may confidently[5] assert, that Pennsylvania has suffered so much within the last 3 years, by her Bank-mania, that she will remember the rod for half a century to come.

I have only to re-iterate my sincere wishes for your health & happiness, and salute you with constant esteem[6] & respect

ELIJAH GRIFFITHS

RC (DLC); addressed: "Thomas Jefferson Esq‍ʳ Monticello virginia"; address partially canceled and redirected successively in two unidentified hands to Lynchburg and Monticello; stamp canceled; franked; postmarked Philadelphia, 11 Dec., and Lynchburg, 29 Dec.; endorsed by TJ as received 31 Dec. 1820 and so recorded in SJL.

The LATE GOVERNOR of Pennsylvania was William Findlay, who had recently been defeated for reelection by Joseph Hiester. AN OLD PARTY: the Federalists. THE NEW-YORK CANDIDATE: DeWitt Clinton.

[1] Manuscript: "goverment."
[2] Manuscript: "mary."
[3] Manuscript: "Shavery."
[4] Preceding two words interlined in place of "a."
[5] Manuscript: "confident."
[6] Manuscript: "esteen."

From Richard Rush

DEAR SIR. London December 11. 1820.

I hasten to acknowledge the receipt of your favor of the 20ᵗʰ of October, enclosing a bill of exchange drawn by[1] Joseph Marx and son, for 40 pounds sterling. It got to hand this day. The list of books enclosed, it will afford me very great satisfaction to procure in the best manner in my power. I shall hope for the pleasure of writing to you again respecting them, and beg permission to offer you, dear sir, in the meantime, with my thanks for all the other contents of your letter, the assurances of my most respectful attachment.

RICHARD RUSH.

Dupl (MHi); at head of text: "Duplicate"; endorsed by TJ as received 22 Feb. 1821 and so recorded in SJL. Dupl (DLC); address cover only; with PoC of TJ to Samuel Williams, 11 June 1822, on verso; addressed: "Thomas Jefferson Monticello. 2"; franked; postmarked Washington, 18 Feb. RC (MHi); endorsed by TJ as received 6 Mar. 1821 and so recorded (as a "Dupl.," adjacent to 22 Feb. entry) in SJL; enclosed in Daniel Brent to TJ, 26 Feb. 1821. RC (DLC); address cover only; with PoC of TJ to Joseph Jones, 14 June 1822, on verso; addressed: "Thomas Jefferson. Monticello. 1."

[1] Preceding two words interlined in Dupl and RC in place of "on."

To Edmund Bacon

DEAR SIR   Poplar Forest Dec. 12. 20.

M[r] Yancey & myself conclude it will be best to send the pork of this place to Monticello before Christmas.[1] hoping you will recieve this letter on Sunday the 17th I wish you to send off the waggon the next mornin[g][2] Monday 18[th.] being empty, & with a good team it may be here in 3. days [that][3] is by Wednesday night, by which time the pork will be ready, and the waggon may start Thursday morning with that of this place & be at Monticello Christmas eve. send a spare mul[e] also if you please for Johnny Hemings who cannot perform the journey on foot. if the weather permits I shall be at home on Sunday myself to dinner, as I propose starting on Friday the 15th. if you recieve this before I get home be so good as to send up immediately to Edy to have us some sort of a dinner ready: for I expect there is none of the white family at home. I salute you with my best wishes

TH: JEFFERSON

PoC (CSmH: JF); on verso of RC of Archibald Robertson to TJ, 6 Sept. 1819; edge trimmed; at foot of text: "M[r] Bacon"; endorsed by TJ.

[1] Omitted period at right margin editorially supplied.
[2] Word faint.
[3] Word faint.

To Samuel Garland

SIR   Poplar Forest Dec. 12. 20.

I had counted on sending you an additional order for 200.D. before my leaving this place, my grandson having promised to see to the sending down some flour to give me notice of it. not having heard from him I presume the state of our river has not yet permitted it: I must therefore defer the draught to my return home and the moment my flour can be sent off I will take care to forward you the order to Lynchburg. accept the assurance of my esteem & respect.

Th: Jefferson

PoC (MHi); on verso of reused address cover of Thomas Ewell to TJ, 16 Aug. 1819; at foot of text: "Mr Saml Garland"; endorsed by TJ.

MY GRANDSON: Thomas Jefferson Randolph.

From John A. Robertson

SIR: RICHMOND, December 12th, 1820.

"Ne quid falsi, dicere audeat, ne quid veri non audeat."[1]

It may be presumed, that some apology for thus obtruding on you, a communication from a private individual, in whose interest, perhaps, you have no concern, ought to be made. The sequel must substitute that apology.

Endued by nature, with the outlines and confirmed by education in, at least, some of the *minutiæ* of that dignity of feeling and independence of sentiment, concomitant characteristics of honorable men, possessing also a consciousness of my integrity of character and perfect equality, with any gentleman, in whatever sphere he moves, it cannot be, reasonably, supposed, that this respectful communication to *you*, in vindication of *myself*, has any other origin, than what is truly ascribable, in common, to every man, similarly situated. *Disdaining* to *solicit* the good opinion of any man, and holding perhaps, in too much indifference, that of many others, it ought not and cannot, fairly, be suspected upon this occasion, that even disingenuity, much less sycophancy or dissimulation is resorted to.

It is, nevertheless, incumbent on every member of society, to obviate and, if he can *dispel*, impressions, erroneously, entertained against him, by those, who, but for the delusion and imposition, under which, they, *honestly* labor, would spurn, with indignation and contempt, from their presence, the authors of that slander, leading to such impressions. As a member of the Virginian Bar, and consequent, frequent association with gentlemen of the same profession, it would give me pleasure, upon terms *perfectly reciprocal*, to be always, at least, in the polite interchange of those civilities so essentially necessary, to the feelings and comfort of all. But it is discovered, that the *poison* supposed to have been subdued by its *specific antidote, long since*, has at this moment its influence *here*, in the widely extended ramifications,

[450]

most assiduously given this *turbid current*. From information,[2] not to be questioned, it appears that some members of the bar of Richmond, suppose me capable of all or *some* of the charges and *enormities*, showered down upon me, by a petition for divorce (never seen by the pretended petitioner) out of which grew a report of "the committee for Courts of Justice," following and expatiating on the acrimony of the petition, and terminating, ultimately, in an act of the Legislature, in favor of the petitioner.

Let it be remembered that this was, *intentionally*, a case *ex parte*, that the petition was drawn by the *only* witness* in the case, that he gave an affidavit almost *verbatim* with the petition upon which was founded the report of the committee, in almost the *identical* language. Let it be also recollected, that this witness was *flatteringly* interested in a *pecuniary* point of view, then in expectancy on such event, was the only brother of the *nominal* petitioner, and was at the time, and had been for years, *previously* a most malignant and malicious enemy of mine. Let it be borne in mind, also, that so far from opposing (after the term of *six years* separation, from this unfortunate lady had elapsed, without any previous complaint on her part) I, purposely, withheld all evidence from the committee, and strongly enjoined on every member of the Legislature, with whom the liberty could be taken, by letters and personal conversation, not to oppose, but *aid the bill in all its stages;* unless some *other* witness should appear of a character sufficient to command my attention. This, as was presumed, did not happen, and the case was permitted to pass, *sub silentio*, on my part, relying on the statement which would, thereafter immediately be made, for my *complete exculpation*. The exposure of *this witness*, in my[3] several publications, afterwards, his *present* standing, in the estimation of the *honorable* part of the community, near him, and the *volume* of testimony of the most respectable and impartial gentlemen, of that part of the country, then given to the public, it was supposed had, forever, silenced my defamers. I was deceived. *Compelled* to resort to a public print, not generally circulated in the state, the denunciations contained in, and promulgated by the "Enquirer" were not fully met. Hence it is, that whilst, throughout Virginia, my reputation was defamed, the *true* or counteracting statement was confined to a very narrow sphere. This is the only solitary charge, ever, by even my most inveterate enemies, levelled against me. Should this, however, from the *evidence* adduced, as above characterised, be *partially* true only, it is unhesitatingly admitted, as sufficient *for all their purposes*.

But this charge and specifications, were to me as entirely *new* and *astounding*, as base, *infamous* and *false*. To establish this assertion, there is now in my possession, a *series* of evidence of the most credible witnesses, who, from the very nature of things, *cannot* be mistaken. A small portion of this testimony is subjoined, the whole being too voluminous, here to insert, and which can be further augmented to any amount, either in number or respectability of witnesses. I have confined this address, with a few exceptions, to such *members of the bar* here, as in my estimation, would properly receive it, or to whom this communication was supposed due, meaning no disrespect to those omitted.

In conclusion, I shall simply remark, that, as no other charge, *throughout my life*, thus far, worthy of the least notice, has, to my knowledge, been urged against me; that *he* who can, after the perusal of this letter, &c., entertain the *least doubt* of the truth of this assertion: *that of all and every charge against me, contained in the petition for divorce, before referred to, and the statement of the witness, I am entirely innocent*, must, indeed, be sceptical in the *extreme*, or *predisposed* to a contrary opinion.

I have now performed what was conceived a duty to myself, and shall feel entirely satisfied, in any result.

I am, sir, very respectfully, your most obedient servant,

J. A. ROBERTSON.

NOTE. *The five libellers excepted. Their paper was drawn by the *same* person; they were and had been, from my earliest life my personal enemies, carried and sent this paper through the state for signatures, but could obtain *no other* name.—One out of the five, (Capt. W. Fitzgerald) now dead, has recanted in the most formal manner *in writing*, drawn and certified by a gentleman of the bar, of his own selection, in which he states, not only the imposition practised on him, but his own regret for such an act.

This paper is in my possession, certified, and duly attested. The libel was never heard of, by me, until the law had passed—had it been known, the petitioner would not have had *a single* vote in her favor *at any stage* of the bill.

Printed circular (ViW: TC-JP); on a sheet folded to form four pages, with letter on p. 1, enclosure on pp. 2–3, and address on p. 4; addressed by Robertson: "Thomas Jefferson, Esqʳ Monticello Albemarle" by "Mail"; franked; postmarked Richmond, 22 Dec.

John Archer Robertson, attorney, was a native Virginian raised in Amelia County, part of which became Nottoway County in 1789. He wed Elizabeth Royall in the latter county in 1795, but the Virginia General Assembly granted her a divorce in 1814, stipulating that neither party could remarry during the other's lifetime. In 1802 Robertson moved to Richmond to practice law, and in 1807 he served as a captain in the Virginia militia. For an unspecified amount of time, probably in about 1819, he reportedly edited the Richmond *Virginia Patriot*, a Federalist newspaper. By 1822 Robertson was in Baltimore, where he denied a report that he had penned an essay by a "Native of Virginia" accusing TJ of fraud. As a resident of Kent County, Maryland, he received only a handful of votes when he ran for a seat in the United States House of Representatives in 1824. Two years later the Maryland legislature upheld a Baltimore County Court ruling that denied Robertson a license to practice law in that county. By 1829 he again resided in Baltimore, and in 1834 he practiced law there (Landon C. Bell, *Cumberland Parish: Lunenburg County, Virginia, 1746–1816, Vestry Book, 1746–1816* [1930; repr. 1994], 314; *Acts of Assembly* [1813–14 sess.], 143 [22 Jan. 1814]; Richmond *Virginia Argus*, 31 July 1802; TJ's List of Militia Officers Sent Circular Letter, [8 July–6 Sept. 1807] [DLC: TJ Papers, 168:29677–8]; *Lynchburg Press*, 24 May 1822; Burlington, Vt., *American Repertory & Advertiser*, 27 Aug. 1822; *Baltimore Patriot & Mercantile Advertiser*, 17 Aug. 1824, 17 Jan. 1826, 28 Oct. 1834; *Journal of the Proceedings of the House of Delegates of the State of Maryland* [1828–29 sess.], 359 [19 Feb. 1829]).

NE QUID FALSI, DICERE AUDEAT, NE QUID VERI NON AUDEAT is adapted from Cicero's laws of history in *De Oratore*, 2.62, that one should "not dare to tell anything but the truth" and should also "make bold to tell the whole truth" (Cicero, *De Oratore*, trans. E. W. Sutton and Harris Rackham, Loeb Classical Library [1942; rev. ed., 1948; undated reprint], 244–5). SUB SILENTIO: "under silence; without notice being taken; without being expressly mentioned" (*Black's Law Dictionary*).

On 11 Jan. 1814 the Richmond ENQUIRER printed the report of the Committee for Courts of Justice regarding Elizabeth Robertson's petition for divorce, which had been read in the Virginia House of Delegates on 29 Dec. 1813 (*JHD* [1813–14 sess.], 94). It stated that "shortly after their union," John A. Robertson "gave proofs of a most malevolent and cruel disposition, by breaking out into personal violence that will render the petitioner a cripple the balance of her life—In the course of a few years thereafter

his enormities became insupportable—By communicating to her a disease contracted in his intercourse with the dissolute and abandoned, he reduced her to the last degree of disease and wretchedness; in which situation he not only denied her the aid of a physician, but destroyed a prescription and medicine which had been procured for her, and declaring she should have no relief, prevented the servants from rendering her their assistance." The report went on to say "that while the petitioner was in this emaciated condition, & in a state of high salivation, her said husband caused her to be dragged from her bed into a cold room, where she remained entirely exposed, until she had lost all appearance of life, and this for the avowed purpose of giving her a cold which might terminate her existence; from which situation the petitioner was relieved by the interposition of a neighbouring lady— Shortly after this occurrence, the petitioner was driven from her home by her husband, who declared that if she ever returned he would put her to death in a *short way*. Under these circumstances the petitioner sought refuge with her father, who has sustained her ever since." In addition, "after detaining from the petitioner for several months, all her children for the sole purpose of increasing her miseries, the said John A. Robertson turned them out of doors, telling the eldest boy, who was about eleven or twelve years old, that if their grand father would not receive and support them, they might go to the woods and live as they could." Finally, the committee reported that "it appears to be the common opinion of the neighbourhood, not denied by the said John A. Robertson . . . that he is now living in open adultery with a woman upon whom it is believed he depends for subsistence." Robertson wrote a lengthy rebuttal for the *Enquirer*. When that paper refused to print his manuscript he sent it instead to the *Virginia Patriot*, which published it on 23 Apr. 1814.

[1] Latin phrase between dateline and salutation.

[2] Printed circular: "informrtion."

[3] Word added in margin by Robertson in place of "many."

Testimonials to John A. Robertson's Character

Nottoway County, 20th January, 1814.[1]

We the undersigned, have been long acquainted with John A. Robertson, Esq., and have *always* and *do* view him as a gentleman of *unquestionable honor, probity, and integrity.*

JAMES H. MUNFORD,
High Sheriff, Nottoway,
A. ROBINSON,
Coroner and Magistrate,
Nottoway,
ROBt. DICKINSON,
Com. Rev.[2] and Magistrate,
Nottoway.
DANIEL E. JACKSON, Constable,
Nottoway.
ISAAC WINFREE, Major,
1st Battallion, 49th Regiment,
Nottoway County, and Magistrate.
EDWARD ROBINSON,
Capt. Cavalry, Nottoway Cy.
PETER BLAND, Attorney at Law,

P. R. BLAND, Attorney at Law,
JOHN BLAND,
J. B. HOLMES.
V. B. HOLMES.
JOSEPH J. FOWLKES,
Capt. Cavalry.
PLEASANT CRADDOCK.
CHRISTIAN ROBERTS, &c.
&c.
Many others equally respectable, all of the county.

Nottoway County, 8th February, 1814.

I DO CERTIFY, that I have been long acquainted with John A. Robertson, Esq., and that any charge against him of ill-treatment to his children, whilst in a state of separation from his lady, I have no knowledge of. He had them some short time with him, subsequent to this event, immediately in my neighborhood, and I never heard a whisper of ill-treatment, and so far from "*turning them out of his house*," they were, as I have heard and *believe*, in his absence, taken away by their mother and carried to her father's. The eldest son remained and was sent to Hampden Sidney College, at the sole expence of the father, and when he took a tour to the western and southern country, he left money with me to pay for several sessions, and left the youth in all respects under my care and protection. I have frequently visited Mr. Robertson, *whilst married* and afterwards, and never saw him treat any member of his family *even indecorously.* He married the *only* daughter of my *only* full brother. Given under my hand the date above.

(SIGNED)   LITTLEBURY ROYALL.

[EXTRACT FROM MR. COMER'S AFFIDAVIT.]

The affidavit of Thomas Comer of lawful age, and first duly sworn, &c. This affiant saith that he has been long acquainted with John A. Robertson, Esq. and lived as a neighbor to him many years, whilst he was a married man; their houses were about a quarter of a mile apart, in full view, and that almost *daily* an interchange of visits was had between them or some members of their families; that the most perfect harmony subsisted between said

Robertson and his lady; so far from any thing like mal-treatment or ill-nature manifested towards her, the very reverse, in the estimation of this affiant, was the course pursued by Capt. Robertson.—Had any other been the case, it is almost impossible it should be unknown to this affiant, whose intimacy with and contiguity to this family, preclude the supposition of ignorance of family grievances. This affiant viewed Capt. Robertson as an affectionate husband, a tender and indulgent father, and kind and benevolent neighbor. Why Mrs. Robertson left her husband this affiant cannot undertake to say. Upon the whole, this affiant cannot but suppose, that this separation of man and wife, was brought about by some of Mrs. Robertson's *nearest* relations, founded upon *pecuniary* considerations and resentment against Capt. Robertson. This affiant concludes by stating, that in his opinion (and perhaps he knows more upon this subject than most persons) Mr. Robertson stands *wholly* blameless, touching his separation from his wife, and because the well known character of this gentleman, as a man, a neighbor, and a magistrate, preclude a contrary opinion, in the minds of all who know him, who cordially and really love and respect him; and he is moreover, in his humble conception, justly entitled to a divorce; and further this affiant saith not.

(SIGNED)   THOMAS COMER.*

Nottoway County, Ss.

This day, Thomas Comer personally appeared before me, a magistrate for the county aforesaid, and made oath to the truth of the foregoing affidavit in due form, and subscribed his name in my presence. Given under my hand and seal, at Nottoway Court-House, this 2nd August, 1810.

PR. B. JONES. [*Seal.*]

*NOTE. Mr. Comer being at this time in a low state of health, and intending then to apply to the legislature for a *divorce*, I gave notice and had the above affidavit taken, which was done in my absence, and in presence of the agent of the adverse party.—Mr. Comer is now dead; was a man of undoubted veracity and honor, and married the sister of Mr. John Royall, the father of Mrs. Robertson.[3]

Nottoway, 27th February, 1814.

THIS IS TO CERTIFY, that I lived as overseer for Capt. John A. Robertson in the year 1805, ate and slept in the dwelling-house, and *never* did I discover any thing, like ill-treatment to his wife, or any member of his family, but on the contrary, great tenderness and politeness to all around him.[4] Given under my hand the date above. (SIGNED,)

Teste, A. OLD.   PETERSON OLD.

Nottoway County, January 25th, 1814.

I, WILLIAM BEVILL, DO HEREBY CERTIFY, that during the years 1810, '11 and '12, I lived as overseer for Mr. John Royall, father of Mrs. E. Robertson, that this lady was then in a state of separation from her husband, residing with her father, that from what I frequently *saw* and *heard* from this family (boarding in the house) in relation to this separation, I have no hesitation in stating as my *firm conviction*, that Mr. Royall's family, particularly Mrs. Royall,

[455]

were the *sole* causes in producing and perpetuating this state of things. Given under my hand the date above.

  Teste,   (SIGNED) WILLIAM BEVILL.
  JAMES H. MUNFORD.
  EDWARD MUNFORD.

I DO HEREBY CERTIFY, that I lived as overseer, for Capt. John A. Robertson, about five years, (whilst he was married) during a part of which time, my house was not more than one hundred yards from his residence and family, that I was almost *daily* through his yard and in the house, and that during *the whole time*, I hesitate not, to say, that the said Robertson treated his family, *particularly his lady*, with all the attention and respect that any gentleman could do, nor did I ever have the smallest cause to *suspect* him of acting *otherwise*. Given under my hand, 14th March,[5] 1814. (SIGNED,)

  Teste, JAMES ROYALL VAUGHAN.   JOHN SLEDD.

I, SARAH SLEDD, wife of John Sledd, join in the truth of the above statement being equally well informed on the subject—1814.

  Teste, JAMES R. VAUGHAN. (SIGNED,) SARAH SLEDD.

I lived several years, as overseer, for John A. Robertson, Esq. subsequent to Mr. Sledd, and do with pleasure confirm his statement as strictly true, knowing Mr. Robertson and lady at the time he speaks; and further, that the same continued to be the case whilst I resided with him. Given under my hand, this 14th March, 1814.

  Teste, WILLIAM FORLINES. (SIGNED,) JOHN BRIGGS.

            Nottoway County, 5th April, 1814.
  I have lived as a neighbor to Capt. John A. Robertson several years whilst he was a married man, and very frequently visited this gentleman's family, and do say, without the hazard of contradiction, that to his wife, family and neighbors, he always acted with the utmost propriety and politeness, and that I cannot but view a *contrary* statement as false and malicious, because my knowledge of this gentleman and his family affairs, preclude, entirely, a belief in such statement. Given under my hand. JOHN ROBINSON, SR.[6]

            Nottoway County, 14th July, 1814.
  THIS IS TO CERTIFY TO THE WORLD, that John D. Royall, did in the month of June last, apply to me to grant him a certificate, changing in some degree my first (Pat. 23d April) which I not only positively and peremptorily refused, but was compelled (in my own house) to insult him. He observed at the same time, that if *I* would *recant*, the two Mr. Holmes's would do so. This had no other effect, but to render him more contemptible, knowing or believing, that those gentlemen had never agreed to any such *absurdity*. That upon the subject of divorce, there has been but one sentiment, as far as my knowledge extends, that is, *perfect astonishment* at the act of the Legislature, altho' wished by Mr. Robertson and his friends. Given under my hand, the date above.

  Teste,   (SIGNED,) JAMES H. MUNFORD, Sheriff, N. C.
  V. B. HOLMES.

WE DO HEREBY CERTIFY, that we *never* informed Mr. J. D. Royall, that we would alter or *change* our certificate, "of the 20th January last," but on the contrary, *positively* refused, as we viewed it to be an act of justice only, due to Capt. John A. Robertson, to state him to be a *gentleman* and *honorable man*. Given under our hands, this 29th July, 1814.

<table>
<tr><td>(SIGNED,)</td><td>JOHN B. HOLMES.</td></tr>
<tr><td></td><td>VIVION B. HOLMES.</td></tr>
</table>

Teste, WILLIAM F. BROADNAX.

Printed text (ViW: TC-JP); conjoined with covering letter; brackets in original. In an alternate sequence and differing substantially, most of these testimonials previously appeared in the Richmond *Virginia Patriot*, 23 Apr. 1814, with only the most significant variations noted below.

The names A. ROBINSON, DANIEL E. JACKSON, CHRISTIAN ROBERTS, EDWARD ROBINSON, and JOHN ROBINSON, SR., were more accurately printed in the *Virginia Patriot* as A. Robertson, John C. Jackson, Chastain Roberts, Edward Robertson, and John Robertson, Sr., respectively.

[1] Reworked by hand from "1820."
[2] Abbreviation for "Commissioner of the Revenue."
[3] Text from bracketed heading to this point not in *Virginia Patriot*.

[4] *Virginia Patriot* here adds "That during this year Mrs. Robertson was very sick a considerable time, Mr. Robertson not only had Dr Patterson to attend her, but sent me to Petersburg for Dr. Gilliam, with a letter and offer of 20 guineas, if he would come, he however did not come but wrote Mr. Robertson—That during this time Mrs. Robertson had an infant at the breast (born the summer of this year) who was an uncommonly healthy and fine child. Mr. Robertson's conduct to every member of his family, appeared very correct and proper."
[5] Instead of preceding six words, *Virginia Patriot* reads "Mrs Robertson was healthy and well during this time and appeared *in all respects* well satisfied."
[6] Remainder of text not in *Virginia Patriot*.

To Francis Eppes

DEAR FRANCIS   Poplar Forest Dec. 13. 20.

Yours of Oct. 31. came to me here Nov. 28. having first gone to Monticello. I observe the course of reading at Columbia which you note. it either is, or ought to be the rule of every collegiate institution to teach to every particular student the branches of science which those who direct him think will be useful in the pursuits proposed for him, and to waste his time on nothing which they think will not be useful to him. this will certainly be the fundamental law of our University to leave every one free to attend whatever branches of instruction he wants, and to decline what he does not want. if this be not generally allowed at Columbia, I hope they may be induced to indulgence in your case, in consideration of the little time you have left, & which you cannot afford to waste on what will be useless to you, or can be acquired by reading hereafter without the aid of a teacher. as

I do not know any professor at Columbia but Doct[r] Cooper, request, in my name, his interest & influence to be permitted to adapt your studies to your wants.

Reviewing what you say are the courses of the 4. classes, I pass over the 1st and 2[d] which you are done with, and should select for you from the 3[d] Algebra, Geometry, trigonometry and Natural philosophy, & from the 4th Logarithms and chemistry to which I should add astronomy, Botany[1] & natural history, which you do not mention in any of the classes. I omit Blair's Rhetoric, Watt's logic, Kaims, Paley, Butler E[t]c which you can read in your closet after leaving College as well as at it. and in Mathematics I do not think you have time to undertake either Conic sections or fluxions. unless you can be indulged in this selection I shall lament very much indeed the having advised your going to Columbia: because time is now the most pressing & precious thing in the world to you; and the greatest injury which can possibly be done you is to waste what remains on what you can acquire hereafter yourself, & prevent your learning those useful branches which cannot well be acquired without the aids of the College.

Whether our University will open this time 12month or be shut up 7. years, will depend on the present legislature's liberating our funds by appropriating 100,000 D. more from the Literary fund. if you watch the newspapers you will see what they do, and be able to judge what may be expected.

Ellen & Virginia are here with me. we leave this the day after tomorrow for Monticello, where we hope to meet your aunt, who will be returning at the same time from Richmond. we learn by your letter to Virginia that Wayles is with you. to him and to yourself I tender my affectionate attachments. to D[r] Cooper also give my friendly souvenirs. the difficulty with which I write puts that much out of my power   TH: JEFFERSON

RC (DLC); addressed: "M[r] Francis Eppes at the College of Columbia S.C."; franked; postmarked Lynchburg, 29 Dec. PoC (CSmH: JF); on William Daniel to TJ, 4 Sept. 1819, with some obscured and polygraphically misaligned text rewritten by TJ; edge trimmed; endorsed by TJ.

Citing letters of 24 Dec. 1820 just received from ELLEN W. Randolph (Coolidge) and VIRGINIA J. Randolph (Trist), Elizabeth Trist reported to her grandson Nicholas P. Trist on 1 Jan. 1821 that while returning to Monticello from Poplar Forest "they had a most terrible journey

rain and bad roads bad accomadations, and M[r] Jefferson had the Rheumatism very bad travilling." Earlier in the letter Trist stated that she had learned from a letter of 20 Dec. from Cornelia J. Randolph that "M[r] Jefferson and the two young Ladies return'd from Poplar Forest in good health a week before xmass, the family had not assembled, only five in family but they expected M[rs] Randolph up at xmass." In a previous communication Trist informed her grandson that "Monticello is still solitary not one of the white family there but they expected to begin to rally about xmass but that I suppose will depend on the state of the weather and the roads" (Elizabeth Trist to Nicholas P. Trist, Farmington, 16 Dec. 1820, 1 Jan. 1821 [RCs of both in ViU: Trist, Randolph, and Burke Family Papers]).

YOUR AUNT: Martha Jefferson Randolph. WAYLES: John Wayles Baker.

[1] Word interlined.

From Peter S. Du Ponceau

Philadelphia 14 Dec[r] 1820

M[r] Du Ponceau presents his respects to M[r] Jefferson, & has the honor of Sending to him at the request of M[r] Pickering a corrected sheet of his Essay on an uniform Orthography of Indian languages, to be Substituted for the Same Signature in the copy formerly Sent, which is now cancelled.

RC (DLC); dateline at foot of text; endorsed by TJ as received 21 Dec. 1820 and so recorded in SJL. Enclosure: portion, not found, of John Pickering, *An* *Essay on a Uniform Orthography for the Indian Languages of North America* (Cambridge, Mass., 1820).

Sawing Instructions for James Martin

Sawing for paling a garden 250.f. square
1500. pales 4.I. wide $\frac{3}{4}$ I. thick. 6.f. long
1500.f. 1 I. plank to cut to 6.f. lengths.
100. pr of rails 10.f. long, to wit 100 pieces
 first cut 5 I. sq. clear. & then split diagonally thus
all of yellow poplar.

TH:J.
Dec. 14. 20.

MS (Anonymous, 1991; photocopy in TJ Editorial Files); entirely in TJ's hand; adjacent to signature: "left for Cap[t] Martin."

From Thomas Gimbrede

SIR U.S. Militarry Academy West Point 18th December 1820.
I was appointed two years ago professor of Drawing to this Institution; the Situation is highly respectable, but the Climate of Virginia would be more Congenial to my feelings & no doubt better for my familly.

I Take the Liberty to bring myself to your recolection, for that University which rises under your Protection; as a Draftman Painter & Engraver. a Communication from you on that Subject will be thankfully recieved.

with the highest consideration I have the honour to be your Obedient Serv[t]   THO[s] GIMBREDE

RC (ViU: TJP); adjacent to closing: "to the Hon[ble] Tho[s] Jefferson"; endorsed by TJ as received 28 Dec. 1820 and so recorded in SJL.

From John Mantz

DEAR SIR,   Fred[k] Town Maryland Dec[r] 19 1820
I send you by M[r] Elijah Brown—one side upper leather tanned alltogether with wood—and no Bark in any way whatever has there been applyed—to Complete it—you will please to accept the same— and remain yours respectfully—   Ob H S   JOHN MANTZ

RC (MHi); endorsed by TJ as received 31 Jan. 1821 and so recorded in SJL. RC (MHi); address cover only; with PoC of TJ to David Hosack, 5 Mar. 1821 (second letter), on verso; addressed: "Thomas Jefferson Esq[r] Near Charlotts Vill Albermarle County Virg ℔r E Brown."

John Mantz (1767–1839), merchant and tanner, owned a general store with Isaac Mantz by 1797 in Fredericktown (later Frederick), Maryland, and in 1801 he was compensated for "supplies furnished French prisoners at Fredericktown." By 1803 the Mantzes had also entered the tanning business, which John Mantz conducted on his own by 1819.

He served as a Frederick County commissioner in 1820 (Philadelphia *Porcupine's Gazette*, 12 Oct. 1797; *Accounts of the Treasurer of the United States, of payments and receipts of Public Monies, From the first of October, 1800, to the thirtieth of June, 1801, inclusive* [Washington, 1801], 101; MdHi: Quynn Family Collection; Fredericktown *Bartgis's Republican Gazette*, 29 Apr. 1803; Fredericktown *Bartgis's Republican Gazette, and General Advertiser*, 22 May 1819; Scharf, *Western Maryland*, 1:482; Hagerstown *Torch Light & Public Advertiser*, 22 Apr. 1823; gravestone inscription in Mount Olivet Cemetery, Frederick).

From Joseph C. Cabell

DEAR SIR,   Senate Chamber 20th Dec: 1820.
I thank you sincerely for your favor of Nov: 28. which I received on my arrival here on 5th ins[t]. I should have written you before now, but that my whole time has been taken up by the scandalous attack on Governor Randolph's character. Thank Heaven! we were fortunate enough to make the blow recoil on the heads of his accusers, and I trust we shall never again be insulted by the intrusion of such abominable subjects. You will hear the whole affair from your family. I have

shewn your letter to Gen[l] Breckenridge & some other friends. M[r] Johnson will not be here till christmas. We have agreed, for reasons I will more fully detail hereafter, to let the subject of the University lie over till after christmas. I am going to spend the Holidays with M[rs] Cabell in W[ms]burg, from which I will write you at leisure. For the present I will[1] only say that we shall probably have to fall down in our petition for a sum sufficient to finish the buildings, and let the rest lie till another session. We shall have the academies to contend with this year. Our difficulties are great, but every effort will be used to carry the bill. Some objections are made to the mode in which our accounts are presented. Some ask why the items are not more detailed: others, why m[r] Garrett's accounts do not go back farther than April. I would advise the fullest & freest[2] rendition of accounts. There lies our hold on the public affections. The affair of the payment to Doctor Cooper is known to our enemies.

Yours faithfully

JOSEPH C. CABELL

RC (ViU: TJP-PC); endorsed by TJ as received 24 Dec. 1820 and so recorded in SJL. RC: left half of address cover only (CSmH: JF), with PoC of TJ to Francis Eppes, 8 Apr. 1821, on verso; right half of address cover only (MHi), with PoC of TJ to Louis H. Girardin, 8 Apr. 1821, on recto; addressed (trimmed): "M[r] Jefferson M[o]nticello"; franked; inconsistently postmarked Richmond, 19 Dec.

In his 4 Dec. 1820 annual address to the Virginia legislature, Governor Thomas Mann Randolph advocated religious tolerance, expressed his own preference for seeking the divine in the natural world, and warned against the "indirect legislative sanction" of sectarianism. He also proposed a system of gradual emancipation that would use taxes on slaves to purchase enslaved youths and send them abroad. While the speech was somewhat controversial, potentially far more damaging was a SCANDALOUS ATTACK on Randolph's personal character, the details of which are not now known. Through the efforts of Cabell and other supporters, those charges were refuted and the General Assembly elected Randolph to another one-year term on 16 Dec. 1820 (*JHD* [1820–21 sess.], 6–12, 48; William H. Gaines Jr., *Thomas Mann Randolph: Jefferson's Son-in-Law* [1966], 123–7; Elizabeth Trist to Nicholas P. Trist, 16 Dec. 1820 [ViU: Trist, Randolph, and Burke Family Papers]; Cabell to TJ, 22 Dec. 1820).

[1] Cabell here canceled "content."
[2] Manuscript: "freeest."

From Edwin Lewis

SIR   Mobile 20 Dec[r] 1820

read the enclosed and See how you have ruined a native american a Child of a firm patriot of 76 to promote a vile foreign partizan

Your deeply injured   E LEWIS

RC (MoSHi: TJC-BC); dateline at foot of text; addressed: "The Hon[l] Thomas Jefferson Monticella Virginia"; franked; postmarked Mobile, 23 Dec.; endorsed by TJ as received 19 Jan. 1821 and so recorded in SJL.

Edwin Lewis, merchant, attorney, and land speculator, was raised in North Carolina and conducted business in Savannah, Georgia, before moving by 1803 to the eastern portion of Mississippi Territory that became the state of Alabama in 1819. The new town of Franklin was laid out in 1807 on land of his in Washington County on the Tombigbee River near Saint Stephens, where he had formerly had a store. Lewis served as deputy marshal of Mobile County in 1819, was commissioned a justice of the peace there in 1820 and 1823, and was authorized to construct a turnpike near Mobile in 1821. Over an extended period continuing as late as 1829, Lewis presented formal complaints against public officials and sought recognition of various land claims (*Terr. Papers*, 5:282, 6:265–7, 18:401–5; Madison, *Papers, Pres. Ser.*, 3:21; Clay, *Papers*, 4:701; Jacqueline Anderson Matte, Doris Brown, and Barbara Waddell, comps., *Old St. Stephens: Historical Record Survey* [1997; rev. ed. 1999], 29–32, 101–2; Harry Toulmin, comp., *A Digest of the Laws of the State of Alabama* [Cahaba, 1823], 422, 424, 773–4; *JHR*, 8:26, 10:55, 128–9, 11:133 [18 Nov. 1811, 14 Dec. 1815, 2 Jan. 1817, 12 Jan. 1818]; *Mobile Gazette & Commercial Advertiser*, 15 Dec. 1819; A-Ar: index to the secretary of state's commissions and civil appointments register; Jackson, *Papers*, 7:768–9).

E N C L O S U R E

Edwin Lewis to Harry Toulmin

Sir— [by 7 Nov. 1820]

I should not deem it necessary to address you, nor the public, after you have retired from office with the consent of both the state and United States government, and by almost every persons consent, except your own, but for some vouchers which you sent to Washington City to disprove the truth of my charges vs. you, in congress. Among them is a letter of Abner S. Lipscombe,[1] (now promoted to the bench) in which he makes a number of false assertions, which it is my right and a duty which I owe to myself to expose, to prevent any impressions being made by them, or their authors, prejudicial to my character. He thus commences his address to you: "Dear Sir—Some time ago I saw the copy of a letter, said to have been addressed to the Honorable Henry Clay, Speaker of the House of Representatives, from E. Lewis, now of the state of Mississippi, replete with the most infamous calumny against your personal and public character. It is a fact well known to every gentleman of the bar in this country, that the delays complained of in the suits where E. Lewis was concerned, either as attorney, or as a plaintiff, was produced and necessarily grew out of his want of a sufficiency of professional knowledge for the management of his suits, whenever he has attempted to conduct a suit in his own way, without the controul of any other person, the consequence has been delay by non suits, abatements and writs of error, &c."[2] Now, Sir, you and Mr. Lipscombe both knew this statement was wholly false—the cases I complained of being delayed, were myself vs. Figures Lewis; Peince vs. myself and Malones, injunctions.—Now, sir, produce the record, that will prove there never was an abatement, or non suit or writ of error, except a writ of error, I brought in the case of F. Lewis, in which your decree was reversed, and all your proceedings set aside, down to the original bill, answer and replication. So that at the end of nine years delay, and[3] a long time spent, and I struggling with the deepest distress, my suit stood as at the beginning. I call on you and Mr. Lipscombe to produce the records in any cases wherein I managed a suit, and that a non suit or abatement took place, or a writ of error sustained[4] against me for want of legal knowledge, or acknowledge yourselves convicted of falsehood.[5] He again says, "the case of capt Swain, refered to by Mr. Lewis, was an action of trespass for cutting lumber to build barracks for the troops on Lewis' land; it being a case sounding in damages, the defendant could not be legally held to bail, without an order from one of the judges of the Superior Court; and it appears that no such order was applied for on the part of the plaintiff—but the defandant was held to bail without, and of course was discharged on motion, as one that had been illegally bound." Nothing can be more false than every word of this, for the case of captain Swain was not an action of trespass—you have a copy of the charges which will prove this false—you know it was an indictment for false imprisonment of Cole, in which I had no concern; on which, after a true bill was found, the party (a countryman of yours) was arrested and bound over to court, where he attended; and on motion, you discharged him without trial; when, if tried, he would have been unquestionably convicted; thus exercising a power of suspending the law; a power which the king of England could not exercise; then refer to the case of trespass, and the records and writ will prove all Mr. Lipscombe said on that subject is false, as on the back of the writ a proper affidavit was made, and you made, sir, order on the writ for bail in your own hand writing, and he never was discharged on that case, in which he was convicted, & the jury gave a verdict for me for $200 damages. Mr. Lipscombe makes several other assertions equally false, and concludes his address to you thus—"I have thought this expression of my sentiments due to your public character, and I hope to have the pleasure of always esteeming your private virtues."

I am, sir, respectfully, &c.

(Signed)   A. S. LIPSCOMBE.

Now, sir, I have no objection to Mr. Lipscombe's esteeming your private or public character. I said nothing about your private virtues, although I do not esteem them. I attacked your public character, your official acts only. Sir, I could transcribe other statements, some under oath, equally false, and you knew they were false, when you sent them on; but I presume you were ignorant of my being in Washington City, and had no expectation of my seeing them. It is my object to do away any false impression on the minds of those who have read them, or who are in the habit of hearing your partizan's stories, by thus shewing Mr. Lipscombe's statement is false, and denouncing every affidavit and statement which you sent on to disprove my charges, to be equally false; and I am ready to enter into a fair investigation, which will prove their falsehood. I should not consider you entitled to this notice; but as some of your partizans are in situations which enable them to bias those ignorant of the truth, this statement will enable them to form just opinions of men and things. The following is the Certificate given by col. James Caller to Chief Justice Johnson, in which he stated that you said you had been in a party in England and in Kentucky, and had been injured by it, and had determined not to enter into a party again; but that you found it necessary to form a party here; that you insinuated that the party was to be sworn in for the purpose of sticking together. Your certificate men, it is reasonable to suppose, belong to this sworn in party.

What but the malice of Hell could induce you, after you had pursued me with your judicial vengeance for twelve or fourteen years, on all occasions, to call your sworn in partizans and disciples around you, and get them to make such a set of false statements; some under oath, and send them on to Washington City to stab my reputation in this dark, secret, inquisitorial and illegal manner? Had you not injured me enough to have glutted the appetite of a demon of night and of hell, by keeping me 14 years attending your court in vain; by delaying me justice, when you knew it would ruin me to be delayed; during which time I was reduced to the most cruel hardships and sufferings, being often obliged to walk 150 miles and back on foot, in attending your court, to witness further delay, insult and oppression from you; thus depriving me of the means of carrying on any profitable business, and wasting my time and spending my money.?* No! you must cap these innumerable wrongs by attempting in this clandestine manner to destroy my reputation; or was my destruction a part of the object of your forming and swearing in your party agreeable to col. Caller's certificate? Sir, I think the pirates are not so detestable as the wicked judge who robs a man of his time in attending courts and spending money, and keeping him in suspense for fourteen years, by delaying and denying him justice.   E. Lewis.

> "*Ah! little knowest thou, who hast not try'd
> What hell it is in suing long to bide,
> To loose good days that might be better spent,
> To pass long nights in pensive discontent;
> To speed to-day, to be put back to-morrow,
> To feed on hope, to pine with fear & sorrow,
> To fret thy soul with crosses and with care,
> To eat thy heart through comfortless despair,
> To fawn, to crouch, to wait, to ride, to run,
> To spend, to give, to want, to be undone;
> Unhappy wight! Such hard fate doom'd[6] to try,
> That curse God send unto mine enemy."

Broadside (MoSHi: TJC-BC); undated, but printed by 7 Nov. 1820 when Lewis enclosed copies in a letter to John Quincy Adams (DNA: RG 59, MLR); at head of text: *"Truth is not Calumny"*; between heading and salutation: **"To Harry Toulmin, former Judge on Tombeckbe."**

Harry Toulmin (1766–1823), educator, public official, and jurist, was born in Taunton, England, and was a Unitarian minister in Lancashire from 1786 until 1792. In the face of disapproval of his political and religious views, Toulmin moved to the United States the next year and settled in Kentucky. He was president of Transylvania Seminary (later Transylvania University), 1794–96, and Kentucky's secretary of state, 1796–1804. In the lat-

ter year TJ appointed him to a federal judgeship in Mississippi Territory, which he held until Alabama achieved statehood in 1819, with Toulmin serving in the new state's constitutional convention. He also compiled the legal codes of Kentucky, Mississippi Territory, and Alabama between 1802 and 1823. Toulmin died at his plantation in Washington County, Alabama (*ANB*; *DAB*; *PTJ*, 27:270–1; Sowerby, nos. 2175, 2181, 3313; *JEP*, 1:472, 474 [12, 22 Nov. 1804]; Washington *Daily National Intelligencer*, 13 Dec. 1823).

The Committee on the Judiciary of the United States House of Representatives examined and discharged accusations of misconduct by Lewis against Toulmin in both 1817 and 1818, first reporting on 27 Feb. 1817 of "sundry documents furnished by Edwin Lewis" that "there is no evidence whatever contained in these documents which could warrant any proceedings against Judge Toulmin" (*ASP, Miscellaneous,* 2:443; *Annals,* 15th Cong., 1st sess. [18 Apr. 1818], 1768).

Lewis adapted AH! LITTLE KNOWEST THOU . . . UNTO MINE ENEMY from Edmund Spenser's poem entitled "Prosopopoia. Or Mother Hubberds Tale,"

originally printed in his *Complaints. Containing sundrie small Poemes of the Worlds Vanitie* (London, 1591), n.p.

[1] Broadside: "Lipsccmbe."
[2] Broadside: "error,&c."
[3] Broadside: "delay,and."
[4] Broadside: "sustaintained."
[5] Broadside: "offalsehood."
[6] Broadside: "doom d."

From John A. Robertson

SIR,   Richmond 20th December 1820.

After much reflection and indecision on the subject, I have concluded to make this communication, sensible, however, that it must necissarily present to you, not only an instance, of the versitility of human character, but of that peculiarity in relation to the writer, a parellel to which is not, very readily, to be adduced—

To one like you, however, so well versed in the character of man, in a national as well as individual point of view, the causes of particular effects and general motives of action, in the one or the other character, are analised with a facility of reasoning & perspicuity of discernment, amounting, very nearly, to absolute certainty—I have no wish to conceal my motives on this occasion—

Science and literature have, from my earliest life, been objects of my most ardent pursuit, at intervals only—The volitility of my disposition, whilst engaged in scholastic research, and the imprudent and extravagant course, in pecuniary matters, attendant on my early manhood, combined prevented the attainment so fondly wished for, from that complete consummation, which under other circumstances, would have been easily effected, at least, to a much greater extent—After the fiery age of youth was a little softened, politics engrossed my whole attention and in both writing & haranguing my course, for some years, was marked with a warmth and zeal rarely equalled, never surpassed— Frequently was I a candidate for a seat in the state legislature and once for congress—I was as often disappointed and always upon the ground of my opposition to your administration and those with whom you acted, for such was the weight of your political character in this section of the state, that no open opponent to your course stood the least chance of election. I was however candid and honest in my course and was one among the first, after the attack upon the Chessapeake, by the British frigate Leopard (1807) who tendered the services of a well trained volunteer company which I had the honor to command and received, from you, on the occasion, a very flattering letter of thanks &c.

I never permitted myself to be ranked with any other political sect but the republican, yet with the opinions and principles of many honorable gentlemen, termed federalists, mine perfectly corresponded on many important occasions—It is, however, unnecessary to state to you that <u>names</u> are nothing, but are too frequently resorted to, with selfish views, as terms of crimination & recrimination by contending demigogues and factionists; suffice it therefore to say on this head, that of politics and <u>mere</u> politicians I am really tired, and find, after all, that we must look to the <u>heart</u> & not always the <u>professions</u> of men to distinguish the patriot from the <u>impostor</u>—

It is due to candor, here, to remark, that upon a review of your whole public life, the outlines of which I have known from the dawn of manhood, it must be acknowledged that our common country is deeply indebted to you, for the many and signal services you have rendered, with an ability and zeal too not falling to the lot of one individual in a <u>million</u> and that your name will descend to posterity with that approbation & applause, stamping with immortality the man, for whose labors America is so much indebted, whilst some who have had a momentary exaltation, will be forgotten and not a few will live on the historic page, as lamentable <u>mementos</u> of political and moral depravity—These facts, the result of much reflection, have, at length, taught me the necessity of <u>moderation</u>, in my intercourse with man and proved the impropriety of hasty denunciations of any particular system and it's supporters; especially in politics & more especially, before the understanding is sufficiently expanded and the judgment somewhat matured by age and experience; but it is hoped that recent events have smoothed those political asperities, too common here in times past and that we shall never again witness those disagreeable occurrences, recollected by all, to disturb the quiet of this august Republic—

I have some intention of residing in your <u>salubrious</u> section of the state and would feel much gratified to be often in your company—A veneration for your great acquirements, is here the motive—

I am in the prime of life, healthy & temperate, am a member of the bar of the <u>superior</u> courts here and a few of the inferior of the country, was raised in the county of Amelia & descended from one of the oldest families of the state, I have been married & was unhappy, in that state and after six years separation, the legislature divorced us; I have four fine children, handsomely seated, on their own property in Not-

toway, well educated, to their ages, & who are in fact wealthy inde-
pendantly of me. Mrs R. is dead and consequently, altho' my family
are dear to me, I am entirely unincumbered in that respect, having,
six years ago after paying my debts, given them every thing, relying
on my own exertions, for a support—The accompanying letter will
give you a correct idea of the subject of separation and divorce—I am
called industrious in my profession and am flattered with the possession of talents, by my friends, am what is generally called a classical
scholar; of those things however, others will judge for themselves, I
feel strongly my own deficiency—I write a good hand, of which this
is a pretty fair specimen, and with great facility & dispatch and can
compose, on any given subject, with tolerable ease and in a stile of
which you may form, perhaps, a correct estimate & have been all my
life, I trust, entirely above a single mean or dishonorable act—My
great object is to write the history of Virginia at times when not professionally engaged, for we have as yet no authentic history of our
native state—Until very lately, I have intended to go to the Southwest-
ern parts of the Union to reside and have gradually, for two years,
lessened my professional business—That idea is now abandoned, but
my business now is so arranged as to enable me to take a new stand
& your neighborhood for the aforegoing reasons is the place contemplated—I could to you, Sir, in your declining years, render I think,
some services, in various ways &c &c. I wish you to favor me with an
answer to this, stating my prospects your views &c and do so, if you
please, as soon as your convenience will admit—I hope Sir that, in
any event, you will consider this letter as confidential and that should
you reciprocate my views, your friendship & reasonable patronage,
may be calculated on.   I am Sir: with profound respect & esteem y^r mo: ob^t &c   JOHN A. ROBERTSON

☞ Direct to me Richmond

RC (ViW: TC-JP); addressed: "Thom-
as Jefferson, Esqr Monticello Albemarle"
by "mail"; franked; postmarked Rich-
mond, 22 Dec.; endorsed by TJ as received 28 Dec. 1820 and so recorded in
SJL.

TJ's VERY FLATTERING LETTER OF
THANKS to Robertson of 25 Aug. 1807,
not found, is recorded in SJL as concerning the light infantry company of the
49th regiment in Nottoway County. The
ACCOMPANYING LETTER was Robertson's
circular of 12 Dec. 1820.

From Joseph C. Cabell

Dear Sir,   Williamsburg 22 Dec: 1820.

On consultation with Gen[l] Breckenridge & others it was decided that we should bring forward nothing in regard to the University till after Christmas. I got leave of absence till 29th and left town on 20th. The evening before my departure I was informed that M[r] Griffin of York had brought in a set of Resolutions the evident effect of which would be[1] to embarrass the disposable[2] part of the Literary Fund so as to defeat the claims of the University: & these resolutions were warmly supported by the friends of Hampden Sidney, but particularly by M[r] Miller of Powhatan. They give the right to the counties to draw out the Derelict part of the fund, provide against the recurrence of a similar state of things, and make an appropriation to W[m] & Mary, Hampden Sidney, Washington College, New London, the University &[c]. I went immediately to see Gen[l] Breckenridge and spent the evening in conversing with him on this subject. He was glad the opposite party had come forward so early in the session. Instead of getting an advantageous start of us, he thought they would only defeat themselves, by disclosing their plans & conflicting with each other: & our friends, he thought, should attend the committee & let them run on for a time. M[r] Bowyer & M[r] Gordon seemed to be fearful of the consequences of this course. I got leave of absence with the intention of carrying M[rs] Cabell up on 29th; but owing to this movement of the opposition, I had determined to leave her in W[ms]burg and to return in the steam boat on 26th. I left your letter with Gen[l] Breckenridge, and had shewn it to many of our friends. There was a general concurrence in the opinion that we should not succeed in an attempt at a general system of schools, and that we should aim at only so much money as would finish the buildings, leaving the mortgage for the present on our funds. It will be a hard struggle to get even this. The hostile interests are strong, & well conducted this session. I have looked over the accounts since I last wrote you. I am now satisfied that M[r] M. was only seeking for materials of opposition: & I think it unnecessary[3] for M[r] Garrett to send down the detailed account before 1st April. The summary statement covers the whole ground. Should it be necessary, I will hereafter call for explanation as to any part of the accounts. Gen[l] Breckenridge thinks Gen[l] Blackburn will run with us. M[r] Doddridge comes down in a good humor, has candidly acknowledged that I was in the right as to the great litter of banks: and avowed himself a friend to the University. He is anxious for an endowment of the Randolph Academy. But I hope he will ultimately unite with us. Bowyer of Rockbridge is my intimate friend & heartily with us. Otey of Bedford advocates an appropriation to New London Academy, but I believe will in the end go right. Mʳ Watson of Louisa is our zealous friend. I fear Mʳ Crump of Cumberland will be induced to insist on an appropriation to Hampden Sidney: yet I hope he will ultimately cooperate with us. His local position is unfortunate. D. S. Garland & party will be violently opposed to the University: but I hope that influence is now but small. I am advised by Genˡ Breckenridge not to stir the question relative to the old charters but as a dernier resort. Some have thought it a dangerous weapon inasmuch as it would divide the friends of Science: and throw the majority against us. Morris, Breckenridge, Bowyer, Genˡ Taylor—Coalter—all—think the principle sound, and that it cannot ultimately be resisted. Our object now is to finish the buildings. If this could be done without resort to this doctrine, I would willingly put it aside for the present—but I do not see how we can avoid calling it in; unless they should defeat themselves, & leave the field⁴ open to us. I will keep you fully informed from time to time. Let me urge you to write to Judge Roane & one or two other friends: but at least, to Judge Roane.—The Governor's triumph over his enemies was compleat. Never was overthrow more brilliant & galling. His friends regretted greatly the introduction of some topics into his message; the parts respecting slavery & religion would have done him great injury, but for the attack on his character, which united the country in his support.

I am, dear sir, faithfully yours   Jos: C: Cabell

RC (ViU: TJP-PC); endorsed by TJ as received 31 Dec. 1820 and so recorded in SJL. RC (MHi); address cover only; with PoC of TJ to Lancelot Minor, 31 Mar. 1821, on verso; addressed: "Mʳ Jefferson Monticello," with "Charlottsville" added in an unidentified hand; franked; postmarked Williamsburg, 25 Dec.

On 19 Dec. 1820 Thomas Griffin presented a SET OF RESOLUTIONS on the Literary Fund to the Virginia House of Delegates, which referred them to the Committee of Schools and Colleges. In addition to providing for the disbursement to each county of its share of THE DERELICT PART OF THE FUND, they proposed to MAKE AN APPROPRIATION to the state's academies and to the colleges and university named by Cabell above, required that a still-to-be-determined number of poor and promising students be

given scholarships at institutions receiving state aid, and allocated to county primary schools any funds remaining after payment of the specified appropriations (*JHD* [1820–21 sess.], 51–2; *Richmond Enquirer*, 23 Dec. 1820).

A 31 Dec. 1787 statute of the Virginia General Assembly chartered the RANDOLPH ACADEMY in Clarksburg (later West Virginia) and allotted it a share of the fees paid to public surveyors. A building was constructed and the school opened in about 1795, but it seems only to have lasted for a couple of decades (*Acts of Assembly* [1787–88 sess.], 46; Henry Haymond, *History of Harrison County, West Virginia* [1910], 287–90).

Cabell did later raise THE QUESTION RELATIVE TO THE OLD CHARTERS, reportedly arguing "that an appropriation of public money to the uses of either of the old colleges ought not to be granted by the

Legislature, except upon the express condition that such college should, like the
University of Virginia, be at all times and
in all things subject to the control of the
Legislature" (Cabell to TJ, 4 Jan. 1821;
quote from Cabell, *University of Virginia*,
194n). DERNIER: "last."

[1] Reworked from "evident object of
which was."
[2] Manuscript: "disposabble."
[3] Manuscript: "unnessary."
[4] Manuscript: "feald."

To James Leitch

Dec. 22. 20.

half a sack of salt or as much as the bearer can bring on his mule
1.℔ pepper.   TH:J.

RC (DLC: George Frederick Holmes
Papers); written on a small scrap; date-
line beneath signature; at foot of text: "M^r
Leitch." Not recorded in SJL.

Leitch's records indicate that on this
date TJ purchased by order "2½ Bushels

Salt" at "9/–" for a total of $3.75. In an
earlier entry for the same day, Leitch recorded selling TJ, per Edmund Bacon,
"2 Sets Knitting needles 4½^d. 1^℔ Pepper
3/– ℔ Order" for $0.63 (Leitch Daybook,
p. 181).

From Joel Yancey

DR SIR   Poplar Forest Decr 22. 1820

Jery arriverd here last Evening about 4 oClock, with one of his
Mules[1] very lame and complains much about badness of Roads, I had
every[2] thing ready, and shoud have loaded wednesday night, had
Jery came, but they now will be a day later than you expected, I hope
to get them off this morning by sun rise, the pork turn,^d out very well,
and has been destributed as you derected, the 23 hogs picked out for
Monticello, and which you will receive[3] by the waggons, weighed
3020^℔ nett and very nice, the face, back bone, and leaf fat, will average 30^℔ to each hog, so that you will not receive more than about
2300, exclusly of the lard, 2 Kegs butter 85^℔ and 102^℔ Gross, 150^℔
lard, 18 ps old bacon, 51^℔ Soap and 2 beeves, the Dft Steer, could not
be taken, the overseer (Miller) with 3 or 4 hands, was in pursuit of
him yesterday and the day before constantly, but could do nothing
with him, I will have him taken, and broke, if possible, and sent down
in march, with the other beeves and Muttons, the waggons will have
about 2000^℔ each wich will be as much as the teams can Draw in bad
roads, please send our people off immediately after the hollidays, as

we shall be in great want of the waggon till its return, a list of each load at the bottom. I am with Highes respect

y[r] mo o[bt] ser[vt]   JOEL YANCEY

Deck		℔	
1 Barrel pork 88 ps.		1257	
1 cask of lard, (half full)		150	
2 firkins butter gross		187	Decks load
1 Box containing 18 ps old Bacon & 51℔ Soap		150	

Jery		℔	
1 barrel pork 73 ps		1050	
all The articles Johny Heming charge, supposed to be		700	Jerys load

RC (MHi); endorsed by TJ as received 25 Dec. 1820 and so recorded (with mistaken 25 Dec. composition date) in SJL. RC: left half of address cover only (MHi), with PoC of TJ to Bernard Peyton, 3 [Apr.] 1821, on verso; right half of address cover only (MHi), with PoC of TJ to Robert Mayo, 5 Apr. 1821, on verso;

addressed: "M[r] Thomas Jefferson Monticello" by "Deck."

JERY: Jeremiah (Jerry) (b. 1777). DECK: Dick (b. 1767).

[1] Manuscript: "Males."
[2] Manuscript: "very."
[3] Manuscript: "recive."

To Joseph C. Cabell

DEAR SIR   Monticello Dec. 25. 20.

Your letter of the 20th was the first intimation that I had omitted to inclose, with the documents of our Report, the first half year's account of the Bursar, which had been duly rendered in April and filed away. I now correct that error by inclosing it to the Governor with a letter of explanation, to be communicated to the legislature.   You may have observed an apparent difference of 38,364.D between the Proctor's[1] estimate of what is wanting to compleat the buildings, and our estimate embodied in the Report. with the Report and letter inclosing it, I wrote an additional one to the Governor, shewing that this difference was merely apparent. as the evidence of this on the face of the two estimates, if closely observed, rendered it's communication to the legislature not absolutely necessary, I observe it has not been sent to them with the other papers. I inclose you however a copy of it, in the handwriting of one of my grandaughters, for my dislocated wrist is failing so fast that I apprehend the loss of the power of writing altogether. this explanation may be necessary in both houses, but may be given verbally as well as by the formal letter. I lately saw in a newspaper an estimate in square miles of the area of each of the states, of which the following is an extract. 'Virginia 70,000. sq. mi. Massachusets 7,250. Connecticut 4,764. Delaware 2,120. Rhode island 1,580.'[2] by this it appears that there are but 3. states smaller than Massachusets; that she is the 21st only in the scale of size, and but $\frac{1}{10}$ of that of Virginia. yet it is unquestionable that she has more influence in our confederacy than any other state in it. whence this ascendancy? from her attention to education unquestionably. there can be no stronger proof that knolege is power, and that ignorance is weakness. quousque tandem will our legislators be dead to this truth? ever & affectionately yours. TH: JEFFERSON

RC (ViU: TJP); edge torn, with missing text supplied from PoC; addressed: "Joseph C. Cabell esq. of the Senate of Virginia now in Richmond"; franked; postmarked Milton, 26 Dec.; endorsed by Cabell. PoC (DLC); on verso of a reused address cover from John Barnes to TJ; signature trimmed; endorsed by TJ. Enclosure: FC of TJ to Thomas Mann Randolph, 9 Nov. 1820.

The Washington *Daily National Intelligencer* listed the AREA OF EACH OF THE STATES on 29 Nov. 1820. QUOUSQUE TANDEM: "how much longer."

[1] Word interlined in place of "Bursar's" (with the "'s" left uncanceled by TJ).
[2] Omitted closing quotation mark editorially supplied.

To George Alexander Otis

SIR[1]   Monticello Dec. 25. 20.

I have to thank you for the 2^d vol. of your translation of Botta which I recieved with your favor of the 5th on my return home after a long absence.[2] I join mr Adams heartily in good wishes for the success of your labors, and hope they will bring you both profit & fame. you have certainly rendered a good service to your country; & when the superiority of the work over every other on the same subject shall be more known, I think it will be the common Manual of our revolutionary history.[3] I have not been sensible of the Southern partiality imputed by mr Adams to the Author. the Southern states as well as Northern did zealously whatever the situation or circumstances of each or of their sister states required or permitted, and a relation of what they did is only justice.[4] I disapprove, with mr Adams, of the factitious speeches which Botta has composed for R. H. Lee & John Dickinson, speeches which he and I know were never made by these gentlemen. they took a part indeed in that great debate, and I believe we may admit mr Dickinson[5] to have been the prominent debater against the measure. but many acted abler parts than R. H. Lee, as particularly mr Adams himself did. mr Lee was considered as an Orator & eloquent, but not in that style which had much weight in such an assembly of men[6] as that Congress was. frothy, flimsy, verbose, with a musical voice and chaste language, he was a good pioneer but not an efficient reasoner. this mr Adams can tell you as well as myself. with regard to Botta, I have understood that he has taken some occasion to apologise for these suppositious[7] speeches by pleading the example of the antient historians. and we all know that their practice was to state the reasons for and against a measure in the form of speeches, & put them into the mouths of some eminent character of their selection who probably had never uttered a word of them. I think the modern practice better of saying it was argued on one side by A. B. C. & others, so and so, and on the other by D. E. F. & others, so and so; giving in this form the reasons for and against the measure. I do not recollect whether Botta has repeated the fault on other occasions. with respect to the speeches in the British parliament I have taken for granted that he copied or abridged them from the Parliamentory debates.[8] M[r] Adams's criticism on Davila and Hume is just; that the former is an apology for Catharine of Medicis, and the latter of the Stuarts, to which might be added Robertson's Mary, queen of Scots. and these odious partialities are much to be lamented: for otherwise they are three of the finest models of historical composition which have been produced since the days of Livy & Tacitus.[9]

Wishing you a full remuneration, either by the profits of your work, or by the evidence it may have furnished the government of the degree in which they may avail the public of your services, I salute you with sentiments of esteem & respect.   TH: JEFFERSON[10]

P.S. I have just dispatched your two volumes to mr Botta, to whom I am sure they will be a gratification.[11]

RC (MBBS: Jeremiah Colburn Autograph Collection, on deposit MHi); endorsed by Otis. PoC (MHi); on reused address cover of Andrew Smith to TJ, 18 June 1819; at foot of first page: "M[r] George Alexander Otis"; endorsed by TJ. Tr (MHi: Adams Papers); undated extracts copied by Otis into his letter to John Adams of 4 Jan. 1821. Tr (MHi: Adams Papers); extracts dated 25 Dec.

1820 copied by Otis into his letter to John Quincy Adams of 27 Jan. 1821.

[1] Tr to John Quincy Adams begins with this word.
[2] Tr to John Adams begins here, preceded by salutation.
[3] Trs end here.
[4] Trs resume here.
[5] Manuscript: "Dickenson."

[6] Preceding two words interlined.
[7] All texts: "supposititious."
[8] Tr to John Quincy Adams ends here.

[9] Tr to John Quincy Adams resumes here.
[10] Tr to John Adams ends here.
[11] Tr to John Quincy Adams ends here.

To Thomas Mann Randolph

SIR   Monticello Dec. 25. 20.

Casting my eye over a printed copy of the late Report of the Visitors of the University, I discovered that the statement of the Bursar's account for the first half of the year, from Oct. 1819. to Mar. 1820. inclusive, was wanting, and turning to the papers on file, I found I had omitted it in making up the documents for the report. this first part of the statement had been duly rendered by the Bursar to the Visitors at their April meeting, and had been filed among the papers in my possession. the second-half-year from Apr. to Sep. inclusive, was rendered in like manner to the October meeting, and was inclosed with the report, without adverting, at the moment, to the date of it's commencement, or recollecting the part on file, which should have accompanied it. I now inclose that part for the inspection of the Literary board and of the legislature, with the expression of my regret & apology for this oversight, which I trust will be believed to have been without intention, as without motive. I have the honor to be
    with the highest consideration, Sir your most obed^t & most hble serv^t TH: JEFFERSON

PoC (ViU: TJP); on verso of reused address cover of Bernard Peyton to TJ, 21 June 1819; at foot of text: "Govr Randolph"; endorsed by TJ.

Randolph conveyed the enclosed BURSAR'S ACCOUNT to the Virginia General Assembly in a letter of 29 Dec. 1820 to Linn Banks, Speaker of the House of Delegates, in which Randolph noted that he had received the above item on 28 Dec. 1820 (Vi: RG 79, House of Delegates, Speaker, Executive Communications).

Alexander Garrett's Account with the University of Virginia

Dr — The University of Virginia — In acc't with — Alexander Garrett Bursar — Cr

Date (1819)	Particulars		Amount (In acc't with)
Sep 30	To ballance per report due the bursar this date	$	50 99
Octo 4	" John Gorman per Draft & Receipt		50
	" Robert Lindsay "		392 33
1	" John M Perry "		100 00
	" James Dinsmore "		50 00
	" Nelson Barksdale "		50 00
	" Arthur S. Brokenbrough " for M & J Raggi per Draft & Receipt		
	" Andrew Jameson		10 00
5	" James Oldham in part		7 72
	" William Phillips "		100 00
	" ditto in part "		36 00
11	" Thomas Stone "		64 00
	" ditto "		18 00
15	" Archibald Stuart "		10 00
29 & 30	" John M Perry "		5 00
30	" Richard Ware "		500 00
30	" John Winn for Richard Ware "		370 00
	" Cowden & Campbell "		50 00
	" P. Laporte "		100 00
	" Robert Gentry "		25 00
	" Andrew McKee for Richard Ware "		181 00
	" ditto for George Miliway		40 00
Nov 1	" Carter & Phillips ballance		30 00
	" William Garth "		436 00
			64 96

Date (1819)	Particulars		Cr Amount
Octo. 4	By Jeremiah A Goodman in part his 2d Install[t]	$	5 00
7	" President & directors of the Literary fund ditto		1,000 00
16	" ditto		3.156 81[1]
	" A S Brokenbrough for Subscriptions paid him to Wit	Henry Chiles 1 & 2d Installments $50:00; John M Perry 2d Installment 50:00; James Dinsmore 2d Installment 50:00; Nelson Barksdale 2d Installment 50:00	200 00
Nov 1	" William Garth 2d Install: his subscription		37 50
2	" A S Brokenbrough for subscriptions paid him to Wit	Richard Duke in part of 1 & 2d Install: $88:74; Wm H. Merewether in part 2d Install: 16:64; Robert Gentry in full 2d Install: 25:00; A B Harvie in full 2d Install: 125:00	255 38
8	" A S Brokenbrough draft on James Monroe in favour of John Winn 2d Install:		250 00
20	" John H Cocke for Jno Fuqua's 2d Instal:		10 00
Dec 13	" James Leitch this sum borrowed of him		40 00
Feby 2d	" President & directors of the Literary fund 2d State donation		15.000 00
1820	" Bank of Virginia for Jno Pleasants jr Instal:		25 00
	" ditto for J Baker Instal		30 00
March 6	" David Watson for James Michies Subscription 1818 & 1819		30 00
	" ditto for Wm Ragland 1818		25 00
	" Samuel L Hart 2d Instalment		25 00

Dr — **The University of Virginia** — **In acc't with** — **Alexander Garrett Bursar** — **Cr**

Debit side — The University of Virginia, In acc't with

	Description	In acc't with
2	" James Black	38 00
	" Nelson Barksdale in part	50 00
	" Wm D Merewether for Richard Duke	12 48
	" William D. Merewether	86 06
	" ditto	6 84
	" Brokenbrough & Harvie	125 00
3	" Nelson Barksdale in full — per Draft & Receipt	
	" Henry Chiles for Richard Ware	150
	" Henry Stone for James & Thomas Stone	80
	" J & M Raggi ballance	25
4	" Robert Gentry	20
	" A S Brokenbrough	20
5	" Fanny Barnett	177 08
	" James Leitch	5
7	" Adam Shuey	300
8	" Bramham & Jones	18 50
	" Bramham & Jones for Richard Ware	58
	" Same for Same	65 52
	" Same for Js & Tho Stone	69 45
	" Same for James Stone	42 10
	" Same for Geo W Kinsolving	30 00
	" John Winn in part	25 00
	" Same by A S Brokenbrough	22 69
	" Draft on James Monroe for his 2d Instal: Subs:	300 00 / 250 00

Credit side — Alexander Garrett Bursar, Cr

	Description	Detail	Cr
21	" A S Brokenbrough for Subscriptions paid him to Wit		
	" John H Craven part of 2d Installment	$108:16	
	" Nimrod Bramham 2d Installment	125:00	
	" Joseph Coffman 2d Installment	12:50	245 66
	" A S Brokenbrough for Subscriptions paid him to Wit,		
	" John Rogers 1 & 2 Installment	$100:00	
	" Peter Minor 2d	100:00	
	" Francis W Gilmer 2d	25:00	
	" John Fretwell 2d	25:00	
	" James Minor 1st	75:00	
	" Dabney Minor 2 & 3d	200:00	
	" John Minor 3d	50:00	
	" A Whitehurst 1 & 2d & part 3d	34:66	
	" Allen Dawson 2d	25:00	
	" Opie Norris 2d	75:00	709 66
22	" Reubin Lindsay per Mr Jefferson 3 & 4th Install:		500 00
27	" A S Brokenbrough for Jno Dyer part 2d Inst	$31:93	
29	" Same for Samuel Dyer 2d Inst:	100:00	
	" Same for James Leitch 2d Instal.	125:00	256 93
	" James O Carr 2d Installment	125:00	75 00
	" A S Brokenbrough for Jno H Craven part 2d Inst	$16:84	
	" Same for Geo W Kinsolving 2d Inst	12:50	29 34
	" Alexander Garrett 2nd Installment		125 00

		Description		$	c
1820	Decemʳ 13	" John Massie in part	per Dft & Recᵗ	40	00
	Janʸ 25	" George W Spooner	"	7	50
		" Richard Ware	"		92
		" Phillips & Carter	"		60
		" Richard Ware	"		25
	Febʸ 2	" Joseph Carter for James Oldham	"	300	
		" Same for Same	"	200	
		" Same for Same ballance	"	78	57
		" Same for Same	"	138	21
		" Same for Richard Ware	"	21	83
		" John M Perry	per Draft & Receipt.	600	00
			"	3615	90
		" Same for James Dinsmore	"	400	00
		" Same for Same	"	500	00
		" Same for Geo. W Spooner	"	200	00
		" Same for Johnson Pitts	"	100	00
		" Same for John H Craven	"	20	70
		" Same for Same ballance	"	11	36
		" Same for Same	"	109	88
		" Carter & Phillips	"	183	00
		" Same	"	400	00
		" Same	"	622	28
		" John Winn & Co	"	344	68

			In acct with	Amount	Cr
" John Winn	for Richard Ware	"		15 00	
" Same	for Nelson Barksdale	"		1383 51	
" Same	for Robert Gentry	"		40 00	
" Same	for John Gorman	"		55 00	
" Same	for James Leitch 2 Drafts	"		168 60	
" Same	for Daniel Davis	"		21 49	
" Same	for David Fowler	"		12 64	
" Same	for James Leitch	"		211 22	
" Same	for Same	"		39 00	
" Same	for Dabney Gooch	"		237 28	
" Same	for Campbell & Cowden	"		112 00	
" Same	for James Leitch	"		40 00	
3 " Edmund Anderson for James Dinsmore		"		20 00	
" Same	for Richard Ware	"		60 00	
" Same	for John Pollock	"		17 85	
3 " Thomas Jefferson for M & J Raggi		per Dft & Receipt		400 00	

8	" Jesse Garth for David Owens	"	179 65
	" Jesse Garth	"	28 97
	" Edward Collard for Quin & Harkins	"	55 45
	" Same for Nicholas Basset	"	39 00
	" William Garth	"	57 00
	" William Pitt for Joseph Pitt	"	97 33
	" Richard Ware for Cowden & Campbell	"	38 00
11	" Bramham & Jones for Peter Laporte	"	25 50
	" Same for John Herrin	"	106 00
	" M & J Raggi	"	20 00
	" David Isaacs	"	24 00
12	" A S Brockenbrough for P. Boxley	"	670 00
	" Same for John Nunn	"	290 00
	" Same for Jos: Sandridge	"	119 00
	" Abia Thorn	"	86 50.
	" Richard Shackleford	"	4 00
	" Negroe Charles for Richard Ware	"	14 00
	" Benjamin Austin for Frank Burkhead	"	4 16
14	" Willis Garth	"	67. 50.
16	" David Summers for John Lawrance	"	161. 76
18	" John Winn for Richard Ware	"	70 00
21	" Fanny Barnett	"	6 00

The University of Virginia   In acc.ᵗ with   **Alexander Garrett Bursar**

March	4	" A S. Brockenbrough	"	400 00
		" Same for Jno Van Lew & Co	"	500 00
	6	" John D Foster for John Massie ball[ce]	"	44 28
		" John Slaughter	"	211 00
		" Same for Charles Harper	"	120 00
	18	" Isaac Moore	"	46. 50
		" Nelson Barksdale per Dft & Receipt	"	40 00
		" Same	"	22 00
		" Same for Manual Reese	"	4. 30
		" Nathaniel Thacker	"	5 64
		" John H Craven	"	108 16
		" John M Perry	"	137 50
		" James Leitch	"	100 00
		" Peter Minor	"	125 00
		" John Fretwell	"	25 00
		" Dabney Minor	"	325 00
		" John H Craven	"	34 66
		" Nelson Barksdale	"	25 00
		" John M Perry	"	75 00
	22	" A S Brockenbrough for general expences	"	30 00

Date		Description		Amount	
25		" M & J Raggi	"	40	00
27		" John M Perry	"	400	00
		" A S Brokenbrough for P A Sabbaton	"	70	60
		" Same for D W & C Warrick	"	37	00
		" John Dyer for Dudly Richardson	"	31	93
		" John C Wells for Albemarle Sheriff	"	14	25
		" Same for Wm Ramsey	"	20	52
28		" Kelly & Norris	"	33	17
		" Ira Harris for Sheriff Albemarle	"	9	27
		" Same for Richard Ware	"	45	00
		" Same for Daniel Davis	"	14	92
29		" James Leitch	"	225	00
		" A S Brockenbrough paid Jno H Craven ball: Dft	"	18	84
		" Same for George W Kinsolving	"	12	50
		" Alexander Garrett	"	250	00
Ap^{l} 1		" Ballance remaining in the Treasury[2] this date	"	643	20.
			$	22031	28.

The Foregoing is an account of the reciepts & disbursements of money, by the Bursar of the University[3] of Virginia from the first day of October one thousand eight hundred and nineteen, to the thirty first day of March One thousand eight hundred and twenty, (inclusive) shewing a ballance remaining in the Treasury (on the last mentioned date) of Six hundred and forty three[4] dollars twenty cents: All of which is respectfully reported to the Visitors of the University of Virginia, this third day of April One thousand eight hundred and twenty: ALEX: GARRETT Bursar

MS (Vi: RG 79, House of Delegates, Speaker, Executive Communications); entirely in Garrett's hand; page numbers, internal headings, and running totals at breaks of pages editorially omitted; endorsed by Garrett: "Bursar University Vᵃ Account & Report 3ᵈ April 1820." Possibly originally enclosed in a missing letter from Garrett to TJ, 3 Apr. 1820, for which see note to TJ to John Vaughan, 24 Apr. 1820.

JNO PLEASANTS JR: probably James Pleasants. EDWARD COLLARD: Edward Callard. FRANK BURKHEAD: Francis Birckhead. D W & C WARRICK: D. W. & C. Warwick.

[1] Reworked from "3.156.00."
[2] Manuscript: "Treasuary."
[3] Manuscript: "Uneversity," here and below.
[4] Manuscript: "thee."

To Thomas Ritchie

DEAR SIR   Monticello Dec. 25. 20.

On my return home after a long absence, I find here your favor of Nov. 23. with Colᵒ Taylor's 'Construction construed,' which you have been so kind as to send me, in the name of the author as well as of your self. permit me, if you please, to use the same channel for conveying to him the thanks I render you also for this mark of attention. I shall read it, I know, with edification, as I did his Enquiry to which I acknolege myself indebted for many valuable ideas, and for the correction of some errors of early opinion, never seen in a correct light until presented to me in that work. that the present volume is equally orthodox, I know before reading it, because I know that Colᵒ Taylor and myself have rarely, if ever, differed in any political principle of importance. every act of his life, & every word he ever wrote satisfies me of this. so also as to the two presidents, late and now in office, I know them both to be of principles as truly republican as any men living. if there be any thing amiss therefore in the present state of our affairs, as the formidable deficit lately unfolded to us indicates, I ascribe it to the inattention of Congress to it's duties, to their unwise dissipation & waste of the public contributions. they seemed, some little while ago to be at a loss for objects whereon to throw away the supposed fathomless funds of the treasury. I had feared the result, because I saw among them some of my old fellow laborers, of tried and known principles, yet often in their minorities. I am aware that in one of their most ruinous vagaries the people were themselves betrayed into the same phrensy, with their Representatives. the deficit produced, & a heavy tax to supply it will, I trust, bring both to their sober senses. but it is not from this branch of government we have most to fear. taxes & short elections will keep them right. the Judiciary of the US.[1] is the subtle corps of sappers & miners constantly working under ground to undermine the foundations of our confederated fabric. they are construing our constitution from a coordination of a general and special governments to a general & supreme one alone. this will lay all things at their feet, and they are too well versed in English law to forget the maxim 'boni judicis est ampliare jurisdictionem.' we shall see if they are bold enough to maintain the daring stride their 5 lawyers have lately taken. if they do, then, with the Editor of our book, in his address to the public, I will say that 'against this every man should raise his voice,' and more, should uplift his arm. Who wrote this admirable address? sound, luminous, strong, not a word too much, nor one which can be changed but for the worse. that pen should go on, lay bare these wounds of our constitution, expose these decisions seriatim, and arrouse, as it is able, the attention of the nation to these bold speculators on it's patience. having found from experience that impeachm[t] is an impracticable thing, a mere scare-crow, they consider themselves secure for life; they sculk from responsibility to public opinion the only remaining hold on them, under a practice, first introduced into England by L[d] Mansfield. an opinion is huddled up in Conclave, perhaps by a majority of one, delivered as a crafty Chief judge, as if unanimous, and, with the silent acquiescence of lazy or timid associates, he sophisticates the law to his mind by the turn of his own reasoning. a judiciary law was once reported by the Attorney Gen[l] to Congress, requiring each judge to deliver his opinion seriatim & openly, and then to give it in writing to the clerk to be entered on the record. a judiciary independant of a king[2] or Executive alone, is a good thing; but independance on the will of the nation is a solecism, at least in a republican government.

But to return to your letter. you ask for my opinion of the work you send me, and to let it go out to the public. this I have ever made a point of declining (one or two instances only excepted.) complimentory thanks to writers who have sent me their works have betrayed me sometimes before the public, without my consent having been asked. but I am far from presuming to direct the reading of my fellow citizens, who are good enough judges themselves of what is worthy their reading. I am also too desirous of quiet to place myself in the way of contention. against this I am admonished by bodily decay, which cannot be unaccompanied by a corresponding wane of the mind. of this I am, as yet, sensible, sufficiently to be unwilling to trust myself before the public, and when I cease to be so, I hope that my friends will be too careful of me to draw me forth and present me, like a Priam in armour, as a spectacle for public compassion. I hope our political bark will ride thro' all it's dangers; but I can in future be but an inert passenger. I salute you with sentiments of great friendship and respect.

TH: JEFFERSON

RC (MHi: Washburn Autograph Collection). PoC (DLC); at foot of first page: "Mr Thos Ritchie."

The FORMIDABLE DEFICIT LATELY UNFOLDED TO US was detailed in Secretary of the Treasury William H. Crawford's annual report, which he submitted to the United States Senate on 5 Dec. 1820 (*ASP, Finance*, 3:547–53; *Richmond Enquirer*, 12 Dec. 1820). BONI JUDICIS EST AMPLIARE JURISDICTIONEM: "It is the role of a good judge to enlarge (or use liberally) his jurisdiction (or remedial authority)" (*Black's Law Dictionary*).

In a case that would be decided by the United States Supreme Court in *Cohens v. Virginia* (1821), regarding the constitutionality of efforts by legislatures to prohibit the sale in their states of tickets for a federally sanctioned lottery to benefit the city of Washington, the 5 LAWYERS, William Pinkney, David B. Ogden, Thomas Addis Emmet, John Wells, and Walter Jones, argued on 27 June 1820 that "it would be monstrous if any state legislature could impede the execution of a law made for national purposes" (Baltimore *Niles' Weekly Register*, 2 Sept. 1820; *Richmond Enquirer*, 5 Sept. 1820).

John Taylor's *Construction Construed, and Constitutions Vindicated* (Richmond, 1820; Poor, *Jefferson's Library*, 11 [no. 652]), opened with an ADDRESS TO THE PUBLIC in which the work's anonymous editor criticized the Supreme Court for infringing on states' rights and declared "Against such a decision, it becomes every man, who values the constitution, to raise his voice" (p. i). The failure of the 1804–05 attempt to remove Samuel Chase from the Supreme Court persuaded TJ THAT IMPEACHMᵀ IS AN IMPRACTICABLE THING (*ANB*).

TJ was referencing John Marshall as the CRAFTY CHIEF JUDGE under whose leadership Supreme Court decisions were first debated internally and then often delivered as UNANIMOUS opinions. In a report on the judiciary system that he submitted to the United States House of Representatives on 31 Dec. 1790, ATTORNEY GENᴸ Edmund Randolph unsuccessfully proposed that Supreme Court justices be required to give their opinions SERIATIM & OPENLY (*ASP, Miscellaneous*, 1:31).

[1] Preceding three words interlined.
[2] Preceding three words interlined.

To Boissy d'Anglas

DEAR SIR   Monticello Dec. 26. 20.

It is long since I ought, if I had been able, to have acknoleged your obliging letter of April of the last year: but severe and continued ill health has long suspended in me the power of acknoleging the kind attentions of my friends generally as it has that with which you had honored me, accompanying it with a copy of your Memoirs of M. de

Malesherbes. no better subject could have been chosen for the exercise of your pen, for no honester, and few abler men ever adorned our nature. his writings and his administration, jointly with those of his friend and colleague Turgot, were the dawn ushering in that blaze of light on the world, which has so wonderfully affected the destinies of man. in recording his principles, moral and political, you have developed those on which you have so worthily acted yourself; and on late as well as former transactions. of the councils of your country, I have sought your name as the index which, to distant spectators, would point to what was right. I congratulate you then, dear Sir, on the final result of the struggles of your country, and the honorable part you have maintained thro' the whole of them. the pleasure which the reading your book afforded me, by passing in review the virtues of a man I so much admired as M. de Malesherbes,[1] has been the more gratifying, as it recalled to my mind the advantages I had of enjoying your society and acquaintance at his house, and at those of other cherished friends. the result of the agitations of that day we foresaw with exactness enough, but not the deplorable sacrifices, as unnecessary as cruel, which were to rend our hearts in the progress towards that result. I hope you are now landed in the safe harbor of representative government where the waters, always a little rough, will only experience such agitation as is necessary to keep them pure. be assured, Sir, that no one more sincerely than myself wishes this to your country, nor to yourself longer blessings of life, health and happiness.

Th: Jefferson

PoC (DLC); on a reused address cover from Arthur S. Brockenbrough to TJ; at head of text: "thro' depmt of state"; at foot of first page: "M. le comte Boissy d'Anglas, Pair de France"; endorsed by TJ. Recorded in SJL with the additional notation: "inclosed to mr D. Brent of the depmt of state." Enclosed in TJ to Albert Gallatin, 26 Dec. 1820, and TJ to Daniel Brent, [ca. 27 Dec. 1820], not found (see note to Brent to TJ, 26 Feb. 1821).

[1] Manuscript: "Malesherbe."

To Destutt de Tracy

Monticello. Dec. 26. 20.

Long ill health, dear Sir, has brought me much into default with my corresponding friends, and it's sufferings have been augmented by the remorse resulting from this default. I learnt with pleasure from your last letter, and from a later one of M. de la Fayette, that you were mending in health, and particularly that your eye-sight was sensibly improved.

I have to thank you for the copy of your Commentary on Montesquieu accompanying your letter, and a second thro mr Barnet. the world ought to possess it in it's native language, which cannot be compensated by any translation. the edition published here is now exhausted, and the copy-right being near out, it will be reprinted with a corrected translation. for altho the former one was sent to me for revisal, sheet by sheet, yet the original not being sent with them (for the printer was 100. leagues distant) I could correct inaccuracies of language only, and not inconformities of sentiment with the original. the original MS. was returned to me afterwards, and I hold it as testimony against the infidelities of Liege, or of another country.   A second edition of your Economie Politique will soon also be called for here, in which Milligan's error on the freedom of your press will not be repeated. when he first printed the Prospectus of that work, the observation was true, as it was some time before your original was published in Paris. but he was so slow in getting it thro' the press that the original appeared before his translation. he ought certainly after that to have omitted or corrected his Prospectus. the knolege however of your charter has corrected the error here, by it's sanction of the freedom of the press: and the publication of the work there, and still more that of the Commentary on Montesquieu are a full vindication of the character of the Charter. these two works will become the Statesman's Manual with us, and they certainly shall be the elementary books of the political department in our new University. this institution of my native state, the Hobby of my old age, will be based on the illimitable freedom of the human mind, to explore and to expose every subject susceptible of it's contemplation.

I still hold and duly value your little MS. entitled 'Logique.' being too small to make a volume of itself, I had put it into the hands of a very able editor of a periodical publication which promised to be valuable. it would have made a distinguished article in that work; but it's continuance having failed for want of the encoragement it merited, I was disappointed in the hope of giving to the world this compendious demonstration of the reality & limits of human knolege. I am still on the watch for a favorable opportunity of doing it. I am not without the hope that the improvement in your health may enable you still to compleat your Encyclopedie Morale, by adding the volume which was to treat of our sentiments and passions. this would fill up our moral circle, and the measure of our obligations to you.

We go with you all lengths in friendly affections to the independance of S. America. but an immediate acknolegement of it calls up other considerations. we view Europe as covering at present a smoth-

ered fire, which may shortly burst forth and produce general confla-
gration. from this it is our duty to keep aloof. a formal acknolegement
of the independance of her colonies, would involve us with Spain certainly, and perhaps too with England, if she thinks that a war would
divert her internal troubles. such a war would hurt us more than it
would help our brethren of the South: and our right may be doubted
of mortgaging posterity for the expences of a war in which they will
have a right to say their interests were not concerned. it is incumbent
on every generation to pay it's own debts as it goes. a principle which,
if acted on, wou[ld] save one half the wars of the world; and justifies,
I think our present circumspection. in the mean time we recieve &
protect the flag of S. America in it's commercial intercourse with us,
on the acknoleged principles of neutrality between two belligerant
parties in a civil war: and if we should not be the first, we shall certainly be the second nation in acknoleging the entire independance of
our new friends. what that independanc[e] will end in, I fear is problematical. whether in wise governments or military despotisms. but
prepared however, or not, for self-government, if it is their will to
make the trial, it is our duty and desire to wish it cordially success.
and of ultimate success there can be no doubt, and that it will richly
repay all intermediate sufferings. of this your country, as well as ours,
furnishes living examples. with the expression of hopes for them, accept my prayers for the perfect restoration of your health, & it's continuance thro' a life as long as you shall wish it.

TH: JEFFERSON

PoC (DLC); first two pages on reused
address cover to TJ; final page on verso
of reused address cover of otherwise
unlocated letter from Francis Eppes to
TJ, 27 Aug. 1819 (see note to TJ to
John Wayles Eppes, 9 July 1819); edge
trimmed; at head of text: "thro depmt of
State"; at foot of first page: "M. le Comte
Des-tutt de Tracy. pair de France"; en-
dorsed by TJ. Recorded in SJL with the
additional notation: "inclosed to mr D.
Brent of the depmt of state." Enclosed in
TJ to Albert Gallatin, 26 Dec. 1820, and
TJ to Daniel Brent, [ca. 27 Dec. 1820],
not found (see note to Brent to TJ, 26
Feb. 1821).

Among TJ's papers is an undated letter from Destutt de Tracy to Isaac Cox
BARNET, the United States consul at
Paris: "Mr De Tracy fait mille Complimens à Mr Barnett. Il le prie de vouloir

bien faire parvenir à M. Jefferson & à la
Societé philosophique de Philadelphie
les deux Volumes, cì joint en remplace-
ment de Ceux qui ont été perdus Sur le
factor. Mr De Tracy aurait bien Voulu
ecrire Sur le premier feuillet hommage
respectueux de l'auteur mais le papier boit
trop pour que Cela Soit possible" ("Mr.
de Tracy gives a thousand compliments
to Mr. Barnet. He asks him to please have
delivered to Mr. Jefferson and to the
American Philosophical Society of Philadelphia the accompanying volumes, to
replace those that were lost on the Factor. Mr. de Tracy would have liked to
write 'with the author's respects' on the
first page, but the paper is too absorbent
for that to be possible") (RC in DLC:
TJ Papers, 215:38321; in an unidentified
hand; endorsed by TJ: "Tracy to Barnett";
translation by Dr. Roland H. Simon). On
3 Dec. 1819 the American Philosophical

Society recorded receiving a donation to its library from Destutt de Tracy (APS, Minutes [MS in PPAmP]).

The PRINTER was William Duane. TJ had himself written the prospectus for Joseph Milligan's edition of Destutt de Tracy, *Treatise on Political Economy* (ECONOMIE POLITIQUE) (see TJ's Title and Prospectus for Destutt de Tracy's *Treatise on Political Economy*, [ca. 6 Apr. 1816]).

A previous reference to the University of Virginia as TJ's HOBBY is in Hore Browse Trist to Nicholas P. Trist, 26 Jan. 1819, commenting on the recent passage of the bill chartering the institution: "Mr Jefferson will go now full tilt on his hobby you may depend he is infinitely delighted" (RC in DLC: NPT).

Robert Walsh was the VERY ABLE EDITOR of the short-lived PERIODICAL, the *American Register; or Summary Review of History, Politics, and Literature*. ENCYCLOPEDIE MORALE: Destutt de Tracy's *Élémens d'Idéologie*.

To Albert Gallatin

DEAR SIR   Monticello Dec. 26. 20.

'It is said to be an ill wind which blows favorably to no one.' my ill health has long suspended the too frequent troubles I have heretofore given you with my European correspondence. to this is added a stiffening wrist, the effect of age on an antient dislocation, which renders writing slow and painful, and disables me nearly from all correspondence, and may very possibly make this the last trouble I shall give you in that way.

Looking from our quarter of the world over the horizon of yours we imagine we see storms gathering which may again desolate the face of that country. so many revolutions going on, in different countries at the same time, such combinations of tyranny, and military preparations and movements to suppress them, England & France unsafe from internal conflict, Germany, on the first favorable occasion, ripe for insurrection, such a state of things, we suppose, must end in war, which needs a kindling spark in one spot only to spread over the whole. your information can correct these views which are stated only to inform you of impressions here.

At home things are not well. the flood of paper money, as you well know, had produced an exaggeration of nominal prices and at the same time a facility of obtaining money, which not only encouraged speculations on fictitious capital, but seduced those of real capital, even in private life, to contract debts too freely. had things continued in the same course, these might have been manageable. but the operations of the U.S. bank for the demolition of the state banks, obliged these suddenly to call in more than half their paper, crushed all fictitious and doubtful capital, and reduced the prices of property and produce suddenly to $\frac{1}{3}$ of what they had been. wheat, for example, at the distance of two or three days from market, fell to, and continues at from one third to half a dollar. should it be stationary at this for a while, a very general revolution of property must take place. something of the same character has taken place in our fiscal system. a little while back Congress seemed at a loss for objects whereon to squander the supposed fathomless funds of our treasury. this short frenzy has been arrested by a deficit of 5 millions the last year, and of 7. millions this year. a loan was adopted for the former and is proposed for the latter, which threatens to saddle us with a perpetual debt. I hope a tax will be preferred, because it will awaken the attention of the people, and make reformation & economy the principles of the next election. the frequent recurrence of this chastening operation can alone restrain the propensity of governments to enlarge expence beyond income. the steady tenor of the courts of the US. to break down the constitutional barriers between the coordinate powers of the States, and of the Union, and a formal opinion lately given by 5. lawyers of too much eminence to be neglected, give uneasiness. but nothing has ever presented so threatening an aspect as what is called the Missouri question. the Federalists compleatly put down, and despairing of ever rising again under the old division of whig and tory, devised a new one, of slave-holding, & non-slave-holding states, which, while it had a semblance of being Moral, was at the same time Geographical, and calculated to give them ascendancy by debauching their old opponents to a coalition with them. Moral the question certainly is not, because the removal of slaves from one state to another, no more than their removal from one county to another, would never make a slave of one human being who would not be so without it. indeed if there were any[1] morality in the question, it is on the other side; because by spreading them over a larger surface, their happiness would be increased, & the burthen of their future liberation lightened by bringing a greater number of shoulders under it. however it served to throw dust into the eyes of the people and to fanaticise them, while to the knowing ones it gave a geographical and preponderant line of the Patomac and Ohio, throwing 14. states to the North and East, & 10. to the South & West. with these therefore it is merely a question of power: but with this geographical minority it is a question of existence. for if Congress once goes out of the Constitution to arrogate a right of regulating the condition of the inhabitants of the states, it's majority may, and probably will next declare that the condition of all men within the US. shall be that of freedom. in which case all the whites South of the Patomak and Ohio must evacuate their states; and most fortunate those who can do it first. and so far this crisis seems to be advancing.[2] the

Missouri constitution[3] is recently rejected by the House of Representatives. what will be their next step is yet to be seen. if accepted on the condition that Missouri shall expunge from it the prohibition of free people of colour from emigration to their state, it will be expunged, and all will be quieted until the advance of some new state shall present the question again. if rejected unconditionally, Missouri assumes independant self-government, and Congress, after pouting awhile, must recieve them on the footing of the original states. should the Representatives propose force, 1. the Senate will not concur. 2. were they to concur, there would be a secession of the members South of the line, & probably of the three North Western states, who, however inclined to the other side, would scarcely separate from those who would hold the Misisipi from it's mouth to it's source. What next? conjecture itself is at a loss. but whatever it shall be you will hear from others and from the newspapers. and finally the whole will depend on Pensylvania. while she and Virginia hold together the Atlantic states can never separate.[4] unfortunately in the present case she has become more fanaticised than any other state. however useful where you are, I wish you were with them. you might turn the scale there, which would turn it for the whole. should this scission take place, one of it's most deplorable consequences would be it's discoragement of the efforts of the European nations in the regeneration of their oppressive and Cannibal governments.   Amidst this prospect of evil, I am glad to see one good effect. it has brought the necessity of some plan of general emancipation & deportation more home to the minds of our people than it has ever been before. insomuch that our Governor has ventured to propose one to the legislature. this will probably not be acted on at this time. nor would it be effectual; for while it proposes to devote to that object one third of the revenue of the state, it would not reach one tenth of the annual increase. my proposition would be that the holders should give up all born after a certain day, past, present, or to come, that these should be placed under the guardianship of the state, and sent at a proper age to St Domingo. there they are willing to recieve them, & the shortness of the passage brings the deportation within the possible means of taxation aided by charitable contributions. in these I think Europe, which has forced this evil on us, and the Eastern states who have been it's chief instruments of importation, would be bound to give largely. but the proceeds of the land office, if appropriated to this would be quite sufficient. God bless you and preserve you Multos años.

TH: JEFFERSON

RC (NHi: Gallatin Papers); endorsed by Gallatin. PoC (DLC); at head of text: "thro' depmt of State"; at foot of first page: "Albert Gallatin." Tr (ViU: TJP); extract in Nicholas P. Trist's hand. Recorded in SJL with the additional notation: "inclosed to mr D. Brent of the depmt of state." Enclosures: (1) TJ to Boissy d'Anglas, 26 Dec. 1820. (2) TJ to Destutt de Tracy, 26 Dec. 1820. (3) TJ to Marc Antoine Jullien, 26 Dec. 1820. (4) TJ to Lafayette, 26 Dec. 1820. (5) TJ to Marc Auguste Pictet, 26 Dec. 1820. (6) TJ to David Bailie Warden, 26 Dec. 1820. Enclosed in TJ to Daniel Brent, [ca. 27 Dec. 1820], not found (see note to Brent to TJ, 26 Feb. 1821).

For the 5. LAWYERS, see note to TJ to Thomas Ritchie, 25 Dec. 1820. On 13 Dec. 1820 the United States HOUSE OF REPRESENTATIVES rejected by a vote of 79–93 "the resolution declaring the admission of the state of Missouri into the Union" (*JHR*, 14:70; Washington *Daily National Intelligencer*, 14 Dec. 1820). OUR GOVERNOR: Thomas Mann Randolph. MULTOS AÑOS: "many years."

[1] TJ here canceled "reality."
[2] Tr begins here.
[3] Word interlined in place of "question."
[4] Tr ends here.

To Francis W. Gilmer

Monticello Dec. 26. 20.

I thank you, very dear Sir, and cordially for your little treatise on Usury, which I have read with great pleasure. you have justified the law on it's true ground, that of the duty of society to protect it's members, disabled from taking care of themselves by causes either physical or moral: and the instances you quote where this salutary function has been exercised with unquestionable propriety, establish it's vindication in this case beyond reply. macte virtute esto, curaque ut valeas, et me, ut amaris, ama.   TH: JEFFERSON

RC (CLU-C). PoC (MHi); on verso of reused address cover of Gabriel Crane to TJ, 24 May 1819; at foot of text: "Francis W. Gilmer esq."; endorsed by TJ.

MACTE VIRTUTE ESTO, CURAQUE UT VALEAS, ET ME, UT AMARIS, AMA: "Well done. Take care that you fare well, and love me as you are loved."

To Marc Antoine Jullien

SIR   Monticello. Dec. 26. 20.

Long continued ill health, and a slow & uncertain convalescence have put it out of my power to acknolege sooner your favors of Feb. and March of the last year, and particularly to than[k] you for the several tracts you were so kind as to send me. the duplicate copies were disposed of as you wished to our societies, academies, and literary characters. I read them all with pleasure, and especially the Nº of the Revue encyclopedique, and it's interesting views of the new works of science in Europe.

I rejoice indeed that the commemoration of the life & virtues of my friend Kosciuzko is undertaken by a person so able to present them worthily to the world. the connection too which the several scenes of his services furnished between the three great revolutions of Poland, France and America, cannot fail to render the work of great interest to those three countries. a citizen of the US. some time since informed me he wished to undertake this work. but I discoraged the attempt by assuring him it was already in hands fully qualified for the task, in a situation to learn better the incidents of his early as well as latter life (to which I knew my fellow citizen had no means of access) and that the short interval Kosciuzko had past in America could hardly authorise the account of that to be entitled the History of his life. he has consequently declined it and will, I am sure have cause to felicitate himself on having avoided a competition for which he was so little prepared.

I read with great pleasure the views you present of the progress of France towards a rational government. some late incidents, I had feared, portended trouble; but the earth will as soon reverse it's course in it's orbit, as the mind of man fall back from the lights recently shed on it, to the darkness of Monkish ages and impositions. the general insurrection of the South will bid defiance to the tyrants of the North, and their armies will catch the flame they are sent to extinguish, and spread it's salutary purifications over their native soil. man has for countless ages been enveloped in darkness, civil and religious. the lights of science have at length found their way into his mind. he had always the power, and needed only the will to resume his rights and be free. he now has that will, and the world will at length be free. at the age of 77. years I cannot expect to see this. it is comfortable however to foresee it; and to pass the few days remaining to me in prayers for it's speedy consummation, to which I add those for the continuance of your useful labors thro' long years of health & happiness.

Th: Jefferson

PoC (DLC); edge trimmed; at head of text: "thro depmt of State"; at foot of first page: "M. Jullien. rue d'Enfer. St Michel. N° 18. à Paris"; endorsed by TJ. Recorded in SJL with the additional notation: "inclosed to mr D. Brent of the depmt of state." Enclosed in TJ to Albert Gallatin, 26 Dec. 1820, and TJ to Daniel Brent, [ca. 27 Dec. 1820], not found (see note to Brent to TJ, 26 Feb. 1821).

The CITIZEN OF THE US. was John H. James.

To Lafayette

It is long indeed, my very dear friend, since I have been able to address a letter to you. for more than two years my health has been so entirely prostrate, that I have, of necessity intermitted all correspondence. the dislocated wrist too, which perhaps you may recollect, has now become so stiff from the effect of age, that writing is become a slow and painful operation, & scarcely ever undertaken but under the goad of imperious business. in the mean time your country has been going on less well than I had hoped. but it will go on. the light which has been shed on the mind of man thro' the civilised world, has given it a new direction from which no human power can divert it. the sovereigns of Europe who are wise, or have wise councellors, see this, and bend to the breeze which blows. the unwise alone, stiffen and meet it's inevitable crush. the Volcanic rumblings in the bowels of Europe from North to South, seem to threaten a general explosion, and the march of armies into Italy cannot end in a simple march. the disease of liberty is catching: these armies will take it in the South, carry it thence to their own country spread there the infection of revolution & representative government, and raise it's people from the prone condition of brutes to the erect attitude of man.   Some fear our envelopment in the wars engendering from the unsettled state of our affairs with Spain, and therefore are anxious for a ratification of our treaty with her. I fear no such thing, and hope that if ratified by Spain it will be rejected here. we may justly say to Spain 'when this negociation commenced, 20. years ago, your authority was acknoleged by those you are selling to us. that authority is now renounced, and their right of self-disposal asserted. in buying them from you then, we buy but a war-title, a right to subdue them, which you can neither convey nor we acquire. this is a family quarrel in which we have no right to meddle. settle it between yourselves, and we will then treat with the party whose right is acknoleged.' with whom that will be no doubt can be entertained. and why should we revolt them by purchasing them as cattle, rather than recieving them as fellow men? Spain has held off until she sees they are lost to her, and now thinks it better to get something than nothing for them. when she shall see South America equally desperate, she will be wise to sell that also.

With us things are going on well. the boisterous sea of liberty indeed is never without a wave, and that from Missouri is now rolling towards us: but we shall ride over it as we have over all others. it is not a moral question, but one merely of power. it's object is to raise a geographical principle for the choice of a president, and the noise will be kept up till that is effected. all know that permitting the slaves of the South to spread into the West will not add one being to that unfortunate condition, that it will increase the happiness of those existing, and by spreading them over a larger surface, will dilute the evil every where and facilitate the means of getting finally rid of it, an event more anxiously wished by those on whom it presses than by the noisy pretenders to exclusive humanity. in the mean time it is a ladder for rivals climbing to power.

In a letter to M. Poirey of Mar. 18. 19. I informed him of the success of our application to Congress on his behalf. I inclosed this letter to you, but hearing nothing from him, and as you say nothing of it in your's of July 20. I am not without fear it may have miscarried. in the present I inclose for him the Auditor's certificate, and the letters of General Washington and myself, which he had forwarded to me, with a request of their return. your kindness in delivering them will render unnecessary another letter from me, an effort which necessity obliges me to spare myself.

If you shall hear from me seldomer than heretofore ascribe it, my ever dear friend, to the heavy load of 77 years and to waning health, but not to weakened affections. these will continue what they have ever been, and will ever be, sincere and warm, to the latest breath of yours devotedly   TH: JEFFERSON

RC (NNPM); endorsed by Lafayette as answered 1 July 1821. PoC (DLC: TJ Papers, 218:39039, 216:38558); first two pages on reused address cover to TJ; third page on verso of reused address cover of Thomas Cooper to TJ, 28 July 1819; edge chipped and trimmed; torn at seal; at head of text: "thro' Depmt State"; at foot of first page: "M. de la Fayette." Recorded in SJL with the additional notation: "inclosed to mr D. Brent of the depmt of state." Enclosures: (1) auditor's certificate, not found (see note to John C. Calhoun to TJ, 20 Mar. 1819). (2) enclosures to TJ to Calhoun, 31 Dec. 1817. Enclosed in TJ to Albert Gallatin, 26 Dec. 1820, and TJ to Daniel Brent, [ca. 27 Dec. 1820], not found (see note to Brent to TJ, 26 Feb. 1821).

TJ's letter to Joseph Léonard Poirey was dated 8 Mar. 1819, not MAR. 18. 19.

To Marc Auguste Pictet

DEAR SIR   Monticello. Dec. 26. 20.

Your favor by mr Terril was duly recieved, but ill health has long suspended with me the power of acknoleging the attentions of my friends, and a slow and chequered convalescence renders writing still difficult. I owe, and return you with pleasure, many thanks for your multiplied kindnesses to mr Terril. these have been, in his mind too, as seeds sown in a fertile soil, and have produced a rich harvest of affections to you, and of gratitude for the many obligations you have heaped upon him. we have recieved him on his return with great joy, and the more we have seen of him, the more we have found cause of contentment. his conversations prove how well his time has been employed, and leave us nothing to regret but his fond recollections of the happiness he enjoyed with you which prey too much on his mind. time may weaken these; but not a little time will be necessary, and no time will efface them. the thoughts of returning to Europe may yield by degrees to the obstacles opposed to them. after passing the summer in my neighborhood he has returned to Kentucky to prepare himself for the bar, and for the functions of civil life. we miss him much in our society, as he had made himself among the most acceptable of it's members. this specimen of improvement would be a great encouragement to a repetition of the experiment with others of our youthful subjects; but we think it a duty to provide for them a nearer resource, by transplanting to our own country the sciences you have reared. the state in which I live is now engaged in the establishment of an University, in which all the sciences will be cultivated which the circumstances of our country would as yet render useful. this institution will employ the remaining days and faculties of my life, and will be based on the illimitable freedom of the human mind.

Altho' your Geneva is but a point, as it were, on the globe, yet it has made itself the most interesting one perhaps on the globe. industry, honesty, simplicity of manners, hospitality & science seem to have marked it as their own, and interest all mankind in prayers for the continuance of it's freedom and felicity. it has mine most sincerely, and for nothing in it more especially than your personal happiness and prosperity.   —I recieve with pleasure the information you give me respecting the families Delessert & Gautier. a period of 30. years since I left Europe has withdrawn from me the knolege of much which has happened to my friends there. with mr Gautier of the house of Grand in Paris, I was intimately acquainted, and much attached to his worth. I know not whether I have gained or lost by ignorance of the fortunes of my friends in the unparalleled convulsions amidst which they have been placed. nor do I know that these are yet over. there seem to be something more than specks in the horison of Europe, which may renew the desolations of that country, fated to eternal war. God preserve you from it's evils, whatever are portended, and grant you as many years of life, health and happiness as yourself may desire.   Th: Jefferson

RC (Frédéric Rilliet, Geneva, Switzerland, 1947). FC (MHi); in the hand of Ellen W. Randolph (Coolidge), with date and signature by TJ; at head of text in TJ's hand: "thro' Depmt of State"; at foot of first page in TJ's hand: "M. Pictet. Professeur à Geneve"; endorsed by TJ.

Recorded in SJL with the additional notation: "inclosed to mr D. Brent of the depmt of state." Enclosed in TJ to Albert Gallatin, 26 Dec. 1820, and TJ to Daniel Brent, [ca. 27 Dec. 1820], not found (see note to Brent to TJ, 26 Feb. 1821).

To David Bailie Warden

DEAR SIR   Monticello Dec. 26. 20.

Your acceptable letters of Mar. & Apr. 20. and of May 15. of the present year, have not been sooner answered, nor the brochures you so kindly sent me, acknoleged because the state of my health has in a great degree interdicted to me the labors of the writing table. add to this a stiffening wrist, the effect of age on an antient dislocation, which is likely to deprive me entirely of the use of the pen.

We are expecting to see you all involved in war, in Europe. revolutions going on in so many of it's countries, such military movements to suppress them, the intestine borborisms of Engl^d France, and Germany, seem impossible to pass away without war; in a region too where war seems to be the natural state of man.

Nor are we much at our ease here. the mischiefs of bank paper, catastrophe of our commerce, sudden and continued reduction of the nominal value of property & produce, which has doubled and trebled in fact the debts of those who owed any thing, place us in a state of great depression. but nothing disturbs us so much as the dissension lately produced by what is called the Missouri question: a question having just enough of the semblance of morality to throw dust into the eyes of the people, & to fanaticise them; while with the knowing ones it is simply a question of power. the Federalists, unable to rise again under the old division of whig and tory, have invented a geographical division which gives them 14. states against 10. and seduces their old opponents into a coalition with them. real morality is on the other side. for while the removal of slaves from one state to another adds no more to their numbers than their removal from one county to another, the spreading them over a larger surface adds to their happiness and renders their future emancipation more practicable.

Mr Botta, when he published his excellent history of our revolution, was so kind as to send me a copy of it, for which I immediately, & before I had read it, returned him my thanks. a careful perusal as soon as I had time made me sensible of it's high value, and anxious to get it translated & published. after some time I engaged a very competent person to undertake it, & lent him my copy. he proceeded however very slowly, & had made little progress when a mr Otis sent me a first volume of a translation he had made, and lately a 2^d the 3^d and last being now in press. it is well done, and I am anxious to send a copy to mr Botta, if I can find the means. the 1st difficulty is to keep it out of the French post office, which would tax it beyond it's value: and you know my situation among the mountains of the country, & how little probable it is that I should meet with a passenger going to Paris. I will therefore address a copy thro' my friend John Vaughan of Philadelphia and request him to deliver it to some passenger from that place to Paris. would it be asking too great a favor of you to mention this, with my great respect, to mr Botta, supplying my inability to write? and could you even go further, should you at any time find yourself in the book shop of Messrs Debures, and say to them that I shall take care in the spring to remit them the 38 ƒ–40 c balance of their last envoi, which arrived safely, to which I shall add a further call for some books.

Our family, all present at least, join in friendly remembrances of you. mr Randolph is at present our Governor, & of course at Richmond. he has had the courage to propose to our legislature a plan of general emancipation & deportation of our slaves. altho this is not ripe to be immediately acted on, it will, with the Missouri question, force a serious attention to this object by our citizens, which the vicinage of St Domingo brings within the scope of possibility. I salute you with constant & affectionate respect and attachment.

TH: JEFFERSON

RC (MdHi: Warden Papers); addressed: "Mr David B. Warden Paris." PoC (DLC); on reused address cover of Richard Ware to TJ, 17 June 1819; damaged at seal; at head of text: "thro' depm^t of state"; endorsed by TJ. Recorded in SJL with the additional notation: "inclosed to mr D. Brent of the depmt of state." Enclosed in TJ to Albert Gallatin, 26 Dec. 1820, and TJ to Daniel Brent, [ca. 27 Dec. 1820], not found (see note to Brent to TJ, 26 Feb. 1821).

BORBORISMS: "borborygmi." The VERY COMPETENT PERSON was Louis H. Girardin. ENVOI: "parcel; package."

To Maria Cosway

Monticello. Dec. 27. 20.

'Over the length of silence I draw a curtain,' is an expression, my dear friend, of your cherished letter of Apr. 7. 19. of which, it might seem, I have need to avail myself; but not so really. to 77. heavy years add two of prostrate health during which all correspondence has been suspended of necessity, and you have the true cause of not having heard from me. my wrist too, dislocated in Paris while I had the pleasure of being there with you, is, by the effect of years, now so stiffened, that writing is become a most slow and painful operation, and scarcely ever undertaken but under the goad of imperious business. but I have never lost sight of your letter, and give it now the first place among those of my transatlantic friends which have been laying unacknoleged during the same period of ill health.

I rejoice in the first place that you are well; for your silence on that subject encorages me to presume it. and next that you have been so usefully and pleasingly occupied in preparing the minds of others to enjoy the blessings you have yourself derived from the same source, a cultivated mind. of mr Cosway I fear to say any thing, such is the disheartening account of the state of his health given in your letter. but here or wherever, I am sure he has all the happiness which an honest life ensures. nor will I say any thing of the troubles of those among whom you live. I see they are grea[t] and wish them happily out of them, and especially that you may be safe and happy, whatever be their issue. I will talk about Monticello then, and my own country, as is the wish expressed in your letter. my daughter Randolph whom you knew in Paris a young girl, is now the mother of 11. living children, the grandmother of about half a dozen others, enjoys health and good spirits and sees the worth of her husband attested by his being at present Governor of the state in which we live. among these I live, like a patriarch of old. our friend Trumbull is well, & profitably & honorably employed by his country in commemorating with his pencil some of it's revolutionary honors. of mrs Cruger I hear nothing, nor, for a long time, of Mad^e de Corny. such is the present state of our former coterie, dead, diseased & dispersed. but 'tout ce qui est differé n'est pas perdu,' says the French proverb, and the religion you so sincerely profess, tells us we shall meet again, and we have all so lived as to be assured it will be in happiness. mine is the next turn, and I shall meet it with good will. for after one's friends are all gone before them, and our faculties leaving us too, one by one, why wish to linger in mere vegetation? as a solitary trunk in a desolate field, from which all it's former companions have disappeared. you have many good years remaining yet to be happy yourself and to make those around you happy. may these, my dear friend, be as many as yourself may wish, and all of them filled with health and happiness will be among the last & warmest wishes of an unchangeable friend.

Th: Jefferson

PoC (MHi); on reused address cover of Samuel J. Harrison to TJ, 25 Aug. 1819; edge trimmed; at head of text: "thro' depmt of state"; at foot of first page: "Mrs Maria Cosway"; endorsed by TJ. Recorded in SJL with the additional notation: "inclosed to mr D. Brent of the depmt of state." Enclosed in TJ to Rich-ard Rush, 27 Dec. 1820, and TJ to Daniel Brent, [ca. 27 Dec. 1820], not found (see note to Brent to TJ, 26 Feb. 1821).

TOUT CE QUI EST DIFFERÉ N'EST PAS PERDU: "not all that is postponed is lost."

To William Roscoe

DEAR SIR   Monticello. Dec. 27. 20.

Your letter recieved more than a twelvemonth ago, with the two tracts on penal jurisprudence, and the literary institution of Liverpool, ought long since to have called for the thanks I now return, had it been in my power sooner to have tendered them. but a long continuance of ill health has suspended all power of answering the kind attentions with which I have been honored during it: and it is only now that a state of slow and uncertain convalescence enables me to make acknolegements which have been so long and painfully delayed. the treatise on penal jurisprudence I read with great[1] pleasure. Beccaria had demonstrated general principles: but practical applications were difficult. our states are trying them with more or less success: and the great light you have thrown on the subject will, I am sure, be useful to our experiment. for the thing, as yet, is but in experiment. your Liverpool institution will also aid us in the organisation of our new University, an establishment now in progress in this state, and to which my remaining days and faculties will be devoted. when ready for it's Professors, we shall apply for them chiefly to your island. were we content to remain stationary in science, we should take them from among ourselves; but, desirous of advancing, we must seek them in countries already in advance: and identity of language points to our best resource. to furnish inducements, we provide for the Professors separate buildings in which themselves & their families may be handsomely and comfortably lodged, and to liberal salaries will be added lucrative perquisites. this institution will be based on the illimitable freedom of the human mind. for here we are not afraid to follow truth wherever it may lead, nor to tolerate any error so long as reason is left free to combat it.

We are looking with wonder at what is passing among you. it
'Resembles ocean into tempest wrought,
    To waft a feather, or to drown a fly.'

there must be something in these agitations more than meets the eye of a distant spectator. your queen must be used in this, as a rallying point merely, around which are gathering the discontents of every quarter and character. if these flowed from theories of government only, and if merely from the heads of speculative men, they would admit of parley, of negociation, of management. but I fear they are the workings of hungry bellies which nothing but food will fill and quiet. I sincerely wish you safely out of them. circumstances have nourished between our kindred countries angry dispositions which both ought long since to have banished from their bosoms. I have ever considered a cordial affection as the first interest of both. no nation on earth can hurt us so much as yours; none be more useful to you than ours. the obstacle, we have believed, was in the obstinate and unforgiving temper of your late king, and a continuance of his prejudices kept up from habit after he was withdrawn from power. I hope I now see symptoms of sounder views in your government; in which I know it will be cordially met by ours, as it would have been by every administration which has existed under our present constitution. none desired it more cordially than myself, whatever different opinions were impressed on your government by a party who wished to have it's weight in their scale as it's exclusive friends.

My antient friend and classmate, James Maury, informs me by letter, that he has sent me a bust which I shall recieve with great pleasure and thankfulness, and shall arrange in honorable file with those of some cherished characters. will you permit me to place here my affectionate souvenirs of him, and accept for yourself the assurance of the highest consideration and esteem.   Th: Jefferson

RC (UkLi: Roscoe Papers); addressed: "William Roscoe esquire Liverpool"; endorsed by Roscoe, in part, as received 12 Feb. 1821 at Liverpool "under cover from Mr Rush ℔ his friend J. Maury." FC (DLC); in the hand of Virginia J. Randolph (Trist), with date, internal address, and notation at head of text in TJ's hand (trimmed): "[thr]o depmt of State." Recorded in SJL with the additional notation: "inclosed to mr D. Brent of the depmt of state." Enclosed in TJ to Richard Rush, 27 Dec. 1820, and TJ to Daniel Brent, [ca. 27 Dec. 1820], not found (see note to Brent to TJ, 26 Feb. 1821).

RESEMBLES OCEAN . . . DROWN A FLY is from the first part of Edward Young's poem, *The Complaint: or, Night-Thoughts on Life, Death, & Immortality* (London, 1742; see also Sowerby, no. 4548), lines 152–3. YOUR QUEEN: Caroline of Brunswick, whose husband George IV attempted to divorce her on grounds of adultery and deny her the title of queen when he inherited the British throne in 1820. She received a great deal of popular support during her subsequent politicized "trial" in Parliament (*ODNB*). YOUR LATE KING: George III, king of Great Britain, who was adjudged insane and WITHDRAWN FROM POWER during his last years, 1811–20, with his son and successor George made regent.

[1] Reworked from "recieved with equal."

To Richard Rush

DEAR SIR   Monticello Dec. 27. 20.

I took the liberty, in October last, to request you to put a catalogue of books, which I inclosed, into the hands of an honest bookseller, one to whom I might address myself with confidence hereafter without troubling you; and at the same time desired my correspondent in Richmond Capt Bernard Peyton to remit a bill of 40.£ sterling to be delivered to the Bookseller to be placed by him to my account.

I now avail myself of the protection of your cover for the two inclosed letters. that to mr Roscoe will readily find it's destination. mrs Cosway's address I do not know. mr Cosway her husband, about 31. or 32. years ago when I knew them both in Paris, was the most celebrated miniature painter in England & perhaps in Europe. his house in London & Cabinet was the fashionable daily resort of the diplomatic corps,[1] of foreigners & distinguished natives. he was living a year ago but paralytic. I think their residence will be known to the gentlemen of that art.

I will say nothing to you of politics because I know no more of them than from the newspapers which you get. we are laboring hard under the portentous Missouri question. the preceding generation sacrificed themselves to establish their posterity in independent self-government, which their successors seem disposed to throw away for an abstract proposition. they have a right to do it, as we have to lament it. in all events I salute you with friendship & respect.

                                                        TH: JEFFERSON

RC (ICN: Thomas Jefferson Letters); addressed: "His Excellency Richard Rush Minister Plenipotentiary of the US. of America London"; endorsed by Rush; with notations by Rush mentioning the enclosed letters and " *<His felicitous>* The happy brevity of his allusion to the 'Missouri question.'" PoC (DLC); on verso of reused address cover of Chapman Johnson to TJ, 17 June 1819; damaged at seal; at head of text: "thro depmt of State";

endorsed by TJ. Recorded in SJL with the additional notation: "inclosed to mr D. Brent of the depmt of state." Enclosures: (1) TJ to Maria Cosway, 27 Dec. 1820. (2) TJ to William Roscoe, 27 Dec. 1820. Enclosed in TJ to Daniel Brent, [ca. 27 Dec. 1820], not found (see note to Brent to TJ, 26 Feb. 1821).

[1] Word interlined in place of "court."

[501]

From Robert Barnard

SIR.   George Town D.C. 28th Decr 1820

SIR.   George Town D.C. 28th Dec[r] 1820

I have observed the report of the Trustees or Committee of the College or Institution about to be formed in the state of Virginia for the purpose of Education—Altho' your name does not appear, your well known Character for literary & Scientific acquirements Would lead me to suppose that you are neither indifferent to the success of the Institution, nor decline to take An active part in promoting it.—Under that impression[1] Sir permit me to make the Enquiry of you Whether there will be wanted a Teacher of the Classics & the learned Languages— If so, might I be permitted Also to state to you that I am acquainted with one who is fully Competent to be a Tutor in both Hebrew— Greek & Latin; in all of which he is conversant Grammatically

I am not recommending myself in making this Enquiry but should such a person be wanted in the Institution, the man for whom I am (unknown to him) Making this application w[d] be found upon investigation fully Equal to any recommendation that Can be given of him— He is at present Engaged in A situation far below his Talents, & the remuneration for which is barely sufficient for the support of his numerous family. The knowledge of these circumstances, has induced me to take this liberty & may perhaps be deemed by You a good reason for noticing this application. Should you honor me so far & require further information I shall have great Satisfaction in rendering it, Assured that I shall be Assisting in promoting the interest of learning & in Elevating to a situation more worthy of his Education & literary acquirements, a man at present placed far below his deserts—

Any reply You may favor me with may be addressed as below, Waiting which

I remain Sir Your very obed Ser[t]   ROB[T] BARNARD
                                          care of Tho[s] C. Wright
                                          George Town D.C.

RC (DLC); at foot of text: "To Tho[s] Jefferson Esq &c &c"; endorsed by TJ as received <5> 4 Jan. 1821 and so recorded in SJL.

Robert Barnard (1786–1852), clerk, was born in Boston, Lincolnshire, England. In 1819 he moved to Georgetown, D.C., and four years later to nearby Washington, where he became a naturalized United States citizen in 1824. Barnard was treasurer and clerk of the Potomac Company in 1825 and secretary of the same when it merged in 1828 with the Chesapeake and Ohio Canal Company, of which he then became assistant clerk. He went on to serve as treasurer of the company, 1834–40, 1841, and 1841–46. A founding member of the Columbian Horticultural Society in 1833, Barnard was elected its president in 1840. His real estate in Washington was valued at $7,000 in 1850 (DCHi: Barnard Family Papers; Barnard's naturalization record, 28 Dec.

1824 [DNA: RG 21, DIDC]; *Acts of the States of Virginia, Maryland, and Pennsylvania, and of the Congress of the United States, in relation to the Chesapeake & Ohio Canal Company* [1828], 51, 53, 148; Harlan D. Unrau, *Historic Resource Study: Chesapeake & Ohio Canal* [2007], 624; *Constitution and By-Laws of the Columbian Horticultural Society, in the District of Columbia* [1833], 8; Washington *Daily*

National Intelligencer, 11 Sept. 1840, 11 Oct. 1852; DNA: RG 29, CS, D.C., Georgetown, 1830, Washington, 1840, 1850; gravestone inscription in Oak Hill Cemetery, Washington).

Barnard made THIS APPLICATION on behalf of his brother Samuel Barnard (see Samuel Barnard to TJ, 12 Feb. 1824).

[1] Manuscript: "inpression."

To Peter S. Du Ponceau

DEAR SIR   Monticello Dec. 28. 20.

This letter is strictly confidential. some time ago a mr John Sanderson, of Philada, addressed a letter to me, informing me he was engaged in a biographical work which embraced the life of our late Chancellor Wythe, of whom however his materials were scanty, & requesting me to supply him. of the Mentor of my youth I felt the duty of bearing witnesses to his virtues, and furnished what I knew. lately he sent me his 1st vol. and indeed I found it superiorly written; exhibiting mind, information & polish. a little too florid perhaps for the sober style of history, of which however he had a great example in Robertson; perhaps also a little too speculative, in which history should indulge with the brevity of Tacitus. as it is possible he may apply to me as to other characters of his work, & these communications may be delicate, it is material I should know something more of him. what is his character moral and political, does he write for money or fame, E^{t}c? information as to these particulars must govern my confidences, and with a view to regulate them alone I ask the favor of your information, with an assurance it shall be used for no other purpose, and that your letter shall be burnt the moment it is perused. with my thanks for this kind office accept my friendly and respectful salutations.   TH: JEFFERSON

RC (ViU: Albert H. Small Declaration of Independence Collection); addressed: "Peter S. Duponceau esq. Philadelphia"; franked; postmarked Charlottesville, 30 Dec. PoC (DLC); on verso of reused address cover of Ezra Stiles Ely to TJ, 14 June 1819; endorsed by TJ.

To D. Mariano

Sir   Monticello Dec. 28. 20.
    Your favor of Aug. 7. 19. was recieved in due time and answered by
mine of Sep. 10. 19. that of Nov. 26. of the present year came during
a long absence from home which must apologise for the date of this.
when our University will be opened, and what will be the emoluments
of the Professorships are entirely undecided. on the latter subject the
Visitors have come to no determination, & the time of opening will
depend entirely on the further[1] aids the legislature may give. if none,
the buildings will be shut up several years until the present funds
shall have redeemed the debt contracted in erecting them.
I am sorry that in this state of uncertainty it is not in my power to
answer the enquiries of your letter and with my regrets I must pray
you to accept the assurance of my great respect.
                                                      Th: Jefferson

PoC (ViU: TJP); on verso of reused   [1] Word interlined.
address cover of Arthur S. Brocken-
brough to TJ, 1 July 1819; at foot of text:
"D. Mariano"; endorsed by TJ.

To Frederick A. Mayo

Sir   Monticello Dec. 28. 20.
    I was very sorry to learn that you had suffered in the common ca-
lamities of the times, and still more so on seeing your stock in trade
advertised by trustees. I have two considerable boxes of books, packed
some time ago, containing upwards of 100. vols, which want binding.
but not knowing whether you still carry on the binding business, I
have suspended the sending them to you, until I can be informed by
yourself whether you can bind them, and shall govern myself by your
answer with every assurance of my best wishes & respect.
                                                      Th: Jeff[erson]

PoC (MHi); on verso of reused address   Kanawha County (later West Virginia)
cover of Daniel Brent to TJ, 4 July 1819;   and of his STOCK IN TRADE, including "a
mutilated at seal; at foot of text: "Mr   large collection of Law and other BOOKS,
Frederic A. Mayo"; endorsed by TJ.   in the various departments of literature,"
                                            and "a variety of STATIONERY, SUR-
Trustees advertised the 13 Dec. 1820   VEYOR'S INSTRUMENTS, &c." (Rich-
auction in Richmond of Mayo's land in   mond Enquirer, 17 Nov. 1820).

To Charles Willson Peale

DEAR SIR   Monticello Dec. 28. 20.

'Nothing is troublesome which we do willingly' is an excellent apophthegm, and which can be applied to no mind more truly than yours. on this ground I am sure you will be so good as to exchange the pair of inkglasses you sent me, & which the furnisher will doubtless exchange. they are a little too large to enter the sockits of the polygraph I keep in Bedford, as I found on a late visit to that place. I return them to you in a box of wood, in the bottom of which I have had a mortise made of the true size. glasses which will enter that freely will exactly answer.   Knowing the friendly interest you take in my health, I will add that it is not quite confirmed, but is improving slowly. my stiffening wrist in the mean time gets worse, & will ere long deprive me quite of the use of the pen. ever & affectionately yours   TH: JEFFERSON

RC (TxU: Thomas Jefferson Collection); at foot of text: "Mʳ Peale." PoC (MHi); on verso of reused address cover of Arthur S. Brockenbrough to TJ, 5 July 1819; torn at seal; endorsed by TJ.

TJ appears to have learned the maxim that NOTHING IS TROUBLESOME WHICH WE DO WILLINGLY from George Wythe, and he incorporated it into his so-called Canons of Conduct (*PTJ*, 34:421; enclosure to TJ to Thomas Jefferson Smith, 21 Feb. 1825). INKGLASSES: "vessels or receptacles for holding writing or printing ink" (*OED*).

From William Davis Robinson

SIR,   Washington December 28ᵗʰ 1820—

Permit me to request your acceptance of my Memoirs of the Mexican Revolution—

Should I learn that any thing therein containd, compensates you for the trouble of perusing the book, it will afford me much pleasure—

The rules of literary composition I am unacquainted with—my habits and career have afforded me only casual opportunities of making a few gleanings in the field of literature, but as I disclaim all pretensions to the character of a professional author, I trust my fellow Citizens will overlook any inaccuracies in point of style—

Respectfully I have the honor to be
Your obedᵗ Servᵗ   WILLIAM DAVIS ROBINSON

RC (MHi); dateline at foot of text; endorsed by TJ as received 28 Jan. 1821 and so recorded in SJL. RC (MHi); address cover only; with PoC of TJ to William J. Coffee, 5 Mar. 1821, on verso; addressed: "Thomas Jefferson Esqʳ." Enclosure: Robinson, *Memoirs of the Mexican Revolution: including a Narrative of the Expedition of General Xavier Mina. with some observations on the Practicability of Opening a Commerce between the Pacific and Atlantic Oceans* . . . (Philadelphia, 1820; Poor, *Jefferson's Library*, 4 [no. 118]).

William Davis Robinson (1774–1824), merchant, was a native of Philadelphia. From 1799 he operated out of Caracas, in what became Venezuela, where he traded extensively with Spanish authorities. Robinson began to oppose them, however, following a trade dispute over poor-quality tobacco, and in 1806 he and other foreigners were forced to leave the Spanish colonies in America. Between 1810 and 1814 he returned to South America, using his status as a neutral merchant to trade with and support members of various revolutionary movements in the region. In the latter year Robinson went to Washington, D.C. He soon published *A Cursory View of Spanish America, particularly the neighboring vice-royalties of Mexico and New-Granada, chiefly intended to elucidate the policy of an early connection between the United States and those countries* (Georgetown, D.C., 1815). Bearing a passport from Secretary of State James Monroe, in 1816 Robinson went via New Orleans to Mexico. There royalists turned him over to Spanish officials, who imprisoned him for two-and-a-half years as a revolutionary spy. Robinson wrote to the United States Department of State several times during his captivity, seeking aid in obtaining his release and sharing information on Spanish activities in Mexico. He finally escaped and returned to the United States late in 1819, publishing his *Memoirs of the Mexican Revolution* the following year. In 1821 Robinson unsuccessfully requested a federal appointment to South America or Florida. The next year, after moving to Colombia to pursue mercantile activities in Cartagena, he fruitlessly sought an appointment at that port city. Robinson visited New York briefly in 1824 before traveling to Caracas, where he died (Eduardo Enrique Ríos, *Robinson y su Aventura en México* [2d ed., 1958], esp. 5–41; Robinson, *Memorias de la Revolución Mexicana*, trans. and ed. Virginia Guedea [2003], esp. vii–xxiii; *City of Washington Gazette*, 24 Sept. 1818; Robinson to Monroe, 2 Oct. 1816, and Robinson to John Quincy Adams, 6 Oct. 1817 [DNA: RG 59, MLR]; *New-York Evening Post*, 1 Dec. 1819; DNA: RG 59, LAR, 1817–25; New York *National Advocate*, 8 July 1824; Portland, Maine, *Eastern Argus*, 6 Jan. 1825).

On this date Robinson sent James Madison a similar letter and enclosure (Madison, *Papers, Retirement Ser.*, 2:196).

To Thomas Gimbrede

SIR   Monticello Dec. 29. 20.

I am favored with your letter of Dec. 18. and am sorry it is not in my power to give any satisfactory answer to it's enquiries. the walls of our buildings are not yet compleated and the entire finishing of the structures necessary is to be accomplished before we proceed to procuring professors. when this will be must depend altogether on the aids which the legislature may give to this object. with my regrets that I can say nothing more definite accept the tender of my respectful salutations   TH: JEFFERSON

PoC (ViU: TJP); on verso of reused address cover of Maria Cosway to TJ, 7 Apr. 1819; at foot of text: "M. Gimbrede"; endorsed by TJ.

To William Paxton

SIR   Monticello Dec. 29. 20.

I should long ago have answered your friendly lette[r] of Aug. 4. but that it was my intention soon after that to go to Bedford, and while there to visit the Natural bridge. but my journey was retarded till late in November and the winter set in so early, that in my state of feeble health, I was obliged to decline crossing the mountain. in the summer & autumn of the ensuing year I intend to pass 3. or 4. months in Bedford and shall then certainly go to the bridge. I know it is difficult to trace lines while the leaves are out, but that difficulty must be surmounted by patience. with my thanks for the kindness of your attention, which to one at such [a?] distance is a real charity I tender you the assurance of [my?] esteem & respect.

TH: JEFFERSON

PoC (MHi); on verso of reused address cover of Henry Dearborn to TJ, 24 June 1819; edge trimmed; torn at seal; at foot of text: "Mr Wm Paxton"; endorsed by TJ.

To John H. Rice

SIR   Monticello Dec. 29. 20

I recieved yesterday by the hands of Dr Carr your favor of Oct. 30. with a copy of the new edition of Smith's history of Virginia which you are so kind as to present to the University of Virginia. in behalf of that in[sti]tution I return you thanks for the donation and also for the friendly interest you are pleased to express for it's success. the want of such an establishment, in our quarter of the Union, has been long felt and regretted, and it's consequences are but too sensibly seen. parents especially have lamented it, who know the efficacy of sound and useful education towards forming the morals, the characters & habits of youth. should the legislature view in the same light the importance of this institution to the character and prosperity of our state, and aid it accordingly, I hope it will be so constituted and conducted as to merit the continuation of your friendly dispositions towards [it.?] Accept, I pray you, my thanks for the kind wishes you are so good as to express towards myself, and the assurance of my high respect & esteem.   TH: JEFF[ERS]ON

PoC (ViW: TC-JP); on verso of reused address cover of Jeremiah Greenleaf to TJ, 23 June 1819; mutilated, edge trimmed, and signature faint; at foot of text: "The revd John H. Rice"; endorsed by TJ.

To John A. Robertson

Sir Monticello Dec. 29. 20.

I have duly recieved your favor of the 20th and see in it a great proof of your candor and justice. of the two great parties which divided our nation in it's early stage, the one wished to strengthen the hands of the Executive, the other of the Representative branch of the government. the latter was my own disposition, resulting from reading, experience and reflection; and my election to the Executive functions was considered as evidence that such was the wish of the majority of our citizens. that the course I pursued should not be immediately satisfactory to the Minority, was to be expected: but I have ever hoped that, like yourself, others, on a calm and dispassionat[e] review of my administration, would do justice to the integrit of my course, if not to it's wisdom, and would acquit my errors of any obliquities of intention.

I learn with pleasure your election of this part of our country for your future habitation. it has certainly the advantages of a ferti[le] soil, navigation, healthy and temperate climate, and of an industrious, independant and orderly population; and the neighborhood of the University will ensure a choice addition to our society. our bar is pretty much crouded, not defective in talent, and one member of it particularly of great eminence, now a representative in Congress. still talent in a new comer will make it's way.

Towards the enterprise you propose, of writing the history of our country, the first object will be the obtaining materials. of these you have no doubt satisfied yourself of the resources. I formerly possessed[1] some store of that kind: but all which were printed, and much of what was MS. went to Congress with my library, and the few loose notes I retained were communicated to mr Girardin while writing his volume of our latter history. if any aids remain however within my power, they shall be freely furnished.

I am bound particularly to thank you for the kind sentiments expressed towards myself, and I tender you the assurance of my great respect. Th: Jefferson

PoC (DLC); edge trimmed; in left margin near bottom of first page: "Mr John A. Robertson."

The attorney of great eminence was probably Philip P. Barbour.

[1] Manuscript: "possesses."

To Edmund Bacon

TH:J. TO MR BACON Dec. 30. 20.

the pork delivered mr Minor according to the entry in my book was 10. hogs weighing 1067 ℔ @ 8.50 D = 90.69½ D

RC (ViU: TJP); written on a small scrap; dateline at foot of text. Not recorded in SJL.

TJ made this PORK sale in December 1818 to Samuel Overton Minor, from whom he received $70 through Bacon "in part payment" on 2 Mar. 1819 (Betts, *Farm Book*, pt. 1, p. 161; *MB*, 2:1351).

To George Long (ca. 1782–1843)

SIR   Monticello Dec. 30. 20.

I have duly recieved your favor of the 20th inst. and with it miss Palmyra Johnson's poetic tale of Rosalie, and I beg leave, thro' the same channel to return her my thanks for it. I have read it with great pleasure, and that is saying much for it from a reader of 77. but the effusions of a feeling heart and delicate fancy, expressed in smooth numbers, make their impression even on the dull sensibilities of that age, and the sympathies with the fate of a Constance, & fortune of a Rosalie can still be felt. I have more especially to thank her for the partialities towards myself, which she has been pleased to express in her dedication, in which she has ascribed to me much more than I have merited or claimed, and I pray you, Sir, to accept the assurance of my great respect   TH: JEFFERSON

RC (NNGL); bottom corner torn, with missing text supplied from PoC. PoC (CSmH: JF); on verso of reused address cover of otherwise unlocated letter from John Wayles Eppes to TJ, 28 June 1819 (see note to TJ to Eppes, 9 July 1819); damaged at seal; at foot of text: "Mr George Jones"; endorsed by TJ as a letter to "Jones George" and so recorded in SJL; additional notation by TJ beneath endorsement: "qu. Long George." Tr (Glenn Horowitz Bookseller, New York City, 2019); in Palmira Johnson's hand; at head of text: "To printer of Rosalie."

George Long (ca. 1782–1843), printer and bookseller, was a British citizen who worked as a printer in New York City by 1802. Long partnered with Monteith McFarlane by 1806, and he continued on

his own after McFarlane's death in 1809. By 1812 Long included bookselling in his enterprise, which he continued until his death in New York (*Printer and Bookmaker* 24 [1897]: 48; U.S. Marshal's Returns of Enemy Aliens, DNA: RG 59, PW1812; *Longworth's New York Directory* [1802]: 253; [1806]: 250; [1810]: 256; [1812]: 188; [1840]: 398; New York *Commercial Advertiser*, 4 Oct. 1809; *New-York Daily Tribune*, 11 Jan. 1843).

Long's FAVOR of 20 Dec. 1820, not found, is recorded in SJL as a letter from "Jones George" received 28 Dec. 1820 from New York. Long printed and published an epic poem by Palmira Johnson entitled *Rosalie, a Tale* (New York, 1821), which included a printed DEDICATION from the author: "*To Thomas Jefferson.* In the lively sense I have been taught to cherish for thy talents and virtues, permit me Sir, to dedicate to thee this small work. May health, ease, and happiness attend thy age; as the setting Sun, thou wilt descend to thy grave, with thy honors, as a glory, beaming around thy head; and thy memory will be deeply engraven on the hearts of thy grateful Countrymen, never to be obliterated, but by the tear of expiring Liberty."

To Joel Yancey

[Monticello, 30 Dec. 1820. SJL entry reads "a chair. 2 doz. wine. trees." Letter not found.]

From Joshua Dodge

My Dear Sir,   Marseilles 1 Jany 1821

I had the honor of writing to you per Brig Union of Marblehead informing you of my having Shipped per that Vessel Sundry articles on your account & consigned them, agreeable to your orders, to the Collector of the first Port in the United States not South of the Chesapeak at which Said Vessel would arrive at.

The Ledanon Wine having Since arrived, I have Shipped Same on the Cadmus Capt Ives bound for Boston consigned to the Collector of that Port to be forwarded to you, I have Sent him the Invoice amounting to two hundred eighty nine francs & thirty centimes, he will forward the same to you with this letter which I recommend to his care— I hope you will be pleased with the articles per Union & Cadmus, to the procuring & conditioning of which I have paid every attention in my Power. I respectfully request you to accept my best & warmest wishes on the renewal of the year and that the Almighty may long preserve those days which you have rendered So highly useful to your grateful Country is the Sincere wish of your most respectful & most grateful Servant,   Josh^a Dodge

RC (MHi); at foot of text: "To Thomas Jefferson Esqr Monticello, Virginia"; endorsed by TJ as received 11 Apr. 1821 and so recorded in SJL. Enclosed in Henry A. S. Dearborn to TJ, 3 Apr. 1821.

From Peter S. Du Ponceau

Dear Sir   Philad^a 3^d Jany 1821

I have received the Letter you have done me the honor to write to me, dated the 28th ult^o which shall be treated as it is meant, as Strictly private & confidential. I am well acquainted with Mr Sanderson. Some

Years ago a Mr Carré, a planter from St Domingo, & a refugee here from that Island, being an excellent Latin Scholar, & possessing other literary qualifications, established an Academy in the vicinity of this City, & took Mr Sanderson as his Usher—Sanderson had had an University Education, & having given satisfaction to Mr Carré, he married his only daughter & became his partner, in which station he still continues. From his Father in law he imbibed an enthusiastic fondness for ancient literature, & following Horace's precept <u>Vos</u> <u>exemplaria</u> <u>Græca</u> &c, he acquired the style & manner which has obtained your approbation. He is still a young Man, & begins to have a growing family, which his profession of a Schoolmaster is not sufficient to Support. In this situation, he accepted the offer of a Bookseller to write the lives of the signers to the declaration of Independence, which Subject was not his choice. Thus you see he writes for money as well as fame, tho' the love of the latter strongly predominates. He Spent more time in writing his first Volume than pleased the Bookseller, & would have spent more, could he have followed his own inclination. As to character & disposition, he is ingenuous, diffident & modest; he is a young Man of perfect integrity & may be trusted. He places great confidence in my advice, & has none of that Self Sufficiency So disgusting in young Authors.

This is my candid opinion of Mr Sanderson. I should have added that he lives much retired, tho' of late, Some of our[1] principal characters, & among others Chief Justice Tilghman, have taken notice of him & endeavoured to draw him from his retirement, by inviting him to mixed parties—He knows very little of the world, tho' his manners are neither rustic nor aukward.

When I said that M^r sanderson places great confidence in my advice, I said it with this view, that if you wish any thing to be indirectly communicated to him, I believe it will have its effect. But, perhaps, you need not have recourse to this mode, for it is my firm opinion, that Mr Sanderson is incapable of betraying any confidence that you may honor him with.

I have the honor to be With the greatest veneration & respect Sir   Your most obedient humble servant

PETER S, DU PONCEAU

RC (DLC); at head of text: "Thos Jefferson, Esqr"; endorsed by TJ as received 10 Jan. 1821 and so recorded in SJL.

In his *Ars Poetica*, 268–9, Horace advised poets: "VOS EXEMPLARIA GRÆCA nocturna versate manu, versate diurna"

("For yourselves, handle Greek models by night, handle them by day") (Fairclough, *Horace: Satires, Epistles and Ars Poetica,* 472–3).

[1] Manuscript: "out."

To Tarlton Saunders

SIR   Monticello Jan. 3. 21.

As soon after my return home as other business would permit, I took up the papers which you put into my hands with a view to compare them with those I possessed here. I found that they were in a different form, and not being myself familiar with accounts[1] I could not[2] readily accomodate them to my comprehension, altho' undoubtedly quite regular in their form. they appeared to me to re-open the old accounts, & go far beyond the date of the settlement between mr Lyle and myself. this was on the 4th of Mar. 1790. when we settled the balance due from me to Kippen & co. and Henderson & co. at 1402 £–11 s–2 d sterling, for which I gave 6. bonds payable successively with English interest, from Apr. 19. 1783. besides these there was a bond of mine to R. Harvie and co. assigned to Kippen or Henderson & co. (partners of Harvie) on which, after proper credits 132 £–12 s sterl. was agreed to be due.

about 2. years after, to wit, in 1792. mr Lyle sent me an account of my mother's amounting to £94–17–1½ which I agreed to take on myself, and gave a bond for it accordingly July 30. 1792. payable after the others, with interest from Sep. 1. 1771. (deducting the 8. years war[)]

I proceeded on the discharge of these bonds, and in May. 1808 I recieved from mr Lyle a statement of the application of the payments down to that of 1000.D. July 1. 1806. which overpaid the 5th bond by £ 217–7–8. which balance he carried to the credit of the 6th bond, leaving due on that

	£ s d
Principal	402–11–2
Interest	248–18–3

d° from July. 1. 1806. until paid

With respect to the bond to Harvie & co. mr Lyle in 1811. became very anxious to have it paid in preference to the others; because he observed that some other accounts could not be closed until that payment was made. subsequent to his statement of July 1. 1806. to wit 1808. Nov. 23. I had made a payment of 500.D without saying on account of which bond, and July 6. 1811. I paid 1000.D. particularly on account of this bond. applying both of these payments to Harvie's bond, the last overpaid it 18 £–6 s–6 d which sum may be carried to the interest of the 6th bond.

My mother's debt being the last to be paid, the payments have not reached it as yet.

It appears then that my bonds N° 1. to 5. inclusive, and the one to Harvie are discharged, and should be returned to me; and that on the two others, to wit, N° 6. and mrs Jefferson's debt I shall still owe as follows.

N° 6. Principal   £402–11–2
Interest due and unpaid to July 1. 06.   £248–18–3
1811. July 6. overpaid on Harvie's bond   18– 6–6   230–11–9
                Interest on £402–11–2 from July 1. 06 until paid

Returning me therefore the six other bonds, and retaining these two, the state of the debt stands as clear as any thing can make it.

It remains therefore to speak of payment. I am sure you are sensible that during the present convulsionary crisis (wheat @ 2/6 here) no farmer can make his plantation expences, nor consequently have a dollar of disposable surplus. how long this state of things may continue we cannot foresee; and therefore a promise now to make payment at a fixed epoch could convey no certainty, and might only produce on both sides the pain of disappointment. in the mean time I hold property in readiness for sale. but until produce rises there can be no purchasers. I think you mentioned to me in conversation that the youngest of mr Lyle's legatees or distributees, would not be of age until 7. years hence: and it occurred to me at the time that possibly a full payment within that term might answer for the youngest legatee or distributee. not that I would ask that term absolutely; but only to give time for the restoration of prices to their future level, whatever that is to be. when that shall take place, I shall not delay one moment making a sale and payment of this debt: whereas to sell now would certainly double the debt. in the mean time I speak from a consciousness that the money would not be at interest in safer hands than mine, or bottomed on a clearer or more abundant mass of property. on this subject I shall be happy to hear from you, to relieve me from inquietude.

John Bolling's bond for 52 £–19 s–8 d with interest from 1793. Dec. 1 was assigned to mr Lyle I think about³ 1792, to whom his estate owed a considerable debt of his own. by a letter of Mar. 23. 1811. mr Lyle informed me he should be obliged to bring suit; and my memory decieves me exceedingly if he did not get a judgment and if there was not a sale of negroes under execution, to satisfy it. in which belief I am strengthened by mr Lyle's silence from that time, and his never having returned the bond to me that I might take measures myself for it's recovery. the estate I know was solvent. but as that subject is under your investigation, the application of this credit will await it's result. in the mean time I tender you the assurance of esteem and respect.   TH: JEFF[ERSON]

	£	s	d
1783. Apr. 19. Harvie's bond Principal	132	12	0
1808. Nov. 23. Int. to this date 25 Y–7 M–4 D	169	3	6
	301	15	6
By order on Gibson at this date	112	10	0
	189	5	6
1811. July 6. Int. on £132–12 to this date 2 Y–7 M–13 D	17	8	
	206	13	6
By order on Gibson 1000.D.	225	0	0
overpaid of this bond & to be credited to Nº 6.	18	6	6

PoC (MHi); edge trimmed; signature faint; at foot of first page: "Mʳ T. Saunders"; endorsed by TJ, in part (brackets in original): "Saunders Tarleton. [for Jaˢ Lyle]." Recorded in SJL as a letter to "Saunders Thoˢ" for Lyle. Enclosed in TJ to Bernard Peyton, [ca. 3 Jan. 1821], not found (see note to Peyton to TJ, 8 Jan. 1821).

Tarlton Saunders (d. 1831), agent, dissolved his Richmond commission-business partnership with C. H. Saunders in 1806. The following year he married Sally Bland Goode Lyle, the widow of James Lyle (d. 1806). Saunders served in Chesterfield County companies of the Virginia militia during the War of 1812, and he bought flour from TJ through Patrick Gibson in 1815. He owned ten slaves when he appeared in the 1810 census as a resident of Manchester, Chesterfield County, but had none the following decade when he was listed as a resident of Richmond, where he died (Nathaniel Claiborne Hale, *Roots in Virginia: An Account of Captain Thomas Hale, Virginia Frontiersman, His Descendants and Related Families* [1948], 75, 78; Richmond *Enquirer*, 28 Nov. 1806, 29 Aug. 1809; *Virginia Militia in the War of 1812: From Rolls in the Auditor's Office at Richmond* [2001], 2:224, 824; Gibson to TJ, 10 May 1815; DNA: RG 29, CS, Chesterfield Co., 1810, Richmond, 1820; *The Richmond Directory, Register and Almanac, for the Year 1819* [Richmond, 1819], 67; *Daily Richmond Whig*, 9 June 1831).

For JOHN BOLLING'S BOND, see note to Saunders to TJ, 15 Sept. 1821.

[1] Manuscript: "acounts."
[2] Word interlined.
[3] Reworked from "in."

From Joseph C. Cabell

DEAR SIR,   Richmond 4ᵗʰ Jan: 1821.[1]

I thank you sincerely for your letter of Dec: 25ᵗʰ which I found here on my arrival on 30ᵗʰ. Indisposition confined me in Williamsburg rather longer than I expected when I last wrote you. Since my arrival I have been incessantly engaged on the subject of the University. We have a powerful combination to oppose, & the result is extremely doubtful. If you will examine the enclosed Resolutions of mʳ Griffin you will find them drawn with great art; and on full consultation[2] I have put forth boldly the doctrine relative to the old charters which I announced to you & mʳ Madison at the Spring meeting, & to the

Board in the autumn. It seems to be spreading rapidly among our friends, and doubtless disconcerts our enemies. My time is spent entirely in endeavoring to rekindle the flagging zeal of our friends, to drill them on the subject, & to prepare them well for the struggle. I fear Johnson may be averse to go with us in the attempt to annex terms of admission to the Colleges. He is expected to-day. But all the rest are for it. And I hope he will join. My health is not good owing to a bad cold: and I beg you to excuse the manner in which I write. Rest assured that my best exertions will be used to carry the appropriation, and if we fail, the opposition shall feel our strength. Could you point my attention to any tract on the policy of the new charters in preference to the old. I am now endeavoring to shake the W^m & mary party by offering the Lower Country an equal participation in the Academical fund (hereafter to be distributed) leaving W^m & mary out of the System. The leaders of that party were not prepared for this, and will try to divert the funds to the College. But I think we will disconcert their combination by this proposition. Mr Watkins of Prince Edward has resigned, & m^r Richard Venable, a man of talents & influence, offers in his place. Doddridge is with the opposition. Blackburn has gone home, for a season. It is reported he is against us: but I hope not. Bassett, Griffin, Smith, Garland, Miller, Doddridge— are leaders on the other sides. You may rest assured that every exertion will be made to keep down the University: and you must be prepared for a failure this session. We hope to get $50,000; but that is extremely doubtful. I find my collection of documents & my knowledge of facts of great use to me at this time. I have shewn your last letter to m^r Miller & he is satisfied <u>as to that point</u>. Should I be silent, ascribe it to my engagements here. faithfully yours

JOS: C: CABELL

RC (ViU: TJP); endorsed by TJ as received 8 Jan. 1821 and so recorded in SJL. RC (ViU: TJP); address cover only; with TJ's Notes on D. Mariano, [ca. Mar. 1821], on verso; addressed (trimmed): "Mr Jefferson Montic[e]ll[o]"; franked; postmarked Richmond, 4 Jan.

For the ENCLOSED RESOLUTIONS, see note to Cabell to TJ, 22 Dec. 1820.

[1] Reworked from "1820."
[2] Superfluous period editorially omitted.

From Frederick A. Mayo

HONO: SIR   Richmond the 4 Janu: 1820 [1821]
Haveing received your kind letter, and with pleasure inform, your honour, that I am still carrieng on the Book binding, and shall be happy
to execute any work, which you wish to have done,—I shall soone
take the liberty of sending you a letter, and a speciment of Binding
       Your most humble Servant   FREDERICK A MAYO

NB. The box of books, you will pleas to have directed to the Care of
    Mess[1] S. & M Allens Office,—or the Compiler Office—as on either
    of those places work or Orders for my Bindry are received—

RC (MHi); misdated; endorsed by TJ   COMPILER: *Richmond Commercial Com-*
as a letter of 4 Jan. 1821 received four   *piler.*
days later and so recorded in SJL.

                                [1] Word interlined.

From George Alexander Otis

SIR,   Philadelphia 4th January 1821.
    I beg to acknowledge the receipt of your respected and benign let-
ter of 25th Ult°: and especially, the signal honour you have deigned
to confer on me in transmitting my translation to the Author. It is
assuredly the most flattering, and altogether the most grateful to my
feelings of any circumstance that could have befallen me. Though I
have been several years in different parts of Europe, it was not my
good-fortune to make the acquaintance of a man whose writings have
inspired me with more enthusiasm than those of any other modern
European; and to be thus introduced to him, is a gratification of no
common magnitude. The plan of his History seemed to exact a specimen of American deliberative eloquence; if the genuine speeches of
those who took part in the great debate upon the question of indepen-
dency, have been preserved, it has not been my fortune to meet with
them. If they exist, they might be given in the form of notes to the next
edition, should another be called for. The subject of History has appeared to me, from youth upwards, the most useful as well as delightful branch of literature; and with a faint hope of being Some day in
a situation to exercise my pen upon that of my own Country, I have
made a long study of the fine models you have indicated, and especially of Livy, Tacitus, Sallust and Thucydides. Xenophon &c.
    The greatest happiness that could fall to my lot, would be that of
contributing to turn the attention of my young fellow citizens to a

subject which I have regretted to remark that they are generally very superficially acquainted with; and that in consequence of the insupportable dullness of our vernacular writers, with some honorable exceptions. Belknap &c. The wide extent over which American readers are dispersed, preventing frequent and easy communication, except for Newspapers, is certainly rather a discouraging circumstance for domestic literary enterprises of considerable moment and difficulty. But the unworthy reflections upon our national character, found in most of the British writers, seems a motive for encouraging the feeble attempts which may be made to substitute, little by little, Books of our own production, at least in a degree sufficient to correct the false[1] impressions that must be the inevitable result of an exclusive reading of English Books. Their books of travels in a particular manner, appear calculated to give an unfavourable idea of all the nations they visit, from the contempt they have for all foreigners. And these would seem to have a more extensive circulation among us than most others, excepting their novels and romances.

I find it impossible to express the grateful emotions which are awakened in my breast, by the extreme goodness with which you are pleased to express your good wishes for my Success; but your habitual benevolence Renders it Superfluous; for the being that does good to his fellow being well knows the effect it must produce upon his heart.

I have the honour to be with the highest veneration and sincerity sir, Your obliged humble Servant

GEORGE ALEXANDER OTIS.

RC (DLC); between dateline and salutation: "Honble Thomas Jefferson"; endorsed by TJ as received 10 Jan. 1821 and so recorded in SJL.

In a preface to his translation of Botta, *History of the War*, 1:vii, Otis made the REMARK that "He has been told that his countrymen have no taste for literature, with the exception, however, of Poesy, and the Tales of my Landlord; and that a HISTORY OF THE WAR OF AMERICAN INDEPENDENCE, has no better fate to hope for than to continue to incumber the shelves of the bookseller. But his impressions are different: he thinks, on the contrary, that, as the Tales of my Landlord, themselves in a degree historical, and penned with talent, are in universal request, the existence of *a* taste in literature among American readers is a thing demonstrated." Otis was referencing Sir Walter Scott's *Tales of My Landlord*, a set of seven historical novels published in four series between 1816 and 1832.

[1] Word interlined.

From Charles Willson Peale

DEAR SIR   Belfield Jany 4th 1821.[1]

Yours of 28th Ul^t received, yesterday, and coming home last night, I thought of my small Polygraph, which was made for a traveling conveniency, I find are exactly what you want, therefore it gives me pleasure to send them.

I have long thought on the means to preserve health, and have made many experiments to assertain what would be the best food, as well as drink—and as I enjoy perfect health, many of my acquaintance ask me, what I eat &c my answer is, that it is not so much the quality as the quantity, yet a choise is to be made, and that which is not so easily digested I use very sparingly. And although I drink only water, I do not take great draughts of it—but sip of it on going to bed, when I rise in the morning, and after every thing I eat—because it helps digestion better than any other liquid—therefore a cure for colick, if colick is caused by indigestion. I masticate well all my food, by which much saliva is thus mixt with it.

All this is only a preamble to what I wish to say to you. About 14 years past, I was waken'd by severe pain in my foot, as I had frequently removed triffling pains by rubing the part effected—I now determined to make tryal of rubing although at the moment the pain was tormenting to touch it—however I began to rub, first lightly,[2] then more violently, (I mean with my hand) and continued it so long that all the pain was driven away, and I sleep the remainder of the night. in the morning I found my foot a little[3] swelled with redness on the Skin, and totally free of pain. This was so satisfactory, that ever since I have been in the practice of driving away pain, when ever I have felt it, on my limbs or Body. As I observe that as Animals grow old, that their teeth become more Solid, the cavities where the nerve or marrow is, it becomes very small, and thus perhaps may be the case with all our bones in extreme old-age. I have not examined the bones of various ages for want of opertunity, and leisure, nor have I read any author on the subject. this is however a little[4] foreign to my subject, that of rubing. Many People complain of Rheumatic pains, The rubing as I direct I have prooved in some instances to be an effectual cure—Not with a flesh brush, that only frets or irritates the Skin—but with one or both hands, pressing and rubing the Mustles and all the internal struture togather, by which not only the circulation of the blood is promoted, but also obstructions in the smaller fibers is removed, and a warmth of the parts are obtained of an agreable nature. Exercise we all know is of vast importance to obtain health, especially

[518]

in the open air. But at times we can rub our limbs or Body, more especially when stripted of our garments. therefore before I get in Bed I rub my feet, leggs, thighs, hips, Body, Shoulders & Arms. with one hand, but where I can with both hands, the harder the better, as it warms me. rubing the abdomen while in Bed, And as often as I get up in the night, I have recourse to the same exercise. Now my Dear Sir may not such a practice be servicable to you—Your wrist I hope would be made better—This is more than passive exercise, it is real exercise, or rather active exercise, that will give energy to the whole System. A perseverance in rubing must be practiced with complaints of long standing—I hope what I [have][5] written may induce you to a tryal with your wrist. as I conceive you must lament the loss of useing it. I cannot help believing that much of my present abilities to do any kind of work or exercise may have been from the above practice—for I do assure you that I feel as active as I have ever been in my younger days. can this be a delusion?

My Son Rembrandt on reading your letter on the receipt of the drawing from his Picture, conceived it would be useful to him, therefore I let him have it, and at New york he had it put into a news paper, and I am inclined to think that it drew the attention of the Corporation, for since the publication of it, the Mayor & Corporation in a body visited his exhibition, paid him high compliments, and it has led to an important Visitation to him—I had some reluctance in parting with said letter, yet I hope you will not regret my giving it to him, since such has been his benefit.   I am as ever your obleged freind   C W Peale

PS. My next will be to give you some account of my Museum

RC (DLC); at foot of text: "Tho[s] Jefferson Esq[re] Monticella"; endorsed by TJ as received 10 Jan. 1821 and so recorded in SJL. PoC (PPAmP: Peale Letterbook); edge trimmed.

[1] Reworked from "1820."
[2] Manuscript: "lighly."
[3] Manuscript: "alittle."
[4] Manuscript: "alittle."
[5] Omitted word editorially supplied.

To Joel Yancey

DEAR SIR   Monticello Jan. 4. 21.

I have for sometime been becoming sensible that[1] age was rendering me incompetent to the management of my plantations. failure of memory, decay of attention and a loss of energy in body & mind convince me of this; as well as the vast change for the better since my plantations here have been put under the direction of my grandson

T. J. Randolph. his skill, his industry and discretion satisfy me that it will be best for me to place all my plantations, in Bedford as well as here, under his general care instead of my own. as myself therefore he will consult and plan with you on the course of our crops and plantation proceedings generally, and in all things you may consider him as myself and I am sure you will have more satisfaction in consulting with him who will understand the subject than with myself who did not. be so good as to hurry your flour & tobacco down and always to drop me a line when either goes off, that I may know how to draw.[1] I shall pay my visits to Pop. Forest as usual for the sake of change of position. I salute you with affectionate esteem and respect.

Th: Jefferson

PoC (MHi); on verso of reused address cover of Chapman Johnson to TJ, 1 July 1819; mutilated at seal, with five words rewritten by TJ; at foot of text: "Mr Yancey"; endorsed by TJ.

[1] Manuscript: "that that."

To Robert Barnard

Sir   Monticello Jan. 5. 21.

Your favor of Dec. 28. was recieved the last night. the buildings for the accomodation of the Professors and students of our University will not be ready until next autumn. but when we shall be able to call for Professors and open the institution will depend on the aid our legislature may give. until this be ascertained, we can say nothing on the subject of Professors. but the opening, whenever it may be fixed will be announced in the papers so as to notify all who may be disposed to apply.

Accept the assurance of my respect.   Th: Jefferson

RC (DCHi: Barnard Family Papers); at foot of text: "Mr Robert Barnard." PoC (DLC); on verso of a reused address cover from John Adams (in Louisa C. Smith's hand) to TJ; endorsed by TJ.

From Emile de Vendel

Sir,   Newburgh Jany–5th. 1821.—

Having understood that a college is about to be established in Virginia under your Patronage and that it will embrace a Professorship of the French language, I beg leave to enquire of you (if the above is correct) whether a selection of a Professor of the French language has been made; I am anxious to offer myself as a candidate for the office, and trust that satisfactory testimonials of my character and abilities can be produced.

I am a native of France; I have been in this country five years, and when I left home, was honored with recommendatory letters, among others from the Marquis La fayette to Mr. Monroe, now President of the United States, and to Mr Crawford, Secretary of the treasury.

May I ask of you the favor of informing me whether there is a vacancy in the office and in the college above alluded to.—

With Sentiments of the highest respect and esteem, I have the honor to be, Your most obed[t] Serv[t].—

DE VENDEL

(Newburgh, Orange County, N.Y. State)

RC (DLC); at foot of text: "Mr. Jefferson"; endorsed by TJ as received 28 Jan. 1821 and so recorded in SJL; with FC of TJ to de Vendel, 30 Jan. 1821, on verso.

Emile (Emilius) de Vendel (ca. 1793–1857) was born in Paris. While young he served as a secretary in Napoleon's army, and he was later in the National Guard. After the emperor's exile to Elba in 1814, de Vendel joined three other young men in covertly delivering him despatches, for which service Napoleon personally thanked them after his escape from that island. With the restoration of the Bourbon monarchy, however, de Vendel was imprisoned for six months. He afterwards moved to the United States, arriving in New York City late in 1815. The next year his wife opened a boarding school in Schenectady, which she moved to Newburgh in 1820. By 1828 de Vendel lived in Huntsville, Alabama, where he was a manager of the Huntsville Theatre. His

home was also the site of a female academy until he moved permanently to Mobile County around 1832. There his wife continued to run a boarding school for girls. De Vendel owned nine slaves in 1850 (*Gulf States Historical Magazine* 1 [1903]: 333–6; [de Vendel], *Liberté Individuelle sous le Regne des Bourbons* [Paris, 1815]; New York *Commercial Advertiser*, 28 Nov. 1815; *Albany Advertiser*, 28 Sept. 1816; New York *Mercantile Advertiser*, 23 May 1820; *Louisville Public Advertiser*, 23 July 1828; Huntsville *Southern Advocate*, 23 June 1832; *Pensacola Gazette*, 23 May 1840; DNA: RG 29, CS, Ala., Huntsville, 1830, Mobile Co., 1840, 1850, 1850 slave schedules; Mobile Co. Will Book, 3:1–3; *Ballou's Pictorial Drawing-Room Companion* 13 [1857]: 399).

Lafayette recommended de Vendel to James MONROE and William H. CRAWFORD from La Grange in separate letters dated 8 Oct. 1815 (NN: Monroe Papers; ICU).

To Elijah Griffiths

DEAR SIR   Monticello Jan. 5. 21.

Your favor of Dec. 11. has been recieved, and certainly no one would more gladly be useful to you than myself. but from the time of my retiring from office, so multitudinous were the applications to me to sollicit appointments from government that I should have had to submit to a total prostration of all self respect, or to[1] decline interfering generally. I have done so rigorously,[2] but in a very few & very special cases. I shall willingly make application in your case, if there shall be ground [fo]r it. but as I much doubt the passage of a bankrupt law [a]fter our own experience as well as that of England, I am unwilling to make an useless breach of my rule. the interval between it's [p]assage[3] thro' the 1st & 2d house will be quite sufficient to warn me of the possibility of it's passing the 2d as the papers come to me in 3. days. for this I will be on the watch, and take care that my letter shall be recieved before the final passage. in the mean time accept the assurance of my great esteem & respect   TH: JEFFERSON

PoC (DLC); on verso of reused address cover of Mathew Carey to TJ, 23 June 1819; two words faint; at foot of text: "Dr Elijah Griffith"; endorsed by TJ.

[1] TJ here canceled "refuse."
[2] Manuscript: "rigorusly."
[3] Word damaged at seal.

To Edward Wiatt

SIR   Monticello Jan. 5. 21.

It is not in my power to give any satisfactory answers to the enquiries of your letter of Dec. 4. the buildings for the accomodation of the Professors and 200. students will be compleated by the ensuing autumn: but when we shall be able to call [for] Professors and open the institution will depend on the aid the legislature will give. boarding at Charlottesville is about 125.D. (without bed, washing, wood or candles) the tuition fees may perhaps raise that to 150 or 175.D but their amount is not yet fixed. Accept the assurance of my respect.

TH: JEFFERSON

PoC (DLC); on verso of reused address cover of John Hollins to TJ, 25 June 1819; one word faint; at foot of text: "Mr Edward Wiatt"; endorsed by TJ.

Notes on Early Career
(the so-called "Autobiography")

[*Ed. Note*: During the first seven months of 1821, TJ composed a lengthy description of his early political life. He began writing on 6 January and returned to the work on at least sixteen subsequent days before finally laying down his pen in the summer. TJ did not provide the resulting ninety-three-page manuscript with a title. It was first published in 1829 as his "Memoir" (TJR, 1:1–89). After Henry A. Washington's edition of TJ's writings appeared early in the 1850s, scholars have usually followed his lead and called it TJ's "Autobiography," which probably exaggerates his intentions for the work (HAW, 1:1–110). Covering the period from his birth in 1743 until his arrival at New York City in 1790 to take up his duties as George Washington's secretary of state, the piece contains little introspection and focuses almost entirely on TJ's public actions, goals, and achievements. It will be printed in its entirety at the date of its last entry, 29 July 1821.]

From Horace H. Hayden

Dear Sir.   Baltimore Jany 6th 1821—

I am happy to have it in my power to offer for your perusal the result of my[1] observations and remarks, on some of the geological phenomena of this continent, as well as those of some others—

Since the publication of this work (in octob^r) I have been anxious to forward it to you by private conveyance; but no opportunity offering, I was induced to apply to Mr Skinner, P.M—who kindly offere'd to forward it to you by Mail; through the medium of which I hope you will receive it safe and without injury—

This work, Sir, has been written under all the inconveniences and disadvantages inseperable from a professional Vocation, in which, I may say, nearly the whole time allotted for active pursuits, has been engross'ed; consequently, subject to almost constant interruptions— To these may be attribut'ed many inaccuracies which, under more favourable circumstances, would not have escaped detection—These, however, it is hoped, will not lessen the importance of the subject, nor diminish the pleasures which the various phenomena[2] of Nature are calculated to afford to the contemplative and phylosophic min'd—

Accept, Sir, the homage of unfeign'd respect and esteem from Your Very Ob^dt Servt   Horace H Hayden

RC (DLC); endorsed by TJ as received 19 Jan. 1821 and so recorded in SJL. RC (DLC); address cover only; with PoC of TJ to John H. Cocke, 12 Mar. 1821, on verso; addressed: "Thos Jefferson Esqr Monticello Va"; franked; postmarked Baltimore, 7 Jan.

Horace H. Hayden (1769–1844), dentist, was born and educated in Windsor, Connecticut. At the age of fourteen he made two trips to the West Indies as a cabin boy on a brig. Two years later Hayden's father began to teach him carpentry and architecture, and in his early twenties he made two more voyages to the West Indies before working as an architect in Windsor. Having moved to New York City, in 1792 Hayden decided to pursue a career in dentistry, a discipline in which he was largely self-taught. In 1800 he began a dental practice in Baltimore, and a decade later the state of Maryland licensed him as a dentist. During the War of 1812 Hayden served as a sergeant and assistant surgeon in the state militia. He gained respect in Baltimore both as a dentist and more broadly as a medical professional, and he published extensively in medical journals. In addition to dentistry, Hayden studied and published works on geology and botany, and he obtained patents for a tanning oil in 1823 and a dentifrice the following year. Having long advocated a professional dental association, he became the first president of the American Society of Dental Surgeons in 1840. Building on his own experience teaching dental students privately, that same year Hayden helped found the Baltimore College of Dental Surgery (later the University of Maryland School of Dentistry), reputedly the world's first dental college. He served it both as president and as a professor until his death (*DAB*; Charles R. E. Koch, ed., *History of Dental Surgery* [1909], 2:58–65; William M.

Marine, *The British Invasion of Maryland, 1812–1815* [1913], 317; *List of Patents*, 259, 266; Baltimore *Sun*, 27 Jan. 1844).

Hayden apparently sent separately for TJ's PERUSAL his *Geological Essays; or, An Inquiry into some of the Geological Phenomena to be found in Various Parts of America, and Elsewhere* (Baltimore, 1820; Poor, *Jefferson's Library*, 6 [no. 285]), because TJ acknowledged it on 15 Jan. 1821, before this letter reached him.

[1] Word interlined.
[2] Manuscript: "phemomena."

To John Vaughan

DEAR SIR   Monticello Jan, 6. 21.

I have a great desire to send to mr Botta of Paris a copy of his best of all our histories of the revolution, as translated by mr Otis. the difficulty is to get it to him without it's passing thro' the French post office, which would tax him beyond it's cost. this can be done only thro' a passenge[r] and I think it must be a gratification to any passenger to deliver it to him in person, & I should pray him to accompany it with my particular respects to mr Botta. from hence no opportunity of a passenger ever occurs; but from your city I presume they are frequent enough to enable you to forward it for me without difficulty & with the less as dispatch is not material. add this to your multiplied favors to me, & accept the assurance of my constant & respectful friendship.   TH: JEFFERSON

P.S. I shall forward the volumes by distinct mails, not to overload[1] our village mail.

PoC (MHi); on verso of reused address cover of Thomas Cooper to TJ, 13 Sept. 1819; edge trimmed; mutilated at seal, with one word rewritten by TJ; adjacent to signature: "John Vaughan esq."; endorsed by TJ.

[1] Manuscript: "ouerload."

From James Madison

DEAR SIR   Montpellier Jany 7. 1821

In the inclosed you will see the ground on which I forward it for your perusal.

In the late views taken by us, of the Act of Congress, vacating periodically the Executive offices, it was not recollected, in justice to the President, that the measure was not without precedents. I suspect however that these are confined to the Territorial Establishments, where they were introduced by the old Cong^s in whom all powers of Gov^t were confounded; and continued by the new Congress, who have exercised a like confusion of powers within the same limits. Whether the Congressional code contains any precedent of a like sort, more particularly misleading the President I have not fully examined. If it does, it must have blindly followed the territorial examples.

We have had for several months a typhus fever in the family, which does not yield in the least, to the progress of the season. Out of twenty odd cases, there have been six deaths, and there are several depending cases threatning a like issue. The fever has not yet reached any part of our White family; but in the Overseers, there have been five cases of it including himself. None of them however have been mortal.

Health & every other blessing   JAMES MADISON

RC (DLC: Madison Papers); endorsed by TJ as received 11 Jan. 1821 and so recorded in SJL. Enclosure: Tench Coxe to Madison, Philadelphia, 28 Dec. 1820, stating that he is still looking for the copies of Congressional debates desired by Madison; reporting on his researches into matters relevant to the Missouri question, noting that "My materials have been historical, constitutional & statutory; and I have satisfied myself, that as the black & colored people were not, in 1774. 1776. 1781. (the Confederation) 1787 the date of the constitution, parties to our social compacts (provincial or state) so that cannot <u>have entered</u> or <u>be admitted</u> without <u>grave and customary form</u>," enclosing one of his "mild and calm addresses" to Quakers on the subject, and requesting Madison to forward it to TJ; remarking that in Pennsylvania, "Our <u>electors</u> are all <u>citizens</u> paying taxes. We have <u>native</u> blacks and yellows, <u>not taxed lest they should apply to vote</u>, excluded by the Commissioners from <u>all juries and from arbitrations</u>; by <u>law</u> from the Militia; by the courts from all retail sales of wine & distilled spirits; from the benefit of <u>tuition</u> ordained, without notice of color, for 'the poor, gratis' but tho arranged under a law <u>not excluding blacks & yellows</u>, so dispensed by <u>eminent quakers, members of the abolition society, that</u> no black or mulattoe <u>has ever</u> been admitted!"; complaining that "some are for an abolition, <u>without compensation</u>, of all Penns^a slaves and servants of 28 years, of slave parents, increasing the free suddenly, at a moment of Haytian civil war, extensive black & red armaments in Spanish & Portuguese America, and of great embarrassment from our own 200.000 free colored people"; and concluding that, inasmuch as free blacks are clearly "a messy, increasing <u>unmanagable</u> evil" in Philadelphia, and even more so in New York City, "from whose workhouses, common Gaols and penitentiaries we have detailed accounts," it remains to be determined how African Americans can best be "disposed of with justice and policy" (RC in DLC: Madison Papers; docketed by Madison; printed in Madison, *Papers, Retirement Ser.*, 2: 193–5).

The enclosure to Coxe's letter to Madison, which was probably also conveyed to TJ at this time, was the proof sheet of Coxe's essay no. XII written as "A Democratic Federalist" and addressed "To the Friends of Truth," which appeared in the Philadelphia *Democratic Press*, 4 Jan. 1821 (Madison's copy in DLC: Madison Papers, ser. 7, newspaper file).

Madison was probably recalling the provision in the "Ordinance for the government of the territory of the United States North West of the river Ohio," passed by the Continental Congress (OLD CONG[s]) on 13 July 1787, which allowed Congress to appoint territorial governors and secretaries with limited terms (Worthington C. Ford and others, eds., *Journals of the Continental Congress, 1774–1789* [1904–37], 32:335–6).

From Bernard Peyton

D[R] SIR,   Rich'd 8 Janu[y] 1821

I rec[d] a few days since by M[r] Johnson's Boat 64 Blls: your Flour, which was then dull sale at $3\frac{1}{4}$—owing however to the prospect of a freeze, the article become more in request, & I was enable to effect a sale at $3.37\frac{1}{2}$, as per ⅔ sales above, which was the very best I could do with it, & which hope will be satisfactory to you.   Nett proceeds as above, say $184.42, at your credit.

I am favor'd this morning with yours covering a letter to M[r] T. Saunders, which shall be delivered as soon as possible—

Your draft favor A. Robinson Esq[r] of Lynchburg for thirty $30 Dollars has been presented & paid.

With sincere affection Yours   B. PEYTON

RC (MHi); subjoined to enclosure; mistakenly endorsed by TJ as a letter of 1 Jan. 1821 received ten days later and so recorded in SJL. RC (MHi); address cover only; with PoC of TJ to Joel Yancey, 19 Mar. [1821], on verso; addressed: "M[r] Thomas Jefferson Monticello near Charlottesville"; stamped; postmarked Richmond, 8 Jan.

TJ's letter to Peyton COVERING TJ to Tarlton Saunders, 3 Jan. 1821, has not been found and is not recorded in SJL. On 13 Dec. 1820 TJ recorded having received $30 from Archibald Robertson (ROBINSON) and giving him an order on Peyton for the same amount (*MB*, 2:1371).

ENCLOSURE

Account with Bernard Peyton for Flour Sales

Sales 51 Blls: super, 10 fine, & 3 x midlings Flour by B. Peyton
                                        for ⅔ M[r] Tho[s] Jefferson

1821 Rich'd
5 Janu[y]   To Lewis Ludlum for Cash in store
                  51 Blls: super fine Flour at $3.37\frac{1}{2} $172.12
                  10 do fine   do "   3.12\frac{1}{2}   31.25

3 do x midlings do "		2.25	6.75	
				$210.12

Charges

Cash paid on ⅗ freight	$6.00	
Canal Toll $6.67. Drayage $1.38	8.05	
storage $5.12—Inspection $1.28	6.40	
Commission at 2½ pʳ Cᵗ on $210.12	5.25	$ 25.70

Nett proceeds at Cʳ Mʳ T. Jefferson $184.42

MS (MHi); in Peyton's hand; with
covering letter subjoined; calculations by
TJ at foot of text:

```
"64. 184.42 (2.88
     128
     564
     512
     522."
```

From Patrick Gibson

SIR   Richmond 9ᵗʰ Janʸ 1821—

Since I last wrote you on the 9ᵗʰ ultᵒ I have received 62 bls: of your flour, which I have this day sold to Messʳˢ Lucke & Sizer at 3⅜$, this is a better price than I was able to obtain on its arrival, and is indeed as high as is warranted by any foreign market—I am,

With much respect Your obᵗ Servᵗ   PATRICK GIBSON

RC (DLC); between dateline and salutation: "Thomas Jefferson Esqʳᵉ"; endorsed by TJ as received 13 Jan. 1821
and so recorded in SJL; with calculations
by TJ at foot of text regarding the payment of a portion of his debt to Gibson
through the sale of the above flour (see
Gibson to TJ, 12 Sept. 1820):

```
              "3.375
                  62
               6.750
              202 50
              209.25
              262.72
               53.47
3 discᵗˢ of 60 180."
```

From William Thornton

DEAR SIR   City of Washington Janʸ 9ᵗʰ 1821.

I have never been honoured with a line from you since your favor of the 9ᵗʰ of May 1817—which I answered on the 27ᵗʰ relative to the College about to be established in your Vicinity.—I am in hopes my Letter reached you, not so much from any advantage it could possibly offer you, as to shew my desire to fulfil to the utmost of my ability every wish with which you have honored me.—I am in hopes that your long silence may arise more from your retirement from active life, than from any disinclination to preserve my name in the list of your friendship: for it has been almost the only consolation of my life that I have been honored with the friendship of the good & great.—

I write now to solicit from you a favor.[1]—I have always been a Friend to Revolutions, & at the time the French revolution began I was so ardent an admirer of the general plan, which had commenced, of overturning all kingly & priestly Governments, knowing them to be oppressive, that I hoped for the progress of the arms of France; thinking that in a few years there would not be a King on Earth: but the French were not well versed in the true principles of national Governments, & failed in the establishment of their Constitution. The most absolute Tyranny succeeded, & finally the restoration of one of the Bourbons.—

While I was a Student at the University of Edinburgh, also in London & Paris, I was anxious to see the commencement of the Revolution of the South Americans, for I thought them under the most miserable & despotic Government.—The celebrated Countess de Beauharnois solicited for me, through the medium of the Duke de Penthievre, from the Court of Spain, Letters to Mexico. But I was refused admission into the Spanish Territories. At that time there were many Jealousies against admitting Foreigners into the Spanish Dominions, especially mineralogists, & I was engaged in the Study of mineralogy, under the celebrated Faujas de St Fond.—I have[2] been always considered, by the South Americans, an active[3] Friend; & they have made me several offers of high appointment in their Service; but though I was engaged only in the trivial office I still hold, which does not give support to my Family, I have invariably refused every temptation to enter into the patriot Service; wherein I was offered the immediate rank of Colonel of horse; & a high office in their Civil Service; with land enough whereon to settle a Colony. I refused every thing, but rendered them, as a friend, every Service in my power,[4] & all the great revolutionary Characters of South America have considered my House, as a place of friendly Consultation.—Several Individuals have been sent to South America, as agents from this Government, & I was in hopes that I might have been honored by such a mission. It is indeed but a minor appointment, but I am sincerely of opinion that I could render not only efficient Services to this Government, but also to any Republic in South America to which I could be sent, particularly to the Republic of Columbia. Colonel Todd, an amiable young Gentleman, was however sent there; but if he should after visiting that Country prefer any other Situation, I should be happy to be permitted to succeed him.—I am induced to think I could be of service there, because I was intimately acquainted with the principal Chiefs of the Republic: viz, with Señ^r Jose R: Revenga, who is Sec^y of State & Finance; with the celebrated Rossio, who is now Vice Pres-

ident of the Republic; with the renowned[5] Orator & excellent Pedro
Gual L.L.D. who was Govr of Carthagena &c—and by these & other
Individuals I have been urged to settle in that Country.—These Considerations have induced me to be particularly desirous of a mission
there: for I do not wish to change my Allegiance after having lived so
long in this highly respected Republic, & yet I am desirous of rendering myself useful to them, not only in endeavouring to cement their
friendship with this Government, but in what might be beneficial in
the establishment of their republic, which I know is desirous to pursue the excellent principles that have so long distinguished this.—I
have applied to the President on this Subject, & he has spoken of me
favourably; but I have heard that he thinks the public voice would be
against my having such an appointment. I know not why; for some of
the most worthy Senators Colonel Johnson & others,[6] have, without
my knowledge, waited on the President, & requested him to appoint
me thither: many other Friends have also recommended me in the
most particular manner to him. I am well known to the President, &
in writing this I solicit your kind & friendly aid in recommending me
as a proper person, if I should be so happy as to possess your good
opinion, & you should deem me not unfit for such an agency. One of
the great objects I have in view is to write the general & natural History of that almost unknown Country; & I think I could serve this
Government in any negotiations with that, because I have been so
long considered as the Friend of that Government, that if any thing
can be advantageously done I am in hopes I could effect it; and certainly much will be required if any public Business is to be performed
of any moment with that rich powerful & extensive Republic.—I shall
consider it of the utmost importance to obtain from you a Letter of
Recommendation to the President; who seems very friendly to me;
but as this is a Govern^t which is regulated in some measure by public opinion, it would not be unavailing to obtain as many Evidences
of the public Sentiments in my favor as possible: I know however of
none that can produce such an Effect as a Recommendation from you.
I should consider any thing favourable from you[7] as a host in my behalf.—If I could render as much Service to the Government as another,
I think I could render still more benefit to this Country at large by
giving an account of all the valuable[8] vegetable and other Productions
of that fertile region, especially as I am capable of drawing them.—
The celebrated Franklin offered me the most honorable Employm^t
without Solicitation, that was perhaps ever offered, in the same stile,
from one so renowned to one so young as I then was. He offered while
Governor of Pennsylvania, if I would travel in the Service of the

United States, & only keep a regular Journal of every thing which I might think worthy of Observation, & which should be delivered to the Government, he would obtain for me such a Salary as would be deemed worthy of any Gentleman; & to shew how much he was in earnest in this appointment, he promised as his individual Subscription, the whole of his Salary as Governor of Pennsylvan[a] for one year, which amounted to one thousand pounds Penn[a] Currency.—He stated too, that I was not to be controuled in any respect, as he would trust solely to my honor.—He had known me formerly, when I was a Student in Paris (he being then minister) through an Introduction to him from my Guardian[9] Doctor Lettsom of London.—My delicate State of health soon after prevented me from accepting this noble this generous offer from one of the greatest men living, but I should otherwise have chearfully accepted it, & I have never ceased to cherish in my most grateful remembrance, this highly honorable proof of his devotion to the advancement of Science, & this proof of confidence so very flattering to one so young.—

The famous Doctor Ratcliff left £800 Sterlg. ℞[r] annum for ever to be given to four young travelling Physicians £200 Sterlg. each for which they were required to write twelve Letters[10] annually in latin on any Subjects of Science. They were equally without restraint in residence or Country.—

I take the liberty of enclosing for your perusal, the Copy of a very kind Letter, written in my behalf, by the Honor[ble] Joseph Anderson 1st Comptroller of the Treasury of the United States, with whom I have been acquainted for many years. I have some others that are very friendly on the same Subject, & I hope if the President see so many Testimonies in my favor he will think himself authorized by the public opinion to accord what I so earnestly wish.—My time of life will not permit any delay; for what I wish to undertake would require all my Exertions, were I even younger in Life.—

I am dear Sir with the highest respect & consideration Y[rs] &c

WILLIAM THORNTON—

P.S.—Since writing the foregoing, I have this Day, viz on the 16th Jan[y] heard that Colonel Todd means to return.—The sooner therefore I can be favoured with a few Lines to the President, the more you will oblige me   W.T.

RC (DLC); between full signature and postscript: "Honorable Thomas Jefferson"; pages numbered by Thornton; endorsed by TJ as received 28 Jan. 1821 and so recorded (mistakenly as a letter dated 28 Dec.) in SJL. Tr (DNA: RG 59, LAR, 1817–25); entirely in Thornton's hand; lacking postscript; endorsed by Thornton: "Copy of a Letter from William Thornton to the Hon: Thomas Jefferson."

John Coakley Lettsom wrote Thornton a letter of INTRODUCTION to Benjamin Franklin on 28 Jan. 1784 (Franklin, *Papers*, 41:514–6). The British physician John Radcliffe (RATCLIFF) endowed two traveling medical fellowships through Oxford University in his 1714 will (*ODNB*; Joseph B. Nias, *Dr. John Radcliffe: A Sketch of His Life with an account of his Fellows and Foundations* [1918]).

The enclosed COPY OF A VERY KIND LETTER was probably Joseph Anderson to James Monroe, Washington, 22 Feb. 1820, which noted Anderson's long association with Thornton; recommended him as an agent to South America, preferably Colombia; and explained that "his personal acquaintance with Some of the first Characters in South America, and the confidence I have been informd they have in the Doctor, woud give him great advantages in the contemplated Mission— and the great circumspection and caution, Which he advised those Characters to Observe Whilst in the United States, and thereby avoid commiting our Gov-

ernment, may be considered as an evidence of the prudent manner, in Which he woud deport himself as an agent of the United States" (RC in DNA: RG 59, LAR, 1817–25; with one repeated word editorially omitted; endorsed by Daniel Brent: "In Doctor Thornton's of 24th feb: 1820").

[1] Remainder of paragraph in Tr reads "I have always been a friend to the revolutions of Kingly & priestly Governments, knowing them to be oppressive."
[2] Tr here adds "since the commencement of their Revolution."
[3] Tr: "as a sincere."
[4] Tr here adds "compatible with my Duties."
[5] RC: "renouned." Tr: "renowned."
[6] Preceding four words interlined.
[7] Tr here adds "with whom I have been so long acquainted, & under whom I have so long served the Public."
[8] Word not in Tr.
[9] Tr here adds "the late."
[10] Tr here adds "(one each month)."

From William S. Cardell

DEAR SIR,   New York 11th Jan 1821

I had the honor to address you in[1] February last, in behalf of a number of Gentlemen, on the subject of an institution for promoting the literature of our country. The correspondence on the subject has been extensive and interesting, and the society is organised under very encouraging prospects. The enclosed[2] circular which is in part an amplification of my former letter will explain the leading principles and objects.

The officers elected are John Quincy Adams President—Judge Livingston, Judge Story and Hon. William Lowndes, Vice Presidents.— Alex. M[c]Leod D.D. Rec. Sec. John Stearns MD. (President N.Y. State Med. Society) Treasurer.—Counsellors, Chancellor Kent, Daniel Webster, Boston, Bishop Brownell Con. John M. Mason, D.D. Joseph Hopkinson N. Jersey, P. S. Du Ponceau LL.D. Phil. John L. Taylor, North Carolina, H. Clay, Kentucky—There are 2 vacancies. D[r] Smith of William & Mary Col. is proposed to fill one, and Doct Dana President of Dartmouth the other.

Among other transactions of this institution, it is made my duty, Sir, respectfully to communicate to you thier unanimous election of you as an honorary member. The other honorary members are Hon John Adams James Madison, James Munroe, C. C. Pinckney, John Jay and John Trumbull.

The society of course can have no expectation of exalting the dignity of men who have passed thro all forms and degrees of honor which a nation can confer: but it is the highest tribute of respect in our power to offer, and the cordial approbation expressed by those distinguished citizens gives to the institution the means [of]³ additional usefulness to our country.

There is more coincidence of opinion and more⁴ concert in action than were anticipated on a subject so new and among men so widely scattered.

The only publication made by the society is the offer of a premium of 400 Dollars and a gold medal for the best American History, calculated for a class book in Academies and schools. Several other premiums are proposed copies of which will be printed and circulated in a few days to obtain the opinions of members respecting the selection of objects.

Accept Sir this renewed assurance of my highes[t] consideration and respect.

W. S. CARDELL
Corresponding Sec.
Am. Acad. of Lang. & B. Lettres.

RC (DLC); torn at seal; addressed: "Hon. Thomas Jefferson Monticello (Virg.)"; franked; postmarked New York, 11 Jan.; endorsed by TJ as received 19 Jan. 1821 and so recorded in SJL.

Cardell sent a longer letter with the same enclosures to John Adams on this day, and on the next he wrote one to James Madison very similar to the one to TJ. His letters to Adams and Madison included Washington Irving, "now in London," among the COUNSELLORS of the American Academy of Language and Belles Lettres, and he named William Allen, president of Bowdoin College, as a potential candidate for one of the VACANCIES (MHi: Adams Papers; Madison, *Papers, Retirement Ser.*, 2:207–16).

¹ Manuscript: "in in."
² Manuscript: "enlosed."
³ Omitted word editorially supplied.
⁴ Word interlined.

I

Circular from American Academy of Language and Belles Lettres

DEAR SIR,   *New-York, October* 1, 1820.

YOUR attention is respectfully requested to an association of Scholars for the purpose of improving American literature. This association, though yet at its commencement and unknown to the public, has been the subject of an interesting correspondence for some months past; and it is believed will not be deemed unimportant as connected with the best interests of our country.

To settle at once a point on which some difference might exist, it is not designed, independent of England, to form an American language, farther than as it relates to the numerous and increasing names and terms peculiarly American; but to cultivate a friendly correspondence with any similar association or distinguished individuals in Great Britain, who may be disposed to join us in an exertion to improve our common language.

The objects of such an institution which directly present themselves, are, to collect and interchange literary intelligence; to guard against local or foreign corruptions, or to correct such as already exist; to settle varying orthography; determine the use of doubtful words and phrases; and, generally, to form and maintain, as far as practicable, an English standard of writing and pronunciation, correct, fixed, and uniform, throughout our extensive territory. Connected with this, and according to future ability, may be such rewards for meritorious productions, and such incentives to improvement, in the language and literature of our country, and in the general system of instruction, as from existing circumstances may become proper.

These objects will not be thought trifling, by those who have spent much time in the cultivation of literature, or attended to its influence on society. Such persons need not be told how directly they are connected with our progress in general knowledge, or our public reputation; or that their influence may extend from social to national intercourse, and to our commercial prosperity. Perspicuity in language is the basis of all science. The philosophy that professes to teach the knowledge of *things*, independent of *words*, needs only to be mentioned among enlightened men to be rejected.

Most of the European nations have considered the improvement of language as an important national object, and have established academies, with extensive funds and privileges, for that purpose. An interference of the government has, perhaps, been omitted in England, from a singular and rather accidental reliance on the acknowledged superiority of a few leading individuals; and so long as all the literature in the English language had its origin and center in London, there was less danger in thus leaving it to the guidance of chance. Science may be comparatively recluse; but literature is social; and American scholars, spread over 2,000,000 square miles, are not to be drawn to a virtual and national association, without the form.

It is very properly said of France that its literature has frequently saved the country when its arms have failed. The advantages resulting to that nation, from the exertions of a few academicians, have been incalculable, and may serve to show, in some degree, what such a confederacy of scholars is capable of performing. The effect of their influence was not barely to elevate France in the literary world, and to improve its learning within itself; but to extend their language throughout Europe; to introduce, at the expense of other nations, their books, their opinions, and, in aid of other causes, their political preponderance. The Philological Academies of Italy and Spain, though unaided by the same powerful co-operation, have effected very great improvements in the language and literature of their respective countries. The great work now performing by the German scholars, in addition to what they have before done, is a noble example to other nations, and calculated to elevate the condition of our nature. With how much greater force does every consideration connected with this subject, apply, in a free community, where all depends upon the virtue and intelligence of the great body of the people.

Without dwelling a moment on invidious comparisons between England and the United States, the time appears to have arrived, in reference to ourselves, when, having acquired a high standing among nations, having succeeded in a fair trial of the practicability and excellence of our civil institutions, our scholars are invited to call their convention and to form the constitution of national literature.

We have some peculiar advantages in an attempt to establish national uniformity in language. Happily for us, our forefathers came chiefly from that part of England where their language was most correctly spoken, and were possessed of a good degree of intelligence, according to the learning of that time. Though in a country as diversified as ours, there are, from various causes, many particular corruptions, we hardly find any thing that can properly be called a provincial dialect. We have at present no very inveterate habits to correct, where gross barbarisms, through large districts, are to be encountered. The attempt therefore, seasonably and judiciously made, presents a prospect not only of success, but of comparative facility. Our scattered population seem only to want from a competent tribunal, a declaration of what is proper, to guide them in their practice. The present appearances are more favorable than the most sanguine among the projectors of the plan dared to predict. There is the best reason to expect the general concurrence of our distinguished literary men in favor of a measure which promises so many advantages, so nationally important in its principles and effects, and to which so little can be objected. It is deemed unnecessary at present to dwell minutely on the details of the plan, which probably will not be difficult to settle, if the leading principles are generally approved. It is equally useless to enter upon a train of arguments to prove the advantages of such an association under the present circumstances of our country. The commanding influence of literature upon national wealth and power, as well as morals, character, and happiness, especially in free communities, will not be doubted by those whose minds have been most directed to this interesting branch of civil policy. Perhaps there never has been, and never may be, a nation more open to the influence of moral causes, than the American Republic at the present[1] time. In every country truly free, public opinion is in effect the governing law; and public opinion, and all the complicated interests of society, greatly depend on the state of national literature. That independence which is our boast must consist in the proper independence of the mind. Without contemning the experience of past ages, we ought not too slavishly to follow the path of others.

It is enough to respect the Europeans as honorable competitors, without regarding them as absolute masters. American ambition should aspire to noble objects, if we mean to rise to excellence: for, besides that the imitator is almost necessarily inferior to his model, the old world can furnish no model suited to the circumstances and character of our country. We are a world by ourselves. Our privileges, resources, and prospects, are of the highest order. Happily exempt from hereditary despotism or bigoted hierarchies, from jealous and powerful bordering nations; the professed advocates of rational freedom, the world may justly claim from us an example worthy of such a situation and such a cause. Our numbers and wealth are greater than those of England were, when the last of her splendid colleges was erected; we may have the learning of Europeans in common stock, with an exemption from their burdens, and the highest eminence which others have attained, ought to be the American starting point in the career of national greatness.

And is there any thing impossible, or even particularly difficult, in reducing these ideas to practice? Without expecting to render human nature perfect, or to fix an unalterable standard for living language and literature, may there not be some regulation which will place the decisions of the wise in preference to the blunders of the ignorant? When can a more favorable time be expected, to correct the irregularities yearly multiplying upon us, and becoming more and more embodied with the literature of our country? Why should chance be expected to accomplish, what, from its nature, can result only from well-regulated system? It would indeed be imprudent to attempt too much. Sound discretion will point out a middle course between a wild spirit of innovation and a tame acquiescence in obvious error. Language is too important an instrument in human affairs to have its improvement regarded as useless or trifling. Of all the objects of national identity, affection, and pride, national literature is the most laudable, the most operative, and the most enduring. It is to the scholars of antiquity we owe all we know of their statesmen and heroes, and even their distinctive national existence. In the long train of ages their tables of brass have mouldered away, and their high-wrought columns crumbled to dust. Cities have sunk, and their last vestige been lost. The unconscious Turk half-tills the soil manured with decayed sculpture: but the monuments of genius and learning, more durable than marble and brass, remain the subject of undecreasing admiration and delight. The fame to which great minds aspire, is, to soar above the local contentions of the day, and live to after ages in the esteem of their fellow men. The thought of this animates the patriot's hope and nerves his arm, in danger, toil, and want. Shall it not be the ambition of Americans to proclaim the honor of their benefactors, and transmit the glory of their country to the latest age of the world? We are not here to awe the ignorant by the splendor of royal trappings, but to command the respect of the wise and good by moral greatness. These objects are neither above the capacity, nor beneath the attention, of our countrymen. They are interwoven with our individual happiness, our national character, and our highest interests. When we survey this vast assemblage of States, independent, yet united; competitors in useful improvement, yet members of one great body; the world has never prepared such a theatre for the exhibition of mental and moral excellence: and if the men of all ages, whom we most delight to honor, have made it their chief glory to advance the literature of their respective countries, shall it be degradingly supposed, that, in this favored land, either talents or zeal will be wanting in such a cause? If it is said, that Americans have not paid that attention to education which the subject demanded; it is true; and neither justice nor sound policy requires us to disguise the fact: but has any fatality ordained that the people most interested in diffusing the light of instruction, *must* be degraded in the republic of letters? Much irritation has been produced by the observations of foreign writers upon the learning and intellect of our countrymen. We ought not to waste time in idle complaint on this subject. Is there not in America enough of genius, of scholarship, and of patriotic spirit, if properly organized and conducted, to raise our literary character above the influence of any combination abroad? Shall our numberless blessings remain an unprized possession? Will foreign pens maintain and elevate American character? Is it not time to make a *national* stand in the *moral* world, as the expositors of our own principles, the vindicators of our institutions, and, under a Beneficent Providence, the arbiters of the destiny of unborn millions? Even if, contrary to all human expectation, such an association should fail in its objects, would it not justly be said, '*magnis tamen excidit ausis*'?

It is not intended to bring the society before the public by a premature and unnecessary parade, but to make it known chiefly by its practical good.

The following is a general outline of the institution alluded to, subject of course to such variations as may be thought to increase the prospect of its utility.

To be called "THE AMERICAN ACADEMY OF LANGUAGE AND BELLES LETTRES."

Its prime object is to harmonize and determine the English language; but it will also, according to its discretion and means, embrace every branch of useful and elegant literature, and especially whatever relates to our own country.

To be located in the city of New-York, where accommodations will be furnished free from expense.

To commence with fifty members; maximum number, one hundred and twenty. More than that would lessen the credit of membership, and diminish rather than increase its authority.

Members to be divided into three classes. Resident, who reside in or near New-York; Corresponding, those whose distance prevents their regular attendance; and honorary, those at home or abroad, whom the body may think proper expressly to admit as such: but, perhaps, it will be thought best to make very few honorary members in the United States. The only reason for making a difference between resident and corresponding members, is to give to the latter all practicable privileges and facilities in communicating their opinions, propositions and votes in writing, as a compensation for the difficulties of personal attendance. In questions requiring a ballot, the written opinions and wishes of distant members are taken as votes on all points to which they directly relate. As most of the questions likely to arise will relate to written language, and as few of them will require haste in the decision, there will be a particular fitness in arriving at a general result through the means of the various opinions in writing.

It will be a standing request, though not absolutely required, that each member shall, within one year after his admission, deliver personally, or by writing, a discourse upon some subject relating to language or general literature, or to the situation and interests of the United States.

The Society, when organized, will send a respectful communication to such literary gentlemen in the British dominions as may be thought proper, explaining to them the design of the establishment, and inviting their co-operation. Public policy, as well as general convenience will point out to them the importance of improving our language, facilitating its acquisition to foreigners as well as native citizens, and preserving its uniformity throughout the extensive regions where it now does, or hereafter may prevail.

The *Modus Operandi* should be the result of the joint wisdom of the body, when formed; but almost every disputed point in language, and in ours they are very numerous, may be made a CASE, subjected to rule as far as possible, and brought to a decision, endeavoring to have this decision concurrent between the British and ourselves.

But besides the acknowledged corruptions which prevail in the language of this country, our peculiar institutions and circumstances; our discoveries and improvements, have given rise to a large class of new words, *Americanisms*, if the critics please; necessary to express new things. To adopt and regulate these is not to alter the English language; but only to supply its deficiencies. This is particularly a work of our own. It is also important that attention should be paid to the numerous names of places, French, Spanish and Aboriginal, which are daily becoming incorporated with our literature, and concerning which so much diversity at present exists.

The unprofitable disputes among teachers and the authors of elementary books, who are often very unskilful advocates of their opposing systems, and whose arguments tend only to increase a difference which ought not to exist, would be in a great degree obviated. *The professors of* RHETORIC *and* LOGICK, *in our best universities, should at least agree in spelling the names of the important sciences they teach.* Our numerous youth would then be left free to pursue the straight course to the knowledge of a language which might be, not only strong and copious, but, to a far greater extent, regular and fixed. In addition to other advantages, there cannot be a rational doubt that such an institution may have a beneficial influence in exciting emulation and national concert, in our literature in general, and that many might be drawn to this interesting subject, who are now less profitably and less honorably employed in other pursuits.

The object here contemplated is certainly of sufficient national importance to merit an adequate fund from the public. Should this fail, it would be improper to lay a burdensome expense on the members. Expenditures to any considerable amount are not considered indispensably necessary; for though individuals may not be able to accomplish all that may be desired, much may be done at a moderate actual expense. Twenty-five dollars at the admission of a member, and two dollars a year afterwards, though trifling to some, is considered enough to impose by any imperative rule.

The only objections which have been made to the proposed plan, are on the ground of its practicability. The difficulties alleged are, the superiority of the British in literature; the contempt with which they will look on our institutions and offers of correspondence; the prejudices of our own people in their favor, and the consequent necessity of waiting for them to lead the way. These difficulties, if correct to the extent that some of our citizens seem inclined to admit, show at least the necessity of TRYING to produce a favorable change. If in literature and science we are greatly inferior to any other people, it is not because we are deficient in natural, political, or moral advantages, or have not as strong reasons as any nation ever had to encourage letters; but because we have hitherto neglected any general or systematic means for their advancement. The arguments are fallacious which attempt to find in the circumstances or dispositions of our people any disqualification for the highest mental attainments. American genius and enterprise properly directed, may as well be displayed in the highest walks of literature and science as in any thing else. One difficulty is our scholars, as such, have very little intercourse, and have too long been strangers to each other. *Homo solus imbecilis.* Concert will excite a generous emulation. This, upon the plan proposed, will operate upon a vast and highly reputable field; it will be identified with the national character and the dearest interests of a great and rising people, and cannot fail to produce excellence and command patronage and respect. The bare circumstance of exciting attention to the subject is an important point gained. '*Aude et faciat.*' A colonial servility in literature is as unworthy of our country as political dependence. The necessary limits of this letter forbid a course of reasoning upon the subject: it may be thought proper to give a fuller exposition in a pamphlet form. The general principles explained above are deemed sufficient as the basis of preparatory arrangement.

Among the respectable persons consulted respecting the proposed institution, the sentiment, as far as ascertained, is very general and zealous in its favor. It is designed to carry it into effect with as little delay as sound discretion, in reference to character and advantageous arrangements for a favorable commencement will admit.

The constitution formed for the Society is purposely a very short one, intended chiefly as the basis for a commencement. A body of scholars, associated for the laudable object of promoting the literature of their country, many of them very familiar with public proceedings, will need fewer legal rules than a bank or a state. Whatever may be the deficiencies of this constitution, experience will be more competent to supply them than any wisdom of anticipation.

From the peculiar circumstances of our country, the institution will have no guide in any thing which has gone before; but liberal criticism will make some allowance for the difficulties necessarily attendant on first attempts. The same regular progress will not be expected in an untrodden field as on a well travelled road; but in pursuing a noble object with good intention, there is the consolation that those best qualified to judge are least inclined to condemn. If our beginning is a small one, so was that of the Royal Society of London; and we can have no reason to dread more obloquy from the illiberal, than they received.

Very generous subscriptions, by a number of gentlemen who are not expected to be members, are volunteered, *pro patria*, and there is an encouraging prospect for funds. If among the variety of character in our country, there is a portion too ignorant, or too grovelling, to depart from their own narrow views of immediate gain, it is hoped that, among ten millions of people, there are enough possessed of talent to estimate, and spirit to maintain, an institution whose aim is to promote the best interests and lasting honor of the United States. In such a cause it is deemed unnecessary for the institution to solicit pecuniary aid, farther than by a fair exposition of its principles and objects. The subscriptions are to be a free-will offering upon the altar of our country: yet it will be no less creditable to the society, than just in itself, to hold in grateful remembrance and transmit to future generations, the names of those generous citizens who, by their donations, become at once, the patrons of learning and the vindicators of the American name. It may be one of the good effects of this society to bring patriotic generosity more into fashion, by causing it to be more honored.

In behalf of the Association, Sir, I have the honor to be, Very respectfully and truly yours,   WILLIAM S. CARDELL.

Printed text (DLC: TJ Papers, 218: 38971–2); with second enclosure on verso of last page. Also printed in *Literary and Scientific Repository, and Critical Review* 2 (1 Jan. 1821): 69–76; *Port Folio* 11 (1821): 397–407.

"Quem si non tenuit MAGNIS TAMEN EXCIDIT AUSIS" ("and though he greatly failed, more greatly dared") is from

Phaëthon's epitaph in Ovid, *Metamorphoses*, 2.328 (*Ovid*, trans. Grant Showerman, J. H. Mozley, and Frank Justus Miller, Loeb Classical Library [1914–29; rev. George P. Goold, 1977–79], 3:82–3). HOMO SOLUS IMBECILIS: "A man alone is weak." AUDE ET FACIAT: "Dare and let him do it."

[1] Printed text: "thepresent."

II

Constitution of the American Academy of Language and Belles Lettres

Constitution of the American Academy of Language and Belles Lettres.

———

WE, the subscribers, impressed with the importance of Literature to the moral habits, character and happiness of individuals and nations; wishing to contribute, collectively, our best exertions for the improvement of ourselves and our country; to give to emulation its exciting impulse, on an extended plan; to control its irregularities, and prevent its divisions; to seek as a united body, those advantages, of which, as individuals we feel the want; do hereby agree with each other, to form a Society for Literary purposes, and adopt the following Rules for the government of our Association:

ARTICLE 1.—The name of this Institution shall be "The American Academy of Language and Belles Lettres."

Its objects are, according to its discretion and ability, to collect, interchange and diffuse literary intelligence; to promote the purity and uniformity of the English language; to invite a correspondence with distinguished scholars in other countries speaking this language in common with ourselves; to cultivate throughout our extensive territory, a friendly intercourse among those who feel an interest in the progress of American Literature, and, as far as may depend on well-meant endeavors, to aid the general cause of learning in the United States.

ARTICLE 2.—The Members of this Institution shall be divided into three classes, Resident, Corresponding, and Honorary.

The class of Resident Members shall include those who reside within twenty-five miles of the city New-York. They shall not exceed one-fourth of the limited number of members.

Corresponding and Honorary Members may be chosen in any part of the world.

Members residing at more than twenty-five miles distance, from the city of New-York, may send in writing, their votes or resolutions upon any subject before the Society, and votes thus sent to the Corresponding Secretary, shall be admitted as fully as if such members were personally present.

During six months from the date hereof, each member shall pay, on his admission to this Society, ten dollars; and each member admitted after six months shall pay, on his admission, twenty-five dollars. The yearly dues from each member shall be two dollars; provided, that, from honorary members, and from those who are neither residents nor citizens of the United States, no payment shall be required.

A member forfeits his right to vote if his payments are in arrear, and two years total neglect of the Society shall be considered a renunciation of membership.

The whole number of members of this Institution, shall not exceed one hundred and twenty at any time within two years from the date hereof, nor two hundred at any time in ten years

The admission of members shall be as follows: the candidate shall be proposed, in writing, by a member, at a regular meeting: a vote shall then be taken whether the Secretary shall enter his name: out of five or more candidates thus entered, the Standing Committee shall select one to propose for membership at the next quarterly meeting: if seven-eighths of the votes taken shall be in his favor, he becomes a member, and not otherwise.

The votes or opinions of a member concerning the admission of a candidate, shall on no account be communicated to any person who is not a member.

ARTICLE 3.—The officers of this Institution shall consist of a President, three Vice-Presidents, Corresponding Secretary, Recording Secretary, and Treasurer; together with thirteen Counsellors; of whom the President and Corresponding Secretary shall be two. They shall be chosen by ballot annually, and shall form the Standing Committee.[1] They may meet from time to time by their own appointment, to attend to the concerns of the Institution; to devise and propose such measures as they may think proper to advance its interests; to settle the accounts, and report the state of the funds at each annual meeting. They may appoint a Librarian, and may select from their own number, or other members of the Society, a Committee to superintend the publications of the Institution, whenever in their judgment such measure shall become expedient.

A vacant office may be filled at any quarterly meeting.

ARTICLE 4.—The meetings of this Institution shall be on the first Monday in each of the four seasons of the year. Meetings may take place by adjournment, as often as may be thought proper. The annual election shall be the first Monday in June.

ARTICLE 5.—A member shall be selected to deliver a public address before the Society at each annual meeting. The Standing Committee will make arrangements for this purpose.

ARTICLE 6.—Any addition or amendment may be made to this Constitution, if a proposition in writing for that purpose shall be adopted for consideration, at a regular meeting of the Society, and carried by two-thirds of the votes taken upon it at a subsequent quarterly meeting, and in no other manner.

ARTICLE 7.—This Constitution shall become valid when signed, or, in writing agreed to, by fifty persons, whom the members engaged and the committee appointed for that purpose shall accept.

Done at New-York the 15th day of June, 1820.

Printed text (DLC: TJ Papers, 218: 38972); on verso of final page of first enclosure. Also printed in *Port Folio* 11 (1821): 407–9.

[1] Comma editorially altered to a period.

From Archibald Thweatt

DEAR SIR   Eppington 11 Jany 1821

I have without consulting him, inclosed a letter from my friend Judge Roane: I pray you to comply with his request: finish off your character by saving us again.—   with affectionate attachment
    yrs &c   ARCHIBALD THWEATT
                                                    Wilkinsonville post office
                                                    —my address.—

RC (ViU: TJP-ER); addressed: "Thomas Jefferson esq: Monticello Milton vᵃ"; stamp canceled; franked; postmarked Richmond, 11 Jan.; endorsed by TJ as received 13 Jan. 1821 and so recorded in SJL. Enclosure not found.

To James Madison

DEAR SIR   Monticello Jan. 13. 21.

I return you mr Coxe's letter without saying I have read it. I made out enough to see that it was about the Missouri question, and the printed papers told me on which side he was. could I have devoted a day to it, by interlining the words as I could pick them out, I might have got at more. the lost books of Livy or Tacitus might be worth this. our friend would do well to write less and write plainer.

I am sorry to hear of the situation of your family, and the more so as that species of fever is dangerous in the hands of our medical boys. I am not a physician & still less a quack but I may relate a fact. while I was at Paris, both my daughters were taken with what we formerly called a nervous fever, now a typhus, distinguished very certainly by a thread-like pulse, low, quick and every now and then fluttering. Dr Gem, an English physician, old, & of great experience, & certainly the ablest I ever met with, attended them. the one was about 5. or 6. weeks ill, the other 10. years old was 8. or ten weeks. he never gave them a single dose of physic. he told me it was a disease which tended with certainty to wear itself off, but so slowly that the strength of the patient might first fail if not kept up. that this alone was the object to be attended to[1] by nourishment and stimulus. he forced them to eat a cup of rice, or panada, or gruel, or of some of the farinaceous substance of easy digestion every 2. hours and to drink a glass of Madeira, the youngest took a pint of Madeira a day without feeling it and that for many weeks. for costiveness, injections were used; and he observed that a single dose of medecine taken into the stomach and consuming any of the strength[2] of the patient was often fatal. he was attending a grandson of M^{de} Helvetius, of 10. years old at the same time, & under the same disease. the boy got so low that the old lady became alarmed and wished to call in another physician for consultation. Gem consented. that physician gave a gentle purgative, but it exhausted what remained of strength, and the patient expired in a few hours.

I have had this fever in my family 3. or 4. times since I have lived at home, and have carried between 20. & 30. patients[3] thro' it without losing a single one, by a rigorous observance of Gem's plan and principle. instead of Madeira I have used toddy of French brandy about as strong as Madeira. Brown preferred this stimulus to Madeira. I rarely had a case, if taken in hand early, to last above 1. 2. or 3. weeks, except a single one of 7. weeks, in whom, when I thought him near his last, I discovered a change in his pulse to regularity, and in 12. hours he was out of danger. I vouch for these facts only, not for their theory. you may, on their authority, think it expedient to try a single case before it has shewn signs of danger.

On the portentous question before Congress, I think our Holy alliance will find themselves so embarrassed with the difficulties presented to them as to find their solution only in yielding to Missouri her entrance on the same footing with the other states, that is to say with the right to admit or exclude slaves at her own discretion. ever & affectionately yours   TH: JEFFERSON

P.S. I should have observed that the same typhus fever prevailed in my neighborhood at the same times as in my family, and that it was very fatal in the hands of our Philadelphia Tyros.

RC (DLC: Madison Papers, Rives Collection); postscript added separately to RC and PoC. PoC (DLC); on reused address cover to TJ; edge trimmed; at foot of first page: "Mʳ Madison." Not recorded in SJL. Enclosure: enclosure to Madison to TJ, 7 Jan. 1821.

MY DAUGHTERS: Martha Jefferson (Randolph) and Maria Jefferson (Eppes).

[1] Manuscript: "do."
[2] Manuscript: "strengh."
[3] Manuscript: "patitients."

From Peachy R. Gilmer

Dᴿ Sɪʀ   Liberty 14ᵗʰ Jany 1821

Mrs Trist some time ago presented me a campeachy chair, which had been sent for her, to Monticello and informed me that you had been so obliging, as to offer to send it to Poplar Forest. I have since heard nothing of it and should be glad to get, it, If at Poplar Forest you will do me the favour, to direct Mr Yancey, to deliver it to me—If at Monticello I will request Mr Minor to forward it by his boat, to James River, and have it sent to Lynchburg: I should not have troubled you with any notice of the matter, but presume that amongst concerns of so much more importance, it has been forgotten.

Very Respectfully yr obt servt.   P. R Gɪʟᴍᴇʀ

RC (MHi); endorsed by TJ as received 21 Jan. 1821 and so recorded in SJL. RC (DLC); address cover only; with PoC of TJ to Daniel Brent, 9 Mar. 1821, on verso; addressed: "Thomas Jefferson Esqʳ Monticello By Mail"; franked; inconsistently postmarked Liberty, 13 Jan.

Peachy Ridgeway Gilmer (1779–1836), attorney, was the son of TJ's friend George Gilmer (d. 1795) and brother of Francis W. Gilmer. Born in Albemarle County, he received a private education before attending the College of William and Mary for one session, 1797–98. Gilmer afterwards studied law with his brother-in-law William Wirt, and he was admitted to the Albemarle County bar. In 1803 he married Mary House, the niece of Elizabeth Trist. Three years later Gilmer moved to Henry County and prac-

ticed law. In 1818 he moved to the town of Liberty (later Bedford), where he was admitted to the Bedford County bar and appointed commonwealth's attorney later the same year. Gilmer returned to Albemarle County permanently in 1830. He owned five slaves in 1820 and fifty in 1830 (ViU: Gilmer Family Correspondence, including Gilmer's memoir; John Gilmer Speed, *The Gilmers in America* [1897], 72–91, 151–2; *William and Mary Provisional List*, 19; Woods, *Albemarle*, 207–8, 381, 402; *PTJ*, 42:494–5; *Historical Sketch, Bedford County, Virginia* [1907], 23; DNA: RG 29, CS, Bedford Co., 1820, 1830, Albemarle Co., 1830; *Richmond Whig & Public Advertiser*, 15 Apr. 1836; Washington *Daily National Intelligencer*, 22 Apr. 1836; Albemarle Co. Will Book, 12:187–9).

From Thomas Mann Randolph

DEAR SIR, Richmond Jany 14. 1821

I was informed yesterday that Mr Johnson of the Board of Visitors of the University had become disqualified by "failure to act for the space of one year" Sect. 7. C. 34. Vol. 1. p. 91. General Cocke, who informed me, is of that opinion; and I believe the other Visitors, now here, are likewise disposed to give that construction, as he failed to attend both the "stated meetings" in the last year. My opinion is that he will not be disqualified untill 28th February, the termination of the first year of the four, for which he has been by law appointed. He can attend a meeting by "special call" in time to remedy the defect likely to occurr. I beg leave to recommend the 22^d February, as the day, and that it should be advertised immediately. The Legislature may be up in time, or the Visitors may leave it without inconvenience at that period of the session. The Annual Report of the Literary Fund is to be brought down to Dec. 31. 1820, to give a view of the School branch of the system, the appropriation to which is applicable throughout the Calendar, not the Fiscal year. It only needs copying now. Some of the results are: accession to Capital stock from all sources from Oct. 1st '19. to Dec. 31. 1820. 63.000.54^cts am^t of income for same period 58.293.86. Increase of Permanent Funds, in Paper, since last report, 68.977.49. The Cash in the Treasury on Oct. 1st 1820 was only 36.505.70. The am^t of current expenditure exclusive of investments for the same period 67.855.95.^x of which to University for annuity 19.156.81. to schools 46.584.96. The difference between the Auditors ballance^++ last year to credit of Fund, and the Cash in the Treasury this year is now openly declared to be another defalcation of J^no Preston. It is supposed to have been an error in the settlement of his acct for purchase of stocks during his^1 last year. He presented it in July, the Lieut. Govr & At^ty Gene^l were appointed to examine it; they reported on Dec. 22^d; 5 months after, and omitted a Warrant for 50.000 $. issued to him the preceding year; for which sum it is believed he was credited on the final settlement. I have still hope it may be explained, but such has been the effect of the belief to the contrary, that the Lieut. Govr had 96 votes for removal from the Council, while Martin of Nelson who has not been in Richmond since July, and beged by letter to be removed, had only 103. I have yesterday got pos-

---

^x1279.38 more paid back: fines remitted by law: expences of process &C. the Board expences have been only 834 $ salaries and all.

^++91.619.53.

session of the Journal, and mean to investigate the matter if possible. But no account for purchases of stocks, with prices, has been written in it ever; and my only hope is to find the detached papers, to compare with the Warrants issued. I am of opinion that the friends of the University should only ask leave to make another loan, and to have the period of reimbursement of both made the same with that of the James River Company viz. 20 years. The sum required will still leave nearly half their annuity free and the increase of the Literary Fund will perhaps allow an augmentation of it next year to that amount.

Patsy is at Tuckahoe. I was just seting out to join them at dinner today when the propriety of making the communication concerning Mʳ Johnson, (immediately,) occurred to me. I shall go this evening. She only waits for the Roads to be passible to go home.

    with very sincere and affectionate attachment you &c

                                                    Tʜ M Rᴀɴᴅᴏʟᴘʜ

RC (CSmH: JF); endorsed by TJ as received 19 Jan. 1821 and so recorded in SJL. RC (MHi); address cover only; with PoC of TJ to Peter Minor, 9 Mar. 1821, on verso; addressed: "Thomas Jefferson Esqʳ Monticello near Charlottesville"; franked; postmarked Richmond, 14 Jan.

A member of the University of Virginia Board of Visitors could ʙᴇᴄᴏᴍᴇ ᴅɪsǫᴜᴀʟɪꜰɪᴇᴅ under the provisions of the 25 Jan. 1819 "act for establishing an University" (*The Revised Code of the Laws of Virginia* [Richmond, 1819], 1:91; Poor, *Jefferson's Library*, 10 [no. 572]). The ʟɪᴇᴜᴛ. ɢᴏᴠᴿ & ᴀᴛᵀʸ ɢᴇɴᴇᴸ were Peter V. Daniel and John Robertson, respectively.

In its constitutionally mandated triennial replacement of two members of the Council of State, the Virginia General Assembly voted on 8 Jan. 1821 for the ʀᴇᴍᴏᴠᴀʟ of John M. ᴍᴀʀᴛɪɴ and William Yates (*JHD* [1820–21 sess.], 100).

The stipulations governing the loan to the ᴊᴀᴍᴇs ʀɪᴠᴇʀ ᴄᴏᴍᴘᴀɴʏ were specified in the 17 Feb. 1820 "act to amend the act, entitled 'an act for clearing and improving the navigation of James river,' and for uniting the eastern and western waters, by the James and Kanawha rivers" (*Acts of Assembly* [1819–20 sess.], 45–6). ᴘᴀᴛsʏ: Martha Jefferson Randolph.

[1] Preceding two words interlined.

From Joel Yancey

Dᴇᴀʀ Sɪʀ   Bedford Jan 14ᵗʰ 21

Your letter by Mʳ Randolph[1] I received a few days since, and have particularly observed the contents. in transfering your authority over your plantations here to your grandson, I presume you did not include me even the present year, and that your motive was, to give me an opportunity to withdraw, which I without hesitation did immediately to Mʳ Randolph, and I can asure you, that no man in Virginia will be better pleased, should he succeed here as well as he has done in your estimation in Albemarle, I have done the best I could, and I know I could do no better under the direction of Mr Randolph or any other person, I have long been sensible, that my attention to your affairs, took me too[2] much from my own, and that I have been by no means a gainer by it. I am satisfied also, notwithstanding more might have been done, and Acts of providence have happen^d, that you, when you come to make a[3] comparison, with the appearance of your plantations now—and their producing order five years ago, you will acknowledge, that some improvements have been made here also, (tho not equal to those in Albemarle) independent of the increase and condition of the stock, I promised Mr R. upon his insisting, and saying, that the business, and consequently you, would be injured, by my withdrawing immediately, as he was not provided with a manager, to continue to do what I can for your Interest & happiness till he can procure one which I hope will be with as little delay as possible. My family is still very Ill. scarcly any hopes of the recovery of my Daughter, lost 2 of my best House survants, which I had raised and five more negroes dangerously sick, I remain with the Highest respect

y^r mo ob^t ser^{vt} JOEL YANCEY

RC (MHi); endorsed by TJ as received 21 Jan. 1821 and so recorded in SJL. RC (MHi); address cover only; with PoC of TJ to Andrew Cock, 9 Mar. 1821, on verso; addressed: "Mr Thomas Jefferson Monticello."

[1] Manuscript: "Randolp."
[2] Word interlined.
[3] Manuscript: "to a make a."

From Peter Stephen Chazotte

SIR   Philadelphia 15th Jany 1821.

Permit me again to trouble you, and allow me, to do myself the honour of presenting you with a pamphlet, containing facts and observations, on the policy of immediately introducing the rich culture of coffee, cocoa, vines, olives, capers, almonds, &^{a} &^{a} In East Florida and in the Southern States, and which, I flatter myself, you will do me the honour to accept and give to it a moment's perusal. On a subject of such national importance, and which may raise the United States to the highest degree of power, riches and commerce, the opinion of your Excellency will be received with perfect defference and respect by:

your Excellency,   most humble & obed^t Servt
                                            P^R STEPHEN CHAZOTTE

RC (DLC); dateline at foot of text; endorsed by TJ as received 28 Jan. 1821 and so recorded in SJL; with FC of TJ to Chazotte, 29 Jan. 1821, on verso. RC (DLC); address cover only; with PoC of TJ to Lafayette, 22 Mar. 1821, on verso; addressed: "To his Excellency Thomas Jefferson, Esqʳ Montecello Virginia." Enclosure: Chazotte, *Facts and Observations on the Culture of Vines, Olives, Capers, Almonds, &c. in the Southern States, and of Coffee, Cocoa, and Cochineal, in East Florida* (Philadelphia, 1821).

From Joseph Delaplaine

DEAR SIR,   Philadelphia 15 Janʸ 1821

I had the honour, some considerable since, of sending to you, for your kind acceptance, in the name of the author, a poem by my friend Mʳ Charles Mead.—

From a gentleman of your distinguished[1] character, and well known cultivated taste, I know it Would be gratifying to Mʳ Mead to receive an opinion[2] of this little production, which I hope it will not be very[3] inconvenient to you to give.—

With every assurance of respect & consideration[4] I am D sir Your obed sᵗ   JOSEPH DELAPLAINE

RC (DLC); endorsed by TJ as received 28 Jan. 1821 and so recorded in SJL. RC (ViU: TJP); address cover only; with TJ's Notes on Capitals for University of Virginia Buildings, [after 6 Mar. 1821], on verso; addressed: "Thomas Jefferson Esqʳ Monticello Virginia"; stamp canceled; franked; postmarked Philadelphia, 15 Jan.

[1] Manuscript: "distingushed."
[2] Manuscript: "opinin."
[3] Manuscript: "vey."
[4] Manuscript: "consderation."

To Horace H. Hayden

Monticello Jan. 15. 21.

Th: Jefferson presents his thanks to mr Hayden for his Geological essays, which he has been so kind as to send him. he has indulged himself but little in that branch of science, deterred by the magnitude of the object, and shallowness of our means. yet the pursuit is worthy of encouragement as it may produce other utilities. he prays mr Hayden to accept his respectful salutations.

RC (ViU: TJP); dateline at foot of text; addressed: "Horace H. Hayden esq. Baltimore"; franked; postmarked Charlottesville, 16 Jan.; endorsed by Hayden.

From Thomas Eston Randolph

DEAR SIR   Ashton 15th Jany 1821

By Col° Wood (the Surveyor) I received a letter from Mr Randolph from Richmond dated 11th Jan^y—inclosing the halves of sundry Bank notes amounting to $470.—the other halves he says "are sent under cover to Jefferson through Mr Jefferson"—I presume you must have received that letter on Saturday—it is very important to me to get that mony, it being particularly appropriated, and should have been paid away on Saturday last—   Jefferson is not yet return'd—but I apprehend the Governor's letter to his son, was merely to serve as an envelope for the safe conveyance of those notes—If you will have the goodness to open that letter and send its contents to me (the halves of the notes) it will greatly accomodate me—   It will be satisfactory to you to see Mr Randolph's letter, and I have therefore sent it by my Son—   with respect and affectionate regards

THO^S ESTON RANDOLPH

RC (MHi); dateline at foot of text; addressed: "Thomas Jefferson Esq^e M°Cello"; endorsed by TJ as received 15 Jan. 1821 and so recorded in SJL.

To Daniel Raymond

Monticello Jan. 15. 21.

Th: Jefferson returns his thanks to mr Raymond for the copy of his Thoughts on Political economy which he has been so kind as to send. retired entirely from Political concerns, he reads little now in that line: yet he rejoices to see the public attention drawn to it. no nation has ever suffered more than ours from the want of knolege in that branch of science, as the errors of our public functionaries on that subject have solely produced the revolution in property now taking place. he prays mr Raymond to accept his respectful salutations.

PoC (MHi); on verso of portion of re-used address cover to TJ; dateline at foot of text; mistakenly endorsed by TJ as a letter to "Robert" Raymond and so recorded in SJL.

Daniel Raymond (1786–1849), attorney and author, was born in Connecticut and studied law under Tapping Reeve and James Gould in Litchfield. By 1814 he was a member of the Baltimore city bar, and the next year he was admitted as an attorney and counsellor-at-law of the United States circuit court there. Raymond authored *Thoughts on Political Economy* (Baltimore, 1820; Poor, *Jefferson's Library*, 12 [no. 715]), which he reprinted with variations several times over the next twenty-five years. He opposed the extension of slavery in *The Missouri Question* (Baltimore, 1819), and he ran unsuccessfully as an antislavery candidate from Baltimore for the Maryland House of Delegates in 1825, 1826, 1827, and 1829, and as a Whig from Allegany County in 1836. Raymond moved permanently to Cincinnati by 1842, where he published a newspaper, the *Western Statesman*, until the following year. He continued to practice law until his death (*DAB*; Charles Patrick Neill, *Daniel Raymond: An Early Chapter in the History of Economic Theory in the United States* [1897], esp. p. 14; *Litchfield Law School*, 12; *The Baltimore Directory and Register, for 1814–15* [Baltimore, 1814], 160; *New-York Courier*, 16

May 1815; Baltimore *Genius of Universal Emancipation*, 24 Sept. 1825, 16 Sept. 1826, 28 July 1827, 2 Oct. 1829; *Richmond Enquirer*, 20 Sept. 1836; Cincinnati *Philanthropist*, 10 Sept. 1842; *Western Law Journal*, new ser., 1 [1849]: 527–8).

As he did for John Adams, Raymond presumably had his publisher send TJ directly his *Thoughts on Political Economy* (Adams to Raymond, 8 Feb. 1821 [Lb in MHi: Adams Papers]).

From Thomas B. Parker

SIR   Boston Jany 16th 1821

You doubtless have heard that the citizens of massachusetts deemed it necessary, on the seperation of Maine, to alter and amend their state constitution. Accordingly, delegates were chosen from every town and have met in convention, and have made alterations and amendments which are to be submitted to the people for acceptance or non-acceptance. Two important questions have been decided by this convention, namely, "that the Senate shall be proportioned according to valuation" and "that every taxable person shall pay a tax for the support of publick teachers of religion."

Under the impression, Sir, that you will excuse me, I make bold to ask your opinion on those two questions, as I am in doubt whether it be most consistant to base the senate on valuation or on population. It is said "that taxation and representation should go together" and that "there should be a check on the popular branch.["] Would there not be a sufficient check were the senate proportioned on population and chosen by districts?—If the senate are proportioned on valuation it seems to me to operate unequally; for, on that principle, the county of Suffolk with a population of 43,000 are entitled to six Senators and middlesex county, adjoining, with a population of 50,000, are entitled to only four. As to the second question, has civil goverment a right to interfere with religious matters and to compel men to aid in support of publick teachers of religion? Is it expedient, is it good policy so to do? Is it not a violation of the rights of conscience which every one pretends to hold sacred? I am in doubt, and still more so when I find a man like the venerable Mr Adams, supporting principles which, apparently, are aristocratical and, consequently, opposed to genuine republicanism. I wish to act deliberately and consistantly and therefore do not wish to give my humble support to measures that coincide not with the fundamental principles of republicanism and equal rights. It is my sincere disire that all should equally enjoy their rights and priviliges and be protected and defended by goverment in that enjoyment.

I hope Sir I do not intrude too much upon you sensible as I am of your goodness to oblige. Your opinions if I shall be so happy as to receive them will be considered a favor of much value. Hoping you still continue to enjoy good health

With great Respect I subscribe myself Your ob^t & obliged Hum^l Servt Thomas B Parker

RC (DLC); edge trimmed; endorsed by TJ as received 28 Jan. 1821 and so recorded in SJL. RC (MHi); address cover only; with PoC of TJ to Joseph Wilson, 12 Apr. 1821, on verso; addressed: "To the Hon'le Thomas Jefferson Monticello Virginia."

According to 1810 census data referenced by the delegates to the Massachusetts constitutional convention, the population of the COUNTY OF SUFFOLK was actually 34,381, while that of MIDDLESEX COUNTY was 52,789 (*Journal of Debates and Proceedings in the Convention of Delegates, chosen to revise the Constitution of Massachusetts, Begun and holden at Boston, November 15, 1820, and continued by Adjournment to January 9, 1821* [Boston, 1821], 231). John ADAMS represented Quincy at that convention.

From Arthur S. Brockenbrough

Dear Sir, University V^a Jan 17^h 1821

Captain Perry wishes to raise about $2000.00 to meet his engagements with a Mr Lewis a gentleman of Kentuckey who is now in the neighbourhood waiting on him—the Bursar being without funds he has no chance of obtaining that sum unless you will be so obliging as to give the Bursar a draft on the President & Directors[1] of the Literary fund for the am^t wanted, I have no wish to draw the balance of the annual appropriation as yet, as most of the claims of large am^t against the institu[tion are] paid off except about $1000 due for the last years Negro hire— I am Sir respectfully

your Ob^t Sev^t A. S. Brockenbrough

P.S.

When you can conveniently ride up here should be glad to consult with you on puting up some of foundations on the western street with stone—& that as soon as the weather will permit A.S.B

RC (CSmH: JF); mutilated at seal; addressed: "Thomas Jefferson Esqr Monticello"; endorsed by TJ as received 17 Jan. 1821 and so recorded in SJL.

[1] Manuscript: "Diretors."

From Joseph C. Cabell

Dear Sir, Richmond. 18th Jan: 1821.

I am sorry to inform you that it seems to be the general impression here that we shall be able to effect nothing for the University during the present session. It is with the most heartfelt grief that I acknowledge this to be my own impression. The Reports relative to the Literary Fund are not yet before us, and this delay operates against us. The Governor has done all in his power, but the delay seems to be unavoidable. This serves as an excuse for the inactivity of our friends. I must confess that it seems to me that there is not the desirable zeal, activity, or concert on the occasion. I foresaw this result two weeks ago, but was told I was over anxious, & unnecessarily alarmed. yesterday Mr Morris came to me in the Lobby and with much concern told me all seemed to be going against us in the House of Delegates, & urged the necessity of a meeting among the leading friends of the University. This measure I earnestly pressed a fortnight ago. A time was fixed, but bad weather intervened, & the want of a Report being stated as an impediment, I suffered the measure to lie. We shall get the Report next week: but now gentlemen are alarmed, and tomorrow evening some half dozen of our leading friends are to meet at my Lodgings. In the mean time the state of the fund is understood to be very unfavorable. The annual Revenue falls short of the appropriation: the school fund cannot be touched: & the small surplus of uninvested revenue, & capital, will be a bone of contention. Mr Johnson told me to-day, he saw no prospect of success, from the state of the fund. But I do not despair, and all that I can do, shall be done. I am turning my attention to a future & better Assembly. I shall endeavor to get back Taylor of Chesterfield, (to whom I spoke yesterday) Broadnax of Brunswic, Genl Taylor &^c &^c. We have many [vocal?], or secret, powerful influences to oppose, of which I will say more to you in future. Whilst we do every thing in our power to stem the torrent, it would be well if you & Mr Madison would aid in getting some efficient friends into the next assembly. In haste,

I remain, Dr Sir, faithfully yours. Joseph C. Cabell

RC (ViU: TJP-PC); one word illegible; endorsed by TJ as received 28 Jan. 1821 and so recorded in SJL.

THE GOVERNOR: Thomas Mann Randolph.

To John Wayles Baker

DEAR WAYLES   Monticello Jan. 19. 21.

Yours of Dec. 8. came safely to hand and I was glad to learn you were seated at Columbia. that institution will have sustained a great loss in mr Elliot; but I still think you will be better there than[1] any where else that I know of. with respect to your pursuits I cannot advise them with precision; because I do not know whether you are so far advanced in classic science as that you may withdraw from that school. I may say however in general that the object of the first importance you have to acquire is the French language, and the 2^d Mathematics, Astronomy and Natural philosophy. I do not know how far the rules of your college will permit you to divide your time among the classes which teach these particular articles; but it is so much the right of the parent, and not of the faculty, to say what the student shall learn & what he shall not, that I presume the rules of your college say the same thing. you know my difficulty of writing, and will therefore accept here the assurances of my affectionate attachment

TH: JEFFERSON

PoC (CSmH: JF); on verso of reused address cover of John Steele to TJ, 3 July 1819; at foot of text: "J. W. Baker"; endorsed by TJ.

South Carolina College (later the University of South Carolina) SUSTAINED A GREAT LOSS when Stephen Elliott re-signed its presidency shortly after his election. Thomas Cooper was then chosen as president pro tem, an appointment that later became permanent (New York *American*, 3 Jan. 1821).

[1] Manuscript: "thant."

To James Clarke

DEAR SIR   Monticello Jan. 19. 21.

On my return from Bedford lately I had the misfortune to lose the rod and ratchet wheel which communicates motion from the wheel of the carriage to the Odometer; and I had not been thoughtful enough to note the number of teeth in that wheel, their form, or the size of the wheel. I am obliged therefore to request you to draw for me on paper, or on a card the exact diagram of that wheel [wh]ich,[1] as well as the rod on which it is put, I expect my smith could make. or perhaps you can save me half the doubt by stitching between 2 cards the little wheel itself, which in that way will come safely under a letter cover by the mail. my trial of the machine in going to Bedford, and in returning until the loss, was very satisfactory. accept my friendly & respectful salutation[s]

TH: JEFFERSON

PoC (DLC); on verso of reused address cover to TJ; edge trimmed; adjacent to signature: "Col° James Clarke"; endorsed by TJ; with notation by TJ at foot of text: "Mar. 22. 21. sent a duplicate" (see note to Clarke to TJ, 2 Apr. 1821).

[1] Word faint.

To Francis Eppes

[D]EAR FRANCIS   Monticello Jan. 19. 21.

Your letter of the 1ˢᵗ came safely to hand. I am sorry you have lost mr Elliot; however the kindness of Dʳ Cooper will be able to keep you in the tract of what is worthy of your time.

You ask my opinion of Lᵈ Bolingbroke and Thomas Paine. they were alike in making bitter enemies of the priests & Pharisees of their day. both were honest men; both advocates for human liberty. Paine wrote for a country which permitted him to push his reasoning to whatever length it would go: Lᵈ Bolingbroke in one restrained by a constitution, and by public opinion. he was called indeed a tory: but his writings prove him a stronger advocate for liberty than any of his countrymen, the whigs of the present day. irritated by his exile, he committed one act unworthy of him, in connecting himself momentarily with a prince rejected by his country. but he redeemed that single act by his establishment of the principles which proved it to be wrong. these two persons differed remarkably in the style of their writing, each leaving a model of what is most perfect in both extremes of the simple and the sublime. no writer has exceeded Paine in ease and familiarity of style; in perspicuity of expression, happiness of elucidation, and in simple and unassuming language. in this he may be compared with Dʳ Franklin: and indeed his Common sense was, for awhile, believed to have been written by Dʳ Franklin, and published under the borrowed name of Paine, who had come over with him from England. Lᵈ Bolingbroke's, on the other hand, is a style of the highest order: the lofty, rythmical, full-flowing eloquence of Cicero. periods of just measure, their members proportioned, their close full and round. his conceptions too are bold and strong, his diction copious, polished and commanding as his subject. his writings are certainly the finest samples in the English language of the eloquence proper for the senate. his political tracts are safe reading for the most timid religionist,[1] his philosophical, for those who are not afraid to trust their reason with discussions of right and wrong.

You have asked my opinion of these persons, and, <u>to you</u>, I have given it freely. but, remember, that I am old, that I wish not to make new enemies, nor to give offence to those who would consider a difference of opinion as sufficient ground for unfriendly dispositions. God bless you, & make you what I wish you to be.

TH: JEFFERSON

PoC (DLC); salutation faint; lower corner torn away, with two words rewritten by TJ; at foot of first page: "Francis Eppes."

Eppes's LETTER of 1 Jan. 1821, the address cover only of which has been found, is recorded in SJL as received 11 Jan. from Columbia (RC in MHi; with PoC of TJ to Bernard Peyton, 16 Mar. 1821, on verso; addressed: "Thomas Jefferson Esqr near Charlottesville Albemarle virginia";

stamped; postmarked Columbia, S.C., 2 Jan.).

The PRINCE REJECTED BY HIS COUNTRY was James Francis Edward Stuart, nicknamed "the Old Pretender," a claimant to the British throne in whose shadow government Henry St. John, Viscount Bolingbroke, served as secretary of state, 1715–16 (*ODNB*).

[1] Manuscript: "religinist."

To John Wayles Eppes

DEAR SIR   Mon[ticello] Jan. 19. 21.

Your favor of the 7th has been recieved & I sincere[ly] congratulate you on the resolution of all your complaints into a regular & fixed gout. a severe fit now [and][1] then with clear intervals of health is certainly preferable to a perpetual half sickness. it will relieve you too from medecine, as we all know there is none for the gout but patience and flannel.

I really think your allowance to Francis is abundant. of the expence of clothing I am not a judge; but experience has reduced to an axiom with teachers that with students their progress in learning is in the inverse proportion of their pock[et]-money. yet I think Francis will be more likely to lay out his surplus in books than in objects of dissipation. I am sorry they hav[e] lost Elliot; but the favor in which he seems to be with Dr Cooper, will fill all his time with what is useful. whether we shall open at the end of this year or 7. years hence will depend on the determination of the legislature to give us what is wanting, or throw it away on an impracticable plan of primary schools.   We have a severe winter. 33.I. of snow have already fallen, and the thermometer was this morning at $12\frac{1}{2}$.   ever & affectionately yours   TH: JEFFERSON

PoC (CSmH: JF); on verso of a reused address cover from Thomas Appleton to TJ; dateline faint; edge trimmed; at foot of text: "J. W. Eppes esq."; endorsed by TJ.

Eppes's missing FAVOR OF THE 7TH Jan. 1821 is recorded in SJL as received four days later from Mill Brook.

[1] Omitted word editorially supplied.

From James Monroe

DEAR SIR   Washington Jany 19. 1821

m^r Lawrance & m^r Jones, two young gentlemen of new york, lately presented to me by m^r Sandford a Senator from that State, & otherwise highly recommended, intending to visit you and m^r madison, I have taken the liberty to give them this introduction. It is their object to visit Europe in the Spring, & I am satisfied, that it will afford them much pleasure, to convey any letters there for you, or to be in any respect useful to you. I hear with great interest, through many channels, that you continue to enjoy very good health. with my best wishes & affectionate regards, I am dear Sir

your friend & servant   JAMES MONROE

RC (MHi); endorsed by TJ as received 25 Jan. 1821 and so recorded (with additional bracketed notation: "Lawrance & Jones") in SJL.

William Beach Lawrence (1800–81), attorney, public official, and author, was born in New York City. He graduated from Columbia College (later Columbia University) in 1818 and studied law the following year under Tapping Reeve and James Gould in Litchfield, Connecticut. Lawrence visited Monticello in 1821 before spending two years in Europe, after which he practiced law in New York City. President John Quincy Adams appointed him secretary of the American legation to Great Britain in 1826, and the following year he was made chargé d'affaires at London. Lawrence returned in 1829 to New York, where he continued to practice law and served as a trustee of the College of Physicians and Surgeons (later merged with Columbia University), 1837–51, and first vice president of the New-York Historical Society, 1840–44. In 1850 he moved to Newport, Rhode Island. Lawrence was elected lieutenant governor of Rhode Island in 1851, and the next year he became acting governor until the incumbent's term expired later in 1852. He lectured and wrote widely on legal matters, with one of his best-known works being an annotated edition of Henry Wheaton's *Elements of International Law* (1855; 2d ed., 1863). Lawrence died during a visit to New York City for medical treatment (*DAB*; *The Biographical Cy-*clopedia of Representative Men of Rhode Island [1881], 287–9; Milton Halsey Thomas, *Columbia University Officers and Alumni, 1754–1857* [1936], 69, 133; *Litchfield Law School*, 19; *JEP*, 3:543, 545, 4:52 [14, 19 Dec. 1826, 3 Feb. 1830]; Robert W. G. Vail, *Knickerbocker Birthday: A Sesqui-Centennial History of the New-York Historical Society, 1804–1954* [1954], 76, 382, 476; *New-York Times*, 26 Mar. 1881).

John Quentin Jones (1803–78), merchant and banker, was born in New York City and graduated from Columbia College (later Columbia University) in 1815. Two years later he studied law under Reeve and Gould in Litchfield, and he was listed as an attorney in New York City in 1820. The following year Jones visited Monticello before traveling to Europe. He eventually returned to New York and worked as a merchant, 1833–38. He was appointed factory agent of New York's Chemical Bank in 1834 and cashier in 1839. When the bank was rechartered in 1844, Jones became its president, holding the position until his death. He also served as chairman of the Clearing House of New York City, 1865–71. In his will Jones left specific bequests amounting to $145,000, in addition to other real and personal estate and stock shares (Thomas, *Columbia University Officers and Alumni*, 130; *Litchfield Law School*, 18; *Mercein's City Directory, New-York Register and Almanac* [New York, 1820], 265; *New-York Evening Post*, 11 Apr. 1821; *Longworth's New York Directory* [1833]: 355;

[1838]: 358; *History of the Chemical Bank, 1823–1913* [1913], esp. 87–92; William J. Gilpin and Henry E. Wallace, *Clearing House of New York City: New York Clearing House Association, 1854–1905* [1904], 47, 50; *New-York Times*, 3 Jan. 1878; New York Co. Surrogate's Court Will Book, 257:95–8).

Monroe wrote a similar letter of introduction to James Madison on this day (Madison, *Papers, Retirement Ser.*, 2:232).

To Archibald Thweatt

DEAR SIR   Monticello Jan. 19. 21.

I duly recieved your favor of the 11th covering Judge Roane's letter, which I now return. of the kindness of his sentiments expressed towards myself I am highly sensible; & could I believe that my public services had merited the approbation he so indulgently bestows, the satisfaction I should derive from it would be reward enough. to his wish that I would take a part in the transactions of the present day I am sensible of my incompetence. for first I know little about them, having long withdrawn my attention from public affairs, and resigned myself with folded arms to the care of those who are to care for us all. and, next, the hand of time pressing heavily on me, in mind as well as body, leaves to neither sufficient energy to engage in public contentions. I am sensible of the inroads daily making by the federal, into the jurisdiction of it's co-ordinate associates the state-governments. the legislative and executive branches may sometimes err, but elections and dependance will bring them to rights. the judiciary branch is the instrument which working, like gravity, without intermission is to press us at last into one consolidated mass. against this I know no one who, equally with Judge Roane himself, possesses the power & the courage, to make resistance; and to him I look, and have long looked, as our strongest bulwark. if Congress fails to shield the states from dangers so palpable and so imminent, the states must shield themselves and meet the invader foot to foot. this is already half done by Col° Taylors book: because a conviction that we are right accomplishes half the difficulty of correcting wrong. this book is the most effectual retraction of our government to it's original principles which has ever yet been sent by heaven to our aid. every state in the Union should give a copy to every member they elect as a standing instruction, and ours should set the example.   Accept with mrs Thweatt the assurance of my affectionate & respectful attachment.

TH JEFF[ERSON]

PoC (DLC); signature faint; at foot of text: "Archibald Thweatt esq." Enclosure: enclosure to Thweatt to TJ, 11 Jan. 1821.

From James T. Austin

Sir   Boston 20^{th1} January 1821

The kindness with which you have noticed some former communications, induces me to submit the enclosed remarks to the disposal of your leisure—

I need not say that when a practising Lawyer finds it necessary to offer an opinion at variance with the interests of high officers in his profession he lays himself liable to some recrimination—

I trust the opinions here advanced are not such as are in opposition to the results of your experience—At any rate they offer me an occassion to repeat the declaration of

My highest consideration And profound Respect

JAMES T AUSTIN

RC (DLC); dateline beneath signature; at foot of text: "Hon⁰ T Jefferson"; endorsed by TJ as received 8 Feb. 1821 and so recorded in SJL. Enclosure not found.

[1] Reworked from "21."

From John R. Cotting

Dear Sir   Boston Jan 20 1821

Your liberal mind and the high estimation in which you[1] are held by the literary & philosophical World, and your great experience in scientific pursuits[2] will I presume render an apology unecessary for troubling you with this address. Inclosed I send you a prospectus of a new work the only one of the kind ever proposed for publication in America. A work which has long been wanted by the scientific public, and is almost indispensable to the readers of modern travels and history. I have endeavoured to render it as perfect as the progressive state of chemistry and natural history will permit; in this I have been assisted by the excellant professor of chemistry in Harvard University. The work has already received considerable patronage by all classes of citizens in this section of the country. A specimen[3] of the type, form and paper accompanies the prospectus. My object in writing to you, is to avail myself of your superior advice in regard to the manner of treating the subjects, and also of any information you may please to afford me with regard to the mineral productions of our own country especially in your section of it, concerning which, I know of no man so well calculated to gratify me. Any hints or observations you may see fit to furnish me will be gratefully received and shall be duly noticed in the work.

Wishing you every blessing and comfort to which a mind devoted to science and the good of his fellow citizens is entitled,

I am With sentiments of much esteem and respect Your most devoted and very humble Sirvant^2 J. R COTTING.^{3}

RC (MHi); endorsed by TJ as received 5 Feb. 1821 and so recorded in SJL. RC (MHi); address cover only; with PoC of TJ to Craven Peyton, 5 Mar. 1821, on verso; addressed: "Hon. Thos Jefferson Monticello. Virginia"; franked; postmarked Boston, 22 Jan.

John Ruggles Cotting (1784–1867), educator and geologist, changed his surname from "Cutting" early in adulthood. He was born in Acton, Massachusetts, and apparently attended Harvard University briefly before graduating from Dartmouth College in 1802. Cotting was ordained a Congregational minister in 1807 and pastored a church in Waldoborough (later Waldoboro), Maine, before resigning in 1811 and becoming an Episcopalian. He spent the next twenty-four years teaching in a number of different schools in Massachusetts and lecturing on the physical sciences. Cotting taught chemistry for one term at the Berkshire Medical Institution, 1824–25, and served as an instructor at Amherst Academy while editing the *Chemist and Meteorological Journal* at Amherst College in 1826. He published *A Synopsis of Lectures on Geology* in 1835, and later that year he moved to Augusta, Georgia, where he conducted a geological survey of Burke and Richmond counties. Cotting's report on his survey having gained the attention of state authorities, in 1836 he was appointed geologist of Georgia and commissioned to conduct a survey of the entire state. Delays in the work and waning legislative support led to the termination of his official position in 1840, but the General Assembly allowed Cotting to retain the uncompensated title of state geologist. He published *An Essay on the Soils and Available Manures of the State of Georgia . . . founded on a geological and agricultural survey* in 1843 but never received enough support to publish the report of

his full survey. Neither the report nor Cotting's field notes survive. He moved permanently in about 1840 to Milledgeville, Georgia, where he operated a female academy beginning in 1842. Cotting was one of the first members of the Association of American Geologists in 1840 and of its successor, the American Assocation for the Advancement of Science, eight years later. He hosted the British geologist Charles Lyell during the latter's 1846 visit to Milledgeville. In 1860 Cotting's combined real estate and personal property were valued at $350 (Lester D. Stephens, "John Ruggles Cotting and the First State Geological Survey of Georgia," *Georgia Historical Quarterly* 97 [2013]: 296–321; *General Catalogue of Dartmouth College and the associated schools, 1769–1925* [1925], 108; DNA: RG 29, CS, Ga., Baldwin Co., 1850, 1860; Milledgeville *Southern Recorder*, 15 Oct., 5 Nov. 1867; gravestone inscription in Memory Hill Cemetery, Milledgeville).

The enclosed PROSPECTUS and accompanying sample have not been found. Late the previous year Mathew Carey & Son took subscriptions in Philadelphia for Cotting's *Dictionary of Chemistry and Mineralogy*, which was projected to run to 750 pages and cost $3 for subscribers and $4 for nonsubscribers. The advertisement included the endorsement of John Gorham, Harvard's PROFESSOR OF CHEMISTRY (Philadelphia *Franklin Gazette*, 30 Nov. 1820). The work seems never to have been printed, but Cotting soon published a 420-page volume entitled *An Introduction to Chemistry, with Practical Questions designed for beginners in the science. from the Latest and Most Approved Authors. to which is added A Dictionary of Terms* (Boston, 1822).

^{1} Manuscript: "your."
^{2} Manuscript: "pusuits."
^{3} Manuscript: "speimen."

Account with Thomas G. Watkins

[after 20 Jan. 1821]

Mr Jefferson

      To Th G Watkins   D^r

1820

June	28.	Prescription for negro woman [Doley?]	$2.00
Sep^r	11.	Call and presc^n negro Criddy	2.00
	15.	Presc^n &^{c} when at Monticello (negro Wom^n)	2.00
Nov^r	7.	visit last evenning & attention to y^r legs & presc^n & preparing medc^n for stomach }	3.00

1821

Jan^y	1.	Riding by Tufton to see negro Gill	1.00
	20.	Calling by & extracting a tooth for you	2.00
			$12.00

MS (MHi); written by Watkins on one side of a small scrap; undated; one word illegible; with note by TJ at foot of text: "July 28. sent by Dr Watson 12.D." Probably enclosed in Watkins to TJ, 7 June 1821.

From John M. Perry

S$_{IR}$ university. Jan. 21. 1821

I have to beg the favour of you to Reconsider the proposition made by the proctor last wednesday m^r Lewis has become quite impatient to get home in truth it has become[1] the Subject of Conversation for the neighbourhood—that he is waiting here solely on me—if you Can without injorey to the univer'ty permit the sum <u>wanting for him</u> to be drawn—its accomodation to me would be beyond Calculation I do not wish Sir, to be understood in any wey as Complaining to you I have no Cause of Complaint of any sort earthly

    Respectfully Sir y^r ob Stet   J$_{OHN}$ M. P$_{ERRY}$

RC (CSmH: JF); addressed: "Thomas Jefferson Esquire Monticello"; endorsed by TJ as received 21 Jan. 1821 and so recorded in SJL.

[1] Manuscript: "beome."

To John M. Perry

DEAR SIR   Monticello Jan. 21. 21.

When I gave the order for the last of the loan-money I understood it would discharge every thing we owe, & actually demandable, and mr Brockenbrough did not say that what you request was of that character. still I would not have hesitated to authorise an advance if there[1] were any monies left of the former funds. but the annuity of this year is meant by the Visitors for a particular application which I do not think myself at liberty to interfere with, unless I could see some determination of the legislature to supply other funds. I really regret the obstacle to your request, and that I am not free to remove it. Accept assurances of my esteem & respect.

TH: JEFFERSON

PoC (DLC); at foot of text: "Capt [1] Manuscript: "their."
Perry"; endorsed by TJ.

To Thomas Mann Randolph

DEAR SIR   Monticello Jan. 21. 21.

Our last mail brought us your favor of the 14th. the case of mr Johnson is thus. his last attendance was on the 4th of Oct. 1819. at the meeting of Apr. 1820. he was prevented by the preceding[1] day being one of very close snow. at our meeting of Oct. 1820. he was confined in Amherst by a dangerous illness. this was known to the board and became a matter of consultation; and the words of the law being that 'on failure of a visitor[2] to act for the space of one year, the Governor with the advice of council shall appoint a successor' they were of opinion (unanimously I believe) that the case had arisen as to mr Johnson, altho' entirely without voluntary default, and they instructed me to apply for a reappointment, all of us considering that his loss to the board would be very serious. as there was time yet before the next meeting, I let the matter lie, until he called on me the other day when I mentioned it to him. he had not before been apprised of the terms of the law; and it is now my duty to ask his reappointment. I am aware that the loose use of the word <u>successor</u> in the law might be understood to exclude the person failing.[3] I know it was not the intention in drawing it (because I drew it myself) nor can I suppose the legislature had such intention. the word was used as the proper one in the other two cases of death & removal and importing nothing

[560]

more in the other case than a new commission. and as this case must frequently happen, I think we had better at once adopt a liberal construction best suited to practice. but if yourself & the board should think yourselves obliged to adhere to the letter of the law, I would[4] propose that a commission be given to any body, who will first accept it and resign the next day, when a 2^d commission may be given to mr Johnson as his successor. this will only give the trouble of two commissions instead of one to produce the same effect: altho' I think myself that the other is quite within the rules of construction, which allow much weight to convenience and a rational presumption of the intention of the legislature.

With respect to the loan you suggest, three of our colleagues being on the spot and so much better judges of the circumstances which govern the case, that I shall acquiesce with perfect satisfaction in whatever they may do. accept the assurance of my great affection & respect.   TH: JEFFERSON

P.S. Jan. 22. I kept my letter open in hopes that I might announce to you Martha's arrival the last night when we thought we might expect her. but she is not arrived, nor have we any information later than your letter of the 14th

Jefferson got back from Bedford the night before last. he was gone there when the letter to him under cover to me was recieved. on application by mr T. E. Randolph I broke the seal and gave to him the sealed paper within, which was addressed to him.

RC (DLC); postscript on a separate scrap; addressed: "His Excellency Thomas M. Randolph Govr of Virginia Richmond"; franked; postmarked Charlottesville, 23 Jan.; endorsed by Randolph as received 30 Jan. PoC (DLC); on reused address cover of William J. Coffee to TJ, 4 July 1819, not found (see note to Bernard Peyton to TJ, 28 July 1819); lacking postscript; endorsed by TJ.

THREE OF OUR COLLEAGUES: James Breckinridge, Joseph C. Cabell, and Chapman Johnson.

[1] RC: "precedin." PoC: "preceding."
[2] Preceding three words interlined.
[3] Preceding three words interlined and reworked from "him," also interlined.
[4] Manuscript: "woud."

From Robert H. Rose

SIR,   Silver Lake, P^a Jan 21. 1821.

I do myself the honour of sending you the enclosed Address, hastily composed and delivered at the Organisation of an Agricultural Society, in a new County. You have furnished the author with a theme for his eulogium; and have exhibited to Statesmen an example worthy of their imitation, and greatly to the honour of Agriculture.

I am, Sir with great respect
Your obed^t & humble serv^t ROB^T H ROSE

RC (MHi); addressed: "Thos. Jefferson Esq late Pres^t of the U.S. Monticello Virginia"; franked; endorsed by TJ as received 8 Feb. 1821 and so recorded in SJL. Enclosure: Rose, *An Address delivered before the Agricultural Society of Susquehanna County, At its Organization, December 6, 1820* (Montrose, Pa., 1820; reprinted in Baltimore *American Farmer* 3 [1821]: 101–4), emphasizing the importance of scientific knowledge in successful agriculture; encouraging farmers to maintain attractive homes and gardens; advising against the indiscriminate clearing of timber; urging farmers to procure the best agricultural implements, seeds, and livestock; recommending that more attention be paid to plowing and manuring farmland; touting the benefits of domestic manufacturing; and expressing the hope that the Pennsylvania legislature will support internal improvements.

Robert Hutchinson Rose (1776–1842), land developer, was born in Chester County, Pennsylvania, and spent the winters of his youth in Philadelphia. He received a medical education, though he apparently did not practice in that field. Rose served as agent of the Susquehannah Company, 1803–04. Around that time he reportedly also visited Italy. Rose wrote several poems that appeared in the *Port Folio* between 1802 and 1805, and

he later published a volume of poetry, *Sketches in Verse* (Philadelphia, 1810). In 1809 he bought a large tract of about one hundred thousand acres in Pennsylvania in a section of Luzerne County that became Susquehanna County the next year. Rose's property included the township of Silver Lake. He encouraged the settlement and development of the area thereafter and served as the town's postmaster from 1810 until his death at his home in Silver Lake. In 1817 Rose was elected president of the newly established Silver Lake Bank, and in 1820 he became the president of the Agricultural Society of Susquehanna (Emily C. Blackman, *History of Susquehanna County, Pennsylvania* [1873], 445–51, 457–9, 544–5; Rhamanthus M. Stocker, *Centennial History of Susquehanna County, Pennsylvania* [1887], esp. 28, 196, 500–1, 505; NBiSU: Rose Family Papers; Julian P. Boyd and Robert J. Taylor, eds., *The Susquehannah Company Papers* [1930–71], vol. 11; Randolph C. Randall, "Authors of the *Port Folio* Revealed by the Hall Files," *American Literature* 11 [1940]: 406–7; *Lancaster Journal*, 27 Jan. 1817; Philadelphia *North American and Daily Advertiser*, 25 Mar. 1842).

On this day Rose also sent a copy of the enclosure to James Madison (Madison, *Papers, Retirement Ser.*, 2:250).

To John Adams

Monticello Jan. 22. 21.

I was quite rejoiced, dear Sir, to see that you had health & spirits enough to take part in the late convention of your state for revising it's constitution, and to bear your share in it's debates and labors. the amendments of which we have as yet heard prove the advance of liberalism in the intervening period; and encourage a hope that the human mind will some day get back to the freedom it enjoyed 2000 years ago. this country, which has given to the world the example of physical liberty, owes to it that of moral emancipation also. for, as yet, it is but nominal with us. the inquisition of public opinion overwhelms in practice the freedom asserted by the laws in theory.

Our anxieties in this quarter are all concentrated in the question What does the Holy alliance, in and out of Congress, mean to do with us on the Missouri question? and this, by the bye, is but the name of the case. it is only the John Doe or Richard Roe of the ejectment. the real question, as seen in the states afflicted with this unfortunate population, is Are our slaves to be presented with freedom and a dagger? for if Congress has a power to regulate the conditions of the inhabitants of the states, within the states, it will be but another exercise of that power to declare that all shall be free. are we then to see again Athenian and Lacedemonian confederacies? to wage another Peloponnesian war to settle the ascendancy between them? or is this the tocsin of merely a servile war? that remains to be seen: but not I hope by you or me. surely they will parley awhile, and give us time to get out of the way. What a Bedlamite is Man!—But let us turn from our own uneasinesses to the miseries of our Southern friends. Bolivar & Morillo it seems, have come to a parley with dispositions at length to stop the useless effusions of human blood in that quarter. I feared from the beginning that these people were not yet sufficiently enlightened for self-government; and that after wading through blood & slaughter, they would end in military tyrannies, more or less numerous. yet as they wished to try the experiment, I wished them success in it. they have now tried it, and will possibly find that their safest road will be an accomodation with the mother country, which shall hold them together by the single link of the same chief magistrate, leaving to him power enough to keep them in peace with one another, and to themselves the essential powers of self government and self-improvement, until they shall be sufficiently trained by education and habits of freedom to walk safely by themselves. representative government, native functionaries, a qualified negative on their laws, with a previous security by compact for freedom of commerce, freedom of the press, habeas corpus, and trial by jury, would make a good beginning. this last would be the school in which their people might begin to learn the exercise of civic duties as well as rights. for freedom of religion they are not yet prepared. the scales of bigotry are not sufficiently fallen from their eyes to accept it for themselves individually, much less to trust others with it. but that will come in time, as well as a general ripeness to break entirely from the parent stem.— you see, my dear Sir, how easily we prescribe for others a cure for their difficulties, while we cannot cure our own. we must leave both,

I believe, to heaven, and wrap ourselves up in the mantle of resignation, and of that friendship of which I tender to you the most sincere
assurances.   TH: JEFFERSON

RC (MHi: Adams Papers); addressed: SCALES . . . FALLEN FROM THEIR EYES
"President Adams Montezillo Quincy";   references the Bible (Acts 9.18).
franked; postmarked Charlottesville, 23
Jan. PoC (DLC).

From Thomas Law

DEAR SIR—   Washington Jany 23 1821—
     m^r Crommelin & Mr Van Lenwep two very intelligent & respect-
able travellers will present to you some hasty remarks published in
the Washington Gazette & formed into a pamphlet by Mr Dupont
one of the most amiable judicious & useful adopted citizens—
     Your polite attention to the Bearers which they would be sure of
even without an introduction will oblige
     y^{rs} with unabated
     Esteem regard & respect   THOMAS LAW—

RC (DLC); dateline at foot of text; en-   his own until his death in Arnhem, the
dorsed by TJ as received 31 May 1821   Netherlands (Johannes H. Scheffer, ed.,
and so recorded in SJL; with additional   *Genealogie van het Geslacht Crommelin*
notation by TJ beneath endorsement: "by   [1879], 123; NeAA: Crommelin Family
Van Lenwep." RC (ViU: TJP); address   Papers; *Baltimore Patriot & Mercantile Ad-*
cover only; with PoC of TJ to James E.   *vertiser*, 11 May 1821; Providence *Rhode-*
Heath, 15 Aug. 1821, on verso; addressed: *Island American, and General Advertiser,*
"To Thomas Jefferson Esqr Montecello."   18 May 1821; Providence *Rhode Island*
                                               American, 10 Dec. 1824; *Letter and Ac-*
     Claude Daniel Crommelin (1795–1859),   *companying Documents from the Hon.*
merchant, was born into a prominent   *Richard Rush to Joseph Gales, Esq., Mayor*
Dutch mercantile family in Amsterdam.   *of the City of Washington; respecting the*
In 1819 he traveled to the United States   *Loan of a Million and a Half of Dollars,*
on behalf of his family's firm, Daniel   *negotiated by the former, in Europe, for the*
Crommelin & Sons. American newspa-   *said city and the towns of Georgetown and*
pers announced in May 1821 that, with   *Alexandria, under the authority of An Act*
a small group of European men that in-   *of Congress of the United States, passed on*
cluded Jacob van Lennep, Crommelin   *the 24th of May, 1828* [1830], esp. 153;
was "on a visit to the western part of the   Ne: Nederlandsche Bank Papers; Joost
United States." He subsequently returned   Jonker, *Merchants, Bankers, Middlemen:*
to Amsterdam. In 1829 Crommelin was   *The Amsterdam Money Market During*
named as a trustee when his firm loaned   *the First Half of the 19th Century* [1996],
$1.5 million to the cities constituting the   39–41, 194–200).
District of Columbia. He served as a di-   Jacob van Lennep (1769–1855), mer-
rector of the Nederlandsche Bank, 1838–   chant and diplomat, was born into a
49, and as one of its commissioners,   family of Dutch traders in Smyrna (later
1851–59. In 1854 Crommelin dissolved   Izmir, Turkey). In 1784 he joined the
the family firm he had come to head but   firm of his father, David George van Len-
remained in the mercantile business on   nep, and he took over the concern's man-

agement in 1792. Five years later van Lennep established the firm of Jacob van Lennep & Company, which he directed until 1848. The company traded in a variety of merchandise, including opium. Van Lennep made business trips to Europe and the United States in 1790, 1815–17, and 1819–22, and in 1823 his firm gave the city of Boston an Egyptian mummy as a token of appreciation for the profitable trade conducted there. In 1825 van Lennep was named the Dutch consul general at Smyrna, a position he held until his death in that city (Henrick S. van Lennep, *Genealogie van de Familie van Lennep* [2007], 332, 338–40; Jan Schmidt, *From Anatolia to Indonesia: Opium Trade and the Dutch Community* *of Izmir, 1820–1940* [1998], esp. 87–108; *Boston Daily Advertiser*, 3 May 1823; Washington *Daily National Journal*, 2 Aug. 1826; gravestone inscription in Alsancak Dutch Protestant Cemetery, Izmir).

The PAMPHLET was likely *An Address to the People of the United States, drawn up by order of the National Institution for the Promotion of Industry, established in June, 1820* (New York, 1820; possibly Poor, *Jefferson's Library*, 11 [no. 689]), which was also printed in installments in the *City of Washington Gazette*, 23, 27, 28 Dec. 1820. Eleuthère I. du Pont de Nemours sat on the board of the new institution (*New-York Statesman*, 27 June 1820).

From Joseph C. Cabell

DEAR SIR,   Richmond 25 Jan: 1821.

Since the date of my letter of 18th ins[t] the meeting therein alluded to has taken place. I find Mr Johnson[1] averse to any expression of opinion on the subject of the Ancient[2] charters. Our meeting broke up without any valuable result. The want of a Report on the state of the Literary fund, retards our movements.[3] There is a current constantly setting against us on Richmond Hill.[4] It scatters discord in our ranks, & undermines the zeal of our friends. Preston's last deficiency falls on the literary fund, and augments our difficulties. The counties that neglected to draw, insist pertinaciously on their "equal rights." That claim I suspect will nearly exhaust the surplus on hand. Even some of our friends, Johnson, Breckenridge &[c] think we should not touch the principal of the fund: & the balance still due from the Gen[l] Gov[t] forms a part of the principal. The annual Revenue falls short of the annual appropriation. There is no prospect that we shall be able to get into the poor school fund. In this situation, hemmed in by difficulties & obstacles on all sides, one only prospect opens itself to my view. I presume that it is in every case proper to finish the buildings. To get the necessary funds for this object, must be our polar star. For this purpose, we must get our credit for the existing loan of $60,000, put on one of the two bases which I proposed last spring: and obtain a power to make another loan of $50,000, on similar terms. This would give us the buildings & a clear income of about $7000. Future assemblies must be looked to for the balance. I spoke of this plan to Genl Breckenridge & Mr Johnson, yesterday: & spoke of it as a dernier resort. They seemed to approve it. We shall first, however, ask for further funds in some shape or other. Governor Randolph told me some time since, we should have to content ourselves with this. He has gone into the country & I presume will see you before his return.

I will now, touch upon a subject[5] that has engaged my thoughts for a long time past, and been often mentioned to some of my intimate friends. It is that of my withdrawing altogether from public life[6] at the end of my present term of service. Genl Cocke will be with you shortly, and will explain to you the grounds on which I think, with some of my friends, that this measure becomes proper. I pauze to give my friends an opportunity to cast about for a safe depository for the great interests of our district. A Mr Claiborne of Nelson has notified me of his intention to offer. At first I thought it might be improper to retire under the imputations that might be made: & so expressed myself to my friend Governor Randolph. But on further reflection & on consultation with my brother & Genl Cocke, I do not think <u>that</u> circumstance should have the least weight with me. <u>All other reasons</u> apart, I do not suppose that a canvass could be dispensed with, and such is the weakness of my breast, that to ride from Court House to Court House, making speeches to large crouds, exposed to the rigors of the season, might carry me to the grave, or bring on me further & more distressing symptoms of pulmonary affection.[7] Do not suppose, I beseech you, that my feelings & opinions have undergone any change. On the contrary, in retiring, I will do all in my power to bring in such persons as may be calculated to effectuate in future your great views of literary improvement. In the course which I contemplate, I have no view or wish to go to Congress, or into any other public station. I have been here 13 winters. My object[8] now is domestic, rural, & literary leisure. I thank my friends in Albemarle, & the district, but above all yourself, for the confidence so long bestowed on me. The little share which I have had in promoting the establishment of the University & in seconding your views on that subject, will always constitute one of the most agreeable reflections of my life. May you succeed to the utmost of your wishes will ever be my constant & fervent prayer. But that great & valuable institution, I hope, is now on a safe & permanent footing: and altho' its endowment is for the present too small, yet it must & will ultimately triumph over all its enemies.

I presume it is unnecessary to announce my final determination till the close of the session. I remain, Dr Sir, faithfully your friend

JOSEPH C. CABELL

RC (ViU: TJP-PC); endorsed by TJ as received 28 Jan. 1821 and so recorded in SJL. RC (MHi); address cover only; with PoC of TJ to John Graves, 5 Mar. 1821, on verso; addressed: "Thomas Jefferson esq. Monticello"; franked; postmarked Richmond, 25 Jan.

The Richmond neighborhood of RICH-MOND HILL later became known as Church Hill (Mary Wingfield Scott, *Old Richmond Neighborhoods* [1950; rev. ed., 1984], 23–54). In this context, however, Cabell may have been thinking of Shockoe Hill, the site of Virginia's capitol.

DERNIER: "last."

[1] Cabell here canceled "totally."
[2] Preceding two words interlined.
[3] Preceding three words interlined in place of "paralizes every thing."
[4] Cabell here canceled "A certain great man & his friends."
[5] Preceding four words interlined in place of "for the first time, mention to you, about a subject."
[6] Cabell here canceled "for some."
[7] Cabell here canceled "Our friend Mr Gordon would be a safe depository of our interests."
[8] Cabell here canceled "& wish."

From Constantine S. Rafinesque

RESPECTED SIR—   Lexington K^y 25th Jany 1821

I have delayed answering your last favor until I could send you my Ichthyology of the Ohio, and the Western Minerva. The former I have now the pleasure to forward you, and shall be glad to know your opinion on it. But I cannot send you the Western Minerva, although the first number is printed, because this Journal is not to be published at present. It has been condamned before its appearance (upon some proof-sheets) by a new kind of[1] Western Literary Inquisition and Censorship, and forbidden to be published, to which we have been compelled to assent for peace-sake. C'est une cabale nouvelle de l'ignorance contre les lumieres. The principal motives stated in the verbal decree of this new Inquisition, were, that the Journal was too learned, that it dared to inculcate political and moral Wisdom, to surmise that the Sun does not stand still and has an orbit[2] and that the Earth therefore performs a spiral course through Space, to teach Agricultural truths, to employ mystification against ignorance and folly &c &c. You will perhaps hardly believe that this could happen in the U. St. but it is a fact, and although we had 2 or 300 suscribers, we must suppress the work, and are even forbidden or rather prevented to publish the fact in the newspapers—If I can recover some proof-sheets, I will send them to you: they will be a literary Curiosity, and you will judge whether the decree was just, timely or even excusable.—

This is but one of the many difficulties which I experience in the prosecution of my labors; but after a momentary despondency, my courage and zeal overcome them.—

I am however tired of being sequestered in a spot where my labors are but partially appreciated, and I long for a wider field, where I may have an opportunity of enlarging the Sphere of Knowledge without restraint.

I have read your Report to the Legislature of Virginia. I am sorry to perceive that you do not wish to organize immediatly your University. You must be aware that the Professors which are to be called to it; must come from far, some perhaps from Europe (if I am rightly informed) and one or two years, will be requisite for them to prepare themselves, settle their interests and come.—It might perhaps be advisable to name immediatly your Professors, which might only take possession in due time; if some should refuse the appointment, you would then have time to name others. I Say so because it is my wish that a prompt decision might take place and in your lifetime. If I was elected in any branch, it would be greatly beneficial to me, even if I was only to take possession in five years: and meantime I am prevented by this hope from applying any where else.

I have heard it mentioned in conversation that you meant <u>perhaps</u> to send to Europe for all your Professors. I hope that this is not the case, at least for all: and in what relates to me, I do not know a single Individual either in the U. St. or in Europe, who is <u>at the same</u> time <u>equally acquainted</u> with Geology, Mineralogy Meteorology[3] Zoology and Botany as I am—I am in correspondance with the most distinguished Naturalists & Botanists of both continents, and when it will be needful, extracts from their Letters will show how they value my labors and discoveries.—It will be sufficient to name in Europe Dr Leach the best Zoologist of England,

> Prof— Hooker of Glasgow, the best scotch Botanist
> W. Swainson—the author of Zoological Illustrations
> Dr. Sealy—of Cork in Ireland—
> Chevalier Cuvier—of Paris—
> Prof— Decandolle of Geneva, the best European botanist
> Prof Delille of Montpellier—
> Mr. Bory St Vincent Editor of Annals of Phys. Science
> Prof— Gravenhorst, of Breslaw.
> Mr Blainville—Paris—Editor of Journal D'hist. Naturelle

And in the United States, Stephen Elliot of Charleston, Dr. Torrey of Newyork. Dr. Mitchill, Govr Clinton, &c.—

If the Election of your Professors is still delayed, and you may recomend me meantime for some other literary situation, I hope you will remember me. The liberal offer of my Library Museum and Herbarium, ought to show how zealous I am for Science, even against my interest. Whenever I shall have a liberal Salary, I shall not spend it as many of[4] our American Professors have done till now, in giving parties and carousing; but in performing Scientific Travels (in the vacations), publishing important works, purchasing rare books &c

I hope you will excuse whatever may be too personal, and bold in this Letter. I write under some sharp feelings; and wish you could know me thoroughly. Your discernment will perform the task. Believe me Respected Sir, Sincerely Yours

PROF. C. S. RAFINESQUE

PS. Who are the other Trustees of your University

RC (MHi); addressed: "Honble Thomas Jefferson &c &c &c Monticello near Charlotteville Virginia"; stamped; postmarked Lexington, 2 Feb.; endorsed by TJ as received 19 Feb. 1821 and so recorded in SJL. Enclosure: Rafinesque, *Ichthyologia Ohiensis, or Natural History of the Fishes Inhabiting the River Ohio and its tributary streams, Preceded by a physical description of the Ohio and its branches* (Lexington, Ky., 1820).

C'EST UNE CABALE NOUVELLE DE L'IGNORANCE CONTRE LES LUMIERES: "It is a new cabal of ignorance against enlightenment."

[1] Preceding four words interlined in place of "an American or rather."
[2] Preceding four words interlined.
[3] Word interlined.
[4] Preceding two words interlined.

From Edmund Bacon

DEARE SIR.   January 26th 1821—

I have examined the statem^t on the paper Just recieved and believe it contains every article in acc^ts betwen You & myself excepting the three beeves. they was value'd to 40 dollars 13 Dollars & a third each M^r Th J Randolph saw them. the two first killed in the fall was two of them. one being a good cow is kept for milch. If it soots and you think it not improper you may extend the settlement of acc^ts on to the comeing September as I shall not call on you for a dollar untill I leave virginia

I am yours &C   E: BACON

we will be some days imploy^d yet sawing the bar^l stuff we have a smart chame already sawed. will the carpenters still mall it as it is now necessary for it to be malled by some body as the coopers require it.

RC (ViU: TJP-ER); addressed: "Mr Jefferson."

The PAPER JUST RECIEVED has not been found. CHAME and MALL: presum-

ably "chime," here meaning a barrel stave, and "maul," splitting with a maul and a wedge (*OED*).

From Jared Mansfield

SIR, West-Point Jany 26th 1821

The Superintendent, Officers, Professors, Instructors, & Cadets of the U. States' Mil. Academy, impressed, with a high sense of the great services, you have rendered the Nation, & that this Institution, with which they are connected, originated under Your patronage, & presidency, are anxious for some special, & appropriate memorial of your person, which may descend to posterity. They have already in the Academic Library the portraits of the Great Washington the Founder of Our Republic, & of Col. Williams the first Chief of the Mil. Academy, & they wish to add yours to the number, as being alike one of the Founders, & Patrons of both.

Presuming on Your goodness, they have already engaged one of the best Portrait Painters of our Country (Mr Sully of Philadelphia) to wait on You for that purpose, whenever it may suit your convenience.

May I request, Sir, that you would gratify us by sitting to him for your picture, & that you would signify to me as acting in behalf of my Colleagues, the time when Mr Sully may be permitted to attend you for that purpose.

I am with the most profound respect, Your Obed^t & devot^d, humb^{ll} Ser^t

JARED MANSFIELD
Prof^r at Mil. Acad^y

RC (NWM: Mansfield Papers); endorsed by TJ as received 8 Feb. 1821 and so recorded in SJL.

Jared Mansfield (1759–1830), mathematician, surveyor, and educator, was born in New Haven, Connecticut. He attended Yale College (later Yale University) in the class of 1777 but was expelled during his senior year for misconduct. In 1786 Mansfield became rector of New Haven's Hopkins Grammar School, and Yale eventually awarded him a master's degree in 1787. He resigned from Hopkins in 1790 but returned a few months later and continued as its head until 1795. Mansfield afterwards taught briefly in Philadelphia before returning to lead a private school in New Haven. In 1801 he published *Essays, Mathematical and Physical: containing New Theories and Illustrations of some very Important and Difficult Subjects of the Sciences. Never Before Published* (New Haven, [1801]; Sow-erby, no. 3733). This ambitious work brought Mansfield to the attention of TJ, who in 1802 appointed him captain of the United States Army Corps of Engineers and professor of mathematics at the United States Military Academy. Mansfield left West Point the following year when TJ appointed him surveyor general of the United States, a position he held until 1812 and during which time he lived in Marietta and Cincinnati while he surveyed Ohio and the Northwest Territory. He was promoted to major in 1805 and lieutenant colonel in 1808 before resigning his army commission in 1810. President James Madison appointed Mansfield professor of experimental and natural philosophy at West Point in 1812, and after being diverted to supervise the construction of fortifications during the War of 1812, he taught there from 1814 until resigning in 1828. Mansfield moved thereafter to Cincinnati. He died during a visit to New Haven (*DAB*; Dexter, *Yale Biog-*

raphies, 3:644, 691–4; *PTJ*, 37:131–2, 348–9, 40:410–2; *JEP*, 1:422, 424, 453, 455, 2:22, 69, 301 [27 Apr., 3 May 1802, 11, 15 Nov. 1803, 24 Feb. 1806, 19 Feb. 1808, 9 Nov. 1812]; Heitman, *U.S. Army*, 1:688; *The Centennial of the United States Military Academy at West Point, New*

York. 1802–1902 [1904], 2:53–4, 63; Hartford *Connecticut Courant*, 9 Feb. 1830; *New-York Morning Herald*, 13 Feb. 1830).

[1] Manuscript: "hunb[l]."

To William S. Cardell

SIR   Monticello Jan. 27. 21.

I have to make my acknolegements for the honor done me by the American academy of language & belles lettres, in appointing me an honorary member of their society, and I pray you to be the organ of rendering them my thanks. at my age and distance I can be but a very unprofitable associate but I sincerely wish them all the success which the object of the institution merits. the improvement & enlargement of the scope of our language is of first importance. science must be stationary unless language advances pari passu. there are so many differences between us & England of soil, climate, culture productions, laws, religion & government,[1] that we must be left far behind the march of circumstances were we to hold ourselves rigorously to their standard. if, like the French Academicians it were proposed to fix our language, it would be fortunate that the step was not taken in the days of our Saxon ancestors whose vocabulary would illy express the science of this day. judicious neology can alone give strength & copiousness to language and enable it to be the vehicle of new ideas.

I pray you to accept the assurance of my great respect.

TH: JEFFERSON

RC (NNGL); addressed: "M[r] William S. Cardell New York"; franked; postmarked Charlottesville, 30 Jan.; endorsed by Cardell. PoC (DLC); on verso of a reused address cover from Peter Cardelli to TJ. Printed in American Academy of Language and Belles Lettres,

Circular No. III; to the American Members, and Patrons of the Institution, from the Corresponding Secretary (New York, 1822), 10.

[1] Manuscript: "goverment."

To Patrick Gibson

DEAR SIR   Monticello Jan. 27. 21.

Your favor of the 9ᵗʰ was recieved in due time. I do not know the exact date or amount of my note in the bank of Virginia, except that the latter is between 11. & 1200.D. I therefore inclose you a blank, hoping it is in time for renewal. I find myself so much declining by age and ill health in the attention and energy necessary for business that I am turning every thing over to my grandson whose industry and correctness renders him worthy of all confidence. he is now in Richmᵈ and I desired him to explain to you the unfortunate accident just happened to the Shadwell mill; of the main shaft snapping in two which will disable them from delivering flour for a month to come. Capᵗ Peyton being the agent of my grandson in Richmond has been the occasion of my concerns being partly[1] addressed to him: but really if produce is to continue at what it is, we must abandon raising as it does not repay the expence of culture alone, and I see no resource but to clothe & feed ourselves, and to buy nothing, as we can make nothing to pay for it. I hope your health is becoming better and beg you to be assured of my great friendship and respect.

TH: JEFFERSON

PoC (DLC); on verso of reused address cover of James Madison to TJ, 28 Sept. 1819; at foot of text: "Mʳ Gibson"; endorsed by TJ. Enclosure not found.

TJ's GRANDSON was Thomas Jefferson Randolph.

[1] Word interlined.

To Peachy R. Gilmer

DEAR SIR   Monticello Jan. 27. 21.

The chair which is the subject of your letter of the 14ᵗʰ was sent to Poplar Forest the last summer, and has only awaited the order of mrs Trist or of yourself. I write to mr Yancey this day to deliver it to any person under your order. we heard from Farmington three days ago. mrs Trist was well, but mr Divers much otherwise. indeed nothing can be more changeable than the condition of his health from one day to another. accept the assurance of my great friendship and respect

TH: JEFFERSON

RC (ItT: Luigi Nomis di Cossilla Autograph Collection); at foot of text: "Mʳ Gilmer." PoC (MHi); on verso of a reused address cover from Edmund Bacon to TJ; several words rewritten by TJ due to polygraph misalignment; endorsed by TJ.

To Joel Yancey

DEAR SIR   Monticello. Jan. 27. 21.

I recieved by my grandson yours of the 14th and cannot say that I have recieved any thing which has given me more pain[.] nothing on earth was farther from my intention than that it should be considered as intended to give you an opportunity to withdraw. it was sincerely meant, as it was expressed, to be a withdrawal of myself from a super-intendance to which age had rendered me incompetent and transfer-ring it to a younger member of my family, who would have the same interest which I had myself in taking care of every thing for the family. I wished to install him at once into a substitution which the ordinary course of nature must shortly do of itself. and I beg you to be assured that I have been ever so impressed with the assurance of your zeal, care & direction of my affairs that I should have considered your withdrawal at any time as a misfortune, and especially [at?] this time and that it should be brought about by what was so [dif]ferently in-tended. I value your friendship too much to withhold this explanation and I hope you will suffer this misconception to pass off as if it had never happened, and to leave no shadow of impression on either of our minds.

There is an arm-chair at Poplar forest, in the parlour, which was carried up in the summer, and belongs to mrs Trist. it is crosslegged covered with red Marocco, and may be distinguished from the one of the same kind sent up last by the waggon, as being of a brighter fresher colour, and having a green ferret across the back, covering a seam in the leather. be so good as to have it delivered to mr Peachy Gilmer when called for, and to be assured of my sincere friendship & respect.   TH: JEFFERSON

PoC (MHi); on verso of a reused address cover from Wilson Cary Nicholas to TJ; edge trimmed; torn at seal; at foot of text: "Mr Yancey"; endorsed by TJ.

From Edmund Bacon

SIR.   Jany 28th 21

Inclosed is the two papers of acc^{ts} to merely ask the favour if you will look over them and see if you dont discover a small mistake You will find at the bottom of the acc^t of November 12th 1817. Your acknowlegement of 1102.09 D due on the 22nd of september past. and that on the 31st of December ensueing thare was 145. D 18 C Interest makeing of principal and Interest 1247. D 27 C on the last acc^t the amount of 1102.09 is set down to become due at the 31st of Decr at the time named for the 145. D 18 C Interest to be due this as I understand it takes from me the Interest on the 1102$ from 22nd of Sepr untill the 31st of Dece^r ensueing. perhaps I may not understand it right. but as stated above is the way I do understand it. and I no you will do it right. I therefore send both acc^{ts} to you to examin and will Call in the forenoon tomorrow

  I am yours &C   E BACON

RC (ViU: TJP-ER); dateline between closing and signature; addressed (torn): "[. . .] Jefferson Monticello"; endorsed by TJ as received 28 Jan. 1821. Enclosures not found.

Bacon recorded settling his account with TJ on this day, noting that "the 1st of this present month the sum of $634.71" was due from TJ (ViU: Bacon Memorandum Book, 1802–22).

From Ethan A. Brown

Columbus, Ohio, January 28^h 1821.

  In the accompanying report, the legislature of Ohio have attempted to maintain the principles, on which they have proceeded, in their controversy with the Bank of the United States. With a feeling of anxiety, whether those principles, and the conduct of our legislature, under their influence, will be censured, or approved, by Mr Jefferson, this appeal is transmitted, with the utmost respect, for his perusal, by his obedient Servant,   ETHAN A. BROWN

RC (DLC); dateline at foot of text; endorsed by TJ as received 15 Feb. 1821 and so recorded in SJL.

Ethan Allen Brown (1776–1852), attorney and public official, was born in Darien, Connecticut, and received a private classical education. He became a law clerk in Alexander Hamilton's New York City office in 1797 and two years later was Hamilton's assistant secretary during the latter's tenure as United States inspector general. In 1801 Brown was admitted to practice law in the New York City Mayor's Court. He purchased land in what became Rising Sun, Indiana, and established a law office in Cincinnati in 1804. Brown served as a judge on the Ohio Supreme Court, 1810–18, and was elected to two consecutive terms as governor of Ohio beginning in the latter year. He resigned in 1822 to fill a vacant seat in the

United States Senate. Brown chaired the Committee on Roads and Canals and strongly supported internal improvements. Immediately after his senate term ended in 1825, he spent five years as an Ohio canal commissioner. In 1830 President Andrew Jackson appointed Brown chargé d'affaires to Brazil. After he resigned this post in 1834, he was commissioner of the General Land Office in Washington, D.C., 1835–36. Brown thereafter moved to his Indiana farm. He represented Dearborn County for one term in the Indiana House of Representatives, 1841–43. Brown died in Indianapolis while serving as vice president of a Democratic state political convention (*ANB*; *DAB*; OHi: Brown Papers; Harold C. Syrett and others, eds., *The Papers of Alexander Hamilton* [1961–87], 23:11–2n, 24:302; New York *Commercial Advertiser*, 22 May 1801; *JEP*, 4:107, 109, 427, 498, 500, 579 [25, 26

May 1830, 24 June 1834, 28, 29 Dec. 1835, 15 Dec. 1836]; *Journal of the House of Representatives of the State of Indiana* [1841], 288; [1842], 3; Indianapolis *Indiana State Sentinel*, 26 Feb. 1852; gravestone inscription in Union Cemetery, Rising Sun).

The ACCOMPANYING REPORT, not found, was probably the *Report of the Joint Committee of Both Houses of the General Assembly, on the Communication of the Auditor of State Upon the subject of the proceedings of the Bank of the United States, against the Officers of State, in the United States Circuit Court* (Columbus, Ohio, 1820). Ohio began its CONTRO-

VERSY with the Second Bank of the United States in 1819, when state officials collected taxes from the bank's Chillicothe branch. The United States Supreme Court eventually ruled this action unlawful in its 1824 decision of *Osborn v. Bank of the United States* (Marshall, *Papers*, 10:36–82; Patricia L. Franz, "Ohio v. The Bank: An Historical Examination of *Osborn v. The Bank of the United States*," *Journal of Supreme Court History* 24 [1999]: 112–37).

Two days previously Brown sent James Madison a similar letter and enclosure (Madison, *Papers, Retirement Ser.*, 2:237).

To James Madison

DEAR SIR   Monticello Jan. 28. 21.

My neighbor, friend and physician, Doct' Watkins, being called to Philadelphia, is desirous to pay his respects to you en passant, and asks me, by a line to you, to lessen his scruples on doing so. you will find my justification in his character when known to you. his understanding is excellent, well informed, of pleasant conversation and of great worth. as a Physician I should trust myself in his hands with more confidence than any one I have ever known in this state, and am indebted to his experience and cautious practice for the restoration of my health. recieve him therefore with your wonted kindness and accept the assurance of my affectionate respect.   TH: JEFFERSON

RC (DLC: Madison Papers); at foot of text: "M' Madison." PoC (DLC); on verso of reused address cover of Daniel Brent to TJ, 25 Sept. 1819; endorsed by TJ.

From Theodorus Bailey

DEAR SIR,   Post-Office New york 29. Janu' 1821.

An unclaimed letter under your frank, addressed to M' George Jones—New york, remains in this Office—It was received here on or about the 6th instant—M' Jones is not a Resident of this City; nor do I know where to find him. Will you have the goodness to advise me what direction I shall give this letter?

I avail myself of this occasion to renew to you the assurance of my sincere respect & regard   THEODORUS BAILEY.

RC (MHi); endorsed by TJ as received 8 Feb. 1821 and so recorded in SJL.

The UNCLAIMED LETTER was TJ to George Long (ca. 1782–1843), 30 Dec. 1820.

To Peter Stephen Chazotte

Monticello June [Jan.][1] 29. 21.

Th: Jefferson returns his thanks to mr Chazotte for the pamphlet he has been so kind as to send him on the several cultures proposed to be introduced into the Southern states. he is sensible of the advantages they will produce, but at the age of 77. he must leave the attention to these things to those who are young enough to aid and witness their success. he prays M[r] Chazotte to accept his respectful salutations.

RC (Mrs. Richard D. Nelson, Short Hills, New Jersey, 1949); misdated; dateline at foot of text. FC (DLC); on verso of Chazotte to TJ, 15 Jan. 1821; in TJ's hand; dateline at foot of text. Recorded in SJL as a letter of 29 Jan. 1821.

[1] Reworked in an unidentified hand to "Jany." Dft: "Jan."

To Joseph Delaplaine

SIR   Monticello Jan. 29. 21.

Your favor of the 15th is recieved, as was in due time that of Oct. 11. with the poem of mr Meade, and I did not know that I had omitted[1] to return my thanks for it. this I hope will be kindly imputed to my increasing inability to write letters. when I gave you a written opinion on the biographical work you were engaged in, you will recollect I mentioned that it was the singular case in which I had consented to do so, and that it was for a very special reason. a desire of tranquility & aversion to place myself before the public in any form dictate this law to me, and I hope that mr Meade's indulgence to the inertness of 77. will plead in my favor, and that with yourself he will accept with my thanks the assurance of my great respect.

TH: JEFFERSON

RC (LNT: George H. and Katherine M. Davis Collection); addressed: "M[r] Joseph Delaplaine Philadelphia"; franked; postmarked Milton, 3 Feb.; endorsed by Delaplaine. PoC (DLC); on verso of re-used address cover of Robert Lovett to TJ, 12 Aug. 1819; mutilated at seal; endorsed by TJ.

TJ gave his WRITTEN OPINION of the first number of *Delaplaine's Repository of the Lives and Portraits of Distinguished*

Americans, 2 vols. (Philadelphia, 1816–18; Poor, *Jefferson's Library*, 4 [no. 139]) in a letter to Delaplaine of 25 Dec. 1816, accompanied by a separate letter of the same date pleading his aversion to giving public opinions of literary works.

[1] Manuscript: "omitte."

To William Davis Robinson

SIR   Monticello Jan. 29. 21.

I have duly recieved your letter of Dec. 28. with the volume on the Mexican revolution which you have been so kind as to send me. I shall read it with great pleasure. observing the idle tales and contradictory statements of the newspapers on the subject of the revolutions going on in Spanish America, I have made a point to pass them over unread, except when given under a known name. because I think ignorance nearer to truth than error. having as yet seen nothing of known character on the Mexican revolution your information will be the more welcome to a mind as yet a blank on the subject. with my thanks be pleased to accept the assurance of my great respect.

TH: JEFFERSON

PoC (MHi); on verso of reused address cover of Noah Worcester to TJ, 20 Sept. 1819; at foot of text: "Mr William Davis Robinson"; endorsed by TJ.

To William Thornton

DEAR SIR   Monticello Jan. 19. [29] 21.

Your letter of the 9th was 19. days in it's passage to me, being received yesterday evening only. and now that I have recieved it, I wish that I could answer it more to your satisfaction. I must explain to you my situation. when I retired from office at Washington my intimacy with my successor being well known, I became the center of application from all quarters by those who wished appointments to use my interposition in their favor. I gave into it for a while until I found that I must for ever keep myself prostrate, and in the posture of a suppliant before the government, or renounce altogether the office of an Intercessor. I determined on the latter; and the number of applicants obliged me to have a formal letter printed in blank, to which I had only to put date, signature and address. I inclose you one of these in proof of the necessity I was under of laying down such a law to myself, and of a rigorous adherence to it. I comfort [m]yself however in your case with the unimportance of any interposition. you are so well known to the President and heads of departments that they need no body's information as to your qualifications and means of service. where they know facts themselves they will act on their own judgments; and in your case particularly with every disposition in your favor; and whatever they shall do for you will give no one greater pleasure than myself.

I am much indebted to you for the pamphlet of patents. it is a document which I have often occasion to consult. with my respectful souvenirs to the ladies of your family I pray you to accept the assurance of my continued esteem and attachment   TH: JEFFERSON

PoC (MHi); on verso of reused address cover of Bernard Peyton to TJ, 27 Sept. 1819; misdated; torn at seal, with one word rewritten by TJ; at foot of text: "Dʳ Thornton"; endorsed by TJ as a letter of 29 Jan. 1821 and so recorded in SJL. Enclosure: enclosure to TJ to Samuel H. Smith, 6 Mar. 1809.

The PAMPHLET OF PATENTS was likely the 5 Jan. 1821 *Letter from the Secretary of State, transmitting a List of the Names of Persons to whom Patents have been Issued, for Any Useful Invention, during the year 1820* (Washington, 1821).

From John Vaughan

Dᴿ SIR   Phil. Janʸ 29. 1821

I have your favor of 6 Jany & have recievd Otis' translation of Botta Vol. 1. 2—The 3ᵈ has been published this day & I Shall no doubt soon recieve it from you—I shall Seize the first opportunity of Sending[1] it to Botta—I informed Mʳ Otis who is much pleased with the Circumstance & has adressed a letter to the author which will accompany the Books I shall also write at same time—It is more difficult now to find persons going to France, owing to the species of non Intercourse (as[2] it were) between her & the United States—

I remain Yours sincerly   JN VAUGHAN

RC (MHi); at head of text: "Thomas Jefferson Monticello"; endorsed by TJ as a letter of 24 Jan. 1821 received 8 Feb. 1821 and so recorded in SJL.

For the SPECIES OF NON INTERCOURSE, see note to Joshua Dodge to TJ, 25 Nov. 1820.

[1] Manuscript: "Send."
[2] Manuscript: "at."

To Joseph C. Cabell

DEAR SIR   Monticello Jan. 30. 21.

You will recollect that at the meeting of the Visitors of the University on the 4ᵗʰ of Oct. last, mr Johnson being disabled by sickness to attend and having been prevented at the April meeting by bad weather we were apprehensive his commission might be vacated by a <u>failure to act for the space of one year</u>, and I was requested to apply to the Governor for a renewal of the commission. I accordingly communicated the request to the Governor by letter. he observed to me that mr Johnson could not have failed to act for the space of a year, because he had not been one year in office under the present commission which commenced only on the 29ᵗʰ of Feb. last; and he suggested that a meeting, or any other act <u>as a visitor</u> before the 28ᵗʰ of Feb. ensuing, might yet save the lapse. I know of but one act which the law authorises to the visitors individually & out of meeting to wit the concurrence in the call of a special meeting. this is undoubtedly <u>a visitorial act</u>: and I propose therefore that the visitors shall individually sign such a call, annexing the date of their respective signatures, which will prove it done within the year. I accordingly[1] sign such a paper myself and forward it to mr Madison for his signature with a request to forward it on to you to obtain your's, mr Johnson's, Genˡ Breckenridge's & Genˡ Taylor's. on your returning it to me I will obtain Genˡ Cocke's. I have fixed on the 1ˢᵗ of April because we meet of course at Monticello on or before that day for the preparation of business. it will not be necessary to repair actually to the University, the <u>signature</u> of the call being the essential act, and the actual meeting at the university not necessary to it's[2] validity. a reappointment by the Govʳ & council might have saved us this ceremony but for the use of the unlucky word 'successor' in the law: and altho' I suggested to the Governor that that might be got over by a first appointment and resignation of a John Doe, he thought some might raise scruples on it as an evasion, and that we had better prevent it by an act of our own: and I think myself that, as this accident will frequently happen, we had better keep the remedy within our own power by setting this precedent at once. affectionate salutations to yourself and our colleagues.

                                                            TH: JEFFERSON

RC (ViU: TJP); addressed: "Joseph C. Cabell esq. of the Senate of Virginia now in Richmond"; franked; postmarked Orange Court House, 6 Feb. 1821; endorsed by Cabell as answered 20 Feb. 1821. PoC (DLC); on a reused address cover from Chapman Johnson to TJ; mutilated at seal, with missing text rewritten by TJ; endorsed by TJ. Enclosed in TJ to James Madison, 30 Jan. 1821.

[1] Manuscript: "accordly."
[2] RC: "it'." PoC: "it's."

To Emile de Vendel

Jan. 30. 21

Th:J. begs leave to inform M. de Vendel in answer to his lre of the 5th that the University of this state is as yet little more than in embryo, and that the time of it's opening is distant and uncertain & he prays him to recieve his respectful salutns.

FC (DLC: TJ Papers, 219:39059); on verso of de Vendel to TJ, 5 Jan. 1821; in TJ's hand; dateline at foot of text.

To James Madison

DEAR SIR   Monticello Jan. 30. 21.

The inclosed letter to mr Cabell so fully explains it's object, and the grounds on which your signature to the paper is proposed if approved, that I will spare my stiffening & aching wrist the pain of adding more than the assurance of my constant & affect^{te} friendship.

TH: JEFFERSON

RC (DNT, on deposit ViU: TJP); at foot of text in William B. Sprague's hand: "To James Madison," with Sprague's initialed note on verso indicating that the text was "Sent me by Hon: J. Madison" in August 1828. Not recorded in SJL. Enclosures: (1) TJ to Joseph C. Cabell, 30 Jan. 1821. (2) Call for Meeting of University of Virginia Board of Visitors, 30 Jan.–13 Feb. 1821.

From George Alexander Otis

SIR,   Philadelphia Jany 30th 1821.

While I have the honor of transmitting you the last volume of my translation, I avail myself of that indulgence which you have already so largely extended towards me, to lay before you a criticism of the venerable John Jay: and though somewhat lengthy, in justice to that estimable man, I beg leave to do it in his own words.[1]

"Having as yet received and read only[2] the first volume of the History, I cannot form, and consequently cannot express, an opinion of the whole[3] work.—As to the <u>first</u> volume, there are in it certain assertions, representations, and suggestions, of which there are some which I believe to be erroneous,[4] and others which I suspect to be inaccurate.[5] Being too feeble to write or to read much at a time without fatigue, I forbear to enumerate them.—I will nevertheless for your

[580]

satisfaction, select and notice one of the most important—Viz.—That anterior to the Revolution, there existed in the colonies a desire of Independence.

The following extracts respect this Topic.[6]

Page 10.   'The love of the Sovereign and their ancient country, which the first colonists might have retained in their new establishments, gradually diminished in the hearts of their Descendants.'

11.   'The greater part of the colonists had heard nothing of Great Britain, excepting that it was a distant kingdom, from which their ancestors had been barbarously expelled.'

12   'As the means of constraint became almost illusory in the hands of the Government, there must have arisen[7] in the minds of the Americans the Hope and with it the Desire to shake off the yoke of British[8] Superiority.'
'The colonists supported impatiently the superiority of the British Government.'

15.   'Such was the State of the English colonies in America, such the Opinions and dispositions of those who inhabited them, about the middle of the eighteenth century. . . . It was impossible that they should have remained ignorant of what they were capable; and that the progressive development of national Pride should not have rendered the British yoke intolerable.'

33.   'Already those who were the most zealous for Liberty, or the most ambitious, had formed in the secret of their hearts, the resolution to shake off the yoke of England whenever a favorable occasion should present.[9]—This Design was encouraged by the recent cession of Canada.'

199.   'The colonists looked upon (the Congress of 1774.) as a Convention of men who in some mode or other, were to deliver their country from the perils that menaced it. The greater part believed that their ability &c. . . . would enable them to obtain from the government a removal of the evils that oppressed them, and the reestablishment of the ancient order of things.—some others cherished the belief, that they would find means to conduct the American nation to that Independence, which was the first and most ardent of their aspirations—or rather, the sole object of that intense passion, which stung and tormented them, night and Day.'

314. 'Both (Putnam and Ward) had declared themselves too openly in favor of Independence. The Congress desired indeed to procure it, but withal in a propitious time.'

388. 'Thus ceased, as we have related, the royal authority in the different provinces. It was replaced progressively by that of the People:—that is, by Congresses, or Conventions-extraordinary, that were formed in each Colony.—But this was not deemed sufficient by those, who <u>directed</u> the affairs of America. Their <u>real</u> object being <u>Independence</u>.'[10]

Explicit[11] Professions and assurances of allegiance and Loyalty to the Sovereign (especially since the accession of king William) and of affection for the mother country, abound, continues mr Jay, in the Journals of the colonial Legislatures, and of the Congresses and Conventions, from early Periods to the second petition of Congress, in 1775.[12]

If those professions and assurances were sincere, they afford evidence more than sufficient to invalidate the charge of our desiring & aiming at Independence.

If, on the other hand, those professions and assurances were factitious and deceptive, they present to the world an unprecedented instance of long-continued, concurrent, and detestable Duplicity in the Colonies.—Our country does not deserve this odious and disgusting imputation. During the course of my life, and until after the second petition of Congress, (in 1775.) I never did hear any American, of any Class, or of any description, express a wish for the Independence of the colonies.

Few Americans had more or better means and opportunities of becoming acquainted with the sentiments and Disposition of the colonists relative to public affairs than the late Doct^r Franklin.

In a letter to his Son, dated the 22 March 1775. he relates a conversation which he had with Lord Chatham, in the preceding month of August.　　His Lordship having mentioned an opinion prevailing in England, that America aimed at setting up for itself as an independent state, the Doctor thus expressed himself. 'I assured him, that having more than once travelled almost from one End of the continent to the other, and kept a great variety of company, eating, drinking and conversing with them freely, I never had heard, in any conversation, from any Person, drunk or sober, the least expression of a wish for a separation; or a hint that such a thing would be advantageous to America.'　　It does not appear to me necessary to enlarge further on this subject.—It has always[13] been, and still is, my opinion and belief, that our Country was prompted and impelled to independence by Necessity and not by Choice. They who know how we were then circumstanced, know from whence that necessity resulted.—It would be indeed extraordinary, if a Foreigner, remote like mr Botta, from the best sources of authentic information, sh^d in writing such a History, commit no mistakes. That gentleman doubtless believed his narrations to be true. But [it][14] is not improbable that he sometimes selected his materials with too little apprehension of error; and that some of his Informers were too little scrupulous. This remark derives a degree of weight from the following passage in the History— viz. 'General Montgomery left a wife, the object of all his tenderness, with several children, still infants, a Spectacle for their country at once of pity and admiration. The State, from gratitude towards the father, distinguished them with every mark of kindness and protection.'[15] I have been acquainted with general Montgomery's widow from my youth—the fact is, that she never had a child.[16]

In making the Translation attention has doubtless been paid to the Rule that a Translator should convey into his translation with perspicuity and precision the ideas of his author and no others; and express them, not literally, but in well adapted classical language. How far your Translation is exactly correct I am an incompetent Judge; for, not understanding the language of the original, I cannot examine[17] and compare the Translation with it.

Of the style and manner of the Translation I think well."[18]

Having the intention, in case other Editions should be called for, of writing notes, it is desirable for me, who am permitted to approach the highest and best sources of information to remit no diligence in profiting of my good fortune as far as the motive shall appear an excuse for the liberty.

Wishing from my heart that the evening of your honoured days may be as happy and free from bodily suffering as their course has been glorious and useful to mankind! I have the honor to be, with the highest veneration, Sir, your obliged humble servant

GEORGE ALEXANDER OTIS.

The biographical sketch of mr Botta, was furnished me by the Sardinian Consul, in this city; who has promised to obtain for me a more ample account of his life. But I thought this, imperfect as it is, might excite a curiosity to know more of a man, who was capable of viewing our revolutionary Transactions and events with a philosophic eye, and describing them with a polished and eloquent pen,

RC (DLC); in Otis's hand, with excerpt from John Jay's 13 Jan. 1821 letter to Otis (Dft in NNC: Jay Papers) in an unidentified hand; ellipses in original; repeated "page, 12" at head of second page editorially omitted; postscript on separate sheet; beneath signature: "To the Honble Thomas Jefferson Monticello"; endorsed by TJ as received 12 Feb. 1821 and so recorded in SJL. Enclosure: Botta, *History of the War*, vol. 3.

For the 1775 SECOND PETITION OF CONGRESS, whose signers included Jay and TJ, see *PTJ*, 1:219–23. Benjamin Franklin wrote the lengthy LETTER TO HIS SON William Franklin during his voyage back to Philadelphia from London in 1775 (Franklin, *Papers*, 21:540–99, passage quoted by Jay on p. 549). The discussion of General Richard MONTGOMERY is on p. 433 of the first volume of Otis's translation of Botta, *History of the War*. Otis included a BIOGRAPHICAL SKETCH of Botta in the enclosed volume, pp. xi–xii. The SARDINIAN CONSUL in Philadelphia was Gaspare Deabbate.

¹ Unidentified handwriting begins here.
² Word underscored in Jay's Dft.
³ Word underscored in Jay's Dft.
⁴ Word underscored in Jay's Dft.

⁵ Word underscored in Jay's Dft.
⁶ Line in Otis's hand.
⁷ Botta, *History of the War*, and Jay's Dft: "and gradually increased."
⁸ Botta, *History of the War*, and Jay's Dft: "English."
⁹ Superfluous closing quotation mark editorially omitted.
¹⁰ Quotation marks in above table of extracts all editorially altered from double to single.
¹¹ Superfluous opening quotation mark preceding this word editorially omitted.
¹² Manuscript: "775."
¹³ Manuscript: "alway." Jay's Dft: "always."
¹⁴ Word supplied from Jay's Dft.
¹⁵ Set of double quotation marks editorially altered to single.
¹⁶ Superfluous closing quotation mark editorially omitted.
¹⁷ Manuscript: "examinine." Jay's Dft: "examine."
¹⁸ Unidentified handwriting ends here.

To Thomas B. Parker

SIR   Monticello Jan. 30. 21.

I am indebted to you for your favor of the 16ᵗʰ and for information of the two amendments to your constitution therein noticed, and on which you ask my opinion. in a former letter to you I expressed my entire retirement from every thing political, and my unwillingness to commit myself to controversy or offence, even by expressing opinions: and on the same grounds I must request to be excused in the present case, and especially on subjects respecting other states, so much more capable than I am of judging for themselves. the making your Senate the [re]presentative of wealth instead of men, is a feature which doubtless will be scrupulously questioned by the people, to whom it is to be referred, and who are themselves men, but not wealthy men. the question of a general assesment for the support of the ministers of religion was a very early one in this state. the supporters of the antient establishment of the Anglican church here finding that establishment untenable retreated to a general assesment as a strong hold, on which many rallied to them. but the principle of perfect freedom in religion at length prevailed and we have not since found in experience that the zeal of either pastors or flocks has been damped by this reference to their own consciences; and the proposition of a general assesment, on which, before it was tried, we were almost equally divided, would not now I think get one vote in ten. I pray you to accept my respectful salutations.   TH: JEFFERSON

PoC (DLC); on verso of reused address cover of Chapman Johnson to TJ, 25 Sept. 1819; damaged at seal; at foot of text: "Mr Thomas B. Parker"; endorsed by TJ.

TJ's 1779 "Bill for Establishing Religious Freedom" AT LENGTH PREVAILED in Virginia, becoming law in 1786 (*PTJ*, 2:545–53).

From John W. Taylor

HONORED SIR   Washington January 30^h 1821—
    There has been established in Union College, Schenectady, N.Y. an **A** of the **Φ.B.K.** Society—Chancellor Kent is now its President & I am one of its members—At the annual meeting last July it was greatly desired to have more knowledge of the history of the society than was possessed by any of the attending members—The honor of having introduced it into the United States from England was attributed to yourself—An ardent desire was expressed to ascertain the leading facts connected with its foundation, & progress there, & its establishment in this country—Several members urged upon me the duty of addressing you upon the subject—I have delayed compliance until now unwilling to trespass on your goodness by making what I feared might be considered an unreasonable request—If your engagements should prevent an answer to this letter, you will I doubt not, do justice to the motives by which it is dictated—Impressed from early youth with sincere veneration for your character & eminent services in the cause of liberty & science—Admiring that beneficent <u>Philosophy</u> which has been <u>the governing principle of your life</u>—and wishing you a prolonged enjoyment of signal prosperity & usefulness
    I am Dear Sir Very truly your friend & servant—
                                        JOHN W. TAYLOR

My residence is at Ballston Springs N.Y. to which I shall return after the adjournment of Congress—

RC (ViW: TC-JP); postscript written perpendicularly in left margin; between dateline and salutation: "To Thomas Jefferson Late President of the U.S."; endorsed by TJ as received 8 Feb. 1821 and so recorded in SJL. FC (NHi: Taylor Papers); in a clerk's hand, signed by Taylor; lacking postscript; endorsed by Taylor.

John W. Taylor (1784–1854), attorney and public official, was born in Ballston, Albany County (later Charlton, Saratoga County), New York. He graduated from Schenectady's Union College in 1803, studied and practiced law in Ballston Spa, and was admitted to practice in the New York Supreme Court as a counsellor-at-law in 1810. Taylor was appointed a loan commissioner for Saratoga County in 1808, and he represented the county in the state legislature, 1812–13. He served ten terms in the United States House of Representatives, 1813–33, with two stints as Speaker, 1820–21 and 1825–27. Taylor supported the prohibition of slavery in Missouri in 1819 and attracted attention by speaking out against slavery in Congress, and he supported a national bank and protective tariffs while opposing as unconstitutional federally funded internal improvements. After losing reelection in 1832 he continued to practice law in Ballston Spa. In 1840 Taylor was elected to the New York State Senate, from which he resigned in 1842 due to illness. The following year he retired to Cleveland, Ohio, where he died (*ANB* digital edition, biography added in 2003; *DAB*; NHi: Taylor Papers; Edward F. Grose, *Centennial History of the Village of Ballston Spa* [1907], 238–44; *A General Catalogue of the Officers, Graduates and Students of Union College, from 1795 to 1854* [1854], 13; *Albany Gazette*, 4 Aug. 1806, 22 Feb. 1810; New York *Public Advertiser*, 18 Apr. 1808; Ballston Spa *Advertiser*, 30 Oct. 1810; Franklin B. Hough, *The New-York Civil List* [1858]; *Daily Cleveland Herald*, 19 Sept. 1854; gravestone inscription in Ballston Spa Village Cemetery).

The Alpha chapter of Phi Beta Kappa (A OF THE Φ.B.K.) in the state of New York was chartered in 1817 (*A Catalogue of the New-York Alpha of the Phi Beta Kappa* [1852]). For the society's original foundation, see note to Thomas McAuley to TJ, 19 May 1819.

Call for Meeting of University of Virginia Board of Visitors

We the subscribers, visitors of the University of Virginia being of opinion that it will be to the interest of that institution to have an occasional meeting of the visitors, by special call, on the 1st day of April next, do therefore appoint that day for such meeting, and request the attendance of the sd Visitors accordingly; personal notice being to be given to them respectively one week at least before the said day. witness our hands on the several days affixed to our respective signatures.

TH: JEFFERSON rector. Jan. 30. 1821.

JAMES MADISON Feby 3. 1821

C JOHNSON—10th Feby 1821—

JOSEPH C. CABELL 10 Feb: 1821.

JAMES BRECKINRIDGE 10 Feb. 1821

ROBERT TAYLOR Feby 13th 1821

MS (ViU: TJP); in TJ's hand, signed and dated by him, Madison, Johnson, Cabell, Breckinridge, and Taylor; endorsed by TJ: "Call of Visitors for Apr. 1. 1821." Enclosed in TJ to Madison, 30 Jan. 1821, and Cabell to TJ, 20 Feb. 1821.

To Joseph C. Cabell

Dear Sir Monticello Jan. 31. 21.

Your favors of the 18th and 25th came together three days ago. they fill me with gloom as to the dispositions of our legislature towards the University. I percieve that I am not to live to see it opened. as to what had better be done within the limits of their will, I trust with entire confidence to what yourself, Genl Breckenridge and mr Johnson shall think best. you will see what is practicable and give it such shape as you think best. if a loan is to be resorted to, I think 60,000.D will be necessary, including the library. it's instalments cannot begin until those of the former loan are accomplished: and they should not begin later, nor be less than 13,000.D. a year. (I think it safe to retain 2000.D. a year for care of the buildings, improvement of the grounds, & unavoidable contingencies.) to extinguish this 2^d loan will require between 5. & 6. instalmts. which will carry us to the end of 1833. or 13. years from this time. my individual opinion is that we had better not open the institution until the buildings, Library & all, are finished, and our funds cleared of incumbrance. these buildings, once erected, will secure the full object infallibly at the end of 13. years, and as much earlier as an enlightened legislature shall happen to come into place. and if we were to begin sooner, with half funds only, it would satisfy the common mind, prevent their aid beyond that point & our institution remaining at that forever would be no more than the paltry academies we now have. even with the whole funds we shall be reduced to 6. professors, while Harvard will still prime it over us with her 20. professors. how many of our youths she now has, learning the lessons of anti-Missourianism, I know not; but a gentleman lately from Princeton told me he saw there the list of the students at that place, and that more than half were Virginians. these will return home, no doubt, deeply impressed with the sacred principles of our Holy alliance of Restrictionists.

But the gloomiest of all prospects is in the desertion of the best friends of the institution; for desertion I must call it. I know not the necessities which may force this on you. Genl Cocke, you say, will explain them to me; but I cannot concieve them, nor persuade myself they are uncontroulable. I have ever hoped that yourself, Genl Breckenridge and mr Johnson would stand at your posts in the legislature, until every thing was effected, and the institution opened. if it is so difficult to get along, with all the energy and influence of our present colleagues in the legislature, how can we expect to proceed at all, reducing our moving power? I know well your devotion to your country, and your foresight of the awful scenes coming on her, sooner or later. with this foresight, what service can we ever render her equal to this? what object of our lives can we propose so important? what interest of our own, which ought not to be postponed to this? health, time, labor, on what in the single life which nature has given us, can these be better bestowed than on this immortal boon to our country? the exertions and the mortifications are temporary; the benefit eternal. if any member of our college of Visitors could justifiably withdraw from this sacred duty, it would be my self, who 'quadragenis stipendiis jamdudum peractis' have neither vigor of body or mind left to keep the field. but I will die in the last ditch. and so, I hope, you will, my friend, as well as our firm-breasted brothers and colleagues mr Johnson and Gen¹ Breckenridge. nature will not give you a second life wherein to atone for the omissions of this. pray then, dear and very dear Sir, do not think of deserting us; but view the sacrifices which seem to stand in your way, as the lesser duties, and such as ought to be postponed to this, the greatest of all. continue with us in these holy labors, until, having seen their accomplishment, we may say with old Simeon 'nunc dimittis, Domine.' under all circumstances however of praise or blame, I shall be affectionately your's

TH: JEFFERSON

RC (ViU: TJP); addressed: "Joseph C. Cabell esquire of the Senate of Virginia now in Richmond"; franked; postmarked Charlottesville, 3 Feb.; endorsed by Cabell. PoC (DLC).

In the autumn of 1820, only 9 of Harvard University's 286 undergraduate students and 11 of the 121 students at the College of New Jersey (later Princeton University) were VIRGINIANS (*Catalogue of the Officers and Students of the University in Cambridge. October, 1820* [Cambridge, Mass., 1820], 10–6; *College of New-Jersey. Catalogue of the Officers and Students of Nassau-Hall* [(Trenton, N.J., 1820)]). QUADRAGENIS STIPENDIIS JAMDUDUM PERACTIS: "having already completed forty years of service."

Merit M. Robinson reported to John H. Cocke from Richmond on 22 Feb. 1821 that "Our friend, Cabell, after listening to your advice, and promising, upon conviction of its soundness, to withdraw from public life, has changed his mind, and determined to continue at the labouring oar.

He is wrong: and for several reasons in addition to those advanced by you. Mʳ Jefferson, principally, perhaps solely, has produced the unfortunate change. Cabell shewed me, some days ago, a letter to him from that gentleman; whom, I take pleasure, in saying is an ornament to his country, as a gentleman and man of letters; but in whom, as a practical man, either in state affairs, or the common concerns of life, I have no confidence. The letter, like all from his pen, is flattering, plausible, and persuasive; and by art, and not force, has upset poor Cabell. He recᵈ some other letters, he told me, urging him to be again a candidate for the Senate, and he has consented to be one. I join you in thinking, it would be better, that he should not" (RC in ViU: JHC).

In his own letter to Cocke dated Richmond, 10 Mar. 1821, Cabell wrote that "When I come I will shew you mʳ Jefferson's letter, which chiefly determined me to offer again for the Senate, and if you can stand such a letter, you must be made of steel" (RC in ViU: JCC).

From Martin Dawson

DEAR SIR   Milton 1ˢᵗ Febʸ 1821
   Your Acceptance to Joseph Gilmores order in favour of John Rog-
ers for *Seventy five Dollars due 5ᵗʰ Septʳ last belongs to me—below
you have Sketch your Acceptances Now due Viz
Joseph Gilmore Order Accepted by you *$75—
Interest on the same since 5ᵗʰ Sepᵗ last
   (4. m. 25 d)   1.84   76.84
Edmund Meeks Order Accepted by you   18.35
Interest on the same since 1 Janʸ last
   (1 m)   9   18.44 $95.28
payments of these claims when Convenient will Oblige
   Yo, Ob. Hu. Serᵛ   MARTIN DAWSON

RC (ViU: TJP-ER); addressed (trimmed): "Thomas Jefferson esq[ʳᵉ] Monticello" by "Mr Bacon"; with TJ's Notes on Account with Dawson, [ca. 4 Mar. 1821], subjoined; endorsed by TJ without date of receipt, followed by his note: D
   "Rogers for Gilmore 75.
   Meeks   18.35."

To John Mantz

                                    Monticello Feb. 1. 21.
   Th: Jefferson recieved yesterday Mʳ Mantz's present of very handsomely dressed leather, for which he begs leave to return him his
thanks, and to express the pleasure he recieves from new discoveries
and advances in the useful[1] arts. those who by new processes cheapen
the comforts of life and place them within the reach of a greater portion of mankind may be said truly to deserve well of their country.
with his acknolegements he prays mr Mantz to accept his respectful
salutations.

PoC (MHi); on verso of reused address cover to TJ; dateline at foot of text;
endorsed by TJ.

[1] Reworked from "ar."

From John Adams

DEAR SIR   Montezillo February 3ᵈ 1821
   I have just read a sketch of the life of Swedenborg, and a larger
work in two huge volumes of Memoirs of John Westley[1] by Southey,
and your kind letter of January 22ᵈ came to hand in the nick of time

to furnish me with a very rational exclamation, "What a bedlamite is man"! They are histories of Galvanism and Mesmerism thrown into hotch potch,[2] they say that these men were honest and sincere, so were the Worshipers[3] of the White Bull in Egypt and now in Calcutta, so were the Worshipers of Bacchus and Venus, so were the worshipers of St Dominick and St Bernard. Swedenborg and Westley had certainly vast memories and immaginations, and great talents for Lunaticks.   Slavery in this Country I have seen hanging over it like a black cloud for half a Century, if I were as drunk with enthusiasm as Swedenborg or Westley I might probably say I had seen Armies of Negroes marching and countermarching in the air shining in Armour. I have been so terrified with this Phenomenon that I constantly said in former times to the Southern Gentleman, I cannot comprehend this object I must leave it to you, I will vote for forceing no measure against your judgements what we are to see <u>God</u> knows and I leave it to him, and his agents in posterity. I have none of the genius of Franklin to invent a rod to draw from the cloud its Thunder and lightning. I have long been decided in opinion that a free governme[nt] and the Roman Catholick religion can never exist together in any nation or Country, and consequently that all projects for reconciling them in old Spain or new are Utopian,[4] Platonick and Chimerical. I have seen such a prostration and prostitution of Human Nature, to the Priest hood in old Spain as settled my judgment long ago, and I understand that in new Spain it is still worse if that is possible.

My appearance in the late convention was too ludicrous to be talked of. I was a member in the Convention of 1779 and there I was loquacious enough. I have harrangued and scribbled more than my share but from that time to the convention in 1820 I never opened my lips in a publick debate.[5] after a total desuetude for 40 years I boggled and blundered more than a young fellow just rising to speak at the bar, what I said I know not, I beleive the Printers have made better spee[ch]es than I made for myself. Feeling my weakness I attempted little and that seldom, What would I give for nerves as good as yours? but as Westley said of himself at my age, "old time has shaken me by the hand, and parallized it."[6]

What pictures of Monarchy even limited Monarchy, have the trials of the Duke of York and the Queen of England held up to the astonishment contempt and scorn of mankind, I should think it would do more than the French [or] American revolutions, to bring it into discredit. indeed all human affairs, without your philosophical and Christian mantle of resignation would be deeply melancholy;[7] even that friendship which I feel for you ardent and sincere as it is would be over clouded by constant fears of its termination.

JOHN ADAMS

RC (DLC); in an unidentified hand, signed by Adams; edges chipped, with missing text supplied from FC; endorsed by TJ as received 15 Feb. 1821 and so recorded in SJL. RC (MHi); address cover only; with PoC of TJ to John Vaughan, 11 June 1822, on verso; addressed by Susanna Boylston Adams Clark (Treadway): "Honble Thomas Jefferson. Monticello. Virginia"; franked; postmarked Boston, 6 Feb. FC (Lb in MHi: Adams Papers).

Robert Southey reported in *The Life of Wesley; and the Rise and Progress of Methodism* (London, 1820) that shortly before his death at the age of eighty-seven, John Wesley said that "TIME HAS SHAKEN ME BY THE HAND, and death is not far behind" (2:561). The trial of the DUKE OF YORK likely refers to the 1809 examination in the British House of Commons into the conduct of Prince Frederick, Duke of York and Albany, when it became known that his mistress Mary Anne Clarke had used her connection with him to sell military commissions (*ODNB*). For the trial of the QUEEN OF ENGLAND, see note to TJ to William Roscoe, 27 Dec. 1820.

[1] Adams's amanuensis here inserted an asterisk keyed to a note at foot of first page: "Wesley."
[2] Omitted comma at right margin supplied from FC.
[3] RC: "Worsipers." FC: "Worshipers."
[4] RC: "Eutopian." FC: "Utopian."
[5] Omitted period at right margin supplied from FC.
[6] Omitted closing quotation mark editorially supplied.
[7] RC: "malancloly." FC: "malancholly." Semicolon supplied from FC.

From John Taylor

DEAR SIR Port Royal February 3. 1821

I hope you will excuse the liberty I am about to take, when I assure you that I have no other means of effecting my object.

Is the family of the late Col° Wilson C. Nicholas in destitute circumstances? Did he leave sons whose educations are unfinished? Would a contribution, if such is the case, of one hundred and twenty five dollars[1] annually for four years be beneficial to them? Would you receive and apply that sum to this object, without disclosing to any one from whom it comes? I have strong reasons for wishing that such a thing should be known only to yourself. Is there any person in Charlottesville, connected with some respectable man in Fredericksburg, through whom the money may be safely forwarded to you? I am with great respect and esteem, Sir, Your most ob^t S^t

JOHN TAYLOR

RC (NHi: American Historical Manuscript Collection); endorsed by TJ as received 11 Feb. 1821 and so recorded in SJL. RC (MHi); address cover only; with PoC of TJ to William Barret, 5 Mar. 1821, on verso; addressed: "Thomas Jefferson esq^r Monticello Albermarle"; stamped; postmarked Port Royal, 6 Feb.

[1] Manuscript: "dollars dollars."

From William Barret

SIR   Richmond 6th February 1821

SIR   Richmond 6th February 1821
    The agent of Mr B. Miller in Lynchburg, Mr S. Garland, has forwarded to me your bond, granted to A. Robertson & Co for $4256\frac{8}{100}$, on which there is a credit endorsed of $600—
    Mr Millers situation is such at this moment, as to render it necessary that all the balances due him should be collected, as soon as possible— Mr Miller will therefore be under great obligations to you by the payment of the balances due on your bond to A R & Co—If it sh^d not be convenient, at this moment, to discharge it, will you be so obliging as to name the period when it may be <u>calculated</u> on?   I should not be thus urgent but that Mr Miller is pressed by the Executor of his late partner for payment of the balance due by him—I am Sir
    With great respect Your Ob^t Hb^{le} Servt   WILLIAM BARRET

RC (MHi); endorsed by TJ as received 11 Feb. 1821 and so recorded in SJL. RC (DLC); address cover only; with PoC of TJ to Joseph C. Cabell, 22 Feb. 1821, on verso; addressed: "Thomas Jefferson Esqr Monticello"; franked; postmarked Richmond, 7 Feb.

William Barret (1786–1871), merchant and tobacco manufacturer, was a lifelong resident of Richmond. He joined the Richmond Light Infantry Blues and served with that unit during the War of 1812. In 1816 Barret partnered with David Higginbotham and Boyd Miller in the firm of Higginbotham, Barret & Company, and later he became a successful tobacco manufacturer in his own right. In the 1820s he was active in the American Colonization Society and its local subsidiaries. Barret had a workforce of about one hundred slaves in 1850, roughly half of whom he owned. His slaves included Henry Box Brown, who worked in his tobacco fac-

tory but famously escaped to freedom in 1849 by having himself shipped in a box to Philadelphia. Having become one of the wealthiest men in Richmond, Barret retired just as the Civil War began and preserved much of his wealth through foreign investments. He died when his pipe ignited his dressing gown. At his death Barret's estate was estimated to be worth half a million dollars (*DVB*; Fillmore Norfleet, *Saint-Mémin in Virginia: Portraits and Biographies* [1942], 69, 141; John A. Cutchins, *A Famous Command: The Richmond Light Infantry Blues* [1934], 296, 298, 322; *Richmond Enquirer*, 1 May 1816; DNA: RG 29, CS, Richmond, Industrial Schedules, 1850 and 1860; Brown, *Narrative of the Life of Henry Box Brown* [1851], esp. 15–8; Jeffrey Ruggles, *The Unboxing of Henry Brown* [2003]; Richmond *Daily Dispatch*, 21, 25 Jan. 1871; gravestone inscription in Hollywood Cemetery, Richmond).

To John R. Cotting

SIR   Monticello Feb. 7. 21.
    I have duly recieved your favor of Jan. 20 and am sorry it is not in my power to render any service to your useful undertaking. age and ill health render me no longer equal to the labors of science, and a

disabled wrist making writing slow and painful, has obliged me to abandon even common correspondence. with my regrets be pleased to accept the tender of my great respect.   TH: JEFFERSON

PoC (MHi); on verso of reused address cover of Robert I. Evans to TJ, 2 Oct. 1819; at foot of text: "Mr John Ruggles Cotting"; endorsed by TJ.

From Joseph C. Cabell

DEAR SIR,   Richmond Feb: 8. 1821.

I have received your letter of 31st ult. and return you many thanks for the kind & friendly expressions it contains. It is not in my nature to resist such an appeal. I this day handed into the office of the Enquirer a notification that I should again be a candidate. We will pass on to matters of more importance. I have shewn your letter to Genl Breckenridge & Mr Johnson, who seemed (& particularly the former) to be as much affected by it, as myself. We are all in confusion here about the accounts of the Literary Fund. The statements of our public officers differ, and there seems to be no surplus on hand, altho the auditor says there should be $101,000. The opposite party secretly exult at this state of things, altho' they pretend to be much disappointed. Our plan of a second loan may yet succeed, if the House should not get disgusted by the confusion of the public accounts, & reject every thing. Your letter has kindled great zeal in Genl Breckenridge. Yesterday Genl Blackburn in discussing Selden's Resolutions, spoke of the University as "a great institution highly deserving our patronage." We have great difficulties to contend with. Your name & Hand writing have great effect here. Let me entreat you with the freedom of a friend, immediately to write to Genl Breckenridge a letter on the subject of the University, such as may be shewn generally, shewing no preferences, & making no imputations. He wishes it, & will make powerful use of it. You may rely on our discretion. I write you with his privity & at his instance. Ever & faithfully yours

JOSEPH C. CABELL

RC (ViU: TJP-PC); endorsed by TJ as received 11 Feb. 1821 and so recorded in SJL.

The *Richmond Enquirer* announced on 10 Feb. 1821 that Cabell would be a CANDIDATE for reelection to the Senate of Virginia.

SELDEN'S RESOLUTIONS, which William Selden presented to the Virginia House of Delegates on 9 Jan. 1821 in anticipation of the United States Supreme Court's upcoming decision in *Cohens v. Virginia*, resolved "That the supreme court of the United States have no rightful authority under the constitution, to examine and correct the judgment for which the Commonwealth of Virginia has been 'cited and admonished to be and appear at the supreme court of the United

States:' and that the General Assembly do hereby enter their most solemn protest against the jurisdiction of that court over the matter" (*Report and Resolutions concerning the Citation of the Commonwealth.*

to answer a complaint before the Supreme Court of the United States [Richmond, 1821], quote on p. 24; *JHD* [1820–21 sess.], 102–8).

To Bernard Peyton

DEAR SIR   Monticello Feb. 9. 21.

I expect that my grandson informed you of the misfortune which had stopped for a while the Shadwell mills. it will still be ten days or a fortnight before they will be able to recommence grinding, and consequently before we can be again getting down our flour. in the mean time I was obliged to draw on you yesterday in favor of Wolfe and Raphael for 100.D. which shall be replaced the moment our mills are in motion. I must pray you to render me your account, say to Dec. 31. and thence regularly every quarter, this being my habitual course. otherwise, not knowing all the items here I lose sight of it.   I have a smith's shop which has leisure beyond my own work, and I am thinking of setting them to make nails at their spare time. will you be so good as to inform me of the prices of nail rod in Richmond and also of the prices of <u>wrought</u> nails there of the different sizes sold by the barrel. supposing the time for renewing my notes to be at hand I inclose you blanks & salute you affectionat[ely]

TH: JEFFERSON

P.S. will you send me a sheet or two of blanks of the bk of the US. & of the Farmers.

PoC (MHi); on verso of reused address cover of William Robertson to TJ, 12 Oct. 1819; edge trimmed; at foot of text: "Capt Bernard Peyton"; endorsed by TJ. Enclosures not found.

MY GRANDSON: Thomas Jefferson Randolph. TJ recorded having drawn on Peyton in favor of WOLFE AND RAPHAEL on 8 Feb. 1821 "to pay them groceries 77.79 and cash 22.21 which I now recieve." The next day he recorded enclosing blank NOTES to Peyton "for renewal, to wit 3000 & 2250 to bk. US. & 2500. to Farmer's bank" (*MB*, 2:1372).

From Lewis Williams

Sir. Washington February 10th 1821

When quite a youth I was taught to venerate and admire the principles upon which you so wisely and happily administered the government of this country—Since I attained to maturer age, and particularly since called on to participate in the affairs of legislation I have been more and more confirmed in the opinions entertained in my earlier years—

Our expenditures, it seems to me, are greater than the genius or policy of the government can justify, and lead inevitably to a system of internal taxation—when this state of things shall have been produced, (in time of profound peace) one of the brightest traits in the character of our government will be greatly obscured—with these views I have resisted as much as I could the tendency of the measures which have been adopted for some years past, and have advocated a return to the republican principles of the good old school—But it appears to be unfashionable to advert with any kind of respect to the principles of that period to which I have alluded—Debts, taxes, armies and navies to a great extent, are not now as they once were, objects formidable to men professing to be republicans—

In advocating a reduction of the army I attempted to derive authority from the course pursued under your administration—You will therefore Sir I hope pardon the liberty I take of enclosing to you the remarks I made on that occasion—

with great respect and veneration I am Sir y^r obt & very H^{bl} Servt

LEWIS WILLIAMS

RC (MoSHi: TJC-BC); at foot of text: "Thomas Jefferson Esqr."; endorsed by TJ as received 15 Feb. 1821 and so recorded in SJL.

Lewis Williams (1786–1842), public official, was born in Surry County, North Carolina, and graduated from the University of North Carolina in 1808. He served as a tutor there, 1810–12, and as a university trustee, 1813–42. Williams represented Surry County for two terms in the North Carolina General Assembly, 1813–14, and sat in the United States House of Representatives from 1815 until his death in Washington. He supported William H. Crawford's 1824 presidential candidacy and was in the opposition during the administrations of Andrew Jackson and

Martin Van Buren. Williams chaired the claims committee for several sessions, and thanks to his lengthy congressional service he was nicknamed the "Father of the House" (William S. Powell, ed., *Dictionary of North Carolina Biography* [1979–96], 6:211; *Sketches of the History of the University of North Carolina, together with a Catalogue of Officers and Students, 1789–1889* [1889], 70, 80, 232; Washington *Daily National Intelligencer*, 24 Feb. 1842).

Williams's enclosure, not found, may have been a copy of his 8–9 Jan. 1821 speech in Congress favoring a REDUCTION OF THE ARMY. On 23 Jan. the House of Representatives passed a bill to that effect, which became law on 2 Mar. 1821 as "An Act to reduce and fix the military peace establishment of the United States" (*Annals*, 16th Cong., 2d sess., 767–94, 936–7; *U.S. Statutes at Large*, 3:615–6).

To William Barret

SIR   Monticello Feb. 12. 21.

I recieved yesterday evening your favor of the 5th inst. I am one of those who during the flood of bank-currency which deluged us, unwarily contracted debts, which had the times continued the same, would have given me no trouble; but by the sudden reduction of that, and the fall of produce from tha[t] cause and the failure of market, I am left in the lurch, these debts being now fully trebled. the flour I now send to market clears me but 1.96. D. after paying expences. I have not hesitated, seeing no prospect of change, to give up the idea of depending on crops for payment, and to offer property for sale. but this too requires time. I offer for sale a merchant mill which would pay every dollar I owe in the world, but I know not when I may meet with a purchaser. I offer lands also, but under the same uncertainty. I am now therefore engaged in making some arrangements which may lessen delays to those to whom I owe and give me time to make reasonable sales. it will be about three weeks before I shall know the result of these; and I must therefore ask that time before I can propose to you specific sums & times of payment. the moment I know this result, you shal[l] certainly hear from me on the subject. in the mean time accept the assurance of my great respect.

                                                    TH: JEFFERSON

PoC (MHi); on verso of reused address cover of Bernard Peyton to TJ, 7 Oct. 1819; edge trimmed; at foot of text: "M[r] Barrett"; endorsed by TJ. Barret's letter was dated 6 Feb. 1821, not THE 5TH INST.

To Frederick A. Mayo

SIR   Monticello Feb. 12. 21.

I this day deliver to a boatman to be conveyed to you 2. boxes of books containing about 100. vols to be bound. inclosed is the list directing how they are to be bound, and in each volume you will find similar directions. they will be directed to the Compiler's office. accept my respectful salutations.   TH: JEFFERSON

PoC (MHi); on verso of a reused address cover from James Monroe to TJ; at foot of text: "M[r] Fred. A. Mayo"; endorsed by TJ. Enclosure not found.

From Bernard Peyton

DEAR SIR,   Rich'd 12 February 1821

I am favor'd this morning with yours of the 9th: current.

Agreeable to your request have stated your ℀ to date, which you will find under cover, together with a copy of one stated in July last to Mr Gibson, by your direction, which was not paid, & which you afterwards desired I would deduct out of the sale of Dr Everetts bill on Liverpool, which you will observe is <u>fully</u> credit^d—I hope every item in those accounts will be recognised by you, & found correct, if not, I shall[1] be always happy to make them so.

For the future, will comply with your wishes in furnishing your ℀ quarterly, & if I should, in the hurry of business, omit it at any time, I shall be pleased to be reminded of it—
Your Notes were safely rec'd, but one week <u>too late</u> for the Farmers Bank, your note there, fell due last week, & I put in one for you, intending to remind you of[2] it by this day's mail.   I enclose as you direct several printed blank notes for the U. states & Farmers Banks, which will save you much writing.

The draft you speak of having drawn on me, shall be honor'd with the greatest cheerfulness,[3] as well as any others you may find it necessary to draw from time to time, without regard to the state of your account, feeling it one of my greatest pleasures to be servicable to you.

I have made enquiry as to the price Wrought Nails in this market & find 8^d 10^d 12^d 20^d & 24^d all sell at 12$\frac{1}{2}$¢, & if an assortment of each is taken, 10¢ p^r ℔ is the price—   There are no Nail Rods in this market just now save a few very superior I have myself from the manufactory of the Messrs: Patterson's of Balto:, which are $7 p^r Bundle of 56 ℔—if those would suit, of assorted sizes; I could forward them to you—

I rec^d some time ago bill Lading your Cask Wine from N. Carolina, as well as a bill the cost of the same, say $30:15 without charges.—It has not yet arrived, so soon as it does; will remit the shippers the cost of the same as above, pay the charges here, & forward it on to you by Gilmore or Johnson's Boats—
The engravings of "American Scenery" mentioned to you in a former letter, are still here waiting your order—

With great respect D^r sir Your mo: Obd: Servt.

BERNARD PEYTON

Flour 3\frac{1}{4}$—dull—
Wheat 62$\frac{1}{2}$¢
Tobacco $4 @ 7$\frac{1}{2}$ & $8 declining—

[597]

N.B. since writing the above your draft favor Wolf & Raphael for $100 has been presented & paid, but your ⅗ being closed did not think it necessary to add this sum to it—it will appear in the next.

B.P.

RC (MHi); endorsed by TJ as received 19 Feb. 1821 and so recorded in SJL. Enclosures not found.

[1] Manuscript: "shal."
[2] Manuscript: "if."
[3] Manuscript: "cheefulness."

From Timothy Pickering

SIR,   Salem Feb[y] 12, 1821.

You will recollect that Gibbon, in his history of the decline and fall of the Roman Empire, treats of the Christian Religion; and that he assigns five secondary causes of its prevalence, & final victory over the established religions of the earth. Among these, one was "the miraculous powers ascribed to the primitive church." It seems plain that Gibbon considered the miracles ascribed to Christ[1] & his Apostles, alike destitute of reality as those which are found in the legends of the Church of Rome. In relation to the latter, Bishop Watson, in his letters to the Historian, puts "to his heart" this question—"Whether her absurd pretensions to that very kind of miraculous powers, you have here displayed as operating to the increase of Christianity, have not converted half her numbers to Protestantism, and the other half to Infidels?"—[2]

But absurdities, in relation to Christianity, are not confined within the pale of the Church of Rome. There are some doctrines taught in Protestant Churches, in Europe & America, so repugnant to the ideas I entertain of the perfect wisdom, justice and benevolence of the Deity, as to authorize the opinion, that they could not be the subjects of a Divine Revelation. I have not found them in the books said to contain such a revelation; and I long ago renounced them. They constituted parts of parental and school instruction, from my earliest remembrance: but I never taught them to[3] my children. I believed them implicitly, till I was of an age to think and inquire for myself; and one other doctrine to a later period—that of the Trinity; for I had not heard it called in question in any pulpit; and books on the subject had not fallen in my way. Few, indeed, who can read and understand theological controversies, allow themselves time to investigate the merits of the questions involved in them. Official and professional duties occupy the attention of most; and of numbers of the remaining few of educated men, science & the general pursuits of literature engross the leisure hours. Some of these, to whom doctrines are presented for religious truths which shock their reason,—taking them, without further inquiry, to be the Christian system,—they reject this as an imposture. This was exemplified in a case which has recently come to my knowledge; and of so interesting a nature as to induce me to request a statement of it in writing, from the young gentleman who reported it: and I take the liberty of presenting it to you, in the writer's own words, from his letter to me, dated at Cambridge the 7th instant.

"I was last April in New-Orleans; and took passage on board the P.A. captain H. for New-York: among the passengers were Dr Drake and Mr Townsend, both of New York; and the latter gentleman a member of the new 'Congregational Society'[4]* in that city. This society had been formed during my absence from this part of the United States; and I was happy to find some one who could give me an account of its beginning and its prospects. Mr T. gave me such an account of both as I was glad to hear; and spoke also of the success of Mr Sparks,† in Baltimore; and of other appearances which promised well for the general promotion of Liberal Christianity. He likewise mentioned Mr Channing's sermon preached at the ordination of Mr Sparks, and the first six numbers of the New Series of the 'Christian Disciple;'[5]‡ all of which had been published during my absence, and all of which he had on board.—I asked if Dr Drake belonged to this new[6] society; and learned that he did not; and also, that he was an Infidel. Mr T. brought the above mentioned pamphlets on deck; and while I was looking over a number of the 'Disciple,'[7] I observed Dr Drake to take up the <u>sermon</u>—a circumstance with which I was very much gratified. I had conversed with him a great deal, in the few days we had been acquainted, and was very much pleased with his fairness and candour, the compass of his mind, and the clearness of his views; especially in those subjects which belong to what we call <u>moral reasoning</u>; and I had determined to call his attention to this subject; believing that liberal christianity needs only to be understood, to gain it the approbation of fair and liberal minds."

"I was attentive to every appearance which should show the success of what seemed to me so important an experiment; but I soon observed that the Doctor appeared interested in the sermon: nor did

* Of Unitarians.

† The minister of the Unitarian Church in that City.

‡ A periodical publication ably conducted by some Unitarian Gentlemen in Cambridge and Boston.

he notice any thing else till he had read it all. After reading it, he came immediately to me, and said (nearly in these words)—'This[8] is the first rational exposition of Christianity that I have ever seen. I have taken my views of the Christian Religion from its pretended friends— from those who profess to teach it. I was quite satisfied that the religion which they taught could <u>not</u> be from God: it carried absurdity on its very front. And ever since I was old enough to understand preaching, I have felt that Christianity (for I thought the preachers of Christianity knew best what it was) was an indefensible system. I am pleased with the religion as here represented; and if this is the Christianity of the New Testament, I see no reason for rejecting it.'"[9]

"After this I had occasional conversations with him, on religious subjects; and was always pleased with his good sense, and his desire more fully to understand these subjects. He always spoke in the highest terms of Mr Channing's sermon; and particularly the candour and fairness with which everything is there stated."

"On the first sabbath after our arrival in New-York, he attended the religious exercises of the New Society, and declared his intention of becoming a member. But he was soon confined to his chamber by a sickness from which he never recovered.—But <u>religion</u> does not <u>alone</u> mourn the loss of this eminently promising young man. <u>Literature</u> weeps over his early tomb; and <u>Poesy</u> has hung her harp on the willow!"[10]

I take the liberty, sir, to send you Mr Channing's sermon. Whatever you may think of his views of Christianity, I am sure that the firm and energetic avowal of his opinions, his candour, his ingenuity, and the elegance of his composition, will fully compensate you for the time you shall spend in its perusal.

You cannot be uninformed of a prevalent opinion among your fellow citizens, that <u>you</u> are one of the <u>learned</u> <u>unbelievers in Revelation</u>. Your Notes on Virginia contain expressions which, if they did not <u>originate</u>, have served to <u>strengthen</u> that opinion. You know the influence of a distinguished name over the minds of its warm, and especially of its youthful admirers; and should you become, if you are not now, a Believer, you will deeply regret the effects of that influence.— You can entertain no doubt that eighteen hundred years ago, there appeared in Judea an extraordinary person called Jesus Christ, the founder of a sect which, after him, were called Christians: for Tacitus, Suetonius, and the Younger Pliny speak of him and of this[11] sect. You also strongly appreciate the <u>moral</u> <u>precepts</u> purporting to have been delivered, orally or in writing, by Jesus, and by some of his followers who professed to be ear and eye witnesses of his words, and of the wonderful works ascribed to him. You have called the religion described in the records of those witnesses, "our benign religion": and could you banish from your mind the recollection of the strange tenets which [have][12] been grafted upon that religion, and examine its history and[13] unsophisticated doctrines with the same unbiassed disposition in which you read the histories and other writings of celebrated Romans; you might not think them unworthy to be believed by the most enlightened minds. Certainly, no one can think himself justly exposed to the charge of <u>credulity</u>, for entertaining that religious faith of which Boyle, and Locke, and Newton were sincere professors.

A letter from me, unless on business and the common occurrences of life, you would not expect: for to literature I have no pretensions; and in politics we[14] did not agree: but I can disapprove of the principles and oppose the measures of men in public stations, with an entire exemption from unkind feelings towards them as individuals. By some I have been injured: but I am not conscious of entertaining a particle of resentment or ill-will towards any human being. In all his imitable perfections, Christians believe it to be their duty to imitate God, "who (as St Paul saith) will have all men to be saved, and to come to the knowledge of the truth." In this spirit, and in the simple style of antiquity, I bid you

Farewell.   TIMOTHY PICKERING.

P.S. Mr Channing's Sermon is in a packet accompanying this letter.[15]

RC (MHi); with Pickering's brackets around his footnotes editorially omitted; at foot of text: "Honble Thomas Jefferson"; endorsed by TJ as received 25 Feb. 1821 and so recorded in SJL. 1st FC (MHi: Pickering Papers); in Pickering's hand; lacking author's footnotes. 2d FC (MHi: Pickering Papers); in Pickering's hand; incomplete (see note 10 below); endorsed by Pickering: "To Th: Jefferson Feby 12. 1821. On the Christian Religion. Correspondence with him." Tr (MH: Palfrey Family Papers); lacking author's footnotes.

Timothy Pickering (1745–1829), public official, was born in Salem, Essex County, Massachusetts, graduated from Harvard College (later Harvard University) in 1763, and was admitted to the bar five years later. Between 1766 and 1775 he rose in rank through the Massachusetts militia from lieutenant to colonel, and during the Revolutionary War he served

as colonel adjutant-general to General George Washington, 1777–78, was elected a member of the Board of War in 1777, and served as colonel and quartermaster general of the Continental army, 1780–85. Pickering subsequently moved to Pennsylvania, where he helped organize Luzerne County, supported the new federal constitution at Pennsylvania's ratification convention in 1788, and was a delegate to the state constitutional convention, 1789–90. After selecting him in 1790 to conduct an ultimately successful negotiation with the Seneca Indians, President Washington appointed Pickering postmaster general in 1791, and four years later he made him his secretary of war. In 1795 Pickering was also elected to the American Philosophical Society and became secretary of state, a position he retained until President John Adams fired him in 1800 for his increasingly overt political opposition. After returning to Essex County, Pickering represented Massachusetts as a

Federalist in the United States Senate, 1803–11, and in the United States House of Representatives, 1813–17, where he opposed the Embargo Act of 1807 and the War of 1812. Pickering retired to his farm in Wenham before moving back in 1820 to Salem, where he died (*ANB; DAB;* John L. Sibley and others, eds., *Sibley's Harvard Graduates* [1873–], 15:448–73; Gerard H. Clarfield, *Timothy Pickering and the American Republic* [1980]; MHi: Pickering Papers; *PTJ;* Heitman, *Continental Army,* 440–1; *Doc. Hist. Ratification,* vol. 2; APS, Minutes, 16 Jan. 1795 [MS in PPAmP]; *Salem Gazette,* 30 Jan. 1829).

Edward Gibbon commented skeptically on THE MIRACULOUS POWERS ASCRIBED TO THE PRIMITIVE CHURCH in chapter 15 of *The History of the Decline and Fall of the Roman Empire* (London, 1776–88; Sowerby, no. 101), 1:450, 475–9. Richard Watson, the Anglican bishop of Llandaff, responded to THE HISTORIAN in *An Apology for Christianity, in a Series of Letters, addressed to Edward Gibbon, Esq* (Cambridge, Eng., 1776; Sowerby, no. 1651), quote on pp. 75–6.

The YOUNG GENTLEMAN whose letter of 7 Feb. 1821 Pickering quoted was James Hayward (RC in MHi: Pickering Papers). The P.A. was the brig *Phœbe Ann,* captained by Silas Holmes (CAPTAIN H.) (New York *American,* 26 May 1820; *Hunt's Merchants' Magazine and Commercial Review* 43 [1860]: 770). The CONGREGATIONAL SOCIETY attended by the poet Joseph Rodman Drake may have been New York City's First Congregational Church, established in 1819 (New York *American,* 1 May 1820). HUNG HER HARP ON THE WILLOW is adapted from the Bible, Psalm 137.2.

The controversial EXPRESSIONS concerning scriptural revelation in TJ's *Notes on the State of Virginia* include his rejection of the universal deluge as an explanation for the presence of fossilized shells thousands of feet above sea level (*Notes,* ed. Peden, 31–3, 265–6n). TACITUS, SUE- TONIUS, AND THE YOUNGER PLINY referred to Christians in *The Annals,* 15.44 (*Tacitus,* trans. Maurice Hutton, William Peterson, Clifford H. Moore, John Jackson, and others, Loeb Classical Library [1914–37; undated reprint], 5:282–3), *Lives of the Caesars,* 6.16 (*Suetonius,* trans. John C. Rolfe, Loeb Classical Library [1913–14; rev. ed. 1997–98; repr. 2001], 2:106–7), and *Letters,* 10.96 (*Pliny,* trans. Betty Radice, Loeb Classical Library [1969; undated reprint], 2:284–91), respectively. On 4 Mar. 1801 in his first inaugural address, TJ stated that Americans were "enlightened" by a BENIGN RELIGION, "professed indeed and practised in various forms," but sharing many virtues (*PTJ,* 33:150). The biblical verse from Sᵀ PAUL is 1 Timothy 2.4.

¹ FCs and Tr: "Jesus."
² 1st FC: "infidelity." 2d FC and Tr: "Infidelity."
³ FCs and Tr here add "any of."
⁴ Quotation marks editorially changed from double to single, with omitted closing quotation mark supplied from 1st FC.
⁵ Quotation marks editorially changed from double to single.
⁶ Word interlined.
⁷ Quotation marks editorially changed from double to single.
⁸ Double quotation mark preceding this word editorially changed to single.
⁹ Closing single quotation mark editorially supplied.
¹⁰ Preceding four paragraphs replaced in 2d FC with bracketed notation: "Here was transcribed nearly the whole, being all between the hooks, in the first 2ᵈ & 3ᵈ pages, of Mʳ James Hayward's letter, stating the case of the late Dʳ Drake, above referred to." Preceding two sentences not in Tr.
¹¹ FCs and Tr: "his."
¹² Word, not in RC, supplied from FCs.
¹³ Preceding two words interlined.
¹⁴ Pickering here canceled "always."
¹⁵ Postscript not in FCs or Tr.

To James T. Austin

Monticello Feb. 13. 21.

I thank you, Sir, for the paper inclosed in yours of Jan. 20. I think with you that there is no good in lessening the responsibility of judges. their independance on a king is a good thing; but independence on the nation is a bad one. here we have copied England where we ought not. but we have omitted to copy what ought to have been copied, removability on the simple concurrence of the two other coordinate branches. instead of that we have substituted impeachment, a mere scare crow, & which experience proves impracticable. but from these things I withdraw tendering you my respectful salutations.

TH: JEFFERSON

RC (MHi: Elbridge Gerry Papers); addressed: "James T. Austin esq. Boston"; franked; postmarked Milton, 17 Feb. PoC (DLC); on verso of reused address cover of John H. Cocke to TJ, 11 Oct. 1819; endorsed by TJ.

From Joseph Dougherty

DEAR SIR.   Washington City Feb. 13th —21

I have just time at this present moment to Inform you, that I expect before I can finish this to be obliged to close the eyes of our esteemed friend—W. A. Burwell—Several nights siting with him renders me incapable of writing more

Your Humble Servt.   JOS. DOUGHERTY

Please inform Mr T.M.R.

RC (MHi); endorsed by TJ as received 19 Feb. 1821 and so recorded in SJL. RC (DLC); address cover only; with PoC of TJ to LeRoy, Bayard & Company, 11 June 1822, on verso; addressed: "Thos. Jef- ferson Esqr. Late President of the U. States Monticella va"; franked; post-marked Washington, 14 Feb.

T.M.R.: Thomas Mann Randolph.

To Jared Mansfield

Monticello Feb. 13. 21.

I am favored, Sir, with your letter of Jan. 26. and am duly sensible of the honor proposed of giving to my portrait a place among the benefactors of our nation, and of the establishment of Westpoint in particular. I have ever considered that establishment as of major importance to our country, and in whatever I could d[o] for it, I viewed myself as performing a duty only. this is certainly more than requited by the kind sentiments expressed in your letter. the real debt of the institution is to it's able and zealous professors. mr Sully, I fear however, will consider the trouble of his journey, and the employment of his fine pencil, as illy bestowed on an Ottamy of 78. Voltaire when requested by a female friend to sit for his bust by the sculptor Pigalle, answered 'J'ai soixante seize ans; et M. Pigalle doit, dit-on, venir modeler mon visage. mais, Madame, il faudrait que j'eusse un visage. on n'en devinerait à peine la place. mes yeux sont enfoncés de trois pouces; mes joues sont des vieux parchemin mal collés sur des os qui ne tiennent à rien. le peu de dents que j'avais est parti.' I will conclude however, with him, that what remains is at your service, & that of the pencil of mr Sully. I shall be at home till the middle of April, when I shall go for some time to an occasional and distant residence. within this term mr Sully will be pleased to consult his own convenience, in which the state of the roads will of course have great weight every day of it will be equal with me.

I pray you, Sir, to convey to the brethren of your institution and to accept for yourself also, the assurance of my high consideration and regard. Th: Jefferson

PoC (DLC); on verso of reused address cover of John Barnes to TJ, 12 Oct. 1819; edge trimmed; at foot of text: "Jared Mansfield esq."

Atomy (OTTAMY): "An emaciated or withered living body, a walking skeleton" (*OED*).
Voltaire wrote to his FEMALE FRIEND Suzanne Necker on 21 May 1770 regarding the taking of his bust (Friedrich Melchior, baron von Grimm, *Correspondance littéraire, philosophique et critique* [Paris, 1812–14; Poor, *Jefferson's Library*, 14 (no.

918)], 1:163–4). The resulting full-length nude statue by Jean Baptiste Pigalle is now in the Louvre.

J'AI SOIXANTE SEIZE ANS . . . J'AVAIS EST PARTI: "I am seventy-six years old; and Mr. Pigalle, it is said, must come model my face. But, Madame, for that, I would need to have a face. One can hardly guess where it is. My eyes are sunk in three inches; my cheeks are like old parchment that has been badly pasted on bones that are attached to nothing. The few teeth I had are now gone."

From Craven Peyton

DEAR SIR Monteagle Feby 14ᵗʰ [13] 1821.

My necessity is such as to compel[l] me now to call on You for the amt between us—about $1350—,[1] this I do, with great reluctan[ce] fearing it may not be entirely Convenient to you, to spare that amt at this time, owing I suppose to my misfortune I was not called on at Christmas as was expected, but the call is made now, & undar such

Circumstances as to Compell me to advance the money—in a very short time, or forfeit my word & Credit which I hold more dear then life, Your Draft on Bernerd Peyton at Sixty days wou^d answer every purpose, & I well know with what pleasure it wou^d be receav^d by him.

with the greatest Respect & Esteem   C. PEYTON

RC (MHi); edge trimmed; misdated; endorsed by TJ as a letter of 14 Feb. 1821 received a day earlier and so recorded in SJL; with Dft of postscript to TJ's 5 Mar. 1821 letter to Peyton on verso.

[1] Reworked from "$1354."

To Craven Peyton

DEAR SIR   Monticello Feb. 13. 21.

I am at this moment engaged in making arrangements which may supply the deficit of crops and prices; but it will be two or three weeks before their result will be known. the moment it is, you shall be informed what can be done either from myself, or by Jefferson to whom I am turning over all my concerns.

I informed my sister Marks that I would send for her any day she would name, and I still await her notice.

Accept my friendly salutations   TH: JEFFERSON

PoC (MHi); on verso of reused address cover of James Ewell to TJ, 12 Oct. 1819; at foot of text: "Craven Peyton esq."; endorsed by TJ. JEFFERSON: Thomas Jefferson Randolph.

To Robert H. Rose

Monticello Feb. 13. 21.

Th: Jefferson returns his thanks to mr Rose for his agricultural address which he has read with pleasure, and is particularly sensible of the friendly sentiments expressed in his letter of Jan. 21. which he reciprocates cordially, with the addition of his respectful salutations.

PoC (MHi); on verso of portion of reused address cover to TJ; dateline at foot of text; endorsed by TJ.

To John W. Taylor

Sir   Monticello Feb. 13. 21.

The honor of your letter of Jan. 30. is just now recieved, and I wish it were in my power to answer it's enquiries. but I am an entire stranger to the **ΦΒΚ**. society, it's history and it's objects. it's existence is known to me by hear-say only. the contrary supposition has probably been founded on an **F.H.C.** society which existed at W^m & Mary college, when I was there, of which I was a member. that was confined to the Alumni of that institution

I do not know, Sir, whether I can yet congratulate you on the prospect of a restoration of the right of self-government to the transatlantic nations, and on the consoling reflection that this is our work. it had for some time a flattering appearance. but the Northern bears seem bristling up to maintain the empire of force. we may still however hope that the hosts on which they rely, may catch the disease they are employed to cure, and carry liberty to the North instead of suppressing it in the South. to my prayers for the attainment of that blessing there, & it's preservation here, I add the tender to yourself of my high consideration and esteem.

Th: Jefferson

RC (NHi: Taylor Papers); addressed: "The honorable John W. Taylor Speaker of the H— of Representatives of the US. Washington"; franked; postmarked Milton, 17 Feb.; endorsed by Taylor.

For the F.H.C. SOCIETY, see TJ to Thomas McAuley, 14 June 1819, and note.

To Theodorus Bailey

Monticello Feb. 14. 21.

I am very thankful to you, dear Sir, for the trouble you have been so good as to take with my letter addressed to George Jones. on recurring to his original, to which mine was an answer, I think it very possible I may have read amiss the cypher subscribed to it. it may perhaps be George Long, or some other signature better known in New York. if you cannot decypher truly the signature, then throw this, that, and the detained letter into the fire as not worth further investigation[.] I often recieve letters with signatures totally undecypherable, which of course I am obliged to put by without answering. but I thought I had guessed rightly at this. it has at least given me the pleasure of renewing to you the assurance of my constant friendship and respect.

Th: Jefferson

PoC (DLC); on verso of portion of reused address cover to TJ; edge trimmed; at foot of text: "Theodorus Bailey esq."; endorsed by TJ. Enclosure: George Long (ca. 1782–1843) to TJ, 20 Dec. 1820, not found (see note to TJ to Long, 30 Dec. 1820).

From Andrew Cock

RESPECTED FRIEND   Flushing—Long Island—State of
THOMAS JEFFERSON—   New York—2ᵈ Mᵒ 14ᵗʰ—1821—

Be good enough to excuse the freedom I have taken in addressing thee—being a stranger—and having no right to intrude upon thy time or attention—I have however conceived that the subject which I shall mention may be of vast importance to those States where men are used for cultivateing the Earth instead of animals of a different species—

Being setled on a Farm & finding the expence of cultivateing the ground wᵈ not be in proportion to the fall of the price of the produce, I last season constructed a Machin[e] for planting corn—and almost every kind of seed that Farmers plant—and finding the benefits of it so great, I have concluded to apply for a patent—a model is on the way to the seat of Goverment

The Machine is drawn by a Horse—and is so constructed that it will drop the corn and cover it as fast as the horse can walk—and by my experiments it performs the labour of seven—if not ten men as it will drop[1] & cover an Acre in one hour.

perhaps our modes of planting may differ, therefore I'll[2] describe mine—The ground—of a sod is ploughed deep enough that in marking out for planting the plough will not tear up the sods—this marking out is done only one way (North & South is preferd) from four to five feet asunder—the manure is strewed in the furrow—the horse walks in the furrow—& the corn drops from 6 to 10 Inches apart as is wishd—and a scraper draws the loose soil in again that was thrown out in marking out the ground—from information[3] it is well calculated both for Cotton & rice—or any Seed planted in drills—the dropping Machine is easily made to suit various seeds—one man can tend it— small stone on small sods is of no consequence—the scraper acting in such a manner as will clear itself of them.

There are boxes & machinery for dropping & rolling in small seeds with the same expedition—In all the descriptions of planting or sowing Machines that I have read of, they are not only complex—but very expensive—this will cost twenty five dollars only—and with careful usage will do a great deal of work with little or no expence for several seasons—in dropping the corn I prefer it at 6 to 8 Inches—and when hoeing it out—reduce it with the hoe to 8 to 10 I find it less labour and think it produces more corn than when planted in hills—If leisure permits—may I ask the favour of a line from thee—giveing me your practise & thy opinion respecting the use of such a Machine in your State—& very much Oblige

Thy Friend in the true sense
of the word   ANDREW COCK

Direct to me in New York (City)

RC (Vi: Nathaniel Francis Cabell Papers); edge trimmed; addressed: "Thomas Jefferson Esqr Monticello Virgnia"; franked; postmarked New York, 19 Feb.; endorsed by TJ as received 3 Mar. 1821 and so recorded in SJL; with later notations on address cover, including one by Nathaniel Francis Cabell stating that the letter concerned "A general Seed Drill" and another in an unidentified hand directing it "For Frank G. Ruffin Esq Shadwell." Enclosed in TJ to Peter Minor, 9 Mar. 1821.

Andrew Cock (1769–1832), merchant and farmer, was born on Long Island, New York. By 1789 he worked as a grocer in New York City in a partnership with his brother Isaac Cock that lasted until 1794. He then operated as a merchant with various partners as Andrew Cock & Company, 1794–1803, and on his own until at least 1808. From 1802 to 1804 Cock was active in the "New-York Society for promoting the Manumission of Slaves, and protecting such of them as have been, or may be liberated." He moved by 1810 to a farm in Flushing, Queens, New York, where he remained until about 1824. Cock won a $7.50 premium from the New York Agricultural Society in 1820 for his "machine for planting corn," and he received a patent for it on 20 Mar.

1821. Having returned to New York City, he served as the secretary of the United States Fire Insurance Company from 1824 until his death from cholera (George William Cocks, comp., *History and Genealogy of the Cock-Cocks-Cox Family* [2d ed., 1914], 74; William Wade Hinshaw and others, *Encyclopedia of American Quaker Genealogy* [1936–50; repr. 1969–77], 3:73, 378; *The New-York Directory, and Register, For the Year 1789* [New York, 1789], 21; New York *Daily Advertiser*, 4 Feb. 1794; New York *American Citizen and General Advertiser*, 30 Jan. 1802; *New-York Evening Post*, 3 Feb. 1803, 9 Apr. 1824, 24 July 1832; New York *Mercantile Advertiser*, 9 Jan. 1804, 10 Nov. 1820; *Minutes of the Proceedings of the ninth American Convention for promoting the Abolition of Slavery . . . assembled at Philadelphia* [Philadelphia, 1804], 6; *New-York Gazette & General Advertiser*, 30 May 1805, 12 Oct. 1814; *Ming's New-York Price-Current*, 30 July 1808; DNA: RG 29, CS, N.Y., Flushing, 1810; *List of Patents*, 224; New York *Statesman*, 14 May 1824; *Boston Courier*, 26 July 1832).

[1] Word interlined in place of "plant."
[2] Manuscript: "Ill."
[3] Manuscript: "imformation."

To John Taylor

DEAR SIR   Monticello Feb. 14. 21.

I recieved three days ago your favor of the 3^d with it's benevolent proposition respecting our deceased & unfortunate friend W. C. Nicholas. he left no son under a course of education. of his three sons, the eldest, Col° Robert, is engaged in an enterprise in Louisiana with his brother in law John Smith. the second is hesitating between that and the study of the law. they are both of them remarkably steady, correct young men of sound judgment and understanding. the 3ᵈ son is in the navy. he left 3. married daughters and 3. unmarried. the former are well married; two of them to husbands who are willing but not able perhaps to do much for the family; the other to one who is able, but perhaps not very willing to do much. the widow & 3. unmarried daughters are living on the estate & it's proceeds. but the negroes will all be sold in the winter. there will then remain to the widow her dower in the lands only. if she sells it will probably yield not more than 5000.D. if she rents, the income will be very scanty, and her health such as to threaten that the 3. unmarried daughters may soon be deprived even of that resource.   I recieved some time ago from mr Ritchie, in your name & his, a copy of your late work on the constitution of the US. I returned him my thanks & begged they might be communicated to yourself thro' the same channel. but I am glad to avail myself of this opportunity of doing it directly[1] and with the more pleasure after having read the book, and acquired a knolege of it's value. I have no hesitation in saying that it carries us back to the genuine principles of the constitution more demonstratively than any work published since the date of that instrument. it pulverises the sophistries of the Judges on bank taxation, and of the 5. lawyers on lotteries. this last act of venality (for it cannot be of judgment) makes me ashamed that I was ever a lawyer. I have suggested to a friend in the legislature that that body should send a copy of your book to every one of our Representatives & Senators in Congress as a standing instruction and with a declaration that it contains the catholic faith which whosoever doth not keep whole & undefiled without doubt he shall perish everlastingly.

Our University labors hard to come into existence. I am surprised it finds enemies in the Colleges Academies & private classical schools throughout the state as if inimical to them. but it becomes in truth their foundation, not their rival. it leaves to them the field of classical preparation,[2] not proposing to turn itself into a grammar school. it leaves to them that middle degree of instruction in geography, surveying, grammer Eᵗc which will be called for by the great body of those who cannot afford or who do not wish an University education. we shall recieve only those subjects who desire the highest degree of instruction for which they now go to Harvard, to Princeton, N. York & Philadelphia. these seminaries are no longer proper for Southern or Western students. the signs of the times admonish us to call them home. if knolege is power we should look to it's advancement at home, where no resource of power will be unwanting. this may not be in my day; but probably will in yours. God send to our country a happy deliverance, and to your self health and as long a life as yourself shall wish.   Th: Jefferson

RC (MHi: Washburn Autograph Collection); addressed: "Col° John Taylor Portroyal"; franked; postmarked Milton, 17 Feb.; endorsed by Taylor: "Tho⁸ Jefferson & copy answer 1821."

The late Wilson Cary Nicholas's SEC-OND son was his namesake Wilson Cary Nicholas (ca. 1796–1828) and his 3ᴰ SON was John Smith Nicholas (Albemarle Co. Will Book, 7:84). TJ regarded the United States Supreme Court decision in

McCulloch v. Maryland (1819) as SOPH-ISTRIES OF THE JUDGES ON BANK TAXA-TION (Marshall, *Papers*, 8:254–80). For the opinion of THE 5. LAWYERS ON LOT-TERIES, see TJ to Thomas Ritchie, 25 Dec. 1820, and note. TJ adapted THE CATHOLIC FAITH . . . PERISH EVERLAST-INGLY from the Athanasian Creed.

¹ Word added in margin.
² Reworked from "education."

To Henry Baldwin

Monticello Feb. 15. 21.

Th: Jefferson returns his thanks to mr Baldwin for the able report on the Tariff he has been so kind as to send him. questions on Political economy are certainly among the most complicated of any within the scope of the human mind. that the public should have differed therefore so much on that which is the subject of this report, is not to be wondered at. it will end, it is to be hoped in a compromise of opinion reconcilable to all. he tenders to mr Baldwin his respectful salutations.

RC (PMA: John Earle Reynolds Collection); dateline at foot of text. PoC (DLC); on verso of reused address cover to TJ; endorsed by TJ.

Henry Baldwin (1780–1844), attorney and public official, was a native of New Haven, Connecticut. He graduated from Yale College (later Yale University) in 1797 and studied law under Tapping Reeve and James Gould in Litchfield and Alexander J. Dallas in Philadelphia before opening a practice in Pittsburgh in 1801. During service in the United States House of Representatives, 1816–22, Baldwin supported protective tariffs and chaired the Committee on Domestic Manufactures. Andrew Jackson appointed

Baldwin an associate justice of the United States Supreme Court in 1830. On the bench he was neither a strict constructionist nor a follower of John Marshall. In 1837 Baldwin published his legal theories and dissenting opinions in *A General View of the Origin and Nature of the Constitution and Government of the United States*. Late in life he moved to Meadville, Pennsylvania. Despite his high judicial office, Baldwin was so poor when he died in Philadelphia that a collection was taken to pay for his burial (*ANB*; *DAB*; Dexter, *Yale Biographies*, 5:243–6; Leon Friedman and Fred L. Israel, eds., *The Justices of the United States Supreme Court 1789–1969: Their Lives and Major Opinions* [1969–80], 1:571–80; *Litchfield*

Law School, 7; *JEP*, 4:41, 43 [5, 6 Jan. 1830]; Philadelphia *North American and Daily Advertiser*, 23 Apr. 1844).
Baldwin's REPORT ON THE TARIFF was probably the *Report Of the Committee on Manufactures, on the various Memorials*

praying for, and remonstrating against, an increase of the duties on imports ([Washington, 1821]), which Baldwin as committee chair referred to the United States House of Representatives on 15 Jan. 1821 (*JHR*, 14:138).

To James Breckinridge

DEAR SIR Monticello Feb. 15. 21.

I learn with deep affliction that nothing is likely to be done for our University this year. so near as it is to the shore that one shove more would land it there, I had hoped that would be given; and that we should open with the next year an institution on which the fortunes of our country depend more than may meet the general eye. the reflections that the boys of this age are to be the men of the next; that they should be prepared to recieve the holy charge which we are cherishing to deliver over to them; that in establishing an institution of wisdom for them we secure it to all our future generations; that in fulfilling this duty we bring home to our own bosoms the sweet consolation of seeing our sons rising, under a luminous tuition, to destinies of high promise; these are considerations which will occur to all. but all, I fear, do not see the speck in our horizon which is to burst on us[1] as a tornado, sooner or later. the line of division lately marked out, between different portions of our confederacy, is such as will never, I fear, be obliterated. and we are now trusting to those who are against us in position and principle, to fashion to their own form the minds & affections of our youth. if, as has been estimated, we send 300,000.D. a year to the Northern seminaries for the instruction of our sons, then we must have there at all times 500. of our sons imbibing opinions and principles in discord with those of their own country. this canker is eating on the vitals of our existence, and if not arrested at once will be beyond remedy. we are now certainly furnishing recruits to their school. if it be asked What are we to do? or said, that we cannot give the last lift to the University without stopping our primary schools and these we think the most important. I know their importance. no body can doubt my zeal for the general instruction of the people. who first started that idea? I may surely say myself. turn to the bill in the revised code which I drew more than 40. years ago; and before which the idea of a plan for the education of the people generally had never been suggested in this state. there you will see developed the first rudiments of the whole system of general education we are now urging and acting on. and it is well known to those with whom I have acted on this subject, that I never have proposed a sacrifice of the primary to the ultimate grade of instruction. let us keep our eye steadily on the whole system. if we cannot do every thing at once, let us do one thing at a time. the primary schools need no preliminary expence. the ultimate grade requires a considerable expenditure in advance. a suspension of proceeding for a year or two on the primary schools, and an application of the whole income during that time, to the completion of the buildings necessary for the University, would enable us then to start both institutions at the same time. the intermediate branch of colleges, academies and private classical schools, for the middle grade, may hereafter recieve any necessary aids when the funds shall have become competent. in the mean time they are going on sufficiently, as they have ever yet gone on, at the private expence of those who use them, and who in numbers and means are competent to their own exigencies. the experience of 3. years has, I presume, left no doubt that the present plan of primary schools, of putting money into the hands of 1200. persons acting for nothing, and under no responsibility, is entirely inefficient. some other must be thought of; and during this pause, if it be only for a year, the whole revenue[2] of that year, with what of the last 3. years has not been already thrown away, would place our University in readiness to start with a better organisation of primary schools, and both may then go on, hand in hand, for ever. no diminution of the capital will in this way have been incurred; a principle which ought to be deemed sacred. a relinquishment of interest on the late loan of 60,000.D. would so far also forward the university, without lessening the capital.   But what may be best done, I leave with entire confidence to yourself and your colleagues in legislation, who know better than I do the condition of the literary fund, and it's wisest application: and I shall acquiesce with perfect resignation to their will. I have brooded, perhaps with fondness, over this establishment, as it held up to me the hope of continuing to be useful while I continue to live. I had believed that the course and circumstances of my life had placed within my power some services favorable to the out-set of the institution. but this may be egoism; pardonable perhaps when I express a consciousness that my colleagues and successors will do as well, whatever the legislature shall enable them to do.

I have thus, my dear Sir, opened my bosom, with all it's anxieties, freely to you. I blame nobody, for seeing things in a different light. I am sure all act conscientiously, and that all will be done honestly and wisely which can be done. I yield the concerns of the world with cheerfulness to those who are appointed in the order of nature to succeed to them: and for yourself, for our colleagues, and for all in charge of our country's future fame and fortune, I offer up sincere prayers.

Th: Jefferson

RC (Roger W. Barrett, Chicago, 1947); torn at seal, with missing text supplied from PoC; at foot of first page: "Gen[l] Brackenridge." PoC (DLC).

The BILL IN THE REVISED CODE was TJ's 1778 "Bill for the More General Diffusion of Knowledge" (*PTJ*, 2:526–35).

[1] Preceding two words interlined.
[2] Manuscript: "revenuee."

To Joseph C. Cabell

Dear Sir   Monticello Feb. 15. 21.

I address this day to Gen[l] Breckenridge a letter as you desired; to be shewn if it is thought expedient within the circle of discretion. I doubt much myself whether it's exhibition to members independant in their purposes, & jealous of that independance may not do more harm than good. on this I put myself into the hands of my friends. I am sure you will see the propriety of letting no copy be taken, or possibility occur, of it's getting beyond the limits of our own state; and even within these limits some of it's expressions should not go forth. ever and affectionately yours   Th: Jefferson

RC (ViU: TJP); addressed: "Joseph C. Cabell esq. of the Senate of Virginia now at Richmond"; franked; postmarked Milton, 17 Feb.; endorsed by Cabell. PoC (DLC); on verso of reused address cover to TJ; endorsed by TJ.

From Isaac A. Coles

D[R] Sir,   Clarksville, Pike County, missouri Feby 15th 1821.

I send you enclosed a specimen of <u>Wild Hemp</u> which I find in great abundance on many parts of my Land—We have collected a sufficient quantity of it for all our purposes, and find that it makes a much stronger rope than the Hemp of Virginia—the stem is generally of the size of ones finger, and from 5 to 10 feet in height—it is a perennial Plant delights in low, moist, rich land, and yields fully as well (I think) as the common hemp—The seeds are small, resembling very much the seed of the Yellow Jessamine, but larger and more full, and are contained in pods on the top of the Plant—as these burst open in the early part of winter, I have not been able to procure any of the seed to send you—The specimen enclosed was tressed[1] from a stalk which

I yesterday cut in the woods, and prepared as you see it, by merely rubbing it between my fingers, & then combing it straight with my pocket comb. It has stood out, exposed in the woods the whole winter—As there is now nothing remaining of this Plant, but the naked stem and the roots (which are exceedingly numerous) it will be difficult to class it, but it does not appear to me to resemble atall either Hemp or flax.—Whatever it may be, it must (I think) prove a Plant of great value—the strength, delicacy, softness & whiteness of the fibre, will no doubt be greatly improved by being cut at the proper time, & treated in a proper manner, & being perennial, when once sowed it will last for ages, and, may be cut with as little trouble as a timothy meadow— I do not despair still of being able to procure a few of the seed, and if I succeed, they shall be forwarded to you. an Inch or two of the top of the Plant, with 2 pods are also inclosed.

Notwithstanding the badness of the times I still think that I shall realize great profits from the Speculation in which I am engaged in this Country—The extraordinary firtility of the soil is so tempting that it fills up with great rapidity—there are some Sections of Land near me on which 10 families are settled, & many on which there are five & six—a neighbor yesterday counted up 132 families within ten Miles of my Land,—6 years ago there was not a white man in the County of Pike which now contains about 1000 voters.

In May I shall return to Virginia when I anticipate the pleasure of a Visit to Monticello—I beg to be presented very kindly to Mrs Randolph and the family—and am

Dr Sir with sincere & devoted attachment y^r frn^d & serv^t

I. A. COLES

RC (DLC); at foot of text: "Thomas Jefferson"; endorsed by TJ as received <19> 18 May 1821 and so recorded in SJL.

[1] Manuscript: "trissed."

From Joseph Dougherty

DEAR SIR   Washington City Feb. 15th —21
   Mr Burwell^s case is hopeless—no change Since I wrote you last.
   Your Humble Servt   Jo^s DOUGHERTY

RC (MHi); endorsed by TJ as received 19 Feb. 1821 and so recorded in SJL.

To George Alexander Otis

DEAR SIR   Monticello Feb. 15. 21.

I have just now recieved your favor of Jan. 30. and confirm, by my belief, mr Jay's criticism on the passages quoted from Botta. I can answer for it's truth from this state Southwardly, and Northwardly, I believe, to New York, for which state mr Jay is himself a competent witness. what, Eastward of that, might be the dispositions towards England before the commencement of hostilities I know not. before that I never had heard a whisper of disposition to separate from Great Britain. and, after that, it's possibility was contemplated with affliction by all. writing is so slow and painful to me that I cannot go into details, but must refer you to Girardin's history of Virginia pa. 134. and Appendix N° 12. where you will find some evidence of what the sentiment was at the moment, and given at the moment. I salute you with great esteem & respect.   TH: JEFFERSON

RC (CtY: Franklin Collection). PoC (DLC); on verso of reused address cover of Thomas Appleton to TJ, 23 Aug. 1819; torn at seal, with two words rewritten by TJ; at foot of text: "Mʳ George A. Otis"; endorsed by TJ.

In the fourth volume of *The History of Virginia; commenced by John Burk, and continued by Skelton Jones and Louis Hue Girardin* (Petersburg, 1816; Poor, *Jefferson's Library*, 4 [no. 127]), a discussion of American attitudes about separation from Great Britain starting on PA. 134 is supplemented by APPENDIX N° 12, which prints "extracts from letters tending to prove that the American declaration of Independence was the effect of ministerial oppression, and not the result of a preconcerted plan." TJ wrote all three of the excerpted letters in 1775 (appendix, pp. 5–8, quote on p. 5; *PTJ*, 1:165–7, 240–3, 268–70).

To Henry Wheaton

                                                      Monticello Feb. 15. 21.

I thank you, Sir, for the very able Discourse you have been so kind as to send me on international law. I concur much in it's doctrines, and very particularly in it's estimate of the Lacedaemonian character. how such a tribe of savages ever acquired the admiration of the world has always been beyond my comprehension. I can view them but on a level with our American Indians, and I see in Logan, Tecumseh & the little Turtle fair parallels for their Brasidas, Agesilaus Eᵗc. the difficulty is to concieve that such a horde of Barbarians could so long remain unimproved, in the neighborhood of a people so polished as the Athenians; to whom they owe altogether[1] that their name is now known to the world. all the good that can be said of them is that they were as brave as bull-dogs. I salute you with very great respect.

TH: JEFFERSON

RC (Doyle Auction House, Sale 18BP01, Lot 10, New York City, 25 Apr. 2018); at foot of text: "Henry Wheaton esq." PoC (DLC); endorsed by TJ. Not recorded in SJL.

DISCOURSE: Wheaton, *An Anniversary Discourse, delivered before The New-York Historical Society, on Thursday, December 28, 1820* (New York, 1821; TJ's copy in PPL, inscribed by Wheaton on title page [trimmed]: "To the hon. Thomas Jeffe[rson] with the author's respe[cts]"). Around this time Wheaton sent the same pamphlet to John Adams and James Madison (Adams to Wheaton, 7 Feb. 1821 [NNPM]; Madison, *Papers, Retirement Ser.*, 2:238).

[1] Word canceled in PoC, with "all their fame &" interlined in its place.

From Joseph Dougherty

Washington City Feb. 16th 21
past 2 oclock.

SIR

I have just closed the eyes of our worthy, good friend Mr W. A. Burwell. for mildness and genuine affection he may have left an equal—but his superior is not to be found.

Your Humble Servt

JOS DOUGHERTY

RC (MHi); endorsed by TJ as received 22 Feb. 1821 and so recorded in SJL. RC (DLC); address cover only; with PoC of TJ to James Madison, 12 May 1822, on verso; addressed (one word editorially corrected): "Thos Jefferson Esqr lat[e] President of the U: States Monticello va"; franked; postmarked Washington, 17 Feb.

From James Monroe

DEAR SIR   washington Feby 17. 1821.

I regret to have to inform you of the death of mr W. Burwell which took place on yesterday, after a long & distressing illness. All possible care was taken of him. He was a most virtuous man & estimable member of the H. of Reps.

The treaty with Spain has been ratified by her govt, unconditionally, & the grants annulled in the instrument of ratification. It is before the Senate, on the question, whether it shall be accepted, the time stipulated for the ratification, having expird. It is presumd that little if any opposition will be made to it.

There is also some hope that Missouri will be admitted into the Union, on a patriotic effort from the Senators & other members from Pennsyl[a]. Hope is also entertaind that our commercial difference with France will be adjusted.

very respectfully & sincerely your friend   JAMES MONROE

RC (DLC); endorsed by TJ as received 22 Feb. 1821 and so recorded in SJL. RC (MHi); address cover only; with PoC of TJ to Frederick W. Hatch, 12 May 1822, on verso; addressed: "Thomas Jefferson Monticello Virg[a]"; franked; postmarked Washington, 17 Feb.

For the Florida land GRANTS AN-NULLED under the Adams-Onís Treaty of 1819, see Monroe to TJ, 5 Oct. 1819, and note.

To Ethan A. Brown

SIR   Monticello Feb. 18. 21.

I have been favored by your letter of Jan. 28. and with the very able report you were so kind as to inclose with it. the question between the state of Ohio—and the US. is certainly elucidated in it with a logic which will require powerful means of answering. between such high parties however, it would illy become me to interpose an opinion, nor am I indeed qualified for it. I have so long withdrawn from attention to public affairs that they are in a great degree[1] unknown to me. the same, among other important questions, has been profoundly investigated by Col[o] John Taylor of this state, in a book recently published, which recalls our constitution to it's first principles, from which, in several points, we seem to be wandering. from Congress or the administration we have little to fear. their dependance on the suffrages of the people will keep them right, or change them when wrong. the Judiciary is the dangerous corps of sappers and miners. because they are in place for life and beyond responsibility, impeachment being found in practice a mere scare-crow. yet a respect for the high parties in the particular case in question, and for the public jealousy of the tendency of their decisions to draw all power from the sovereign to the derivative governments will doubtless induce them, on proper occasions, to revise with candor that class of cases which excites alarm at present in so many of the states. indeed their doctrines have been rendered so questionable by this report, and the book of Col[o] Taylor, their arguments brought so closely to the test of reason, that they owe to themselves, as well as to their country, a most scrupulous reconsideration[.] if their conclusions are finally against the sense of the states, the controul rests with Congress in the first instance, and ultimately with the states, as the constituting powers.   but I must repeat, Sir, that I do not permit myself to take any part in these contentions. and should be especially unwilling to be quoted or involved in them. I leave them, with perfect resignation, to those in charge of the public welfare; and have no fear that they will fail to do ultimately what is best for us all. on this pillow I repose my head with the tranquility which the pressure of years renders the most desirable of all blessings; and I pray you to accept the assurance of my great respect & esteem.   TH: JEFFERSON

PoC (DLC); on a reused address cover from James Madison to TJ; faint punctuation supplied from Trs; endorsed by TJ as a letter to "Brown Ethan A." Tr (OHi: Brown Papers). Tr (OClWHi: Tod Papers); embedded in Elisha Whitlesey to George Tod, 16 Dec. 1821; partially dated Feb. 1821. Mistakenly recorded in SJL as a letter of 17 Feb. 1821.

[1] Trs: "measure."

From Edward Postlethwayt Page

Marietta, Ohio. Feb. 18th 1821—

If our post-master is not a perjured man, you will have received two letters from me, & this, in the hope that he does his duty, is my third. I shall find him out if he is true or false to me—He may think to do Jehovah a service by obstructing me in this or in other ways with his tongue of contempt. But had he more sense, more education, and less pride and bigotry—better for him.—He, being a mason may conclude as Herod did, that spiritual murder of the spiritual Baptist should the rather be religiously adhered to for his oath's sake—But Blue-beard awaits the righteous judgment of Pluto—Blind Homer sung the lost Helen—Blind milton the lost paradise, & blind Sampson now sings lost magic—The trinity of Jehovah may not only be exemplified in the <u>Sun, his light, his heat</u>[1] But in <u>Being, Power, Motion</u>.[2]— Sir, Light is continually developing light to my mind—& something whispers me that Franklin discovered more than his magic square of squares & circle of circles but that in the same heaven-born spirit that popery forbade the reading of the Scriptures, has masonry, which is perverted & most carnal Geometry & Astronomy, as opposed to spiritual Astronomy & <u>communicative</u> love,—purchased up his sublimest discoveries, & so, in the old hellish spirit of avarice fraudulently pilfered the light which is the property of the commonwealth.—Sir, 18 months ago when I was a blind <u>aristocrat</u>, I detested your name as

Satan in human form. So much for king-craft.—Now—the scales are off, and in my estimation there lives not in the world a more sublime philosopher than yourself,—connected with your station.[3] Sir—I revere, I venerate the name of Jefferson, & I weep to think that time has smitten you, and that before Universal masonry & sympathetic union prevails, & opposites subside into eternal calm and the tin and the copper becomes brass—& water mixes and is a level, and the fire harmonizes into fire—& the whole world is leavened into light, & in some sublime manner concavity reciprocates convexity—& the images of the dead are restored by energy of the living by the strength as of a chain cable, each man a link.—I say, that ere the Tree of Nebuchadnezzar be plucked from the ground of avarice, by Urim & Thummim lights and perfections—that tree whose roots are pride, whose trunk is ambition, whose branches are worldly lusts, whose fruit are gold, silver, copper & even Licurgus's iron coin, whose leaves are bank-paper—yea, before you can see realized those sacred rights recognized in that <u>magna</u> charta, the constitution—the same birth— the same death & end therefore the same rights—Ah, before the tree of life with 12 fruits, 7 of which are the 7 eyes of Jehovah, namely, <u>Being</u>, <u>Power</u>, <u>Motion</u>, <u>Knowledge</u>, <u>Wisdom</u>, <u>Light</u>, <u>Love</u>[4] & 5 are the wintry months of man or his right hand five fingers or wise virgins of agency obeying the 7 sockets or cavities of his head—namely <u>Perception</u>, <u>Reception</u>, <u>Retention</u>, <u>Cogitation</u>, <u>Perfection</u>[5] you will have gone to <u>hell</u>, for hell is only the grave or darkness, and is a relative word, as the opposite of light; to that bourne whence no traveller returns.[6] Sir, I believe in universal salvation—Sir the Holy Scriptures from beginning to end are one entire allegory, and may I be eternally tormented in calvinistic hell-fire hotter than that which dear heaven born Calvin tortured poor Servetus 2 hours in, if the knowledge of God & the spirit of Jehovah did not indite them.[7] Masonry is the only true platform—God is a mason but as his light shines <u>equally</u> upon every object as he is diffusive—as he says more blessed to give than to receive—so do we indeed find that there is no true joy but in communicating—hence my love for you—for the world is beyond my love for any copy-right—& I impart, before I even[8] digest my matter—eager for the welfare of the whole—aware that fragments are not parts—that Captain Cook was a broken God when his flesh was <u>separated</u>—Jehovah has but one eternal channel—& that is <u>Order</u>.— You never answer me perhaps for your oath's sake—Who made you a slave?—Why any exclusive rights?
I hope to see you before long.—[. . .] [s]hall proclaim the opened books after the order of Melc[hize]dek

36 angles or 2
pillars of Jacob

West variation is
really accounted
for

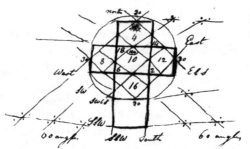

36 angles or 2 pillars
of Esau[9]

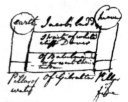

Jarchin or Jachin is hebrew for the moon—11 days difference between a lunar & a solar year—& the glorious $\overline{12}$ between a lunar &
Sidereal year—The 6000 years perhaps are come & the day of judgment begun last year with the Inquisition

Peale's
Allegorical
court of death
will prove a
court of life
to us
Blessed be
Jefferson for
encouraging
it

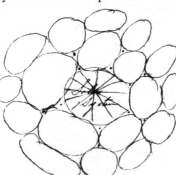

& 19 is the golden
number

Make[. . .]
[. . .]ly all equal
in this form[10]—&
you find 2 systems
beyond the Solar
& wonderful
mysteries of the
Mosaic pavement
&[a] & the 12—&
the trinity Sur-
round the outer
circle by the
Leviathan of
Truth

I could tell you of a thousand other facts hid even from your masonic
research, because in your lodge the word is lost.[11] Aaron's breast-plate
is melted at the mint of avarice.[12] The letter this covers—I had no
need to send—I forward it for your information—See how rapidly we
halcyons move—How different—how incorrect my definition of Urim
& Thummim there—You oath masons have long enough crucified the
light & Geometry to Kings Priests & yourselves—Expand you must—
You are Sampson, Jerico, Noah, Sodom, Absalom, Nathan's David,
Goliah, the prodigal son

RC (DLC); damaged at seal; addressed: "Thomas Jefferson Esqre Late President of the U. States Montecello Varginia," with "Charlottsville" added in an unidentified hand; franked; postmarked Marietta, 21 Feb.; endorsed by TJ as a letter from "Page" received 3 Mar. 1821, with his additional notation: "insane," and so recorded in SJL. Enclosure not found.

THE SPIRITUAL BAPTIST was the biblical John the Baptist, beheaded by order of Herod Antipas (Matthew 14.1–12; Mark 6.16–29). TREE OF NEBUCHADNEZZAR: In the Bible, the Babylonian king Nebuchadnezzar dreamed of the felling of a great tree, which the prophet Daniel interpreted as foreshadowing that king's temporary downfall (Daniel 4). According to Plutarch, Lycurgus replaced all the gold and silver currency in Sparta with heavy and essentially worthless IRON COIN (Plutarch, *Lycurgus*, book 9, in *Plutarch's Lives*, trans. Bernadotte Perrin, Loeb Classical Library [1914–26; undated reprint], 1:228–31). Biblical references to the TREE OF LIFE WITH 12 FRUITS and 7 EYES OF JEHOVAH are in Revelation 22.2 and 5.6, respectively. In the Bible Jesus told the parable of five WISE VIRGINS who were able to attend a wedding banquet because they carried enough lamp oil to last until the bridegroom's arrival (Matthew 25.1–13).

THAT BOURNE WHENCE NO TRAVELLER RETURNS is taken from William Shakespeare, *Hamlet*, act 3, scene 1. Saint Paul relayed Jesus's message that it is MORE BLESSED TO GIVE THAN TO RECEIVE in Acts 20.35. On a voyage to the Hawaiian Islands in 1779, Captain James Cook was reportedly believed at first to be a god by the Hawaiians, but they later killed him and HIS FLESH WAS SEPARATED from his bones according to ceremonial custom (*ODNB*). In Hebrews chapter 7 Jesus is said to be "a priest for ever AFTER THE ORDER OF MELCHIZE-DEK," and Freemasons associate Melchizedek with the order of High Priesthood (Albert G. Mackey, *An Encyclopædia of Freemasonry* [1874], 496).

The story of Jacob's ladder (depicted in the drawing beneath the name of ESAU) is in Genesis 28, where Jacob dreams of a ladder reaching from earth to heaven. In Christian millennial theory the Second Coming of Christ and Judgment Day were anticipated 6000 YEARS after the earth's creation (Stephen D. O'Leary, *Arguing the Apocalypse: A Theory of Millennial Rhetoric* [1994], 120–1). The Temple of Solomon was believed to have been decorated with a MOSAIC PAVEMENT, which masonic lodges sometimes replicate with black-and-white stone flooring (Mackey, *Encyclopædia of Freemasonry*, 510). The biblical parable of THE PRODIGAL SON is in Luke 15.

[1] Beneath his underscoring, Page numbered these phrases 1 through 3.

[2] Beneath his underscoring, Page numbered these words 1 through 3.

[3] Omitted period at right margin editorially supplied.

[4] Beneath his underscoring, Page numbered these words 1 through 7.

[5] Beneath his underscoring, Page numbered these words 1 through 5.

[6] Omitted period at right margin editorially supplied.

[7] Omitted period at right margin editorially supplied.

[8] Word interlined.

[9] Text in graphic beneath reads "earth Jacob's ladder heaven Straits of white cliff Dover Of Babelmandeb or present Christendom Pillar of water Of Gibraltar Pillar of fire."

[10] Text in center of adjacent graphic reads "Solar System."

[11] Omitted period at right margin editorially supplied.

[12] Omitted period at right margin editorially supplied.

To Lewis Williams

Monticello Feb. 18. 20 [1821]

I thank you, Sir, for the able pamphlet inclosed in your favor of the 10th and still more for the kind expressions of that letter. the principle espoused of keeping our expences within our income, in public as well as in private affairs, is of a correctness which cannot be questioned. but of details I am not a judge: having withdrawn myself from all such cares in perfect confidence that Congress and the Administration will take good care of us. I read no newspaper now but a single one, and that chiefly for the advertisements. the war has, no doubt, left us with debts & numerou[s] agents, of which it is difficult to debarras ourselves suddenly, and without a struggle between our feelings and necessities. with respect to debts, whether to be met by loans or taxes, there are two laws of finance which I think should be rigorously adhered to. 1. never to borrow without laying a tax sufficient to pay principal and interest within a fixed period, and I would fix that period at 10. years, & that tax should be solemnly pledged to the lenders. 2. never to borrow or tax without appropriating the money to it's specific[1] object. these rules have been invariably observed by the English parliament and are considered by them as fundamental. but, disposed to do right, as I am sure Congress is, their differences of opinion will, by collision strike out what is right; and if they do not, the people, when they percieve it, will overhaul your proceedings, & bring you to rights. this is our ultimate safety; and with a good [d]egree[2] of confidence that it will not fail us, I tender you the assurance of my great respect & esteem   TH: JEFFERSON

PoC (DLC: TJ Papers, 217:38713); misdated; edge trimmed; at foot of text: "honble Lewis Williams." Mistakenly recorded in SJL as a letter of 17 Feb. 1821.

DEBARRAS: "To disembarrass; to disencumber *from* anything that embarrasses" (*OED*).

[1] Manuscript: "it'specific."
[2] Word faint.

From Bernard Peyton

DEAR SIR,   Rich'd 19 Febru[y] 1821

I am this morning in rec[t] a letter from your Grandson Tho[s] J. Randolph, written at your request, desiring to know whether I would endorse your note for $4,000 proposed to be discounted at one of the Banks in this City, & first endorsed by him: I have by this mail replied to him, as I now do to you, that it will afford me on this, as it has on all former, & will on all future occasions, the greatest pleasure to be servicable to you, & regret that you should have felt any hesitation in making the application yourself. my affectionate attachment for both of you, as well as the most perfect confidence in each, renders it impossible I could have the least hesitation in making myself responsible for any amount you would ask, or in any way contributing to your ease & cumfort in your declining years.

Should you effect the loan, I will with great cheerfulness undertake to attend to the renewal of the note from time to time as it falls due, in addition to those already under my management.
I beg you will never fail to command my name, funds, or services whenever they can be useful to you—

With sincere affection Yours very Truely   B. Peyton

RC (MHi); endorsed by TJ as received 23 Feb. 1821 and so recorded in SJL. RC (MHi); address cover only; with PoC of TJ to Archibald Robertson, 7 June 1822, on verso; addressed: "Mr Thomas Jefferson Monticello near Charlottesville"; stamp canceled; franked; postmarked Richmond, 19 Feb.

From Elizabeth Trist

My Dear Friend   Farmington 19th Feby —20 [1821]
Miss Polly Marks has procured from her Aunt, some of the Mountain Raspberry which she heard you express a wish to have they were brought this morning and shall be coverd till it is convenient for you to send for them—and I enclose a few beautiful flowering beans which John Marks brought from the Mississippi[1] some time since— as the Spring advances I feel some hope of seeing [you][2] at Farmington, I dont think Mr Diverses health has been quite as bad it was last Winter tho he has undergone copious bleedings and blistering—with love to Patsy and the young Ladies who I beg you will remind of their being in my debt, may God preserve you many years in health and happiness and believe me ever your sincere obliged Friend
                                                    E, Trist

RC (MHi); misdated; endorsed by TJ as a letter of 19 Feb. 1821 received the same day and so recorded in SJL.

Patsy: Martha Jefferson Randolph.

[1] Manuscript: "Nississippi."
[2] Omitted word editorially supplied.

From James Brown

SIR Charlottesville Feby 20th 1821

I call^d on you last Spring for the payment of your Bond to Thomas F. Lewis for which I had advanced Cash, It probably has Slipt your Memory, that "I Said would deposit the Bond with Mr. James Leitch to whoom you would please make payment" (as you were not prepared to discharge it at the time I call^d on you) haveing no particular use for the Money untill now, I have applied to Mr. Leitch for it to day & find it has not been paid: You will very much oblige me by either depositing the Money or a drft: on Richmond by the next Albemarle Court.—

Yr. Ob^t Servt JAMES BROWN

RC (MHi); addressed: "Mr. Thomas Jefferson Monticello"; endorsed by TJ as received 28 Feb. 1821 and so recorded in SJL.

On 11 Dec. 1819 TJ recorded his purchase from Thomas Fielding LEWIS of "a chesnut sorrel horse (Peacemaker)" for $125 (*MB*, 2:1359).

From Joseph C. Cabell

DEAR SIR, Richmond 20th Feb: 1821.

I return you the enclosed paper calling a meeting of the Visitors of the University, having procured the signatures of Mr Johnson & Genl Taylor, and annexed my own, as requested in your favor of 30 ult. I have also shewn the paper to Governor Randolph, & the course pursued is satisfactory to him & the Executive.

A Bill in favor of the University has been reported by the Committee of Schools & Colleges. It proposes to authorize a loan by the President & Directors of $60,000, to be paid out of the balance due from the Genl Government, or any other part of the uninvested[1] principal of the fund. It puts the principal on the footing on which my first proposition to the President & Directors of last spring would have placed the loan then proposed, with a small variation. The Bill was drawn by m^r Johnson, on consultation with Genl Breckenridge & myself. Its fate will be decided in a few days. It will be powerfully opposed: but I hope it will get thro', & if it does, I trust the money will finish the buildings, & if it should not, that the people of Albemarle will make up the deficiency. Garland has at last thrown off the mask, and avowed his hostility to the bill. Like many others, he calls himself a friend to the institution. Our worst enemies are pretended friends.

I have written a very urgent letter to Genl Taylor, begging him to come into the Assembly. He declines the proposition. So does Broadnax of Greensville. I enclose you their letters. I have written again to the latter, enclosing for his perusal, your letter to me on the subject of my continuance, and proposing to him to come for one session. I shewed your letter to Mr Taylor of Chesterfield. He had before declined, but when he saw your letter he promised me to think of it. I shall endeavor to get Chancellor Taylor to use his influence with him. Mr Wm Archer of Powhatan has promised me to offer, and we shall get rid of Miller of that county, who declines. Mr Mallory of Orange has becom[e a] very active friend. I have written to m^r Currie of Lancaster inviting him to join us. This is the only effectual way to break down the opposition. W^m & mary, Hampden Sidney, & Washington Colleges, are in my opinion deadly hostile. Mr Venable will oppose our bill: but thinks himself a warm friend. I am almost worn out with anxiety, and wish the matter settled. We have got our James River Bill thro' the House of Delegates. It is of vast importance, and the whole country will soon be alive from Richmond to the mouth of the Kenhawa.

faithfully yours

JOSEPH C. CABELL

RC (ViU: TJP-PC); two words faint; endorsed by TJ as received 23 Feb. 1821 and so recorded in SJL. Enclosures: (1) Call for Meeting of University of Virginia Board of Visitors, 30 Jan.–13 Feb. 1821. (2) William H. Brodnax to Cabell, Greensville, 12 Feb. 1821, expressing his support for the University of Virginia and regret that the Virginia General Assembly is not providing it additional financial aid; remarking that "I have always been aware of the hostility felt towards the University by the ignorant—the prejudiced—& the hunters of popularity by addressing themselves to the pecuniary feelings of the lower orders in Society—and these classes unfortunately usually include a large majority"; declining to run for the legislature because doing so would harm his legal career, submitting it "to your Judgment whether it would not be the excess of imprudence to leave a practice of between four & five thousand dollars a year which would of course be much impaired, when the prospect of rendering any service whatever would be So very doubtful"; and looking with hope to a future when the University will be "a proud and grand institution—an ornament to the State, and an honor to the country" (RC in ViU: JCC). (3) Robert Taylor to

Cabell, Norfolk, 13 Feb. 1821, returning first enclosure above and TJ to Cabell, 30 Jan. 1821; observing that "I am glad that Mr Jefferson has been able to devise this plan of retaining Mr Johnson, whose importance on the board, we all so well know"; but refusing to swerve from his personal rule "never to solicit any publick appointment; nor to accept any, but a military one," having previously determined "that I should not advance my private happiness, and certainly not promote any publick object by entering into political life" (RC in ViU: JCC).

Burwell Bassett presented "A Bill, Concerning the University of Virginia" to the Virginia House of Delegates on 16 Feb. 1821. The measure provided for A LOAN of up to $60,000 from the Literary Fund "for the purpose of completing the buildings and making the necessary preparations for putting the said university into operation" (*JHD* [1820–21 sess.], 197; copy of printed bill in ViU: JCC).

On 15 Feb. 1821 the Virginia HOUSE OF DELEGATES passed "An act to amend the act, entitled, 'an act to amend the act for clearing and improving the navigation of James River, and for uniting the Eastern and Western Waters, by the

James and Kanawha Rivers.'" The Sen-
ate added its approval on 28 Feb. 1821
(*JHD* [1820–21 sess.], 195, 224; *Acts of
Assembly* [1820–21 sess.], 48–52).

[1] Manuscript: "uninvisted."

From Fernagus De Gelone

Sir.   New York february 20th 1821.

from your last honour, I was induced to believe that You were sick
and that Your age had obliged you to renounce to public affairs and
to Study. I verily hope that it is no longer the case. Not from any idea
of interest personal to myself, but from a Sense of devoutedness to
you, Sir, I beg you to let me know how You enjoy your health.

My normal school Succeeds well. You will feel happy to hear of it.

Should You like to have one copy of Mentelle's and Malte-Brun's
(The Géographe Danois) geography, published in 1816 in Paris, 16.
vol. octavo, folio atlas, I would Send it to you.

I have a fine copy of Pausanias, description de la Grèce, Greek &
french, by Clavier. 2. 8vo —

Very respectfully Sir. Your most humble obedient Servant

FERNAGUS DE GELONE
30. Pine Street—

RC (MHi); at head of text: "Thomas
Jefferson"; endorsed by TJ as received 3
Mar. 1821 and so recorded in SJL.

THE GÉOGRAPHE DANOIS: "The Dan-
ish geographer."

To Bernard Peyton

Dear Sir   Monticello Feb. 20. 21.

I recieved yesterday only your favor of the 12th. I find all in it right.
I am in want of some earthen pots for covering plant[s] of Sea-kale in
the garden. I am told they are made at a Pottery, in or near Richmond,
and that mr Wickham particularly has them of the proper size and
form which were made there. will you be so good as to get me half a
hundred & send them by the first boat, or if they have not them ready
made at the Pottery to get them made as soon as possible and forwarded as the season presses. I must also request you to get from
some of the seed-dealors 1. oz. green curled Savoy seed and forward
it by mail in a letter. yours affectionately   TH: JEFFERSON

PoC (MHi); on verso of reused address cover of Delamotte to TJ, 7 July 1819; edge
trimmed; at foot of text: "Cap[t] Peyton"; endorsed by TJ.

From Frederick A. Mayo

HONORABLE[1] SIR   Richmond the 21 Febr 1821
The two boxes of Books have been received[2] in good Order—I find
after some little examination that in the Analectic Magazine the number (November 1819) is wanting, and that a Number of the Port
Folio, (April 1815) was in place of it, which no doubt your honour
had overlookt, as we did not [r]eceive any more of the P. Folio accept
this number—All the different Directions respecting the Books, shall
be most particular observed, and they all will be ready for delivery[3]
in the course of three weeks the furthes
    Your humble Servant   FREDERICK A MAYO

RC (MHi); mutilated at seal; at foot of   [1] Manuscript: "Honarable."
text: "The Hono: Tho: Jefferson"; en-   [2] Manuscript: "recived."
dorsed by TJ as received 25 Feb. 1821   [3] Manuscript: "delervey."
and so recorded in SJL.

To Elizabeth Trist

                                  Monticello Feb. 21. 21.
    I am very thankful, my dear Madam for Miss Polly Marks's kind
attention to my wishes for the Mounta[in] raspberry, and I pray you
to give her that assurance. I now send for them, and I hope mr Divers
will endeavor also to raise them. mrs Randolph is to try the flowering
bean[.] we were so unlucky as to fail the last year in saving the seed
of the green curled Savoy. if mr Divers has any to spare I shall be
much obliged to him for a little. Ellen promises to write to you towards the discharge of the epistolary balance, and as soon as the roads
and weather admit me to visit the University, I shall go on & ask family fare with mr Divers. a letter from Washington of last Thursday
informs me that the situation of our dear friend mr Burwell was totally hopeless. heaven never took to it's bosom a better man. ever and
affectionately your's   TH: JEFFERSON

PoC (MHi); on verso of a reused ad-   ELLEN: TJ's granddaughter Ellen
dress cover from Thomas Cooper to TJ;   Wayles Randolph (Coolidge).
edge trimmed; at foot of text: "Mʳˢ Trist";
endorsed by TJ.

From Elizabeth Trist

Farmington 21ˢᵗ Febʸ

I participate in your sorrow for the critical Situation of our worthy Friend but while there is life there is hope, tho mine is not very sanguine that we shall ever see him again, His friendly and kind attention not only to my self but my Grand Sons has made an indelable impression on my mind and the Idea of losing such a friend is a severe pang to my heart—I shall always remember him with gratitude and affection The best wishes of the family for your health and preservation and believe me ever your

    Sincere and devoted Friend   E, Trist

RC (MHi); partially dated; dateline at foot of text; endorsed by TJ as a letter of 21 Feb. 1821 received the same day. Recorded in SJL as received the following day.

OUR WORTHY FRIEND: William A. Burwell.

To Joseph C. Cabell

Dear Sir   Monticello Feb. 22. 21.

I some time ago put into your hands a pamphlet proving indirectly that the Coll. of Wᵐ & Mary was intended to be a seminary for the church of England. it had been so long since I had read their printed statutes that I had forgotten them. looking lately into them, I find they declare that the 3. fundamental objects of the institution are 1. learning & morals. 2. to prepare ministers for the church of England. 3. to instruct Indians. and they require that the Visitors be all of the church of England, that the Professors sign it's 39. articles, and that the scholars be all taught the catechism of that church first in English, then in Latin. wishing to get my copy bound, I have inclosed it to a bookbinder, but open, and under cover to you, that you may turn to pages 121. 125. 131. 147.[1] for the above. when I was a Visitor in 1779. I got the 2. professorships[2] of Divinity & Grammar school put down, & others of Law & police, of Medecine Anatomy & Chemistry and of Modern languages substituted; but we did not then change the above statutes, nor do I know they have been since changed; on the contrary the pamphlet I put into your hand proves, that if they have relaxed in this fundamental object, they mean to return to it. when you have read the passages will you be so good as to reinclose the book, stick a wafer, and have it handed to Mayo?

    ever & affectionately yours   Th: Jefferson

[628]

P.S. Feb. 23. I have this moment recieved your favor of the 20th and finding that things are not in a state to require inclosing the College statutes, I withdraw them, and return the 2. letters you sent me

RC (ViU: TJP); addressed: "Joseph C. Cabell esquire of the Senate of Virginia now in Richmond"; franked; postmarked Milton, 24 Feb.; endorsed by Cabell, in part, as concerning "Charter of W^m & mary." PoC (DLC); on verso of reused address cover of William Barret to TJ, 6 Feb. 1821; edge trimmed; lacking postscript; endorsed by TJ. Enclosures: enclosures 2 and 3 to Cabell to TJ, 20 Feb. 1821.

PRINTED STATUTES: *The Charter, Transfer and Statutes, of the College of William and Mary, in Virginia: In Latin and English* (Williamsburg, 1758; Sowerby, no. 2097; possibly Poor, *Jefferson's*

Library, 10 [no. 586]). On 4 Dec. 1779 the visitors of the College of William and Mary passed a statute that provided for six PROFESSORSHIPS, "The 1st of which shall be, Law and Police; the 2d, Anatomy and Medicine; the 3d, Natural Philosophy and Mathematicks; the 4th, Moral Philosophy, the Laws of Nature and of Nations, and the fine Arts; the 5th, Modern Languages," and a sixth for the college's Indian school (Williamsburg *Virginia Gazette* [Dixon & Nicolson], 18 Dec. 1779).

[1] Manuscript: "247."
[2] Manuscript: "professorship."

From Joseph C. Cabell

MY DEAR SIR, Richmond 22^d Feb: 1821.

The University Bill passed to a second reading in the House of Delegates by a majority of one vote only. It is now on its third reading & will be read to-morrow. Our friends, I think, are encreasing. Genl Blackburn will support it. Mr Garland came over & voted for it. If we lose the Bill in the lower House, we shall hang on upon the Poor school bill. I hope we shall work it thro', in one way or the other. The enemies, seeing its decisive character, have done their best to destroy it. Heaven grant, that I may be able to send you good news in my next. your letters to myself & Genl Breckenridge have arrived, & are thankfully received. Mr Claiborne has withdrawn: and, as I suppose no one else will come forward, I need not come up till the elections. yours faithfully JOS: C: CABELL

RC (ViU: TJP-PC); endorsed by TJ as received 25 Feb. 1821 and so recorded in SJL. RC (DLC); address cover only; with PoC of TJ to Richard Harrison, 31 May 1822, on verso; addressed: "Mr Jefferson Monticello"; franked; postmarked Richmond, 22 Feb.

The POOR SCHOOL BILL was presented to the Virginia House of Delegates on 13 Feb. 1821 as a measure "concerning the appropriation of the Literary Fund" (*JHD* [1820–21 sess.], 191).

From Destutt de Tracy

MONSIEUR   Paris ce 22 fevrier 1821.

Je m'empresse de vous dire le Sensible plaisir que m'a fait eprouver l'arrivée de votre lettre du 26 x^bre dernier que je viens de recevoir. depuis deux ans entiers j'etais privé de cette Satisfaction Si chère a mon cœur, et bien affligé de penser que le mauvais etat de votre Santé pouvait en etre en partie la cause. Je vous remercie Sincerement de m'apprendre qu'elle est meilleure. jamais elle ne peut etre aussi parfaite que je le Souhaite. Je ne vous parlerai pas de la mienne. elle n'en vaut pas la peine. Je Suis assez aveugle pour ne pouvoir ni lire ni ecrire, et quand je le pourrais l'affaiblissement de ma memoire et de toutes mes autres facultés me condamnent pour jamais à une inutilité absolue. mais vous, Monsieur, recevez je vous prie tous mes vœux et agreez comme la Sincère expression de mon cœur le trop court hommage que j'ai pris la liberté de vous rendre à la tête de ce Commentaire que vous traitez avec tant d'indulgence, et qui est enfin veritablement le mien. j'espere que vous y aurez remarqué a la fin du chapitre Second du livre 11, page 211 une note qui est l'expression triste mais bien Sincère de mon opinion pratique Sur l'etat de L'Europe malgré ce que j'ai dit en Theorie pages 196 et 197 et que je pense egalement. J'espere aussi que vous aurez jetté un coup d'œil Sur le petit ecrit ajouté au commentaire dans cette edition.[a] Je desire bien que vous y ayez trouvé un peu de raison.

Je Suis infiniment flatté du prompt Succès qu'a eu chez vous mon Economie politique et je pense avec reconnaissance que je le dois en grande partie a l'approbation dont vous l'avez honorée. j'ai vu avec grand plaisir qu'a la tête de ce traité d'Economie qui est le 4ème Volume de mes elemens d'Ideologie on avait pris la peine de placer le Supplement à la Logique qui n'est proprement que la Suite et le complement de mon 3eme Volume et par la même raison je desirerais bien que dans la nouvelle Edition que vous me faites esperer on voulut faire le même honneur au 1er Chapitre du 5ème volume consacré à la morale. Si telle etait votre avis je Serois bien aise que l'on joignit à Ce 1er Chapitre le Second qui traite de l'Amour. Je n'en ai imprimé dans l'edition française que les premières lignes, mais il est fait tout entier depuis longtems, et si je ne l'ai pas publié c'est par une Sorte de timidité de faire confidence entière a tout ce qui m'entoure de mes Sentimens les plus Secrets Sur certains objets. n'eprouvant pas le même embarras dans l'eloignement, je l'ai laissé imprimer dans la Traduc-

(a) note. on l'a deja traduit en Espagnol et imprimé à Madrid.

tion Italienne et j'avoue que j'y attache quelqu'importance d'abord parce qu'il est une echantillon de la manière dont je voulais parler de toutes nos passions l'une après l'autre[1] et ensuite parcequ'il me parait qu'on en peut tirer des consequences importantes pour la Legislation. Je me figure d'ailleurs qu'il pourrait paraitre moins etrange à votre Sage nation qu'a toute autre. Dans cette confiance je prends la liberté de vous en envoyer ci joint une Copie manuscrite. Si vous l'approuvez je vous la recommande. Si vous la Condamnez je vous prie de la jetter au feu. je l'abandonne.

à propos de manuscrit je Suis tout etonné que vous n'ayez encore qu'en manuscrit mon petit ecrit intitulé Principes Logiques. Il est imprimé depuis 1817 et j'ai pris la liberté de vous l'envoyer deux fois Sous cette forme; apparemment il S'est perdu. C'est pourquoi je vous prie de trouver bien que j'en joigne encore ici deux exemplaires. Cet ecrit est bien peu de chose et je Serais faché que l'on crut qu'il dispense de la peine de lire mes trois premiers volumes, mais je crois qu'il peut Servir de texte à un cours de Logique et aider les eleves à Se rappeller les developpemens que leur auraient donnés leurs Professeurs. Je Serais bien fier Si, Sous ce point de Vue, il pouvait etre de quelqu'usage dans l'admirable etablissement que vous voulez fonder dans votre pays. ah! Monsieur que ce projet est beau et digne de vous et que tous nos Gouvernemens Europeens Sont loin de cette noble et genereuse intention de repandre la lumière. Nous n'avons ici des universités, des colleges et des institutions publiques de toute espece que pour opprimer la raison et arreter l'essor de l'esprit humain, et on ne permet pas même que par des etablissemens particuliers on echappe à ces perfides enseignemens.

Dans ces Circonstances, Monsieur, je ne me permettrai pas de vous reparler de L'Amerique Meridionale. Je crois comprendre bien tout ce que vous m'en avez dit et je vois que votre Politique est encore de la Saine morale comme elle devrait etre partout et comme elle n'est nulle part que chez vous. dailleurs les circonstances Sont bien changées et vous Savez dans quelle crise nous Sommes de ce Coté ci de l'Ocean. Dieu veuille que la force et la Sagesse ne manquent pas au Soutien de la bonne cause. C'est par ce vœu que je termine. il est intimement uni à tous ceux que je fais pour votre Conservation et votre bonheur.   TRACY

P.S. J'espère, Monsieur, Que vous aurez reçu la lettre que j'ai eu l'honneur de vous ecrire le 24 9bre dernier et qui n'etant partie que dans le mois de Decembre doit S'etre Croisée avec celle de vous à laquelle je reponds aujourdhui.

SIR   Paris 22 February 1821.

I hasten to tell you of the considerable pleasure I felt on the arrival of your letter of last 26 December, which I have just received. For two whole years I have been deprived of this satisfaction so dear to my heart, and the thought that your poor health might have been part of the cause worried me. I sincerely thank you for apprising me that your health is better. It will never be as perfect as I wish it to be. I will not speak to you of mine. It is not worth mentioning. I am too blind to read or write and even if I could, the weakened state of my memory and all my other faculties condemn me to absolute uselessness. But you, Sir, please accept all my best wishes and, as the sincere expression of my heart, the too short tribute I took the liberty of offering you at the beginning of the *Commentaire sur l'Esprit des Lois de Montesquieu*, which you have treated with such indulgence and which is finally truly mine. I hope that you will have noticed at the end of the second chapter of book 11, on page 211, a note which is the sad but very sincere expression of my practical opinion about conditions in Europe, despite my theoretical statement on pages 196 and 197, which is my opinion as well. I also hope that you will have glanced at the small piece of writing added to the *Commentaire* in this edition.[a] I hope you will have found some reason in it.

I am infinitely flattered by the rapid success of my *Treatise on Political Economy* in your country, and I gratefully believe that it is owing largely to the approbation with which you honored it. I saw with great pleasure that someone went to the trouble of placing at the head of this economic treatise, which is the fourth volume of my *Élémens d'Ideologie*, the supplement to the *Logique*, which is, in fact, the continuation of and complement to my third volume. For the same reason, I desire that in the new edition, for which you have made me so hopeful, the same honor be given to the first chapter of the fifth volume, which is devoted to morals. If you agree, I would be very happy if this first chapter were joined to the second, which deals with love. I have only had the first lines of it printed in the French edition, but it has been completely finished for a very long time. I have not published it because of my timidity in confiding to everyone around me my most secret feelings on certain topics. At a distance, I do not feel the same embarrassment, and so I have allowed it to be printed in the Italian translation. I confess that I see some value in it, first, because it exemplifies the manner in which I would like to talk about our passions, in sequence, and also because it seems to me that important conclusions with regard to legislation may be drawn from it. I imagine, furthermore, that it might appear less strange to your wise nation than to any other. Trusting in this, I take the liberty of enclosing herein a manuscript copy. If you approve of it, I will entrust it to you. If you condemn it, please throw it in the fire. I will abandon it.

Speaking of manuscripts, I am astonished that you still have only a manuscript version of my little piece entitled *Principes Logiques*. It has been in print since 1817, and I have taken the liberty of sending it to you on two occasions; apparently it was lost. This is why I now ask you to approve of my enclosing here, once again, two copies. This work is of little account and I

(a) Note: it has already been translated into Spanish and printed in Madrid.

would be annoyed if anyone believed they need not read my first three volumes, but I think that it might be used as a textbook for a course on logic and help students to remember the explanations given to them by their professors. Regarding this, I would be very proud if it could be of some use in the admirable establishment you intend to found in your country. Ah! Sir, how beautiful that project is, how worthy of you, and how far all our European governments are from this noble and generous intention of spreading enlightenment. The universities, colleges, and public institutions of every kind that we have here are solely used to oppress reason and arrest the expansion of the human spirit, and private establishments, which might question these perfidious teachings, are not permitted to do so.

Under these circumstances, Sir, I will not allow myself to talk to you again about South America. I think I understand very well what you have told me about it, and I see that your policy still exhibits a judicious morality, as it should be everywhere, but as it is to be found nowhere except in your country. In any case, circumstances have changed greatly, and you have learned about our crisis on this side of the ocean. God grant that strength and wisdom will not be lacking in support of the good cause. I end with this wish. It is closely connected to all my wishes for your preservation and happiness.

TRACY

P.S. I hope, Sir, that you received the letter I had the honor of writing to you last 24 November and which, having only left here in the month of December, must have crossed paths with that from you to which I reply today.

RC (DLC); in an unidentified hand, signed by Destutt de Tracy; endorsed by TJ as received 31 May 1821 and so recorded in SJL. Translation by Dr. Genevieve Moene. Enclosures: (1) manuscript, not found, of Destutt de Tracy's chapter "De l'Amour." (2) two copies of Destutt de Tracy, *Principes Logiques, ou Recueil de Faits relatifs a l'Intelligence Humaine* (Paris, 1817; Poor, *Jefferson's Library*, 8 [no. 455]).

The beginning of the first enclosure, a discussion of love (L'AMOUR), was printed as chapter 2 of the second part of Destutt de Tracy's *Traité de la Volonté et de ses effets* (Paris, 1815; Poor, *Jefferson's Library*, 8 [no. 454]), 568–72. TJ's copy is in ViCMRL, on deposit ViU, inscribed in an unidentified hand: "A Monsr Thomas Jefferson hommage de l'auteur" ("To Mr.

Thomas Jefferson with the author's respects"), with two lines from Homer's *Iliad*, 22.387–8, in TJ's hand beneath the inscription: "—τοῦ δ' οὐκ ἐπιλήςομαι, ὄφρ' ἄν ἔγωγε ζωοῖςι μετέω, καί μοι φίλα γούνατ' ὀρώρη" ("him will I not forget so long as I am among the living, and my knees are quick") (Homer, *Iliad*, trans. Augustus T. Murray, Loeb Classical Library [1924–25; rev. by William F. Wyatt, 1999; repr. 2003], 2:480–1). TJ used the two lines from Homer that followed in composing the epitaph for his wife (Epitaph for Martha Wayles Jefferson, [after 6 Sept. 1782], *PTJ*, 27:728). An Italian translation of the whole of Destutt de Tracy's chapter on love is printed in his *Elementi d'Ideologia* (Milan, 1817–19), 3:63–163.

¹ Preceding three words interlined.

From Caesar A. Rodney

Wilmington
Honored, Revered & Dear Sir,   Feby 24th 1821.

I have lately recovered from a severe attack of fever, which confined me to my bed for ten days; & I propose to visit Philad^a, tomorrow, where I shall see my old friend S. Gerard, & procure from him some of the genuine Maldonado Pumpkin seed, for yourself. I prefer his, because he has taken more pains in the cultivation of this fine vegetable, & has kept it far separated from any other of the same species. He has preserved an ample supply <u>for you, particularly</u>. I presume I may transmit a sufficient quantity, within your <u>Frank</u>, by mail, & with your permission, will enclose you some for our mutual friend Genl Cocke, to whom I must beg the favor of you to transmit to the proper Post-Office, with the necessary directions, the enclosed letter. I would not give you this trouble, but I do not recollect the office to which to direct it; and tho' I took a Memor^m of it, by accident, I have mis-laid it.

We have lost our amiable and estimable friend Mr Burwell, and I sincerely sympathise, with you, on the melancholy event, which I am sure you must feel very sensibly. I had expected to meet him, next winter, in Congress, to which the people have spontaneously elected me, tho' much against my own wishes. I shall go there, with more reluctance, than when at your earnest solicitation, I consented to serve, to support you & your administration. My numerous & still increasing family now require all my time & exertions.

With every sentiment of respect, affection & gratitude
Yours Most Sincerely & Truly   C. A. Rodney

P.S. If you have not the Green Asparagus I can send you some of the seed. I think my bed produces the finest I ever saw.

RC (DLC); endorsed by TJ as received 8 Mar. 1821 and so recorded in SJL. Enclosure: Rodney to John H. Cocke, Wilmington, 24 Feb. 1821, enclosing a catalogue of William Gibbons's fruit trees, suggesting that Cocke order from it in autumn, and proposing to add some specimens from his own farm; offering to send him some of his early beans next spring; informing him that if TJ agrees he will send Cocke some seeds of the green asparagus and maldonado pumpkin under TJ's frank; and advising him of the illness of "Our poor friend Sinclair" (RC in ViU: JHC; addressed: "Genl J. H. Cocke Virginia," with "New Canton" interlined in an unidentified hand; stamped; postmarked Milton, 13 Mar.; endorsed by Cocke).

s. gerard: Stephen Girard.

From John Vaughan

D SIR   Philad. Feby 24. 1821

By the French Consul I sent down to Washington the 3. Vol—
Botta's Translation—he assures me that the conveyance will be a
good one & that as he knows Mr Botta intimately he will do it with
pleasure

I remain sincerely[1] Your friend   JN VAUGHAN

RC (MHi); at head of text: "Thomas   [1] Manuscript: "sincely."
Jefferson Monticello"; endorsed by TJ as
received 6 Mar. 1821 and so recorded in
SJL.

From Joseph C. Cabell

DEAR SIR,   Richmond 25th Feb: 1821.

I have the pleasing satisfaction to inform you that the University
Bill passed yesterday, not exactly in the shape its friends preferred,
yet in one not very exceptionable. The first intelligence of its passage
in the lower House was conveyed to us in the Senate Chamber by a
tumultuous noise below, like that which is usual on the adjournment
of the House. This was the tumult of rejoicing friends coming to bring
us the glad tidings. Genl Blackburn took the floor most zealously in
favor of the measure: & is now fairly enlisted. I wish you could see
him on his way thro' Charlottesville, accompany him to the University, & invite him to return to the Assembly. I am satisfied he is now
very much disposed to support your literary views, but from the
course of his past life, & the pride of his character, he will be shy, and
the first advances must come from yourself. Doddridge also came
over and heartily supported the Bill. Our great friend in that House
is Genl Breckenridge. He is in truth a powerful friend, & you must
insist on his remaining in the Assembly. We are also much indebted
to Mr Johnson of the Senate. In the House of Delegates Mr Gordon,
has shewn himself an able, valuable, & efficient friend. Mr Watson of
Louisa, Mr Crump of Cumberland, Mr Loyall of Norfolk, Mr Bowyer
of Rockbridge,[1] Mr Chamberlayne of Henrico, were zealous & valuable friends. Mr Morris of Hanover, & Mr Stevenson of the City of
Richmond, deserve the most honorable mention. Stevenson will leave
us, but I hope Morris will remain. I wish you could see Morris. He is
a man of considerable talents, and distinguishes himself by his zeal in
support of the University. I hope Mr Gordon will return. The cordiality

& generosity of his nature make him the favorite of a large circle of friends. Mr Hunter of Essex, would have united with us, but he was called home by the illness of one of his family. He talks of not returning: but I will endeavor to prevail on him by letter. I have failed in regard to Currie: whose letter I enclose you. It is the anxious wish of our best friends, and of no one more than of myself, that the money now granted may be sufficient to finish the buildings. We must not come here again on that subject: These successive applications for money to finish the buildings, give grounds of reproach to our enemies, & draw our friends into difficulties with their constituents. The people of Albemarle would consult their own interests by making up any little deficiency. I hope the buildings may be ready by the next winter. Then I hope we shall be able to disencumber the funds. Rest assured, however, that the opposition will not cease. The enemies of the institution will send up their friends to oppose us. In the southern parts of the State, in the quarter of Brunswick, Greensville &^{c} I am informed, it is now the fashion to electioneer by crying down the University. We must cultivate the west, & unite with it, as much of the east as possible.—

My competitor having withdrawn, I propose to[2] accompany Mrs Cabell to W^{ms}burg, & to come up to the elections. Should any new opponent arise, I hope my friends will give me the earliest notice.

faithfully yours   JOSEPH C. CABELL

RC (ViU: TJP-PC); endorsed by TJ as received 3 Mar. 1821 and so recorded in SJL. Enclosure not found.

The UNIVERSITY BILL passed in the Virginia House of Delegates on 24 Feb. 1821 by a vote of 86–77 and later that day received final approval as "An act con-

cerning the University of Virginia" (*JHD* [1820–21 sess.], 214; *Acts of Assembly* [1820–21 sess.], 15–6). MY COMPETITOR: Sterling Claiborne.

[1] Word interlined in place of "Augusta."
[2] Cabell here canceled "carry."

From Spencer Roane

DEAR SIR.   Richmond, Feb. 25. 1821.

Mr Thweatt has sent me your favour to him, of 19th ultimo. As that letter was produced by mine to him, I owe you an apology for having caused you the trouble.—Be assured that no man respects your repose more than I do, or would be more unwilling to disturb it. your claims to that repose, arising from the most eminent services, and from the weight of years, are so strong, and so touchingly pourtrayed, that I am compelled to say—"almost thou persuadest me to be a christian"—. Although, therefore, in losing our Leader, we run the risk of losing our all, not a whisper of my breath shall be raised against it. Your later days ought to be as serene and as happy, as your life has been illustrious, and useful to your fellow men.

The very flattering mention you are pleased to make of me, in your letter, I shall prize, as the highest honour of my life. I have neither power nor leisure to render any political services, to my fellow-citizens: yet I see the Dangers which surround us, and shall be always ready to lift my voice against them.—on account of the last paragraph in your letter, I have taken the liberty to send it, to Col° Taylor. I have done this, under the approbation of Governor Randolph. Col° Taylor will be highly gratified, by your just and strong testimony in favour of his inestimable work. To that work may, already, in a measure, be ascribed, the revival which has taken place, on the subject of state-rights.—I congratulate you on the resolutions of our assembly produced by the citation of the Commonwealth, into the federal Court: and I also congratulate you, most sincerely, on the support which the university has again received.

With sentiments of the highest Consideratio[n,] respect, and Esteem, I am, Dear sir,

your obᵗ Servant   SPENCER ROANE

RC (DLC); edge trimmed; endorsed by TJ as received 3 Mar. 1821 and so recorded in SJL. RC (DLC); address cover only; with PoC of TJ to Samuel Smith (of Maryland), 10 June 1822, on verso; addressed: "Thomas Jefferson Esquire Monticello Albemarle by mail to milton"; franked; postmarked Richmond, 26 Feb.

ALMOST THOU PERSUADEST ME TO BE A CHRISTIAN is from the Bible (Acts 26.28). For the RESOLUTIONS OF OUR ASSEMBLY, see note to Joseph C. Cabell to TJ, 8 Feb. 1821.

From Daniel Brent

Washington, 26 february 1821.

Daniel Brent presents his respectful Compliments to mʳ Jefferson, and has the Pleasure to transmit to him the enclosed Letter, just received at the Depᵗ of State from mʳ Rush.   He takes advantage of the occasion to acknowledge the receipt of a note which mʳ J. did him the honor to write to him some time ago, enclosing Letters for messʳˢ Gallatin and Rush, to be forwarded; which DB did accordingly forward, according to mʳ Jefferson's wish.

RC (DLC); dateline at foot of text; endorsed by TJ as received 6 Mar. 1821 and so recorded in SJL. Enclosure: RC of Richard Rush to TJ, 11 Dec. 1820.

TJ's missing NOTE to Brent, [ca. 27 Dec. 1820], covered his letters to Albert Gallatin of 26 Dec. 1820 and to Rush of 27 Dec. 1820, and their enclosures.

To Robert S. Garnett

Monticello. Feb. 26. 21.

I thank you, dear Sir, for the Report of the Agricultural Committee on the subject of the Tariff, inclosed in your favor of the 14th. I have read it with pleasure. between that and the Report of the committee of Manufactures, the justice and the expediency of the system of protecting duties, is ably discussed. of all the questions which fall within the scope of the human mind, none are more perplexing than those which arise in the branch of Political economy. the facts are so numerous, so various, so entangled & difficult of access, and the combinations of these facts so complicated, that differences of opinion are to be expected. if there be heads in this world capable of seeing all these facts, all their bearings on one another, of making all the combinations into which they enter, and drawing sound conclusions from the whole, no doubt that a wisdom of that grade may form a system of regulations for directing to the greatest advantage the public industry and interest. the difficulty of doing this however has produced the modern & general conviction that it is safest 'to let things alone.' and the nation which has pursued the regulating system with the most apparent success is now proposing it's gradual abandonment. but I leave these puzzling decisions to those who are to live under them, confident that they will do what is best for themselves, & tender you with great sincerity the assurance of my esteem & respect.

TH: JEFFERSON

RC (Forbes Magazine Collection, New York City, 2003); at foot of text: "Robert S. Garnett esq."; endorsed by Garnett. PoC (DLC); endorsed by TJ.

Garnett's FAVOR of 14 Feb. 1821, not found, is recorded in SJL as received 19 Feb. 1821 from Washington. It enclosed the *Report Of the Committee on Agriculture, on the memorial of the Delegates of the United Agricultural Societies of sundry*

counties in the state of Virginia ([Washington, 1821]), which was presented to the United States House of Representatives on 2 Feb. 1821 (*JHR*, 14:191). Garnett sent the same publication to James Madison with a brief covering letter dated 14 Feb. 1821 (Madison, *Papers, Retirement Ser.*, 2:252).

Great Britain was the NATION beginning to deregulate as it moved toward economic liberalism.

To Frederick A. Mayo

Sir   Monticello Apr. [Feb.] 26. 21.

Your letter of the 21st is recieved. the number of the Portfolio, inserted with those of the Analectic magazine has been put in by mistake and may be thrown away. within a week another volume of the
Weekly register will be closed. it will still wait awhile for it's index.
should I not be able to send it to you before you send away the volumes you are binding, be so good as to remember how they are bound,
that you may be able to bind uniformly the one to be sent. I put into
the box a cartoon open at top & one end, being such as all my papers
are arranged in, instead of tying them in bundles. be so good as to
make 2. dozen such, which I forgot to mention in the list I sent you.
they must be packed in a box by themselves to prevent their being
crushed. Accept my salutations.   Th: Jefferson

deliver the boxes when ready to Capt Bernard Peyton who will forward them.

PoC (MHi); on verso of reused address cover to TJ; misdated; adjacent to
signature: "Mr Mayo"; endorsed by TJ as
a letter of 26 Feb. 1821 and so recorded
in SJL.

cartoon: "carton" (see TJ to William
Short, 8 Mar. 1811, 26 April 1812, and
notes).

From Bernard Peyton

Dear Sir,   Rich'd 26 Feby 1821

I received this morning your esteemed favor 20th curt & observe
contents.

I send under cover herewith agreeable to your request 1 oz Green
curled Savoy Cabbage Seed which I hope will reach you safely and
prove good.—   I have seen Mr Wickham relative to the Earthen
Pots you speak of, he tells me they were made to the North, by his
special direction, & that he has never known any of them made at the
Potteries here,—I have his promise however that he will loan me the
most perfect he has, which I will myself carry to the Pottery & endeavour to have fifty moulded immediately like it, & of the success of
my application you shall be apprised.

I this day recd from your Grand Son a note for $4,000 signed by
yourself & endorsed by him, to which I will add my name, and offer
it for discount at the Farmers Bank on Thursday next, & hope it will
be done; you may expect to hear from me touching it by the next mail

to Charlottesville, in the mean time, will converse with the several directors of the Bank on the subject.

With great respect D^r sir Yours very Truely   B. PEYTON

N.B. The University bill has passed both Houses of the Genl Assembly & is a law of the Land—

RC (MHi); endorsed by TJ as received 3 Mar. 1821 and so recorded in SJL; with additional notations by TJ beneath endorsement related to his 4 Mar. 1821 reply to Peyton: "remit to Leroy & Bayard   Rudim. & orb. pict.   Coffee." YOUR GRAND SON: Thomas Jefferson Randolph.

To Dabney C. Terrell

DEAR SIR   Monticello Feb. 26. 21.

While you were in this neighborhood, you mentioned to me your intention of studying the law, and asked my opinion as to the sufficient course of reading. I gave it to you, ore tenus, and with so little consideration, that I do not remember what it was. but I have since recollected that I once wrote a letter to Dr Cooper,[1] on good consideration of the subject. he was then law-lecturer, I believe at Carlisle. my stiffening wrist makes writing now a slow & painful operation: but[2] Ellen undertakes to copy the letter, which I shall inclose herein.

I[3] notice in that letter 4. distinct epochs at which the English laws have been reviewed, and their whole body, as existing at each epoch, well digested into a Code. these Digests were by Bracton, Coke, Matthew Bacon, and Blackstone. Bracton having written about the commencement of the extant statutes, may be considered as having given a digest of the laws then in being, written and unwritten, and forming therefore the textual Code of what is called the Common law, just at the period too when it begins to be altered by statutes to which we can appeal. but so much of his matter is become obsolete by change of circumstances, or altered by statute, that the Student may omit him for the present, and

1. Begin with[4] Coke's 4. institutes. these give a compleat body of the law as it stood in the reign of the 1st James, an epoch the more interesting to us, as we separated at that point from English legislation, and acknolege no subsequent statutory alterations.

2. Then passing over (for occasional reading as hereafter proposed) all the Reports and treatises to the time of Matthew Bacon, read his Abridgment, compiled about 100. years after Coke's, in which they are all embodied. this gives numerous applications of the old

principles to new cases, and gives the general state of the English law at that period.

Here too the Student should take up the Chancery branch of the law, by reading the 1st and 2d Abridgments of the Cases in Equity. the 2d is by the same Matthew Bacon, the 1st having been published some time before. the Alphabetical order, adopted by Bacon, is certainly not as satisfactory as the systematic. but the arrangement is under very general and leading heads; and these indeed, with very little[5] difficulty, might be systematically, instead of Alphabetically arranged and read.

3. Passing now, in like manner, over all intervening Reports, and tracts, the Student may take up Blackstone's Commentaries, published about 25. years later than Bacon's abridgment, and giving the substance of these new Reports and tracts. this Review is not so full as that of Bacon by any means, but better digested. Here too Woodeson should be read, as supplementory to Blackstone, under heads too shortly treated by him. Fonblanque's edition of Francis's Maxims of Equity,[6] into which the later cases are incorporated, is[7] also supplementory in the Chancery branch, in which Blackstone is very short.

This course comprehends about 23. 8vo volumes, and reading 4. or 5. hours aday, would employ about 2. years.

After these the best of the Reporters since Blackstone should be read for the new cases which have occurred since his time. which they are I know not as all of them are since my time.

By way of change and relief, for another hour or two in the day should be read the law-tracts of merit which are many, and among them all those of Baron Gilbert are of the first order. in these hours too may be read Bracton (now translated) and Justinian's Institute. the method of these two last works is very much the same, and their language often quite so. Justinian is very illustrative of the doctrines of Equity, and is often appealed to, & Cooper's edition is the best on account of the analogies & contrasts he has given of the Roman and English law. after Bracton, Reeves's history of the English law may be read to advantage. during this same hour or two of lighter law reading, select and leading cases of the Reporters may be successively read, which the several digests will have pointed out and referred to.[8] one of these particularly may be named as proper to be turned to while reading Coke Littleton on Warranty. it explains that subject easily which Coke makes difficult and too artificial. this is a case in Vaughan's reports, of Gardner & Sheldon, as well as I remember, for I quote by memory, and after an interval of near 60. years since I read it.

I have here sketched the reading in Common law & Chancery which I suppose necessary for a reputable practitioner in those courts. but there are other branches of law in, which, altho' it is not expected he should be an adept, yet, when it occurs to speak of them, it should be understandingly to a decent degree. these are the Admiralty law, Ecclesiastical law, and the Law of Nations. I would name as elementary books in these branches[9] Brown's Compend of the Civil and Admiralty law, 2. 8^{vos} the Jura Ecclesiastica. 2. 8^{vos} and Les institutions du droit de la Nature et des Gens de Reyneval. 1. 8vo

Besides these 6. hours of law-reading, light and heavy, and those necessary for the repasts of the day, for exercise and sleep, which suppose to be 10. or 12. there will still be 6. or 8. hours for reading history, Politics, Ethics, Physics, Oratory, Poetry, Criticism E^{t}c. as necessary as Law to form an accomplished lawyer.

The letter to Dr Cooper, with this as a supplement, will give you those ideas on a sufficient course of law reading, which I ought to have done with more consideration at the moment of your first request. accept them now as a testimony of my esteem, and of sincere wishes for your success: and the family, unâ voce, desires me to convey theirs, with my own affectionate salutations.   TH: JEFFERSON

RC (ViU: TJP-CT); stained, with faint text supplied from PoC. PoC (DLC: TJ Papers, 219:39219, 221:39492); with TJ's Notes on John H. Thomas's Edition of Coke on Littleton, [ca. 4 Jan. 1824], attached with sealing wax at foot of first page (see note 4 below), and with other emendations possibly also made at that time, the most important of which are noted below; in TJ's hand at head of text, probably added in 1824: "Th: Jefferson to Dabney Terrell esq." Tr (MHi). Tr (NjP: Thomas Jefferson Collection); endorsed: "Letters on the Study of the Law." Tr (ViU: TJP); extract in Nicholas P. Trist's hand; misdated 26 Feb. 1824. Tr (ViU: Jefferson Family Correspondence); extract in Trist's hand; endorsed by Joseph Coolidge: "Thomas's systematic arrangement of Coke upon Lyttleton." All Trs derive from the PoC. Enclosure: TJ to Thomas Cooper, 16 Jan. 1814. Enclosed in TJ to Thomas Mann Randolph, 4 Jan. 1824.

ORE TENUS: "orally; by word of mouth" (*Black's Law Dictionary*). ELLEN: TJ's granddaughter Ellen W. Randolph (Coolidge). Edward Coke provided a chapter on WARRANTY in *The First Part of the In-*stitutes of The Lawes of England: or A Commentary upon Littleton* (4th ed., London, 1639; Sowerby, no. 1781), 364–93. Edward Vaughan included the legal case of GARDNER V. SHELDON in his edition of *The Reports and Arguments Of that Learned Judge, Sir John Vaughan, Kt. late Lord Chief Justice of the Court of Common-Pleas* (London, 1706; Sowerby, no. 2061), 259–73. UNÂ VOCE: "with one voice; unanimously" (*OED*).

[1] In PoC TJ added "Jan. 16. 1814" in left margin opposite the line mentioning his letter of that date to Cooper.
[2] In PoC TJ here interlined "my granddaughter."
[3] ViU Trs begin here.
[4] In PoC TJ here interlined an asterisk keyed to the attached MS of his Notes on John H. Thomas's Edition of Coke on Littleton, [ca. 4 Jan. 1824].
[5] TJ here canceled "trouble."
[6] In PoC TJ here interlined "and Bridgman's digested Index."
[7] Reworked in PoC to "are."
[8] ViU Trs end here.
[9] In PoC TJ here interlined "Molloy de jure maritimo."

To Timothy Pickering

I have recieved, Sir, your favor of the 12ᵗʰ and I assure you I recieved it with pleasure. it is true as you say that we have differed in
political opinions; but I can say with equal truth, that I never suffered
a political to become a personal difference. I have been left on this
ground by some friends whom I dearly loved, but I was never the
first to separate. with some others, of politics different from mine, I
have continued in the warmest friendship to this day, and to all, and
to yourself particularly, I have ever done moral justice.

I thank you for mr Channing's discourse, which you have been so
kind as to forward me. it is not yet at hand, but is doubtless on it's
way. I had recieved it thro' another channel, and read it with high
satisfaction. no one sees with greater pleasure than myself the progress of reason in it's advances towards rational Christianity. when we
shall have done away the incomprehensible jargon of the Trinitarian
arithmetic, that three are one, and one is three; when we shall have
knocked down the artificial scaffolding, reared to mask from view the
simple structure of Jesus, when, in short, we shall have unlearned
every thing which has been taught since his day, and got back to the
pure and simple doctrines he inculcated, we shall then be truly and
worthily his disciples: and my opinion is that if nothing had ever been
added to what flowed purely from his lips, the whole world would at
this day have been Christian. I know that the case you cite, of Dʳ
Drake, has been a common one. the religion-builders have so dis-
torted and deformed the doctrines of Jesus, so muffled them in mysti-
cisms, fancies and falsehoods, have¹ caricatured them into forms so
monstrous and inconcievable, as to shock reasonable thinkers, to revolt them against the whole, and drive them rashly to pronounce it's
founder an impostor. had there never been a Commentator, there
never would have been an infidel. in the present advance of truth,
which we both approve, I do not know that you and I may think alike
on all points. as the Creator has made no two faces alike, so no two
minds, and probably no two creeds. we well know that among Unitarians themselves there are strong shades of difference, as between
Doctors Price and Priestley for example. so there may be peculiarities
in your creed and in mine. they are honestly formed without doubt. I
do not wish to trouble the world with mine, nor to be troubled for
them. these accounts are to be settled only with him who made us;
and to him we leave it, with charity for all others, of whom also he
is the only rightful and competent judge. I have little doubt that the

whole of our country will soon be rallied to the Unity of the Creator, and, I hope, to the pure doctrines of Jesus also.

In saying to you so much, and without reserve, on a subject on which I never permit myself to go before the public, I know that I am safe against the infidelities which have so often betrayed my letters to the strictures of those for whom they were not written, and to whom I never meant to commit my peace. to yourself I wish every happiness, and will conclude, as you have done, in the same simple style of antiquity, da operam ut Valeas. hoc mihi gratius facere nihil potes.

TH: JEFFERSON

RC (MHi: Pickering Papers); addressed: "Timothy Pickering esquire Salem. Mass."; franked; postmarked Charlottesville, 3 Mar.; endorsed by Pickering, in part, as received 10 Mar. 1821 "In answer to mine—topic, Christianity." PoC (DLC). Tr (MHi: Pickering Papers).

good care of your health. You can do nothing to please me more" (Cicero to Oppius, letter 335 [XI.29], and Cicero to Cornificius, letter 347 [XII.23], in Cicero, *Letters to Friends*, ed. and trans. David R. Shackleton Bailey, Loeb Classical Library [2001], 3:120–1, 150–1).

DA OPERAM UT VALEAS. HOC MIHI GRATIUS FACERE NIHIL POTES: "Take

[1] TJ here canceled "presented them."

Conveyance of Limestone Tract to Abraham Hawley

This Indenture made on the 28th day of February in the year one thousand eight hundred and twenty one between Thomas Jefferson of Monticello in Albemarle on the one part and Abraham Holly on the other part witnesseth that the said Thomas in consideration of one hundred dollars, to him in hand paid and of the further sum of three hundred dollars secured to be paid hath given granted bargained and sold to the said Abraham—and his heirs a certain parcel of land lying on the road called the three notched road, and on that part of it which is crossed by plumbtree branch otherwise called Scales Creek in the said County of Albemarle which parcel of land was conveyed to the s^d Thomas in feesimple by Robert Sharp by deed bearing date the 5th of October 1773 under the following description, to wit, Beginning where the southern edge of s^d road crosses the northern edge of the said watercourse, and running down the said edge of the road to a white oak saplin marked on three sides thence to a red oak corner to Huckstep thence to a maple a little above a spring thence across the water course before mentioned where it runs nearest to the sd [maple]^1 to the northern edge thereof thence down the sd edge of

the sd water course to the begining including the spring before mentioned, and also a considerable quantity of limestone and being all the
lands at that date held by the said Robert Sharpe on the northern side
of the said road and supposed to contain about four acres with its ap-
purtenances to have and to hold the said parcel of Land so described
in the sd deed to the sd Abraham Holly & his heirs Reserving nevertheless to the said Thomas & his heirs owners of the house at monticello and as an appurtenance to the said house forever a right[2] to take
from the premises for his and their own use and purpose of every kind
(but not to dispose of to others) as much limestone as they shall think
proper for their own uses as aforesaid and at all times when they shall
think proper which right shall be held and remain in them and their
heirs fully and forever unliable to severance by metes and bounds and
the said Thomas & his heirs the said parcel of Land with its appurte-
nances except as to the rights reserved as aforesaid to the said Abraham Holly & his heirs will forever warrant and defend In witness
whereof the said Thomas hath hereto subscribed his name and affixed
his seal on the day and year first above written

Signed Sealed & delivered   TH JEFFERSON
   in presence of
JOHN WATSON
THOS J RANDOLPH
EDMUND BACON

Tr (Albemarle Co. Deed Book, 22:334);
in the hand of Albemarle County deputy
clerk Ira Garrett; with wax from seal adjacent to TJ's signature; Garrett's signed
attestation at foot of text: "In Albemarle
County Court office the 23rd day of March
1821 This Indenture was presented to
me in said office and acknowledged by
Thomas Jefferson party thereto and there-
upon admitted to record"; signed notation
by a deputy clerk Garth in left margin:
"Examined & delivered to Abram Hawly
the 7th Jany 1822."

Abraham Hawley (Holly) (d. 1838)
lived in Albemarle County by 1810 and
served as a private in the Virginia militia
during the War of 1812. He sold lime to
TJ between 1818 and 1822, and in 1820
he was paid for work done at the University of Virginia. Hawley owned no slaves
in 1810 and 1820 and one in 1830. At his
death his personal property in Albemarle
County was valued at $116.64 (DNA: RG
29, CS, Albemarle Co., 1810–30; *Virginia Militia in the War of 1812: From
Rolls in the Auditor's Office at Richmond*
[2001], 1:89; *MB*, 2:1349, 1350, 1377–9,
1383; ViU: PP; Albemarle Co. Will Book,
13:132).

On 29 Mar. 1771 TJ purchased one
acre of Robert Sharpe's limestone land,
and he paid him on 5 Oct. 1773 "in full
for the lands at the Limestone quarry,"
totaling four acres (*MB*, 1:220, 252, 346,
2:938).

A missing letter from Hawley to TJ of
11 Jan. 1822 is recorded in SJL as received
from Milton the day it was written.

[1] Omitted word supplied from Tr of 5
Oct. 1773 deed to TJ in Albemarle Co.
Deed Book, 6:286.
[2] Manuscript: "rigt."

From Samuel Leake

D. SIR   Richmond Febuary 28ᵗʰ 1821—

dureing the life time of my Grandfather Mask Leake (of Abbemarle County) he made me a gift to a claim of Millitary Land which he[1] purchased of a soldier by the nam of Geo. Malcome who faugtht at the battle of the meddows under Washington in the year 1754 It appears from examineing the registers office that on the 15ᵗʰ day of December 1772 In grant to savage and others of 28627 Acres of Land on the Ohio river this Malcome is one of the Grantees, now the object of my Trowbleing you is that my Grandfather when he purchased the claim of Malcom he took a receipt for the money expressive of the Object for which he paid it &ᶜ my Grandfather in his life time told me that Malcome and himself some short time after the purchase went to Albemarle court with a view, to make a transfer of the Title to the Land by Deed or acknowledment in court of the purchase or something of the kind by which to transfer the title in the best possible manner the nature of the case would admit of—If I mistake not he said you were at the time the presideing member of the bench and that you recommended to them to wait till the Grant or pattent Ishued when they might make a formal conveyance by Deed &c which advice was intended to be pursued but Malcome died or went off or something of the kind—That the Troublesome times came on or rather continued and was then succeeded by the revolution this circumstance braught about—and put off his further attention to this business for a great Lapse of years and he being naturally somewhat delitary never saught farther into the subject—some year or two before his death, which took place sepᵗ 1813. he made me a gift of the claim to the Land and papers relating thereto &ᶜ—the matter has been neglected by me untill a short time past seeing a decree of the chancery court for the[2] stanton district. Malcome name mentioned &c. and on examination of the registirs office finding him one of the Grantees and further understanding that there has been claims of a less auspicious nature established and recollecting to have heard my Grandfather relate the above named circumstances relating to you It accured to me to write you requesting you to recur to in memmory and say if you could recollect the circumstances, If the multiplisity of public business and varied senes through which you have passed have not eraced the recollection from your mind, your answer to this after trying to turn your memmory to the subject will be thankfully received and gratefully acknowledged by   Your Ob st.

                                                  SAMUEL LEAKE

P.S. I hope the liberty taken by one who has no personal acquaintanc with you, in the above request will need no farther apology than the circunstances themselv^s presnt

S. LEAKE

RC (MHi); addressed: "Thomas Jefferson Esqr Charlottesville Albemarle County V^a" by "mail"; franked; postmarked Richmond, 5 Mar.; endorsed by TJ as received 8 Mar. 1821 and so recorded in SJL.

Samuel Leake (1790–1858), innkeeper and farmer, was born in Albemarle County and lived in Richmond by 1820. He purchased a tavern and farm at Rockfish Gap in 1826. The property was known as the Mountaintop Hotel when Leake sold it in 1858. In the 1850 census he is listed as an Augusta County farmer with landholdings valued at $2,965. At his death Leake resided in Henrico County and owned real estate and personal property worth over $44,000, including twenty-four slaves (George Warren Chappelear, *Families of Virginia* [1932–34], 1:23, 33–4; Woods, *Albemarle*, 249; Augusta Co. Deed Book, 45:443–8, 48:409–10, 78:167–8; *Richmond Enquirer*, 2 Feb. 1836, 15 June 1852; DNA: RG 29, CS, Augusta Co., 1850; Richmond *Daily Dispatch*, 28 Dec. 1858; Richmond City Circuit Court Will Book [Common Law], 1:398–9, 459–61).

On 23 Dec. 1772 George Washington wrote a public letter to William Rind, the editor of the Williamsburg *Virginia Gazette*, announcing that officers and soldiers of the 1st Virginia Regiment, including Private George Malcomb (MALCOME), who had enlisted prior to the 1754 Battle of Fort Necessity (also known as the Battle of the Great Meadows [MEDDOWS]) could file land claims under Lieutenant Governor Robert Dinwiddie's 1754 proclamation. A survey of 28627 ACRES was patented to John Savage, from which the regiment's privates were each allotted 400 acres (Washington, *Papers, Colonial Ser.*, 9:143–8). Beginning on 28 Dec. 1820, the *Richmond Enquirer* advertised "VALUABLE LAND FOR SALE" along with the Superior Court of Chancery's 21 July 1820 DECREE that money be collected from Malcomb and the several other patentees to cover fees recently incurred in surveying the large tract. Delinquent lots were to be sold at auction.

[1] Manuscript: "he he."
[2] Manuscript: "the the."

List of Bread Distributed to Monticello Slaves

1821. Feb. Bread list.

Betty Brown	Nance
Mary.	Ned
Burwell	Peter Hem.
Critta.	Sally Hem.
Davy jun^r	Beverly
Fanny	Harriet
Ellen	Madison
Jenny	Eston.
Melinda	Thrimston.
Indridge	Wormly

Dolly	Ursula.
Gill	Joe
Israel	Anne
Phill Bedf^d	Dolly
Joe	Cornelius
Edy	Thomas
Maria	Louisa
Patsy	Caroline
Betsy	Critta.
Peter	51. pecks for the people
Isabella.	3. pecks for the House
John Hem.	54. pecks or 13½ bushels.
John gardener.	
Lewis	
Mary. Moses's	
Davy	
Celia	
Tucker	
Zacharia	
Patsy	
Fosset.	
Fontaine	

MS (ViCMRL, on deposit ViU: TJP); on verso of portion of reused address cover to TJ; in TJ's hand; partially dated.

TJ created similar lists in 1795, 1796, 1810, 1815, and 1817. Although he called each one a BREAD LIST, his use of the word "pecks" suggests that cornmeal or flour was actually distributed (Betts, *Farm Book*, pt. 1, 43, 50, 134, 148, 156).

List of Debts

1821. Feb		D	
√ Wayt	about	200	
√ Higgenbotham		150.90	1820. Mar.
√ Dawson for Gilmer 75.			
Meeks 18.35		93.35	
√ Watson. for Meeks		44.85	
√ Rogers John. for Gilmer		75	
√ Leschot		68.	
√ Brown Ja^s for Fielding Lewis		133.25[1]	
√ Graves		250	
√ Johnson & Peyton		100[2]	
√ Leroy & Bayard.		125	
· University		300.	

				£ s d	
√	Mayo Fred. A.	ab^t	100.		
√	Bowling				
·	Robertson Archib.		611.17		
√	Lietch. James		1348.47		
·	Brand Joseph		339.60	1811. Nov. 4	
·	Bacon Edmund		634.71	1821. Jan. 1	
\	Peyton Craven p^d 700		1,220.31	1820. Oct. 26	
√	Pini		444.[3]		
\	Miller B. p^d 750		3836.96	1820. Nov. 22.	
	Yancey Joel.		1750.		
	Ham Elijah		419.61	1819. Jan. 23.	
	Chisolm Hugh.				
	Carden Youen				
	Nielson John		843.50	1820. May 31.	
	Leroy & Bayard.		2083.20	1820. Jan. 1	
	Pini		7400.	1820. Oct. 1	
	Lietch James		5529.	1820. Oct. 28	£ s d
	Henderson & co. or Lyle.				402–11–2. st. 1806. July 1
					+230–11–9 int.
					94–17–1½ 1779. Sep. 1
	Higgenbotham.		2848.67	1815. Aug. 1.	
	Welsh. for mr Wayles				684– 6–3. curr^cy 1810. Jul. 20.
	Hanbury for d^o				
	Bacon John		370.	1813. Aug. 1.	

MS (CSmH: JF); written entirely in TJ's hand on one side of a single sheet; partially dated.

[1] Entry interlined.
[2] Entry interlined.
[3] Entry interlined.

GILMER: Joseph Gilmore.

Appendix

Supplemental List of Documents Not Found

JEFFERSON'S epistolary record and other sources describe a number of documents for which no text is known to survive. The Editors generally account for such material at documents that mention them or at other relevant places. Exceptions are accounted for below.

From Anonymous, 30 June 1820. Recorded in SJL as received 6 July 1820 from Washington, with additional bracketed notation: "with a pamphlet."

From Paul Loise, 12 July 1820. Recorded in SJL as received 16 July 1820 from Washington, with Loise described parenthetically as an Osage interpreter.

From Charles Bulfinch, 1 Aug. 1820. Recorded in SJL as received 7 Aug. 1820 from Washington, with additional bracketed notation: "by mr Hall" (probably David Aiken Hall, Bulfinch's soon-to-be son-in-law [*Washington Gazette*, 28 Sept. 1821]).

To Colin Buckner, 28 Oct. 1820. Recorded in SJL.

To Matthew Brown, 7 Dec. 1820. Recorded in SJL.

From Matthew Brown, 7 Dec. 1820. Recorded in SJL as received 8 Dec. 1820 from Lynchburg.

INDEX

Aaron (Hebrew priest; Moses's brother), 620

Abner, Thomas: and University of Virginia, 313

Abraham (Old Testament patriarch), 165

Absalom (Old Testament figure), 620

Academy of Natural Sciences of Philadelphia: identified, 12:505n; members of, 340

An Act authorising William Waller Hening to Publish an Edition of certain Laws of this Commonwealth, and for other purposes (*1808*), 212

An Act authorizing the Visitors of the University of Virginia to borrow money for finishing the buildings thereof (*1820*), 68n, 298–9

An Act for establishing an Executive Department, to be denominated the Department of Foreign Affairs (*1789*), 433, 434n

An act for establishing an University (*1819*), 295, 298, 301, 545n, 560–1

An Act making provision for the claim of M. Poirey (*1819*), 494

An act to amend the act, entitled, "an act to amend the act for clearing and improving the navigation of James River, and for uniting the Eastern and Western Waters, by the James and Kanawha Rivers" (*1821*), 625–6

An Act to impose a new tonnage duty on French ships and vessels (*1820*), 221, 425, 426n

An Act to limit the term of office of certain officers therein named, and for other purposes (*1820*), 407, 408n, 433, 446, 525

An Act to provide an accurate chart of each county and a general map of the territory of this Commonwealth (*1816*), 99–100

An Act to regulate the sales of Property under Execution (*1820*), 59

Adam (Old Testament figure), 16

Adam, Alexander: *Roman Antiquities*, 5

Adams, John: on aging, 590; and American Academy of Language and Belles Lettres, 532; and C. G. G. Botta's *History of the War of the Independence of the United States of America* (trans. G. A. Otis), 441,

442n, 472–3; and correspondence with TJ, 94; and B. Franklin, 590; D. Fraser's biographical sketch of, 324; friendship with TJ, 225; friendship with F. A. Van der Kemp, 54–5, 94, 225–6; on governmental systems, 590; health of, 54, 225, 562; house of, 94; identified, 4:390–1n; letter from, 589–91; letters to, 193–7, 562–4; and Mass. constitutional convention, 549, 550n, 562–3, 590; as member of Continental Congress, 472–3; and Missouri question, 563; on religion, 589–90; signer of Declaration of Independence, 252n; on slavery, 590; and South America, 563–4; and speeches of the American Revolution, 441, 472–3; works sent to, 43n, 256n, 414n, 435n, 442n, 532n, 549n, 616n; writings of, 94

Adams, John Quincy: and accusations against L. Harris, 31–2, 63; and American Academy of Language and Belles Lettres, 531; and appointments, 51–2, 157n; identified, 12:91–2n; letter from, 22; letter to, 45; as reference, 426; as secretary of state, 411–2; sends works to TJ, 22, 45; works sent to, 43n, 442n

Adams-Onís Treaty (*1819*): ratification of, 493, 616; and U.S. relations with Spain, 250, 493

An Address delivered before the Agricultural Society of Susquehanna County, At its Organization, December 6, 1820 (R. H. Rose), 561–2, 605

An Address to the People of the United States, drawn up by order of the National Institution for the Promotion of Industry, established in June, 1820, 565n

Adversus nationes (Arnobius the Elder), 258

Ælfredi Magni Anglorum Regis (J. Spelman; trans. O. Walker), 364

Ælfredi Regis res gestæ (Asser), 364

Ælfric of Eynsham: *An English-Saxon Homily on the Birth-Day of St. Gregory* (trans. E. Elstob), 364

Aeneid (Virgil), 92n, 381

Aeschylus: works of, 25, 275

Aesop: referenced by T. Ewell, 246; referenced by TJ, 235

INDEX

Ἀνάλεκτα Ἑλληνικὰ Μείζονα sive Collectanea Græca Majora (A. Dalzel), 381, 443

The Analogy of Religion (J. Butler), 381, 458

An Analytical Digested Index of the Reported Cases in the Several Courts of Equity, and the high Court of Parliament (R. W. Bridgman), 642n

anatomy: collegiate education in, 296n, 628, 629n

anchovies, 118, 419

Anderson, Mr. (of Richmond), 122

Anderson, Edmund: and Central College–University of Virginia subscription, 303; G. Milleway's draft on, 124n; and University of Virginia, 478

Anderson, Edmund, & Company (Richmond firm). *See* Edmund Anderson & Company (Richmond firm)

Anderson, Joseph: as comptroller of U.S. Treasury, 530, 531n

Anglo-Saxon (Old English) language: books on, 363–4; instruction in at University of Virginia, 193; TJ on study of, 193–4

Animal Magnetism (E. Inchbald), xlix

Annales Générales des Sciences Physiques, 568

Annals of Nature (C. S. Rafinesque), 355, 396

Anne (TJ's slave; b. *1807*). *See* Hughes, Anne (TJ's slave; b. *1807*)

An Anniversary Discourse, delivered before The New-York Historical Society, on Thursday, December 28, 1820 (H. Wheaton), 615–6

anonymous authors: letter from, 339–40; letter from accounted for, 651

antiquities: Indian burial mounds, enclosures, and fortifications, 15, 155, 156, 171–6, 177, 178, 179, 180; and vases, 155

Antoninus Pius (Roman emperor): column of, 34

Antrim, Joseph: identified, 12:262n; and plastering at Central College–University of Virginia, 307, 309, 311, 313, 315, 316, 317, 319

apes, 181

The Apocryphal New Testament, being all the Gospels, Epistles and other pieces now extant (ed. W. Hone), 364

An Apology for Christianity, in a Series of Letters, addressed to Edward Gibbon, Esq (R. Watson), 598, 602n

apoplexy, 75

An Appeal from the Judgments of Great Britain respecting the United States of America (R. Walsh), 286

Appeal of Joseph Wheaton, late deputy quarter master general and major of cavalry, to the Senate and House of Representatives of the United States of America (J. Wheaton), 413–4

Appleton, Thomas: Agreement to Hire Giacomo Raggi and Michele Raggi, 237, 239n, 254, 255, 282, 283, 331, 335, 336, 337; and capitals for University of Virginia, 4, 113–4, 243, 342–3; and families of G. Raggi and M. Raggi, 3–4, 112, 114, 335, 342; identified, 8:162n; on Italy, 344, 383–4; letters from, 3–4, 342–5, 383–4; letter to, 112–5; and P. Mazzei's estate, 4, 112–3, 114, 342, 344n, 384; and seeds for TJ, 4, 113; and stonecutters for Central College–University of Virginia, 283, 377–8, 437–8; TJ pays, 50, 123, 177; and TJ's European correspondence, 112, 123

Archæologia Americana: Transactions and Collections, 351, 352n

Archer, William: as Va. legislator, 625

architecture: study of, 325; TJ advises J. Monroe, 60. *See also* building materials

Armstrong, John: identified, 1:20n; Notes on Tadeusz Kosciuszko, 87

Army, U.S.: officers' commissions sought, 409; reduction of, 595–6, 622

Arnobius the Elder: *Adversus nationes*, 258

A. Robertson & Company (firm): dissolution of, 30; TJ's debt to, 30, 68–9, 134, 273, 376, 401, 409, 413, 414, 416, 436, 449–50, 592, 596. *See also* Robertson, Archibald

Arrian (Flavius Arrianus): writings of, 330

arrows, 38, 155

Ars Poetica (Horace), 443

art. *See* drawing; paintings; sculpture

Artigas, José Gervasio, 412n

Askew, Samuel: seeks employment at University of Virginia, 294–5, 341

asparagus, 634

Blair, Hugh: *Lectures on Rhetoric and Belles Lettres*, 5, 381, 458
Bland, John, 454
Bland, Peter, 454
Bland, Peter R., 454
Bland, Richard: and manuscript of Va. laws, 241n; and Stamp Act Resolutions, 230
Bland, Theodorick (*1742–90*): as member of Continental Congress, 446
blankets: TJ purchases, 12
Blenheim (Albemarle Co. estate), 104
Bluebeard (fictional character), 618
Blue Ridge Mountains: visible from Monticello, 36–7; visible from Montpellier, 201
boats: carriage to and from Richmond, 21, 41, 45, 47, 216, 224, 240, 281, 323, 328, 366, 376, 389, 410, 413, 416, 526, 596, 597, 626; cost of transportation by, 25n, 216n, 223, 240, 293, 343; steamboats, 281, 468; stolen, 369–70n
Boethius, Anicius Manlius Severinus: *Consolationis Philosophiæ Libri V. Anglo-Saxonice Redditi ab Alfredo* (ed. C. Rawlinson), 364
Boin, William: and University of Virginia, 305, 307, 308, 320
Boissy d'Anglas, François Antoine, comte de: *Essai sur la Vie, les Écrits et les Opinions de M. de Malesherbes*, 484–5; identified, 14:205n; letter to, 484–5; meets TJ in France, 485
Bolingbroke, Henry St. John, Viscount: TJ on, 553, 554n
Bolívar, Simón, 563
Bolling, John (*1737–1800*) (TJ's brother-in-law): and TJ's debt to Henderson, McCaul & Company, 513
Bolling, Lenaeus (Linnaeus): Buckingham Co. residence of, 211, 276
Bombay, India: council of, 15; harbor of, 15
bombazine (textile), 11
Bonaparte, Napoleon. *See* Napoleon I, emperor of France
bookcases: mentioned, 241
books: on agriculture, 151, 169, 187, 364, 406, 546–7, 576; on American Revolution, 27, 42, 91, 93–4, 127, 204, 209, 218, 286, 440–2, 472–3, 496–7, 516, 517n, 524, 578, 580–4, 615, 635; on art, 416, 597; on astronomy, 380n; binding of, 427; binding

of for TJ, 115, 187, 504, 516, 596, 627, 628, 639; biographical, li, 26–8, 86–7, 168–9, 213–4, 228, 272, 273n, 324, 424, 492, 503, 511; on botany, 224, 257; of builders' prices, 115; on chemistry, 150–1, 164, 169, 187, 557, 558n; classical, 25, 40, 56, 58, 115, 164, 190n, 224, 226, 257, 275, 393; of correspondence, 168–9; on criticism (literary), 224, 257; dedicated to TJ, 509–10; dictionaries, 5, 194, 195, 363, 364; on education, 60–1, 86; encyclopedias, 34, 125, 234, 236; on fish, 567; on French Revolution, 115; on gardening, 364; on geography, 125, 547, 626; on geology, 523; on government, 255, 287, 289n, 353–4; on grammar, 5, 10, 73; on history, 5, 27, 42, 58, 91, 93–4, 115, 127, 150, 151, 154, 169, 181, 187, 197n, 204–5, 206, 209, 218–9, 239, 261, 286, 290, 364, 380–1, 441, 503, 507, 516–7, 532; on mathematics, 125, 209, 400n; on mineralogy, 558n; and music, 264; on natural history, 125, 568; novels, 517; packing and shipping of, 361; of poetry, 5, 74, 75, 346, 509, 517n, 547, 576; on politics, 22, 42, 45, 93, 256n; price of, 361; on rhetoric, 5; on spelling, 262; on stenography, 287; tariffs on, 497, 524; on U.S. Constitution, 168–9, 419–20, 482–4, 556, 609, 617–8, 637; on zoology, 568. *See also* Jefferson, Thomas: Books and Library; law: books on; political economy: works on; religion: works on; subscriptions, for publications; Virginia, University of: Books and Library
Bory de St. Vincent, Jean Baptiste G. M.: edits *Annales Générales des Sciences Physiques*, 568
Boston, Mass.: glass from, 192–3, 370
Boston Glass Manufactory, 192–3, 370
Bostwick, John: New Orleans merchant, 54, 110, 134; as potential purchaser of Lego, 110
botany: books on, 224, 257; collegiate education in, 159–60, 329, 374, 458, 568; scholars of, 568; study of, 199, 329
Botta, Carlo Giuseppe Guglielmo: *History of the War of the Independence of the United States of America* (trans. G. A. Otis), 42, 91, 93–4, 127, 204, 440–2, 472–3, 497, 516–7, 524, 578,

Daniel, Peter Vyvian: identified, 2:88n; as lieutenant governor of Va., 397n, 544; as member of Va. Council of State, 544

Darien, Isthmus of. *See* Panama, Isthmus of

Dartmouth College: mentioned, 531

David, king of Israel, 17, 620

Davie, William Richardson: as founder of University of North Carolina, 339–40; minister plenipotentiary to France, 339, 340n

Davila, Enrico Caterino: *Istoria delle guerre civili di Francia*, 441, 473

Davis, Daniel: identified, 1:419n; and University of Virginia, 304, 478, 481

Davis, John W.: and University of Virginia, 310, 311, 313, 314, 315, 316

Davy (TJ's slave; b. *1784*). *See* Hern, David (Davy) (TJ's slave; b. *1784*)

Davy (TJ's slave; b. *1803*). *See* Hern, David (Davy) (TJ's slave; b. *1803*)

Dawson, Allen: and Central College–University of Virginia subscription, 476

Dawson, Martin: identified, 2:281–2n; letter from accounted for, 138n; letters from, 375, 589; letter to, 137–8; as merchant, 366n; TJ pays, 366; TJ's account with, 138, 375, 589, 648; and TJ's promissory note to E. Bacon, 138

Dayton, Jonathan, 252n

Deabbate, Gaspare, 583

deafness: education of deaf and mute, 28–9, 46, 61, 86

Dearborn, Henry: identified, 1:280n; and G. Stuart's portraits of TJ, 192

Dearborn, Henry Alexander Scammell: as Boston customs collector, 510; identified, 4:197n; letter to, 191; and G. Stuart's portraits of TJ, 192, 389–90; TJ introduces B. Peyton to, 191, 192

Death: A Poetical Essay (B. Porteus), 74, 75

debt, private: laws regarding, 59

de Bure Frères (Paris firm): identified, 10:232n; invoices from, 56, 58, 223; letter from, 56–8; TJ purchases books from, 56–7, 58, 89, 223, 497; TJ's account with, 56, 58, 497

Declaration of Independence: debate on, 295; mentioned, 615n; signers of, li, 213–4, 228, 230, 251, 252n, 511; TJ as author of, 42, 110–1

De errore profanarum religionum (J. Firmicus Maternus), 258

Defence of Usury; Shewing the Impolicy of the Present Legal Restraints on the terms of Pecuniary Bargains (J. Bentham), 445

De Jure Maritimo et Navali: or, a Treatise of Affairs Maritime and of Commerce (C. Molloy), 642n

Delambre, Jean Baptiste Joseph: and weights and measures, 234n

De La Motta, Jacob: *Discourse, delivered at the Consecration of the Synagogue, of the Hebrew Congregation, Mikva Israel, in the city of Savannah, Georgia*, 235; identified, 235n; letter from accounted for, 235n; letter to, 235

Delaplaine, Joseph: *Delaplaine's Repository*, 576–7; identified, 3:51n; letters from, 346, 547; letter to, 576–7; sends work to TJ, 346, 547, 576

Delaware: size of, 472

Delaware Indians, 85n, 108, 109, 132–3, 261, 415n

Delaware River: survey of, 357

Delessert, Étienne, 495

Delile, Alire Raffeneau, 568

Democratic party. *See* Republican party

Democratic Press (Philadelphia newspaper), 526n

De Monomachia, sive Duello. . . . Lines, on Duelling. Addressed to the Legislative Assemblies of America (L. H. Girardin), 290n

Demosthenes: works of, 330

Deneale, James: identified, 72n; letter from, 70–2; letter to, 89; surveying instrument and method of, 70–1, 89

de Pradt, Dominique Dufour, baron. *See* Pradt, Dominique Dufour, baron de

Derbigny, Pierre (Peter) Augustin Bourguignon: as gubernatorial candidate, 146; identified, 4:632n

De Re Publica (Cicero), 226

DeSaussure, Henry William: and T. Cooper, 50, 50; identified, 51n; letter from, to J. Vaughan, 50–1; opposes J. Wallace, 381–2

Destrehan, Jean Noël, 146

Destutt de Tracy, Antoine Louis Claude: and American Philosophical Society, 487–8n; *Commentaire sur l'Esprit des Lois de Montesquieu*, 420–1, 423n, 486, 630; *Commentary and Review of Montesquieu's Spirit of Laws*, 486;

Gordon, Robert: identified, 1:369n; and
tin for TJ, 274
Gordon, William Fitzhugh: and Central
College–University of Virginia subscription, 304; and establishment
of University of Virginia, 430, 468;
identified, 5:270n; as Va. legislator,
430, 567n, 635–6
Gorham, John: professor at Harvard
University, 557, 558n
Gorman, John: identified, 14:557–8n;
letter from, 69; letter from accounted
for, 69n; as stonecutter, 69; and University of Virginia, 303, 304, 308,
309, 310, 311, 316, 317, 319, 475, 478
gout, 75, 554
government. *See* politics
Graham, George, 234n
Graham, John (*1774–1820*): and closure
of port of New Orleans, 250; identified, 1:161n
Graham, Michael: and University of
Virginia, 305
grammar: collegiate education in, 296n,
609, 628; study of, 72–3
*Grammatica Anglo-Saxonica ex
Hickesiano Linguarum Septentrion-
alium Thesauro Excerpta* (G. Hickes),
363
Grand, Ferdinand: as banker, 495
Granet, François Marius: *The Choir of
the Capuchin Church in Rome*, 75, 76n
granite, 198
grapes. *See* viticulture; wine
grass: timothy, 353
Gravenhorst, Johann Ludwig Christian,
568
Graves, John: TJ's debt to, 648
Gray, Francis Calley: identified, 8:237n;
TJ sends greetings to, 183
Gray, Thomas: "Elegy Written in a
Country Churchyard," 387; quoted,
202
Gray, William: identified, 183–4n; letter
to, 183–4; TJ introduces B. Peyton to,
183, 192
Great Britain: J. Adams on, 590; Board
of Agriculture, 151n; and common
law, 640, 642; constitution of, 553;
financial system of, 638; House of
Commons, 229, 591n; House of
Lords, 229; judicial system in, 603;
laws of, 196, 640–2; ministers to U.S.,
37; and parliamentary investigation

of Queen Caroline, 363n, 500;
parliament of, 229, 473, 622; political
unrest in, 361, 488, 496, 499–500;
rainfall in, 97; and recruitment of
faculty for University of Virginia,
499; Revolution of *1688* ("Glorious
Revolution"), 230, 231–2n; and
Stamp Act (*1765*), 229–30; Stuart
dynasty of, 473; taxes in, 622; and
U.S., 37, 412n, 487, 500, 517, 533,
534, 537, 571. *See also* American
Revolution; George III; George IV;
Jefferson, Thomas: Opinions on;
Rush, Richard; War of *1812*
*A Greek and English Manual Lexicon to
the New Testament* (J. H. Bass), 364
*Greek Exercises, in Syntax, Ellipsis,
Dialects, Prosody, and Metaphrasis*
(W. Neilson), 10
Greek language: applicants to teach at
University of Virginia, 502; gram-
mars, 10; and neology, 195; study
of, 280, 329–30; thesauri, 224, 257;
works in, 224, 229, 236–7, 257, 258,
330, 393
Gregory, George: *Dictionary of Arts and
Sciences*, 34
Grehon, José Amado: as Portuguese
chargé d'affaires, 412
Griffin, Thomas: as Va. legislator, 468,
469n, 514–5
Griffiths, Elijah: on banks, 448; identified, 1:237n; letter from, 447–8; letter to, 521–2; on Missouri question,
447–8; on politics, 447–8; seeks
appointments, 447, 521–2
Griswolds & Coates (New York firm),
216n
groceries: purchased by TJ, 116, 594n;
suppliers of, 363. *See also* food
gruel, 542
Gual, Pedro: as governor of Cartagena,
529
Guegan, Henry (Louis Henri Guégan):
and books for TJ, 224, 236–7, 257–8,
366, 393, 394, 401; identified, 224n;
letter from, 257–60; letters to, 224,
236–7, 393
Guibert, François Apollini de, Comte,
325
gunpowder: for Navy Department, 246;
TJ orders, 13; TJ purchases, 6
guns. *See* firearms
gutters: at University of Virginia, 18–9

INDEX

Principles of Political Economy, considered with a view to their practical Application (T. R. Malthus), 421

The Private Correspondence of Benjamin Franklin, LL.D. F.R.S. &c. (ed. W. T. Franklin), 205–6

Proceedings and Report of the Commissioners for the University of Virginia (Thomas Jefferson): distributed by TJ, 220

Proposals, For Publishing, By Subscription, An Original Work, entitled "The Biographical Compendium, and Patriot's Mirror" (D. Fraser), 324

protractor, 70, 89

Providence, R.I.: churches in, 266–8; contagious disease in, 268

Psalterium Davidis Latino-Saxonicum vetus (J. Spelman), 364

public health. *See* health; medicine

Publius, James: letter from, 390; requests money from TJ, 390

pumpkins: from Maldonado, 294, 341, 634; seeds for TJ, 294, 341, 634

Purviance & Nicholas (firm): failure of, 4

Putnam, Israel: and snakes, 15–6; supports American independence, 582

putty, 11, 14

Pyrläus, Johann Christoph: and Indians, 109

Pythagoras: teachings of, 278–9

Quakers: and antislavery, 525n

quarries: in Va., 645n

quartz: mentioned, 198

Quatuor D. N. Jesu Christi Evangeliorum Versiones perantiquæ duæ, Gothica scil. et Anglo-Saxonica (F. Junius; ed. T. Marshall), 364

Quin & Harkins (firm): and University of Virginia, 479

Radcliffe, John, 530, 531n

Rafinesque, Constantine Samuel: and Alligewi antiquities, 153–6, 171–6, 177–81, 355, 396; *Annals of Nature*, 355, 396; edits *Western Minerva, or American Annals of Knowledge and Literature*, 355, 356n, 396, 567; *Ichthyologia Ohiensis, or Natural History of the Fishes Inhabiting the River Ohio and its tributary streams*, 567, 569n; identified, 15:41n; on *Jeffer-*

sonia diphylla (twinleaf), 355–6; letters from, 153–7, 171–6, 177–82, 355–6, 567–9; letter to, 396; seeks professorship, 355, 396, 568–9

Raggi, Giacomo: family of, 3–4, 19, 39, 112, 114, 243, 254, 335, 342; identified, 14:67n; letter from, 237–9; as stonecutter for University of Virginia, 19, 39, 237–8, 239n, 243–4, 254, 254–5, 309, 319, 336, 337n, 377, 475, 476, 478, 479, 481; Thomas Appleton's Agreement to Hire Giacomo Raggi and Michele Raggi, 237, 239n, 254, 255, 282, 283, 331, 335, 336, 337

Raggi, Michele: family of, 3–4, 19, 39, 112, 114, 237, 243, 254, 283, 335, 337, 342, 377, 437; financial situation of, 331; health of, 243, 283, 331, 336, 437, 438; identified, 14:67n; letters from, 237–9, 282–5, 331–2, 377–9, 437–9; letter to, 335–7; requests assistance from TJ, 331, 377–8, 437–8; returns to Italy, 331, 377–8, 437; as stonecutter for University of Virginia, 19, 39, 237–8, 239n, 243–4, 254, 254–5, 282–3, 305, 311, 312, 316, 319, 331, 335–7, 377–8, 437–8, 475, 476, 478, 479, 481; Thomas Appleton's Agreement to Hire Giacomo Raggi and Michele Raggi, 237, 239n, 254, 255, 282, 283, 331, 335, 336, 337

Ragland, John C.: identified, 7:502n; and University of Virginia, 303

Ragland, Thomas: and Charlottesville Academy, 65, 187; identified, 15:468n

Ragland, William: and Central College–University of Virginia subscription, 475

Railey, Daniel Mayo: and Central College–University of Virginia subscription, 304

The Raleigh (Buckingham Co. ordinary), 276

Ramsden, Jesse: scientific-instrument maker, lii

Ramsey, William: and University of Virginia, 481

Randolph: and University of Virginia, 311

Randolph, Miss, 9

Randolph, Benjamin Franklin (TJ's grandson): education of, 338

Randolph, Cornelia Jefferson (TJ's granddaughter): correspondence with siblings, 264n; correspondence with

Stuart, Archibald: identified, 2:93–4n; introduces A. Hodgson, 35, 35; letter from, 35; and University of Virginia, 475

Stuart, Gilbert: identified, 7:526–7n; portraits of TJ by, 192, 389–90

Stuart, James Francis Edward ("The Old Pretender"), 553, 554n

Sturz, Friedrich Wilhelm: edits works of Cassius Dio, 56

subscriptions, for publications: art, 416; biographies, 324; history, 94; on interest, 435; journals, 217, 219, 293, 294, 567; maps, 99, 101; newspapers, 251. *See also* books; Jefferson, Thomas: Books and Library

subscriptions, nonpublication: for Central College–University of Virginia, 152, 170, 220, 269, 282, 300, 431, 432

Suetonius: and Christianity, 600

sugar: mentioned, 337n

Sugarloaf Mountain (Md.), 200

suicide: artistic depictions of, 75

Sully, Thomas: identified, 4:356–7n; portraits of TJ by, 570, 604

sumac (plant), 199

Summers, David: and University of Virginia, 479

Superior Court of Chancery for the Staunton District, 646, 647n

Supreme Court, U.S.: and *Cohens v. Virginia*, 484n, 593–4n, 637; criticized, 484n; and impeachment, 483, 484n, 603; and *McCulloch v. Maryland*, 609, 610n; and *Osborn v. Bank of the United States*, 575n, 617; procedures of, 483, 484n; TJ on, 483, 617–8

surveying: of Delaware River, 357; J. Deneale's instrument and method of, 70–1, 89; and dividers, 70; instruments for sale, 504n; and Natural Bridge, 163, 507; plotting table, 357; and protractor, 70, 89; and scale, 70; study of, 325, 609; and sweep, 70; TJ provides instructions to L. H. Girardin on, 89. *See also* scientific instruments

Swain, Capt., 463

Swainson, William: *Zoological Illustrations*, 568

Swan Tavern (Charlottesville), xlix–l

Swedenborg, Emanuel: J. Adams on, 589–90; and theology, 16, 17n

Swedish language: and spelling of Indian words, 109–10; works in, 109

sweep (surveying instrument), 70

Swift, Jonathan: TJ references, 291

Swift, William Roberdeau: and J. Corrêa da Serra, 142; identified, 142n; letter from, 142

Synopsis Plantarum, seu Enchiridium Botanicum (C. H. Persoon), 224, 257

A Systematical View of the Laws of England (R. Wooddeson), 641

Tableau des Saints (Holbach), 190n

Tables of Interest and Discount, calculated on the only true principle of 365 Days to the Year (L. Chapman), 435

Tachy-Graphy. The Most exact and compendious methode of Short and swift writing that hath ever yet been published by any (T. Shelton), 287

Tacitus: and Christianity, 600; lost works of, 541; writings of, 330, 473, 503, 516

Tales of My Landlord (W. Scott), 517n

tallow, 151

Tama, Diogène: *Transactions of the Parisian Sanhedrim, or Acts of the Assembly of Israelitish Deputies of France and Italy*, 74, 93

tanning: bark for, 460

Tarleton, Sir Banastre: military activities of in Va., 35–6, 39n

Tatian (early Christian author), 189, 196

taverns: plays performed at, xlix–l

taxes: on carriages, 242n; collected from Second Bank of the U.S. branches, 575n; customs, 4, 25n, 58, 216, 223, 240, 293; on horses and mules, 242n; on imports, 158, 221, 249–50, 252n, 291; on land, 242n, 281; and religion, 549–50, 584–5; and representation, 549, 584; on slaves, 242n, 461n; TJ on, 483, 489, 622; TJ pays, 366; on tobacco, 242n; in Va., 242, 281, 328; on wine, 52, 117

Taylor, Creed: and establishment of University of Virginia, 625

Taylor, John (of Caroline): *Construction Construed, and Constitutions Vindicated*, 419–20, 482–4, 556, 609, 617–8, 637; donation to W. C. Nicholas's family, 591, 608–9; identified, 10:89–90n; *An Inquiry into the Principles and Policy of the Government of the United States*, 482; letter from, 591; letter to, 608–10; and University of Virginia, 609–10

Taylor, John Louis: and American Academy of Language and Belles Lettres, 531

Taylor, John W.: as candidate for Speaker of U.S. House of Representatives, 158, 159n; identified, 585–6n; letter from, 585–6; letter to, 606; and Missouri question, 606; and Phi Beta Kappa, 585, 606

Taylor, Joseph: as builder for University of Virginia, 313

Taylor, Robert Barraud: encouraged to run for Va. legislature, 551, 624, 625n; identified, 14:94n; as member of University of Virginia Board of Visitors, 297, 396, 469, 579, 586, 624

Taylor, Samuel: as Va. legislator, 551, 625

Tazewell, Littleton Waller: identified, 2:350n; and manuscript of Va. laws, 239, 240

tea: drinking of, 16; Paraguay (maté), 294

Tecumseh (Shawnee chief): belt and shot pouch of, 38; leadership of, 615

telescopes: pocket, li–lii, 348 (*illus.*)

Terence (Publius Terentius Afer), 330

Terrell, Dabney Carr (TJ's grand-nephew): identified, 9:482n; letter to, 640–2; studies in Geneva, 494–5; studies law, 495, 640–2

Tertullianus, Quintus Septimus Florens: writings of, 189, 196, 258

textiles: baize, 11; for bolting, 376, 389, 401; bombazine, 11; calico, 6; cambric, 6; cassimere, 6; cotton, 9; ferret (fabric tape), 14; flannel, 9, 12, 13; hemp, 12; holland, 6, 8, 10, 11; jean, 8; Kendal, 12; kersey, 12; linen, 7, 12; lutestring, 9; muslin, 6; nankeen, 6; osnaburg, 12; plain cloth, 11, 12, 13; ribbon, 9; shirting, 13; silk, 6, 8, 9; Ticklenburg, 8, 12, 14; velvet, 12; and weaving, 36; wool, 10, 11. *See also* manufacturing; thread

Thacker, Martin: and Central College–University of Virginia subscription, 303

Thacker, Nathaniel: and University of Virginia, 309, 480

theodolites, 99

theology: collegiate education in, 628

Théorie Générale des Equations Algébriques (É. Bézout), 400n

thermometers: and meteorological observations, 97, 251, 400n, 554

Θησαυρὸς τῆς Ἑλληνικῆς Γλώσσης. *Thesaurus Graecae Linguae* (ed. H. Estienne), 224, 257

Thesaurus Linguæ Romanæ & Britannicæ (T. Cooper), 364

Thiene, Adriano, 343

Thiene, Marcantonio, 343

Thomas (TJ's slave; b. *1813*). *See* Hughes, Thomas (TJ's slave; b. *1813*)

Thomas, Isaiah: and American Antiquarian Society, 351; identified, 352n; letter from accounted for, 352n; letter to, 351–2

Thomas, James: employee of J. Milligan, 427; identified, 14:39n; and J. Milligan's bookselling business, 427

Thomas M. Randolph & Company (Shadwell mills, Va.). *See* Randolph, Thomas Eston (TJ's cousin); Randolph, Thomas Mann (*1768–1828*) (TJ's son-in-law; Martha Jefferson Randolph's husband)

Thompson, S. J. & Company (Baltimore firm). *See* S. J. Thompson & Company (Baltimore firm)

Thomson, Charles: *The Holy Bible, containing the Old and New Covenant*, 115; identified, 9:342n

Thomson, James: quoted, 203; *The Seasons*, 203n

Thorn, Abia B.: as brick-mason for University of Virginia, 19, 303, 313, 314, 319, 479

Thornton, Anna Maria Brodeau (William Thornton's wife): TJ sends greetings to, 578

Thornton, William: and design of Central College, 527; on France, 528; health of, 530; identified, 1:466n; letter from, 527–31; letter to, 577–8; as patent office superintendent, 528; 578; seeks appointment, 528–31, 577–8; and South America, 528–30, 531n

Thoughts on Political Economy (D. Raymond), 548–9

Thoüin, André: identified, 1:202n; sends seeds to TJ, 46

thread, 6, 8, 11, 12, 13, 14

Thrimston (Thrimson) (TJ's slave; b. ca. *1799*). *See* Hern, Thrimston (Thrimson) (TJ's slave; b. ca. *1799*)

Thucydides: works of, 330, 441, 516

THE PAPERS OF THOMAS JEFFERSON are composed in Monticello, a font based on the "Pica No. 1" created in the early 1800s by Binny & Ronaldson, the first successful typefounding company in America. The face is considered historically appropriate for The Papers of Thomas Jefferson because it was used extensively in American printing during the last quarter-century of Jefferson's life, and because Jefferson himself expressed cordial approval of Binny & Ronaldson types. It was revived and rechristened Monticello in the late 1940s by the Mergenthaler Linotype Company, under the direction of C. H. Griffith and in close consultation with P. J. Conkwright, specifically for the publication of the Jefferson Papers. The font suffered some losses in its first translation to digital format in the 1980s to accommodate computerized typesetting. Matthew Carter's reinterpretation in 2002 restores the spirit and style of Binny & Ronaldson's original design of two centuries earlier.